DATE DUE

DEMCO 38-296

CONTEMPORARY
Jewish-American Novelists

A Bio-Critical Sourcebook

Edited by
JOEL SHATZKY AND MICHAEL TAUB

With a foreword by Daniel Walden

Emmanuel S. Nelson, Advisory Editor

Greenwood Press
Westport, Connecticut
London

Library of Congress Cataloging-in-Publication Data

Shatzky, Joel.
    Contemporary Jewish-American novelists : a bio-critical sourcebook
/ edited by Joel Shatzky and Michael Taub : with a foreword by
Daniel Walden.
        p. cm.
    ISBN 0–313–29462–3 (alk. paper)
    1. American fiction—Jewish authors—Bio-bibliography—
Dictionaries.   2. American fiction—20th century—Bio-bibliography—
Dictionaries.   3. American fiction—Jewish authors—Dictionaries.
4. American fiction—20th century—Dictionaries.   5. Jews in
literature—Dictionaries.   I. Taub, Michael.
PS374.J48C66   1997
813'.54098924'003—dc21   96–37047

British Library Cataloguing in Publication Data is available.

Library of Congress Catalog Card Number: 96–37047
ISBN: 0–313–29462–3

First published in 1997

Greenwood Press, 88 Post Road West, Westport, CT 06881
An imprint of Greenwood Publishing Group, Inc.

Printed in the United States of America

The paper used in this book complies with the
Permanent Paper Standard issued by the National
Information Standards Organization (Z39.48–1984).

10 9 8 7 6 5 4 3 2 1

For Dorothy Shatzky, who through our thirty years together has always been my best editor.

—Joel Shatzky

For Patricia Hecht, who taught me more about American Jewry than all the books I've ever read.

—Michael Taub

Contents

Contents

Foreword

Daniel Walden

Some years ago Leslie Fiedler said to me that American Jewish literature was moribund. Having been at the inception, out of which came Bellow, Malamud, and Roth (Philip, that is), he now saw the end. When I suggested a Modern Language Association session that would examine his claim, he agreed. Subsequently, when he could not attend, at the last minute, I was fortunate enough to get Cynthia Ozick to appear. It was in New York City. The ballroom was jammed. On the program were Bonnie Lyons, Cynthia Ozick, and myself. As the program progressed, it became crystal clear not only that was American Jewish literature not moribund, but that it was alive and well, changing, and evolving.

The fact is that while at one time Abraham Cahan, Anzia Yezierska, and Henry Roth, the pioneers, wrote about their lives in Russia-Poland, the transition to the New World, and their traumas and pains growing up in New York City, they were succeeded by Saul Bellow, Bernard Malamud, Philip Roth, and many others, who wrote mainly of their adjustment in the New World, in New York City and places like small-town New Jersey or Corvallis, Oregon. For many of the writers in the first or second generation, leaving the Old Country and trying to cope with the powers of Americanization, the struggle with anti-Semitism, the difficulty with the rigors of making a living, and the trauma of being an "other" and "making it" were fit subjects for book after book, short story after short story. Abraham Cahan wrote of David Levinsky's "rise" from immigrant to millionaire, and yet at the beginning of the book and at the end he complained that he wasn't happy and if he had it to do over again, he'd choose an academic path. Hah. His Eastern European Jewish past pulled him to the City College of New York. Americanization and its attractions and excitement pulled him in the direction of the American Dream of Success. Meanwhile, Anzia Yezierska told us what it was like to be a poor woman early in the century and what her female immigrant response was.

With Bellow, Malamud, Roth, Ozick, Nissenson, Potok, and many others, American Jewish literature came of age. Bellow won two National Book Awards, a Pulitzer Prize, and the Nobel Prize in literature. Ozick and Philip Roth have been justly celebrated for their pathbreaking books and short stories. Millions of Americans have seen *Goodbye, Columbus*, the movie, and millions know *The Chosen*, the film. Probably more have seen *The Natural*, with Robert Redford, or Malamud's *The Fixer*. The point is that with the passing of time, American Jewish writing has been able to penetrate middle America, for better or worse. In *Goodbye, Columbus*, the novella, we can see how Philip Roth balances the excesses of the Patimkins with the thoughtfulness of Neil and his aunt. In Malamud's *The Natural*, the book, even though it does not have any Jewish "*tam*" (flavor), it is possible to discern Malamud's Jewish sensibilities, his concern for suffering and redemption. For Ozick and Potok, whose creative work included a traditional belief in Judaism, versus the skepticism of almost all of the others, the agonies of Potok's Danny and Reuven as they grew up and evolved were matched by the extraordinary and exquisite and convoluted agonies of being Rabbi Kornfeld in Ozick's "The Pagan Rabbi."

However, as life moves on, so culture changes, and socioeconomic and psychological changes impact on an alive, bubbling American Jewish literary culture. As I put it in introducing *New Voices in an Old Tradition* in *Studies in American Jewish Literature* 13 (1994), which I edited, "The fact is that contrary to Irving Howe's pronouncement that 'American Jewish fiction has probably moved past its high point,' and Leslie Fiedler's claim that American Jewish fiction ended with Bellow, Malamud and Roth, American Jewish fiction is alive and well." Not only has a new generation emerged, but several generations have been seen, and among them are significant new critical voices and new authorial, imaginative voices.

There is a new spirit of pluralism in the American Jewish community. In a new collection of short fiction, *Writing Our Way Home*, edited by Ted Solotaroff and Nessa Rapoport, we see children and grandchildren of Holocaust survivors, converts to Judaism, Sephardim, descendants of *conversos*, and lesbians and gay men. As Ludger Brinker pointed out in *SAJL* 13 (1994), reflecting the new mix, Jyl Lynn Feldman, Judith Katz, and Leslea Newman all ask questions arising out of the nexus of acculturation and assimilation but also out of their ability to reinterpret the Jewish tradition from the point of view of Jewish lesbian writers. These writers, together with Melvin Bukiet, Rebecca Goldstein, and Thane Rosenbaum, who have won the Edward Lewis Wallant Award, as well as Bellow, Malamud, Henry Roth, Philip Roth, Chaim Potok, Cynthia Ozick, Allen Ginsberg, Woody Allen, Charles Bernstein, Arthur Miller, Laura Hobson, Grace Paley, Jo Sinclair, and so many others from the 1940s on, exemplify Alan Wald's statement that today there is no such thing as one American culture, that the United States is the home of many cultures, "each internally riven by class, gender, religion, and in some cases color stratification'' (*MELUS* 14:2, Summer 1987). Or, as Werner Sollors put it in *The Invention of Ethnicity* (xv), ''Texts are not mere reflections of existing differences but also . . . productive forces in nation-building enterprises.''

The situation that surrounded the statement and the claims that American Jewish fiction died with Bellow, Malamud, and Roth is no longer relevant. A new wind is blowing. We are at the dawn of new literary creations, today and tomorrow and then more tomorrows. *L'chaim* and *mazel tov*.

Preface

This book attempts to address the need for a comprehensive reference guide to Jewish-American novelists whose major works, for the most part, were written after World War II. Briefly put, our definition of Jewish imaginative literature is fiction written by Jews on Jewish themes or involving Jewish interests and concerns.

Since the end of World War II, the Jewish community in America has been transformed from a predominantly immigrant population in which most adults still spoke or certainly understood Yiddish as the *mamaloshen* (mother tongue) into a culture so thoroughly assimilated into mainstream America—wherever that might be located now—that today approximately half of all American-born Jews marry out of the faith. The Jewish culture of Europe, particularly the Yiddish-speaking world, that was obliterated by the Nazis is now only found in faint echoes of Jewish-Americana, expressed vividly in that wonderful story by Cynthia Ozick, "Envy: Or Yiddish in America." In it, Edelshtein, a Yiddish poet bedeviled in America without a translator, tells the tale of a funeral cortege passing through the Bronx and lower Manhattan to bury an old Jew in Staten Island and going by the office of the last Yiddish daily in New York. "There were two editors, one to run the papers off the press and the other to look out the window. The one looking out the window saw the funeral procession passing by and called to his colleague: 'Hey Mottel, print one less!' "

This kind of gallows humor evokes the sense of loss expressed by many Jewish-American authors of the Old World destroyed and a new one bereft, with little of substance to replace what had been lost. Perhaps what accounts for the popularity of the works of Isaac Bashevis Singer, whose celebrity is only explicable through English translations of his work, is his link with that lost past and his skill in using the vernacular of the present in bringing it to life. The special burden of the Jewish-American novelists of today is to find a substantial subject that is inherent in a culture that has become so fragmented and vitiated by the descent into soulless commercialism that perhaps the satire of Ozick and Phillip Roth has become the most logical response.

A dilemma we have had to face is the publication of a volume several years ago by Greenwood Press, edited by Ann Shapiro, that was devoted exclusively to Jewish-American women authors. This presented us with a problem: replicate or exclude. We chose to include a selected number of Jewish-American women writers whom we consider essential in any reference work of this kind also found in the Shapiro volume, but we also included in the Appendix brief biographical entries and cross-referencing of those postwar writers found in her volume. We hope that this is a satisfactory compromise, but we also would like to note that a significant number of Jewish women novelists not included in the Shapiro volume are introduced here, many for the first time in any major reference work.

Our focus on those works of authors of Jewish origin not noted for ethnic concerns, such as Norman Mailer, is on those specific writings that would be of interest to students and scholars of Jewish-American literature, with brief reference to their other publications. The majority of novelists represented here are noted primarily for their fiction involving Jewish themes and characters. We have departed, however, from limiting our entries to American-born or American-based writers by including the Canadian novelist Mordecai Richler.

We have aimed for inclusion of a number of figures who have been marginalized in the past, particularly Jewish women and gay authors, with the hope that a greater diversity of Jewish experience will be exposed to a wider readership than in the recent past. We have also included such up-and-coming younger writers as Steve Stern and authors who might be considered controversial such as Art Spiegelman. If we have erred in some instances both in matters of inclusion and exclusion, we also believe that we have given into the hands of scholars and students of Jewish-American literature a valuable reference of the broadest selection of novelists yet published.

Acknowledgments

The editors wish to thank Emmanuel Nelson, who initially suggested and encouraged this project; David Shapiro, Richard Kostelanetz, and Burt Kimmelman for their invaluable service in providing us with the names of numerous contributors; Dan Walden, whose footsteps as a pioneer in Jewish-American bio-bibliography we follow; Alan Berger, Sarah Blacher Cohen, and Ellen Schiff for their incisive advice; David Ritchie, J. Keith Ostertag, Patricia Viele, and the rest of the library staff at the State University of New York, Cortland, for their help in the research; and Martin Taub, who helped finance some of the expenses of putting this work together.

Introduction

Sanford E. Marovitz

Fifty years ago the way to identify Jewish-American fiction was not yet a critical issue. If a novel or story was written by an American Jew about Jews, whether American or not, it was generally considered to fall into that category. If a Jewish author in America wrote chiefly about non-Jews, however, as did Edna Ferber and Nathanael West, their fiction was held to be simply American. Even today only Jewish readers are likely to think of *Showboat* and *The Day of the Locust* as Jewish-American fiction, notwithstanding the subjects of show business and Hollywood. As for Christian authors writing sympathetically about Jews, like Myra Kelly at the beginning of this century, classifying her stories about Jewish schoolchildren on the Lower East Side as Jewish-American fiction would be dubious at best. One of the most notorious examples of a non-Jew who wrote "realistic" novels about the Jewish community is that of "Sidney Luska" in the 1880s; most readers assumed that he was Jewish, not knowing that his name was actually Henry Harland and that he was writing under a pseudonym. At the end of the decade Harland traveled to England, converted to Catholicism several years later, and published increasingly anti-Semitic novels there under his real name. Were all of these writers then considered as being contributors to Jewish-American literature? The answer must be "No," because if such a designation existed at all around the turn of the century, it was certainly not in common usage. Only now do we look back upon these authors from the 1880s through roughly World War II in an attempt to classify them and their fiction definitively in terms of religion or ethnicity, but all such categorizations are relative to particular applications.

For *Contemporary Jewish-American Novelists: A Bio-Critical Sourcebook*, postwar Jewish-American fiction is fiction that has been written by American Jews, native-born or naturalized, and it has been left to the authors of each entry to determine how much—if any—attention should be given to novels and stories in which Jewish characters appear minimally or not at all. Some authors, like Norman Mailer, have conscientiously detached themselves from focusing on specifically Jewish subject matter in their work,[1] but this collection contains an entry on Mailer. Saul Bellow and Bernard Malamud occasionally published fiction devoid of Jewish characters—*Henderson the Rain King* and *The Natural*, for example—yet critics have probed these novels seeking recognizably Jewish themes or images, attempting thereby to place these works in the total pattern of each author's canon. The same holds true of Edward Lewis Wallant's *Children at the Gate*, Joseph Heller's *Catch-22*, and Chaim Potok's *I Am the Clay*, among numerous others.

Saul Bellow has attempted to characterize Jewish writing by seeing it in terms of *story*. For him, Jewish literature goes back to the Hebrew Scriptures, of which the ''message . . . cannot be easily separated from its stories and metaphors. . . . For there is power in a story. It testifies to the worth, the significance of an individual.''[2] Cynthia Ozick believes that the Jewish writer is typically more concerned with reality than aesthetics. For her, Jewish literature will not endure unless it is ''centrally Jewish,'' meaning that it ''touches the liturgical,'' not specifically prayer, but ''a communal voice, the echo of the voice of the Lord of History.'' For Ozick, because in her view secular Judaism is oxymoronic, Jews detached from faith cannot write Jewish literature.[3] Robert Alter, in contrast, can point to no key that identifies ''the Jewish character of all Jewish writers. . . . [O]ne must always attend to the particular ways in which Jewish experience impinges on the individual.''[4]

According to Richard J. Fein, Jewish writers are linked by an internalized sense of insecurity.[5] Bonnie K. Lyons perceives in Jewish authors four attitudes on man's ''moral nature'' and identifies eight themes particularly in Jewish-American life and art that appear in their fiction.[6] With copious examples, she persuasively discusses each of these items so as to reveal the underlying relations that exist among them, the authors, and their work. Although Lyons's essay deals specifically with postwar Jewish-American fiction, her observations may be extrapolated for insight into values and themes that are shared with earlier writing by American Jews as well.

The foregoing suggests that common elements may be found in Jewish literature from the biblical era to our own, but it may also be a mistake to depend upon them as a basis for insisting upon its uniqueness, for to do so would only be to narrow its scope and thereby reduce the universality that it surely enjoys. Moreover, because considering any period or genre of Jewish literature entails seeing the whole of it by virtue of its elements in common, it would be more useful to discuss postwar American Jewish fiction by placing it in the cultural context of the past century or so rather than in isolation. These novels and stories did not simply emerge with the end of the war; they evolved collectively, and without reference to the sources that brought them into being, they can be understood and appreciated only in a limited way. As the sculpture requires a base and the painting a frame for accentuation and support, so does the fiction by American Jews of the past half century need its historical context, "the communal voice," in Ozick's phrasing, "the echo of the God of History."

From its origin in the late nineteenth century to the present, Jewish-American fiction may be divided and subdivided into a wide variety of topical categories. Chronologically, it may be conveniently approached by considering it in terms of four main divisions that overlap the necessarily elastic boundaries: first, from the post–Civil War period through the mid-1920s, when issues pertaining to immigration and problems of resettlement dominated much of American Jewish life; second, from about 1925 through World War II, which encompasses the proletarian era and the rise of the first generation of American Jews born into citizenship to Eastern European immigrant parents; third, the three decades that immediately followed the close of the war from about 1945 through the early 1970s, when awareness of the Shoah and the establishment of Israel as an independent Jewish nation led to an expanded interest in and sympathy for the Jewish people and their culture, which in turn hastened both assimilation and secularization; and fourth, from the early-to-middle 1970s to date.

This contemporary period is surely the most complex of the four for Jewish literary study, and the reasons are manifold. Easier assimilation fostered divisiveness in the Jewish community through increased intermarriage, a turning from religion, and the consequent attenuation of *kehila* (community) on the one hand. On the other was a return to faith by the offspring of secularized parents, a broadened intellectual and liturgical role for women in the synagogue, a revitalization of orthodoxy and Hasidism in the United States, and a burgeoning interest in learning Hebrew and Yiddish, especially among young people. No longer were these tongues regarded as "dead" languages, for they were rapidly gaining recognition as essential to promote a more intimate linkage between prodigal Jews and their heritage as represented by both Israel, where Hebrew is the national language, and *yidishkayt*, in which Yiddish is fundamental to the heart and spirit.

Obviously, the oppositions that exist among the Jewish people of the current period have generated tremendous tension. To a large extent, this tension is repressed by many Jews unwilling to face their contemporary role as Jews in a historic community, and it is simply disregarded by others who believe that they have severed themselves from the spiritual and cultural taproots that had once nourished them. For Jews in both of these large segments, emotional calls to bond anew by speakers for major Jewish organizations as well as by rabbis and temple presidents, all echoed by the Jewish press, remain either unheard and unread or simply dismissed by unaffiliated Jews as irrelevant to their own lives. Hence the tension within the Jewish community at large increases.

What does this all mean for a fuller understanding and appreciation of fiction by Jewish-American authors published after World War II? A new sense of liberation developed among American Jews from the changes provoked by the war, and this provides a partial but substantial basis for perceiving how and why Jewish-American fiction reached its highest peak in the next two and a half to three decades. That it has remained there since then is a heavily debated question despite the preponderance of Jewish-American women who have achieved recognition and acclaim in the past quarter century and the fact that some of the best among the preceding generation of authors have continued to produce and publish admirable work. I believe that the bio-critical essays in this volume will do much to support that positive view.

Of course, the Shoah and the restoration of Zion in Israel inevitably changed the direction of Jewish-American fiction from what it had been through the years of World War II, but the transformation constituted less a detachment than a reversal of priorities, for to a large degree, what American Jews had been seeking earlier was being realized. Anti-Semitism was no longer fashionable, and the "Restricted" notices that had proliferated earlier in the century—"Restricted," meaning "Jews Not Welcome!" or "No Jews Need Apply!"—were rapidly disappearing. It would be naive to suggest that anti-Semitism itself in the United States was disappearing with them, as several novelists of these decades suggest, but it was certainly no longer the barrier it had been in preceding decades, and what remained of it was seldom overt. American Jews, especially those of Eastern European heritage, were moving into the suburbs from the ethnic urban areas in which their parents or grandparents had originally settled, mostly on the East Coast and in Chicago. Vital new Jewish communities were being established in and around cities across the country, often amid Christians already residing there rather than apart from them in homogeneous neighborhoods of their own. Indeed, the Americanization and assimilation of immigrant Jewry to which Abraham Cahan had devoted much of his life—and the *Forward*, which he edited for nearly fifty years—had largely come to pass.

Although *Contemporary Jewish-American Novelists* deals with postwar fiction, Cahan is an earlier author who warrants momentary attention here because in several important ways both he and his writing were prophetic. As already noted, he anticipated the acculturation of Jewish immigrants and understood that through it they would be absorbed into the mainstream of the American economy. From there, he knew that they could establish a foundation of economic stability, education, and self-assurance that would enable them to realize for themselves "the American Dream." In Cahan's eyes that phrase was not an empty one but a promise. As he himself had made it, so could those Jews who had followed him through the gates of Castle Garden and Ellis Island.

That this process of Americanization would generate ill results as well as benign ones he could also foresee, and he represented both the good and bad of it in much of his journalism and fiction, most notably in the novel for which he is best known, *The Rise of David Levinsky*, published in 1917. Whereas an earlier serialized version of that work was written by request of *McClure's Magazine* to illustrate the remarkable success of the immigrant Jew in American business, the final complete novel did much more: it adumbrated the secularization of those Jewish immigrants who turned from divinity to dollars as their center of worship, a conversion made by Levinsky himself. Remaining is the shell of a Judaism devoid of spirit but accompanied by nostalgic recollections of *yidishkayt*, a romanticized version of an oppressive and insecure existence in the Pale and elsewhere in Eastern Europe for centuries. To be sure, the Old Country lost its hold on the immigrants as early as the second generation when Yiddish gave way to English through public education, and Jewish laws and traditions succumbed to a new way of life.

Through the character of Levinsky, Cahan also prophesied the alienation of American Jews since they had become socialized anew and comfortably en-sconced in an environment no longer hostile but even supportive of their in-dependent, capitalist enterprise. Indeed, the gospel of work that had come to the New World and thrived among the Puritans and their descendants corresponded well with the Jews' own ethic and drive for success. But because they had lived for centuries according to a pattern of existence chiefly governed by a combi-nation of law and tradition, the past left a residue that could not be easily sloughed off and forgotten.

In consequence, like Levinsky, modern assimilated postwar Jews could no longer be certain of their identity. The struggle for acculturation and assimilation was over, but nothing came through it to replace the historic values and guide-lines left behind in the *shtetlech* and the ghettos. For many, indeed, most, the ties to the past were severed. Comfortable materialism and self-indulgence left second- and third-generation Jews divorced from a meaningful past, and without it, they could no longer be certain how to identify themselves except by name. "Am I an American in a secular community, or am I a Jew?" the bewildered alien might ask, and if the latter, "How do I know it?" automatically followed because a reflection, an image, a shell of the past no longer sufficed to confirm an identity.

As I suggested earlier, however, the end of the war did not effect a clean and total break with themes and approaches to narrative that typified fiction of pre-vious decades. Writers such as Meyer Levin and Jerome Weidman who had established themselves in the 1930s and 1940s continued to publish and sell their fiction. Whereas Levin had left novels dealing with Chicago's West Side behind with the war years, however, Weidman still looked back upon the years and repercussions of immigration that he knew firsthand from the Lower East Side, where he was reared; this he did with powerful effect in one of his most popular stories, "My Father Sits in the Dark" (1961). Gerald Green also drew from his early years amid the poverty and hostility of Brooklyn during the 1930s in *The Last Angry Man* and *To Brooklyn with Love*, set in the old neighborhood of the city where his family had lived.

Social criticism remained a presence in Jewish-American fiction after the war, though it did not predominate as it had earlier, in the 1920s and 1930s. Anti-Semitism continued to appear in such early postwar novels as Laura Z. Hobson's *Gentleman's Agreement* and Weidman's *The Enemy Camp*. In *The Heartless*

Light, Green described the unethical aggressiveness of the media, and in the early 1970s Philip Roth satirized the then-current Nixon administration in *Our Gang* before demythologizing through parody an array of American cultural icons in *The Great American Novel*, including professional baseball, on which the novel focuses. In *The Tenants*, the most violent novel that Bernard Malamud had yet published, he presented a stark vision of deteriorating racial relations through the conflict of two writers, an African American and a Jew, living in the same condemned tenement. A decade later, Saul Bellow incorporated inter-racial violence as a subtheme in perhaps his most pessimistic novel, *The Dean's December*.

That Roth's hilarious satire in *The Great American Novel* centers on baseball, "the great American game," confirms that Jewish authors have not been im-mune to the appeal of popular sport, including commercialized national athletics. Malamud's first novel, *The Natural*, is also devoted to baseball, though only metaphorically can it be categorized as a Jewish novel; although no character identifiable as a Jew appears in it, Malamud himself once said that "all men are Jews,"[7] so by right of inclusion, all of his team members and the rest of his cast are sons (and daughters) of Abraham as well. A year after *The Natural* was published, Mark Harris's baseball novel *The Southpaw* met a favorable reception. Chaim Potok, another lover of baseball, introduced his first novel, *The Chosen*, with a game between Jewish teams, one Hasidic and the other not, which brought two central figures together and thus created the grounds for a thematic conflict that would dominate the work.

As baseball represents one aspect of the popular culture incorporated into Jewish-American fiction, a more historic one dating to Abraham Cahan's first novel, *Yekl, A Tale of the New York Ghetto* in 1896, is the caustic, ironic humor that evolved from an element of *yidishkayt*, a way of finding an aspect of com-edy in virtually anything, including oppression, despair, and suffering. Even Yekl—Jake the Yankee—recent immigrant that he is, takes pride in his professed expertise in baseball and prizefighting, but the humor goes beyond his foolish vanity when the Yiddish spoken by all of Cahan's characters in that short novel is salted with pictorial observations and curses that reflect the bitter outlook of its speakers, Eastern European Jews who refuse to be cowed. In postwar fiction, Grace Paley's sensitive stories, mostly about women with chil-dren and occasional husbands in New York City, are saturated with such humor, even at times controlled by it, as is much of Saul Bellow's fiction, *Herzog*, for example. Stanley Elkin's mix of comedy with pathos in *Criers and Kibitzers, Kibitzers and Criers* also falls into this category, as does the humor in Joseph Heller's most acclaimed novel, *Catch-22*, a satire on life in the Army Air Force that transcends the military and reflects broadly on American culture and values. A particularly innovative form of self-denigrating Jewish humor appears in Har-vey Pekar's *American Splendor*, a series of comic books that began in the 1970s, with new issues still being published from time to time. Only an occasional anecdote or story focuses on a Jewish theme among these realistic depictions of lower-middle-class life in Cleveland, but the humor in nearly all of them has its source in Yiddish and a clearly Jewish frame of mind.

Pekar is but one of several contemporary American writers who have converted the comic-book format into a medium for serious representation. Among Jewish Americans, none has gained higher acclaim in that genre than Art Spiegelman, whose powerful tracing of his parents' experience through the Shoah appears in *Maus: A Survivor's Tale*, originally a series of episodic sketches in the underground press and now available in two-volume hardbound and paperback editions. Spiegelman's rendering of the Holocaust has been accomplished by means of a device usually associated with fable: he has transformed humans into different types of animals, each representing a particular nationality or ethnic group: Nazis are pictured as cats, Poles as pigs, and Jews as mice. Threaded among the atrocities is a subtheme of fierce generational conflict between Spiegelman and his father, an unresolved conflict that exposes the artist's anger lying near the surface of his consciousness.

Probably because the Shoah was a shattering, almost incredible episode in modern, especially Jewish, history, and the fear that such catastrophic horror could only be trivialized as a setting or subject in fiction, few Jewish-American authors immediately employed it as a focal subject in their work. Beginning with the 1960s, however, a change occurred. One of the most moving early novels to include the Holocaust as a major theme is *The Pawnbroker* by Edward Lewis Wallant, published at the beginning of that decade. It portrays Sol Nazerman, the pawnbroker, as a psychologically warped and divided survivor who can neither confront nor come to terms with himself for his own role among the victims, including those members of his family who did not survive and those of his sister's liberal Jewish family with whom he lives in suburban New York. Late in the same decade, Richard Elman's trilogy deals with the struggle of Hungarian Jews as the Nazis gain control, and in Norma Rosen's *Touching Evil*, enduring psychological effects of the Shoah are seen to continue long beyond the physical brutality and carnage.

Early in the 1970s several more novels were published in which the Holocaust prominently appeared, often through recollection, as in *The Pawnbroker*. In *Mr. Sammler's Planet*, Saul Bellow employed it to portray Sammler as an aging survivor who continues struggling, on the one hand, with the dark, fearful days of his past in Poland after the Nazis had taken over the country, and on the other, with the chaos of contemporary New York City amid racial tension, crime, apathetic police, and student radicals. Within the next few years, too, came Gerald Green's controversial *Holocaust* along with major novels by Isaac Bashevis Singer and Susan Fromberg Schaeffer, both with a Holocaust theme woven through a complex web of love relationships: *Enemies: A Love Story* and *Anya*, respectively. In 1979 Roberta Silman represented in *Boundaries* a developing relationship between a Jewish-American widow and the son of a Nazi, problematic, of course, because of the Holocaust background, and three years later

Norma Rosen published *At the Center*, her second novel with important reference to the Shoah.

Despite the rapidity with which news of the Holocaust traveled among American Jews after the camps were liberated, then, an interim period had to pass between knowledge of the recent historical facts and an understanding of them that was at least sufficient to alert Jews to their vulnerability in a world of "others" and to awaken them to the truth that no Jew can remain untouched by the Shoah. Jewish-American authors responded in different ways to such recognitions. Some employed a Holocaust theme in their fiction, as did those just mentioned. Others turned to messianism. For example, a messianic theme is central in Arthur Cohen's fantastic novel *In the Days of Simon Stern*; seeing himself as *the* Messiah, Simon attempts to fulfill his mission amid incidents and thoughts drawn from Jewish history. Some fifteen years later, Cynthia Ozick based *The Messiah of Stockholm* in part on the writings of Bruno Schulz, slain on the street during the Shoah. In two collections of stories by Hugh Nissenson, messianism is also prominent, this time, however, with particular reference to Israel, a land that he feels as part of himself despite his acknowledged atheism. In this respect, he and Ozick stand at opposite ends of the spectrum of Jewish belief, for she denies even the possibility of a secular Judaism.

In fact, no contemporary American writer has been more outspoken than Ozick in favor of a return to the sources for a Jewish literature that she believes simply cannot be true without the vital connection that joins all Jews through history back to the original covenant that God made with Abraham. For most Jews the world over, despite their own existence among the nations of the Diaspora, the roots of their lives as participants in that covenant are deeply embedded in the land of Zion. Since the establishment of Israel as an independent Jewish state, Jewish-American authors have incorporated it into their fiction, not necessarily as the principal setting but at least as a resonant presence. Limited space permits mentioning only a few examples here.

Transforming history into fiction, Meyer Levin brought out two panoramic novels in the 1970s, *The Settlers* and *The Harvest*, dealing with the problems of emigration from Europe, settlement in Palestine, and finally the establishment of Israeli independence. Many of Nissenson's stories, as mentioned earlier, are set in Israel, and in *The Counterlife*, possibly Philip Roth's strongest novel to date, the scenes of argument among Israelis themselves over which side has the best solution to the Jewish-Arab dilemma are among his best. From these monologues and dialogues alone, it would be difficult to tell where Roth himself stands on the issue. An altogether different approach to the use of Israel as a setting for fiction occurs in E[sther] M[asserman] Broner's novel *A Weave of Women*, where a minyan of ten international women gather to reconstitute Jewish history from a feminist perspective.

Broner's novel exemplifies the fact that over the past three to four decades women authors have been increasingly visible as contributors to the rapidly expanding canon of Jewish-American fiction. A glance through the list of subjects in the table of contents to the volume in hand testifies to their major auctorial role in contemporary Jewish letters. Although not all of them are represented in this collection, Tillie Olsen, Susan Fromberg Schaeffer, Norma Rosen, Lynn Sharon Schwartz, Cynthia Ozick, Anne Roiphe, Joanne Greenberg (Hannah Green), and Grace Paley, some already named in this Introduction with examples of their fiction, are among those authors whose work has been receiving justifiable praise from a wide reading public. Olsen's *Tell Me a Riddle* and her later *Silences* assert the rights to be free of oppression and to be heard, but if she expresses this insistence forcefully, she also does it without hostility. Paley's feminism, too, is assertive, even defiant at times, though she writes as she speaks, manifesting a strong commitment not only to women but to humanity. Yet in her life as in her stories she recognizes the special value to be gained from a community of women offering mutual support. Although she often speaks through one of her central figures, Faith Darwin, Paley acknowledges that their views may be similar, but each is her own person.

As often understated as not, on the order of Gertrude Stein's *Three Lives*, the suffering of Paley's female characters reflects the agony induced by externally imposed suppression and by mental and physical abuse. The characters in her stories are ethnically diverse, and only the older Jewish generation in them has adhered to traditions of *yidishkayt*. Among the younger Jewish women, like Faith herself, Judaism seems more a memory than a vital link to the past. The same is not true, however, among many of Paley's contemporaries in whose fiction serious attempts to regain history are being made. As early as only one year after the war, for example, Jo Sinclair brought out *Wasteland*, her prize-winning novel on the life of Jake Braunowitz, who bitterly rejects his Jewish past, anglicizes his name to John Brown, and after a long ordeal returns to Judaism with his original name restored. In a magnificent novel that he himself called "intensely Jewish,"[8] *The Stolen Jew*, Jay Neugeboren's hero, Nathan Malkin, also returns to accept his responsibility to family, memory, and the Jewish people.

With this theme of rejection and return in mind, one might say that in earlier Jewish-American fiction in which identity is a major issue among the immigrants, as it often is, the question raised is "Am I a Jew or an American?" In the postwar novels, however, it has changed to "What kind of a Jew am I?," or "Am I a Jew at all?" In her first novel, *Joy to Levine!*, Norma Rosen portrayed a *shlemiel* who is fearful of marrying outside the faith, but enjoying a stroke of unusual luck, he discovers that his destined one with an Italian-sounding name is Jewish after all. Two decades later in *At the Center*, she dealt more seriously with rejection and return, especially regarding Hannah's return to the Hasidic community she had left.

As S. Lillian Kremer has recently observed, much contemporary Jewish-American fiction is Jewish "in its moral insistence and its reference to Jewish texts."[9] Of course, "moral insistence" has long been a central mission of Jewish writing, but her perception that many current authors have returned to Hebrew

Scripture and commentary from a detached concern with their Jewish heritage points to a dramatic change recently in Jewish values among the fiction writers, one that surely reflects a similar restoration in the heretofore secularized members of the Jewish community itself. In a whimsical story dealing with this desire for acquaintance—not necessarily reacquaintance—with their textual heritage, for instance, the male characters in Joanne Greenberg's "Things in Their Season" become so disturbed over their aging rabbi's decision to end his Talmud sessions that they conspire to convert time into a commodity and steal it for him to extend his years of teaching.

But the contemporary author who has done most to bring an awareness of Hebrew texts not only to the larger Jewish community but to a vast Christian readership as well is surely Chaim Potok, whose novels on particularly Jewish themes introduce conflicts among different groups of believers, each adhering to books, interpretations, and patterns of behavior that in some cases allow for little or no compromise. In Potok's fiction, ideas come to life in such a way that the ancient confronts the modern, the traditional opposes the mystical, the books of faith conflict with those of the secular world, and so forth. In his masterful fifth novel, *The Book of Lights*, Potok subtly employed light imagery based on Jewish mystical texts to enrich and deepen his fictionalized account of Gershon Loran's rabbinical training and practice amid the religious conflicts between traditional talmudic study and mystical revelation, and between holy and profane light, especially that created by nuclear bombs.

Gershon's intensity as a student and chaplain in Korea resembles that of the protagonists in Potok's earlier four novels. All go through a period of uncertainty and severe alienation, though in each case Potok brings the issue to some manner of favorable resolution. Such alienation, whether self-imposed or provoked by external circumstances, is a common theme in much postwar fiction. It is central in Philip Roth's work from his early *Goodbye, Columbus* and the stories published with it in that first volume through most if not all of his later fiction. Portnoy, Kepesch, Zuckerman, and other characters in his work are isolated souls regardless of their rampant sexual activities and strange, often perverse, social relationships. Whereas in Roth's fiction such isolation always has its grotesque comic aspects, among other authors it is rendered as a dreadful, frightening experience, such as those suffered by Wallant's pawnbroker and Bellow's Tommy Wilhelm in *Seize the Day*.

J. D. Salinger's Franny dwells in an extended coma, and almost a decade after the publication of "Franny" in 1955, Joanne Greenberg's popular *I Never Promised You a Rose Garden* portrays Deborah Blau living in two altogether separate and incompatible worlds, the material one of her family and the mental hospital in which she is institutionalized, and the other in her imagination. Each is frightening as it attempts to pull her away from the other until she is finally restored to psychological integrity. Throughout his writing career, Bernard Malamud, too, often turned to the theme of alienation, as is evident in such early stories as "The Mourners" and "The Magic Barrel." Nowhere in his canon is this theme more striking, however, than in his final and most pessimistic novel, the futuristic *God's Grace*, in which only one human survivor exists in a world that has passed through nearly total nuclear destruction. Another type of alienation occurs in the fractured mother-daughter relationship of Anne Roiphe's *Lovingkindness*, which was also published in the 1980s. Despite setbacks, a tentative reconciliation is suggested near the conclusion.

In earlier paragraphs, including but not limited to those immediately preceding, I introduced a number of novels in which characters exist in a psychologically divided state. Other well-known works not yet mentioned but that present variations on the same problem are Bellow's second novel, *The Victim*; Roth's "Eli the Fanatic"; Ozick's "The Pagan Rabbi"; Levin's *The Fanatic*; Doctorow's brilliant *The Book of Daniel*, undoubtedly his finest work to date; and Schaeffer's *The Madness of a Seduced Woman*. The neurotic, in some cases psychotic, states of mind suffered by the principal figures and others in much of this fiction, as in Roth's novels published over roughly the past two decades, manifest distinctive characteristics that Sander L. Gilman has identified with Jewish self-hatred.

According to Gilman, when Jews are disturbed and feeling alienated from being categorized as outsiders, they respond to their consequent anxiety over such marginalization by projecting it onto fellow Jews and thus externalizing it. Struggling to become what they are not and cannot ever be, that is, members of the majority society that distinguishes them unfavorably, Jews only confirm what they are in the eyes of that majority. Simultaneously, they turn hostile toward other Jews, whom they see through their own imagined identity with the majority as the majority themselves do. In other words, their view of other Jews is but a projected unfavorable self-image.[10]

Among Gilman's profuse illustrations of Jewish self-hatred, historic and contemporary, his most intricate and complex analysis of modern fiction occurs in his explanation of Roth's Zuckerman novels, especially the *Zuckerman Bound* trilogy, completed in 1983. His penetrating analysis is difficult to follow at times, but it is persuasive, and through illuminating Roth's fiction from the perspective of Jewish self-hatred, Gilman casts light over and into the novels and stories of many other Jewish-American authors as well, particularly during the postwar period.[11]

Roth's work since *My Life as a Man* (1974) has been discussed by many of his critics with special attention given to his apparent use of postmodernist techniques because of the complications and uncertainties he introduces through manipulating his narrative point of view. If, as Gilman proposed, however, the manipulation is not simply indicative of an aesthetically complicated and purposely ambiguous methodology, but serves instead as a meticulously constructed system by which conflictive inner Jewish voices are traced through the author's own consciousness to expose rather than conceal his struggle for a satisfactory Jewish identity, then Roth is more clearly a Jewish writer and his novels more clearly Jewish in content than he would have us believe.

Be that as it may, Roth's fiction cannot be separated from postmodernist aims and methods. In such recent works as *Deception* and *Operation Shylock*, both of the 1990s, unidentifiable conversationalists in the one and a confusing doppelgänger in the other are devices by which he purposely obfuscates the narrative point of view and thus leaves readers to flounder among understandings and misunderstandings of their own. Although Doctorow, Cohen, and Neugeboren, among other Jewish-American authors of the period, had gained various special effects through their manipulation of narrative perspective in earlier years, Roth's method in these novels leads to greater uncertainty of meaning beyond the level of craftsmanship and technique.

Moreover, Roth, like other Jewish-American novelists, especially in the 1970s and after, has turned attention in his work to the theme of writing about writing. This idea is hardly a new one, but in recent years, again through the use of postmodernist methods, it has been developed in different ways. Malamud's *Dubin's Lives*, Doctorow's *Lives of the Poets*, Roth's Zuckerman novels, Paley's "A Conversation with My Father," Neugeboren's *The Stolen Jew*, and Ozick's *The Messiah of Stockholm* are all works in which writers are reflectively engaged either in discussing or writing about literary art, and particularly, through unmistakable personae, their own.

S. Lillian Kremer sees "a vibrant, flourishing" Jewish-American literature in existence today, a "renaissance" of Jewish writing in the United States as we rapidly approach the twenty-first century.[12] *Contemporary Jewish-American Novelists: A Bio-Critical Sourcebook* confirms her glowing assessment of the fiction being written and published by Jewish-American authors. Nor is this fiction all of a kind. Indeed, the diversity in both form and content of fiction brought out over the past half century precludes reductive categorization beyond a few immediately evident truths.

First, the overpowering facts of the Shoah and Israel's independence as a Jewish state resonate through much of the writing. Second, the identity theme that had been prominent in Jewish-American novels and stories since before the turn of the last century is still a major concern, though in the more recent period one's status as an American is no longer a question, but only one's status as a Jew. Third, the uncertainty over one's sense of Jewish *being*—of either retaining a vital connection not only to covenantal Judaism but also to the traditions of *yidishkayt* or of detaching oneself from this presumed burden of the past and declaring sovereignty in a secular culture—has made alienation and psychological instability prominent themes in postwar fiction by Jewish Americans. Fourth and finally, the entry of many outstanding women authors as contributors to the Jewish-American canon in a field heretofore dominated by men has sensitized readers to new ways of understanding both relations and divisions within the Jewish community and, no less important, of facing the responsibilities of their own role within it as well. This all augurs well for Jewish-American fiction in the century soon to come.

NOTES

1. Sanford Pinsker, *Jewish-American Fiction, 1917–1987* (New York: Twayne, 1992), 105.

2. Saul Bellow, "On Jewish Storytelling," in *What Is Jewish Literature?*, ed. Hana Wirth-Nesher (Philadelphia: Jewish Publication Society, 1994), 15.

3. Cynthia Ozick, "America: Toward Yavneh," in *What Is Jewish Literature?*, 25, 28.

4. Robert Alter, "Jewish Dreams and Nightmares," in *What Is Jewish Literature?*, 66.

5. Richard J. Fein, "Jewish Fiction in America," *Judaism* 24 (Fall 1975): 407. Quoted in Bonnie K. Lyons, "American Jewish Fiction since 1945," in *Handbook of American-Jewish Literature: An Analytical Guide to Topics, Themes, and Sources*, ed. Lewis Fried (Westport, Conn.: Greenwood Press, 1988), 2.

6. Lyons, "American Jewish Fiction since 1945," 64.

7. Quoted by Irving Malin in *Jews and Americans* (Carbondale and Edwardsville: Southern Illinois University Press, 1965), 176.

8. Quoted by Cordelia Candelaria, "Jay Neugeboren," in *Twentieth-Century American-Jewish Fiction Writers*, ed. Daniel Walden, vol. 28 of *Dictionary of Literary Biography* (Detroit: Gale Research, 1984), 187.

9. S. Lillian Kremer, "Post-alienation: Recent Directions in Jewish-American Literature," *Contemporary Literature* 34:3 (Fall 1993): 571.

10. Sander L. Gilman, *Jewish Self-Hatred: Anti-Semitism and the Hidden Language of the Jews* (Baltimore: Johns Hopkins University Press, 1986), 11–12.

11. Ibid., 354–60.

12. Kremer, "Post-alienation," 589.

WALTER ABISH   (1931–   )

Leonard Orr

BIOGRAPHY

Walter Abish's life reads like an imaginative novelist's work of fiction. He was born in Vienna, Austria, on December 24, 1931, the son of a businessman. Before the end of the decade, the Abish family had managed to escape to Shanghai, where they spent the war years in a curious limbo of community exile, distrust in the complacent acceptance of permanence and solidity, and a fascination with language. Abish repeatedly turns to this Shanghai period in his autobiographical statements and "self-interviews."

As with Roland Barthes's reading of Japan in *Empire of Signs* as a semiotically generative land filled with signifiers with no signifieds, so Abish was stunned, bewildered, confused, and entranced by Shanghai. There was tremendous violence and brutality that remained "invisible" simply because the middle and upper classes, and Abish's own exiled community, learned not to see it. Abish has remarked that his "reluctance to employ straightforward explanatory action in my work stems in part from growing up in a world that was bewildering in its profusion of stylized drama, a drama that remained forever highly elusive" (quoted in Klinkowitz, *The Life of Fiction*, 70). The wartime refugees in Shanghai did not assimilate at all into Chinese life or even do more than maintain the uncomprehending distance of the tourist. Abish attended an English-language school where China was not mentioned, read indiscriminately in three lending libraries, and noted how the Europeans, though cut off, usually permanently, from their native lands, maintained all their old habits and rituals, all the social hierarchies, as if they were still in their own land.

After the war, Abish made his way to the new nation of Israel and served in the Tank Corps in the Israeli Defense Forces. "I was crossing the parade ground in Ramle during my second year in the Tank Corps when quite suddenly the idea of becoming a writer flashed through my mind. A moment of pure exhilaration" (Abish, "The Writer-to-Be," 112). But he took many years to develop as a writer and meanwhile studied architecture and urban planning. His life seems often to have followed skewed or unpredictable paths in much the same manner as his fictional characters. It is hard to say how reliably we should see his many reminiscences about these early days. For example, Abish mentioned that while in Israel he entered into a marriage of convenience:

[H]er convenience, since as a married woman she would not have to serve in the army and postpone her intention to study law. . . . The awareness of what I had done intensified and heightened my "impression of living." I chose to interpret my impulsive act as a poetic gesture. Arrabal defined a poet as someone who doesn't necessarily write poetry, but was a terrorist or provocateur. . . . Am I being quite truthful? Am I being carried away by the text? Am I permitting the theory that a love affair represents the ideal first text-to-be to distort what actually took place? (Abish, "The Writer-to-Be," 111)

Abish moved to the United States and became an American citizen in 1960. He soon began publishing in the sort of small and experimental literary magazines in which his work still appears (*Extensions, Fiction, New Directions in Prose and Poetry, Conjunctions, TriQuarterly, Transatlantic Review*, and so on). He married a sculptress, Cecile Abish (who also supplies photographs for several of his books), taught at Columbia University for ten years, was one of the editors of both *Fiction* and *Conjunctions*, participated in the Fiction Collective anthologies, and so became identified with the avant-garde fiction writers of the period, Donald Barthelme, Robert Coover, Ronald Sukenick, and Gilbert Sorrentino. He published a collection of poems, *Duel Site* (1970), two collections of stories, *Minds Meet* (1975) and *In the Future Perfect* (1977), and three novels, *Alphabetical Africa* (1974), *How German Is It* (1980), and *Eclipse Fever* (1993), along with the unclassifiable prose experiment *99: The New Meaning* (1990). He has received a number of major awards, including the Guggenheim Fellowship, the PEN/Faulkner Award for the Most Distinguished Work of American Fiction (1980, for *How German Is It*), and a MacArthur Prize Fellowship.

MAJOR WORKS AND THEMES

Prior to *How German Is It*, Abish's fiction is both cerebral and technically challenging, often focusing on clashes between one illusion and another, or on the idea that things are very different in reality than they appear on the surface. Jerry Varsava traced this to Abish's wartime experiences: "Unknown to him, there lurked below Vienna's surface decorum, concealed by the refinement and prosperity of a former imperial center, a most virulent ethnoracial hate. And how did such a world appear to a boy of seven or eight? Life, Abish tells us, was very much an affair of surfaces for him, a mistaking of the *apparent* for the *real*. Reassured by the props of his childhood—favorite toys, a comfortable home, a supportive family—Abish viewed life as a harmonious arrangement of people and objects'' (295).

Abish's early works are experimental in the manner of European and Latin American fabulists (such as Jorge Luis Borges, Juan José Arreola, Raymond Roussel, and Henri Michaux) and the writers of constrained and generative forms such as the Oulipo writers Raymond Queneau and Georges Perec or the *nouveaux romanciers*, particularly Alain Robbe-Grillet. In his first novel, *Alphabetical Africa*, Abish employs the technique of lipogrammatism, a form of authorial self-constraint in which the author decides arbitrarily to avoid the use of one or more letters (so Oulipo writer Georges Perec has written an entire mystery novel, *La Disparition*, without the use of the letter *e*, the most common letter in French as it is in English). *Alphabetical Africa* has fifty-two chapters titled with letters in order from A to Z, then Z to A. All of the words in chapter ''A'' start with the letter *a* (''Are all archaeologists arrogant Aristotelians, asks author, as Angolans abduct Alva. Adieu Alva. Arrivederci''), chapter ''B'' admits words that start with either *a* or *b*, and so on. Each chapter adds the use of one letter, so that the prose becomes increasingly free of constraint and reads more like ''normal prose.'' But after the double *z* chapters in the middle of the novel, the process is reversed: the use of one letter is removed with each chapter, until the last chapter is once again made up only of words that start with *a*.

What seems at first to be merely a mechanical and pointless exercise can soon be seen to be a humorous, reflexive, and generative device, at least in Abish's hands. Each new letter admitted into use unleashes new plot and character potentials. If the ''A'' chapter predisposes the plot toward African armies advancing, annihilating antelopes, alligators, and ants, if it means that the plot will have characters named Alex, Alva, Allen, and Albert and have its ostensible setting in Angola, the ''F'' chapter predisposes the novel toward French, flags, flying, the Fulani, and the introduction of a character named Ferdinand (''Ferdinand, another African freak, flies Eastern frequently, first class, . . . forgetting French flag, forgetting everything but decadent French entrees, fried frogs, for example.''). It is not until the ninth chapter that the first person can be used, and we are introduced to a first-person narrator writing a book about Africa, constructing countries and characters like Alva.

Alphabetical Africa also dislocates the reader by the postmodern technique described by Brian McHale as misattribution in zone construction (47–48). Abish's Africa has some of the qualities of the actual Africa, enough to seem to set it within the everyday world (reminders of French colonialism, jungles, and tribes). At the same time, Abish's Chad has a coastline and so clashes with the reader's understanding of the world. The constraints have led to the generation of the plot, countries, and characters, and the collaboration and anticipation of the involved reader is needed for this to work.

Abish's short stories show a variety of innovations and employ the same sly humor as *Alphabetical Africa*. In "Minds Meet," the theme is messages missent and misunderstood. The Chappe brothers develop a system of semaphore signals on tall masts on rooftops ("in this form 192 signals could be sent simultaneously, although 192 signals were a bit much for a man to absorb at one time"). They are commissioned by Napoleon to send to the Dutch the message "Is there any other way to live?" Tzar Nicholas I wanted to build a series of towers encircling the world and reaching into the pre-Columbian pyramids because of his hopeless romanticism about the Mayans ("though it is doubtful to this day whether he could pronounce the word 'Tlahuizcalpentecutli' "). The story is broken into small sections, each with thematic headings ("Taken Aback by the Message," "The Abandoned Message," "Abashed While Receiving the Message," "The Abbreviated Message," and so on). In "This Is Not a Film This Is a Precise Act of Disbelief," the Godard-like film director Michel Bontemps is gathering information centering on "the familiar" in the town of South Tug from the Ite family about the Mall they developed. In "The Istanbul Papers," an American Consulate employee who is a scholar of Mao and medieval Latin texts and an old friend of Jack Kennedy and Norman Mailer from Harvard days falls in love with a woman who claims to be Hitler's daughter, and he can't understand "Norman's" hostility to this idea ("Some people can't seem to rid themselves of all that old film footage of World War II").

But Abish's most important book to date, and the one most germane to this guide, is *How German Is It/Wie Deutsch Ist Es*. If many of Abish's works can be slighted by those who do not see the importance of postmodernist "game playing," this novel utilizes many of the same concerns and techniques of narrative fragmentation and foregrounding of language to make a solid and serious confrontation with the Holocaust, with national stereotyping, and with attempts to repress both the memory and the recognition of atrocity.

The difficult and critically admired German novelist Ulrich Hargenau returns after a long period in Paris to his hometown of Brumholdstein, but the return to Germany is a return to "the edge of forgetfulness," as the first section is titled, a place where guilt, complicity, and collaboration in the concentration camps has been repressed in a massively organized attempt at a "state of the forgetting of being" (Martin Heidegger's *Seinsvergessenheit*). This is symbolized by the town of Brumholdstein itself, named after the still-alive and much-honored philosopher Brumhold (a Nazi sympathizer, based on Heidegger, not allowed to teach during the Allied Occupation and Denazification Program). The new name of the town conceals that of Durst, the old name unfortunately associated with death camps and forced labor, and Brumholdstein is even built over the ruins of Durst to eradicate the Nazi past completely. The emphasis now, as the mayor and other boosters of the town's image argue, must be on the New Germany, freed from the messiness of history. The mayor prefers the works of the popular novelist Bernard Feig to those of the angst-ridden Ulrich Hargenau. "His novels, the mayor said, are not immersed in the past, and the characters in his books are all happily free of that all too familiar obsession with the 1940–45 period of our life. Great applause'' (82).

The New Germany is that of the economic miracle, of the Mercedes and the Autobahn, of leather Euro-fashions and multinational corporations. It is embodied by the beautiful couple Egon and Gisela in their tight-fitting, black leather clothes on the cover of a *People*-type magazine. As the omniscient narrator notes, ''It is pleasant to contemplate . . . this attractive couple, especially knowing there is no overwhelming reason to suspect or doubt their political affiliation (they are *echt Deutsch*).'' But no amount of change and renaming and rebuilding can actually cover the past fully enough; it keeps reasserting itself.

Ulrich's father (Ulrich von Hargenau, Sr.) was executed after becoming involved in the 1944 attempt to assassinate Hitler. Ulrich's ex-wife, Paula, is currently involved with antigovernment terrorists (they bomb post offices and drawbridges). When workers attempt to repair a sewerpipe below the streets downtown, they discover a mass grave, bringing unpleasant world attention to the small town. The old family servant of the Hargenaus, the waiter Franz, insistently takes every opportunity to address the Hargenaus with their prewar *von* restored to their name. Franz is building a matchstick model of the camp at Durst, and when he seeks the plans, he is rushed out of the public library.

The brilliance of the omniscient third-person narrator undercutting everything related to the New Germany by constant reference to the Nazi years makes every set of innocent questions seem like the interrogation of prisoners. Every attempt to honor Brumhold recalls his collaboration (''it was only five minutes brisk walk to the university, where old Brumhold was still teaching philosophy after an enforced period of idleness, the result of too many speeches in the '30s and early '40s, speeches that dealt with the citizen's responsibilities to the New Order''). How German is the German language? ''Has it not once again, by brushing against so many foreign substances, so many foreign languages and experiences, acquired foreign impurities?'' The refrain of ''a glorious German summer'' combines the present summer of the story with the summer of 1944 when Hargenau's father was executed (''What was the summer of 1944 like? Active. Certainly, active.''). *How German Is It* is a powerful and chilling book about the Holocaust, about memory and forgetting, about Germany, and about the desire to repress. It has affinities with the fiction of Israeli novelist Aharon Appelfeld (especially *Badenheim 1939*).

CRITICAL RECEPTION

Because Walter Abish is a writer of experimental, highly allusive, innovative texts, his work has not engendered much of a response in the popular press, and reaching a mass readership does not seem to have been Abish's goal. Except for his most recent book, *Eclipse Fever*, published by Knopf, his books were all published by New Directions and smaller presses (Burning Deck and Tibor de Nagy Editions). Despite this marginal place in the marketing of contemporary fiction, Abish's work has always been very positively received by other well-known experimental writers. Richard Howard hailed *Alphabetical Africa* in the *New York Times Book Review*, focusing on the foregrounded language as carrying the emotional charge of erotic obsession (19), and John Updike aptly noted in the *New Yorker* that calling the book " 'a masterpiece of its kind' does not seem too strong an accolade for a book apt to be the only one of its kind" (112).

How German Is It garnered a great many enthusiastic reviews; it was seen at once as a turning point for Abish's writing, his finest and most accessible book, and the one most connected to history and serious debate. Beyond the reviews and the PEN/Faulkner Award, beyond the MacArthur Prize Fellowship, a number of scholarly, critical essays were devoted to the novel (see the articles of Saalmann, van Delden, Varsava, and Wotipka; especially interesting are the responses by German critics such as Milich and Schopp). It is clear that Abish's reputation will grow and he will be more clearly seen as a major American writer.

BIBLIOGRAPHY

Works by Walter Abish

Duel Site. New York: Tibor de Nagy Editions, 1970.
Alphabetical Africa. New York: New Directions, 1974.
Minds Meet. New York: New Directions, 1975.
In the Future Perfect. New York: New Directions, 1977.
"Self-Portrait." In *Individuals: Post-Movement Art in America*, ed. Alan Sondheim. NY: Dutton, 1977, 1–25.
How German Is It. New York: New Directions, 1980.
"The Writer-to-Be: An Impression of Living." *SubStance* 27 (1980): 104–14.
"Wie Deutsch Ist Es" (interview with Sylvere Lotringer). *Semiotext(e)* 4 (1982): 160–78.
"The Fall of Summer." *Conjunctions* 7 (1985): 110–41.
"Just When We Believe Everything Has Changed." *Conjunctions* 8 (1985): 125–31.
99: The New Meaning. Providence, RI: Burning Deck Press, 1990.
Eclipse Fever. New York: Knopf, 1993.

Studies of Walter Abish

Arias-Mission, Alain. "The Puzzle of Walter Abish: *In the Future Perfect*." *SubStance* 27 (1980): 115–24.
Butler, Christopher. "Scepticism and Experimental Fiction." *Essays in Criticism* 36 (1986): 47–67.
———. "Walter Abish and the Questioning of the Reader." In *Facing Texts: Encounters between Contemporary Writers and Critics*, ed. Heide Ziegler. Durham, NC: Duke University Press, 1988, 168–85.
Durand, Regis. "The Disposition of the Familiar (Walter Abish)." In *Representation and*

Performance in Postmodern Fiction. ed. Maurice Couturier. Montpellier: Delta, 1983, 73–83.

Howard, Richard. Review of *Alphabetical Africa, New York Times Book Review*, Dec. 29, 1974, 19.

Klinkowitz, Jerome. "Experimental Realism." In *Postmodern Fiction: A Bio-Bibliographical Guide*, ed. Larry McCaffery. Westport, Conn.: Greenwood Press, 1986, 63–77.

———. *The Life of Fiction.* Urbana: University of Illinois Press, 1977, 59–71.

———. *The Self-Apparent Word: Fiction as Language/Language as Fiction.* Carbondale: Southern Illinois University Press, 1984.

———. "Walter Abish and the Surfaces of Life." The *Georgia Review* 35 (1981): 416–20.

Martin, Richard. "Walter Abish's Fictions: Perfect Unfamiliarity, Familiar Imperfection." *Journal of American Studies* 17 (August 1983): 229–41.

McHale, Brian. *Postmodernist Fiction.* London: Routledge, 1987.

Milich, Klaus J. "Lekture der fremden Zeichen: Walter Abishs Literarisierung der Wahrnehmung im intertextuellen Diskurs mit der postmodernen Anthropologie." *Amerikastudien/American Studies* 38:2 (1993): 181–202.

Saalmann, Dieter. "Walter Abish's *How German Is It*: Language and the Crisis of Human Behavior." *Critique: Studies in Modern Fiction* 26 (1985): 105–21.

Schirato, Anthony. "Comic Politics and Politics of the Comic: Walter Abish's *Alphabetical Africa.*" *Critique: Studies in Contemporary Fiction* 33:2 (Winter 1992): 133–44.

Schopp, Joseph. "Das Bilderbuch-Deutschland des Walter Abish oder: Vom Beunruhigungswert literarischer Stereotypen." *Amerikastudien/American Studies* 31:4 (1986): 441–52.

Siegle, Robert. "On the Subject of Walter Abish and Kathy Acker." *Literature and Psychology* 33:3–4 (1987): 38–58.

Updike, John. Review of *Alphabetical Africa. New Yorker.* March 24, 1974, 112.

van Delden, Maarten. "An Interview with Walter Abish on *Eclipse Fever.*" *Annals of Scholarship* 10:3–4 (1993): 381–91.

———. "Walter Abish's *How German Is It*: Postmodernism and the Past." *Salmagundi* 85–86 (Winter–Spring 1990): 172–94.

Varsava, Jerry A. "Walter Abish and the Topographies of Desire." *Thought* 62 (September 1987): 295–310.

Wotipka, Paul. "Walter Abish's *How German Is It*: Representing the Postmodern." *Contemporary Literature* 30:4 (Winter 1989): 503–17.

MAX APPLE (1941–)

Jerome Klinkowitz

BIOGRAPHY

Born in Grand Rapids, Michigan on October 22, 1941, Max Apple was raised by his grandparents in traditions more appropriate to a writer such as Isaac Babel. "Grand Rapids, Mich., in the 1950's was not an East European ghetto," Apple explained to readers of the *New York Times Book Review* in 1981, "although my grandma did her best to blur the distinctions." In subsequent essays and interviews, this appealingly comic writer has clarified what such an upbringing meant. For one thing, it meant learning Yiddish before English. For another, it involved "observing all those strange cultural things that I am still amazed at," as Apple told critic Larry McCaffery in 1987: "My family was always fascinated by what the *goyim* did. *Goyim* were marvelous creatures to me— we'd go to the supermarket and watch *goyim* shop, watch them eat, all sorts of things. The analogy that comes to mind is the way Isaac Babel describes the Cossacks." Yet most important in Max Apple's background is that all this observing took place not in early twentieth-century Russia, Poland, or Lithuania, but in an America gearing up for a decidedly different style of revolution in the 1960s. This latter decade Apple experienced as a graduate student in English literature (he received his Ph.D. in 1970).

Not that the author of *The Oranging of America* (1976), *Zip* (1978), and other works that have helped define how recent culture has changed wanted to be an academically directed writer. Getting his doctorate, he told Larry McCaffery, "was just something I did that would maybe get me a job" (36), which is how his unexceptional university career developed. Unlike some innovative fiction writers with doctorates (Ronald Sukenick, Raymond Federman, or William H. Gass), Apple has not written extensive analyses and commentaries. Unlike other widely published writers (such as John Barth and Clarence Major), he did not make career improvements by seeking better jobs: after an initial appointment in 1970–1971 at Reed College in Portland, Oregon, he accepted an assistant professorship at Rice University in Houston, Texas, where he climbed the traditional ladder at the customary pace of promotion to associate professor (1976) and full professor (1980). As opposed to the style of writers Richard Kostelanetz has described as ''grants-mongerers,'' Apple has never exploited the feeding trough of government and private foundation support. Like his grandfather, a fervently antiunion baker who never earned a good living until he retired, Max Apple has succeeded by mastering the slow grind of good teaching and responsible publishing, qualities that critics have distinguished in his work.

MAJOR WORKS AND THEMES

There is a gently instructive quality to Max Apple's fiction at its best. As one who has experienced history from both sides of the fence—having watched mainstream events as an outsider and then having become part of a dominant new current himself—he has been able to recast the evolving nature of American life in terms that are at once fantastic and realistic. In his fiction, ''Howard Johnson'' is not a motel but a living person; ''Disneyland'' is less an amusement park than an actual nation that can make treaties with Taiwan; and Fidel Castro is not just a revolutionist and a dictator but a sports enthusiast who quite literally pitches in to help an old White Sox player and (in the novel *Zip*) backs a prizefighter as a way of publicizing revolutionary politics in America. To those who would object that such reconstructions of fact exceed credibility, Apple is always ready with an even more ridiculous example, this time taken from actual history. Indeed, one of his major strategies is to blur the distinctions between fact and fantasy as a way of reminding readers that everything is ultimately made up.

Stories collected in *The Oranging of America* advance Apple's overtly fictive strategy. His title piece features Howard Johnson as an icon of popular culture, a man who revolutionizes motor travel by divining exactly where people need to stop and rest. As a reminder to readers that real people are not involved, the author introduces another supposedly real person, the poet Robert Frost, who serves as the inspiration for painting these pioneering motels orange. A similar tactic motivates ''My Real Estate,'' in which a very real Houston Astrodome is transformed, in subtle steps, into a model city that might otherwise be expected to exist only on another planet. With ''Inside Norman Mailer,'' Apple portrays himself as what he is, a young, untested author whose first efforts will be measured against the heavyweights of our time. But to make a story of it, he casts this confrontation as a boxing match, all of which makes eminent sense once the mythical author of *The Naked and the Dead* agrees to take him on. ''You have given dignity to my challenge,'' Apple writes; ''like a sovereign government you have recognized my hopeless revolutionary state and turned me, in a blink, credible, at least to you, at least where it counts. I slap my fists together and at the bell I meet you for the first time as an equal.''

Prizefighting is a central metaphor in Max Apple's first novel as well. *Zip* is narrated by Ira Goldstein, a young man caught between two cultures. One is his mother's, that of Jewish immigrants from Eastern Europe who still resist easy assimilation into mainstream American culture. The other is his girlfriend's, the politically and sexually radicalized 1960s. To negotiate his way between these two realms, Ira manages the career of a boxer named Jesús who is himself caught up in iconic struggles between Cuban Premier Fidel Castro and the Federal Bureau of Investigation's J. Edgar Hoover. Each side has its stories, many of which inform Ira's life and direct his aspirations. Yet as in the boxing ring, there is an ultimate conflict, one that leaves the narrator with little more than an understanding of how so much human existence is based on the interactions of rituals. Written in the rarely used second person of direct address, *Zip* speaks to fighter Jesús Martinez directly; as a textual record of Ira Goldstein's excuse for all that has gone wrong during their partnership, it encompasses styles of behavior that during the 1960s became virtual realities themselves.

With the short fiction gathered in *Free Agents* (1984), the author takes a step toward postmodern historicity by deliberately comingling autobiography and imagination. ''Free Agents'' itself features his internal organs striking for autonomy, insisting that they and not others should have the right to decide where, if ever, they are to be transplanted. In ''An Offering,'' he turns himself into a publicly held company. Both stories anticipate critical theory of the 1990s, in which the writer textualizes his or her body as a method of expression. Yet in this collection, Max Apple shows that he can be sentimental as well, particularly in the story ''Bridging,'' where a ritual for the transition from Brownies to Girl Scouts allows a widowed father to accept the necessarily altered relationship with his daughter. It is ''Walt and Will,'' however, that indicates the clearest direction in Apple's evolving, for here he is able to take two well-known characters from popular history—the Disney brothers of cartoon and amusement-park fame—and plumb their experiences for the depth of poetic truth.

This method is used even more extensively in Apple's major novel, *The Propheteers* (1987). This narrative takes the commercial history of America and animates it in the characters of its figurehead founders: Walt Disney, Howard Johnson, C. W. Post, and Clarence Birdseye. How a product like Post Grape-Nuts influences behavior is a matter for sociological study, but in terms of personifying American behavior, it fits right in with how certain breakfast-cereal companies decide how people begin their days, just as other corporate concerns direct how these same Americans will most typically spend their vacations. Apple's genius is to bring this semiology to life in both an entertaining and instructive way.

The ultimate test of Max Apple's method is seeing if he can textually objectify his own life. He succeeds with *Roommates* (1994), the book-length story of how his 103-year-old grandfather stabilized the author's family in the face of tragedies dealt with previously in "Bridging." Because it incorporates so much of what Apple had already published as fiction, *Roommates* has been received as a novel; in fact, it qualifies as postmodern autobiography, where the life of the imagination shares equal prominence with the events of history.

CRITICAL RECEPTION

As a writer in the 1970s crafting fictions about the previous decade, Max Apple found himself being celebrated as a satirist and dismissed as a clown. Unhappy with both characterizations, the author proposed a better reading in "On Realism," a brief essay published at the decade's end in the *Nation*. "I am a fiction writer," he insisted to this magazine's literate yet socially committed readership. "I make things up. I stand accused of a quirky imagination." To his dismay, he had to admit that "my publisher sends out a flyer suggesting that my work is zany. Book reviewers have called me crazy. My friends ask me where I get my strange ideas" (117).

To answer these questions and refute such charges, Apple does what comedian Mort Sahl did half a generation before him: he takes the daily newspaper and within its first few pages documents reported events that far exceed the presumed extravagances of his own writing. These events, including such matters of the times as the Shah of Iran househunting in Palm Springs and the People's Republic of China signing a marketing deal with Coca-Cola, are solid evidence that reality is "zanier" than anything in *The Oranging of America*. In a perceptive review of Max Apple's first collection, critic Joe David Bellamy had made the same observation: that the author "creates fabulous fantasies within which few of the laws of nature are suspended except the laws of probability, and for the utterly improbable he makes us grateful" (66).

Apple's reputation among scholars of contemporary American fiction rests on his ability to write without imposing a formal unity on what Alan Wilde has called the "highly prized complexities" that motivate his work. In Wilde's pioneering article from *Contemporary Literature* (Fall 1985), one finds that "Apple's tactics manifest, instead, a very postmodern acceptance and, more, a welcoming of diversity, contradiction, tension, friction, and conflict—a confirmation of these things, moreover, for their own sake and not for the ultimately satisfying unity ('an achieved harmony,' as Cleanth Brooks describes it [in *The Well Wrought Urn*]) they can in theory be made to subserve" (278).

By 1996, with the success of *Roommates* as both the ethical and aesthetic justification of his literary method, Apple could be appreciated as a major writer. It is thus that he appears in Marc Chénetier's definitive study of the era, *Beyond Suspicion: New American Fiction Since 1960* (1996). "In this way," Chénetier established, "the most desperate, the most unremarkable, and the most popular images of American everydayness are given imaginary depth" (86) and allowed to function as new "mythologies," as postmodern theorist Roland Barthes has proposed.

BIBLIOGRAPHY

Works by Max Apple

The Oranging of America and Other Stories. New York: Grossman, 1976.
Zip. New York: Viking, 1978.
"On Realism." *Nation* 228:4 (February 3, 1979): 117.
"My Love Affair with English." *New York Times Book Review*, March 22, 1981, 9, 24–25.
"On Persisting as a Writer." *Michigan Quarterly Review* 21:1 (Winter 1982): 21–25.
Free Agents. New York: Harper and Row, 1984.
The Propheteers. New York: Harper and Row, 1987.
Roommates. New York: Warner, 1994.

Studies of Max Apple

Bellamy, Joe David. *Literary Luxuries: American Writing at the End of the Millennium.* Columbia: University of Missouri Press, 1995.
Chénetier, Marc. *Beyond Suspicion: New American Fiction since 1960.* Philadelphia: University of Pennsylvania Press, 1996.
Glausser, Wayne. "Spots of Meaning: Literary Allusions in Max Apple's 'Vegetable Love.'" *Studies in Short Fiction* 20:4 (Fall 1983): 255–63.
Klinkowitz, Jerome. *Structuring the Void: The Struggle for Subject in Contemporary American Fiction.* Durham, NC: Duke University Press, 1992.
McCaffery, Larry, and Linda Gregory. *Alive and Writing: Interviews with American Authors of the 1980s.* Urbana: University of Illinois Press, 1987.
Wilde, Alan. "Dayanu: Max Apple and the Aesthetics of Sufficiency." *Contemporary Literature* 26 (Fall 1985): 254–85.
———. "Max Apple and the American Nightmare." *Critique: Studies in Contemporary Fiction* 30:1 (Fall 1988): 27–47.

PAUL AUSTER   (1947–)

Martine Chard-Hutchinson

BIOGRAPHY

Paul Auster was born in Newark, New Jersey, on February 3, 1947, in a Jewish family of Russian and Polish origins. The story of his family is one of violence—his grandmother shot her husband—and loss: the fathers are the missing elements that Auster's literary imagination systematically tries to re-create one way or another. His literary fathers then acquire a special dimension; they are called Kafka, Borges, Jabès, and Beckett. At Columbia University, where Auster got his M.A. in 1970, he discovered French poets, whom he translated while writing poems himself. Then he became a merchant seaman, a census taker, and a tutor before going to France, where he stayed from February 1971 to July 1974. There he mostly did translations (Blanchot, Sartre, Mallarmé), but was also a telephone operator for the Paris bureau of the *New York Times* and even the caretaker of a farmhouse in Provence. Back in the United States he wrote articles and went on translating, this time with Lydia Davis, his new wife, who bore him a son, Daniel, in 1977. In a relatively short time came a divorce and almost a renunciation of writing. Yet chance, a major factor of recomposition of both his life and his fiction, intervened three times. The first time was in December 1978, when he was reconciled with the idea of being a writer; the second time was on January 14, 1979, when his father's death miraculously opened up the gates of fiction to him: "In some sense, all the novels I've written have come out of that money my father left me" (*The Art of Hunger*, 295). Finally, in early 1981, he met Siri Hustvedt, a writer herself (*The Blindfold*, 1993), whom he later married; they have a daughter, Sophie, who was born in 1988, and live in Brooklyn.

Facts and fiction seem constantly to overlap with Paul Auster, who indeed often makes novels out of the very facts of life (*Leviathan*, for instance), not to say of his own life; he can even appear in his novels (as in *City of Glass*) or in his movies, much in the Hitchcock manner. For Auster uses autobiographical material as an opportunity to play with images, to renew genres, and to mystify his readers. His fans are mostly French and Japanese since he tends to be regarded as an elitist writer with a European turn of mind by the American reading public in general, though New Yorkers have recently developed a passion for him.

He was awarded two poetry grants by the Ingram Merrill Foundation (1975, 1982) and one by PEN Translation Center in 1977. He also received literary fellowships from the National Endowment for the Arts for poetry in 1979 and for creative writing in 1985. Some of his novels have been nominated for other major awards: *City of Glass* for an Edgar Award for best mystery novel (1986) and *The Locked Room* for a Boston Globe Literary Press Award for fiction. In 1990 he received the Morton Dauwen Zabel Award from the American Academy of Arts and Letters. In France he was awarded the Prix France-Culture de Littérature Etrangère in 1989 and the Prix Médicis Etranger in 1993 for *Leviathan*.

MAJOR WORKS AND THEMES

Jewishness for Paul Auster may appear more metaphorical than literal, and yet all his works—fiction and nonfiction—are concerned with the "difficulty of being Jewish, which is the same as the difficulty of writing" (Edmond Jabès, *The Book of Questions* 36) in a post-Holocaust world. These are the very lines that haunt his essays, which were later collected in *The Art of Hunger* (1982) and in *Ground Work* (1990), and more particularly the beautiful essay about Edmond Jabès called "Book of the Dead" or "Poetry of the Exile," the one he wrote on Paul Celan, or "The Decisive Moment," in which he speaks of Charles Reznikoff's *Testimony* and *Holocaust*.

Like Edmond Jabès, the Jewish poet, his "comrade in solitude," Auster has tried first as a poet and then as a fiction writer to "create a poetics of absence" (*Ground Work*, 189). For him, writing poetry, like translating, requires a slow process of reaching the self in a mineral world from which it was first dug up (*Unearth* [1974]) and then confronted with the translation of the chaotic experience of *Wall Writing* (1976). Like the poem, the self goes through a phase of fragmentation, in *Fragments from Cold* (1977), to the point of despair: "I believe, then, in nothing," in *Facing the Music* (1980). Loss of self, or the paradoxical location of self in "the impossibility of words" ("Interior"), is the theme that haunts his poetic pieces. The poetic voice disintegrates in silence, yet the experience of solitude as the ultimate paradox born out of the seeds contained in "Covenant" ("Something lost / became / something to be found") is the mark of potential rebirth for the persona's self: "Out of solitude, he begins again" ("Disappearances," the eponymous poem that opens the first edition of his poems, *Disappearances: Selected Poems 1970–1979* [1988], and is still to be found in the latest edition, *Ground Work: Selected Poems and Essays 1970–1979* [1990]).

His writings, which are all deeply rooted in the active search for the father in a Kafkaian sense, testify to an evolution from the metaphysical detective story with occasional Jewish undertones to a more tradition-bound novel with more overtly Jewish characters like the rabbi in *Mr Vertigo* (1994), his latest novel. Yet all his characters are submitted to the same type of experience, in which they are confronted with loss and are condemned to eternal wandering before having a chance of being reinitiated to their Jewishness. "He wanders toward the promised land. That is to say: he moves from one place to another, and dreams continually of stopping. And because this desire to stop is what haunts him, is what counts most for him, he does not stop. He wanders. That is to say: without the slightest hope of ever going anywhere" ("Pages for Kafka," in *The Art of Hunger*, 23). Hence the problematical relationship with "New York Babel," and with America, as the impossible re-presentation of the Promised Land. The Jewish self hides behind the masks that the writer keeps creating for the sake of protection and elusiveness, forcing the reader to engage in a game of hide-and-seek.

Strangely enough for a writer playing with masks, Auster's first prose book, *The Invention of Solitude* (1982), looks like an autobiographical essay, but is not, if we are to believe its author: "I don't think of it as an autobiography so much as a meditation about certain questions, using myself as the central character" (*The Art of Hunger*, 266). Its peculiar composition, namely, two books written separately with a gap of about a year, as well as its fragmentary quality, do not contribute to creating the usual mood of revelation. Yet the first book, called *Portrait of an Invisible Man*, which was written in response to his father's death and uses the first person, has very personal, not to say intimate, accents. *The Book of Memory*, the second book, is as personal as the first even though it is written in the third person, a way of exploring the depth of solitude and the interaction of alterity and identity. Right from the beginning, Paul Auster's split literary voice appears to bear the tension of duality: the son and the father, the biblical and the literary doubles, America and Europe. It seeks fusion with other voices and yet retains its singularity as if to defy "the shipwreck of the singular," one of the major obsessions of the book.

From then on, Paul Auster has never ceased to play with mirrors, doppelgängers, and masks. Under the pseudonym of Paul Benjamin he wrote a popular detective novel called *Squeeze Play*, a potboiler reminiscent of Chandler or Hammett with a few personal touches, like the character of Max Klein, a private eye more inclined to paper the walls of his office with engravings of the Tower of Babel than with posters of naked pinups. This atypical private eye, with a smack of metaphysical preoccupations, announced Quinn, the main protagonist of *City of Glass* (1985), Auster's first metaphysical-autobiographical detective novel, which is the first volume of *The New York Trilogy* (1987), the other two being *Ghosts* (1986), a one-act play that was reworked into a piece of prose fiction, and *The Locked Room* (1986). All three were first published separately, but read as a whole, they appear like texts that mirror each other, variations on the same theme, namely, the "question of who is who and whether or not we are who we think we are" (*The Art of Hunger*, 270) and the search for the absent—lost, dead, missing—f/Father. God literally remains a dead letter for Quinn, a dead color in *Ghosts* or a dead historical/literary figure in *The Locked Room*. All literature is a palimpsest, though, and all writers are vampires, as is illustrated by the name of Fanshawe, actually borrowed from Hawthorne's first novel.

Hawthorne is summoned again in the epigraph of Auster's next novel, *In the Country of Last Things* (1987), which deals with the search for a missing brother this time. Like Quinn, Anna Blume wanders through "New York Babel," but here the vision is apocalyptic. Though the fiction is supposed to refer to the near future, it can be read as a chronicle of the twentieth century and of the Holocaust in particular. It has a definite historical basis, with specific references to the Warsaw Ghetto and the siege of Leningrad. "A very difficult book to write," Auster confessed, this is a story of survival, recalling another *Journal* by another Anna, who did not survive; no wonder that here the failure of language is total: "The words get smaller and smaller, so small that they are not even legible anymore" (*In the Country of Last Things*, 183).

With *Moon Palace* (1989), Auster's fiction suddenly became more enjoyable to the American reading public. Less metaphysical? Less metafictional? Less intertextual? Less Jewish? Perhaps more openly American. American history is brought to the fore: first 1492, like the number of books in Uncle Victor's library, like a spiritual testament; then all those historical events that contributed to shaping America's identity, like the war against the Native Americans or the atom bomb or the Vietnam War. The character is called Marco Stanley Fogg; he is the quintessential traveler and a most learned man to boot, who takes care of a blind man in a wheelchair and becomes his biographer. Like Quinn, he has become a bum in search of a missing father, whom he "imagined as a space-traveler who had passed into the fourth dimension and could not find his way back" (*Moon Palace*, 4). The moon, then, is connected with the father figure, that of Victor and his Moon Men, with Moon Palace, whose "magic letters . . . hung there in the darkness like a message from the sky" (*Moon Palace*, 17), and it becomes the protean metaphor of the American spirit of adventure and of the quest for both national and personal origins.

The Music of Chance (1990) begins "with Nashe sitting behind the wheel of a car," exactly where *Moon Palace* ends, with Fogg's car being stolen and his having to continue his journey on foot. Jack Kerouac looms large here, too, and the novel's road-movie quality did not escape the attention of a young movie director named Philip Haas, who was to make a moderately successful movie out of it in 1993. Auster told the story of Jim Nashe, a fireman, the story of an Austerian "hero" bound to measure himself up with loss: his wife left him, he left his daughter with his sister, his father was a blank also until he inherited $200,000 from him, which was a mixed blessing for sure. Once again, as in Auster's life, the central figure of the father appears as the main purveyor of money and of freedom but as an unstable sign of identity. The music of chance is the music of memory, a connection that had long been established in "the Book of Memory," but it is also the music of death, which is poetically described as "an avalanche of whiteness" bound to engulf the hero.

In Auster's eighth novel, *Leviathan* (1992), which he dedicated to his friend Don DeLillo, he dramatizes the confrontation of Peter Aaron, an American Jew (?), alias Paul Auster, with American history, or rather with the dual image of biblical and political chaos, that of Leviathan. The man of chaos is Benjamin Sachs, Peter Aaron's friend, who was born the very day Hiroshima was bombed and dies on July 4, 1990, after becoming a terrorist and bombing the Statue of Liberty. The novel is fraught with historical references and is supposed to explore the question of freedom at the various stages of American history from its origins to the post-Hiroshima age. But it also serves an aesthetic purpose, that of showing that fiction and facts constantly overlap.

Auster's latest novel, *Mr Vertigo* (1994), is radically different from his other books, being a major step in terms of genre and of inspiration, even though it looks like another modern road movie. First, it is a magic tale: "I was twelve years old the first time I walked on water" (*Mr Vertigo*, 3). Then it has overtly Jewish characters like a new Messiah and a rabbi, and Jewish overtones. What is at stake here is not only spiritual initiation, but initiation to flight or, if correctly understood as levitation, initiation to being a Jew. Indeed, Walter Clairborne Rawley will fly. He may have been modeled after Philippe Petit, the French high-wire walker, whose book Auster translated. In the preface to *On the High Wire* Auster said, "The high-wire is an art of solitude, a way of coming to grips with one's life in the darkest, most secret corner of the self. When read carefully, the book is transformed into the story of a quest, an exemplary tale of one man's search for perfection" (*The Art of Hunger*, 255). Whether it is transposed from a true character or not, *Mr Vertigo* is that exemplary tale of man's search for perfection, which (post)modern man will never reach if he discards the Jew in himself, as the cover illustration playing on the juxtaposition of tradition and modernity in the form of a second cover embedded in the first seems to suggest. The designer is no less than Art Spiegelman, Pulitzer Prize–winning author/artist of the graphic novel *Maus*, who has also supervised the adaptation of *City of Glass* into a graphic novel.

Paul Auster's latest contribution to art is the script of *Smoke*, a movie directed by Wayne Wang and featuring William Hurt and Harvey Keitel, among others. It is based on "Augie Wren's Christmas Story," a story he wrote for the *New York Times* (December 25, 1990). The movie is a comedy that deals with storytelling, another word for smoke, or, if we are to believe Paul Auster, "a hymn to the Grand Social(ist) Republic of Brooklyn." Brooklyn is also at the heart of another movie, called *Blue in the Face*, that Wang and Auster have just codirected in the wake—in the curls?—of *Smoke*.

CRITICAL RECEPTION

In general, Paul Auster is very popular with French critics and has been experiencing more and more success in France and in Japan. He has been translated into fifteen languages, a fact that testifies to his world renown. Yet even if he has always been favorably received in New York, he is considered a fringe writer in the United States. However, *The Invention of Solitude* did not go unnoticed in America: "Titles, pictures, quotations, clippings.... Fragments. Literary bits of thought. Old self, new self, self as parent as self. These are items which form a journal . . . which turns out not to be a journal, but a literary evocation of one" (Austin, 23). *The New York Trilogy* has been better received; Dennis Drabelle, referring to *City of Glass*, clearly stated the issue: "In his detectives who degenerate beyond the standard seediness into self-jailing voyeurs and bagpersons in the cramped streets of New York City, Auster has provided a striking vision of contemporary American stasis" (9). Geoffrey O'Brien, speaking of *Ghosts*, praised "this stripped-down generic story" (46), while Stephen Schiff suggested that *The Locked Room* was "a brilliant leap forward" (12). But it seems that *Smoke* is winning Paul Auster new fans and that he is suddenly seen in a different light, praised now for the garrulous fluency of his writing. Even the graphic version of *City of Glass* has been highly acclaimed: "Auster's Bret-Easton-Ellis-with-brains darkness and stripped-down narrative lend themselves superbly to graphic interpretation" (Plages, 70).

BIBLIOGRAPHY

Works by Paul Auster

Poetry

Unearth: Poems, 1970–1972. Weston, CT.: Living Hand Publications, 1974.
Wall Writing: Poems, 1971–1975. Berkeley: The Figures, 1976.
Fragments from Cold. Brewster, N.Y.: Parenthèse, 1977.
Facing the Music. Barrytown, N.Y.: Station Hill Press, 1980.
Disappearances: Selected Poems. Woodstock, N.Y.: Overlook, 1988.
Ground Work: Selected Poems and Essays 1970–1979. London: Faber and Faber, 1990.

Nonfiction, Autobiography, and Essays

White Spaces. Barrytown, N.Y.: Station Hill Press, 1980.
The Art of Hunger. 3 editions: the shorter one, London: Menard Press, 1982; the longer one, Los Angeles: Sun and Moon Press, 1992; the longer one including two essays, "The Death of Sir Walter Raleigh" and "The Red Notebook," New York: Penguin Books, 1993.
The Invention of Solitude. Los Angeles: Sun Press, 1982.

Translations

A Little Anthology of Surrealist Poems. New York: Siamese Banana Press, 1972.

Dupin, Jacques. *Fits and Starts: Selected Poems of Jacques Dupin*. New York: Living Hand, 1974.

With Lydia Davis. Friedlander, Saul, and Mahmoud Hussein. *Arabs and Israelis: A Dialogue*. New York: Holmes and Meier, 1975.

The Uninhabited: Selected Poems of André Du Bouchet. New York: Living Hand, 1976.

With Lydia Davis. Sartre, Jean-Paul. *Life Situations*. New York: Pantheon Books, 1977.

With Lydia Davis. Chesneaux, Jean. *China: The People's Republic, 1949–1976*. New York: Pantheon Books, 1979.

With Lydia Davis. Chesneaux, Jean, and Paul Auster, Lydia Davis and Marie-Claire Bergère. *China from the 1911 Revolution to Liberation*. New York: Pantheon Books, 1979.

Mallarmé, Stéphane. *A Tomb for Anatole*. San Francisco: North Point Press, 1983.

Petit, Philippe. *On the High Wire*. New York: Random House, 1985.

Blanchot, Maurice. *Vicious Circles*. Barrytown, N.Y.: Station Hill Press, 1985.

With Margit Rowell. Miro, Joan. *Selected Writings and Interviews*. Boston: G. K. Hall, 1986.

Novels

City of Glass. Los Angeles: Sun and Moon Press, 1985.

Ghosts. Los Angeles: Sun and Moon Press, 1986.

The Locked Room. Los Angeles: Sun and Moon Press, 1986.

In the Country of Last Things. New York: Viking Penguin, 1987.

The New York Trilogy (composed of *City of Glass, Ghosts, The Locked Room*). London: Faber and Faber, 1987.

Moon Palace. New York: Viking Penguin, 1989.

The Music of Chance. New York: Viking Penguin, 1990.

Leviathan. New York: Viking Penguin, 1992.

Mr Vertigo. London: Faber and Faber, 1994; Paris: Actes Sud, 1994.

Graphic Novel

City of Glass. Adapted by Paul Karasik and David Mazzuchelli. New York: Neon Lit, 1994.

Editor

The Random House Book of Twentieth-Century French Poetry. London: Random House, 1982.

(And translator) Joubert, Joseph. *The Notebooks of Joseph Joubert: A Selection*. San Francisco: North Point Press, 1983.

Screenplays

Smoke, Blue in the Face, The Making of Smoke. London: Faber and Faber, 1995.

Works Cited and Studies of Paul Auster

Austin, Jacqueline. ''The Invention of Solitude.'' *American Book Review* 6:1 November–December 1983): 23.

Barone, Dennis, ed. *Beyond the Red Notebook: Essays on Paul Auster*. Philadelphia: University of Pennsylvania Press, 1995.

Drabelle, Dennis. "Mystery Goes Post-Modern." Review of *City of Glass*. *Book World, Washington Post*, June 15, 1986, 9.

Drenttel, William, ed. *Paul Auster: A Comprehensive Bibliographic Checklist of Published Works, 1968–1994*. New York: Trade and Ltd. Editions, 1994.

Duperray, Annick, ed. *L'Oeuvre de Paul Auster* (collected essays). Paris: Editions Actes Sud, 1995.

Jabés, Edmund. *The Book of Questions*. Hanover, New Hampshire: University Press of New England, 1991.

O'Brien, Geoffrey. "And Then What Happened?" Review of *Ghosts*. *Village Voice* 31: 29 (July 22, 1986): 46.

Plages, Peter, and Yahlin Chang. "Drawing on the Dark Side." Review of *City of Glass*. *Newsweek*, September 5, 1994, 70.

Schiff, Stephen. "Inward Gaze of a Private Eye." Review of *The Locked Room*. *New York Times*, January 4, 1987, 11–12.

JONATHAN BAUMBACH (1933–)

Marilyn Metzcher Smith

BIOGRAPHY

Jonathan Baumbach was born on July 5, 1933, in New York City, where he has lived most of his life. Baumbach earned his A.B. at Brooklyn College (1951–1955) and his M.F.A. at Columbia University (1955–1956). Service in the U.S. Army brought him west to Stanford University, where he gained a Ph.D. in 1961. Baumbach then taught English at Ohio State University, and in 1964, he returned to New York, where he directed the freshman English program and taught at New York University. Since 1972, he has been a professor of English at Brooklyn College, City University of New York.

Since 1966, Baumbach has been on the board of directors for the Teachers and Writers Collaborative, and in 1974, he became a film critic for *Partisan Review*. He is also a member of the National Society of Film Critics and served as chair from 1982 to 1983. Baumbach has received the New Republic Young Writers Award (1958), Yaddo summer grants (1963, 1964, 1965), National Endowment for the Arts Fellowships (1967, 1969), a Guggenheim Fellowship (1978), and an Ingram-Merrill Fellowship (1983) and contributes to periodicals such as *Chicago Review, Esquire, Kenyon Review, Nation, New York Times Book Review, Partisan Review, Saturday Review*, and *TriQuarterly*.

A writer and teacher, Baumbach enjoys not only teaching but also the accompanying financial freedom that allows him to follow his intuition as a writer. When he could not find a publisher for his third novel, Baumbach became frustrated with a commercial publishing industry whose excessive concern with salability impeded the development of new writers and new techniques. In response, Baumbach and several colleagues formed the Fiction Collective in 1974 to publish the innovative fiction rejected by commercial publishers. Baumbach served as a codirector from 1974 until 1978, and he is still on the board of directors. Many of his works since 1974 have been published through the Fiction Collective.

MAJOR WORKS AND THEMES

Jonathan Baumbach's critical study *The Landscape of Nightmare: Studies in the Contemporary American Novel* was based on his doctoral dissertation and published in New York in 1965 and London in 1966. It examines one novel each of nine postwar novelists: *All the King's Men* by Robert Penn Warren, *The Victim* by Saul Bellow, *The Catcher in the Rye* by J. D. Salinger, *Invisible Man* by Ralph Ellison, *Wise Blood* by Flannery O'Connor, *The Assistant* by Bernard Malamud, *Lie Down in Darkness* by William Styron, *The Pawnbroker* by Edward Lewis Wallant, and *Ceremony in Lone Tree* by Wright Morris. All nine illustrate Baumbach's idea that "the modern world is a nightmare, and the best contemporary novelists know it, and tell us what it is like to realize the fact" (McCabe, 704). In the nightmare landscape of the human psyche exist "adamic falls" and "quixotic redemptions," fathers and sons contesting for an impotent power, and minorities drawing on their alienated status in society to produce "a comedy of horrors" (Malin, *American Literature*, 349). Each protagonist "contemplates his own secret spiritual history, his 'exemplary passage from innocence to guilt to redemption' " (McCabe, 704), a redemption defined by self-knowledge (Gossett, 157).

Baumbach's fiction takes that human psyche and its search for redemption through self-knowledge and, through these themes, explores postmodern ideas. The insanity of everyday life and the blurring of boundaries between apparent oppositions such as fantasy and reality, sanity and insanity, and self and other become vital in a world where memories, dreams, perceptions, and pop-culture images merge to form identity.

Baumbach's first novel, *A Man to Conjure With* (1965), presents "an ingenious portrait of a schlemiel-Everyman cracking up" (Resnik, 41). Peter Becker, a middle-aged man attempting to reconcile a failed marriage, tries to find the life he believes himself to have lost, the potential self he was at twenty. But the roots of that lost self are difficult to find as he searches mostly in his dreams, which color his world, allowing Baumbach to explore imagination and its interactions with language and identity. Ultimately, reality shifts into the language of dream (Klinkowitz, "Super Fiction," 181).

The scene darkens with Baumbach's second novel, *What Comes Next* (1968), for if Becker is the "schlemiel-Everyman" trying to recapture his twenty-year-old potential, this novel follows the development of a twenty-year-old madman. Surrounded by the violence of American society during the Vietnam War, Christopher Steiner perceives his reality through nightmarish fantasy, and the merging of the two leads to alienation, paranoia, and more violence as Steiner transforms from victim into victimizer. That all individuals and society itself create this violence is illustrated in Steiner's double. Originally, Steiner seems the opposite of his history tutor, professor Curtis Parks, but the two begin to merge through desire for Rosemary (another of Parks's students), their alienation in general, and their eventual destructive and self-destructive acts. Thus Baumbach portrays his protagonist's madness as ordinary, even inevitable.

By Baumbach's third novel, *Reruns* (1974), characters who perceive life disjointedly are no longer insane, for disjuncture is the state of the postmodern world. The protagonist-narrator, Jack, undertakes the apparently identity-stabilizing task of autobiography, but instead illustrates the flexibility of identity in a world filled with pop-culture icons. Jack tries to reinvent his present life by reliving his memories, including his dreams of his past as the "Jewish American domestic nightmare" (Agar, 130), reworking each experience several times in different ways. No longer tucked away in dreams, fantastically impossible events happen so logically that reality and imagination commingle. But no longer does the confusion madden; it brings "a surprisingly optimistic ending. . . . green leaves on a dead tree" (Agar, 130).

Babble (1976) too mixes fantasy, reality, pop culture, and identity by presenting a baby as the narrator-hero who relates his surreal adventures. The adventures and the images that accompany them repeat, producing "an ingenious series of themes-with-variations" that "reverse themselves to show us how absurd they are" (Selz, 168). The device of the baby-narrator reappears in some of Baumbach's short fiction in *The Return of Service* (1979), "a collection that is entirely tongue in cheek. . . . There is a story about a story, a parody of a detective novel, an essay on a nonexistent ridiculous novel, a retelling of Hollywood's King Kong myth and an overall impression that Baumbach, like one of his characters, will do anything 'if it seems like fun' " (Winch, 14). The stories present "numerous parodies of famous stories, situations, films, characters, and their emblematic powers" (Skiles, 15).

Filmlike *Chez Charlotte and Emily* (1979) also explores the constructions of pop culture and their effect on the combination of fantasy and reality that make up human identity. Characters' names parody the icons of pop culture; Francis Sinatra is the "main character." Meanwhile, situations fantastically do the same; Sinatra's life parodies soap operas and spy thrillers, among other genres, but his adventures are revealed as occurring within his imagination, and then he is revealed as an invention of someone else's imagination. In a slightly less layered variation, *My Father, More or Less* (1982) explores a father-son relationship when Tom Terman visits his estranged father, Lukas, a novelist writing a movie script. Three life stories are presented: son's, father's, and screenplay's. Again there are "mirrors and movies, stories within stories" (*Kirkus Review*, 50).

Similarly, Baumbach's next collection of short stories, *The Life and Times of Major Fiction* (1987), presents various people who "retell tales, veering from the truth, resculpting it to fit their mood or their audience" (*Publishers Weekly*, 65). *Separate Hours* (1990) examines the marital breakup of psychotherapists Yuri and Adrienne Tipton. Each presents opposing views of the same events despite repeating patterns in one another's lives, demonstrating communications breakdown and the unreliability of narration as well as narrator. Baumbach's latest novel, *Seven Wives* (1994), repeats an earlier pattern by reintroducing the protagonist-narrator of Reruns. Having married seven different women, Jack again relives his past, this time to figure out which of his wives wants to kill him. Eventually, Jack finds that each of his succession of wives is another version of the same woman.

Indeed, Baumbach's fiction brings his characters (more or less successfully) through the process he described in *The Landscape of Nightmare*, but adds important postmodern explorations. Each protagonist attempts to gain (and communicate) redemptive self-knowledge, but the task is complicated by the fantastic realities of postmodern experience. Baumbach rejects the false order of modernism by merging fantasy, dream, reality, pop culture, and language into the flexible but ultimately intertextual, indefinable, and incommunicable postmodern identity.

CRITICAL RECEPTION

Because of its innovation, Jonathan Baumbach's work elicits strong reactions. On the one hand, Bernard McCabe called *The Landscape of Nightmare* "honest and valuable" (704), and Granville Hicks said that Baumbach "has read carefully and intelligently, and each of his nine chapters is stimulating" (31). In the middle, Louise Gossett considered his readings "essentially accurate," but worried that "it is confusing to equate redemption with self-knowledge" (157), and Irving Malin noted that Baumbach "rebels against the apparent clichés of his introduction" to "contribut[e] many exciting, brave, and helpful readings" (*American Literature*, 349). On the other hand, James Harvey saw *The Landscape of Nightmare* as an exercise in justifying a literary critic's theories rather than pushing readers to deeper understandings of either the specific literature discussed or larger theoretical concerns in general.

In *A Man to Conjure With*, Baumbach, claimed Emile Capouya, skillfully refrains from manipulating readers with a potentially sentimental situation. In the delicate business of *What Comes Next*, C.D.B. Bryan noted, "Baumbach's value as a writer is that he makes the insanity of his hero seem appallingly sane" (32), but H. S. Resnik protested that Baumbach's "moral sledgehammer" attempt to show the reader to be "deeply implicated in a wave of inhuman brutality" was "so tedious that one is tempted to conclude that nobody, not even a mass murderer, is that guilty" (46).

Reactions to *Reruns* were mixed as well. Although Irving Malin praised Baumbach's ability to make the reader identify with the protagonist (25–26), Beverly Gross called it "an overly long conceit. . . . just the same joke reworked too many times" (602). Michael Menshaw feared that Baumbach "is spinning his wheels," but looked forward to his future development, praising his "technical ability" and his prose's "energy and acuity" (27). Thalia Selz claimed that in *Babble*, "few can rival Baumbach in wit, invention, and breadth of understanding," and that despite the sentimental danger of babies, the novel "is never strained and almost never private or cute" (168). But Joseph Epstein found the novel such "a silly game" that "to attempt criticism . . . can only be viewed as becoming an accessory to a crime" (595).

Don Skiles noted that "the quality that makes for marvels in [*The Return of Service*] is a Brooklyn sense of humor," explaining, "Parody always runs the risk of being sophomoric, pointless, and simplistically egotistic, and there are times when this occurs in Baumbach, but not often. Instead, he's able to keep the reader, if the reader will stay with him, on a very fine dividing line between satire with a sharp bite, and parodic invention that enriches that which it parodies" (15). But Evelyn Toynton feared that Baumbach "seems at times to be merely straining after significance, hoping to arrive at an epiphany through luck alone" and hoped that he would "stop obsessing so contentiously about art and life, art and illusion, the problems besetting the creator of fiction" (22).

In response to *Chez Charlotte and Emily*, Peter Quartermain apprehended that Baumbach's lack of trust leads him to adopt a voice that "continually points things out to the reader lest he be too ignorant or blind to spot them," a flaw that not only alienates readers, but also "mislead[s] the writer himself into thinking he is doing something he isn't," such as rejecting the concept of narrative but using it to structure his text (70–71). Brian Geary called *Seven Wives* "cleverness-for-its-own-sake stuff" in which "Baumbach just grabs pieces out of reality out of the pedestrian consciousness" (96), while Catherine Bush complained of a "flatness of tone and a limited emotional palette" juxtaposed with "moments of witty ingenuity" (10).

Jerome Klinkowitz provided the most inclusive and positive discussion of Baumbach's work. In "Jonathan Baumbach's Super Fiction" and *The Life of Fiction*, he traced Baumbach's development through the writer's first several works, focusing first on his interest in guilt and the redemptive process in *The Landscape of Nightmare*. Turning to the fiction, Klinkowitz explored the patterns of the first novel as relatively conventional and each later work as abandoning more conventions in order to mix fantasy and reality and to focus more attention on language itself as the real medium of the art. Seeing Baumbach as a vital author because he mixes the roles of academic, teacher, critic, writer, and even publisher, Klinkowitz placed him "in the company of our most serious experimentalists. The very fact that his progress to this style has been a studied, conservative, step-by-step process makes his work one of the best indices to fiction in our time" ("Super Fiction," 178).

BIBLIOGRAPHY

Works by Jonathan Baumbach

Fiction

A Man to Conjure With. New York: Random House, 1965; London, Gollancz, 1966.
What Comes Next. New York: Harper and Row, 1968.

Reruns. New York: Fiction Collective, 1974.
Babble. New York: Fiction Collective, 1976.
The Return of Service. Urbana: University of Illinois Press, 1979.
Chez Charlotte and Emily. New York: Fiction Collective, 1979.
My Father, More or Less. New York: Fiction Collective, 1982.
The Life and Times of Major Fiction. New York: Fiction Collective, 1986.
Separate Hours. Boulder, Co: Fiction Collective Two, 1990.
Seven Wives. Boulder, Co: Fiction Collective Two, 1994.

Play

The One-Eyed Man Is King. Produced at Theater East, New York, 1956.

Other Works

The Landscape of Nightmare: Studies in the Contemporary American Novel. New York:
    New York University Press, 1965; London: Owen, 1966.
Editor, with Arthur Edelstein. *Moderns and Contemporaries: Nine Masters of the Short
    Story*. New York: Random House, 1968. Revised ed., *Moderns and Contempo-
    raries: Twelve Masters of the Short Story*. New York: Random House, 1977.
Writers as Teachers/Teachers as Writers. New York: Holt, Rinehart and Winston, 1970.
Statements: New Fiction from the Fiction Collective. New York: Braziller, 1975.
With Peter Spielberg. *Statements 2: New Fiction*. New York: Fiction Collective, 1977.

Works Cited and Studies of Jonathan Baumbach

Agar, John. Review of *Reruns*. *Carolina Quarterly* 27 (1975):129–30.
Bryan, C.D.B. "Climate of Violence." Review of *What Comes Next*. *New York Times
    Book Review*, October 13, 1968, 32.
Bush, Catherine. Review of *Seven Wives*. *New York Times Book Review*, May 22, 1994,
    10.
Capouya, Emile. Review of *A Man to Conjure With*. *Bookweek*, October 3, 1965, 19.
Epstein, Joseph. "Is Fiction Necessary?" Review of *Babble*. *Hudson Review* 29 (1976):
    593–604.
Geary, Brian. Review of *Seven Wives*. *Library Journal*, May 15, 1994, 96.
Gossett, Louise Y. Review of *The Landscape of Nightmare*. *South Atlantic Quarterly* 65
    (1966): 156–57.
Gross, Beverly. Review of *Reruns*. *Nation* 219 (1974): 602.
Harvey, James. "In and out of Fashion." Review of *The Landscape of Nightmare*. *Ken-
    yon Review*, January 1966, 108–16.
Hicks, Granville. Review of *The Landscape of Nightmare*. *Saturday Review*, April 17,
    1965, 31.
Klinkowitz, Jerome. "Jonathan Baumbach's Super Fiction." *Chicago Review* 26 (1975):
    178–88.
———. *The Life of Fiction*. Urbana: University of Illinois Press, 1977.
Review of *The Life and Times of Major Fiction*. *Publishers Weekly*, April 3, 1987, 65.
Malin, Irving. Review of *The Landscape of Nightmare*. *American Literature* 37 (1965):
    349.
———. Review of *Reruns*. *New Republic*, October 19, 1974, 25–26.

McCabe, Bernard. Review of *The Landscape of Nightmare*. *Commonweal*, September 24, 1965, 704–5.

Menshaw, Michael. Review of *Reruns*. *New York Times Book Review*, October 13, 1974, 26–27.

Review of *My Father, More or Less*. *Kirkus Reviews*, February 1, 1982, 148.

Quartermain, Peter. "Trusting the Reader." Review of *Chez Charlotte and Emily*. *Chicago Review* 32 (1980): 65–74.

Resnik, H. S. Review of *What Comes Next*. *Saturday Review*, October 26, 1968, 41, 46.

Selz, Thalia. Review of *Babble*. *Fiction International* 6/7 (1976): 167–68.

Skiles, Don. Review of *Charlotte and Emily* and *The Return of Service*. *American Book Review*, March 3, 1981, 15.

Toynton, Evelyn. "Dream and Variations." Review of *The Life and Times of Major Fiction*. *New York Times Book Review*, June 7, 1987, 22.

Winch, Terence. "Short Stops on the Reading Railroad." Review of *The Return of Service*. *Book World*, March 30, 1980, 14–15.

SAUL BELLOW (1915–)

Pirjo Ahokas

BIOGRAPHY

Saul Bellow was born on June 10, 1915, in Lachine, near Montreal, in the province of Quebec. His parents had emigrated to Canada from St. Petersburg, Russia, in 1913, and he was the youngest of their four children. Bellow's father, an onion importer in Russia, was involved in several unsuccessful business ventures in Canada, and Bellow spent the first nine years of his life in one of the poorest sections of Montreal. In the polyglot world of his Jewish childhood, Bellow learned Hebrew, Yiddish, French, and English. At about the age of four he began to read the Old Testament as part of his traditional religious Jewish education.

In 1924 the family moved to Chicago, a city that was to become one of the favorite settings of Bellow's subsequent fiction. During his formative years, Americanization and assimilation were very important issues to the family, even if they were divisive. Immersed in literature from an early age, Bellow was educated at the University of Chicago and at Northwestern University, from which he graduated with honors in sociology and anthropology (B.S., 1937). Late in 1937 Bellow left the University of Wisconsin at Madison to become an author.

The careers of the Jewish authors of Bellow's generation have often been intertwined with the activities of a loosely connected literary group called the New York Intellectuals. After having been employed for a brief period with the Writers Project of the Works Progress Administration in 1938 and after having worked in various other short-term jobs, Bellow began his writing career in the pages of *Partisan Review*, the New York Jewish intellectuals' periodical, which published his first story, "Two Morning Monologues," in 1941.

The background of Bellow's literary career is linked with the postwar Jewish breakthrough in letters. Supporters of radical political causes and proponents of modernist fiction, the New York Intellectuals were interested in social justice and also admired authors who in one form or another tended to denounce society. Like the other key representatives of second-generation Jewish-American fiction, Bellow struggled to affirm a secular Jewish identity. Although he had been involved with Trotskyist organizations while he was a high school and university student in the early 1930s, he had severed all links with radical political groups by the early 1940s. In 1943 Bellow worked on Mortimer Adler's Great Books project for the *Encyclopaedia Britannica*. In 1944 Bellow's *Dangling Man*, a novel of introspection and existential anxiety, was published. It managed to capture the atmosphere of political disillusionment and serious intellectual probing. In a fairly short time, the New York Intellectuals, who had supported radical political causes, also reached a point of crisis. Many perceptive critics of this circle identified with the disoriented protagonist's sense of displacement and linked his anguish with that of the heroes in much of modernist European literature. *Dangling Man* was followed by *The Victim* (1947).

The conscious effort to win back vital elements of the ethnic past in America is noticeable in the Jewish-American novelists' turn toward Jewish materials in the 1950s—sometimes called the Jewish decade. According to some critics, it was Saul Bellow who ushered in the new period with his vividly imagined third novel, *The Adventures of Augie March* (1953). Affirmative in tone, this free-wheeling picaresque book embodies the protagonist's expansive search for identity. Written while Bellow was traveling on a Guggenheim Fellowship in Europe, in New York, and at Princeton University, the novel paralleled the New York Jewish intellectuals' breaking out of their previous confinement. In 1952 the *Partisan Review* staged a symposium on "Our Country and Our Culture." Sharing Bellow's background, the majority of the postwar New York Intellectuals publicly renounced their earlier radicalism and joined society at large. Augie, at least on the surface, imagines himself as a present-day Columbus with as unproblematic a relationship to the past as to the future. *The Adventures of Augie March* brought Bellow the 1954 National Book Award and established his reputation as one of the major young American authors of his generation.

In addition to writing novels for half a century, Bellow has written five plays, two published collections of short stories as well as a good number of uncollected stories, and a book-length journalistic account of his trip to Israel. *It All Adds Up: From the Dim Past to the Uncertain Future* (1994), his most recent book, is a nonfiction collection including literary essays, travel pieces, and remembrances of friends.

Bellow has been the recipient of numerous honors and awards, including the National Book Award (three times), the Pulitzer Prize, and the Croix de Chevalier des Arts et Lettres. He holds honorary degrees from Harvard and Yale universities and from several other institutions. In 1976 he was awarded the Nobel Prize in literature.

For most of his professional life, Bellow has been associated with colleges and universities. After the war he taught at the University of Minnesota, New York University, Princeton, and Bard College. In 1963 Bellow returned to the University of Chicago after receiving an appointment to the Committee on Social Thought. He has served the committee for the past three decades, acting as chair from 1970 to 1976. Although Bellow claims to be "some sort of liberal," his reputation, especially in recent years, has taken on a more conservative cast, and he has been attacked as reactionary. Bellow's current main affiliation is with Boston University, where he is a professor of literature. Still at the height of his powers, he moved with his fifth wife, Janice Friedman, from Chicago to Boston and continues his writing there.

MAJOR WORKS AND THEMES

All of Bellow's fiction addresses the intellectual, cultural, social, and spiritual problems of the historically troubled modern world. Indeed, Bellow tends to regard the novelist as "an imaginative historian, who is able to get closer to contemporary facts than social scientists possibly can." Due to his wide and eclectic reading, Bellow is capable of synthesizing the most diverse intellectual trends and movements. Also apparent in his works is his vast knowledge and command of Western literature and literary traditions. Not surprisingly, then, the typical Bellovian protagonist is an intellectual hero, generally a male, urban American Jew, who, to quote the words of the Nobel Committee, "can never relinquish his faith that the value of life depends on its dignity, not on its success."

Resisting "the Waste Land outlook" of the earlier modernist tradition in the early stages of his career, Bellow has used his writing as well as his fictional heroes as vehicles for exploring affirmative solutions. Caught up in a spiritual crisis, the typical Bellow hero usually seeks transcendence from his despair and alienation. Until quite recently the critics have chosen to stress the transcendentalist Bellow, but as scholars like Malcolm Bradbury point out, "Bellow has grown more apocalyptic; a doubter of concepts, he has grown more conceptual and abstract" (*Saul Bellow* 33). In many cases, however, the imminence of gloom is alleviated by Bellow's liberating sense of humor, a redeeming quality that also manages to throw further light on the impenetrable complexities of life.

With his first two novels, Bellow consolidated his reputation as an academic author paying his respects to the New Critical formal requirements of well-made fiction. In a mid-1960s interview, he explained that in part, his early choice of form was caused by social inhibitions, by his fear that he "would be put down as a foreigner, an interloper," who "would probably never have the right *feeling* for Anglo-Saxon traditions, for English words." In the 1950s Bellow discarded this repressive attitude and developed a new urban prose style characterized by a freely digressive fusion of a high style and colloquial street English, frequently either energized by underlying intonations of Yiddish speech or spiced by the occasional use of Yiddish phrases. Indeed, Irving Howe has maintained that "Bellow's relation to Yiddish is easy and authoritative though by no means sentimental" (*World of Our Fathers*, 593). According to Howe, Bellow "brought to completion the first major new style in American prose fiction since those of Hemingway and Faulkner" (594).

Bellow's fiction has taken a variety of forms. Some critics divide his canon into two groups: the tightly organized shorter books written in Bellow's "mandarin English" and the expansive works like *Henderson the Rain King* (1959) composed in the looser prose style. Whether this is the case or not, in a novel like *Herzog*, Bellow successfully fused his sweeping exuberance with the disciplined technique of his early novels.

Signaling a change in American literature, *Dangling Man* turns against the ideal of the hard-boiled hero, epitomized in fiction by Hemingway's masculine protagonists. Drawing on Dostoyevsky, whom Alfred Kazin regarded as the "patron saint" of the immediate postwar generation, the novel introduces a Chicagoan "underground man," an outsider and a reflective consciousness called Joseph. Moreover, as if anticipating the intertextual richness of the subsequent works by such Jewish-American authors as Bernard Malamud and Philip Roth, *Dangling Man* contains echoes of Kafka and French existentialism. Bellow's successful dramatization of the alienated protagonist's states of emotion and consciousness enabled him to create a much-needed distance from the native traditions of not only the tough guy but also the proletarian hero.

The Victim recapitulates the note of isolation in depicting a lonely city Jew troubled by his Dostoyevskian double in New York's suffocating summer heat. Based on Dostoyevsky's *The Eternal Husband* and *The Double*, the novel is a complex exploration of the mutually damaging effects of anti-Semitism. Bellow's treatment of the theme gains a great deal of poignancy from the fact that the novel was written and set in the immediate postwar years. Glimpses of recovered responsibility and transcendence are provided by the small Jewish cafeteria community presided over by Schlossberg, the wise old Yiddish theater critic, who notes, "It's bad to be less than human and it's bad to be more than human. . . . Choose dignity. Nobody knows enough to turn it down."

In addition to editing a collection entitled *Great Jewish Short Stories* (1963), Bellow was an early translator of I. B. Singer's classic story "Gimpel the Fool." An unlikely cross between Singer's Gimpel and the good-natured rogue-protagonists of the Spanish *Lazarillo de Tormes* and Fielding's *Tom Jones*, Bellow's American *picaro* in *The Adventures of Augie March* is a gullible self-made intellectual with a penchant for magnifying himself to the proportions of a Greek hero and becoming, in John J. Clayton's words, "a parodic Aeneas, just as Bloom is a parodic Ulysses" (88). Prominent mentors abound in Bellow's novels. In *Augie March*, the instructors, ranging from Einhorn, a would-be philosopher and a petty gangster, to Mintouchian, the wealthy Armenian lawyer whom Augie meets in Mexico, are cunning manipulators whom the protagonist also endows with mythic proportions.

The central thrust of the sprawling novel is an optimistic celebration of force and the multifariousness of American society, but many critics have identified a contradiction inherent in the novel. Born in Jewish Chicago, colorfully depicted at the start of the book, Augie is also trying to discover "what I was meant to be." Considerable difficulty can be detected in Bellow's attempts to combine the narrator-protagonist's formless wanderings with the *Bildungsroman* elements concerned with Augie's moral growth. Gradually, sinister undercurrents of Augie's life turn the exuberance of his American dream into a swan song of loss.

Bellow's other fiction from the 1950s includes the somber novella *Seize the Day* (1956) and *Henderson the Rain King* (1959), a lighthearted comic novel about an energetic and driven millionaire's trip to mythic Africa. Like some of his friends among the New York Intellectuals, Bellow discovered Wilhelm Reich in the late 1940s, and the famous psychotherapist's thinking influenced him strongly, particularly during the period when he wrote these two books.

According to Reich, the false ideals of modern society oppress people in their very bodies, and in Tommy Wilhelm, the protagonist of *Seize the Day*, Bellow shows us a middle-aged Jewish New Yorker suffocated by his physical and spiritual surroundings. A failure in his personal and business relationships, the self-pitying hero lives with his rich and exacting diagnostician-father in a Broadway hotel for retired people. Concerned with many aspects of the American Dream, Wilhelm, rejected by his own father, helplessly throws himself on the mercy of a number of father figures. The most significant among them is Dr. Tamkin, a quack who not only abuses Wilhelm's confidence but also causes him to lose his life's savings in the stock market. A master deceiver and con man, Tamkin also functions as an ironic savior figure in exhorting his ward to "seize the day." The novella focuses on a single day, close to Yom Kippur or the Day of Atonement for the Jews. Having lost all his money, Tommy Wilhelm is finally prepared to loosen up his Reichian muscular armor, symbolized by the great knot he has constantly felt "tied tight within his chest." In the final epiphany of *Seize the Day*, Wilhelm wanders into the funeral of a stranger, and the "therapeutic" release finally allows him to gain a better understanding of himself and his emotions as well as show his sense of compassion for humanity as a whole. Some critics regard *Seize the Day* as Bellow's finest work. In 1986 it was released as a remarkably faithful film directed by Fiedler Cook and starring Robin Williams.

Drawing on Jessie L. Weston's *From Ritual to Romance, Henderson the Rain King* is a comic fertility quest, and Bellow's wealthy pig farmer is his first non-Jewish hero. Trying to find meaning in his life, Bellow's WASP giant with a face like Grand Central Station travels to Africa, where he meets two tribes, the "feminine" and peaceful Arnewi and the masculine Wariri, characterized by "male" energy and dealing in death. To begin with, Eugene Henderson (note

the allusion to Hemingway's initials) is a boisterous egoist fleeing his responsibilities in order to come to terms with an irrepressible voice inside himself
that keeps saying "I want, I want." Fearing death but learning from the Arnewi
that he possesses "*grun-tu-molani*, man want to live," he participates in the
Wariri's rain-making ritual. In a humorous scene, reminiscent of Reich's theories
of rain making, he becomes Sungo, the tribe's Rain King. Finally, Henderson's
therapeutic interaction with King Dahfu, his African mentor well versed in armor
blocks and orgone therapy, renders him capable of going back to America with
a renewed sense of self and a purpose in his life.

Bellow returned from the purely fictive Africa of his parodic novel to Jewish
characters and Jewish milieux in his next novel, *Herzog* (1964). Moses Herzog,
the tormented eponymous hero and scholar of romanticism, is a far more substantial intellectual than any of the main characters preceding him. Moreover,
Bellow has put a great deal of himself into the protagonist, and therefore the
novel contains strong autobiographical components. In part, the charm of *Herzog*
derives from the fact that the scholar-protagonist's suffering is seen against the
backdrop of the ghetto milieu of the author's childhood in Montreal. The vividly
imagined immigrant neighborhood of Napoleon Street comes alive with all its
sordid details in the flashbacks that deal with Moses's boyhood and provide
interesting contrasts to the characters' middle-class lives. Immensely popular
among American readers, *Herzog* appealed, in Bellow's own words, "to Jewish
readers, to those who have been divorced, to those who talk to themselves, to
college graduates, readers of paperbacks, autodidacts, to those who yet hope to
live a while, etc." Beyond the immediate exigencies of the failure of Herzog's
second marriage, which provide the spine for the well-organized and intermittently exciting plot, the novel is about the protagonist's inward journey.

Throughout the novel Herzog is ceaselessly trying to analyze his personal and
historical anguish. A man of the 1960s, he rebels against "the cheap mental
stimulants of Alienation, the cant and rant of pipsqueaks about Inauthenticity
and Forlornness." Paralyzed by the delusion of total explanations, he takes
recourse in his grandiose research plan on "the importance of the 'law of the
heart' in Western traditions," but it is to no avail. Struggling for his sanity at
a point of chaos, Herzog writes unsent letters to recipients ranging from himself
and his near relatives and friends to "Dear Doktor Professor Heidegger," "Dear
Herr Nietzsche," and Martin Luther King. Basically, Herzog is also trying to
answer the question that has haunted the Bellovian heroes from *Dangling Man*
on: "How should a good man live; what ought he to do?" Although the protagonist's reflections are used to prefigure his "change of heart," they alone
cannot free him from his despair. Rejecting mere abstract speculation after his
misguided but sobering visit to Chicago, Herzog allows himself to learn from
his past experiences and begins to forge a humanistic personal ethic linked with
the Jewish code of *menschlichkeit*.

It is never difficult to find virtues in *Herzog*. In addition to exploring the
deeper connections below the protagonist's fragmentary ruminations on Western

thought, Bellow has created a memorable gallery of minor characters. Madeleine Herzog is the catalyst for her husband's unhappiness. Nevertheless, the revenge-ful protagonist's unjust portrait cannot hide Madeleine's vulnerability, intelli-gence, and justified anger, which make her an unusually complex and interesting Bellovian female in her own right.

The relatively optimistic ending of *Herzog* is typical of the main phase of Bellow's career, which also includes his plays and *Mr. Sammler's Planet* (1970). The New York premiere of *The Last Analysis* (1964) took place only a few days before the publication of *Herzog*, and in spite of its satirical intent, the play has broad thematic correspondences with the novel. Reminiscent of the dark comedies of Philip Roth's subsequent fiction, the play centers around its hero, Philip Bummidge, who suffers from an illness called "Humanitis," caused by an overexposure to the human condition. A prototype of the absurd man, Bummidge relies on a therapeutic discipline called *Existenz*-Action self-analysis, and taking his treatment in public, he acts out pivotal moments in his life on closed-circuit television. The play was a failure, and none of Bellow's other plays have generated much interest either, a fact that has discouraged him from writing for the theater.

Bellow left New York in 1962, in part because he resented the "increased politicization" of writers there, and some critics trace the beginnings of his growing cultural conservatism to Herzog's accommodation at the close of the novel. After *Herzog* Bellow turned to elderly protagonists. *Mr. Sammler's Planet* focuses on the internal processes of a Holocaust survivor, an Anglophile Polish intellectual, now in his seventies and as encumbered by his past in Europe as by his present in New York. In an interview in 1975, Bellow admitted, "I think of *Mr. Sammler's Planet* as a sort of polemical thing." With its conservative attack on the New Left and the American youth culture, the novel is highly critical of 1960s America. Nowhere is the rift between Mr. Sammler and con-temporary America more pronounced than in the Columbia lecture scene in which his silent but utterly negative estimate of the student audience elicits their hostility. Sammler's obsession with the black pickpocket has also been cited as a sign of Bellow's conservatism. But *Mr. Sammler's Planet* has a much wider scope. A fine example of the American post-Holocaust immigrant novel, it has also been regarded as Bellow's "most Jewish" book.

A deeply divided character, Artur Sammler, with his unbearable experience of having been buried alive in a mass grave in Poland in 1939, is still ransacking his vast knowledge of Western culture and the meaning of his traumatic past in his attempt to define his position regarding the old Bellovian problem of what it means to be human. Born to a freethinking family, Sammler has had a pe-ripheral relationship to Judaism. An acquaintance of the Bloomsbury group in the 1920s and 1930s, he has maintained his "British" reserve but lost his belief in a politics of civility during the war. As in *Herzog*, the disdainful protagonist's secular learning and philosophical abstractions also seem futile until he denies the importance and moral worth of divorcing the self from other people. Again and again in Bellow's novels the alienated heroes long for a human community. Fond of the nephew who rescued Sammler and his loony daughter from Europe, the protagonist of *Mr. Sammler's Planet* ultimately learns to share his life's legacy with those closest to him. Though many readers have found the book pessimistic, it has an affirmative ending.

Bellow's next book is about the mutual bond between Charlie Citrine, a Pulitzer Prize historian and Broadway playwright, and Von Humboldt Fleisher, a brilliant but manic-depressive avant-garde poet and Greenwich Village celebrity. Based on the life of Bellow's friend from the *Partisan Review* circle, the Jewish-American poet Delmore Schwartz, *Humboldt's Gift* (1975) is told in Citrine's voice and deals with the risks of the writer's life in materialistic American society. A prodigy poet with romantic illusions about the artist's role as a sage, Humboldt has gone under, succumbing to "clownery" in his glory hunting, after having spent his talent. Citrine sees his dead former mentor as the great American scapegoat "who wanted to drape the world in radiance, but he didn't have enough material." Described by Bellow as a "comic book about death," the novel is not only about Citrine's, the successful entrepreneurial intellectual's, guilt about having neglected Humboldt after their estrangement but also about his own fear of dying. Indeed, Citrine's own fate is the flip side of his friend's destiny: he feels that he has slept through his life. The sprawling but highly entertaining novel charts Citrine's way from a "moronic inferno" into a "reflective purgatory" where he finds consolation in Steiner's philosophy.

Bellow was a very prolific writer in the 1980s. In *Mr. Sammler's Planet*, the protagonist considered the dead to be "the one subject the soul was sure to take seriously." Death pervades Bucharest and Chicago, the two necropolises in *The Dean's December* (1982), a novel with a heightened focus on political and social issues. The meditative novel about Alfred Corde (the name suggests a cord, a heart), a journalist-academic in his mid-fifties, recapitulates many of the problems raised by Mr. Sammler. This time, however, the East-West comparisons are made between Communist and capitalist societies, and the bleak book is devoid of Jewish characters and specifically Jewish concerns. Closer to *Humboldt's Gift*, the novel *More Die of Heartbreak* (1987) is recounted by the protagonist's nephew, Kenneth Trachtenberg, a professor of Russian literature. In his estimation, the West suffers from "the ordeal of desire" while the East is subjected to "the ordeal of privation." Unlucky in love, uncle and nephew try to disentangle the hapless botanist-protagonist from the vicious financial scheming of his new father-in-law. Suffused with warm family feeling, the novel has been called "a comedy of overelaboration" (89) by Terrence Rafferty. Embodying a Bellovian spiritual quest, *More Die of Heartbreak* utterly fails in its ambitious task of unfolding "the secret of our being" when the uncle unexpectedly escapes to the North Pole.

Bellow's other works from the mid-1980s on include *Him with His Foot in His Mouth* (1984), a short-story collection, and two novellas, *A Theft* and *The Bellarosa Connection*, both from 1989. *A Theft* is set in New York and in many ways is suggestive of Woody Allen's films with their Manhattan interiors. Clara Velde, a four-times-married fashion executive, is the first female protagonist of Bellow's longer fiction. Like the Bellovian male heroes, she is concerned with the dehumanization of life in big cities like her "Gogmagogsville" and seeks a fully lived life.

The Bellarosa Connection returns to Bellow's previous exploration of the significance of memory. The nameless narrator is the founder of the Mnemosyne Institute, where he has trained important customers in the techniques of memory retention. "A walking memory file" himself, he has dissociated memory from emotion and "would like to *forget* about remembering." The main plot concerns his spontaneous reflections on a Holocaust survivor, Harry Fonstein, Fonstein's American wife, and Fonstein's rescuer, who also wanted to bury the past after the war. The skillful tale maps the Bellarosa narrator's inner transformation and his changed response to the Holocaust through his active participation in the act of remembering.

Epiphanous and life-enhancing transformations also take place in Bellow's meticulously crafted short fiction. Frequently regarded as one of Bellow's best stories, "The Old System" in *Mosby's Memoirs and Other Stories* (1968) is a good example. Assessing the costs of assimilation, the author nevertheless allows the American-born narrator to be revitalized and changed by his long-suppressed memories of his dead Jewish relatives. Essentially a novelist, Bellow is especially given to character sketch, and in the same way in which the narrator of "The Old System" can be seen as a precursor of Mr. Sammler, many other shorter pieces tend either to prefigure or to look backward to the thematic concerns of the novels. It does not come as a surprise, then, that critics have linked certain aspects of the stories in Bellow's second collection *Him with His Foot in His Mouth* with such longer works as *The Dean's December* and *A Theft*.

A brilliant observer of all segments of the modern psyche and society, Bellow has contributed considerably to reshaping American fiction into a rich, multi-ethnic tapestry. Perceiving comedy as one of the powers the self possesses, Bellow remains, to quote Bradbury, "one of our most serious novelists, and our most commanding, because he is a great modern novelist of the attempt to reconcile mind, in all its resource and confusion, its fantastic fertility and unending anguish, with a life that is itself absurd, extravagant, pressing us not only with material forces but with ideas and forms of consciousness, information and concepts, boredoms and rewards" (Saul Bellow 103–4).

CRITICAL RECEPTION

The critical response to Bellow's work has been overwhelmingly positive. Bellow maintains a stature shared by few American authors, and he is also a writer of wide international recognition. His early novels brought him academic and critical acclaim. *Dangling Man*, for instance, was reviewed by such prominent critics as Diana Trilling, Delmore Schwartz, and Edmund Wilson. Though many scholars claim that in retrospect *Augie March* was overvalued in its time, it was highly praised by the majority of contemporary critics. However, it was only with the publication of *Herzog*, which remained on the best-seller lists for many weeks, that Bellow began to receive widespread popular attention in the United States.

Most critics concentrate on two aspects of Bellow's fiction: they are interested in the Bellovian hero and in the author's prose style. It is generally agreed that Bellow's place is inside the humanist tradition, although much attention has been paid to his darkening worldview. While many critics have linked Bellow's affirmative approach to Judaism as a source of spiritual sustenance in his fiction, others have also explored the importance of more specifically American cultural traditions in his work.

Critical debate surrounds many aspects of Bellow's writing. Almost from the outset reviewers have accused Bellow of not distancing himself enough from some of his autobiographical heroes. Moreover, the fact that the protagonists are often inseparable from their ideas has often been noted as an obstacle to Bellow's plots. Most of his protagonist-centered novels are rather straightforward first-person narratives emphasizing dialogue and interior monologue, which has led to predictable charges that they lack technical innovation. Bellow's dramatically unjustified resolutions and ambiguous endings have also been problematic.

For all his achievements, Bellow's reputation began to slide through the late 1960s and early 1970s. He was criticized by the young and by some of the older critics of the *Partisan Review* crowd whom he attacked as advocates of the New Left. Even if *Mr. Sammler's Planet* provoked heated debate, together with *Humboldt's Gift* it also strengthened Bellow's great literary reputation. Bellow's portrayal of female characters has been considered as unconvincing and sexist, and more recently he has been accused of misogynistic attitudes. At the other end of the spectrum are those critics who point out that Bellow's women are mainly experienced through male eyes and who regard female characters like Clara Velde in *A Theft* as a great exception. Many reviewers and scholars refer to Bellow's works after *Humboldt's Gift* as ''late Bellow'' and find signs of fatigue in novels like *The Dean's December*. Yet Charles Michaud wrote in his review of *The Bellarosa Connection*, ''Not since Henry James has an American author of Bellow's age continued to produce such arresting work'' (115).

BIBLIOGRAPHY

Works by Saul Bellow

Dangling Man. New York: Vanguard, 1944.
The Victim. New York: Vanguard, 1947.
The Adventures of Augie March. New York: Viking Press, 1953.

Seize the Day. New York: Viking Press, 1956.
Henderson the Rain King. New York: Viking Press, 1959.
Herzog. New York: Viking Press, 1964.
The Last Analysis. New York: Viking Press, 1965.
Mosby's Memoirs and Other Stories. New York: Viking Press, 1968.
Mr. Sammler's Planet. New York: Viking Press, 1970.
Humboldt's Gift. New York: Viking Press, 1975.
To Jerusalem and Back: A Personal Account. New York: Viking Press, 1976.
The Dean's December. New York: Harper and Row, 1982.
Him with His Foot in His Mouth and Other Stories. New York: Harper and Row, 1984.
More Die of Heartbreak. New York: William Morrow, 1987.
The Bellarosa Connection. New York and London: Penguin, 1989.
A Theft. New York and London: Penguin, 1989.
Something to Remember Me By: Three Tales. New York: Viking Penguin, 1991.
It All Adds Up: From the Dim Past to the Uncertain Future. New York: Viking Penguin, 1994.

Works Cited and Selected Studies of Saul Bellow

Berger, Alan. "The Logic of the Heart: Biblical Identity and American Culture in Saul Bellow's 'The Old System.' " *Saul Bellow Journal* 11–12 (Winter 1993–Fall 1994): 2–15 133–45.

Bloom, Harold, ed. *Saul Bellow*. New York: Chelsea House, 1986.

Boyers, Robert. "Moving Quickly: An Interview with Saul Bellow." *Salmagundi* 106–7 (Spring–Summer 1995): 32–53.

Bradbury, Malcolm. *The Modern American Novel*. New York: Oxford University Press, 1983.

———. *Saul Bellow*. New York: Methuen, 1982.

Breit, Harvey. *The Writer Observed*. Tampa, FL: World Publishing, 1956.

Clayton, John J. *Saul Bellow: In Defense of Man*. Bloomington: Indiana University Press, 1968.

Cohen, Sarah Blacher. *Saul Bellow's Enigmatic Laughter*. Urbana: University of Illinois Press, 1974.

Cronin, Gloria L., and Blaine H. Hall. *Saul Bellow: An Annotated Bibliography*. 2nd ed. New York: Garland Publishing, 1987.

Cronin, Gloria L., and Ben Siegel, eds. *Conversations with Saul Bellow*. Jackson: University Press of Mississippi, 1994.

Detweiler, Robert. *Saul Bellow: A Critical Essay*. Grand Rapids, MI: Eerdmans, 1967.

Dutton, Robert R. *Saul Bellow*. New York: Twayne, 1971.

Eisinger, Chester E. *Fiction of the Forties*. Chicago: University of Chicago Press, 1963.

Fuchs, Daniel. *Saul Bellow: Vision and Revision*. Durham, NC: Duke University Press, 1984.

Furman, Andrew. "Ethnicity in Saul Bellow's *Herzog*: The Importance of the Napoleon Street, Montreal, Memories." *Saul Bellow Journal* 13 (Winter 1995): 41–51.

Galloway, David D. *The Absurd Hero in American Fiction: Updike, Styron, Bellow, Salinger*. Austin: University of Texas Press, 1966.

Geismar, Maxwell. *American Moderns: From Rebellion to Conformity*. New York: Hill and Wang, 1958.

Glenday, Michael K. *Saul Bellow and the Decline of Humanism*. Basingstoke: Macmillan, 1990.

Goldman, L. H., Gloria Cronin, and Ada Aharoni, eds. *Saul Bellow: A Mosaic*. New York: Peter Lang, 1992.

Hall, James. *The Lunatic Giant in the Drawing Room*. Bloomington: Indiana University Press, 1968.

Handy, William J. *Modern Fiction: A Formalist Approach*. Carbondale: Southern Illinois University Press, 1971.

Harper, Howard. *Desperate Faith: A Study of Bellow, Salinger, Mailer, Baldwin, and Updike*. Chapel Hill: University of North Carolina Press, 1967.

Harris, Mark. *Saul Bellow: Drumlin Woodchuck*. Athens: University of Georgia Press, 1980.

Hassan, Ihab. *Radical Innocence: Studies in the Contemporary American Novel*. Princeton: Princeton University Press, 1961.

Hendin, Josephine. *Vulnerable People: A View of American Fiction since 1945*. New York: Oxford University Press, 1978.

Howe, Irving, ed. *Saul Bellow: Herzog: Text and Criticism*. New York: Viking, 1976.

————. *World of Our Fathers*. New York: Harcourt Brace Jovanovich, 1976.

Hyland, Peter. *Saul Bellow*. New York: St. Martin's Press, 1992.

Kazin, Alfred. *Contemporaries*. Boston: Little, Brown, 1962.

Kiernan, Robert F. *Saul Bellow*. New York: Continuum, 1989.

Klein, Marcus. *After Alienation: American Novels in Mid-Century*. Cleveland: World Publishing, 1965.

Kramer, Hilton. "Saul Bellow, Our Contemporary." *Commentary*, June 1994, 37–41.

Kremer, S. Lillian. "An Intertextual Reading of *Seize the Day*: Absorption and Revision." *Saul Bellow Journal* 10 (Fall 1991): 46–55.

Kulshrestha, Chirantan. *Saul Bellow: The Problem of Affirmation*. New Delhi: Arnold-Heinemann, 1978.

Lercangee, Francine. *Saul Bellow: A Bibliography of Secondary Sources*. Brussels: Center for American Studies, 1977.

Malin, Irving. *Jews and Americans*. Carbondale: Southern Illinois University Press, 1965.

————. *Saul Bellow and the Critics*. New York: New York University Press, 1967.

————. *Saul Bellow's Fiction*. Carbondale: Southern Illinois University Press, 1969.

Marovitz, Sanford. "That Certain 'Something': Dora, Dr. Braun, and Others." *Saul Bellow Journal* 12 (Fall 1994): 3–12.

McCadden, Joseph F. *The Flight from Women in the Fiction of Saul Bellow*. Lanham, MD: University Press of America, 1980.

McConnell, Frank D. *Four Postwar American Novelists: Bellow, Mailer, Barth, and Pynchon*. Chicago: University of Chicago Press, 1977.

Michaud, Charles. Review of *The Bellarosa Connection*. *Library Journal* 114 (October 1, 1989): 115.

Moore, Harry T., ed. *Contemporary American Novelists*. Carbondale: Southern Illinois University Press, 1964.

Nault, Marianne. *Saul Bellow: His Works and His Critics: An Annotated International Bibliography*. New York: Garland Publishing, 1977.

Newman, Judie. *Saul Bellow and History*. New York: St. Martin's Press, 1984.

Noreen, Robert G. *Saul Bellow: A Reference Guide*. New York: G. K. Hall, 1978.

Opdahl, Keith. *The Novels of Saul Bellow: An Introduction*. University Park: Pennsylvania State University Press, 1967.

Ozick, Cynthia. "Saul Bellow's Broadway." *New Criterion* 14 (September 1995): 29–36.

Pifer, Ellen. *Saul Bellow: Against the Grain*. Philadelphia: University of Pennsylvania Press, 1990.

Pinsker, Sanford. "Late Bellow and the Literary Scene: Why *More Die of Heartbreak* Works and Why It Doesn't." *Saul Bellow Journal* 11: (Fall 1992): 35–40.

Porter, M. Gilbert. *Whence the Power? The Artistry and Humanity of Saul Bellow*. Columbia: University of Missouri Press, 1974.

Rafferty, Terrence. "Hearts and Minds." *New Yorker*, July 20, 1987, 89–91.

Rodrigues, Eusebio L. *Quest for the Human: An Exploration of Saul Bellow's Fiction*. Cranbury, NJ: Bucknell University Press, 1981.

Rovit, Earl. *Saul Bellow*. Minneapolis: University of Minnesota Press, 1967.

———, ed. *Saul Bellow: A Collection of Critical Essays*. Englewood Cliffs, NJ: Prentice-Hall, 1975.

Rupp, Richard H. *Celebration in Postwar American Fiction, 1945–1967*. Baltimore: University of Miami Press, 1970.

Scheer-Schaezler, Brigitte. *Saul Bellow*. New York: Ungar, 1972.

Schraepen, Edmond, ed. *Saul Bellow and His Work*. Brussels: Free University of Brussels, 1978.

Schulz, Max F. *Radical Sophistication: Studies in Contemporary Jewish-American Novelists*. Athens: Ohio University Press, 1969.

Scott, Nathan A., Jr. *Three American Moralists: Mailer, Bellow, Trilling*. Notre Dame, IN: University of Notre Dame Press, 1973.

Shechner, Mark. *After the Revolution: Studies in the Contemporary Jewish-American Imagination*. Bloomington: Indiana University Press, 1987.

Sokoloff, B. A., and Mark E. Poner. *Saul Bellow: A Comprehensive Bibliography*. Folcroft, PA: Folcroft Library Editions, 1974.

Tanner, Tony. *City of Words: American Fiction, 1950–1970*. New York: Harper and Row, 1971.

———. *Saul Bellow*. Edinburgh & London: Oliver and Boyd, 1965.

Trachtenberg, Stanley, ed. *Critical Essays on Saul Bellow*. Boston, MA: G. K. Hall, 1979.

Walden, Daniel. "Saul Bellow's Paradox: Individualism and the Soul." *Saul Bellow Journal* 122 (Fall 1994): 58–71.

Weinberg, Helen. *The New Novel in America: The Kafkan Mode in Contemporary Fiction*. Ithaca: Cornell University Press, 1970.

Wilson, Jonathan. *On Bellow's Planet: Readings from the Dark Side*. Rutherford, NJ: Fairleigh Dickinson University Press, 1985.

MELVIN BUKIET (1953–)

Sanford Pinsker

BIOGRAPHY

Melvin Bukiet (pronounced boo-KET) was born in New York City on September 21, 1953 to Rose and Joseph Bukiet. Rose's parents, in Bukiet's words, "had the wisdom or dumb luck to flee the Tzar a generation earlier." Thus she was born in Norma, New Jersey, one of the Baron De Hirsch communities. By contrast, Bukiet's father was not so lucky. Born in Proszowice, Poland, a village outside of Cracow, he survived the war and came to this country in 1948.

Bukiet attended New York public schools until his family moved first to Long Island and then to New Jersey. He graduated from Sarah Lawrence College and received an M.F.A. from Columbia University. At that point his history turned into books as Bukiet increasingly became the effect, rather than the "cause," of his works. He came to wide public attention with the publication of *Stories of an Imaginary Childhood* (1992), which received the Edward Lewis Wallant Award and was a finalist for the National Jewish Book Award. The following year he became the fiction editor of *Tikkun* magazine, and in 1993 he returned to Sarah Lawrence College as a visiting professor. A collection of deliciously inventive post-Holocaust stories, *While the Messiah Tarries*, was published in 1995 to a readership increasingly familiar with Bukiet not only as a writer of provocative fiction, but also as a regular book reviewer for the *Boston Globe* and the author of op-ed pieces in the *New York Times*. Bukiet lives in Manhattan with his wife Jill Goodman, an attorney, and his three children.

MAJOR WORKS AND THEMES

Reading Melvin Bukiet's stories, one often feels that if Bernard Malamud and Cynthia Ozick produced a son, he would write exactly like this—that is, with moral gravitas leavened by earthy humor, and with world-weariness forced to share space with messianic yearning. Ozick and Malamud are among Bukiet's more important literary models, but so too is the strange Catholic writer who lived most of her life in rural Georgia and whom we know as Flannery O'Connor. She was perhaps America's first theo-fictionist and, as such, an abiding presence in the theo-fictions that Bukiet writes.

Like all literary categories, theo-fiction has as many liabilities as it does assets, but it can be a useful means to distinguish O'Connor from a more conventionally Catholic writer such as J. F. Powers. That Powers's stories often deal with priests and an insider's sense of convent life is true enough, but one does not think of his fiction as God-obsessed in the powerful, uncompromising ways that O'Connor's is. Moreover, the same observations could be made, with an adjustment here, a modification there, about the essential differences between Jewish theo-fictionists and more secularly minded chroniclers of the Jewish-American scene. Philip Roth, for example, fits easily into the latter camp: his earliest stories were slabs of social realism, filled to the brim with sharp, often satirical jabs at the life assimilated, newly affluent Jews made in the American suburbs. Like J. F. Powers, he knew the details, and even more impressive, he knew how to weave them into high art.

But that said, it is worth remembering that his protagonists tended to quarrel with nagging Jewish mothers (*Portnoy's Complaint*) or overly cautious tribal spokesmen (*The Ghost Writer*) rather than with God, and that the result risked reducing itself to an irritating whine. By contrast, a writer like Cynthia Ozick came to the writing of fiction with a moral gravitas and a much richer sense of what "Jewishness" finally means. As she put it in the introductory remarks to an early story: "I believe that stories ought to judge and interpret the world." The result was fiction that changed the way we define Jewish-American writing and, more important, the way that Jewish-American writing defines itself. Ozick herself talked about creating a "new Yiddish," about the necessity of exploring fiction's "liturgical" dimensions, but what she set in motion with stories such as "The Pagan Rabbi" and "Bloodshed" was writing that riddled about God-as-riddle. That Ozick has been compared to O'Connor is hardly surprising because both writers were as unflinching about consequences as they were inclined toward theology.

Melvin Bukiet's extraordinary tales continue this tradition. In *Stories of an Imaginary Childhood* (1992), he re-creates the world of Proszowice, Poland, as seen through the eyes of an unnamed twelve-year-old protagonist; and in *While the Messiah Tarries*, writes stories that move effortlessly from Manhattan to the Soviet Union. What Bukiet will not (cannot?) do is confront the Holocaust experience directly, but the power his fictions pack may reveal more about the situation of Jewry in our nightmarish century than tales of barbed wire and gas chambers ever could. For Bukiet aims at "revelation" of a peculiarly gritty sort. As he put it in his 1993 Edward Lewis Wallant Prize acceptance speech: "Fiction is the language of revelation in our time, and that may be a modern heresy.

As the Bible ceases to satisfy and Biblical parables to soothe, fiction provides the stories we need to tell ourselves.''

Let me hasten to add, however, that the ''stories we need to tell ourselves'' must take both God and history into full account—and furthermore, that they are likely to be unsettling. In the Wallant speech, Bukiet insisted that fiction is ''the voice of God within us enabling a creation from nothing''; it is, therefore, an attempt ''to make the world as it should be.'' But he also went on to point out that ''as God failed at Auschwitz, fiction becomes the world that is, flawed, degenerated from the first idyll.'' *Stories of an Imaginary Childhood*, then, is a shadowy resemblance to a world that did exist (it was, in fact, the world of his father), an effort to reinscribe what the Nazis obliterated into the Book of Life. Memory, however, often takes peculiar, even disturbing turns in Bukiet's fiction, for he is less concerned about getting the details of social realism exactly right than he is with evoking a shivery, theological brooding. Here, for example, is a selection taken from the collection's concluding tale. ''Torquemada'' is, at its most literal level, a feverish dream in which Bukiet's young protagonist imagines that he is the Grand Inquisitor; but it is also a relentless brooding about history's mortal pang, its bloodthirsty darkness:

''Oh, he was a strange one,'' the [Polish peasant boy says.] ''He actually asked me why I hated Jews. Then when I answered him we started fighting. . . .''

''You need to ask why? Because of me, Chmielnicki, and because of Herod and Haman, and because of Torquemada. Or will you tell me that's how He shows His love?'' (*Stories of an Imaginary Childhood*, ''Torquemada,'' 197)

At this, Bukiet's youthful protagonist begins to cry, and the dybbuk of Torquemada is replaced by a growing sense of his Jewishness. The worried elders who have been clustered around him feel that at last, everything is all right. As one puts it: ''What harm could possibly come to us in 1928?'' (''Torquemada,'' 197). Bukiet, of course, is all too aware of the terrible ways that history will answer such innocent questions. Like Aharon Appelfeld's characters, Bukiet's Eastern European Jews live in a world that cannot imagine the night and fog, the fire and ash, destined to consume them. But Bukiet also cannot help brooding about the place that God plays in the unrolling of the unimaginable.

Fiction is, then, a proper place to raise questions that were once the province of theology. It is one of Maimonides' thirteen attributes—the one many pious Jews recited as they entered the gas chambers—that provides a title for Bukiet's latest collection. In the post-Holocaust world, theo-fiction offers a consolation uniquely its own—not the bromide of sermons or the consolation of answers where none can exist, but, rather, tougher questions and more puzzling puzzles.

''The Library of Moloch'' is a case in point. At one level, it is a devastating critique of a project designed to collect videotapes of Holocaust survivors, and of its earnest, well-meaning director. Bukiet's title is, of course, taken from Jorge Luis Borges's ''The Library of Babel,'' arguably his most representative tale about the labyrinthian world of fictions-within-fictions and the magical realism he spins about them. By contrast, Bukiet's story drives toward more palpable conclusions as the director finds himself tormented by a reluctant witness who accuses him of jealousy ("You are jealous of the Holocaust. Jealous of having a reason to hate. . . . Jealous of those who adhere to a broken covenant. Jealous of the sacred.") and then confronted by a fire that systematically destroys the videotapes he has amassed:

In his delirium, he wondered if fire was the fate of all libraries. First, there was the Library of Alexandria with the wisdom of the ancient world, and now, the Library of Moloch containing what its keeper truly believed was the wisdom of the modern world. Perhaps, he thought crazily amid the mounting flames, the fate was not inappropriate, for Moloch was the god of fire to whom children were routinely sacrificed. Moloch, the Lord of Gehenna, lived outside of Jerusalem in what was truly the valley of the damned, forever exiled in sight of the heavenly city. (*While the Messiah Tarries*, "The Library of Moloch," 196)

Earlier, the director's antagonist had told him that there were two inviolate realms. One is memory. The other—which he only discovers in the story's final word—is theology. Theo-fiction, I would argue, concerns itself with both, and, moreover, in ways that are likely to disturb those accustomed to more conventional Jewish-American fiction. But from Job to Reb Levi Yitzhok, Jewish writers have insisted that God, too, must behave as a *mentsh*; and in the last years of our blood-soaked century, such calls have an increased urgency.

CRITICAL RECEPTION

Reviewer-critics were lavish in their praise of *Stories of an Imaginary Childhood*, but perhaps more important, they competed with each other to find a language appropriate to the collection's extraordinary achievement. Writing in the *Chicago Tribune*, Joseph Coates focused on Bukiet's ability to "remember" that which he had not experienced firsthand: "Working with his refugee father's tales of Jewish shtetl life in Poland before the Holocaust, plus his own sense of an irrevocably lost heritage, Bukiet has created a detailed alternative universe of linked short stories full of familiar elements that have an eerie beauty uniquely their own, deriving from the author's commitment to relive a childhood (his father's) that in a sane world would have been his own as well" (May 28, 1992). Others talked about the elements of magical realism that were intertwined into his reconstructed world. Michael Dirda, editor of the *Washington Post's Book World*, planned to assign *While the Messiah Tarries* to an outside reviewer (one "interested in Jewish fiction, especially the kind tinged with fantasy a la Isaac Bashevis Singer"), only to end up reviewing the book himself. Why? Because after skimming a few stories, he simply could not put the book down: "The assurance of the prose, the entrancing voice of the storyteller . . . and, above all, that feather's touch of humor—all these were quite irresistible'' (August 13, 1995, 2). Arguably the most interesting Jewish voice to emerge in several decades, Bukiet is a writer who will be argued about, and explicated, in the next decades.

BIBLIOGRAPHY

Works by Melvin Bukiet

Sandman's Dust. Las Vegas, Nevada: Arbor House, 1985.
Stories of an Imaginary Childhood. Evanston, Illinois: Northwestern University Press, 1992.
While the Messiah Tarries (short stories). San Diego, California: Harcourt Brace, 1995.
After. New York, N.Y.: St. Martin's Press, 1996.
Bukiet's stories have appeared in *Paris Review, Antaeus,* and other literary periodicals.

Studies of Melvin Bukiet

Coates, Joseph. Review of *Stories of an Imaginary Childhood. Chicago Tribune,* May 28, 1992, n.p.
Dirda, Michael. Review of *While the Messiah Tarries*—Washington Post's Book World, August 13, 1995, 2.

ARTHUR ALLEN COHEN   (1928–1986)

Claire R. Satlof

BIOGRAPHY

Arthur Allen Cohen—novelist, theologian, and art critic—was born in New York on June 25, 1928: the son of Isidore Meyer and Bess Junger Cohen, both second-generation American Jews. However, in interviews, Cohen stressed the greater significance of his "rebirth" as a Jew, even referring to himself as a "convert" (Cohen, "Why I Choose to Be a Jew," 748). Cohen wrote that he grew up in a "fundamentally unobservant home" where his parents were more concerned with success as measured in secular American terms than with Jewish education or observance. The result was that "although the flesh was nourished, the spirit was left unattended" (746). Consequently, when Cohen was confronted with the Christian underpinnings of Western culture during required courses at the University of Chicago, he began to consider converting to Christianity. "I was rushed not to a psychoanalyst but to a Rabbi—the late Milton Steinberg," he recalled (747). What followed was the discovery of Judaism and a conscious decision to be Jewish.

Cohen's lifelong dedication to this defining experience, however, did not preclude his continued investigation of Western/secular issues. Instead, throughout his series of professional and textual activities, Cohen investigated both the "natural" and the "supernatural" Jew, as he characterized the distinction in one of his earliest theological works. The "natural" Jew is historical, "activated" by the specifics of nationality, temporality, and civilization. The "supernatural" Jew is a product of the choice to become part of a covenanted transhistorical community that can visualize redemption. Both, significantly, are vital and present in each individual, according to Cohen, and he saw it as his lifelong task, as a specifically religious obligation, to participate in a culture making that valued each side: "If Judaism is to realize its catholic nature it must rediscover its relation to culture—not merely Jewish culture, but the culture of any time and any society of which it is both creature and creator" (Cohen, *The Natural and the Supernatural Jew*, 305).

Cohen received his B.A. from the University of Chicago in 1946 and his master's degree in 1949. Then, abandoning his proposed dissertation on "The Use of Metaphor and Metaphysical Language in Literature," he left to study first at Union Theological Seminary and then the Jewish Theological Seminary. He subsequently redirected his academic interests, becoming both the author of a number of critical investigations (beginning with one on Martin Buber) and a publisher before writing his first novel. In every category of professional activity, Cohen's adherence to the Sartrean view of the artist's role as remaker of the world merges with his sense of religious vocation, as a brief overview of his work suggests. In addition to his fiction and theological works, Cohen wrote on subjects as diverse yet intrinsically connected as Osip Mandelstam, the artist Sonia Delaunay, and the significance of typography in Dadaism. At the same time, Cohen cofounded Noonday Press in 1951, publishing Louise Bogan, Middleton Murray on Keats, and a relatively unknown I. B. Singer. In 1955 he sold Noonday and founded Meridian Books, where he published Hannah Arendt, Philip Rahv, Erich Auerbach, and Lionel Trilling (Cole, 35). After selling Meridian, Cohen served as director of the religious book department of Holt, Rinehart, and Winston, then as editor-in-chief, and finally as editor of the Documents of Modern Art series at Viking. At the time of his death, Cohen and his wife, painter Elaine Lustig Cohen, owned and operated Ex-Libris, a gallery/bookstore specializing in rare historical art documents. In addition, Cohen was on the board of the PEN American Center and was chairman of the board of the YIVO Institute for Jewish Research. He and his wife had one daughter, Tamar.

MAJOR WORKS AND THEMES

While not a critical success, Cohen's first novel, *The Carpenter Years* (1967), is useful as an introduction to the way ideology informs his fiction. In it, a middle-aged Jewish man who has deserted his Jewish wife, son, and life in New York to pass as a Christian director of the YMCA in a rural Pennsylvania town must now face his son, an analyst-in-training who deliberately interviews for a job in this town so he can force a confrontation with his father. Edgar Morrison, formerly Morris Edelman, says that he left his Jewishness because he was afraid of failure—afraid he would betray what he sees as a "mythic significance" of the Jewish people. Therefore, leaving New York, Morris sets out to become a Christian, an American, who "could fail and fail quietly, unknown and undiscovered. Soul redeemed in Jesus Christ . . . and buried in the vastness of America." As much as Edgar tries, though, he continues to feel that he has betrayed "something so vast and incomprehensible that no single man could properly be asked—even, even by God—to be responsible for it all by himself." To return to Cohen's terminology, he has forsaken his supernaturalness, and so when the carpenter years end (an allusion to Jesus' life before his annunciation) and revelation should shine forth, Edgar has only darkness. His Jewish son, Daniel, a reluctant interpreter of dreams, has no better answers, but at least he has access to the dreams themselves, those simultaneously natural and supernatural mergings of art and personal revelation that Leslie Fiedler has called the American Jewish contribution to literature.

By the later books—*A Hero in His Time* (1976), *Acts of Theft* (1980), and *Artists and Enemies* (1987)—Cohen can more clearly articulate and locate the only potential source of comfort: art. In every book after his first, art and fabulation—the imaginative acts of creating—are at the center of the text. In his most extensive discussion of the role of literature, especially Jewish literature, Cohen identifies the goal of the imagination in Sartre's terms as "a synthetic reconstruction of the world" (*The American Imagination after the War*, 21); he continues to specify the role of Jewish literature as "a redevising of the narrative condition of the people of Israel and the Jewish people" (32). What Cohen seeks to create is a new synthesis for Jewish-American literature and its readers, fully participatory in both worlds, part human and part divine. If Hannah Arendt has correctly identified history as the substitute for authority and the thread of historical continuity as the first substitute for tradition, then Cohen attempts to create a new artistically authentic, historically rooted tradition.

In *A Hero in His Time*, for example, Cohen's first real critical success, a Russian-Jewish poet distinguishes "history" from "story" by differentiating between *historia* and *mythopoesis*. *Mythopoesis* is the real story, he asserts (not surprisingly): "Poesis comes from God. The God, he speak poetry, and when . . . God speak poetry, he tell story." The greatest joy, concludes the poet, is keeping an ear to the ground, where we can hear God himself singing stories that we then tell.

The "artist" books, *Acts of Theft* and *Artists and Enemies*, move on to focus both on the divine nature of the artist's role and on the omnipresent coexisting baseness of his human side. While would-be painters and sculptors use and abuse those around them, ultimately betraying their own talent in the first two novellas of *Artists and Enemies*, "Malenov's Revenge" reveals most profoundly both the malevolence of the artistic ego and its potential. Here is the "prophetic artist" whose frustrated realization "I don't like nature as it is" marks the starting point for "his own visionary breakthrough, a premise of reconstruction."

Similarly, in *Acts of Theft*, a physically and psychically displaced artist steals pre-Columbian art treasures, seeking in them a connection to a past he lacks. The narrator makes clear that the value of these artifacts lies in their cultural status, that they "were not made to beautify or ornament, not even to celebrate, but, quite simply, to keep the universe going." Calling this novel a portrait of "the artist as God," John Leonard singled out Cohen's and his fictional artist's drive to mediate between the natural and supernatural worlds: "Obviously both painting and sculpture are desperate measures in the absence of an acceptable metaphysics of the unseen'' (C9). Ultimately, the artist realizes that he must fabricate his own modern idols, new totem poles, that capture the sense of a collective human past and the specificity of his own world.

An Admirable Woman (1983) approaches the idea of fabrication from a different angle. Here, Cohen has fabricated a not–Hannah Arendt (to quote the reviews) as his central character. A press release that accompanied the publication of this fictional autobiography of an intellectual historian stated (lest reviewers fail to notice the close parallels) that this is not a book about Arendt. It is, though, a book about history and free will, a point Cohen underscores by having Erika (the not-Arendt) tell us that her life-text is Genesis 3, the story of the Fall and Expulsion, as glossed by Heinrich von Kleist. Her point, briefly summarized, is that the divine and human contain elements of one another just as history and eternity do. Humanity must live through (in the psychiatric sense of working through) history, engaging it in a ''divine spirit'' if we are to live meaningful lives.

Despite its uneven reception, Cohen's most frequently discussed novel is *In the Days of Simon Stern* (1973), an intensely ambitious novel that epitomizes the possibility of the self-consciously fabricated transition to a new synthetic mode of seeing, if not being. The work's formal elements—tone, characterization, and plot—certainly suggest a rite of passage, although, at first, the intended destination seems purely supernatural. The details outlined in the text fit the anthropological description of a rite of passage with its formal ritualized behavior taking participants through symbolic death to rebirth as well as through the traditionally conceived birth pangs and functions of the Jewish Messiah. Messiah Simon Stern is going to rebuild the Temple and, in the process, guide his followers through the reenactment of the central Jewish myth of exile and redemption, culminating in a new sanctified self-governing community of Israel. The participants in the ritual, the characters in the novel, are Holocaust survivors and are described in classic terms, as is the process they undergo. These are liminars, to use Victor Turner's terminology, occupants of the betwixt-and-between stage, the truly marginal. With no status or kinship, these survivors have retreated to a compound on the Lower East Side where they are building a structure symbolic of their separation and reintegration into society: the Temple.

As an artifact, though, the text seems to embody the ambiguities of the details it describes; the Temple, for instance, is being made to look like an ordinary building. Parodies abound, with Simon himself being a parody of Sabbtai Zvi, the false seventeenth-century Messiah, Shimon Bar Kochba, whose name translates as ''Simon, Son of a Star'' and who was considered by many in the second century to be the Messiah, and Jesus, whose parents were given the same mystical promise as Simon Stern's. Framed tales, newly invented homilies, and midrashic commentaries that do not always make sense are recounted in recognition of the chaos that accompanies rites of passage and communal restructuring. Since all deviation recalls the norm, the resulting tension between parodic invention and traditional Jewish culture constantly recalls those norms just as the parodic linking of Simon with other possible messiahs suggests that he does belong to that tradition.

At the same time, though, the linking of Simon Stern with specifically false messiahs—false to modern Judaism, that is—points to the inevitable unraveling of the scenario and to the historicity of the synthesis. Simon Stern cannot be the Messiah—at least, not a true, an "ordinary" Messiah. First, he does not rescue all the survivors of the Holocaust, much less all the Jews. In addition, he is much too historically American; an inheritor of the David Levinsky tradition of Jewish Horatio Algers, he has made a fortune in real estate by being a true capitalist and an anti-Semite's dream. He has been stingy and scheming and is physically almost a caricature. His kingdom is in a tenement, and his own experience of exile and Holocaust has been to see his parents die when their house, which he owns, catches fire because he has neglected an electrical problem. Simon is too ordinary, too much a part of the natural order.

Even more to the point are the novel's constant reminders of its fictionality, its textual and so historical nature. Not only is the book written in English, "the language of exchange and intercourse, carnal union, . . . fallen angels," as narrator Nathan Gaza tells the reader, but it is a self-conscious artistic creation. In fact, what makes the Messiah the Messiah is his artistic designation as such: "It is I, finally, who must make the myth and make you believe it," writes Nathan. Finally, Simon's Temple, like the others, is destroyed, the community is dispersed, and the neighborhood is condemned.

Yet, in the end, a Messiah has come: Nathan Gaza is vindicated. The Messiah's function is to redeem history, and history is redeemed here—not in the traditional sense of being subsumed but by being allowed to continue. The supernatural restores the natural, providing the reader access to both. This Messiah re-creates a sense of historical consistency, suggesting that Simon Stern is a historical Messiah, a fictional but not a false Messiah.

If Cohen's fictional canon, however, seems to suggest a view of the artist as hero, Cohen is quick to clarify just who qualifies as "artist" and to whom tribute should be made. Quoting Franz Rosenzweig, he notes the absence of a Prometheus or Faust legend in Judaism, the absence of a single man "who would take upon himself the powers of the mysterium." Instead, he claims that role for the entire Jewish people: "Am Yisrael is indeed for the Jewish imagination both Prometheus and Faust, unwilling to succumb to fate, willing, often obliged by the outrage of history, to take to itself the task it believes God to have forgotten" ("Between Two Traditions," 34). Ultimately, in other words, if the Messiah comes when men are speechless, Cohen affirms the voice of the ordinary community of readers who serve the traditional messianic function of uniting history and ritual, again holding them in careful balance as it echoes the stories of the tradition in the fictions of the present.

CRITICAL RECEPTION

Perhaps the best overview of the criticism on Cohen's fiction is the remark by a reviewer of his final work, *Artists and Enemies*, who wrote that "in a way, he exemplified the Karl Kraus witticism about being a famous person but only a few people knew it" (Philipson 20). Reviewing *A Hero in His Time* for the *Village Voice*, in fact, Doris Grumbach began on a note of surprise that such a prolific novelist should be so relatively unknown (45). One possible explanation for Cohen's lack of "popular" status as well as for frequently lukewarm reviews may lie in his deliberately didactic style, complete with authorial moral intent. When asked about the parables and philosophical monologues that occupy much of his novels, he called these a "bonus" to readers, complaining that often "there is an impatience with intellectual endeavor. . . . We're only concerned with the imagination acting as an immediate sensation" (Lask, C24). But the imaginative transfer of essays into fiction seems heavy-handed to many review-ers. David Daiches, reviewing *The Carpenter Years*, wrote, "The details in this novel are filled in with skill and care and there is some powerful and occasion-ally even moving writing. But the author moves uneasily between realism and symbolism" (95). In a similar vein, Mark Shechner noted in the *New York Times* that *Acts of Theft* "begins in melodrama and ends in philosophy" (10). How-ever, a second reviewer for the *Times*, John Leonard, praised the same book, implicitly comparing Cohen to Rimbaud in his creation of the poet-figure as "thief of fire" (C9). Leonard found the novel compelling and aesthetically grat-ifying, whereas Shechner found it "breathless" instead of "sublime."

While *An Admirable Woman* received the National Jewish Book Award, *A Hero in His Time* has received the most consistently enthusiastic critical re-sponse. For Geoffrey Wolff, Cohen here achieves "a tour de force, bringing the idea of poetry to life" in an authentic account of a *schlemiel* as communicant (4), while Grumbach also focused on the novel's realistic characterization. In her critical overview of Cohen's fiction to date, she validated Cohen's own view of his work when she pointed to his use of "Jewish subject matter, the Jew as paradigm for creative artist surviving the deafness and hostility of the rest of humanity" (45).

As mentioned previously, however, *In the Days of Simon Stern* continues to be the most frequently discussed of Cohen's fictional works, possibly because of continuing interest in issues of the Holocaust and redemption. The wildly enthusiastic review by Cohen's good friend and fellow modern-day midrashist Cynthia Ozick may have helped focus critical interest as well. Ozick's review is full of critical detail and superlatives in its recognition of the natural/super-natural connection: "And yet (here is what is extraordinary) in its teeming par-ticularity every vein of this book runs with a brilliance of Jewish insight and erudition to be found in no other novelist; the sacred texts are mastered, and so also are the more problematic mystical and philosophical texts, all ground to-gether into the grain of the fiction. Arthur Cohen is the first writer of any

American generation to compose a profoundly Jewish fiction on a profoundly Western theme'' (6).

BIBLIOGRAPHY

Works by Arthur Allen Cohen

Fiction

The Carpenter Years. New York: New American Library, 1967.
In the Days of Simon Stern. New York: Random House, 1973.
A Hero in His Time. New York: Random House, 1976.
Acts of Theft. New York: Harcourt Brace Jovanovich, 1980.
An Admirable Woman. Boston: David R. Godine, 1983.
Artists and Enemies: Three Novellas. Boston: David R. Godine, 1987.

Selected Articles

"Why I Choose to Be a Jew." *Harper's* 218 (April 1959): 61–66. Reprinted in *The Judaic Tradition*, ed. Nahum N. Glatzer. Boston: Beacon Press, 1969, 744–55.
"Between Two Traditions." *Midstream* 12 (June/July 1966): 26–35.
"Life Amid the Paradigms, or the Absence of a Jewish Critique of Culture." *Journal of the American Academy of Religion* 54 (Fall 1986): 499–520.
"On Judaism and Modernism." *Partisan Review* 54 (Summer 1987): 437–42.
"Myths and Riddles: Some Observations about Literature and Theology." *Prooftexts* 7 (Fall 1987): 110–22.

Other Selected Works

Martin Buber. New York: Hillary House, 1957.
The Natural and the Supernatural Jew. New York: Pantheon Books, 1962.
The Myth of the Judeo-Christian Tradition. New York: Harper and Row, 1970.
Osip Emilievich Mandelstam: An Essay in Antiphon. Ann Arbor: Ardis, 1974.
Sonia Delaunay. New York: Abrams, 1975.
The American Imagination after the War: Notes on the Novel, Jews, and Hope. Vol. 19. Syracuse: Syracuse University Press, 1981.
The Tremendum: A Theological Interpretation of the Holocaust. New York: Crossroad Books, 1981.

Works Cited and Studies of Arthur Allen Cohen

Baker, John F. "Interview: Arthur A. Cohen." *Publisher's Weekly* 209 (January 19, 1976): 10–12.
Berger, Alan L. *Crisis and Covenant: The Holocaust in American Jewish Fiction.* Albany: State University of New York Press, 1985.
Bilik, Dorothy Seidman. *Immigrant-Survivors: Post-Holocaust Consciousness in Recent Jewish American Fiction.* Middletown, CT: Wesleyan University Press, 1981.
Cole, Diane. "Profession: Renaissance Man: Profile of Arthur A. Cohen." *Present Tense* 9 (Fall 1981): 32–35.

Daiches, David. "Symbolic Dimensions." *Commentary* 44 (April 1967): 94–96.

Gertel, Elliot B. "Visions of the American Jewish Messiah." *Judaism* 31 (Spring 1982): 153–65.

Grumbach, Doris. "Arthur Cohen Catches Fire." *Village Voice*, March 15, 1976, 45.

Kremer, S. Lillian. *Witness through the Imagination: Jewish American Holocaust Literature*. Detroit: Wayne State University Press, 1989.

Lask, Thomas. "Publishing: From Art Books to a Novel about Art." *New York Times*, February 22, 1980, C24.

Leonard, John. "Acts of Theft." *New York Times*, February 12, 1980, C9.

Ozick, Cynthia. "In the Days of Simon Stern." *New York Times Book Review*, June 3, 1973, 6.

Philipson, Morris. "Art Is Not Enough: *Artists and Enemies: Three Novellas*, by Arthur Cohen." *New York Times Book Review*, April 12, 1987, 20.

Rosenfeld, Alvin H. "Arthur A. Cohen's Messiah." *Midstream* 18 (August/September 1973): 72–75.

Shechner, Mark. "Graven Images and Other Temptations." *New York Times Book Review*, March 9, 1980, 10.

Stern, David. "An Introduction to 'Myths and Riddles: Some Observations about Literature and Theology.' " *Prooftexts* 7 (May 1987): 107–9.

———. "Theology into Art: An Appreciation of Arthur A. Cohen." *Response* 21 (Fall 1987): 63–71.

Wolff, Geoffrey. "A Hero in His Time." *New York Times Book Review*, January 25, 1976, 4.

E. L. DOCTOROW   (1931–   )

Sabine Sauter

BIOGRAPHY

Edgar Laurence Doctorow was born on January 6, 1931, in New York City to David Richard and Rose Levine Doctorow, both children of Russian-Jewish immigrants. He grew up in the Bronx and attended the Bronx High School of Science before moving west to study at Kenyon College under the direction of John Crowe Ransom. Guided by leaders of the New Criticism, Doctorow learned to "hear the music in language" and "become an effective editor" (Doctorow, Interview).

In 1952 Doctorow graduated with an A.B. (Honors). The same year he started graduate work in playwriting at Columbia University, but his studies were cut short by the draft board. From 1953 to 1955 Doctorow served with the U.S. Army Signal Corps, mostly in Germany. On August 20, 1954, he married Helen Esther Setzer, and together they have three children: Jenny, Caroline, and Richard. Doctorow currently makes his home in New Rochelle, New York.

While working as a script reader for Columbia Pictures Industries in New York City, Doctorow began his career as a novelist. He has spoken of having to read so many bad westerns that he finally felt compelled to "lie about the West in a much more interesting way than any of these people were lying" (quoted in *Contemporary Authors*, 110). The "falsehood" or invention that grew out of this sense of obligation turned into his first novel, *Welcome to Hard Times* (1960). Since writing his western, Doctorow has established himself as a major American author, writing seven more novels, one drama, a book of short stories, screenplays for two of his novels, the text for a book of American photographs, and a collection of essays. His work has been translated into over twenty languages, and three of his books, *Welcome to Hard Times, Ragtime* (1975), and *Billy Bathgate* (1989), have been made into films.

Throughout his career Doctorow has held many writing-related positions. From 1959 to 1964 he worked as senior editor at the New American Library in New York City. From 1964 to 1969 he was editor-in-chief at Dial Press in New York and from 1968 to 1969 vice president and publisher. Doctorow was writer-in-residence at the University of California at Irvine from 1969 to 1970 and a member of the faculty at Sarah Lawrence College, Bronxville, New York, from 1971 to 1978. He was a creative-writing fellow at the Yale School of Drama from 1974 to 1975. In 1975 he was also visiting professor at the University of Utah; from 1980 to 1981 he was visiting senior fellow at Princeton University. Since 1982 he has been Glucksman Professor of English and American Letters at New York University, New York City.

The numerous honors awarded Doctorow for his fiction confirm his place as one of the most popular authors writing in English today. *The Book of Daniel* (1971) was nominated for a National Book Award in 1972. Doctorow received a Guggenheim Fellowship in 1973 and was a Creative Artists Service Fellow from 1973 to 1974. *Ragtime* earned the National Book Critics Circle Award and the Arts and Letters Award in 1976. Hobart and William Smith colleges awarded him a Litt.D. in 1979. *Drinks before Dinner* was produced by the New York Shakespeare Festival in 1978 and published in 1979. In 1980 *Loon Lake* (1980) was nominated for the National Book Award, and *World's Fair* (1985) won the National Book Award in 1986. *Billy Bathgate* was also nominated for a National Book Award in 1989. In 1990 it won the PEN/Faulkner Award for Fiction, the National Book Critics Circle Award, and the William Dean Howells Medal. Doctorow's latest work, *The Waterworks* (1994), was a national best-seller. Doctorow is a member of the American Academy and Institute of Arts and Letters, a director of the Authors Guild, a director of PEN, and an active participant in the Writers Guild of America.

MAJOR WORKS AND THEMES

Doctorow seldom addresses Jewish themes or customs directly, but he makes an intellectual investment in the common human lot that can be seen as coming out of his cultural heritage. He was raised in a kind of '' 'Jewish-humanist secular milieu,' which valorized a socialist turn of mind and trade unionist sensibilities'' (Doctorow, Interview). Many of his books focus on middle- or lower-class individuals, portraying them as innovative and sympathetic. While several protagonists are Jewish, the stories on the whole tend to emphasize the flexibility of identity and the way an individual must often conform or even radically transform in order to be accepted into American society. Through his prose we find the United States to be a remarkable place, yet hostile to the poor and possessing a questionable history.

In Doctorow's fourth book, *Ragtime*, Houdini makes a heroic effort to liberate himself from a straightjacket while hanging upside down from the Times Building in New York; his spectacle is successful in that he catches the attention of the general public, and yet his act is based on some kind of hoax. The success of many of Doctorow's artistic feats as a novelist similarly relies on the careful fabrication of some kind of illusion. Doctorow demonstrates to the world at large that in novelistic writing it may be possible to get free from something as monumental as the "Times"; for the author this means a version of the past that has been established by a society's politicians and historians. In his books Doctorow often rewrites earlier periods, changing crucial events or the personality traits of well-known individuals. Doctorow's elaborate, sophisticated, and astonishing trick is to make it seem in his verbal performance as though there is no substantial difference between fact and fiction.

That is not to say that Doctorow is careless in his formulations of previous periods. "Doctorow writes from the perspective of a moral consciousness to reexamine the meaning of the American experience and to revivify our moral imagination," according to Sam B. Girgus (161). Indeed, the author is greatly concerned with what kind of record remains after an event takes place. A main purpose of his writing is to show that writing is always subjective, and that one can always change the way the world appears through the telling of a story. "Reality," Doctorow stated at a conference discussion of his work, "is amenable to any construction placed on it" (Friedl and Schulz, 186). According to Doctorow, the novelist's act of storytelling is no less respectable than another's more standard or "factual" system of representation; a creative writer's account of a notable episode is just as valid as a more conventionally construed historical record. "There is no fiction or nonfiction as we commonly understand the distinction," Doctorow maintains, "there is only narrative" (Trenner, 26).

From Doctorow's own narrative accounts there emerges a rather bleak view of American society. His first book, *Welcome to Hard Times*, depicts a variety of individuals, active during the 1800s, who are powerless to escape a dark fate of doom. These people have moved gradually westward in order to evade the hardships imposed by a newly established eastern civilization—poverty, diminished social status, and political impotence. In the wilderness they band together to form a kind of community. The small society's destruction approaches quickly, however. The narrator, Blue, together with his fellow townsfolk, finds that he cannot escape the difficulties associated with the part of the country he thought he had left behind. The message seems to be that some kind of evil force, in this case embodied in the Bad Man from Bodie, will always emerge to disrupt a peaceful community; it will inevitably assert a kind of dreadful control over a population that wants desperately to be free of such constraints.

In Doctorow's next book, *Big as Life* (1966), the main characters are part of a population whose actions are motivated by fear and anxiety, and whose government is secretive and somewhat deceitful. *Big as Life* is a kind of satiric science-fiction tale. Two naked giants suddenly appear in New York harbor, and their inexplicable existence wreaks havoc in the city. Though it enjoyed some critical support, *Big as Life* is probably Doctorow's weakest work: the author has himself requested that it be kept out of print.

The Book of Daniel, a political and historical novel, again presents a sinister view of society. Americans are depicted as self-involved and otherwise apathetic—unconcerned even about the integrity of their country's justice system. As a whole, the novel engages important questions about the production and presentation of public and private "truths." Some critics observe that this is also Doctorow's most obviously Jewish book: the central character in this story bears a striking resemblance to his biblical counterpart, and the novel is greatly concerned with problems of persecution and anguish.

The Book of Daniel is also based to a great degree on the events surrounding the trial of American Jews Ethel and Julius Rosenberg. The names of the historical figures have been altered in Doctorow's novel, and the gender of the younger child has been changed to female, but many of the incidents that Doctorow "creates" nonetheless correspond to well-known "facts" surrounding the case. Daniel, the main character and narrator, provides the text of the story through the dissertation he is writing in the library of Columbia University. His mental agitation drives him to try to find an alternative but plausible version of his parents' death, an account that will fit with his own idea of himself and simultaneously free his parents from culpability. The narrative is typically experimental, testing the validity of various points of view. The overall story line remains relatively straightforward, but Daniel's own research seems entirely haphazard. The narrator is consistently unable to consolidate all of the conflicting evidence. It is appropriate, therefore, that at the end of his endeavors, Daniel titles his thesis "A Life Submitted in Partial Fulfillment of the Requirements for the Doctoral Degree in Social Biology, Gross Entomology, Women's Anatomy, Children's Cacophony, Arch Demonology, Eschatology, and Thermal Pollution."

In *Ragtime* Doctorow again reinterprets, in a way rewrites, a bygone era. He adapts the lives of actual people like political activist Emma Goldman, financier J. P. Morgan, and escape artist Harry Houdini to suit his own narrative. Occasionally he contrives to have these "real" characters interact with imagined ones. Historical figures meet people who are variously part of a middle-class WASP family, a black ragtime musician's family, and a poor Jewish immigrant duo. *Ragtime* is set for the most part in New York during the period preceding World War I. In the novel, where the prose style strives to imitate the syncopated rhythm of ragtime, "real" and fictional people converse, become lovers, quarrel, threaten each others' lives, and, in some rare instances, even live happily ever after.

Drinks before Dinner is Doctorow's one drama. According to Doctorow in his introduction, it is meant to explore a "sense of heightened language." The play's protagonist, Edgar, belongs to a group of rich New Yorkers that meets regularly for dinner parties at which one superficially enjoys one's friends' newest acquisitions and engages politely in intelligent but inoffensive conversation. On the evening of the play there is a special guest, a Nobel Prize laureate, and Edgar takes the opportunity to try to alert his small community to its own ridiculousness. He holds forth on the ills of society while brandishing a gun to reinforce his authority. But after a couple of hours of ranting, Edgar is only frustrated and exhausted. The guests and hosts appear to be frightened by his words and manic gesticulations, but inwardly they are contemptuous of his presumptions. When he realizes that there is no respectable way out of his situation, Edgar resigns by putting down his gun, which, it becomes obvious, had not even been loaded. Once the small party realizes that the gun is empty, it acts as if Edgar's statements were also merely hollow words and blithely goes on with its dinner party, annoyed only that its festivities have been delayed.

In *Loon Lake* the main character, Joseph Korzeniowski of working-class Paterson, New Jersey, departs from his small-minded and poverty-stricken hometown during the Great Depression and travels through the Adirondack Mountains, where he has a fleeting view of a train filled with grandiose elements of elegance. He follows the train to Loon Lake and finds himself at an estate built in the wilderness by a millionaire. He plunges into the mogul's weird community, which includes a femme fatale, a poet, a gangster, and an aviatrix, and emerges totally transformed. At the end of the novel, the protagonist is a newly corrupt but financially successful Joseph Paterson Bennett, the invented son of the ailing but still-affluent landlord and tycoon who owns the estate. The narrative style in *Loon Lake* is more highly experimental than in previous books, switching without warning from the first to the third person and from prose to poetry to computerized data. The result is somewhat chaotic, but the style works somehow to reflect Doctorow's idea about the turbulent nature of twentieth-century existence.

Doctorow's next two novels also take place during the 1930s in New York. *World's Fair* is probably Doctorow's most optimistic work and is often considered to have strong autobiographical elements. It is narrated for the most part by Edgar, who grows up in New York City and is enchanted by things such as comic strips, his father's music store, a zeppelin, and of course the World's Fair of 1939. In *Billy Bathgate* the title character is again a young boy making his way through New York in the 1930s, but this time the protagonist moves in a darker world: he is a street urchin who gets caught up in the gangster world of Dieter (''Dutch'') Schultz.

Doctorow's most recent work, *The Waterworks*, expands upon an idea present in a short story published in *Lives of the Poets* (1984) called ''The Waterworks.'' In the late nineteenth century an old newspaper editor tells the story of the ominous events surrounding the death of a small child thirty years earlier in the city's reservoir. He brings to the fore the dubiousness of the fact that the marvellous technology of 1871 that enabled the mass production of newspapers actually depended on the culture of derelict children to be appreciated and promoted, as well as the notorious point that scientific advancements of the same period were probably achieved through experiments denigrating the value of human life. *The Waterworks* again refashions an older mode of storytelling: it has qualities of the detective story, the mystery tale, and scientific studies, and critics compare the novel to the stories of Henry James, Charles Dickens, and Edgar Allen Poe.

CRITICAL RECEPTION

Doctorow's strength as a novelist lies in his ability continually to reinvent his narrative style. Every new work represents another attempt to find an original form of expression suitable to the subject at hand. It is this experimental aspect of Doctorow's fiction that draws the most critical attention.

In *Welcome to Hard Times* Doctorow redrafts the genre of the western, giving it new depth and life. The main character, Blue, is a chronicler, and the way in which he records events forces the reader to confront hackneyed problems in a fresh way. "*Welcome to Hard Times*," wrote Kevin Stan in the *New Republic*, "is a superb piece of fiction: lean and mean, and thematically significant. . . . [Doctorow] takes the thin, somewhat sordid and incipiently depressing materials of the Great Plains experience and fashions them into a myth of good and evil. . . . He does it marvellously, with economy and with great narrative power" (quoted in *Contemporary Authors*, 110).

In his next book, *Big as Life*, Doctorow again attempts to infuse his characters with a high degree of figurative or metaphoric meaning. Like many of his later works, the story lacks factual truth, but *Big as Life* has the disadvantage of not being quite believable. While the novel received some critical approval, the public remained generally unconvinced. Doctorow's story about two unclothed giants strangely materializing on the New York waterfront did not sell well, and as mentioned earlier, the author has requested that it be kept out of print.

The Book of Daniel and *Ragtime* are probably Doctorow's best-known books. Reviews of *The Book of Daniel* routinely praise Doctorow's ability to reveal the ambiguities associated with historical writing. Susan Brienza commented that in the novel the narrative style exposes important epistemological predicaments. The difficulty "of not being able to learn The Truth," she noted, "is mirrored in a style of multiple points of view" (98). But while enthusiasm is high for *The Book of Daniel*, not everyone accepts Doctorow's efforts as meaningful or valid. Steven Bloom found that episodes in the novel were "truer for never having taken place" (Friedl and Schulz, 177), but Pearl K. Bell contested that the book was an "ambitious failure" because it "fudges the facts of the Rosenberg case." Bell claimed that a "novelist who tampers with details of history can do so with impunity; but one who changes or ignores its essence is indefensibly evading the truth" (118).

The "truth" Doctorow presents in his novels, however, may be of a more paradoxical nature. The primary "fact" that is revealed in novels such as *The Book of Daniel* or *Ragtime* is that "facts" need to be connected and organized;

they need to be narrated and interpreted to be meaningful. Doctorow's books show that a narrative is an artificial construction that is likely to change the significance of particular points every time it is newly developed. *The Book of Daniel*, like *Ragtime* and other Doctorow novels, promotes the author's opinion that our society should strive toward a "democracy of perception." "I think you may hope to reach the objective view with a multiplicity of witness [*sic*]," Doctorow maintained at a conference discussion of his work. "The important thing is to have as many sources of information, as many testimonies as possible" (Friedl and Schulz, 184).

In *Ragtime* Doctorow toys with historical data of the era preceding World War I, and his playful dalliance was a great success with the general reading public. *Ragtime* was on the best-seller list for forty weeks, and the American Booksellers' Association attributed a remarkable rise in book sales (up 30 percent) in July 1975 to the popularity of Doctorow's novel. Academic magazines praised the work as enthusiastically as the more popular presses (Sutherland, 4). Barbara Foley, examining the forms of historical consciousness in modern fiction, wrote that since "Doctorow treats with equal aplomb facts that are 'true' and those that are 'created,' [the author calls] into question our concept of factuality and, indeed, of history itself" (168). Walter Clemons expressed a similar idea in *Newsweek*. "Many, not all 'questions' [of veracity] can be answered by combing through biographies and histories of the period," he noted. "[But] the fact that the book stirs one to parlour-game research is amusing evidence that Doctorow has already won the game" (73).

Drinks before Dinner was performed at a number of festivals and off-Broadway to mixed reviews. Most critics feel that the text is interesting and thought-provoking but agree also that it somehow lacks the verbal force that drives most of Doctorow's novels. Michael Feingold put it bluntly in the *Village Voice*: "As a novelist, Doctorow has been able to invent ferociously dramatic scenes," he wrote. "It seems puzzling that in most of *Drinks Before Dinner* his writing is flat, prosy, and empty, lacking not only the curves of human speech but the sting of his own narrative style. . . . I salute his desire to say something gigantic; how I wish he had found a way to say it fully and dramatically" (quoted in Harter and Thompson, 99).

Loon Lake once again tackles the problem of history, but here the narrative is more fragmented than in previous novels. Critics are at odds about the merits of Doctorow's experiment. Jochen Barkhausen saw the narrative strategy of *Loon Lake* as a reflection of Doctorow's attempt to "capture" the "elusive self" in writing (125). Other critics have been less generous, judging that the narrative style is too ostentatious and distracts the reader from the central issues. A reviewer for the *Chicago Tribune* professed that "we can see that Doctorow is trying to convey rootlessness and social unrest through an insouciant free play of language and syntax," but added that "the problem is that these eccentricities draw disproportionate attention to themselves, away from the characters and their concerns" (quoted in *Contemporary Authors*, 112).

In *World's Fair* Doctorow switches to the more conventional story of a young boy growing up and discovering the mysteries of adolescence. The narrative is less difficult than *Loon Lake*'s and perhaps therefore more readily appreciated. Connections to Doctorow's personal life have been eagerly noted. "It is a lush narrative giving the reader a portrait of the artist as a child," wrote John Parks. "It is a rich time capsule that does not bury its mementoes for some indeterminant future, but rather offers its gifts to the present" (95, 105).

Doctorow's next book, *Billy Bathgate*, received copious praise. Critics delighted in the story about a wily youngster negotiating his way through a world of hardened criminals. Though the plot and characters share certain qualities with those found in so-called formula fiction, critics found that Doctorow's rigorous narrative style kept the story from becoming trivial or predictable. In his review of *Billy Bathgate* for *Newsweek*, Peter S. Prescott wrote that "Doctorow embraces sex and violence, those staples of best-selling fiction that many say cannot be treated explicitly in literary works. He rises to the challenge and succeeds." Part of the accomplishment, Prescott suggested, is due to the way Doctorow presents the protagonists' principles—without any kind of ethical presumptions. "Doctorow brings a nice sense of moral ambiguity and creates characters who develop or deteriorate at an appropriate rate" (76).

Reviews of Doctorow's most recent book have been rather more mixed. The main problem critics have with *The Waterworks* has to do with the inner workings of the novel. There is a pervading feeling that the intrigues of the plot are too calculated, not born out of Doctorow's usual liberal style. John Bemrose wrote of having "a sense that Doctorow is too much on top of his own material, unable to let the flow of fictional life carry him where it would" (54). Paul Gray similarly remarked upon a failed attempt on Doctorow's part to be especially meaningful. "The shocking, Poe-like tale at the centre of the novel," he lamented, "does not achieve the emblematic significance that Doctorow wishes it to have" (56).

But if critics found fault with a too narrowly conceived story line, they also highlighted the superiority of Doctorow's descriptive powers. Malcolm Jones called *The Waterworks* a "piece of literary larceny," but admitted that Doctorow "weaves a spell of genuine creepiness." The book's weaknesses are ultimately redeemed, he held, by Doctorow's characterization of the city of Manhattan, which becomes the novel's "flawed hero" (76). In a similar fashion, Bemrose labeled Doctorow's "love song to the New York City of the 1870s "brilliant." He argued that Doctorow's "obsession with control undermines his book," but he also insisted that "there is no denying the mastery in [Doctorow's] evocations of New York, the contrapuntal blending of themes, his vividly drawn characters" (54).

Doctorow's narrative inventions revitalize the lives of people we have committed to memory and character types we have dismissed as dull. His stories are vivid, and yet they paint a rather grim picture of what it means to be part of the New World, where one must struggle, often in vain, to improve one's situation in a hostile environment. Judging by the high number of his books that consistently make the best-seller list, though, the reading public is more than willing to be both entertained and enlightened by Doctorow's unique, if slightly macabre, versions of American life.

BIBLIOGRAPHY

Works by E. L. Doctorow

Welcome to Hard Times. New York: Simon and Schuster, 1960. Republished as *Bad Man from Bodie*. London: Deutsch, 1961.
Big as Life. New York: Simon and Schuster, 1966.
The Book of Daniel. New York: Random House, 1971.
Ragtime. New York: Random House, 1975.
Drinks before Dinner. New York: Random House, 1979.
Loon Lake. New York: Random House, 1980.
Lives of the Poets. New York: Random House, 1984.
World's Fair. New York: Random House, 1985.
Billy Bathgate. New York: Random House, 1989.
Jack London, Hemingway, and the Constitution: Selected Essays, 1977–1992. New York: Random House, 1993.
The Waterworks. New York: Random House, 1994.

Works Cited and Studies of E. L. Doctorow

Barkhausen, Jochen. "Determining the True Colour of the Chameleon: The Confusing Recovery of History in E. L. Doctorow's *Loon Lake*." In *E. L. Doctorow: A Democracy of Perception*, ed. Herwig Friedl and Dieter Schulz. Essen, Germany: Die Blaue Eule, 1988.
Bell, Pearl. "Guilt on Trial." *New Leader* 54 (1971): 118.
Bemrose, John. Review of *The Waterworks*. *Maclean's* 107 (July 25, 1994): 30, 54.
Bloom, Steven. "The Book of Daniel and the Rosenberg Case, or E. L. Doctorow Meets M. R. Meeropol." In *E. L. Doctorow: A Democracy of Perception*, ed. Herwig Friedl and Dieter Schulz. Essen, Germany: Die Blaue Eule, 1988.
Brienza, Susan. "Doctorow's *Ragtime*: Narrative as Silhouettes and Syncopation." *Dutch Quarterly Review of Anglo-American Letters* 11.2 (1981): 97–103.
Clemons, Walter. "Houdini, Meet Ferdinand." Review of *Ragtime*. *Newsweek*, July 14, 1975, 73.
Contemporary Authors, New Revision Series, 33. Detroit: Gale, 1991, 110–12.
Doctorow, E. L. Interview, "Writers & Co.," hosted by Eleanor Wachtel, broadcast November 1994. Toronto, ON: CBC Radioworks.
———. "A Multiplicity of Witness." In *E. L. Doctorow: A Democracy of Perception*, ed. Herwig Friedl and Dieter Schulz. Essen, Germany: Die Blaue Eule, 1988.
Foley, Barbara. "From *U.S.A.* to *Ragtime*: Notes on the Forms of Historical Consciousness in Modern Fiction." In *E. L. Doctorow: Essays and Conversations*, ed. Richard Trenner. Princeton, NJ: Ontario Review Press, 1983.

Friedl, Herwig, and Dieter Schulz, eds. *E. L. Doctorow: A Democracy of Perception.* Essen, Germany: Die Blaue Eule, 1988.

Girgus, Sam B. *The New Covenant.* Chapel Hill: University of North Carolina Press, 1984.

Gray, Paul. Review of *The Waterworks. Time*, June 20, 1994, 66.

Harter, Carol C., and James R. Thompson. *E. L. Doctorow.* Boston: Twayne, 1990.

Jones, Malcolm. Review of *The Waterworks. Newsweek*, June 27, 1994, 53.

Morris, Christopher. *Models of Misrepresentation: On the Fiction of E. L. Doctorow.* Jackson: University Press of Mississippi, 1991.

Parks, John. *E. L. Doctorow.* New York: Continuum, 1991.

Prescott, Peter S. Review of *Billy Bathgate. Newsweek*, February 13, 1989, 76.

Sutherland, John. "The Selling of *Ragtime*: A Novel for Our Times?" *New Review* 4:4.

Trenner, Richard, ed. *E. L. Doctorow: Essays and Conversations.* Princeton, NJ: Ontario Review Press, 1983.

STANLEY ELKIN (1930–1995)

Peter J. Bailey

BIOGRAPHY

It is in the nature of Stanley Elkin's fiction that one can read the entire oeuvre and come away with only a very limited sense of its author's life or experiences. Born in Brooklyn on May 11, 1930 to Zelda Feldman Elkin and Philip Elkin, a costume-jewelry salesman whose mastery of the rhetoric of commerce significantly influenced the fiction his son would write, Elkin grew up on the South Shore of Chicago. He graduated from South Shore High School and attended the University of Illinois at Urbana-Champaign, where he received his B.A. (1952) and M.A. (1953). In May 1953, he married Joan Marion Jacobson, whose husband he remained for forty-two years, dedicating all but three of his fifteen books to her without ever creating a character remotely like her. (The closest he came was the narrator's wife in one of his late works, "Her Sense of Timing," who disappears from the narrative on the novella's first page.)

Elkin spent 1955–1957 in the army, returned to the University of Illinois following his discharge, and received his Ph.D. in English in 1961. (It was while working on his doctorate that Elkin undertook the yearlong project he often recalled fondly in interviews: he stayed in bed, reading.) His dissertation, "Religious Themes and Symbols in the Novels of William Faulkner," reflected the New Critical assumptions underlying the fiction Elkin had just begun writing. Although the dissertation addresses notions of Christian eschatology in Faulkner's work, it unapologetically secularizes them, perceiving Faulkner's view of the universe as a thoroughly existentialist one. "For all the talk of God in Faulkner's novels," Elkin argued, more aptly prefiguring his work than illuminating Faulkner's, "for all the religious symbolism in those novels, the ultimate character of God, of Fate, lies with the individual." Elkin's reading of the Faulkner canon is predominantly textual rather than contextual, the doctoral candidate manifesting only the most limited interest in the biography or cultural roots of his subject.

In 1960, Elkin accepted an instructorship at Washington University in St. Louis, beginning an institutional commitment that would continue until his death and would see him named Merle King Professor of Modern Letters in 1983. In a 1980 *Esquire* essay, Elkin expounded upon his satisfaction with his life, his friends, and his job in University City, Missouri: "I live where I live because I am comfortable," he wrote, "because the climate is equable, because the movies come on time but the theater is road show, second company, because the teams are dull but we get all the channels, because there can't be four restaurants in the city which require jackets and ties and there's a $25,000 ceiling on what city employees may earn and I make more than the mayor, the head of the zoo. Because I feel no need to take the paper. Because I feel no need." It is probably the central irony of Elkin's work that his University City equanimity made it possible for him to write his "hard histories of singular human beings"—narratives of characters at the end of their ropes, protagonists defined primarily in terms of the extremity of their need.

Upon his return to Champaign-Urbana, Elkin had joined the editorial board of *Accent*, a University of Illinois literary magazine, and had begun circulating to other journals stories—some of them produced for Randall Jarrell's writing workshop—he had written; in 1957 *Epoch* accepted "The Sound of Distant Thunder." Encouraged by the example of William H. Gass, a philosophy professor writing a novel rather than conventional scholarship whom he befriended at Illinois in 1959, Elkin continued producing short stories, selling them in the early 1960s to magazines such as the *Paris Review, Esquire*, and the *Saturday Evening Post*. Most of these stories were collected in *Criers and Kibitzers, Kibitzers and Criers* in 1965. His nascent fiction-writing career was nurtured by what he referred to as a "mother grant," Zelda Elkin bankrolling his 1962 trip to Rome and London, where he began work on the first of his nine novels, *Boswell*. William Gass later characterized Elkin during these years as someone who could tirelessly entertain friends with his grumpy anecdotal history of himself: "Stanley . . . groused a lot. He wanted what he felt were his just deserts, his due, and to that end he kept accounts. Receipts, it seemed, regularly fell short. In addition, he constantly complained about his health, which was precarious; but those complaints were hard to believe, he seemed so robust" ("An Anecdote," 12).

At thirty-eight, Elkin suffered a serious heart attack that irrevocably altered, among other things, the standards by which he judged other writers' fiction: "Is satire itself an appropriate or seemly aspect of the novel?" he asked rhetorically in his review of a novel in *New York Times Book Review* published shortly after his recovery. "Not, I think, since my near fatal heart attack it ain't." In 1972 he was diagnosed with multiple sclerosis, a disease that, as he described it, "kills you by inches but you suffer by yards." The illness gradually incapacitated

Elkin, confining him to a wheelchair in the last years of his life. (Another plus he attributed to University City was being user friendly for the disabled: ''Are the crippled as comfortable in Santa Barbara?'' he wanted to know.) Elkin extracted a small measure of revenge upon physical disease by scrutinizing a number of its manifestations with clinical precision and bleak humor in his three finest novels, *The Franchiser, George Mills*, and *The Magic Kingdom*. In the latter novel, he has a pediatrician accompanying the fatally ill children on their Disney World excursion conclude that ''disease, not health, was at the core of things; his idea of pith and gist and soul obsolete now, revised downward to flaw, nubbin, rift; incipient sickness the seed which sent forth its contaged shoots raging through the poisoned circuits of being'' (64). William Gass wrote in 1983: ''I won't say that the dirty tricks life has played on him have made Stanley a better player of the game; but they have made him a better player of the game. Once his symptoms had surfaced like submarines—about that unmistakable reality, he grew grouseless; he grew brave'' (''An Anecdote,'' 13).

Elkin insisted that *George Mills*, his most ambitious novel and winner of the National Book Critics Circle Award for Fiction in 1983, had been so exhausting to compose that it was the last fiction he'd ever write. But a British television news report about doomed children visiting Disney World inspired *Stanley Elkin's The Magic Kingdom* (1985), which was followed by *The Rabbi of Lud* (1987), *The MacGuffin* (1991), a collection of essays, *Pieces of Soap* (1992), a collection of novellas, *Van Gogh's Room at Arles* (1993), and the posthumously published novel, *Mrs. Ted Bliss* (1995). Elkin died of heart failure on May 31, 1995.

MAJOR WORKS AND THEMES

A question Elkin was often asked in interviews was the Jewish-American writer question: to what extent did he perceive himself writing within the Jewish-American literary tradition? ''I see myself as a writer who happens to be Jewish, happens to be American, and happens to be a writer,'' Elkin explained in a 1976 *Prairie Schooner* interview. ''Judaism is a religion. It also accidentally happens to have certain cultural aspects. Roth, Malamud, Bellow, perhaps myself, to the extent that we are Jewish-American writers are Jewish-American culturalists'' (23).

The annoyance discernible in Elkin's response to this oft-posed question reflects his perception that alignment within that tradition overemphasized the cultural-satire elements of his work while minimizing the aspect of fiction he valued most highly: language. In his fiction, he told Scott Sanders in a *Contemporary Literature* interview, ''I *am* trying to upset the applecarts of expectation and ordinary grammar, and you can only do that with fierce language'' (133). Although Bellow had a major influence on the development of Elkin's fiction, Faulkner's was even stronger, and what Elkin found there was a style his dissertation described as ''religious'': ''This tone of awe which Faulkner manages to work into, which, indeed, is part of his narratives, indicates, I think . . . the general awe in which he stands of the human spirit, and this general awe is, in one context at least, religious. It is my notion that Faulkner's style, his investment in sentence rhythms, his stockpiling of Latinate words, his tightly reined parallelisms and intricate negatives, and, finally, his massive hyperbole, are the result not of being, as he calls himself, 'a failed poet' but of perhaps unconscious devoutness. . . . Faulkner's stylistic excesses represent a lush spirituality'' (''Religious Themes,'' 52) ''Stylistic excesses''—''the aggression of syntax and metaphor,'' as he described them to Sanders—are, correspondingly, as religious as Elkin's fiction ever got, and although his style is permeated by Yiddish inflections and the self-deprecatory tonalities of Jewish-American humor, his work was characterized by a deliberate, self-conscious aestheticism that aligned it more markedly with the work of his metafictionist contemporaries (Barth, Barthelme, Coover, Pynchon, and Gass) than with the Jewish-American tradition.

If Elkin's fiction does not situate itself neatly within that tradition, however, his work is by no means indifferent to cultural issues of Jewishness. A number of his most memorable protagonists—Ben Flesh of *The Franchiser* and Alexander Main of ''The Bailbondsman'' among them—sound Jewish even if their cultural descent never becomes an issue, and his novels with *goyishe* central characters (*The Dick Gibson Show, The Magic Kingdom*) often introduce Jewish figures (such as the latter novel's young Benny Maxine, dying of ''the chosen disease of the chosen people'') for whom being Jewish is a source of anxiety and conflict. Elkin's preferred approach to this cultural issue in his work differs little from his appropriation of other cultural materials such as radio talk shows, the corporate homogenizing of America, small Midwest city politics, or the Christian Bible's creation narrative: Judaism is a source of metaphors and a vocabulary he could exploit for rhetorical effect in fiction. Rather than making categorical assertions about cultural Jewishness (e.g., Malamud's suggestion in *The Assistant* that to be a Jew is to suffer), Elkin chose to work with literary and cultural stereotypes of Jewishness; his fiction seeks less to define characteristics of Jews in America than to create plots out of the interaction between literary/cultural stereotypes of the Jew and conceptions of reality opposing such stereotypes. To put it another way, Elkin had nothing to say about being Jewish that did not help him develop dramatic tension—a plot. (It is telling that the God of *The Living End*, when asked why he created everything the way he did, responds, ''Because it makes a better story is why.'') The works in which Elkin improvises most consistently upon the theme of American cultural Jewishness are *A Bad Man*, ''The Condominium,'' *The Rabbi of Lud*, and *Mrs. Ted Bliss*.

Leo Feldman, the protagonist of Elkin's second novel, is what the warden of the prison in which he is incarcerated terms ''a bad man''—a subverter of order and organization in the name of self, one who, in the world's view, will always stand accused of his character, guilty of his own impulses. Feldman strives in his world to do what his creator does through the language of fiction, in other words—to ''upset the applecarts of expectation and ordinary grammar.'' His antecedents in Elkin's fiction are Push the Bully of "A Poetics for Bullies," who boasts of "the cabala of my hate, of my irreconcilableness," and a different Feldman in another *Criers and Kibitzers, Kibitzers and Criers* story who refuses meekly to submit to the dying-man role that the world imposes upon him, rejecting a dignified hospital expiration in favor of what he perceives as a heroic death "In the Alley," one he can experience fully, however degrading its conditions. Leo Feldman anticipates, similarly, Alexander Main, "The Bailbondsman," who enjoys the power that his job affords "to put killers back on the streets and return lunatics to their neighborhoods, the good power to loose the terrible, to grant freedom where he felt it was due, more magisterial than a king, controlling the sluices and locks of ordinary life, adjusting at whim the levels and proportions of guilt to innocence, poisoning the streets with possibility" (105). In these protagonists, Elkin presents ordinary life's antagonists and combatants: irascible, willful, tenacious, uncompromising protagonists for whom the self is the ultimate value and all external forces that attempt to define, restrict, or otherwise impinge upon that self's freedom are the enemy. What differentiates Leo Feldman from these others is the extent to which his antagonism toward order, organization, and communal values is identified—or perhaps constructed is a better word—as a specifically Jewish trait.

The theme that most clearly links Elkin to the Jewish-American literary tradition is that of the absolute, irreducible significance of self. Distancing his work from that tradition in his *Paris Review* interview, Elkin insisted that "there is no particular religious tradition in my work. There is only one psychological assertion that I would insist upon: the SELF takes precedence" (Le Clair, 60). The notion that, as Moses Herzog explains in *Herzog*, man is capable of taking on his "bone-breaking burden of selfhood and self-development," that he need not utterly surrender his "poor, squawking, niggardly individuality," represents an important point of convergence between the fiction of Elkin and that of Bellow, another related one being their shared penchant for writing novels with central male protagonists/centers of consciousness whose names or descriptors provide the works' titles. Where their work most clearly diverges is in Elkin's abnegation of the realism characteristic of Bellow's work, a difference Bellow may have been invoking in his blurb for Elkin's *Mrs. Ted Bliss*: "Only an artist, the real thing, would wade so far and deep into the commonplace in order to show us how to turn it inside out." In *A Bad Man*, the "turning inside out" takes the form of Elkin's exaggeration of Jewish and Christian characteristics to the point at which the tension between Leo Feldman and Warden Fisher becomes an almost Kafkaesque confrontation between Jew and American WASP.

A self-proclaimed "Fisher of bad men," Elkin's prison warden represents conventional American middle-class notions of goodness and decency: self-denial, generosity, logicality, a belief that human existence is rational and controllable because it is ordinary—that is, predictable, sane, consecutive, reducible to simple explanations, consistent with normal expectations, and thus amenable to the imposition of moral schemes. Feldman is the "bad man" opposed to all this, one dedicated to self-aggrandizement and to the philosophical assumption that the individual's only possible role in a contingent, senseless universe is to keep himself alive through extending his sense of his own extraordinariness, an undertaking that often necessitates the victimization of fellow humans and the recognition that he is the only one in the world capable of perceiving and celebrating his own specialness. Fisher is reasonable, whereas Feldman insists upon his passions and instincts; Fisher advocates compliance and accommodation, while Feldman keeps a weather eye out for what can be resisted; Fisher feels very much at home in the unheroic, unaspiring bureaucratic world of modern mass society, whereas Feldman feels a stronger tie to "a world that might have been charted on an old map, the spiky spines of serpents rising like waves from wine-dark seas . . . a distant Praetorianed land, unamiable and harsh" (42).

Following in the footsteps of his father, an itinerant peddler who made his living traveling through the Midwest hawking his wares to WASPs on street-corners and at county fairs, Feldman, a department-store owner at the time of his arrest, increases business at the prison canteen by selling prisoners merchandise—overseas mail stationery, shoe trees, suntan lotion—they can't possibly use. The scheme prompts Fisher to slap him into solitary confinement, a punishment he deems appropriate to the trespass of selfishly exploiting others. Upon his release from solitary, Feldman is invited to a party in Fisher's home at which the warden offers his public denunciation of his prison's "bad man":

"Say what you will, Feldman . . . but urbanity is a Christian gift. Rome, London, Wittenberg, Geneva—cities, Feldman. The history of us Christians is bound up with the history of great cities. I mean no offense, of course, but yours is a desert sensibility, a past of pitched tents and camps. . . . I've stood beside side-boards and spent Christmas with friends. There's leather on my bookshelves, Feldman. I've been to Connecticut. I know how to sail. What are you in our culture? A mimic. A spade in a tux at a function in Harlem.

"I make this astounding speech to you not out of malice. It's way of life against way of life with me, Feldman. I show you alternatives to wholesale and retail. I push past your poetics, your metaphors of merchandise, and scorn the emptiness of your *caveat emptor*. I, the least of Christians, do this." (156–57)

The "way of life" the novel opposes to this WASPishly self-congratulatory vision of the world is Feldman's father's invocation of the Jew's history: the Jewish Diaspora, or the scattering of Jews throughout the Old World following the Babylonian captivity. "Ours is a destiny of emergency," Isidore Feldman liked to tell the Illinois farmers before moving in for the sale. "You see me sitting here fulfilling God's will. I bring God's will to the Midwest. I don't lift a finger. I have dispersed. Soon the kid is older, *he* disperses. Scatter, He said. To the ends of the earth. Yes, Lord" (35–36). His son will echo this ethic in his confrontation with a land developer whose WASPish visions of expansionism and progress approximate Fisher's: "I won't have it," Leo Feldman snaps, "Fuck your virgin land. . . . We're in the homestretch of a race: your energy against my entropy. The universe is running down, Mr. Developer. It's bucking and filling. It's yawing and pitching and rolling and falling" (235–36). The novel's major tensions—between WASPish decorum and "bad man" willfulness, between competing perceptions of reality that assume it to be tractable, comprehensible, and ordinary as opposed to threatening, senseless, and incommensurable—are thus presented in symbolic shorthand in *A Bad Man* through the novel's two central metaphoric complexes: the organizing, ordering impulses of Fisher's prison juxtaposed against the dispersive, entropic tendencies of Feldman's Diaspora.

The Jewish protagonists of Elkin's fiction are not uniformly endowed with the qualities of irascibility and resistance with which Feldman is, however; in other works, the nihilist egotism that energizes Leo Feldman gets turned inward and becomes a source of self-flagellation and self-hatred. The fiction that results from this process of narrative introversion inevitably resembles a parody of Jewish-American fiction, and thus we have Marshall Preminger of "The Condominium," among whose numerous *kvetches* offered to the condo-complex association committee of the condominium he inherits from his father is that "even here, among Jews, where everybody's Jewish, I feel Jewish" (250). As the one alienated man in a community of the supposedly culturally estranged, Preminger makes every attempt to settle into his new residence and rid himself of the air he exudes of "tourist condition, the unsavory quality of displaced person he gave off." But in his effort to adapt himself to the prevailing dress code, he learns that the community of the condominium complex is pure illusion, that his father's final home was a retreat into realms of fantasy and self-gratification. Despite the complex's surface communality, its poolside neighborliness and appearance of social interaction, it is ultimately a place of withdrawal into the self, somewhere that allows its residents to turn away from the concerns of the world and trivialize themselves so thoroughly that they won't notice their lives slipping away.

"In the Alley," "A Poetics for Bullies," *A Bad Man*, and "The Bailbondsman" dramatize Elkin's notion that "the SELF takes precedence," an affirmation that is enacted through the protagonists' generation of self-assertive languages of their own, their personal versions of "the aggression of syntax and metaphor." "The Condominium" explores the darker side of self-preoccupation, Preminger's complete isolation from others driving him to the ultimate act of self-negation, suicide. In this novella, the language that ultimately prevails is not that of his never-completed anthropological lecture on home building but the sour epistolary prose of Mrs. Riker, a condominium resident whose sexual attentions to Preminger's father led to his death. The letters she sends Preminger are written in a style utterly unconscious of its own effects, a prose chatty and yet artificially bland, a deadly language that constitutes a stylistic denial of individual responsibility and that defuses extremity by trivializing it. Hers is the banally seductive siren song of the condominium, and Preminger must succumb to it because his own sense of self is too crippled for him to resist that voice's tendencies toward trivialization and sameness with its own force of articulation, differentiation, and self-expression. That Preminger associates Mrs. Riker with the upwardly mobile Jewish women who visited his parents when he was a child is as close as the novella comes to allegorizing the condominium complex's ethos as characteristic of secularized American Jewry.

Leo Feldman's identification of his culture with entropy and decline seems to find parodic dramatization in *The Rabbi of Lud* through the town of Lud, New Jersey, an extensive Semitic graveyard that its rabbi, Jerry Goldkorn, characterizes as "a sort of Jewish death farm." Goldkorn earned his congregation-less rabbinate partly through the dubiety of his bar mitzvah (he proved dyslexic in Hebrew) and his training (undertaken through an offshore correspondence yeshiva in the Maldive Islands). Describing himself as "God's little own welfare cheat," Goldkorn expounds upon his unworthiness to his calling: "I had no aptitude for what was finally just another foreign language to me and not the ordinary, conversational vulgate of God himself. The superheroes in those comic books had more reality for me than all the biblical luminaries and shotguns in the Pentateuch. And this is who He chooses to ride shotgun for Him in New Jersey?" (11). The spiritual education Goldkorn undergoes in the course of the novel culminates in his developing a sense of awe for God, one that is ultimately founded in the Almighty's capacity for sowing death among the living, a conception of divinity Elkin had made much of in *The Living End*. (Quiz, trying to determine how he had been ripped from his life and precipitously dispatched to Hell, exclaims, "I make no charges. I've got no proof, but a thing like that, all that wrath, those terrible swift sword arrangements, that's the M.O. of God Himself!" [102].) The moral education Goldkorn experiences in *The Rabbi of Lud* is summarized by his closing prayer, which asks forgiveness for "the sins we have committed against Thee by seeking to lie low and maintain a low profile" (276). Lud, David C. Dougherty argued in his Twayne study of Elkin, "is not only a town of the dead but a refuge for the dead of spirit—those who have been burned once and determine never to be vulnerable again" (105).

In the end, Goldkorn, the work's unreliable narrator, basically learns what the reader of this, the novel Elkin judged his least successful, has understood throughout reading it: that Goldkorn's stylistic self-effacement is the novel's primary symptom of his "lying low," the narrative itself manifesting his symbolic death of spirit, his want of a sense of awe. (Elkin without awe, it could be argued, is like Henry Miller without sex.) The relative absence of what Elkin termed Faulkner's "religious style"—the "ordinary, conversational vulgate of God himself"—in *The Rabbi of Lud* points up how little evidence the novel provides that for Elkin the Judaic materials with which he was working represented for him anything more than "what was finally just another foreign language." For all of its Yiddishisms and rhetorical exploitation of Jewish customs, *The Rabbi of Lud* principally and very eloquently reaffirms the oft-noted sensitivity of Jews to "the immense, twisted tonnage of complex grief in the world at any given time, in any given place, some right amalgam of woe and rue and complicity and fear. Grief like a land mass, like the seas, complicated as weather seen from high space or the veiled, tie-dye smudge of the alloy earth itself" (276–77).

If Elkin's work was to achieve any reconciliation between Jewish culture and faith, *Mrs. Ted Bliss* would have to achieve the trick, and as Saul Bellow suggested, it was through the commonplace that Elkin advanced upon the spiritual in that last novel. That Elkin chose to write a novel from the point of view of an unexceptional Jewish widow living in a Florida condominium is surprising enough; that she has little gift for language makes her an even more unlikely Elkin protagonist. But what makes *Mrs. Ted Bliss* such a remarkable book is the way in which it achieves Elkinian effects through a—for Elkin—consciously muted language: Elkin subjugates style to character without (as arguably happened in *The Rabbi of Lud*) sacrificing expressive energy. Mrs. Bliss recalls her son having refused to say Kaddish for his father:

So Dorothy, who was as innocent of Hebrew as of French, undertook to say the prayers for her dead husband herself. She read the mourner's prayers from a small, thin blue handbook the Chicago funeral parlor passed out. It was about the size of the pocket calculator Manny from the building had given her to help balance her checkbook after Ted lost his life. She read the prayers in a soft, transliterated version of the Hebrew, but came to feel she was merely going through the motions, probably doing more harm than good. If Mrs. Ted Bliss were God, Mrs. Bliss thought, she'd never be fooled by someone simply *impersonating* important prayers. It was useless to try to compensate for her failure by getting up earlier and earlier every morning. God would see through that with one hand tied behind His back. If there even was a God, if He wasn't just some courtesy people politely agreed to call on to make themselves nobler to each other than they were. (173)

CRITICAL RECEPTION

What reviewers and critics typically praised in Elkin's work was the humor and the precision and generosity of his self-consciously literary language; what they often expressed reservations about was his humor and the precision and generosity of his self-consciously literary language. "Stanley Elkin's novels have sometimes been criticized for their disregard of form and organized plot," novelist Lorrie Moore summarized the familiar objection in her review of *The MacGuffin*, Elkin's next-to-last novel, before proceeding to contest the charge, "for what some might see as their overindulgence of the author's poetic gift— his besotted high style" (5).

In 1964, John Ciardi celebrated the narrative voice of *Boswell* as one possessed of "an intellect both learned and honed, a perception forever ready to burst into its own sort of wild and wacky poetry'' ''In point of style and of intellectual grace,'' Ciardi added, ''the author of Boswell is to the author of Catch-22 as a jeweler is to a primitive potter.'' Then came the equivocation that would become a staple even of positive reviews of Elkin's books: ''Or it may be that Boswell is the hoax of the year, though if it is, it would be so only as one more semblance of the world as Elkin sees it'' (6). Ciardi was hardly the last reviewer to wonder whether Elkin's ironizing vision of the world is not somehow inimical to literature's requisite thematic heft, to ask whether Elkin's fiction is not too funny to be serious.

The publication of Criers and Kibitzers, Kibitzers and Criers, with its narratives of urban Jews confronting the cultural dislocations and contradictions of late modernity, led reviewers to categorize Elkin with Malamud, Irwin Faust, James Purdy, and Philip Roth as a writer of Jewish-American stories; the label received wide circulation subsequently because of the frequent anthologizing of ''I Look Out for Ed Wolfe,'' ''The Guest,'' ''In the Alley,'' and the collection's title story. In the first review essay on Elkin's work, ''Stanley Elkin's Orphans'' (597), Allen Guttmann characterized the author of Boswell and the stories as both kibitzer (one who lives to put others on) and crier (one who bemoans a world he never made); Josh Greenfield's front-page review of A Bad Man in the New York Times Book Review seemed to concur: ''Page for page . . . I know of no serious funny writer in this country who can match him'' (1).

The central Jew/WASP conflict in A Bad Man reinforced the perception of Elkin as a Jewish-American tragicomic novelist, but the reviews of this work sounded a new note that would resonate through the responses to nearly all his subsequent novels: ''Obviously Elkin . . . realizes,'' Irving Malin suggested, ''that he can torture us—as the Warden tortures Feldman?—by dispensing with the comfort of plot and motivation'' (341). Raymond M. Olderman, whose chapter on A Bad Man in Beyond the Waste Land: A Study of The American Novel in the Nineteen-sixties represented the first extended analysis of an Elkin novel, defined what would become the central task of Elkin criticism: illuminating the art that organizes Elkin's plethora of one-liners, anecdotes, shtick, and increasingly diffuse and refracted plot lines into aesthetic unities.

Reviews of The Dick Gibson Show and The Franchiser enhanced Elkin's literary reputation even as they reinforced the currency of the ''whole-is-less-than-the-sum-of-the-parts'' Elkin critical thesis. By the middle 1970s, however, Elkin had begun to accumulate a gathering of defenders against the popular press's growing reservations: fellow fictionists William H. Gass, Robert Coover, and John Irving and substantial academic critics such as Olderman, Tony Tanner, Larry McCaffery, Thomas LeClair, and Alan Wilde, who demonstrated how appropriate it was to view Elkin's fiction in the context of the work of those writers and that of Pynchon, Barthelme, Heller, and Vonnegut. Irving's extravagantly admiring review of The Living End in the New York Times Book Review may have been partially responsible for the novella triptych's becoming Elkin's biggest seller to date, and the reviewers' commendation of the book's economy of means reinforced the idea, sounded as well in reviews of both *Searches and Seizures* and *Van Gogh's Room at Arles*, his previous and subsequent novella collections, that Elkin was at his best when limiting himself to smaller canvasses.

Frank Kermode's assessment of *The Living End* in the *New York Review of Books* might be construed as the annunciation by a major critic of Elkin's arrival as a major American literary figure: Elkin is "certainly an original with his sour, manic prose, his cult of outrage," Kermode contended, and although the satiric targets of *The Living End* "seem somewhat too large and easy" on first glance, a more careful reading reveals that "the fine print will stand a lot of attention from anyone who thinks he could get hooked on a taste so wild and bitter" (44).

While Thomas LeClair judged *George Mills* "Elkin's most ambitious and best novel" (146), other reviewers and critics have not shared Elkin's conviction that this novel—seven years in the writing, its plot encompassing ten centuries and four nations—is his most effective and the one to which his literary reputation could be entrusted. The ambitiousness of the novel (it was often likened to 1970s encyclopedic novels such as *Gravity's Rainbow* and *The Public Burning*) was unanimously acknowledged, as was the sheer imaginative richness of the various Millses' experiences in the Crusades, in an Ottoman harem, and in nursing the dying Judith Glazer. Nonetheless, David C. Dougherty's conclusion epitomizes the ambivalence many critics have felt about *George Mills*: "Technically fascinating, the book lacks the Elkin trademark: a central character driven by his design. Inevitably, because of the [Mills family's] curse, Mills is passive. ... While we are fascinated by brilliant techniques, descriptions, and images, we never become engaged in Mills's struggle because he is not a battler" (39).

The gradual diminution of the battler stance among Elkin's protagonists is one of the significant developments of his post-1980 fiction, *The MacGuffin*'s Bobbo Druff alone approaching the combative egocentricity of his early characters. Eddy Bales's despondent perseverance in facilitating the Disney World trip in his son's memory in Stanley Elkin's *The Magic Kingdom* represents but a dim echo of the defiant self-insistence of Boswell, Leo Feldman, and Alexander Main, and a number of critics perceived the dilution of this psychic energy as constituting a decline in Elkin's work. But throughout his career Elkin had been creating plots dramatizing self-effacing, assimilation-tending egos (Marshall Preminger of "The Condominium," Dick Gibson, and franchiser Ben Flesh among them) at least as regularly as he had contrived narratives driven by the irascible wills of rapacious men, and although narrative tension in *The Rabbi of Lud* (Elkin's least critically acclaimed book) does suffer from the passivity and seclusionary impulses of its protagonist, the absence of a single dramatic organizing consciousness in *The Magic Kingdom* did not keep it from being a brilliantly conceived novel affirming the notion that "the SELF takes precedence," or from being the book many reviewers—Robert M. Adams and Max Apple among them—judged Elkin's finest single work.

In 1991 Lorrie Moore offered her defense of Elkin's aesthetic in describing

The MacGuffin as "not only an Elkinesque portrait of the sorrows of the body and the moral perils of work. It is a plea for the power of talk, for talk as its own resolution—even Druff's manic rapid-mouth-movement, all simile and parentheses and searching stammer, the deejay yak of the heart. Even this verbiage, the novel seemed to say, perhaps especially this verbiage, this incoherence, is an intimacy, a negotiation—a prayer against death" (5). For Moore and other critics, Elkin was letting his own irreconcilably Elkinian language become the stand-in for the aggressively self-assertive protagonist he became increasingly less able to imagine or to dramatize.

Reviewers of *Pieces of Soap* unanimously praised Elkin's essays, one of them—David Gregory—designating him "one of our best essayists" (483), and the following year Francine Prose judged *Van Gogh's Room at Arles* "Elkin's best book," noting especially the title story's "sudden, illuminating glimpse of the accidental, visionary, and (for lack of a better word) religious nature of art" (122). Reviewing *Mrs. Ted Bliss*, Elkin's last novel, Michiko Kakutani echoed Lorrie Moore in locating in Elkin's language—"rich, musical and playful, like that of a Joyce who grew up on Yiddish"—"a kind of momentary stay, a protest, against the implacable facts of mortality. In *Mrs. Ted Bliss*, he has used that remarkable language to create one of the most vivid and sympathetic heroines to come along in a long time and to relate a tale that sums up all the qualities that have distinguished his fiction from the start, a tale that's sad, funny and redemptive all at once." "*Mrs. Ted Bliss*," Kakutani concluded, "stands as both Mr. Elkin's most affecting novel and as a wonderful capstone to a distinguished and eloquent career" (27).

BIBLIOGRAPHY

Works by Stanley Elkin

Religious Themes and Symbolism in the Novels of William Faulkner. Urbana: University of Illinois Press, 1961.
Boswell: A Modern Comedy. New York: Random House, 1964.
Criers and Kibitzers, Kibitzers and Criers. New York: Random House, 1965.
A Bad Man. New York: Random House, 1967.
The Dick Gibson Show. New York: Random House, 1971.
Searches and Seizures. New York: Random House, 1973.
The Franchiser. New York: Farrar, Straus, Giroux, 1976.
The Living End. New York: E. P. Dutton, 1979.
Stanley Elkin's Greatest Hits. New York: E. P. Dutton, 1980.
George Mills. New York: E. P. Dutton, 1982.
Early Elkin. Flint, MI: Bamberger Books, 1985.
Stanley Elkin's The Magic Kingdom. New York: E. P. Dutton, 1985.
The Rabbi of Lud. New York: Scribners, 1987.
The Six-Year-Old Man. Flint, MI: Bamberger Books, 1987.
The MacGuffin. New York: Simon and Schuster, 1991.

Pieces of Soap: Essays. New York: Simon and Schuster, 1992.

Van Gogh's Room at Arles: Three Novellas. New York: Hyperion, 1993.

Mrs. Ted Bliss. New York: Hyperion, 1995.

Works Cited and Studies of Stanley Elkin

Adams, Robert M. Review of *Stanley Elkin's The Magic Kingdom. New York Review of Books*, July 18, 1985, 20.

Apple, Max. Review of *Stanley Elkin's The Magic Kingdom. New York Times Book Review*. March 29, 1985, 39.

Bailey, Peter J. *Reading Stanley Elkin*. Urbana: University of Illinois Press, 1985.

Bargen, Doris. *The Fiction of Stanley Elkin*. Frankfort: Peter Lang, 1980.

Chénetier, Marc, ed. *Delta* 20 (February 1985) (Elkin special issue).

Ciardi, John. Review of *Boswell. Saturday Review*, August 15, 1964, 6.

Coover, Robert. "Preface." In *Stanley Elkin's Greatest Hits*. New York: E. P. Dutton, 1980, ix–xii.

Dougherty, David C. *Stanley Elkin*. Boston: Twayne, 1991.

Duncan, Jeffrey L. "A Conversation with Stanley Elkin and William H. Gass." *Iowa Review* 7:1 (Winter 1976): 48–76.

Gass, William. "An Anecdote." *Washington University Magazine* 54:1 (Spring 1984): 12–14.

———. "Stanley Elkin's *The Franchiser*." *New Republic* (June 1976): 27.

Greenfield, Josh. "The World of Leo Feldman." Review of *A Bad Man. New York Times Book Review*, October 15, 1967, 1.

Gregory, David. Review of *Pieces of Soap. America*, December 12, 1992, 483.

Guttmann, Allen. "The Black Humorists." In *The Jewish Writer in America: Assimilation and the Crisis of Identity*. New York: Oxford University Press, 1971, 76–85.

———. "Stanley Elkin's Orphans." *Massachusetts Review*, Summer 1966, 597–600.

Irving, John. Review of *The Living End. New York Times Book Review*, June 10, 1979, 7.

Kakutani, Michiko. "The Wild Times of a Miami Widow." Review of *Mrs. Ted Bliss. New York Times*, September 8, 1995, 27.

Kermode, Frank. "Love and Do As You Please." Review of *The Living End. New York Review of Books*, August 16, 1979, 44.

LeClair, Thomas. "The Obsessional Fiction of Stanley Elkin." *Contemporary Literature* 16 (1975): 146–62.

LeClair, Thomas. Interview *Paris Review*, Summer, 1976, 54–86.

Malin, Irving. Review of *A Bad Man. Commonweal*, December 8, 1967, 341.

McCaffrey, Larry. "Stanley Elkin's Recovery of the Ordinary." *Critique* 21 (1979): 39–51.

Moore, Lorrie. Review of *The MacGuffin. New York Times Book Review*, March 10, 1991, 5.

Olderman, Raymond M. "A Bad Man," Chapter in *Beyond the Waste Land: The American Novel in the Nineteen-Sixties*: New Haven, Conn.: Yale University Press, 1972.

Prose, Francine. Review of *Van Gogh's Room at Arles. Yale Review*, July 1993, 122.

Saltzman, Arthur M. "Ego and Appetite in Stanley Elkin's Fiction." *Literary Review* 32 (1988): 111–18.

————, ed. *Review of Contemporary Fiction* 15:2 (Summer 1995) (Elkin special issue).

Sanders, Scott. "An Interview with Stanley Elkin." *Contemporary Literature* 16:2 (Spring 1975): 131–45.

Wilde, Alan. "A Map of Suspensiveness: Irony in the Postmodern Age." In *Horizons of Assent: Modernism, Postmodernism, and the Ironic Imagination*. Baltimore: Johns Hopkins University Press, 1981, 127–65.

RICHARD ELMAN (1934–)

Joel Shatzky and Michael Taub

BIOGRAPHY

The son of Edward and Pearl Beckerman Elman, Richard Elman was born in Brooklyn, New York, on April 23, 1934. He received a B.A. from Syracuse University in 1955 and an M.A. from Stanford in 1957 and served in the army in the late 1950s. Married twice, first to Emily Schorr in 1956 (they were divorced in 1970) and to Alice Good in 1978, he has two daughters: Margaret from his first and Lila from his second marriage.

Elman has had a career in both media and the academic world. He was public affairs director at WBAI-FM in New York City in 1961–1964 and has subsequently held academic positions at Hunter College, 1966; Bennington College, 1966–1967; and Columbia University, 1968–1976 as a visiting writer. He has been director of the Bennington College Summer Writing Workshop since 1976. He has also been a visiting professor at the University of Pennsylvania, the State University of New York at Stony Brook, the University of Arizona, and the University of Michigan. He was the Abrams Professor at Notre Dame in 1990. Among his awards are a CAPS Fellowship in 1976 and three PEN syndicated short-story awards. Elman makes his home in Tegucigalpa, Honduras.

MAJOR WORKS AND THEMES

A prolific writer, Elman has written over a dozen books under his own name and half a dozen under pseudonyms. He has also produced three books of poetry. Of particular interest for this reference book is his trilogy of novels about the Holocaust: *The 28th Day of Elul* (1967), *Lilo's Diary* (1968), and *The Reckoning* (1969). The trilogy concerns a Hungarian-Jewish family, the Yagodahs, at the end of World War II, each novel consisting of the same story told from a different point of view. *The 28th Day of Elul* is about the family's plans to betray a relative in exchange for escape from Hungary; *Lilo's Diary* is told from the point of view of the relative they are planning to betray, a young woman engaged to her Yagodah cousin; *The Reckoning* is told from the point of view of the father of the family who is trying to deal with the conflict between his moral convictions and the situation with which he is confronted. *Tar Beach*, a recent work (1992), also involves Jewish themes. It is the story of eight-year-old Peter Pintobasco, growing up in Brooklyn shortly after World War II, and the child's relationship with "Uncle" Izzy, who is the child's real father.

Among the variety of Elman's other works are a novelistic adaptation of the Paul Schrader screenplay *Taxi Driver* (1976), two books of reportage on the welfare poor, *The Poorhouse State* (1966) and *Ill-at-Ease in Compton* (1967), and a collection of vignettes and poems resulting from his experiences in Nicaragua during the Sandinista revolution in the 1970s, *Cocktails at Somoza's* (1981), as well as a number of pseudonymous books. The most notable is *Little Lives* (1978), written under the pen name John Howland Spyker and consisting of vignettes about the residents of a small town in New York State in the 1800s.

CRITICAL RECEPTION

Elman's novelistic writings on Jewish themes have met a mixed reception. Of the three books in his Holocaust trilogy, the *Times Literary Supplement* regarded *The 28th Day of Elul* as "remarkable . . . an exercise in moral restraint which 'tells us more' than many head-on confrontations with the abyss, without being any dishonestly easier to bear" (*Contemporary Authors*, 114). One reviewer of *Lilo's Diary* was also very favorably impressed, describing the novel as "an important 20th Century work of fiction," while *The Reckoning* was regarded by Thomas Lask in the *New York Times Book Review* as "picking over the remains" of characters already familiar to readers of the first two novels (*Contemporary Authors*, 114). Finally, *Tar Beach* was both faulted for its "tedious postmodern clichés of contemporary fiction" by Gerald Nicosia in the *Los Angeles Times* and praised by John Domini in the *New York Times Book Review* as "a meaty concoction about fatherhood, motherhood, and learning to live sanely with both" (*Contemporary Authors*, 115).

SELECTED BIBLIOGRAPHY

Works by Richard Elman

Novels

A Coat for the Tsar. Austin: University of Texas Press, 1958.
The 28th Day of Elul. New York: Scribner, 1967.
Lilo's Diary. New York: Scribner, 1968.

The Reckoning. New York: Scribner, 1969.

Freddi and Shirl and the Kids. New York: Scribner, 1972.

Taxi Driver (based on the Paul Schrader screenplay). New York: Bantam, 1976.

Little Lives. Under the pseudonym John Howland Spyker. New York: Grosset and Dunlap, 1978.

Tar Beach. Los Angeles: Sun and Moon Press, 1991.

Poetry

The Man Who Ate New York. New York: New Rivers Press, 1976.

Homage to Fats Navarro. Illus. Neil Greenberg. New York: New Rivers Press, 1978.

In Chontales. Port Jefferson, NY: Street Press, 1980.

Cathedral-Tree-Train and Other Poems. Grand Junction, TN: Junction Press, 1992.

Other Works

The Poorhouse State: The American Way of Life on Public Assistance. New York: Pantheon, 1966.

Ill-at-Ease in Compton. New York: Pantheon, 1967.

Cocktails at Somoza's: A Reporter's Sketchbook of Events in Revolutionary Nicaragua. Cambridge, MA: Applewood Books, 1981.

For further information on Richard Elman, see *Contemporary Authors*, New Revision Series, 47. Detroit: Gale Research, 1995, 112–16.

LESLIE EPSTEIN (1938–   )

Irene C. Goldman

BIOGRAPHY

Leslie Epstein was born in Los Angeles on May 4, 1938, the firstborn son of Philip and Lillian Targen Epstein. As he tells it: "I was born in 1938, in May, the same month the Germans began sending Jews to Dachau. Germans? Jews? Dachau? I saw the light in Los Angeles, and for all I know the nurses in St. Vincent's wore the starched headgear of nuns" (*Contemporary Authors*, 59). A third-generation American, a product of assimilated parents and American schooling, including Christmas trees and plays and Easter-egg hunts, Epstein reports not even being aware of his Jewishness until he was four or five when some friends asked him what he "was." He never lit a Chanukah candle until he was a father and only rarely spent time with the side of the family that had a seder and actively celebrated their heritage.

Epstein's father, Philip, was a Hollywood screenwriter who, together with his twin brother Julius, collaborated on such classic movies as *Casablanca* and *Mr. Skeffington*. The fact that they wrote at home while Epstein was growing up clearly influenced his desire to write and his talent for comedy. Their great success with Warner Brothers ensured that Leslie and his brother Ricky were raised to wealth, popular culture, and the fantasy world that was Hollywood.

Epstein's schooling was excellent, though his record, he likes to tell, was spotty. Two years after his father's death he was sent to the Webb School, from which he was expelled. Actually he was suspended for only three days for making a wisecrack about the food. He went on to Yale, where another wisecrack got him dismissed for two weeks, but did not prevent his earning a B.A. in 1960. He went on as a Rhodes scholar to Oxford, where he resigned his major in a dispute over whether serious intellectual conversation could take place at table. Leaving Oxford, he took a formative trip to Israel, but returned under threat of the draft to take a diploma in anthropology in 1962. While in England, he read extensively about the Holocaust. From England he returned to California to take an M.A. in theater arts at UCLA and then went back to the Yale Drama School, where he earned his D.F.A. in 1967. While he was at UCLA, he wrote a play that won the Samuel Goldwyn Award.

Epstein's career has been spent as a teacher, writer, and critic of theater, film, and literature. He worked from 1965 to 1978 at Queens College, City University of New York, and then went to Boston University as Professor of English and Director of the Graduate Creative Writing Program. He has been a visiting lecturer at Lane College, Yale University, and Johns Hopkins University and was a Fulbright lecturer at Groningen University in the Netherlands in 1972–1973. He has taught various writing workshops, including a stay at Yaddo in 1982 and three weeks in New Delhi, India, in 1992. He has also earned numerous grants for his writing and has won several awards, including the Playboy Editor's Award in nonfiction (1971), a National Endowment for the Arts award (1972), the American Academy and Institute of Arts and Letters' Distinction in Literature Award (1977), and a Guggenheim Fellowship (1977–1978). His book *King of the Jews* won a National Book Critics Circle nomination for Most Distinguished Work of Fiction in 1979 and the American Library Association Notable Book citation in 1980. He is a frequent reviewer of film and contemporary fiction. Epstein married Ilene Gradman in 1969; they have a daughter, Anya, and twin sons, Theo and Paul, and live in Brookline, Massachusetts.

MAJOR WORKS AND THEMES

Epstein has only recently been willing to consider himself a Jewish writer. In a 1992 Harvard symposium on the subject "What Is Jewish in Jewish Literature?" Aharon Appelfeld argued that to be a Jewish writer, one had to have Jewishness "in their bones and the essence of their lives," to be rooted in the Talmud and in Jewish philosophy and movements from all history, and to have a common memory and an abiding interest in the Jewish people. Epstein, as respondent, used Freud's definition of a shared psychic condition, calling Jewishness in literature a neurosis, that is, a compound of "phobias, anxieties, wit, and introspection; . . . this neurosis is in large part caused by being cut off from the very things that Aharon [Appelfeld] argues are necessary for a true Jewish literature, from that common memory which Aharon uses to define the Jewish people" (quoted in *Contemporary Authors*, 59). If, as Epstein argued in a 1994 interview, creativity is "a bit Freudian" and "one writes inevitably about one's childhood," then one could read in his definition of Jewishness the alienation of his own upbringing outside of his tradition as well as the larger cultural issues of the Diaspora.

Most of Epstein's characters are Jewish, and most of them suffer profoundly, even if comically, from the alienation he describes. The Holocaust pervades

Epstein's work as well; one is never without a sense of potential horror, cruelty, and genocide underlying the surface of existence. An intriguing theme implicit in most of Epstein's novels is the relationship between the comic side of life and the disappointment and tragedy, both of which are part of life. Although he does not address the issue directly, Epstein seems to be asking again and again through his ironic, humorous narrators and observers of hideous circumstance what constitutes the comic and what the tragic.

Epstein's first novel, *P. D. Kimerakov* (1975), set the comic, almost schizoid tone for much of his work to date. It was also very much a product of the times, a spy/cold-war farce owing much to Thomas Pynchon, Jules Feiffer, and Joseph Heller. A self-conscious first-person narrator tells the tale of a rumpled, naive Russian professor of science as he is made to play the fool in love, work, and espionage at home and in the United States. The book has many of the traits of Epstein's later, more mature works: exuberance of imagination; the Jewish narrator who is a naif, but potentially noble; a picaresque movement from one improbable adventure to the next; and the experience of cruelty and evil at the hands of others. It is also a very cinematic novel, reflecting Epstein's lifelong interest in plays and film.

His second book, *The Steinway Quintet Plus Four* (1976), is a collection of short stories. Here Epstein introduces one of his most memorable characters, Lieb Goldkorn, who later figures as the protagonist of three novellas, including a revised ''Steinway Quintet,'' in *Goldkorn Tales* (1985). Goldkorn is an elderly Jewish musician, an Austrian who escaped Nazi Europe as a young man and is now nearly destitute, alcoholic, and with a terminally ill wife. Like Kimerakov, he is a good-hearted naif with that same slightly cracked sense of humor we find in much of Epstein's work. His task is to try to reconcile the Old World culture of his Vienna childhood with modern, urban New York City. Other stories in the collection include ''The Disciple of Bacon,'' about a Hungarian scholar who has spent his life trying to prove that Mozart was Jewish, and two stories later reprinted as part of *Regina* (1982).

Epstein's next work was *King of the Jews* (1979), his most important and controversial novel. It is set in the Jewish quarter of a Polish city and chronicles the rise to power of Isaiah Chaim Trumpelman, who became the Elder of the ghetto during the Nazi occupation. The character and situation are based on the Lodz ghetto and its Elder, Mordechai Chaim Rumkowski. The book reflects a wealth of research on the subject, yet it is not at all a realistic depiction. Rather, Epstein uses again a naive narrator who pretends not to understand what he sees and who presents everything in detached, unemotional, even comic terms. It is this narrative voice that has caused the most controversy, along with Epstein's decision never to mention the Nazis by name, substituting instead such terms as ''the Other'' and ''the Blonde Ones.'' Yet we see much of the real-life circumstances: Judenrat members agonizing over the first transport; strikers, smugglers, people pulling wagons of excrement, and the yellow bus at the end of the tracks in which Jews are gassed to death. The novel explores in depth the moral system of the Nazi occupation, asking such profound questions as what constitutes moral behavior in the context of unfathomable evil; how are we to judge the Judenrat President; and what use was Judaism during the Holocaust?

While explicit violence was largely suppressed in *King of the Jews*, Epstein found gore and violence abounding as he worked on his next manuscript, *Pinto and Sons*, which was not completed until 1990. It tells the story of Adolph Pinto, a German Jew who emigrates to the United States in 1845 in order to study medicine. He is dismissed from Harvard for experimenting on a servant, thus beginning a wild, picaresque adventure to the gold mines of California. His experiment is described in gruesome particulars, as are numerous other physical and medical phenomena in the book. Again Epstein's narrator is naive, seemingly unable to reconcile his Old World ideas with the greed, racism, and violence of the New World. Although Epstein considers himself a traditional writer because he still believes in plot and straight narrative lines, the book shares some postmodern traits, being rooted in the techniques and language of nineteenth-century realism with characters and incidents derived more from tall tales than from any plausible attempt at verisimilitude. Young Modoc Indians who learn English from a volume of Robert Burns's poetry and so speak in Scottish dialect and espouse clan values; an infant who can do advanced mathematical calculations; characters who escape near-death experiences and return unscathed—these are the stuff of cartoons rather than realism. The self-conscious narration, the random violence, and the sense that greed and market considerations rule all behavior stem from a late twentieth-century sensibility that we can call postmodern.

While writing *Pinto and Sons*, Epstein produced two other books: *Goldkorn Tales*, already mentioned, and *Regina* (1982). This last is a third-person narrative following a few weeks in the life of Regina Glassman, a middle-aged Jewish actress and arts critic. Here, Epstein returns to the theme of the alienated Jew. Although Regina knows New York well, this particular summer a rapist and murderer is at large in her neighborhood, an unusual drought sends people to camp on the shores of the Hudson and East rivers, she is fired from her job and separated from her husband, and she has been asked to act in Chekov's *The Sea Gull* as Arkadina, the jealous older woman, when she herself still feels like the ingenue. The use of the play not only serves as a metaphor for Regina's life, but also allows Epstein to do something he clearly enjoys, that is, stage a play. In fact, plays are staged in nearly every one of Epstein's books, clearly reflecting his theatrical training and his interest in comparing real life with how it is fictionalized, directed, and staged.

As of this writing, Epstein had just completed another novel, tentatively titled *Von B*, but not yet in press. An excerpt, "Under the Hat," appeared in *Tikkun* (March/April 1994) and suggests that it will follow the life of another European immigrant to the United States, this time one who becomes a movie mogul.

CRITICAL RECEPTION

By far the most criticism generated by Epstein's work, both favorable and not, has been about *King of the Jews*. Reviewers both praised and damned it for its comic tone, which to Ruth Wisse "reduced the Jewish tragedy to a hollow metaphysical joke" (77). Jane Larkin Crain felt strongly that the book trivialized the Holocaust: "It's as if 6,000,000 Jews hadn't really suffered and died at a particular time and place at all, but had merely been conjured up by Leslie Epstein as background for his fanciful exploration of the Eternal Enigma of the Jew" (53). Other reviewers found his unusual technique courageous (Ascherson, 28–29) and "a lesson in what artistic restraint can do to help us imagine the dark places of our history" (Alter, 45).

Alvin Rosenfeld found fault with the tone but explored thoroughly the background and the literary and historical issues raised by the novel (55–58). Beyond reviews, Irene Goldman revisited the book in 1986 to praise its tone as the result of the narrator witnessing horror that permanently skewed his ability to comprehend the world. Ellen Schiff, in "American Authors and Ghetto Kings: Challenges and Perplexities," in which she wrote of three American treatments of Rumkowski and the Lodz ghetto, found flippancy the "unfortunate by-product" of a generally successful literary technique. Her long and thoughtful exploration of these responses to Rumkowski elucidated the Americanness of Epstein's text. Sidney Krome in "Power and Powerlessness in the Judenrat: Chairman M. C. Rumkowski as *King of the Jews*" offered a comparison of the historical Rumkowski with the fictional Trumpelman and an investigation into Epstein's portrayal of the power, morality, and corruption of the ghetto leader in the novel.

Criticism of his humorous treatment of horror has followed Epstein in his other works as well. In reviewing *Goldkorn Tales*, David Evanier commented on his "uneasy commingling of vaudeville and tragedy, this undercutting of horror with absurdity," and ultimately found that Epstein denies his characters their full humanity and "inevitably appears to deny Jewish history as well" (8). Nevertheless, other critics find Goldkorn charming, and all find his stories worthy of some praise. It is important to note that for all of the critical controversy, Epstein is clearly taken seriously by the literary community as a Holocaust writer. He is frequently invited to participate in discussions and to contribute to collections of essays; his essays and speeches about the Holocaust and the imagination are thoughtful contributions to the ongoing debate.

Criticism for *Pinto and Sons* generally appreciates the humor, imagination, and exuberance of the novel, but also finds it too long and at times too mired in detail. Although noting that it does deal with the moral issues of greed and exploitation of the Indians, Michiko Kakutani spoke for most critics in summing up: "In the end, *Pinto and Sons* never achieves the moral resonance of Mr. Epstein's finest fiction, but it remains an interesting addition to the oeuvre of one of this country's most gifted and far-reaching writers" (36).

BIBLIOGRAPHY

Works by Leslie Epstein

P. D. Kimerakov. Boston: Little, Brown, 1975.
The Steinway Quintet Plus Four. Boston: Little, Brown, 1976.
King of the Jews: A Novel of the Holocaust. New York: Coward, McCann, and Geoghegan, 1979.
Regina. New York: Coward, McCann, and Geoghegan, 1982.
Goldkorn Tales. New York: E. P. Dutton, 1985.
Pinto and Sons. Boston: Houghton Mifflin, 1990.

Works Cited and Studies of Leslie Epstein

Alter, Robert. "A Fable of Power." Review of *King of the Jews. New York Times Book Review*, February 4, 1979, 45.
Ascherson, Neal. Review of *King of the Jews. New York Review of Books*, April 5, 1979, 28–29.
Busch, Frederick. "Even the Smallest Position." *Georgia Review* 38 (Fall 1984): 525–41.
Crain, Jane Larkin. Review of *King of the Jews. Saturday Review*, March 31, 1979, 53.
Evanier, David. "Disaster à la Carte." Review of *Goldkorn Tales. New York Times Book Review*, April 7, 1985, 8.
Goldman, Irene C. "King of the Jews Reconsidered." *Midstream*, April 1986, 56–58.
Kakutani, Michiko. "Idealist in the Old West Is Undaunted by Failure." Review of *Pinto and Sons. New York Times*, November 16, 1990, 36.
Krome, Sidney. "Power and Powerlessness in the Judenrat: Chairman M. C. Rumkowski as King of the Jews." *West Virginia University Philological Papers* 38 (1992): 258–69.
Rosenfeld, Alvin. "The Holocaust as Entertainment." Review of *King of the Jews. Midstream*, October 1979, 55–58.
Schiff, Ellen. "American Authors and Ghetto Kings: Challenges and Perplexities." In *Holocaust Studies Annual*, ed. Sanford Pinsker. Greenwood, FL: Penkevill, 1984, 7–34.
Wisse, Ruth. Review of *King of the Jews. Commentary*, May 1979, 77.

IRVIN FAUST

(1924–)

Richard Kostelanetz

BIOGRAPHY

Irvin Faust was born in Brooklyn on June 11, 1924, to Morris and Pauline Henschel Faust. Although his father was an immigrant, on his mother's side he could trace himself back to a grandfather who had actually fought against the Apaches, serving under General George Crook in pursuing Geronimo. Faust attended City College of New York, where he majored in physical education. He began a teaching career in 1949 in Harlem and continued his education at Teachers College, Columbia University, where his dissertation (1960), *Entering Angel's World*, was published in 1963.

It was during the writing of his dissertation that his doctoral advisor, Raymond Patouillet, suggested that Faust had a talent for fiction. After Faust took a class in writing, he published his first piece, ''Into the Green Night,'' in the *Carleton Miscellany*. More stories were published in *Paris Review, Transatlantic Review*, and other magazines. With his first collection of short stories, *Roar Lion Roar* (1965), Faust's literary career was launched. Faust continued his career as a guidance counselor on Long Island until his retirement.

MAJOR WORKS AND THEMES

The name Irvin Faust first appeared in American little magazines in the early 1960s above stunning stories that dealt with crazy narrators in New York City. It may be surprising to note, then, that Faust, in his late thirties, had not only received a doctorate in social psychology, but had also authored *Entering Angel's World*, a book of individual case studies. It is also surprising, perhaps, to consider that by trade, Faust was not a psychologist or even a university professor but a guidance counselor at a suburban New York high school, where his major job was getting the more ambitious students into choice American colleges.

His psychology book advocates that the therapist assume, "wherever possible, the character and personality" of those with whom he deals. Perhaps the most striking quality of Faust's first collection of stories, *Roar Lion Roar*, is the sheer variety of madnesses apparently not the author's own. His narrators include a Puerto Rican boy whose mental existence becomes so entwined with the fate of the Columbia College football team (known as "The Lions") that when they lose to Princeton, he commits suicide; a rather stupid, dreamy fellow who sets out, accompanied by his Sancho, to be the Albert Schweitzer of New York's Central Park; Calvin Coolidge Delaware, a psychopathic egomaniac who regards himself as "The World's Fastest Human"; a fourteen-year-old who takes movies far too seriously and concomitantly suspects that he possesses "a magical substance" that makes him immortal; and a lonely stockroom boy so pathologically attached to his portable radio that a girl who makes a pass at him must first destroy the radio before she can gain his unobstructed attention.

Perhaps the greatest story here, if not one of the masterpieces of recent short fiction, is "Jake Bluffstein and Adolph Hitler," which describes, from the vantage point of an intimate third-person narrator, a mad aging Jew who fondly remembers the time around World War II when Jews found good reason to hate gentiles. After trying to stir antigentile sentiment among his neighbors by scribbling late at night the word "JUDE" on the window of his neighborhood butcher, he comes to believe that all Jews who do not hate gentiles, like his own rabbi, are fundamentally Nazis. In an unforgettable conclusion, Bluffstein imagines himself the Messiah of the Jews and then collapses in a psychotic breakdown. The idea of a Jew inventing anti-Semitism, much as the vulgar anti-Semite fabricates imaginary Jews, struck some Jewish-American critics as offensive, and this story was singled out at the time for particularly denunciatory criticism. Faust would always be a Jewish novelist excluded from the promotional packages of those flacks trying to make writing by Jews more acceptable to book-buying Americans. The resulting scandal is that his name appears in few critical books about modern American fiction, a situation that implicitly raises questions about contemporary literary intelligence.

Roar Lion Roar dealt quite profoundly with various cultural milieus of New York City, and these interests in individual madnesses and urban life appear not only in Faust's subsequent novels, but also in such stories as the brilliant "Dalai Lama of Harlem," which was published first in *Sewanee Review* and then in his second collection of short stories, *The Year of the Hot Jock* (1985). His first novel, which remains his best, may well be the most perspicacious and sustained portrait of a psychotic breakdown in all novelistic literature. The protagonist of *The Steagle* (1966) is Harold Aaron Weissburg, an English professor at a New York City college—ambitious enough to live above his means, yet not particularly devoted to either his work or intellectual pursuits—and the novel relates the fortnight-plus preceding his fall. As in "Jake Bluffstein," which this novel structurally resembles, the theme of incipient breakdown is evident from the fiction's beginning, and the "plot," so to speak, lies in its elaboration to an expected conclusion. However, Weissburg's disintegration is more gradual and varied than Bluffstein's, as well as more sensitively portrayed. Indeed, what is especially impressive is Faust's shrewd and subtle portrayal of a psychotic who, unlike a neurotic (say, Jean-Paul Sartre's Roquentin or Thomas Mann's Tonio Kroger), is barely aware of his imminent fall.

As a psychotic, Weissburg externalizes his fantasies, really believing that he is a movie star named "Bob Hardy" (of the same family as Andy) or a gruff Italian capable of making a stripper fall in love with him. As in "Jake Bluffstein," Faust is also especially adept at rendering with unfailing similitude how a hysterical consciousness distorts the lines between fantasy and reality so that the reader is never fully sure whether certain actions take place in dream or in life; for deeply embedded in Faust's fiction is the psychological truth that the wish can be as significant as the act. Nonetheless, his characterizations are never theoretically mechanical enough to provide "textbook cases," as neither psychological terminology nor conspicuous symbols mar his perceptive descriptions.

The deficiencies of *The Steagle* stem from historical perspective—an increasing preoccupation of Faust's later fiction—that is inadequately developed, as in the amorphous background in the Cuban missile crisis of October 1962. Certain petty details of characterization—Weissburg seems more of a high-school teacher than a college professor—remain unconvincing.

Faust's next project was a historical novel based upon Marinus Willett (1740–1830), a chronic loser who was Mayor of New York City for a year at the beginning of the nineteenth century: he sided with Alexander Hamilton and opposed the development of the steamboat, among other wrong choices. This Faust work has so far remained unfinished. In 1970 appeared *The File on Stanley Patton Buchta* about a fairly sensitive Long Island WASP who, after serving in Vietnam, decides to become a policeman. Being college educated and more sophisticated than his colleagues, Buchta is enlisted to become an undercover agent assigned to spy upon both a militant right-wing group and its leftist antagonists. This more "newsy" subject seems to popularize Faust's earlier virtues—the intimate feelings for New York City, the appreciation of ethnic diversity and language, and occasional passages of acute psychological understanding; but just as the plot here is needlessly confused and less credible, so is the style considerably thinner than before.

Its successor, *Willy Remembers* (1971), has another middle American for its narrator, Willy T. Klienhans, now well into his dotage, whose opening sentences indicate that his recollection is, to say the least, hopelessly scrambled: "Major Bill McKinley was the greatest president I ever lived through. No telling how far he could have gone if Oswald hadn't shot him." This novel is richer in literary excellences than *Stanley Patton Buchta*, and it resembles *The Steagle* in its portrayal of insensitive psychosis. However, though Klienhans, in Faust's portrayal, becomes more imposing than the silly old fool he seems to be at the novel's beginning, he is scarcely as compelling, or resonant, as Weissburg or even Buchta, and the portraiture is extended far too long, suggesting perhaps that the material of *Willy Remembers* would have worked better as a short story or a novella.

Of Faust's last five published novels, the best is *Foreign Devils* (1973), which begins as a first-person narrative by another of Faust's inspired madmen, Sidney Birnbaum, a Jew who imagines himself a war reporter named Norris Blake covering the Boxer Rebellion in China at the turn of the century. This fantasy is mixed with another of Birnbaum as a jazz musician playing with Benny Goodman in the late 1930s. From time to time present mundane reality intrudes, as we learn that he is separated from his wife and currently working as a teacher at Washington Irving High School. (In the background are the May 1968 riots around Columbia University.) The novel concludes with the cinematic image of Birnbaum's wife running toward him, but this too might be illusory. Here, as in other later Faust works, the reader often gets lost. Nonetheless, Faust's best stories, along with *The Steagle*, clearly establish him among the strongest contemporary psychological novelists.

CRITICAL RECEPTION

For his first book of stories, *Roar Lion Roar*, Faust received mixed reviews, but most enthusiastic was Stanley Kauffmann in the *New Republic*: "Mr. Faust must now be included among those new American authors who refute the lazy-minded assumption that the art of fiction is waning in this country. . . . Opening his book is like clicking on a switch; at once we hear the electric hum of talent." Granville Hicks's review of *The Steagle* in the *Saturday Review* showed an even greater appreciation for Faust's talents: "In several of the stories [in *Roar Lion Roar*, the author] portrayed ways in which people act out their fantasies. . . . [This] novel develops the same theme in a more ambitious way. . . . As in the short stories, the writing is vigorous, often surprising, and full of wit. It beautifully serves Faust's purpose, which is the revelation of a man who is completely unique and yet a good deal like the rest of us."

But some of the structural and stylistic problems in the earlier work were noted more prominently in *The File on Stanley Patton Buchta*. "Though the book begins promisingly, it swiftly collapses to the level of a first-rate comic strip" (L. J. Davis in *Book World*). Jerome Charyn in the *New York Times Book Review* called it a "curiously humorless book," but Arthur Cooper in *Newsweek* still found that Faust "has a knack for exposing the hysteria that exists just beneath the apparent unconcern of urban America."

In 1994 Faust's most recently published novel, *Jim Dandy*, was issued by Carroll and Graf. In the last decade, he has published ten short stories, one of which was awarded the Charles Angoff Award by the *Literary Review* as the best work it published in 1993–1994. Presently, Faust is at work on an eighth novel.

Overall, Faust's reputation will probably rest on his earlier works and several later stories such as "Jake Bluffstein and Adolf Hitler." But his unconventional and sardonic view of the insanities of American society and his depiction in a number of his novels of the confusions of the contemporary Jew give him a unique place in Jewish-American literature.

BIBLIOGRAPHY

Works by Irvin Faust

Roar Lion Roar and Other Stories. New York: Random House, 1965.
The Steagle. New York: Random House, 1966.
The File on Stanley Patton Buchta. New York: Random House, 1970.
Willy Remembers. New York: Arbor, 1971, 1983.
Foreign Devils. New York: Arbor, 1973.
A Star in the Family. Garden City, NY: Doubleday, 1975.
The Year of the Hot Jock and Other Stories. New York: Dutton, 1985.
Jim Dandy. New York: Carroll and Graf, 1994.

Studies of Irvin Faust

Bruccoli, Matthew J. "Irvin Faust." In *Conversations with Writers II*. Detroit: Bruccoli Clark/Gale Research, 1978.
Kostelanetz, Richard. "New American Fiction Reconsidered." *TriQuarterly* 8 (1967): 2.

Reviews Cited

Charyn, Jerome. *New York Times Book Review*, June 28, 1970, 30.
Cooper, Arthur. *Newsweek*, July 6, 1970, 76.
Davis, L. J. *Book World*, August 2, 1970, 2.
Hicks, Granville. *Saturday Review* 49 (July 16, 1966): 25.
Kauffmann, Stanley. *New Republic* 152 (January 30, 1965): 22.

BRUCE JAY FRIEDMAN (1930–)

Harold Heft

BIOGRAPHY

Bruce Jay Friedman was born on April 26, 1930, in New York City to Irving and Molly (Liebowitz) Friedman. Raised and educated in the Bronx, where his interest in writing first began to manifest itself while he was in high school, Friedman eventually majored in journalism at the University of Missouri. In the early 1950s, Friedman served as a lieutenant in the U.S. Air Force, where he was a writer and photographer for the magazine *Air Training*. Since the mid-1950s, Friedman has married twice and has emerged as one of the leading American writers of fiction, drama, and screenplays of the postwar era.

His first major publication, the novel *Stern* (1962), earned him a small following and a reputation as an important new voice in American Jewish writing. *Stern* was followed by the novel *A Mother's Kisses* (1964), which received an equally positive critical reception in addition to increased commercial success. Although Friedman has continued to write novels since the 1960s, none of his subsequent works, which include *The Dick* (1970), *About Harry Towns* (1974), *Tokyo Woes* (1985), *Violencia* (1988), and *The Current Climate* (1990), have received as positive a critical response as his two earliest novels. Instead, his greatest successes in recent decades have resulted from the strength of his Off-Broadway plays *Scuba Duba* (1967) and *Steambath* (1971), as well as from his contributions to such comic screenplays as *Stir Crazy* (1980), *The Lonely Guy* (1984) (which was adapted from his 1978 nonfiction book *The Lonely Guy's Book of Life*), and *Splash* (1984), for which he was nominated for an Academy Award.

Friedman has also produced several volumes of nonfiction, including a companion piece to *The Lonely Guy's Book of Life, The Slightly Older Guy* (1995), as well as multiple volumes of his short fiction, much of which has been reissued in the recently published *The Collected Short Fiction of Bruce Jay Friedman* (1995).

MAJOR WORKS AND THEMES

Although Friedman's novels have not attracted as much scholarly or commercial attention as those of certain of his North American Jewish contemporaries, such as Philip Roth, Mordecai Richler, and Joseph Heller, the best of his fiction contains thematic consistencies with their work and forces the experience of their postwar generation in radically new, if not surreal, directions. What Friedman shares with other figures of his generation is the simultaneously humorous and painful awareness of the contradictions of the late twentieth-century American Jew. (It is the humor generated from these contradictions that Friedman and his critics alike have labeled as his ''black humor.'') In Friedman's fiction, as in that of many of his contemporaries, the cultural (if not merely nominal) Jew attempts to assimilate into an ironically idealized vision of mainstream American society, only to be made over and over again to recognize, through a series of real and imagined affronts, both his/her differences and the flawed nature of his/her constructed vision of America. Although the Jewishness of Friedman's characters is rarely an overtly defining trait, archetypal Jewish literary figures, such as the paranoid, craven, hypochondriacal schlemiel and his smothering Jewish mother dominate Friedman's fiction. His plots, though often simplistic, linear, and episodically rendered (which is the reason why his work has translated so well into plays and Hollywood films), gain much of their appeal from the efforts of his protagonists to respond to their commonplace dilemmas in even the most limited ways. Friedman's heroes are antiheroes who are their own cruellest critics, consistently defeating their own best efforts or intentions with worry. His protagonists, like the title character of *Stern*, Joseph of *A Mother's Kisses*, Kenneth LePeters (né Sussman) of *The Dick*, and Harry Towns, inspire admiration on the part of Friedman's readers not for their strength or willingness to attempt to achieve greatness but for their ability to survive despite the flawed nature of the vision they have created. Since the religion that still provides them with an identity can no longer provide spiritual guidance, they must struggle to devise a new set of rules for their survival in order to counter a hostile world and their own self-destructive tendencies.

Where Friedman deviates most from his contemporaries to create an original version of the Jewish-American experience is in his ability to make of his schlemiel protagonists picaresque figures, abandoning their familiar ethnic urban surroundings in order to journey into and confront the unknown American frontier and clash with an ironically romanticized America (or, in the case of *Tokyo Woes*, with Japanese culture). Like Philip Roth's Alex Portnoy, Friedman's protagonists are fascinated by their readings of the ''other,'' more mainstream America, but unlike Portnoy, they take their mothers and children and wives with them into the experience and attempt not only to read the experience against their difference, but to internalize and naturalize it as part of their lives. In other words, such protagonists as Stern, in his vision of suburban American life, and Joseph, in his efforts to conform to university life at Kansas Land Grant Agricultural College, permit themselves to abandon, if temporarily, their urban ethnic bias in an effort fully to engage in their experience of the other America.

These experiments on the part of Friedman's protagonists are, of course, never entirely successful, since his protagonists are never able completely to abandon their cultural bias and because middle America is never confronted mainly in the spirit of exploration but more in the spirit of desperation or escape from the problems of a more familiar world. However, Friedman is usually able, in the process of his picaresque stories, to generate outrageous humor and profound melancholy in the evocation of a directionless, sprawling, quasi-gothic rural American landscape into which the confused, assimilated urban Jew may retreat for a period of time when the demands of the more representative experience prove overwhelming. Friedman's protagonists' project of conforming to the other America and their inability completely to shed some sense of their Jewishness become intimately entwined with their sense of self-worth.

CRITICAL RECEPTION

Max F. Schultz described the title character of *Stern* in his 1974 book *Bruce Jay Friedman* (the only book-length study of Friedman's work to date) in terms that could as easily apply to most of Friedman's protagonists in their attitudes toward cultures to which they cannot belong: "The conflicts in Stern are drawn sharply on both the psycho-sexual and psychosocial levels. Stern wishes to be a big man, a powerful man, a ''Big Jew''—that is, a Gentile. He wishes to be a member in good standing of the WASP club of America . . . and his move to the Gentile suburb is a vital step in his transformation. At the same time, Stern wishes masochistically to remain Jewish; like a mother-dominated boy, he desires to be feminine and persecuted, passively and guiltily suffering punishment as a sign of divine and maternal love'' (44). Friedman's protagonists, then, are not simply caught within the generational contradiction of a religious Jewish past and an assimilation-oriented future, but are actively involved in the struggle to define the terms of that future and are suffering the internal and external repercussions of self-doubt inherent in the project of acting as pioneers in that endeavor.

While the subject matter of much of Friedman's fiction is evidently culled from his own experiences—like Friedman, Stern had served in the air force, Joseph attends college in rural America, and Harry Towns is a writer struggling to deal with his sudden success—there is also a more general sense throughout his fiction, nonfiction, dramatic, and film writings (much of which has very little overtly in common with his life) that Friedman is consistently dominated by a limited number of themes. Although such films as *Splash* and *Stir Crazy*, for example, are not populated by Jews attempting to define themselves in various American experiences, they do suggest a sense of the alienation and terror of individuals caught in an unfamiliar segment of American society, scrambling to improvise rules for survival in this new setting. *The Lonely Guy* does not depict the sense of physical displacement witnessed in Friedman's fiction, but it does reflect the sadness of survival in an America where the individual is constantly confronted with the painful awareness of his or her own difference. Friedman's writing since the 1970s has apparently been more oriented around the need to generate the quick laugh than the profound reading of American society, but it is the nature of those laughs, most often derived from a familiar sense of confusion in finding the correct terms on which to base one's own identity in the absence of any relevance to traditional values, that relates directly to his writings of the 1960s that constitute his major contribution to American Jewish fiction.

BIBLIOGRAPHY

Works by Bruce Jay Friedman

Fiction

Stern. New York: Simon and Schuster, 1962.
Far from the City of Class, and Other Stories. New York: Frommer-Pasmantier, 1963.
A Mother's Kisses. New York: Simon and Schuster, 1964.
Black Angels. New York: Simon and Schuster, 1966.
The Dick. New York: Knopf, 1970.
About Harry Towns. New York: Knopf, 1974.
Let's Hear It for a Beautiful Guy, and Other Works of Short Fiction. New York: Fine, 1984.
Tokyo Woes. New York: Fine, 1985.
Violencia. New York: Grove-Atlantic, 1988.
The Current Climate. New York: Atlantic Monthly Press, 1989.
The Collected Short Fiction of Bruce Jay Friedman. New York: Fine, 1995.

Nonfiction

The Lonely Guy's Book of Life. New York: McGraw-Hill, 1978.
The Slightly Older Guy. New York: Simon and Schuster, 1995.

Plays

Scuba Duba. New York: Simon and Schuster, 1968.
Steambath. New York: Knopf, 1971.

Screenplays

Stir Crazy. Columbia, 1980.
Splash! With Lowell Ganz and Babaloo Mandel. Buena Vista, 1984.
The Lonely Guy (adaptation of *The Lonely Guy's Book of Life*). Universal, 1984.

Works Cited and Studies of Bruce Jay Friedman

Algren, Nelson. "The Radical Innocent." *Nation*, September 21, 1964, 142–43.

Avery, Evelyn. "Bruce Jay Friedman." In *Twentieth-Century American-Jewish Fiction Writers*, ed. Daniel Walden. Vol. 28 of *Dictionary of Literary Biography*. Detroit: Gale, 1984, 69–74.

Gilman, Richard. "Oedipus, Shmedipus, Mama Loves You." *Book Week*, August 23, 1964, 5, 8.

Gold, Herbert. "Even Bachelors Get the Blues." *New York Times Book Review*, February 11, 1979, 10–11.

Greenfield, Josh. "Bruce Jay Friedman Is Hanging by His Thumbs." *New York Times Magazine*, January 14, 1968, 30–42.

Hyman, Stanley E. "An Exceptional First Novel." *New Leader* 45 (October 1, 1962): 22–23.

Merkin, Daphne. "Writers and Writing: Jewish Jokesters." *New Leader* 60 (March 26, 1979): 12–13.

Rood, Karen. "Bruce Jay Friedman." *Dictionary of Literary Biography*, vol. 2. Detroit: Gale, 1978, 157–161.

Schultz, Max F. "The Aesthetics of Anxiety; and the Conformist Heroes of Bruce Jay Friedman and Charles Wright." In *Black Humor Fiction of the Sixties: A Pluralistic Definition of Man and His World*. Athens: Ohio University Press, 1973, 91–123.

———. *Bruce Jay Friedman*. New York: Twayne, 1974.

SANFORD FRIEDMAN   (1928–)

Joel Shatzky

BIOGRAPHY

Sanford Friedman was born on June 11, 1928, in New York City, the son of
Leonard and Madeline (Uris) Friedman. He received a B.F.A. from the Carnegie
Institute of Technology (now Carnegie-Mellon University) in 1949 and began
his involvement in theater when he was barely out of his teens as playwright-
in-residence at University Playhouse in Cape Cod, Massachusetts. After graduation, he moved to London, where he was a clerk for a year.

From 1951 to 1953 Friedman was in the army as a military policeman. He
served in Korea and received the Bronze Star. He returned to theater in 1954
as a producer for the Carnegie Hall Playhouse and then supported himself as a
writer from 1958 to 1975. He was a part-time instructor in reading poetry at the
Juilliard School in New York City from 1975 to 1979. From 1985 until the
present, he has been conducting workshops in creative writing at S.A.G.E. in
New York City. Since 1985, he has also been a member of the Executive Board
of the PEN Center.

In 1965, Friedman received the O. Henry Award from the Society of Arts
and Sciences for "Ocean," a segment of his first novel *Totempole*. In 1984, he
was honored with an award in literature from the American Academy and Institute of Arts and Letters.

Until *Totempole* was published in 1965, Friedman was primarily a playwright,
although many of his works were unproduced. When he was nineteen, however,
his first play, *Dawn from an Unknown Ocean*, was presented at University Playhouse in Mashpee, Massachusetts. Sections of *Totempole* first appeared in the
Partisan Review and *New World Writing*. After *Totempole*, Friedman published
three more novels. The first, *A Haunted Woman* (1968), explored the crisis of

a widowed woman whose late husband's play is about to be produced. In 1975, Friedman's best-received work, *Still Life: Two Short Novels*, examined sexuality in a far more symbolic way than in his first work. His most recently published novel, *Rip Van Winkle* (1980), completely departs from his earlier concerns.

MAJOR WORKS AND THEMES

Friedman's first novel, *Totempole* (1965), focuses on Stephen Wolfe, a young man growing up in a New York Jewish family during the Depression. The novel concerns Stephen's developing self-awareness of his homosexuality. In this respect, Friedman is a pioneer in his introduction of homosexual themes to a Jewish milieu.

Stephen's relationship with a counselor at a boys' camp is sensitively portrayed. In his review of the novel, Granville Hicks stated, ''I do not know of any piece of fiction that deals more perceptively with preadolescent sex'' (21). The approach that Friedman uses, however, is analytical and seems to be a reflection of the earlier forms of gay fiction in which a plea for understanding as much as an assertion of sexual identity is emphasized.

The novel connects Stephen's sexuality from infancy to his psychological neuroses, including the episodes in which his father parades around only in pajama tops to the distress of his mother and the delight of Stephen. But physical description at times predominates over psychological insight, as if Friedman is trying to provide evidence in order to support his protagonist's feelings about his sexuality.

The pressures on Stephen to conform are evident when he attempts a heterosexual affair in college and fails, but he arrives at reasonable emotional stability through male companionship in Korea. What is clear throughout is that Friedman does not try to disguise the sexuality of the protagonist through subtlety or metaphor at a time in which such a novel was still considered daring. Reflecting the climate of opinion in 1965, one reviewer, J. M. Carroll, asserted that the ''perversions and inversions'' of Friedman's sexual descriptions ''seem excessive'' (3309). Where the novel suffers most is a reflection of the time in which it was written. It has the elements of a case study that can be used to advance a cause, a cause that no longer had to be argued by the time Friedman's next novel about gay issues was published a decade later.

Friedman's second novel, however, *The Haunted Woman* (1968), is a depiction of a modern, sensitive woman who is at a crisis in her life concerning her own future and that of her dead husband's work. The author shows his emotional range by not dealing as directly with the subject of his first novel. The interest in psychological analysis that surfaced in *Totempole*, however, remains.

It was in his third book, *Still Life* (1975), two short novels, that Friedman combined his exploration into the deeper elements of the psyche with his sexual concerns. Through the juxtaposition of the two works, the first set in contemporary New York, the second in mythic Greece, Friedman explores the sexual imagination in its physical and symbolic manifestations.

The title work of the book concerns Danny Wahl, the son of a highly cultivated French-Jewish family. He has returned home in order to see if he can adjust to "normal" life after his stay at a mental institution. Danny's inability to accept his sexuality ends with a brutal description of his suicide. The fact that he is only an adolescent points to the pressures toward sexual conformity even in the 1970s that could motivate him to such a terrible act.

Friedman delves into myth in the second novella, "Lifeblood," which tells the story of Agdistis, Dionysus's hermaphrodite half-brother, who is castrated by order of a council of the gods. The beautiful youth Attis, however, becomes Agdistis's lover and eventually his self-castrating, sacrificial victim. The linking of the two novellas occurs not only through the act of denying one's sexuality, one through death, the other through castration, but also through the use of a "council" that Danny imagines and that mirrors the council of Olympians in "Lifeblood."

Thus the novel's two parts, separated though they are by time and imagination, complement one another in exploring the connection between myth and delusion, madness and its symbolic representation. Friedman is attempting to discover in these two works the archetypal forms for the emotional dislocations that homosexuals go through when they do not have the psychological support system that they need to sustain them against social alienation.

It is perhaps significant that after a gap of five years, Friedman's most recently published work, *Rip Van Winkle* (1980), has nothing to do with homosexuality, as if he had laid the subject to rest. Perhaps his desire to explore that theme was more in keeping with the pre-Stonewall era than with the more recent period of sexual liberation. But it is far more likely that Friedman's view transcends any narrow definitions of subject matter. It is in his intellectual daring in presenting a specifically Jewish milieu in his development of gay themes at a time in which few if any Jewish-American writers dealt with this issue that gives his work its distinction in Jewish-American literature.

CRITICAL RECEPTION

Although Friedman's protagonist's sexual experiences were referred to as "perversions" in *Totempole* in J. M. Carroll's review of the book, Granville Hicks praised the novel for its "honest" representation of Stephen Wolfe's sexuality. Hicks specifically admired the way in which "Friedman treats the homosexual theme . . . with great candor and no lubricity" (21).

On the other hand, in the *New York Times Book Review*, Webster Schott criticized the sexual detail as "a guide to technique . . . and a plea . . . for homosexuality as a form of romantic love" (26). Carroll, in fact, did not recommend the novel for fiction collections, and Schott considered it "talent spent on a Cause" (26).

In contrast, the reviews for *Still Life* may reflect the work of a writer who is more confident of his craft, as well as the critics of a different era. W. R. Evans regarded the title story as "a minor masterpiece" (196), and John Hollander in the *New Republic* described the two sections of the novel as "a subtly but powerfully unified work" (30).

The first of the two novellas fared better than the second, however, as Evans regarded much of the talk among the gods in "Lifeblood" as "phony conversation." Bruce Allen also took Friedman to task for "a cloying emphasis on masochistic butchery" in "Still Life" (1153). Yet the sexual nature of the materials was no longer alluded to with any indication of moral censure but merely, in Allen's review, as "ambivalent sexuality."

Overall, the reception of *Still Life* was very favorable, with far less emphasis on the subject itself as controversial and far more upon its artistic merits than in the critical response to *Totempole*. Friedman's interest, however, seemed to move away from gay themes in *Still Life*, in comparison to the earlier novel, and more toward myth and archetype. As a strategy for examining and attempting to come to grips with his sexuality, Sanford Friedman's work deserves careful examination as an arresting example of Jewish-American homophilic literature at a time when the subject itself was a source of great controversy. Yet perhaps the best summation of his fiction was expressed by R.W.B. Lewis when Friedman received the award for literature from the American Academy and Institute of Arts and Letters: "Sanford Friedman's fiction explores the realm of prose romance in which inner states and outward representation enter into allegorical relation" (quoted by Friedman in a telephone conversation with editor).

BIBLIOGRAPHY

Works by Sanford Friedman

Totempole. New York: Dutton, 1965. Reissued by North Point Press, San Francisco: 1984.
A Haunted Woman. New York: Dutton, 1968.
Still Life: Two Short Novels. New York: Saturday Review Press, 1975.
Rip Van Winkle. New York: Atheneum, 1980.

Works Cited and Studies of Sanford Friedman

Allen, Bruce. Review of *Still Life*. *Library Journal*, June 1, 1975, 1153.
Carroll, J. M. Review of *Totempole*. *Library Journal*, August 1965, 3309.
Evans, W. R. Review of *Still Life*. *Best Seller*, October 1975, 196.
Hicks, Granville. Review of *Totempole*. *Saturday Review*, August 21, 1965, 21.
Hollander, John. Review of *Still Life*. *New Republic*, June 14, 1975, 30.
Long, Barbara. Review of *Totempole*. *Book Week*, September 19, 1965, 24.
Schott, Webster. Review of *Totempole*. *New York Times Book Review*, August 29, 1965, 5:35.

THOMAS FRIEDMANN   (1947–   )

Joel Shatzky and Michael Taub

BIOGRAPHY

Thomas Friedmann was born on March 13, 1947, in Debrecen, Hungary, the son of Ferenc and Hedwig Gottlieb Friedmann, both survivors of the Holocaust. Observant Jews, they gave their son a religious education until he was twenty-one. Friedmann came to the United States in 1956 and became a naturalized citizen in 1961. In 1970 he married Chaya Neufeld, and they have two children, Ilana and David.

Friedmann received his B.A. in 1969 from Brooklyn College and his M.A. from New York University in 1970. He has been a member of the faculty of Onondaga Community College in Syracuse, New York, since 1977 and was director of its Writing Skills Center in 1982–1984. Among his awards have been a PEN award in 1976 and a Pushcart Award, while his novel *Damaged Goods* was named among the "top ten novels with Jewish content for 1985" by the Jewish Telegraphic Agency.

MAJOR WORKS AND THEMES

In an interview printed in *Contemporary Authors*, Friedmann explained that although he thinks and writes in English, "I still dream and count in Hungarian, and retain the use of Hebrew and Yiddish for the study of the Bible and commentaries. My fiction, I think, reflects the collisions among these languages and cultures" (168).

Friedmann is fascinated by the stories of such traditional authors as Nathaniel Hawthorne, Herman Melville, and Henry James, especially where they depict the meeting between Americans and foreigners abroad. His first novel, *Damaged*

Goods (1984), has a theme similar to that of a number of other noted Jewish-American authors concerning the rebellion of a young man against the limitations of an Orthodox Jewish background. In a telephone interview Friedmann elaborated on his view that *Damaged Goods* was one of the earliest books by a child of Holocaust survivors who also had to deal with the conflicts of growing up Orthodox in a secular American society. He cited several more recent novels that have pursued this theme.

His earlier collection of short stories, *Azriel*, concerns a character in the title story who is a superhero, but in the Jewish tradition, who triumphs over the enemies of the Jews not through brute strength but through brainpower. Friedmann has been working on a new novel, *The Hartz Treasure*, for the past ten years, and excerpts from it have been printed in a number of literary magazines such as *Black Ice*. He sees a similar theme in both novels, which "seem to be about the attraction as well as the destructiveness of history, ritual, and heritage" (quoted in *Contemporary Authors*, 169).

BIBLIOGRAPHY

Works by Thomas Friedmann

Hero Azriel: A Collection of Tales. Marblehead, MA.: Micah, 1979.
Damaged Goods. Sag Harbor, New York: Permanent Press, 1984.

Works Cited and Studies of Thomas Friedmann

Berger, Alan L. *Crisis and Covenant*. Albany: State University of New York Press, 1985.
For further information about Thomas Friedmann, see *Contemporary Authors*, 118. Detroit: Gale Research, 1986, 168–69.

DANIEL FUCHS (1909–1993)

Gabriel Miller

BIOGRAPHY

Daniel Fuchs was born in New York City on June 25, 1909, the fourth child of Jacob and Sara Fuchs. His father came to America from Russia at the age of seventeen; his mother emigrated at age thirteen from Poland. At the time of Daniel's birth, Jacob Fuchs, suffering from furrier's disease, had to find a new way to support his family. He started selling newspapers near the Whitehall Building, then under construction at 17 Battery Place. When the building was completed, he was given his own stand, where he sold candy and magazines in addition to newspapers.

Daniel Fuchs spent his early childhood on Manhattan's Lower East Side before moving at the age of five to the Williamsburg section of Brooklyn, which was to become the greatest influence on his artistic imagination. His literary bent displayed itself early: he was the editor-in-chief of the *Eastern District High School Daisy* in Williamsburg. He then attended City College, where he remained active in literary affairs, eventually editing the college's literary magazine, the *Lavender*. During his college years, Fuchs spent his summers at camps in New England, serving as a Red Cross swimming examiner and instructor. At a camp in Pittsfield, Massachusetts, he met Susan Chessen, a junior counselor. They were married in 1932.

A year earlier, Fuchs had received his first literary encouragement. He had sent Malcolm Cowley, then editor of the *New Republic*, a piece called "A Brooklyn Boyhood." Impressed, Cowley printed part of it as "Where Al Capone Grew Up" and recommended that Fuchs expand the account into a novel.

Writing required time and leisure that Fuchs did not have, for he was working as a permanent substitute at P.S. 225 in Brighton Beach. In the summer of 1932, however, the Fuchses rented half a cottage in Woods Hole, Massachusetts, and there he expanded "A Brooklyn Boyhood" into his first novel, *Summer in Williamsburg*, which was published by Vanguard in 1934.

Two more novels followed quickly. *Homage to Blenholt*, comic and lighter in tone than its doggedly naturalistic predecessor, was published in 1936. The following year saw the publication of Fuchs's masterpiece, *Low Company*, a grim tale of murder, prostitution, and betrayal. Although the reviews of the three novels were respectful, at times glowing, the books did not sell. Fuchs, who was now a father, grew discouraged. He broke up a fourth novel, tentatively titled *Love in Brooklyn*, and sent parts out as stories.

After not hearing anything for months, he received acceptances and checks from the *New Yorker, Collier's*, and the *Saturday Evening Post*. He also received his first offer from Hollywood. He was unhappy there, however, and returned to New York six months later. The disillusioning experiences of that brief stint were chronicled in a story, "Dream City or the Drugged Lake," published in 1937. But Fuchs returned to Hollywood in 1940, and with the exception of his military service during World War II and two stays in London (1958 and 1962), during which he worked on films, he remained in Southern California for the rest of his life.

During his time in Hollywood, Fuchs was a successful screenwriter, though he never gained a major reputation. His first screen credit was for *The Big Shot*, starring Humphrey Bogart, which was released in 1942. He adapted his novel *Low Company* as *The Gangster*, an underappreciated variation on the gangster-film genre in 1947. Other notable films include *Criss Cross* (1949), *Panic in the Streets* (1950), and *Storm Warning* (1951), which costarred Ronald Reagan. In 1955 Fuchs won an Academy Award for *Love Me or Leave Me*, a crime drama based on the true story of singer Ruth Etting and her stormy relationship with Jimmy "the Gimp" Snyder. The film starred Doris Day, who performed several musical numbers, including the title song, and James Cagney, who called its script the "finest he had ever read."

While in Hollywood, Fuchs continued to write stories, most of which were published in the *New Yorker*. In 1971 he turned an unsold screen story into his fourth novel, *West of the Rockies*, the story of an aging screen star who suffers an emotional breakdown. It was published by Knopf in 1971 to indifferent reviews.

Fuchs stopped working for the movies in the early 1960s and concentrated in his retirement years on writing fiction and autobiographical pieces, many of them published in *Commentary*. His lovely reminiscence of Los Angeles appeared in *Sports Illustrated*'s "1984 Olympic Preview." His last book was *The Apathetic Bookie Joint*, a collection of previously published stories and essays, released by Methuen in 1979. This volume also featured the never-before-published novella "Triplicate," Fuchs's most overtly autobiographical work and one of the best Hollywood stories ever written. Daniel Fuchs died in Los Angeles on July 26, 1993.

MAJOR WORKS AND THEMES

Fuchs's critical reputation rests primarily on the three novels he wrote in the 1930s. These three works are dissimilar in form and style, but they are linked by Fuchs's distinctive perspective on life and human behavior.

Summer in Williamsburg is very much a first novel, narrated by a young man who seeks to understand the small world he lives in. The plot follows his quest, triggered by the suicide of a neighbor, to make a "laboratory out of Williamsburg" and thus to make sense out of all the individual struggles that surround him.

The novel is ambitious, perhaps overly so, as Fuchs attempts to depict the Williamsburg life as he knew it in its entirety. The book suffers from an occasional loss of control, but it is nonetheless remarkable for what it does accomplish. Few novels reflect immigrant and tenement life with the dramatic immediacy of *Summer in Williamsburg*, and fewer can match its stunning accuracy in representing the rhythms and drudgeries of daily life. The attempt to capture life fully in a novel, however, ultimately defeats both the young narrator and the author.

These were people as God made them and as they were. . . . No novel, no matter how seriously intentioned, was real. The progressive development, the delineated episodes, the artificial climax, the final conclusion, the setting, the characters at rest and out of the lives of the readers, these were logical devices and they were false. People did not live in dramatic situations.

Despite the disclaimer, this first novel is an extraordinary effort, offering a poignant and profoundly realistic record of a rich experience.

Homage to Blenholt abandons the episodic structure of its predecessor, as Fuchs examines the comic contradiction between dreams and reality in his most focused and rigorously patterned novel. The character of Blenholt was based on Leo T. Holst, a major figure on the Brooklyn political scene in the 1930s. Writing about the novel many years later in the introduction of the 1990 edition, Fuchs remembered, "For the people in the tenements he was what they craved, a champion—someone to stand up for them . . . and in the nature of things he failed them" (viii). As in many modernist works that teeter on the edge of tragedy, Fuchs's vision finally turns away from the comic. The brilliant climactic scene at Blenholt's funeral anticipates the surreal power of Nathanael West's *The Day of the Locust*, as Fuchs's *luftmensch* dreamer is brought face-to-face with the sordid reality of his hero's life.

In his final novel of the decade, *Low Company*, Fuchs drops the questioning, lovable innocents who populated his first two books. Even the questioning tone is gone, as Fuchs, no longer searching for solutions, presents a bitter and disillusioned worldview, a portrait of a society on the verge of collapse, a nightmare landscape with no hope of redemption. *Low Company* is a surely plotted novel that combines the dominant realist mode of the decade with a surreal perception that replaces the comic sensibility of the earlier works.

In this last of his "Williamsburg novels," Fuchs actually departs from Williamsburg to locate his characters in Brighton Beach, here called Neptune Beach, a grim wasteland of vice, corruption, and murder, where escaping misery is man's only goal. Prostitution is a big business and violence the chief occupation of the novel's characters. Fuchs bends his characters into grotesques embodying his vision of mob anger and individual loneliness. Unlike Nathanael West, however, whose depiction of mob violence he anticipates, Fuchs remains tolerant and engaged by his people, whose humanity still surfaces from beneath the grotesque exterior.

Fuchs did not publish another novel for almost thirty-five years. *West of the Rockies* is a minor effort, focusing on Adele Hogue, a movie star whose antics have forced the film she is working on to close down. The novel takes place in Palm Springs, where, despite their greater wealth, the inner despair and moral bankruptcy of Fuchs's characters remain unchanged; they are still "low company."

Fuchs's most important work after *Low Company* was "Triplicate," a novella combining the stream-of-consciousness style of much of his Hollywood fiction with the realism of his earlier works. The story takes place at a Hollywood party, where the various characters come and go and talk. Using his protagonist to meditate on his own art and life, Fuchs echoes Joyce's "The Dead": he captures the fleeting, ephemeral moments of living even while providing a meditation on dying. Typically for Fuchs, however, "Triplicate" dwells most movingly on the small joys of living.

CRITICAL RECEPTION

Summer in Williamsburg received solid, if unspectacular, reviews. The *New York Times* called Fuchs's style "competent and incisive" and added that "he writes with vigor and freshness" (6). Its critic's complaint focused on the novel's muddled theme. The *New Republic* also praised the book's writing scope, but pronounced its cynicism a sign of immaturity (81).

Homage to Blenholt received stronger notices. The *New Republic* admired Fuchs's ability to switch from the naturalistic tone of *Summer in Williamsburg* "to a racy, caricaturing manner" and predicted that Fuchs might develop into an "outstanding satirist" (229). Stanley Young in the *New York Times* objected that the book lacked "order" but praised the writing, claiming that "the date of . . . Fuchs's next novel should appear in red on the calendar" (6). The *Saturday Review of Literature* was less enthusiastic, declaring the satire a failure because "neither hero nor background is genuine enough to judge the other by" (18).

The reviews for *Low Company* were more mixed. The novelist James Farrell, writing in the *Nation*, stated, "I know of few novelists writing in America today of Fuchs's age who possess his natural talent or his sense of life'' (244). Despite some minor reservations, Harold Strauss of the *New York Times* found the novel ''impressive and unusual'' (6). But the *Saturday Review of Literature* found both the character and the plot ''absurd'' (22).

When the novels were rereleased by Basic Books in 1961 as *Three Novels by Daniel Fuchs*, they received more attention and more respectful reviews. American Jewish literature was suddenly receiving major critical evaluation, and Henry Roth's *Call It Sleep* had just been reissued to great acclaim, while Fuchs had not published any novels since 1937. His silence and the previous critical neglect had seemingly accorded him additional stature.

Robert Gorham Davis gave the *Three Novels* a lengthy review in the *New York Times Book Review*, finding much to praise and comparing Fuchs to James T. Farrell and Saul Bellow (8, 22). Hollis Alpert in the *Saturday Review* found the Williamsburg novels ''more readable and compelling today'' than they had been in the 1930s and, disputing the dismissive designation as minor classics, declared them novels of great power and scope (17–18).

When Fuchs finally published *West of the Rockies* in 1971, it received significant critical attention but mostly lukewarm reviews. Richard Ellman in the *New York Times* felt that the novel suffered from avoiding direct confrontation with experience: ''If he [Fuchs] has ever lived, he's not telling anybody about it here'' (7). Irving Howe dissented; reviewing the novel in *Harper's*, he called it ''fierce [and] grimly absorbing.'' Furthermore, he judged, ''Simply as a writer of narrative, he is more skillful than ever'' (88–89).

The Apathetic Bookie Joint also received major critical attention. *Kirkus Reviews* said that the effect of the stories ''is one of the most extraordinary in American writing'' and went on to label Fuchs ''superb'' and the book ''wonderful'' (811). Irving Howe in the *New York Review of Books* and Harold Beaver in the *Times Literary Supplement* devoted major reviews to the collection. Bucking the tide of critical opinion, Beaver asserted that the move to California had in fact enriched Fuchs's imagination and called him a ''master of the antics of despair'' (431). Howe compared Fuchs to John O'Hara, terming him a ''pure novelist'' (10–11). Mordecai Richler in the *New York Times* was more critical, but he still proclaimed that ''Fuchs will always occupy an honored place in the pantheon of Jewish writers in America'' (9–10).

BIBLIOGRAPHY

Works by Daniel Fuchs

Novels

Summer in Williamsburg. New York: Vanguard, 1934; London: Constable, 1934.
Homage to Blenholt. New York: Vanguard, 1936; London: Constable, 1935.
Low Company. New York: Vanguard, 1937; republished as *Neptune Beach*. London: Constable, 1937.

Stories (Fuchs and others). New York: Farrar, Straus, and Cudahy, 1956.
Three Novels by Daniel Fuchs. New York: Basic Books, 1961. Reprinted as *The Wil-liamsburg Trilogy*. New York: Avon, 1972 (includes *Summer in Williamsburg, Homage to Blenholt,* and *Low Company*).
West of the Rockies. New York: Knopf, 1971; London: Secken and Warburg, 1971.
The Apathetic Bookie Joint. New York: Methuen, 1979; London: Secken and Warburg, 1980.

Selected Screenplays

The Big Shot. With Bertram Millhauser and Abem Finkel. Warner Bros., 1942.
The Hard Way. With Peter Viertel. Warner Bros., 1943.
Between Two Worlds. Warner Bros., 1944.
The Gangster. ABC–Allied Artists, 1947.
Hollow Triumph. Eagle Lion, 1948.
Criss Cross. Universal, 1949.
Panic in the Streets (adaptation). 20th Century-Fox, 1950.
Storm Warning. With Richard Brooks. Warner Bros., 1951.
Taxi. With D. M. Marsham, Jr. 20th Century-Fox, 1952.
The Human Jungle. With William Sackheim. ABC–Allied Artists, 1954.
Interlude. With Franklin Coen. Universal, 1957.

Works Cited and Studies of Daniel Fuchs

Alpert, Hollis. Review of *Three Novels*. *Saturday Review*, September 22, 1961, 17–18.
Review of *The Apathetic Bookie Joint*. *Kirkus Reviews*, July 15, 1979, 811.
Beaver, Harold. Review of *The Apathetic Bookie Joint*. *Times Literary Supplement*, April 18, 1980, 431.
Davis, Robert Gorham. Review of *Three Novels*. *New York Times Book Review*, September 10, 1961, 8, 22.
Ellman, Richard. Review of *West of the Rockies*. *New York Times*, June 13, 1971, 7.
Farrell, James. Review of *Low Company*. *Nation*, February 27, 1937, 244.
Review of *Homage to Blenholt*. *New Republic*, April 1, 1936, 229.
Review of *Homage to Blenholt*. *Saturday Review of Literature*, May 2, 1936, 18.
Howe, Irving. Review of *The Apathetic Bookie Joint*. *New York Review of Books*, December 6, 1979, 10–11.
———. "Daniel Fuchs: Escape from Williamsburg." *Commentary*, July 6, 1948, 29–34.
———. Review of *West of the Rockies*. *Harper's*, July 1971, 88–89.
Krafchik, Marcelline. *World without Heroes: The Brooklyn Novels of Daniel Fuchs*. Rutherford, NJ: Fairleigh Dickinson University Press, 1988.
Review of *Low Company*. *Saturday Review of Literature*, February 18, 1937, 22.
Michelson, Paul. "Communal Values in the Fiction of Daniel Fuchs." *Studies in American Jewish Literature* 5 (1986): 69–79.
Miller, Gabriel. *Daniel Fuchs*. Boston: Twayne, 1979.
———. *Screening the Novel: Rediscovered American Fiction in Film*. New York: Ungar, 1980.
———. "Williamsburg in Wonderland: Daniel Fuchs's 'Triplicate.' " *Studies in American Jewish Literature* 7 (1988): 80–89.

Richler, Mordecai. Review of *The Apathetic Bookie Joint*. *New York Times*, November 11, 1979, 9, 18.

Strauss, Harold. Review of *Low Company*. *New York Times*, February 28, 1937, 6.

Review of *Summer in Williamsburg*. *New Republic*, November 24, 1934, 81.

Review of *Summer in Williamsburg*. *New York Times*, November 18, 1934, 6.

Young, Stanley. Review of *Homage to Blenholt*. *New York Times*, February 23, 1936, 6.

MERRILL JOAN GERBER　　　(1938–)

Becky Spiro Green

BIOGRAPHY

Merrill Joan Gerber was born in Brooklyn, New York, on March 15, 1938, to William and Jessie Soblum Gerber. Her father supported the family with a series of small business ventures, and when Gerber was still a small child, he opened a shop to buy and sell antiques. She began publishing early: poems in the literary magazines of Brooklyn's P.S. 238 and Lafayette High School. When Gerber was fourteen, the family moved to Florida. At Miami Beach High School, she published stories for the first time, in the school magazine called *Embryo*, and there she met Joseph Spiro, whom she would marry in 1960.

Gerber originally attended the University of Miami, where she had won a scholarship, but she soon transferred to the University of Florida, where she studied with Andrew Lytle. She submitted a poem to the *Writer* about this time, and one morning in the university library she discovered her poem in print. In June 1960, Gerber married Joe Spiro, and both began work toward master's degrees at Brandeis University. Feeling that she would be discriminated against as a woman, she declined to take the oral exam for her degree, which, incidentally, she finally received in 1981. She therefore took a job as an editorial assistant at Houghton Mifflin while she continued to write. Gerber studied with Wallace Stegner at Stanford at the time that her first child, Becky, was born in 1962. Within the first months of the Stanford writing workshop, she had sold two stories, one to *Redbook* and one to the *New Yorker*.

By 1965, the year her second daughter, Joanna, was born, she had produced the body of work that comprised her first book of short stories, *Stop Here, My Friend*. In 1967, her third daughter, Susanna, was born, and Gerber published her first novel, *An Antique Man*.

Through the 1960s and 1970s, balancing the demands of a writing career and a family, she published the novels *Now Molly Knows* (1974) and *The Lady with the Moving Parts* (1978), sold stories to such varied publications as *Good Housekeeping*, the *Saturday Evening Post*, and the *Sewanee Review*, and began a run with *Redbook* that culminated in a record number of stories: forty-two Gerber stories appeared in *Redbook* from 1964 to 1991, twenty-five of which were later collected and published as *This Old Heart of Mine: The Best of Merrill Joan Gerber's Redbook Stories* (1993).

Gerber taught writing classes, first at writer's conferences and in local adult-education programs, and later at Pasadena City College, UCLA Extension, and the California Institute of Technology. In the 1980s, she turned her attention to books for teenagers and wrote nine young-adult novels, including *Name a Star for Me* (1983) and *Handsome as Anything* (1990). Another collection of short stories, *Honeymoon*, appeared as part of the Illinois Short Fiction series in 1985.

Gerber published her next novel for adults in 1989, *King of the World*. A collection of stories, *Chattering Man*, came out in 1991, and another novel, *The Kingdom of Brooklyn*, in 1992. In the early 1990s, her mother's declining health and the arrival of a stray Manx kitten led to Gerber's first work of nonfiction, the 1995 memoir *Old Mother, Little Cat: A Writer's Reflections on Her Kitten, Her Aged Mother, and Life*.

Merrill Joan Gerber's awards include the Andrew Lytle Fiction Prize in 1985 for "At the Fence"; the Fiction Network Fiction Competition Prize in 1985 for "Hairdos"; an O. Henry Prize Stories award in 1986 for "I Don't Believe This"; Special Mention of Important Works in Small Presses in 1988 for "Comes an Earthquake" and "Night Stalker"; the *Prairie Schooner* Readers' Choice Award in 1989 for "Chicken Skin Sandwiches"; the Pasadena Arts Council Gold Crown Award for Literary Arts in 1990; and a Best American Short Stories award in 1992 for "Honest Mistakes."

MAJOR WORKS AND THEMES

Merrill Joan Gerber's work has predominantly centered on family life in all its manifestations, including love, conflict, and sometimes terror. Her families are Jewish families; her characters' commitment to their Jewish identity varies as widely as does the commitment of American Jews in all walks of life. Her families have problems ranging from lost Brownie pins to domestic violence, from arguments over the wedding guest list to suicide. Throughout her career, Gerber has employed a wide range of styles: her fiction published in popular magazines such as *Redbook* and *Ladies' Home Journal* is often light in tone, sometimes humorous; her novels and many stories published in literary journals are usually more serious in theme and manner; always, the style fits the substance. However, almost none of Gerber's work can be categorized as "happy" or "sad": much of her work's intensity is in its realism, its refusal to simplify even as it distills.

In 1963, with her first *New Yorker* story, "We Know That Your Hearts Are Heavy," Gerber introduced the characters of Janet, her husband Danny, and her parents Abram and Anna Goldman. Janet and Danny and their family make frequent appearances throughout Gerber's work. In the first *New Yorker* story, Janet is twenty-two and recently married. In "This Old Heart of Mine," the title story in the 1993 collection, Janet and Danny are alone in the house again, their third and youngest daughter having departed for college several stories earlier. In the years between, Janet and Danny experience the joys and crises of family life: births and deaths, arguments and reconciliations, illnesses, pets, and travel.

Janet is the narrator of Gerber's 1967 novel *An Antique Man*. Though Gerber has dealt with weighty matters in all her work, her themes have grown more serious through her career: her most recent novels, *King of the World* and *The Kingdom of Brooklyn*, are intense explorations of the fine lines between love and dysfunction. Some themes, however, have been in her work since the beginning: her first *Mademoiselle* story, "The Cost Depends on What You Reckon It In," is set largely in a place called Sherman's Rest Home, and much of her later work, including the memoir *Old Mother, Little Cat* and the eight "Anna" stories that make up the novella in *Chattering Man*, deal with the physical and psychological consequences of old age. Anna is Anna Goldman, the mother of Gerber's recurring protagonist Janet; but while most of Gerber's Janet and Danny stories are told from Janet's point of view—the character Anna is in her fifties in her first appearances—the Anna stories (which sometimes touch on the same incidents Janet has already related in earlier stories) are seen through Anna's eyes, beginning in her seventies and ending with a story that opens on her eightieth birthday.

CRITICAL RECEPTION

The critic and novelist Cynthia Ozick reviewed Gerber's first book of short stories, *Stop Here, My Friend*, in *Midstream* in June 1965. She called the stories skillful and successful, the prose accurate and restrained, but disapproved of the characters' relative un-Jewishness: despite Yiddish-speaking grandmothers, rabbis, and challah, the "stories are without . . . Jewish consciousness," and the characters are "mildly touching, in our small bland American way" (108). In later years, however, Ozick's criticism of Gerber's work changed to strong and vocal support. When *King of the World* won the 1990 Pushcart Press Editor's Choice Award, Ozick had nominated it. When *The Kingdom of Brooklyn* won Hadassah's Harold U. Ribalow Award in 1993, Ozick spoke at the award ceremony, recanting her earlier criticism, admitting that Gerber's books "reveal the lives of contemporary Jews as they sometimes really are," and calling Gerber's work "a strong plain prose that shines with the clarity of absolute probity, mixed with all the rubble, pain, and debris of things-as-they-are."

From the earliest reviews, most of Gerber's work has drawn praise from critics. Maggie Rennert, writing about Gerber's first short-story collection in 1965, declined to describe the work as "promising": "I don't know what she can promise that she hasn't delivered already, and I can't imagine how she could possibly blow it later" (20). *Stop Here, My Friend* was warmly received by many other critics, and reviews of her subsequent novels remained largely, though not exclusively, favorable.

An Antique Man was described as "full of warmth, honesty, and insight" (Simon, 23) and "as relentless in observing the symptoms of the spirit as a doctor must be in observing the symptoms of the body" (Epstein, 57). Walter Sullivan, however, writing in the *Sewanee Review*, while describing the novel as "almost flawless in its execution," saw the characters as "homeless and without faith" and felt that "Miss Gerber makes nothing of these signs of spiritual decline" (155).

Reaction to *Now Molly Knows* varied considerably, from a "poignant and funny novel of adolescence and the first discovery of sex and love, by a brilliant young Jewish novelist" (*Hadassah Magazine*) to "too timid and drab to be moving" (Shulman, 33). The character of Molly was mentioned by Mary Jean DeMarr and Jane S. Bakerman in the study *The Adolescent in the American Novel since 1960*: Molly, they felt, resembled male adolescent protagonists "who define themselves so narrowly, relying primarily upon their sexuality to grant them adult power" (132).

Gerber's most recent novels have garnered the highest and most consistent praise. Of *King of the World* Susan Brownmiller wrote, "This could be a text-book case of wife battery and child abuse. But novelist Merrill Joan Gerber puts it on paper with greater eloquence, ambivalence and compassion than I would have thought possible" (3). Susan Koppelman noted, "In this brilliantly written novel, the reader follows Michael and Ginny from their passionate courtship through the many years of a marriage replete with schlamazeldich—bad luck—to Michael's dangerous descent into craziness and Ginny's escape with their young son to a new life. Two of the novel's many layers of complexity have to do with disability and intermarriage. Ginny . . . is an alienated Jew. . . . Michael . . . is a denominationless secular Gentile white man with . . . a sense of the entitlement he has inherited as a heterosexual white Gentile man in the sexist, racist anti-Semitic homophobic world. He has been taught that he is entitled to be a king" (6).

Of *The Kingdom of Brooklyn* Lynne Sharon Schwartz wrote, "Merrill Joan Gerber's superb evocation of an anguished child's faltering steps toward consciousness is set in a house divided. . . . Below is the cellar, dark realm of terror to Issa, the child narrator, where the house's entrails, especially the fiery furnace, personify the ancient furies that shape the fates lived out above. . . . Issa's mother . . . rules the passive family by her headaches, tantrums, and suicide threats . . . a figure whose misery exceeds her circumstances; readers who require a neat post-Freudian etiology of neuroses and family dysfunction will be dissatisfied" (8).

BIBLIOGRAPHY

Works by Merrill Joan Gerber

Short Story Collections

Stop Here, My Friend. Boston: Houghton Mifflin, 1965.
Honeymoon. Illinois Short Fiction. Urbana: University of Illinois Press, 1985.
Chattering Man: Stories and a Novella. Atlanta: Longstreet Press, 1991.
This Old Heart of Mine: The Best of Merrill Joan Gerber's Redbook Stories. Atlanta:
     Longstreet Press, 1993.

Novels

An Antique Man. Boston: Houghton Mifflin, 1967.
Now Molly Knows. New York: Arbor House, 1974.
The Lady with the Moving Parts. New York: Arbor House, 1978.
King of the World. Wainscott, NY: Pushcart Press, 1989.
The Kingdom of Brooklyn. Marietta, GA: Longstreet Press, 1992.
The Anna Stories: Syracuse, NY: Syracuse University Press, 1997.

Novels for Young Adults

Please Don't Kiss Me Now. New York: Dial Press, 1981.
Name a Star for Me. New York: Viking Press, 1983.
I'm Kissing As Fast As I Can. New York: Fawcett Juniper, 1985.
The Shimmer of My Indian Prince. New York: Fawcett Juniper, 1986.
Also Known as Sadzia! The Belly Dancer! New York: Harper and Row, 1987.
Marry Me Tomorrow. New York: Fawcett Juniper, 1987.
Even Pretty Girls Cry at Night. New York: Crosswinds, 1988.
I'd Rather Think about Robby. New York: Harper and Row, 1989.
Handsome as Anything. New York: Scholastic, 1990.

Memoir

*Old Mother, Little Cat: A Writer's Reflections on Her Kitten, Her Aged Mother, and
     Life.* Atlanta: Longstreet Press, 1995.

Works Cited and Studies of Merrill Joan Gerber

Brownmiller, Susan. Review of *King of the World. Chicago Tribune*, January 19, 1990,
     3.
DeMarr, Mary Jean, and Jane S. Bakerman. *The Adolescent in the American Novel since
     1960.* New York: Ungar, 1986.
Epstein, Seymour. Review of *An Antique Man. Saturday Review*, September 30, 1967,
     57.
Koppelman, Susan. Review of *King of the World. St. Louis Jewish Light*, July 18, 1990,
     6.
Review of *Now Molly Knows. Hadassah Magazine*, October 1976, 22.
Ozick, Cynthia. Review of *Stop Here, My Friend. Midstream*, June 1965, 106–8.

Rennert, Maggie. Review of *Stop Here, My Friend. Book Week, New York Herald Tribune*, March 7, 1965, 20.

Schwartz, Lynne Sharon. Review of *The Kingdom of Brooklyn. Los Angeles Times*, October 11, 1992, 8.

Shulman, Alix Kates. Review of *Now Molly Knows. Ms.*, April 1974, 33–35.

Simon, Marion. Review of *An Antique Man. National Observer*, October 23, 1967, 23.

Sullivan, Walter. Review of *An Antique Man. Sewanee Review*, Winter 1969, 154–64.

HERBERT GOLD (1924–)

Joel Shatzky and Michael Taub

BIOGRAPHY

Herbert Gold was born on March 9, 1924, in Cleveland, Ohio, to Samuel S. and Frieda (Frankel) Gold. Raised in Cleveland, Gold was the son of immigrant parents who ran a fruit and vegetable store. His younger life was very much like the one so memorably described in his short story "The Heart of the Artichoke." His father was assimilated, if not in his way of pronouncing English, in his attitude toward the United States as the land of success and toward a past that he was determined to forget. Young Herbert had little if anything that might be considered a "Jewish" background, even refusing to have a bar mitzvah, and it was not until later in life that he began to explore some of the aspects of Judaism that he knew little of in his childhood.

Often, Gold's response to Judaism in his work is in the reaction others have to Jews, as when in an episode as a young writer in *My Last Two Thousand Years* he insists that his name be spelled correctly as "Gold," not the anglicized "Gould" the editor suggests. Gold saw service during World War II as a member of army military intelligence from 1943 to 1946. He received a B.A. and M.A. from Columbia in 1946 and 1948 in philosophy and a degree from the Sorbonne in 1951. Gold has been married twice, first in 1948 to Edith Zubrin; they were divorced in 1956. In 1968 he married Melissa Dilworth; they were divorced in 1975. He has two children, Ann and Judith, by his first marriage and three by his second, Nina, Ari, and Ethan.

Gold has been quite successful as a writer, with twenty novels and five story collections as well as half a dozen other published books over a forty-year period, but he also has an extensive career in the academic world. He has been a lecturer in philosophy and literature at Western Reserve University and in the

English departments at Wayne State University, the University of California at Davis, Cornell, Berkeley, Harvard, Stanford, and Ohio University.

Among his many awards are a Fulbright Fellowship at the Sorbonne, an Inter-American Cultural Relations grant to Haiti, a Guggenheim Fellowship, a National Institute of Arts and Letters grant in literature, a Longview Foundation Award, a Ford Foundation Theater Fellowship, the Sherwood Anderson Prize for fiction, and an L.H.D. from Baruch College of the City University of New York. Gold's experiences in Haiti in the 1950s had a profound impression on him, but he has made California his home for over twenty-five years.

MAJOR WORKS AND THEMES

Although Gold is known for a number of novels that do not specifically involve a Jewish milieu, such as *The Man Who Was Not with It* (1956), of particular interest for readers of this volume are his short story "The Heart of the Artichoke" (1951), a collection of short stories, *Love and Like* (1960), and three novels that are heavily autobiographical: *Fathers* (1967), *My Last Two Thousand Years* (1972), and *Family: A Novel in the Form of a Memoir* (1981).

Gold has often found his subject in these works, the earliest of which anticipated Philip Roth's "fictional" autobiographies by several years, through a "Negative Jewish Identity." This is best illustrated in "The Heart of the Artichoke," Gold's most widely anthologized and deservedly celebrated short story. In it, a young boy rebels against his father's ambitions for him to take over his fruit and vegetable store. The father reacts by attempting to evoke the memory of a past that he has tried all his life to forget: He "swayed over the soup, food breathing back into his body the prayers he had forgotten in leaving his own father. His swaying shoulders sloped and remembered" (*Love and Like*, 40). Yet the father is not able to find in what is left of his heritage sufficient sustenance for himself or his son. It is all but gone. In this work and many others, Gold seems to be attempting to find for himself a definition of identity through the absence of both a cultural and religious tradition. In fact, it was through his experiences in Haiti, as one of the very few Jews on the island, that he began to become more curious about his heritage.

Gold is dissatisfied in *My Last Two Thousand Years* with "Chicken soup Judaism, country-club Judaism" (233), but, like Philip Roth, he does not seem willing or able to probe beyond the superficial level of a Jewish milieu that has been Americanized almost to the point of oblivion. There are references to the Holocaust, to anti-Semitism, and to Israel. In a *Playboy* interview in the 1970s, Gold saw himself as a Zionist, but the most profound sense of his identity comes, paradoxically, through his quest for it, centered on the relationship between a father and son.

A physical conflict between them in "The Heart of the Artichoke," the father's inability to remember correctly a prayer when the two of them go into a synagogue in the old neighborhood in *My Last Two Thousand Years*, the father's reminiscence of life in Kamenets-Podolsk in *Fathers*: all are forms of the limited communication between the generations, unable to find in their heritage sufficient common ground to meet and connect. But it is this very "Negative Jewish Identity," which is only filled through identification with Israel, that makes Herbert Gold's work, brilliantly written as it is, problematic in its expression of the plight of the contemporary American Jew.

CRITICAL RECEPTION

Many of Gold's works have received highly favorable criticism. Reviewers of an early novel like *The Man Who Was Not with It* praise Gold's excellent ear for dialogue and colorful language. His ability to imitate the phrases and rhythms of different forms of speech is also evident in his novels and stories that have elements of Yiddish-English in them. Favorable reviews of *Fathers* by Bernard Bergonzi in the *New York Review of Books* and Granville Hicks in the *Saturday Review* pointed to Gold's Whitmanesque and affirmative stance toward life. On the other hand, William Abrahams in the *Saturday Review* accused Gold of being too assimilated in *My Last Two Thousand Years*, as if being Jewish was of no greater consequence than being Unitarian. This is not an entirely fair evaluation, considering that Gold's character's struggle to define his Judaism in this novel provides far more of a key to an understanding of the tensions within the work than had he passively accepted assimilationism. Thomas Edwards in the *New York Times* regarded the quest for identity as a tribal experience that is precisely what enriches the resonance of the novel.

The final novel of this series, *Family*, which is about the women in the saga, has been the most warmly received. Jerome Charyn in the *New York Times Book Review* thought of it as a homage to Gold's mother, but the overall view of some critics that the three novels are the best of Gold's work shows that even the absence of a clear sense of his Jewish identity was a way for the author to discover much of what is most substantial in himself. Yet this element of Negative Jewish Identity, evident in many of the writers in this volume, is in itself one of the greatest challenges to the future of both Jewish identity and Jewish literature in America.

BIBLIOGRAPHY

Works by Herbert Gold

Selected Novels

Birth of a Hero. New York: Viking, 1951.
The Man Who Was Not with It. Boston: Little, Brown, 1956.
The Optimist. Boston: Little, Brown, 1959.
Salt. New York: Dial, 1963.
Fathers: A Novel in the Form of a Memoir. New York: Random House, 1967.

My Last Two Thousand Years. New York: Random House, 1972.
Waiting for Cordelia. New York: Arbor House, 1977.
He/She. New York: Arbor House, 1980.
Family: A Novel in the Form of a Memoir. New York: Arbor House, 1981.
A Girl of Forty. New York: Donald I. Fine, 1986.

Selected Short Story Collections

Love and Like. New York: Dial, 1960.
The Magic Will: Stories and Essays of a Decade. New York: Random House, 1971.
Lovers and Cohorts: Twenty-seven Stories. New York: Donald I. Fine, 1986.

Selected Nonfiction

A Walk on the West Side: California on the Brink. New York: Arbor House, 1981.
Travels in San Francisco (memoirs). Berkeley, CA: Arcade, 1990.
Best Nightmare on Earth: A Life in Haiti. Intro. Jan Morris. New York: Prentice Hall, 1991.
Bohemia: Where Art, Angst, Love, and Strong Coffee Meet. New York: Simon and Schuster, 1993.

Works Cited and Studies of Herbert Gold

Abrahams, William. Review of *My Last Two Thousand Years*. *Saturday Review*, November 11, 1972, 69.
Bergonzi, Bernard. Review of *Fathers*. *New York Review of Books*, June 1, 1967, 29.
Charyn, Jerome. Review of *Family*. *New York Times Book Review*, December 13, 1981, 12.
Contemporary Authors, New Revision Series, 45. Detroit: Gale Research, 1994.
Edwards, Thomas. Review of *My Last Two Thousand Years*. *New York Times Book Review*, October 15, 1972, 4.
Hicks, Granville. Review of *Fathers*. *Saturday Review*, March 25, 1967, 25.
Shatzky, Joel. ''Herbert Gold's Search for Identity.'' *Jewish Currents*, February 1988, 26–30.

GLORIA GOLDREICH (1934–)

Lois Rubin

BIOGRAPHY

Born in New York City in 1934, Gloria Goldreich grew up in Brooklyn in a three-generational family whose values and experiences influenced her and permeate her writings. It has been her goal to re-create in her writing this world for future generations who cannot experience it directly. There are many autobiographical elements in her fiction. Characters often reflect her family members: the aunts in *That Year of Our War* are her mother's sisters; many of the child characters in the short stories are based on her own children. Events in the books are sometimes drawn from her experience; collecting money for Israel in the subway ("Reunion") was something she did as a young teenager.

Goldreich always knew she wanted to be a writer. As a small child, she wrote in black-speckled composition notebooks what were, in her view, full-length books. Her writing skills developed further at Abraham Lincoln High School in Brooklyn, where she was given the opportunity to publish in a literary magazine and was taught by a skillful creative-writing teacher, Samuel Lapedos. His adage "Recreate it; don't tell it" still comes to mind when she gets blocked in her writing. While she was attending Brandeis University, she won the *Seventeen Magazine* short-story contest, and her first published work appeared in that magazine. After that, she published many short stories and articles in popular women's magazines (*McCall's, Redbook*) and Jewish periodicals (*Hadassah, Commentary*). She wrote a series of career books in the 1970s for young women entitled *What Can She Be?* and two adolescent novels, *Lori* and *Season of Discovery*.

Two of her stories represented breakthroughs in the use of Jewish content in a popular American magazine. "Gift of Light" (December 1975, a Chanukah story) and "Rachel" (February 1975, a Holocaust story) were among the first stories on these subjects to be published by *McCall's*.

Her first adult novel, *Leah's Journey*, published in 1978, won the National Jewish Book Award for Fiction and was chosen as a Literary Guild selection for September 1978. Since then, she has published many novels on both women's and Jewish themes, the most recent being *That Year of Our War* (1994). Her articles and short stories have recently appeared in such journals as *Lilith, Commentary, Midstream*, and *Congress Monthly*, and several of her stories are found in collections of American Jewish fiction.

Over the years, her stories and novels have reflected her own interests and experiences as she moved through the life cycle: raising children and engaging them in Jewish traditions ("Gift of Light," "Symbol of Love"), reflecting on youthful dreams from the perspective of middle age ("Reunion, "The Shofar"), and dealing with incapacity and death of elderly parents ("The Prayer Shawl," "Eight Candles of Hope," "My Mother's Secret Drawer"). Married to an attorney, she is the mother of two daughters and a son and lives in Westchester County, New York.

MAJOR WORKS AND THEMES

The double focus in Goldreich's fiction is women's issues and the American Jewish experience. Although one or the other is the primary focus, both elements are intertwined in her fiction. In her presentation of women's issues, she particularly dramatizes women's ability to take control of their lives, their sexual and reproductive choices, and their sense of community with other women.

Goldreich's female characters take control of their lives. Most have careers outside the home and are decisive, capable women in their professional and private lives. Although Leah is victimized in the first scene of *Leah's Journey*, we see her taking charge and making decisions throughout: leaving her shtetl to move to the freer atmosphere of Odessa, refusing to cut her hair and wear the ritual wig when she marries, deciding to marry David Goldfeder and move to the United States, deciding to go to work as a designer in the garment industry so that David can go to medical school, traveling alone to Paris and Russia in prewar 1936 Europe, and returning by herself after David's death to what remains of her native village.

Ina (*Four Days*, 1980) has her own computer consulting business, and we see her, even in her hospital bed, capably designing computer programs. Independent and in control, she is portrayed as stronger than her husband, a gentle orphan who arouses maternal feelings in women.

Emma Coen in *West to Eden* (1987) is another high achiever. Deprived of her wealthy birthright (and the fiancé who was attracted to it) by the death and financial ruin of her father, she decides to start a new life in the United States where she establishes a successful boardinghouse in Galveston, Texas. Insisting on full partnership, Emma, with her husband, Isaac Lewin, founds Lewin's Emporium and participates in building the Jewish community of Phoenix and in Arizona's efforts toward statehood. We see Emma using her skills and imagination both in business and in community life.

The four women whose friendship forms the basis of *Years of Dreams* (1992) are all accomplished: Anne is a physician, Merle a musician, Nancy a psychoanalyst, and Rutti an artist. Coming of age in the early days of the women's movement, they move from deferring to the needs of their husbands and children to asserting their own powers and developing their own talents. Nancy finally realizes her goal of becoming a psychoanalyst, abandons a failed marriage, and moves to Israel to start a new life. Merle, protected and controlled for years by a powerful husband, finally breaks away and starts making decisions on her own. Anne puts off marriage until her medical career is established and chooses to be a single parent.

In *That Year of Our War* (1994), Sharon's aunts—Lottie, Edna, and Dina—are "articulate and powerful women" (7), more forceful personalities than their husbands, whom they fondly tolerate. These women go to work, raise children, care for aging parents, and prepare holiday dinners. Without hesitation, they cooperatively take on the role of mother to Sharon after her mother (their sister Miriam) dies and while her father is serving overseas in World War II. They make the necessary decisions and provide the needed nurturing. In that year of maturing Sharon too asserts herself, helping family members through several difficult situations.

Goldreich's women are faced with choices about sexuality and motherhood. In the confined hospital setting of *Four Days*, characters experience various health problems and make reproductive decisions: Marnie suffers a miscarriage and hemorrhage, young Tina awaits treatment for ovarian cancer, Miriam worries about her struggling premature baby, and the protagonist, Ina, awaits diagnosis of a breast tumor and debates whether to abort an unwanted pregnancy. As Ina makes this difficult decision, women with a variety of perspectives give her input.

Mothers (1989) deals with another reproductive issue, the controversial surrogate motherhood. To give her family a financial boost, Stacey agrees to bear a child for David Roth, a man who longs for fatherhood as a way to perpetuate his family and culture, but whose wife Nina can no longer bear children. All aspects of the difficult issue—the desires and reactions of the birth mother, the father, and their spouses and children; the claims of financial reward versus emotional needs—are dramatized through the lives of the two families connected by the conception and birth of Felicia Miriam.

In *Years of Dreams*, reproductive choices become moments of conflict for characters: despite misgivings, Anne chooses to have an abortion and later to become pregnant without marrying; Merle decides to have another child in spite of her husband's opposition. The women's relationships with lovers and husbands are major elements in the plot. Developing sexuality is the focus of *That Year of Our War*, where Sharon Grossberg matures from girl into woman, gaining knowledge and experience about sexuality and women's roles by observation and participation. She makes some uncomfortable discoveries about sex (Uncle Robert's philandering) and experiences intercourse for the first time with Peter. Sexuality, while depicted in a positive fashion, is shown to have its dangers.

Goldreich's books draw attention to the sense of community that exists among women—the support and friendship that are sources of their strength. The hospital floor for women's health problems in *Four Days* serves as a compact female community in which the women encourage and advise each other as they cope with their various medical problems. Another community is that made up of Ina's female friends and relatives, all of whom offer input into her decision about abortion. Likewise, *Years of Dreams* is the story of the friendship of four women who share personal and historic events over three decades of American life. Meeting regularly on Fridays, in the early years the women monitor the play of their children and help each other juggle career and family; later on, they advise each other on personal decisions, glory in each others' successes, and respond immediately in times of crisis.

In *West to Eden*, Natalya advises Emma often on her troubled relationship with Isaac throughout their lifelong friendship. In *Mothers*, the two "mothers" of Felicia Miriam, despite the inherent conflict of their positions, manage to form a bond; they shop for maternity clothes for Stacey together and share holiday dinners.

In *That Year of Our War*, three sisters form a community, banding together to take the place of Sharon's natural mother so effectively that the girl never feels unprotected. Goldreich perceptively renders the relationship of sisters: the mixture of affection and irritation in their interactions, their loyalty to each other in the face of criticism from others, and their control of their resentments to maintain family unity. Likewise, Sharon forms a community with her female cousins, Beth and Heidi, and helps each of them through a crisis.

Women's decisions, problems, and accomplishments are played out against the backdrop of public events, in particular, American Jewish history. In presenting her second focus, the American Jewish experience, Goldreich dramatizes events of American and European history: immigration to the United States from Russia, the development of the American West, World Wars I and II, the Depression, the McCarthy era, the Holocaust, and the founding and development of Israel.

In *Leah's Journey*, the public events against which the lives of the characters develop span a broad time frame, 1919 to 1956. The plot is initiated by the pogrom in 1919 in which Leah is raped and her husband Yaakov murdered. Leah and her new husband, David Goldfeder, then become part of the wave of emigrants leaving Russia for the United States. Leah participates in unsuccessful efforts to improve conditions in Rosenblatt's clothing factory and barely escapes death in the fire that kills her lover Eli Feinstein. She gains firsthand knowledge of the plight of German Jews on a 1936 trip to Europe. Information about the Holocaust is provided by Joe Stevenson's firsthand account of liberating the camps. A view of the early years of Israel is provided through Rebecca's (Leah's daughter) experience helping Jewish refugees illegally enter the country and making a life in the harsh conditions of a desert kibbutz. The book ends sadly with Leah's husband David being shot as he raises the alarm to stop an Arab from entering the children's house in Rebecca's kibbutz.

In *Four Days*, the Holocaust plays a key role in the characters' actions and behavior, although the novel is set in the 1970s. The most private of decisions— to terminate an unwanted pregnancy—is made in the context of Ina's and her family's experience in the Holocaust. Ina, a child survivor who witnessed first-hand the deaths of many Jews, is told about her mother's abortion in the camps at the time when she herself is deciding whether to have an abortion. Her mother appeals to her not to terminate the pregnancy, arguing that "every Jewish baby born is a slap in Hitler's face" (130). When Ina finally decides to have the baby, her decision is expressed as a response to the Holocaust: "She could vanquish their death-sperm of hate by transforming the seed of love into life" (353). References to the Holocaust pervade the book, both in flashbacks to Ina's and her mother's experiences in the camps and in illustrations of the long-range effects of the trauma on the survivors.

This Burning Harvest (1983) has an equally strong historical focus: relations between Arabs and Jews in Palestine in the 1930s and 1940s. The tragic outcome of the love affair between Elana Maimon and Achmed Ibn-Saleem illustrates the destructive implications of Jewish/Arab tensions. Also portrayed are events in Europe under Hitler's growing power and the inadequate reactions of European Jews, the British, and Americans to Hitler.

In *West to Eden*, the accomplishments of Emma and her family are connected to the events of the day, in this case events in American history in the early decades of the twentieth century. The success of Lewin's Emporium reflects the growth of Phoenix. The family participates in Arizona's quest for statehood, helps out in the war effort in World War I, witnesses a run on a bank in 1929, and assists in the rescue of relatives from Hitler's prewar Germany.

The backdrop to the lives of the four women in *Years of Dreams* is the events of the 1960s in America: the assassination of John F. Kennedy (which brings them together initially), the civil rights movement, the women's movement, and the Vietnam War. Jewish events play a role in the book through their impact on the lives of Rutti and Nancy. Rutti, herself a survivor of the Holocaust, endures a painful relationship with Werner, so damaged by his wartime experience that he cannot lead a normal life. Through Nancy and her husbands Dov and Ari, we see life in Israel, in particular, the wartime experiences of the Sinai campaign and the Yom Kippur War.

In *That Year of Our War*, the intertwining of personal and public occurs against the backdrop of the last year of World War II. During the summer in which she learns so much about female sexuality, Sharon also becomes aware of the war and participates in the war effort by sorting goods at a civil defense collection center and raising funds in a craft sale for the war effort. Events of the war are brought to life as family members discuss them and as some relatives—Sharon's father and Beth's husband—participate in them. Information about the Holocaust is provided in the form of firsthand accounts written by a cousin serving in Europe and by a refugee whose wife and daughter have been killed by Nazis.

CRITICAL RECEPTION

Most of the commentary on Goldreich's novels has taken the form of short pieces appearing primarily in book-review guides and Jewish periodicals. Her first novel, *Leah's Journey*, the story of the achievement of an immigrant Jewish woman, was well received. It was praised by *Publisher's Weekly* for its absorbing story line, skillfully drawn characters, and wealth of historical information. Jesse Zel Lurie in *Hadassah* observed, "The lives of the vividly drawn protagonists are portrayed against the panorama of history—the shadows of the Great Depression, the nascent labor movement, the dread days of World War II, the horrors of the concentration camps and the wondrous birth of the State of Israel" (24). The book was chosen as a Literary Guild fiction selection for September 1978.

Four Days was also praised by Barbara Trainin in *Hadassah* for its memorable use of history—as a way to illuminate current ethical dilemmas rather than as a description of events consigned to the past. In particular, Holocaust memories influenced Ina's decision about whether to terminate her pregnancy. On the other hand, Trainin also observed that the book was somewhat slow paced and at times heavy-handed. The book won the Federation Arts and Letters Award.

This Burning Harvest and *Leah's Children* received more mixed reviews. *This Burning Harvest*, the story of a doomed love affair between a Jew and an Arab in Palestine of the 1930s and 1940s, received contradictory estimates, with *Publisher's Weekly* praising it for effective portrayal of historical events and lack of sentimentality, but the *Middle East Journal* criticizing it for stereotyped Arab characters and unsympathetic portrayal of Palestinian nationalism. Two reviewers praised *Leah's Children*, the sequel to *Leah's Journey*, for narrative skill and use of history, but *Kirkus Reviews* criticized it for unrealistic characterizations and sentimentality.

Receiving mostly favorable attention, *West to Eden* was complimented, like the other historical novels, for effectively depicting a time and place (in this case the American Southwest in the first forty years of the twentieth century) and for offering a readable story. On the other hand, critics noted its similarity to the Goldwater family story and the familiarity of the rags-to-riches theme. *Mothers*, a story of surrogate motherhood reminiscent of the Baby M situation, received more mixed evaluations, two reviewers commending its sensitive treatment of a controversial issue, two others finding it overwritten and implausible.

Years of Dreams, the story of the friendship of four women who moved from traditional to more ''liberated'' views of female roles in three recent decades of this century, was applauded by Barbara Rogan (*Hadassah*) for its value as ''a meditation on women's adaptations to an evolving society,'' for its relevance to women's lives, and for strong characterization of the women in their inter-actions with each other, but faulted for its less convincing male characters and occasional overwriting (42). Other reviewers echoed these views, praising the book's treatment of contemporary issues, especially the effects of women's lib-eration, but noticing some sentimentality (*Kirkus Reviews*).

Of all the novels, Goldreich's most recent one, *That Year of Our War* (the story of the last year of World War II on the home front as seen through the eyes of a young girl) has received the most extensive and the most positive critical evaluation. Reviewers valued its skillful evocation of time and place, the convincing portrayal of the viewpoint of a young girl, and the girl herself, ''a smart, observant heroine'' (Quinn, 1514). Even *Kirkus Reviews* usually critical of Goldreich's fiction, had only compliments for this novel: ''There's no lack of emotion in this story of WWII's effect on a large, cohesive Jewish family in Brooklyn, but its pervasive, touching warmth never seems overdone'' (233). The book is also cross-listed as adolescent fiction and was chosen as a Literary Guild alternate selection.

BIBLIOGRAPHY

Works by Gloria Goldreich

Leah's Journey. New York: Harcourt Brace Jovanovich, 1978.
Four Days. New York: Harcourt Brace Jovanovich, 1980.
This Burning Harvest. New York: Berkley Books, 1983.
Leah's Children. New York: Macmillan, 1985.
West to Eden. New York: Macmillan, 1987.
Mothers. Boston: Little, Brown, 1989.
''The Prayer Shawl.'' In *''The Safe Deposit'' and Other Stories about Grandparents, Old Lovers, and Crazy Old Men*, ed. Kerry M. Olitzky. New York: Markus Wie-ner Publishing, 1989, 323–39.
''Z'mira.'' In *America and I: Short Stories by American Jewish Women Writers*, ed. Joyce Antler. Boston: Beacon Press, 1990, 167–78.
Years of Dreams. Boston: Little, Brown, 1992.
That Year of Our War. Boston: Little, Brown, 1994.

Works Cited and Studies of Gloria Goldreich

Christison, Kathleen. ''The Arab in Recent Popular Fiction.'' *Middle East Journal*, Sum-mer 1987, 402.
Lurie, Jesse Zel. Review of *Leah's Journey*. *Hadassah Magazine*, August/September 1978, 24.
Review of *Leah's Journey Publisher's Weekly*, June 5 1978, 85.

Quinn, Mary Ellen. Review of *That Year of Our War. Booklist*, Apr. 15 1994, 1514–15.

Rogan, Barbara. Review of *Years of Dreams. Hadassah Magazine*, June/July 1992, 42–43.

Review of *That Year of Our War. Kirkus Reviews*, March 1 1994, 233–34.

Review of *This Burning Harvest. Publisher's Weekly*, August 1983, 85.

Trainin, Barbara. Review of *Four Days. Hadassah Magazine*, August/September 1980, 25.

Review of *Years of Dreams. Kirkus Reviews*, February 1 1992, 131–32.

PAUL GOODMAN (1911–1972)

Leonard Rogoff

BIOGRAPHY

Paul Goodman had a varied career as poet, dramatist, novelist, and essayist. A New York intellectual, he rose to national prominence as a leading spirit of the youth rebellion of the 1960s.

Goodman was born in Greenwich Village on September 9, 1911, the youngest of three children of immigrant parents, Barnett and Augusta Goodman. Abandoned by his father while still an infant, Goodman was raised in poverty on Manhattan's Upper East Side. He received a Hebrew school education and was well versed in the classical Jewish texts. In 1927 he graduated first in his class from Townsend Harris Hall High School, an elite public school, and enrolled at City College of New York. There he fell under the influence of Morris Raphael Cohen, the philosopher who mentored a generation of young Jews of immigrant ancestry into Western culture. After receiving his B.A. in 1931 with a nearly perfect academic record, Goodman began auditing classes at Columbia University. The philosopher Richard McKeon recognized Goodman's abilities and later invited Goodman to the University of Chicago. Goodman taught literature there while he was enrolled in the Ph.D. program. From 1934 to 1936 he spent his summers as a drama counselor at a Jewish youth camp. During World War II Goodman, a pacifist, was a conscientious objector. Twice married, he was the father of three children.

With McKeon's encouragement, Goodman published "Neo-Classicism, Platonism, and Romanticism" in the *Journal of Philosophy* in 1934. Shortly thereafter, his essays, poems, and short stories began appearing in reviews and little magazines, including the New Directions anthologies, *Symposium*, and the *Partisan Review*. He became a regular contributor to such periodicals as the

Nation, Poetry, Commentary, Dissent, Kenyon Review, and *Black Mountain Review.* He served as editor of *Liberation.*

Goodman was a man of enormous paradoxes, at once a skeptic and a visionary, a traditionalist and an iconoclast. He called himself a "conservative anarchist" and cited both Aristotle and Kropotkin as intellectual antecedents. A self-professed guardian of Western civilization, he prowled the city streets in search of sex or a game of handball. A quintessential New Yorker, Goodman found spiritual succor in his New Hampshire farmhouse. His open bisexuality resulted in his dismissal from the University of Chicago. Teaching positions at the Manumit School of Progressive Education in Pawling, New York, and Black Mountain College in North Carolina ended on similar notes of scandal. Goodman insisted on the congruity of private and public selves, and his politics of sexual liberation brought him into conflicts with institutions that he saw as bourgeois and hypocritical.

A polymath, Goodman wrote learnedly on literature, psychology, education, and urban design. By his own count the author of some forty books, Goodman suffered from professional disregard in each of his chosen fields because of his refusal to specialize. In the late 1960s he found himself thrust into the forefront of the antiestablishment movements with the publication of *Growing Up Absurd: Problems of Youth in the Organized System* (1960) and later *Compulsory Mis-Education* (1964).

Goodman's attacks on the dehumanizing effects of institutions, his characterization of students as "the major exploited class," and his utopian advocacy of decentralized, libertarian communities based on voluntary associations resonated among a youth disaffected by the counterculture and the Vietnam War. Goodman soon found himself uncomfortably cast as a guru figure. Though he attacked the educational bureaucracy of American universities, he became a popular campus speaker and taught at Columbia, Sarah Lawrence, Hawaii, Wisconsin, and San Francisco State and as a Fellow of the Institute for Policy Studies in Washington.

MAJOR WORKS AND THEMES

Poetry

Goodman called himself "a man of letters, primarily a poet." Goodman's poems appeared in a number of little magazines, and he also privately printed several small volumes. A sign of his growing recognition was his inclusion in New Directions' *Five Young American Poets* (1941). He published five verse dramas based on the Japanese Noh in *Stop-Light* (1941). His first volume of poetry, *The Lordly Hudson* (1962), was not published until he was past fifty. This volume was followed by *Hawkweed* (1967), *North Percy* (1968), and *Homespun of Oatmeal Grey* (1970). In his last years Goodman, estranged from the violence, anti-intellectualism, and leftist dogmas of the youth culture, turned to poetry for succor. His *Little Prayers and Finite Experience* (1972) is a collection of thirty-five years of religious musings and meditations, its tone set by his own failing health and unrelieved grief over the death of his son Matthew in a climbing accident. *Collected Poems* (1973), with some late textual revisions, appeared posthumously.

Goodman did not adhere to any poetics, although he was personally and professionally associated with a number of literary movements including the Beats, the Chicago school of critics, and the Black Mountain Poets. In defiance of contemporary literary taste, Goodman often wrote in fixed forms. He experimented with hokku, songs, ballads, and sonnets. A favorite form was a metrically irregular, rhymed or unrhymed lyric written in quatrains consisting of two couplets, the second of which is indented. His poetic effects were largely achieved through diction and syntax, rather than through metaphor, sometimes imitating the fractured rhythms of Yinglish while at others aspiring to a Wordsworthian sublimity. He spoke often and longingly of "our lovely English language" and would easily blend medieval archaisms into his "homespun" vernacular, rhyming "pardon" with "hard on." A favored device was the inversion, a mannerism intended to give his vernacular a poetic effect: "Step back his soldiers from him."

As an anarchist and universalist, Goodman was too skeptical of ideology and too catholic in his tastes to subscribe to any one dogma or school, Jewish or otherwise. He wrote of Adam, Noah, and David as well as the gamelan of Bali, Leon Trotsky, and Richard Nixon. His was a romantic imagination that would draw no lines between the Bible and the Buddha, courtly love and bathroom sex. For Goodman, literature was scripture, and in his early study *Kafka's Prayer* (1947) he spoke of writing as a religious vocation.

Goodman wrote familiarly of biblical figures, who were rendered as representations of himself. The David of his "Ballad of David and Michal" is a mad poet, a light to the "common folk," who dances naked before the proud Michal. David chastises her "who won't put out when music it has got me hot." In "Adam" Goodman saw the exile from paradise of his primeval "ancestor" as the archetype for his own estrangement from America. When Goodman called upon Americans to realize their ideals, he cited Rabbi Tarfon: "I do not need to carry my task through, neither am I free to give it up." This aspiration toward the ideal and confession of failure recurred in Goodman's writings.

Goodman repeatedly invoked his "Creator Spirit, come." He spiritualized sexuality, finding in lust the wellspring of creativity. References to Lord, God, or Buddha abound. Despite his recurrent use of God language, Goodman insisted in *Little Prayers and Finite Experience* that he did not "believe' these theological sentences. . . . I don't have a 'faith,' " "sacred stories," or a "congregation to join." He used "the language of orthodox theology" because it was "a poetic convention, a traditional jargon." In prayer "I disown by experience and again come face to face with nothing." Goodman professed that "God is not a body and I know only about bodies." Whatever his skepticism, Goodman wrote in

Little Prayers and Finite Experience that he liked "the safeguard of the Negative Theology of Jewish and Islamic philosophers . . . that whatever we say, is not true of God, nor is the contrary true." Like Kant, he would find religion "within the limits of mere reason."

Though Goodman was a universalist, the reader will see a recognizably Jewish sensibility. For Goodman, the nothingness he existentially confronted was a voice encountered in dialogue. As Jews typically do, he addressed God personally and familiarly, and he validated his doubts and estrangement in tradition: "My Bible text, when I grew / old enough to be a Jew," Goodman wrote, "was God to Abraham did say / Lech lcha, 'Go Away!' "

Goodman's debt to Martin Buber, which he acknowledged, can be seen in an untitled poem that expresses a classically Jewish encounter between a questioning man and an enigmatic, hidden God: "I ask the Lord, 'Who are You?' / though I know His name is 'Spoken to.' " An "answer" to this question "never yet came to pass"; still, the interlocutor, cursed with "hope," proclaims, "with certain faith let me continue / my dialogue with Spoken-To."

After the death of his son Matthew, Goodman wrote in "Noah's Song," "So religiously I live on in rituals . . . my way is conservative and pious." But Goodman's ritual was not to recite Kaddish, but to hoe a field, pick a sprig of dogwood, and stare longingly at a vanishing rainbow. A nature poet, he drew inspiration from the English romantics and the New England transcendentalists. Goodman saw God as a spiritual immanence embodied in nature. His exultations often echo the psalmist or the prophet: "This is a day which the Lord hath made / rejoice in it and be glad."

Like the New York Intellectuals, Goodman founded his values not in religious orthodoxy, but in modernism. His political radicalism, impassioned intellectuality, and moral gravity were typical of second-generation urban Jews. Kafka and Freud served as models of Jewish rebellion and marginality, writers who broke the constraints of tradition without leaving the fold. Wilhelm Reich, a renegade Jew, offered a politics of sexual liberation. In "A Diary of Makapuu," Goodman identified with this meritocracy: "A white American New Yorker / talented Jew, I am by birth / the royal family." His sexuality, however, undercut any parochial claims or pretensions: "Since my lust / is democratic and pan-humanist / inevitably I come on *noblesse oblige*."

Goodman spoke of himself as perpetually in exile. Jewish youth of his generation, Goodman noted, were eager to rid themselves of "superstitious beliefs"; theological language was considered "moronic." A lay therapist, Goodman described the practice of psychotherapy as being "the nearest I know to formal religious exercises." In *Gestalt Therapy*, which he coauthored with Frederick Perls and Ralph Hefferline, Goodman wrote of poetry as therapy, a way of creating a self. Poetic verbalizing is "an organic problem-solving activity" that addresses an "inner conflict." Borrowing from Buber, he spoke of poetry as "good speech" that brings into contact "three grammatical persons, I, Thou, and It." The best poetry was occasional, tailored to "the motion of my thought.'' An intuitive poet rather than a craftsman, he refused to revise, which he thought would spoil the immediacy that occasioned the poem.

Fiction

Paul Goodman published half a dozen novels and four collections of short fiction. His masterwork was *The Empire City* (1959), the vaguely autobiographical, highly improbable misadventures of the street urchin Horatio Alger. Loosely structured, if at all, the novel is picaresque, allegory, fable, and polemic; the characters are less full-blooded figures than aggregates of positions. The novel's episodes are occasions for the narrator to ruminate on the World War II draft, Wagnerian opera, poetry readings, urban design, the aging process, educational reform, and social welfare, among other issues. Published in four parts, beginning with ''The Grand Piano'' (1942), the novel ostensibly focuses on Horatio's coming of age in a surrealistically rendered New York. It begins with a citation from the *Mishneh Torah* on creation, idolatry, and punishment. The impoverished Horatio's adoptive father is Eliphaz, a sage, Jewish capitalist who runs a madhouse department store from his home, intending to ''undo the work of Creation.'' Eliphaz describes war, which will kill his son Arthur, as ''Goyim Nachus . . . Gentile Pleasures.'' The mysterious Mynheer, a philosophizing Dutchman, marries Horatio's sister Laura. He attempts to educate Horatio into the mores of society and civilization, but the orphan dropout, who has destroyed all records of his existence, prefers to live on ''the dole'' with Laura, an architect, and his brother Lothair, a talented pianist.

''The State of Nature'' (1946) is a discourse on id and ego, a dialogue on primitive impulse and the social compact, all set on the domestic scene during World War II. The adolescent Horatio confronts his draft board while his sister Laura camouflages houses, schools, and churches, creating a Garden Village that returns civilization to a chaotic state of nature It ends in conflagration. Lothair, after being imprisoned as a conscientious objector, opens the cages of a zoo, and an escaped tiger eats his young nephew, the incestuous offspring of Eliphaz's children. Natural aggression is pitted against the American obsession with peace and stability. There is a prolonged debate on whether lust can be civilized and how to restore community after the destruction of war. The section ends with the Voice of Eliphaz's prophecy that a consumerist, conformist American ''Sociolatry'' will result in the ''Asphyxiation'' of feeling and desire. ''Everywhere there will be personal and public peace,'' the Voice inveighs, ''nowhere will there be love or community.''

''The Dead of Spring,'' the third section, failed to find a publisher and was privately printed in 1950. Set ''after a war,'' it focuses on the circle of New Yorkers ''hungry and thirsty and lonely to live in a community of human relations.'' Goodman's answer, deriving from Gestalt therapy, is for them to form ''A Community of Human Relations.'' To raise a child, the Community requires twenty-two character types. The role of the Jew is to be ''outsider, the Scapegoat.'' Emily and Lothair aspire to such a love community, giving birth to a child, St. Wayward. Horatio is blinded ''because there was nothing to see in the world up to his hope,'' but his power is restored by Eros, a homosexual boy of the streets, and he becomes a hustler for love. Horatio is pursued by Rosalind, but the ''urban pastoral romance'' seems doomed by Horatio's arrest for treason as an anarchist without official records. Freed by a wise judge, Horatio marries Rosalind. The characters cope with the paradox of their relationship, whether to join a society gone mad or to risk their sanity by living outside it. Laura hangs herself, and Horatio mourns her with poetry and a ritualistic game of baseball. The ritual is intended to heal the community as the ''gathered soul'' of players prays, ''Creator Spirit, Come.''

''The Holy Terror,'' written in the 1950s, appeared with the publication of *The Empire City* in its entirety. Subtitled ''modern times,'' it is a ''register of reconciliation,'' the narrator tracing how ''our truth'' has transformed America. The final chapters are a series of polemics on the liberating effects of dancing, concert music, eating, relaxing, and play. The narrative gets lost in fantasy. Horatio wakens one morning in a ''haze of insane clarity'' and begins to ''follow the folkways of the Americans.'' He reads the *Herald Tribune*, decides to vote for General (Eisenhower), and joins the PTA. He is redeemed by therapy. St. Wayward, in an Oedipal ritual, slays his father. Wayward emerges as a messianic figure, a moral, unrepressed child who brings healing. Flying off on horseback, he plans to ''rescue the Irish.'' A utopian society is projected free of repression, and the characters gather to affirm that they will work for community. Emily becomes a ''little Jewish old lady,'' lapsing into a Yiddish accent, who invokes the spirit of her father Eliphaz. The last epigraph comes from I Samuel, describing David's putting off the armor of war that Saul has placed upon him. In the end Horatio addresses a prayer, ''Father, guide and lead me stray for I stumble . . . I do not notice the pleasant bypaths.''

The Empire City includes citations from Maimonides, Buber, Moses, Kafka, the Psalmist, and Goodman himself, among countless others, but little else evokes Jewish themes. Those characters who are nominally Jewish lack ethnic identity: they are Jews only because the narrator says they are. Although the book was written against the background of World War II, it says nothing about the Holocaust or the Jewish state.

Goodman's other novels failed to win a wide readership. *Parents Day* (1952) was a semiautobiographical account of a bisexual schoolteacher whose pursuit of boys results in his resignation from the school. *Making Do* (1963) deals with street people whose marginality contrasts with the smugness of suburbanites. Set against the background of the drug culture, sexual liberation, and political violence, the novel focuses on the narrator's homosexual relationship with a twenty-year-old dropout. *Don Juan, or, The Continuum of the Libido*, written in the 1940s, appeared posthumously; it too is an experimental novel with a homosexual theme, a modern version of the Don Juan legend as a love triangle set in the Empire City.

Goodman wrote some sixty short stories published in four collections: *The Facts of Life* (1945), *The Break-up of Our Camp* (1949), *Our Visit to Niagara* (1960), and *Adam and His Works* (1969). Like his novels, the stories are in a variety of forms, inconsistent in voice, tone, and character; they tend to break down into ruminations on the issue at hand. Jewish themes and characters frequent the stories. "Noah's Vineyard" is a biblical retelling that features a horny, drunken Noah trying to till a "senseless landscape" while his sons compose lyrics. The story ends with a digression, a therapeutic analysis, on how we search for antediluvian bones to explain our "inadmissible . . . incomprehensible" life in the modern city. "Adam" is a prose-poem that depicts primeval man as an idealized self of the narrator. He traces renderings of Adam from biblical times through Michelangelo and Milton. The punning—Adam as red, blood, earth, and man—plays on Hebrew etymology.

The title story of Goodman's first collection, "The Facts of Life," describes Ronnie and Martha Morris, a moneyed, highly assimilated Jewish family whose nine-year-old daughter comes home from the "University P'rgressive School" mystified as to why her classmates called her an "old time shoe," a "Joo," or a "Juice." Irish kids from the Holy Name Academy taunt the rich private-school kids with shouts of "Jew School," rendering the Jewish kids defenseless. The child's questions force the mother to confront her Jewishness proudly, while the father protests, "What's the use of *pretending* you're a Jew, when you're *not* a Jew?" The poet and connoisseur Louis, who traces his lineage to Joseph Karo, author of the *Shulchan Aruch*, recommends that Ronnie read Maimonides' *Mishneh Torah* to clarify the "relation of God and Man in a way helpful to the Modern Age." Louis claims to have gotten his rhythms from the Chasidim and describes himself as "like Judah ha-Levi, an allegorical Zionist." Ronnie would punch him in the nose. Yet Ronnie, who denies that Jews are a race, argues with his mistress that Jews tend to be geniuses. "A Prayer for Dew" is set in a synagogue on Passover. A "moonfaced" Rabbi Horn invokes the Tefilas Tal while a "shfartse" changes a light bulb. A yeshiva student debates the halacha of work while the congregants crack Borscht-belt jokes. The bidding for alyiot is depicted as "playing auction-pinochle." The noise of the synagogue Jews satirically contrasts with the beauty of the cantor's "flowing line." The springtime renewal of an "agricultural people" is lost on these vulgar, urban Jews.

The Break-up of Our Camp consists of a roughly autobiographical series of stories told by a drama counselor at a Jewish summer camp on Lake Champlain. The narrator Matthew marvels at the Eastern European children singing in Yiddish, Russian, and Hebrew in northern Vermont. The Zionist marching song, "V'im lo Achshav Eimatai!" (And if not now, when!) sets the theme of the stories. Armand, a French-Canadian canoeist, wanders into the campfire, a Culture Hero who teaches the urban children new rituals of outdoor derring-do. Armand is entranced by the Jews and attracted to the girls, but the Yiddish-speaking Matthew discomfits him with his sense of unbelonging, and Armand paddles off into a lightning storm while the narrator gazes at him, jealous of the canoeist's freedom. The camp goes bankrupt, done in by its unscrupulous owners. Matthew hangs on, drawn by a homosexual desire for a French-Canadian boy and by the need to make a minyan for the remaining counselors who are closing the camp. Local farmers strip the "Jew camp" bare. In "A Congregation of Jews" the narrator joins the minyan—which includes halachic discussions on what to do if there are only nine. While one mourner chants "Ribvon kal ha'olamim," another Jew counts mattresses. The narrator mediates on Nachmanides' commentary on the Shemoneh Esreh while Ostoric, the arts and crafts counselor, disrespectfully struggles to close his overflowing trunk. Matthew is habitually Jewish, shaving and dressing for Shabbat, but he is not a believer. Returning to New York after a series of near disasters, he passes out handbills for "A Memorial Synagogue" for the Jews' "own recent disasters and the disasters of all peoples." He tells his friends, who are derisive, that he has not suddenly become "religious," but "the city is full of Jews." One friend reproves him that rather than make a "recurrence" of Yom Kippur, he should try to prevent it. Matthew answers, "You're right, . . . the thing to do is to make a change. But when I try to do it . . . it comes to nothing but sighing." To those who would want only a Jewish memorial, he also quotes—in Hebrew—Hillel's "Im ein ani li, mi li." The story ends with the commentary of a sculptor, an artist, and an architect on building the synagogue. The architect demurs that in a religion without sacraments, "there is nothing else to see . . . except the Congregation itself." The people, however, are crying, and "people crying can't see much." Many of these stories' tensions focus on the contrast between contemporary Jews as moneyed, bourgeois, and unbelieving and the sacredness of their religion. The narrator validates the spiritual authority of the tradition—he follows its rituals by habit, if not by conviction, and quotes its spiritual masters—while emphasizing his alienation from the Jews.

In his journal *Five Years* Goodman attempted to "universalize and up-date" three articles of Jewish faith: "that there is a Creation, that God is not a body, that the Messiah will come." He pointedly eschewed a fourth article, that the Jews are a Chosen People. He admitted that he was "ambivalent to this idea" as a believer in "egalitarian democracy." In "Terry Fleming—or, Are You Planning a Universe?" the narrator cautions repeatedly, "Don't have any 'chosen people,' " claiming that the complications outweigh the benefits. In *Five Years* Goodman stated that "modern Zionism is not a return to sacramental glory, but the engine of survival" and questioned whether as an "idea" it was strong enough to endure. He also complained that "American Jews have become Establishment," arguing that "suburbanite Jews have sunk into spiritual degradation."

Drama

Paul Goodman published some eighteen plays, all in experimental modes; several were produced by Judith Malina and Julian Beck at the Living Theater in New York. *The Young Disciple* is a martyr play about a horny Christ-like "master." The dramatic theme and characters, according to Goodman's notes, are "grounded in the method of textual criticism of Martin Buber, especially his *Moses*," though he "came to this play through a psychological analysis of the Gospel of Mark." Goodman wanted the protagonist of *Jonah* (1941) to be played as "the little old man who tells Jewish jokes and is always angry and who wants to die." Jonah is given to Yiddishisms like "nebich" and "weh iz mir" to enhance his jokes, some of which Goodman lifted from Lou Holtz and Freud. A Borscht-belt Angel pulls an Easter bunny from his hat for Jonah's daughter; Jonah is sure that the Captain of his ship is anti-Semitic and explains, "Oh, we Jews have special kind of jokes. They consist in happy little anecdotes founded on absolute despair." Jonah recites the Shema before being thrown overboard and in the whale's belly becomes a little Jewish tailor. Jonah has "to make allowances for these Gentiles. They are such nice people." He sings his psalms "in the name of the Father and the son." At Nineveh's court he tells shatchan jokes, though he aspires to be prophet to the gentiles.

In 1959 the Living Theater performed Goodman's *The Father of Abraham*, a dramatic series that he started in 1935. *Abraham and Isaac* is a poetic rendering of the sacrifice as a test of simple faith. Goodman pointedly rejects more complex interpretations. *Hagar and Ishmael* depicts a defiant Ishmael arguing with the angel. In *The Cave at Machpelah* (1958) Ishmael meets with Isaac to arrange the burial of Abraham, setting the stage for Jewish and Arab reconciliation. Goodman returned repeatedly to the Bible, drawing upon its rituals and folk elements. In Goodman's plays, as in the biblical text, the simplicity of the characters contrasts ironically with the grandeur of God's plan for them.

CRITICAL RECEPTION

Goodman's work, often unpolished and uneven in quality, did not enter the academic canon, nor was it widely anthologized in collections of American Jewish writing. Goodman's critical defenders commonly begin by deploring the neglect that settled over his work even before his death in 1972. Goodman's difficult personality cast a shadow on his literary reputation. He continued to be praised by a coterie of admirers, led by his literary executor, Taylor Stoehr, who prepared posthumous editions of Goodman's work, while others pronounced him as unreadable or worse.

Kingsley Widmer savaged Goodman as a "failed litterateur," a "muddy writer" and "muddled thinker," whose reputation is owed chiefly to his role as a cultural icon of the libertarian 1960s. He saw Goodman as a "Jewish agnostic anarchist devoted to the Tao." Widmer acknowledged the trenchancy of Goodman's social thought, but found his poetry to be highly mannered and described *The Empire City* as pompous, awkward, and shapeless, the work of a "literary hobbyist" (8, 106, 138).

Goodman's writing was championed by a number of leading critics, including Adrienne Rich, Nat Hentoff, Richard Howard, George Dennison, Harold Rosenberg, Hayden Carruth, M. L. Rosenthal, and Susan Sontag, although often with qualification. At Goodman's death, Sontag wrote in the *New York Review of Books* that she lamented the silencing of his "direct, cranky, egotistical, generous American voice," labeling him the most singular talent since D. H. Lawrence. Acknowledging Goodman's sloppiness and graceless style and his persistent didacticism, she still found him to be "simply the most important American writer" of the past twenty years (10, 12). Rich admired Goodman's honesty and his unmistakable voice, adding that he had a "beautiful ear" for the vernacular (16–17). Rosenthal praised the "originality" of Goodman's drama as "extraordinary," citing his ability to create a lively language from "pure idea." He saw Goodman's versifying as a romantic "throwback." Goodman's confessional poetry was entirely modern in its "dislocations of syntax" and "shifts of focus" (313–16). Alicia Ostriker in *Partisan Review* saw Goodman's indecorum, his "formal originality," as liberating, but complained that he lacked a true poet's "metaphoric imagination" (292).

In 1983 Hayden Carruth argued at length in the *American Poetry Review* that Goodman was undeservedly neglected, calling him a "poet of intuition" with a "natural facility" who was also a "superb technician" (25, 27–28). Carruth noted Goodman's paradoxes as an American romantic, a New York Jew, and a European man of letters. He described Goodman as "the tough existential man . . . the Jewish Yankee" (22, 27).

Though Goodman resisted categories, several critics recognized a distinctly Jewish voice. George Steiner wrote in *Commentary* that Goodman's "moral choice and the statement of defeat are deeply Jewish" (163), while Richard Howard noted that Goodman was popularly viewed as a "Jewish rhetorician" given to "Old Testament moralizing" (158). Theodore Roszak referred to Goodman's spirituality as "Hassidic magic" (10). Edouard Roditi saw Goodman's subjects as marginal Jews who have shed God and tribe as they melt in the American pot (114–15).

As a New York intellectual, Goodman's associations were largely Jewish. He identified strongly with an urban culture that was heavily Judaized, though he expressed contempt for the materialism of bourgeois Jews. Goodman was among the Jewish intellectuals who made their marginality, their sense of alienation, a central theme of American letters. An assimilated Jew, he found value in Freud. Goodman's open homosexuality anticipated the gay liberation movement. What was recognizably Jewish in Goodman was a secularized messianic zeal that expressed itself as a passionate, relentless pursuit of social justice. Goodman, often accused of megalomania, had a sense of his own chosenness as the agent who would repair the world. Although he is championed by devoted followers and some prominent critics, Goodman remains in reputation as he lived, an outsider.

BIBLIOGRAPHY

Works by Paul Goodman

Stop-Light: 5 Dance Poems. Harrington Park: 5 × 8 Press, 1941.

The Facts of Life. New York: Vanguard, 1945.

Art and Social Nature. New York: Vinco, 1946.

Communitas—Means of Livelihood and Ways of Life. With Percival Goodman. Chicago: University of Chicago Press, 1947.

Kafka's Prayer. New York: Vanguard, 1947.

The Break-up of Our Camp and Other Stories. New York: New Directions, 1949.

Gestalt Therapy: Excitement and Growth in the Human Personality. With Frederick Perls and Ralph Hefferline. New York: Julian Press, 1951.

Parents Day. Saugatuck, CT: 5 × 8 Press, 1951.

The Structure of Literature. Chicago: University of Chicago Press, 1954.

The Empire City. Indianapolis: Bobbs-Merrill, 1959.

Growing Up Absurd: Problems of Youth in the Organized System. New York: Random House, 1960.

Our Visit to Niagara. New York: Horizon, 1960.

The Community of Scholars. New York: Random House, 1962.

The Lordly Hudson. New York: Macmillan, 1962.

Utopian Essays and Practical Proposals. New York: Random House, 1962.

Making Do. New York: Macmillan, 1963.

Compulsory Mis-Education. New York: Horizon, 1964.

The Young Disciple, Faustina, Jonah: Three Plays. New York: Random House, 1965.

Five Years: Thoughts During a Useless Time. New York: Brussel and Brussel, 1966.

Hawkweed. New York: Random House, 1967.

North Percy. Santa Rosa, CA: Black Sparrow Press, 1968.

Adam and His Works. New York: Vintage, 1968.

Homespun of Oatmeal Gray. New York: Random House, 1970.

Tragedy and Comedy: Four Cubist Plays. Los Angeles: Black Sparrow, 1970.

Speaking and Language: Defence of Poetry. New York: Random House, 1971.

Little Prayers and Finite Experience. New York: Harper and Row, 1972.

Collected Poems. New York: Random House, 1973.

Don Juan, or, The Continuum of the Libido. Santa Barbara, CA: Black Sparrow Press, 1979.

Studies of Paul Goodman

Carruth, Hayden. "Paul Goodman and the Grand Community." *American Poetry Review* 12:5 (September–October 1983): 22–32.

Dennison, George. "A Memoir and Appreciation." In Paul Goodman, *Collected Poems.* New York: Random House, 1973.

Horowitz, Steven. "The Poetry of Paul Goodman." Ph.D. diss., University of Iowa, 1986.

Howard, Richard. "Paul Goodman." In *Alone with America: Essays on the Art of Poetry in the United States since 1950.* New York: Atheneum, 1969, 153–63.

Kostelanetz, Richard. *Master Minds*. New York: Macmillan 1969.

Ostriker, Alicia. "Paul Goodman." *Partisan Review* 43:2 (1976): 286–95.

Parisi, Peter, ed. *Artist of the Actual: Essays on Paul Goodman*. Metuchen, NJ: Scarecrow Press, 1986.

Rich, Adrienne. "Caryatid: A Column." *American Poetry Review*, January–February 1973, 16–17.

Roditi, Edouard. "*The Empire City*: A Work in Progress." In *Artist of the Actual: Essays on Paul Goodman*, ed. Peter Parisi. Metuchen, NJ: Scarecrow Press, 1986.

Rosenthal, M. L. *The New Poets: American and British Poetry since World War II*. New York: Oxford University Press, 1967.

Roszak, Theodore. "Portrait of a Tolerably Unhappy Man." *Book World, Washington Post*. October 15, 1972, 3, 10.

Sontag, Susan. "On Paul Goodman." *New York Review of Books*, September 21, 1972, 10, 12.

Steiner, George. "On Paul Goodman." *Commentary* 36 (August 1963): 158–63.

Widmer, Kingsley. *Paul Goodman*. Boston: Twayne, 1980.

GERALD GREEN   (1922–)

James Berger

BIOGRAPHY

Gerald Green was born in Brooklyn on April 8, 1922, the son of Dr. Samuel Greenberg and Anna Matzkin Greenberg. He received a B.A. from Columbia University in 1942 and then served in the U.S. Army Ordnance Corps from 1942 to 1946. After his discharge, Green received an M.S. in journalism from Columbia and then began work as a writer and editor for the International News Service, during which time he also started his career as a novelist. In 1950, he began working for the National Broadcasting Company, where he wrote for a variety of news programs and documentaries, as well as authoring the scripts for *Holocaust* (1978) and *Kent State* (1980). Green has been married twice, first to Maria Pomposelli in 1950 (she died in 1979) and then to Marlene M. Eagle in 1980. He has two children from his first marriage.

MAJOR WORKS AND THEMES

While not a master of prose style or of novelistic form, Gerald Green is a prolific writer who should be of great interest and value to students of Jewish-American cultural history of the late twentieth century because his work takes as its themes the major concerns of secular American Jews from the 1950s through the 1980s: the experiences of the generation of immigrants and their children, the State of Israel and its impact on American Jews, and the revival of interest in the Holocaust since the late 1970s. Green's writing explores—or perhaps more accurately, exemplifies—those widespread forms of contemporary American Jewish life in which Judaism is a cultural rather than a religious identity. Green writes for, of, and from the position of Jews in an uneasy state of assimilation who look first into the histories of their immigrant parents and grandparents, then to the experiences of Israeli Jews, and finally to the victims of the Nazi genocide for proofs of a Jewish identity from which they feel increasingly distant.

Thus Green's most highly praised novel, *The Last Angry Man* (1956), as well as *To Brooklyn with Love* (1968), treat the vanishing or vanished world of urban immigrant communities in New York. *The Stones of Zion: A Novelist's Journal in Israel* (1971) documents Green's responses to Israeli life in the wake of the Six-Day War. *The Artists of Terezin* (1969) and especially his most widely known and most controversial novel, *Holocaust* (1978; subsequently broadcast as an NBC miniseries also written by Green), attempt to reimagine Jewish identity in relation to the Shoah as well as to represent this Jewish catastrophe to a wider American and international audience. Finally, Green's work consistently (indeed, one might say presciently) addresses a less specifically Jewish, more broadly American, modern or postmodern concern: the effects of mass media in shaping public consciousness and affecting private lives. Green spent a long career as a television scriptwriter (where he won one Emmy and was nominated for two others), and he reveals his misgivings about the uses and consequences of this work particularly in *The Last Angry Man* and *The Heartless Light* (1961).

In Gerald Green's career as a writer, the three pivotal and most illustrative works are *The Last Angry Man, The Stones of Zion*, and *Holocaust*. These three works all seek to construct, in quite different settings, what for Green is a new, more assertive, more "muscular" kind of Jewish identity. His protagonists invariably turn against what Green considers the stereotypical Jewish identity of the *shtetl*: passive, pious, and scholarly. Green's heroes are athletes and fighters. Their Judaism is always an open or unstated Zionism that resists oppression and strives for autonomy. It is necessary to observe also that Green's conception of a revived Jewish identity is in all his works a conception of *male* identity. Even in his book on Israel, his heroic Sabras (contrary to historical fact) are almost all men.

Sam Abelman, the aging Brooklyn doctor (based on Green's father) in *The Last Angry Man*, seems to combine Moses (receiver of the law, who sees but cannot enter the Promised Land) with James Dean's "rebel without a cause." The son of pious and passive immigrants, a combative physical education teacher who studies medicine at night, filled with moral anger against the privileges of the undeserving rich, the violence committed by and against the poor, and the phoniness of the growing American media culture, Abelman never stops fighting for an ideal of absolute integrity and loyalty that he can never fully articulate. He is a transitional figure, an anachronism standing between what Green sees as an outmoded Jewish life based on Eastern European models and an active, as-yet-unrealized, Jewish life of the future.

In *The Stones of Zion*, Green sees this Jewish future—a future now connected to a heroic Jewish past—in the State of Israel after the Six-Day War. Sam Abelman cannot enter the future he begins to imagine in part because the only

Jewish past he knows is that brought from Europe by his parents, a past destroyed (and thus, for Abelman and for Green, discredited) by the Holocaust. The new Jewish identity for Green in this travel book is the self-reliant, battle-tested, victorious Sabra, an identity linked through biblical archaeology to those warrior Sabras and nation builders of the Jewish past: Joshua, David, Solomon, and even Herod (though not, in Green's masculinist vision, Sara, Judith, or Esther). Green's tour of Israel, then, combines archaeological sites with sites of battles in the recent war. What is elided, of course, in Green's reconstruction of Jewish history and identity is nearly two thousand years of rabbinic Judaism, the cultures of Diaspora, and—crucially, for a contemporary Jew—the Holocaust.

Green's mixture of pride and shame regarding his Orthodox Eastern European parents and grandparents and his adoption of Israel in the late 1960s and early 1970s as a locus of Jewish pride represented the feelings of a large proportion of secular American Jews of his time. Just as representative was his focus in the late 1970s back toward the Shoah. In fact, Green's novel and television miniseries *Holocaust* were not merely representative but even, in part, constitutive of the widespread revival of interest in the Shoah and the use of that catastrophe as a source of Jewish identity.

Holocaust tells two stories, the Jewish story and the Nazi story, and attempts to answer two major questions, how the Germans, as human beings, could have been capable of the genocide, and why the Jews did not resist more strenuously. In telling the stories of the German-Jewish Weiss family and of the SS officer Erik Dorf, alternating the narrative between the survivor Rudi Weiss's memories and entries from Dorf's diary, Green includes an enormous amount of historical information. It seems as though almost no significant event is left out, as one or another character witnesses or participates in Kristallnacht, the early euthanasia program, Babi Yar, the Wannsee Conference, the Jewish councils, the Warsaw Ghetto uprising, the role of German corporations in the genocide, and so on. In his selection and division of material, Green seems clearly indebted to Lucy Dawidowicz's *The War against the Jews*, and while his historical inclusiveness is helpful as an introduction to a study of the Holocaust (perhaps for high-school students), the novel does suffer from what James Lardner in the *New Republic* called the attempt "not just to tell one story of Jews under Nazism, but *the* story."

With regard to Green's ongoing effort to redefine Jewish identity, in *Holocaust* he continues his series of portrayals of the Jew as fighter. Rudi Weiss, the sole survivor of his family, is an athlete, not a scholar. Unlike the rest of his family, he does not wait for the Nazis to crush him, but leaves home and spends the war engaged in resistance movements. After the war, he moves to Israel. Rudi is the successor and culmination of the other "muscular" Jews of Gerald Green's oeuvre—and like Sam Abelman and the Sabras of *Stones of Zion*, I would argue, a product of Green's ambivalence about his own Judaism, an ambivalence quite typical of assimilated postwar American Jewry.

The miniseries *Holocaust* will remain Green's best-known and most controversial accomplishment. Although it drew an enormous audience, it was widely criticized for trivializing its subject, reducing the central cataclysm of the twentieth century to the format of a glamorized soap opera. *Holocaust* did, however, help reintroduce the Shoah into American public discourse at that crucial, transitional moment when the generation of survivors and witnesses was being silenced by age and natural death. It stands, therefore, as an important document in a complex cultural development—the rediscovery, or reimagining, of the Holocaust after the end of direct witnessing—that is still ongoing in American and Jewish life.

CRITICAL RECEPTION

The critical reception of Gerald Green's writing has been mixed. He has generally been praised for his characters and dialogue and for what has been perceived as the moral and social power of his work; and he has often been criticized for the formal awkwardness of his novels and for, as Robert Molloy wrote in his *Chicago Sunday Tribune* review of *The Last Angry Man*, ''a lack of stylistic elegance'' (4). In a similar vein, James Kelly wrote in the *New York Times Book Review* that *The Heartless Light* is ''as sprawling, as full of force and faults, as Niagara Falls'' (4). As a modern American novelist, Green is obviously closer to Theodore Dreiser than to Henry James; as a postwar Jewish-American novelist, his work more resembles the sagas of Chaim Potok than the fabulations of Malamud or Roth or even Bellow, although his social and cultural concerns often overlap theirs. As a novelist, Green is a storyteller and an earnest explorer of social and moral issues, not a formal innovator.

BIBLIOGRAPHY

Works by Gerald Green

Nonfiction

His Majesty O'Keefe. With L. Klingman. New York: Scribner, 1950.
The Sword and the Sun. New York: Scribner, 1953.
The Last Angry Man. New York: Scribner, 1956.
The Lotus Eaters. New York: Scribner, 1959.
The Heartless Light. New York: Scribner, 1961.
The Portofino PTA. New York: Scribner, 1962.
The Legion of Noble Christians; or, The Sweeney Survey. New York: Trident, 1965.
The Senator. With Drew Pearson. Garden City, NY: Doubleday, 1968.
To Brooklyn with Love. New York: Trident, 1968.
The Artists of Terezin. New York: Hawthorn, 1969.
Faking It; or, The Wrong Hungarian. New York: Trident, 1971.
The Stones of Zion: A Novelist's Journal in Israel. New York: Hawthorn, 1971.

Blockbuster. Garden City, NY: Doubleday, 1972.
Tourist. Garden City, NY: Doubleday, 1973.
The Hostage Heart. New York: Playboy Press, 1975.
An American Prophet. Garden City, NY: Doubleday, 1977.
Girl. Garden City, NY: Doubleday, 1977.
The Healers. New York: Putnam, 1979.
Holocaust. New York: Bantam, 1978.
Cactus Pie. Boston: Houghton Mifflin, 1979.
The Chains. New York: Seaview, 1980.
Murfy's Men. New York: Seaview, 1981.

   Screenplays

The Last Angry Man. Columbia Pictures, 1959; Columbia Pictures Television, 1974.
Holocaust. Titus Productions, National Broadcasting Company, 1978.
Kent State. Interplanetary Productions, National Broadcasting Company, 1980.

Studies of Gerald Green

With the exception of a special issue of *New German Critique* (Winter 1980) on the impact of the broadcast of *Holocaust* in West Germany, no scholarly work has yet been done on Gerald Green, but his work has been widely reviewed.

Kelly, James. Review of *The Heartless Light. New York Times Book Review*, April 23, 1961, 4.
Lardner, James. Review of *Holocaust. New Republic*, May 13, 1978, 27–29.
Molloy, Robert. Review of *The Last Angry Man. Chicago Sunday Tribune*, February 10, 1957, 4.

JOSEPH HELLER   (1923–)

David Buehrer

BIOGRAPHY

Joseph Heller was born to Russian immigrant parents in the Coney Island section of Brooklyn, New York, on May 1, 1923. At age five, he experienced the loss of his father, a bakery-truck driver who died during an operation; hence Heller, his older brother, and his mother were left to struggle on their own in the carnivalesque enclave of Coney Island, at the time a heavily Jewish community. Such early experiences and environments may account, as other critics have noted, for Heller's unique brand of acerbic cynicism and street-smart humor that permeate much of his fiction.

Heller attended Coney Island's Public School 188 and then Abraham Lincoln High School, from which he graduated in 1941. After high school, he worked for short stints in an insurance office and as a blacksmith's assistant at the Norfolk Navy Yard before enlisting in the U.S. Army's Twelfth Air Force Division in the fall of 1942. Stationed in Corsica during World War II, Heller flew some sixty combat missions as a wing bombardier and was discharged as a first lieutenant in 1945. His first and still most highly regarded novel, *Catch-22* (1961), stemmed from Heller's war experiences in Italy and France and includes many characters and events drawn from real life. After the war, Heller married Shirley Held of Brooklyn (they have two children, Erica Jill and Theodor Michael) and enrolled in college under the GI Bill, attending the University of Southern California before transferring a year later, in 1946, to New York University, where he received his B.A. in English in 1948. A year later, he earned an M.A. from Columbia University; his first published short stories also began appearing about this time in magazines such as *Esquire* and the *Atlantic*. Heller then spent 1949–1950 as a Fulbright Scholar at Oxford University, returning to teach at Pennsylvania State University from 1950 to 1952. During the next several years, he established a career as an advertising copywriter for *Time* and *Look* before serving as promotion manager at *McCall's* (1958–1961). Heller continued to write short fiction and occasionally scripts for movies and television (some under the pseudonym Max Orange) at this time, but he returned to academia in 1961 in order to teach fiction and dramatic writing at Yale and the University of Pennsylvania.

Because of the phenomenal success of *Catch-22*, however (it has sold nearly ten million copies in the United States alone and has been translated into more than a dozen languages), Heller has been able to pursue his craft of writing full-time, though he has intermittently over the years taught creative writing at the City University of New York and other schools. Heller is a member of the National Institute of Arts and Letters and currently lives with his wife in East Hampton, New York.

MAJOR WORKS AND THEMES

Any discussion of Heller's abiding themes and motifs in his fiction must start with, and often circle back to, *Catch-22* (1961), a darkly sardonic antiwar novel like none other preceding it and a text that came to be critically acclaimed both within academe and without. The term ''Catch-22'' has even passed into common parlance (and into most American English dictionaries), meaning a kind of double bind or paradox in a law or regulation that makes one a victim no matter what option is chosen. It has become the postmodern tag phrase for existential man's predicament in an ambiguous, absurd world.

In *Catch-22*, Heller parodies the military establishment as a perfect metaphor for the illogical ''systemization'' of a contemporary society hell-bent on alienating and subsuming the individual—here, John Yossarian, a lead bombardier (like Heller himself) stationed on the fictional island of Pianosa during the Italian campaign of World War II. Yossarian's main objective while fighting ''the enemy . . . within, . . . the power brokers who gain from the war'' (Scotto, xxiii) at the expense of all sides involved, including their own (Milo Minderbinder is the caricatured embodiment of this attitude in the novel), is merely to stay alive. In simplistic terms, then, the main theme of Heller's first novel and most of his subsequent ones is death, or at least the antihero's struggle to withstand the monolithic, irrational forces (bureaucracies, governments, corporations, and so on) that can precipitate his demise. But Heller works with other related themes in *Catch-22* as well: what he has called ''the closeness of the rational to the irrational mind'' (Searles, *DLB*, 103), the comic dislocations and black humor endemic to social reality, and the parodic manipulation of language to mimic the confused and absurd vision of the world he perceives, to mention just a few.

Beneath all these obfuscations of plot, disjunctions in chronology, and black-humor foibles, however, remains the protagonist's determination to cheat death and to revolt rationally against the irrational conformity that drives the military and, Heller implies, society at large. In confronting his "loss of self," a theme endemic to much contemporary American fiction, Yossarian has few positive, humanistic options to choose from or models to follow in his quest for survival. But there are plenty of negative examples, "cartoon-strip caricature[s]" (Tanner, 72) of human beings whose self-amalgamation into the mindless military bureaucracy ironically ensures their survival: Scheisskopf, whose sole interest in life is organizing parades; Aarfy, a human form without any human responses, who terrifies Yossarian with his zombielike behavior; and, of course, Minderbinder, who exploits the absurd logic of "Catch-22" to create a corrupt international corporation, even at one point bombing his own men for profit. For Yossarian, only Orr (whose very name suggests an alternative to the system, an "either/or" choice), whose successful desertion to Sweden motivates the protagonist's later escape, offers a model of rational revolt whereby the individual opts for self-preservation over the determinism of an absurd world. Underneath the novel's radical narrative technique and labyrinthine structure, therefore, Heller presents a rather orthodox moral critique against the hypocrisy and egoism of an increasingly bureaucratic contemporary reality. With Yossarian choosing life at the novel's close, Heller reveals his finally humanistic mandate, one based on an at least contingent hope for the future human condition.

During the late 1960s and early 1970s, Heller exploited the immense popularity of *Catch-22* by publishing several dramatic versions of the novel, including *We Bombed in New Haven* (1968), *Catch-22: A Dramatization* (1971), and *Clevinger's Trial* (1973). Finally, in 1974, Heller returned to the novel genre with *Something Happened*, a book markedly different, in both form and content, from *Catch-22*. In his second novel, Heller employs a first-person narrator, Bob Slocum, to show both the dehumanizing weight of the business world and the "bankruptcy of the contemporary middle-class American experience" (Searles, *DLB*, 105) for the individual. The dull monotone of Slocum's voice throughout the novel suggests this protagonist's psychological and moral paralysis, a depressing, obsessive insecurity (reflected in chapter titles like "My Wife Is Unhappy" or "My Boy Has Stopped Talking to Me") that poisons all aspects of his personal and professional life. According to Robert M. Scotto, Slocum's interior monologue reflects two connected themes in *Something Happened*: the individual's "self-loathing and stasis internally and the entropy of America in the twentieth century outside" (xxvii). Hence gone is the comic relief, the black- and sick-humor antics of *Catch-22*, and in its place Heller has substituted a disturbing and unmitigated vision of the emptiness of life for the average American "company man." For Slocum, who for some five hundred pages of bland reflections seems to be going nowhere, something does finally "happen": his son, the only thing in his world he seems to care about, dies. Yet this tragic event, ironically, produces no moral epiphany in Slocum, but rather an increased apathy and coldness that he converts into a drive to "take command" on the corporate ladder of success. As if his son were his last tenuous tie to emotional life, Slocum chooses to incorporate himself into the deadening milieu of the business world, convinced that the only self-realization is in upward mobility. A darker, if more mature, work than Heller's first novel, *Something Happened* may yet "convey an implied affirmation," since the novel "functions not only as an indictment but also as a recommendation for something better" (Searles, *DLB*, 106). But just what that "something" is remains ominously ambiguous by the novel's close.

With *Good as Gold* (1979), however, Heller exploits for the first time in his fiction particularly Jewish themes and motifs. Bruce Gold, the novel's protagonist, in fact shares much in common with Heller: he also grows up in Coney Island, goes to college under the GI Bill and later to Oxford, is an author and college professor, and writes in an apartment near Central Park. But these autobiographical parallels with the book's author presage a broader subtheme, too: "Gold's attempts to come to terms with his Jewish background," with a "racial and religious identity he often wishes to disavow" (Wall, 374). This subtheme becomes even more pronounced because of the novel's conflicting plot sequences: Gold aspires to a career as a government bureaucrat in Washington, which he soon discovers means gaining entrance into "the restricted enclaves of WASP privilege" (Searles, *DLB*, 106), yet at the same time he has been commissioned to write a book about "the Jewish experience" in America, for which he has received a large advance. In many ways, too, the book is a study of Jewish family life, a subject common to the novels of other modern American fiction writers, such as Saul Bellow and Philip Roth, although Gold seems to use his Washington ambitions more as a convenient escape from a marriage that has gone stale, children who constantly disappoint him, and a father and siblings who mock him for his WASPish affectations.

Heller complicates the book's ethnic-identity issues even more, however, by making the New York Jewish intellectual community itself a target of satire; even a real-life Henry Kissinger is thrown into this melee, a man whom Gold despises personally but whose Washington career he would be proud to emulate. These paradoxes, coupled with Heller's "self-conscious use of Yiddish and Yiddish-influenced sentence-structure" (Searles, *DLB*, 106), certainly work to foreground Jewish issues and motifs in *Good as Gold*, if sometimes at the expense of the academic and political satire portrayed in other parts of the novel. This lack of a clear or consistent focus for the book may be one of its faults, yet its depiction of the "ironic, double-bind situations" (Wall, 374) that plague the individual on the American landscape helps us to place the novel in the thematic company of Heller's earlier works.

During the 1980s, Heller published two more novels, *God Knows* (1984) and *Picture This* (1988), which treat the biblical figure of King David and the artistic personage of Rembrandt, respectively. Both books take as their main theme the unreliability of history and the absurd twists of its written record, with Heller wielding his satiric barbs at everything from French Jewish exegesis to post-1945 Cold War politics. Other recent Heller works include *No Laughing Matter* (1986), a biography written with Speed Vogel, and a 1993 compilation of interviews with the novelist, *Conversations with Joseph Heller*, edited by Adam J. Sorkin. But it was Heller's sixth novel, *Closing Time* (1994), touted by its publisher as a "sequel to *Catch-22*," that finally brought the novelist back into the popular limelight. The new book also brings back Yossarian and some of his friends from the war, although now they are old men possessing little of the vitriolic anger or comic absurdity displayed in *Catch-22*. Instead, a tone of "resigned disgust" (M. Adams, 128) permeates their postwar lives in America. This theme is especially true for Yossarian: now sixty-eight, having drifted from one unfulfilling relationship and career move to another (separated from his second wife, he has tried his hand at teaching, investment banking, public relations, and advertising and presently serves as "a semi-retired semi-consultant" for, of all people, the absurd Milo Minderbinder of *Catch-22* infamy), the former antihero is spiteful that his life, like the civilization around him, is running down.

The physical and moral decay of New York City serves as the backdrop for this protagonist's outrage, with his only ray of hope being his young girlfriend, Melissa MacIntosh, who is pregnant with his child. *Closing Time* may continue, as Michael Adams contended, a theme present in much of Heller's fiction of the "conflict between the individual's responsibilities for his fate and the forces willingly or accidentally out to destroy his individuality" (134), only now there seems less satire and optimism and more anguish and pessimism in his characters' battles with the modern world. The novel's other old men, such as Sammy Singer (who made a minor appearance in *Catch-22*), Lew Rabinowitz, and Albert Tappman (Yossarian's wartime chaplain), also waver between passion and passivity, most finally resigning themselves to the idea that democracy in the "land of the free" is a farce. Heller's trademark absurdist humor is again showcased, however, especially in the Milo sections and those dealing with "Little Prick," the President of the United States, who at one point accidently launches a nuclear attack while playing video games in the White House. But if for Yossarian, as before in *Catch-22*, "the proximity to death makes life more valuable," and "making the best out of the worst of situations" (M. Adams, 131) becomes his saving grace, it is clear that such naive optimism within the postapocalyptic milieu of *Closing Time*'s "new world order" is foolish at best. Time is "closing" out on both Yossarian and his America, with little defense left against that ticking clock except bemused resignation.

CRITICAL RECEPTION

The initial reviews of *Catch-22* (1961), despite its later cult and critical status, culminating in a popular film version of the book in 1970, were decidedly mixed. Perhaps this was due, as George Searles postulated, to the novel's "highly experimental treatment of chronology, its absurdist vision, and its madcap energy," making it "a few years ahead of its time" (*DLB*, 103). On the negative side, for instance, Alan Cheuse argued that beneath its "tough, flashy, comic mask," *Catch-22* is a "sentimental novel" that fails as "coherent fiction'' because of the intersection of the comic and tragic, a ''deep and destructive flaw'' to the narrative (82). A bit nastier, Douglas Day called the book ''derivative, poorly edited, repetitive and overlong, . . . a mixed bag, a hash'' and saw Yossarian as an ''anarchist'' of the worst sort (88). But the novel was not without its early admirers, too, who praised it, ironically, for many of the same reasons that others had trashed it. Alexander Cockburn, for instance, lauded Heller's satire and the book's ''slick technique of paradox and dead-pan follow-through'' (90); fellow novelist Norman Mailer dubbed Heller's first novel ''original'' yet ''maddening'' and wide open for ''virtuoso performance[s]'' of critical interpretation, concluding that ''Heller may yet become Gogol'' (69). Over the past quarter century, however, *Catch-22* has received almost entirely positive critical accolades, and its popular resurrection was due in large part to its publication in paperback during the late 1960s when young readers, finding parallels between its black humor and the absurd escalation of the war in Vietnam, ''responded to its antiestablishment theme'' (M. Adams, 128). Now the critical community has caught up, too, and *Catch-22* is generally regarded as one of the most influential American novels published since 1950.

While Heller's dramatic adaptations of his first novel, especially *We Bombed in New Haven* (1968) and *Catch-22: A Dramatization* (1971), also met with generally favorable critical notice, the reviewers seemed disappointed with his long-awaited second novel, *Something Happened* (1974). Its gloominess and flat, realistic delivery alienated many initial critics who expected more of the vaudevillian tone highlighted in *Catch-22*. Reviewers found the book's long lists of mundane facts and the protagonist's psychological quirks both boring and unconvincing. But critic George Searles contended that while the ''extremely limited mode of narration, the unheroic nature of the protagonist, and the ostensibly pessimistic quality of the novel's message'' were features of *Something Happened* that made it a hard sell for reviewers, it might also be a ''more mature book'' than its predecessor, *Catch-22* (''Something Happened,'' 81).

With his second novel, Heller turned from the ''boisterous exaggeration'' and ''hyperbole'' of his first book to ''implication . . . opting for a less strident, less obvious statement'' (''Something Happened,'' 75), yet one that confronted ''some of the most unpleasant truths about . . . contemporary America'' with a tone of ''disquieting verisimilitude'' (Aldridge, 18). This lack of a message in *Something Happened*, leaving only, as Kurt Vonnegut put it, ''a depressingly ordinary fact'' (1)—that of Slocum's ''success'' within the corrupt bureaucracies of corporate America—certainly differentiates the book from *Catch-22*, which has made the overall critical evaluation of it less than unanimously favorable.

Good as Gold (1979), Heller's third novel, was also found to be disappointing by commentators, chiefly because of its unclear focus and perhaps hasty composition. Searles felt that its three narrative strands of ''Jewish family comedy, . . . academic satire, and . . . political lampoon'' were ''too loosely intertwined,'' resulting in a ''rambling, shapeless, nearly 450-page novel that contains many sections of good material but fails as a whole'' (*DLB*, 106). John N. Wall, again comparing it to *Catch-22* with its black-comedy vision, claimed that *Good as Gold* was a ''thin book,'' although this might have stemmed from Heller himself sensing ''the inherent futility of his central character's situation'' (372). Yet the novel's lukewarm, generally mixed reception as a whole did not distract some critics from concentrating on the ''sections,'' such as those dealing with Gold's Jewish-identity struggles, that did work or revealed thematic innovations for Heller. At the very least, *Good as Gold* began to establish Heller as a ''Jewish writer'' to a degree that his previous fictions had not suggested to many critics.

Both *God Knows* (1984) and *Picture This* (1988), Heller's next two novels, also met with rather mixed, bewildered critical reviews. Centering on the last days of King David's life with his bitter frustrations and self-pitying demeanor, *God Knows* was found by Earl Rovit to be in ''shockingly bad taste . . . , deliberately exploit[ing] Samuel 1 and 2 in the worst possible'' way (1772). Galen Strawson felt that the book was a ''frivolous embroidery on a biblical theme,'' although he conceded that it was an ''at least partly accurate and covertly acute psychological illumination of the biblical figures themselves'' (1330).

Heller's next novel, *Picture This*, a contemporary revamping of Aristotle, Rembrandt, and Western cultural history in general, was similarly received. John Leonard found Heller's debunking of history overdone at best: ''Democracy is fraudulent, man is vile, and Heller's contemptuous'' in *Picture This*. ''Never mind that Heller seems . . . to have looked into a cracker barrel instead of the abyss'' (124). Robert M. Adams cited Heller's emphasis on the ''absurd disparit[ies]'' of Western history in the novel, but faulted the author for listing ''a lot of unrelated events,'' which made for its ''chief effect'' narrative ''incoherence'' (9). This line of criticism was also followed by Christopher Hitchens, who called the novel a ''rather doughy satire'' in which ''we get long and ill-sorted chunks of reconstituted narrative'' without thematic focus (1155).

A common complaint against these two novels, already voiced with the publication of *Good as Gold* in 1979, is Heller's maybe-too-hasty composition process, a gripe that has surfaced as well in reviews of his most recent book, *Closing Time* (1994). This ''sequel'' to *Catch-22* has been panned by several influential critics, most notably for the author trying to cash in on the earlier novel's success, though Heller himself does not regret writing *Closing Time* and denies that it is simply a work of ''autobiographical fiction'' (Gelb, 3). Michael Adams believed that, again compared to its predecessor, *Closing Time* ''does little to advance Heller's observations about age, death, and the decline of civilization,'' that the book's ''conflicting tones work against rather than with each other,'' and that ''Heller's criticisms of modern life do not seem particularly fresh'' (130–31). Despite these recent rough reviews of his work, however, Heller remains a major contemporary American novelist, garnering both popular success and a plethora of scholarly attention as he ''continues to probe with the skill, the patience, and the precision of the scientist beneath the camouflage of everyday life'' (Kutt, 236).

BIBLIOGRAPHY

Works by Joseph Heller

Catch-22. New York: Simon and Schuster, 1961.
We Bombed in New Haven. New York: Knopf, 1968.
Catch-22: A Dramatization. New York: French, 1971.
Clevinger's Trial. New York: French, 1973.
Something Happened. New York: Knopf, 1974.
Good as Gold. New York: Simon and Schuster, 1979.
God Knows. New York: Knopf, 1984.
No Laughing Matter. With Speed Vogel. New York: Putnam, 1986.
Picture This. New York: Putnam, 1988.
Conversations with Joseph Heller. Ed. Adam J. Sorkin. Jackson: University Press of
    Mississippi, 1993.
Closing Time. New York: Simon and Schuster, 1994.

Works Cited and Studies of Joseph Heller

Adams, Michael. Review of *Closing Time. Magill's Literary Annual*, 1995, 128–34.
Adams, Robert M. Review of *Picture This. New York Times Book Review*, September
    11, 1988, 9.
Aldridge, Alan. "Vision of Man Raging in a Vacuum." Review of *Something Happened.
    Saturday Review*, October 18, 1974, 18–21.
Cheuse, Alan. "Laughing on the Outside." Review of *Catch-22. Studies on the Left* 3
    (Fall 1963): 81–87.
Cockburn, Alexander. Review of Catch-22. *New Left Review* 18 (1963): 87–92.
Day, Douglas. "Catch-22: A Manifesto for Anarchists." Review of *Catch-22. Carolina
    Quarterly* 15 (Summer 1963): 86–92.
Gelb, Barbara. "*Catch-22* Plus: A Conversation with Joseph Heller." *New York Times
    Book Review*, August 28, 1994, 3.
Hitchens, Christopher. Review of *Picture This. Times Literary Supplement*, October 14,
    1988, 1155.
Keegan, Brenda M. *Joseph Heller: A Reference Guide*. Boston: G. K. Hall, 1978.
Kiely, Frederick T., and Walter McDonald, eds. *A Catch-22 Casebook*. New York: Crow-
    ell, 1973.
Kutt, Inge. "Joseph Heller." In *American Novelists since World War II*. Vol. 2 of
    Dictionary of Literary Biography. Detroit: Gale Research, 1978.
Leonard, John. Review of *Picture This. Ms.*, January–February 1989, 124.
Mailer, Norman. "Some Children of the Goddess." Review of *Catch-22. Esquire*, July
    1963, 63–69.
Merrill, Robert. *Joseph Heller*. Boston: Twayne, 1987.
Miller, Wayne C. "Ethnic Identity as a Moral Focus: A Reading of Joseph Heller's *Good
    as Gold*," *MELUS* 6:3, 1979: 3–17.
Nagel, James, ed. *Critical Essays on Catch-22*. Encino, CA: Dickenson, 1973.
———. *Critical Essays on Joseph Heller*. Boston: G. K. Hall, 1984.
Pinsker, Sanford. *Understanding Joseph Heller*. Columbia: University of South Carolina
    Press, 1991.

Potts, Stephen W. *Catch-22: Antiheroic Antinovel*. Boston: Twayne, 1989.

———. *From Here to Absurdity: The Moral Battlefields of Joseph Heller*. San Bernardino, CA: Borgo Press, 1982.

Rovit, Earl. Review of *God Knows. Library Journal*, September 15, 1984, 1772.

Scotto, Robert M. *Three Contemporary Novelists: An Annotated Bibliography of Works by and about John Hawkes, Joseph Heller, and Thomas Pynchon*. New York: Garland, 1977.

Searles, George. "Joseph Heller." In *Twentieth Century American-Jewish Fiction Writers*, ed. Daniel Walden. Vol. 28 of *Dictionary of Literary Biography*. Detroit: Gale Research, 1984, 103–6.

———. "Something Happened: A New Direction for Joseph Heller." *Critique* 18 (1977): 74–81.

Seed, David. *The Fiction of Joseph Heller: Against the Grain*. New York: St. Martin's, 1989.

Strawson, Galen. Review of *God Knows. Times Literary Supplement*, November 23, 1984, 1330.

Tanner, Tony. *City of Words: American Fiction, 1950–1970*. New York: Harper and Row, 1971.

Vonnegut, Kurt. Review of *Something Happened. New York Times Book Review*, October 6, 1974, 1–2.

Wall, John N. Review of *Good as Gold. Magill's Literary Annual*, 1980, 374.

MARK HELPRIN   (1947–   )

Joel Shatzky and Michael Taub

BIOGRAPHY

Mark Helprin was born on June 28, 1947, in New York City, the son of Morris and Eleanor Lynn Helprin. He received his B.A. and M.A. from Harvard University in 1969 and 1972 and did postgraduate study at Magdalen College, Oxford University, in 1976–1977. He was a member of the Israeli Infantry and Air Corps in field security from 1972–1973 as well as the British Merchant Navy. In 1980 he married Lisa Kennedy. They have two daughters, Alexandra Morris and Olivia Kennedy.

Helprin has told a number of interviewers that he began getting interested in writing at the age of seventeen when, while staying in Paris, he wrote a description of the Hagia Sophia in Istanbul without ever having seen it. He also claimed that at home he was not permitted to sit down to the dinner table to eat unless he told his father a new story each night, a description he later admitted was something of an exaggeration. Among the awards Helprin has received are the PEN/Faulkner Award, the National Jewish Book Award, and an American Book Award nomination. He is a member of the American Academy and Institute of Arts and Letters and has received a Prix de Rome and a Guggenheim Fellowship.

Helprin began submitting stories as an undergraduate at Harvard and finally had two accepted at the same time from the *New Yorker* in 1969. Since then, he has written three novels and two collections of short stories, for the second of which, *Ellis Island and Other Stories*, he received a PEN/Faulkner Award, the National Jewish Book Award, and an American Book Award nomination.

WORKS, THEMES, AND CRITICAL RECEPTION

Helprin's first book of fiction, a collection of short stories, *A Dove of the East* (1975), received generally good reviews, particularly in terms of Helprin's distinctive, "dream-like" style. In an interview by Ann Cunniff, Helprin admitted, "All my life I've allowed what I dream to influence me. My dreams are usually very intense and extremely detailed and always in the most beautiful colors. . . . Frequently, I will dream, and simply retrace that dream the day after when I write. It's like planning ahead, only I do it when I'm unconscious" (quoted in *Contemporary Authors*, 184).

His initial novel, *Refiner's Fire: The Life and Adventures of Marshall Pearl, a Foundling* (1977), also received very positive reviews, but it was with *Ellis Island and Other Stories* that Helprin gained the recognition with which he established his reputation. In one of the stories, "North Light," Helprin reaches into his own life in a riveting description of a group of Israeli soldiers facing battle.

Although his next novel, *Winter's Tale* (1983), received mixed reviews, the following work, *A Soldier of the Great War* (1991), was given very positive responses from such critics as Theodore Solotaroff in the *Nation* and Geoffrey Stokes in the *Village Voice*. For readers interested in Jewish literature, however, Mark Helprin's most noted work remains *Ellis Island and Other Stories*.

BIBLIOGRAPHY

A Dove of the East and Other Stories. New York: Knopf, 1975.
Refiner's Fire: The Life and Adventures of Marshall Pearl, a Foundling. New York: Knopf, 1977.
Ellis Island and Other Stories. New York: Seymour Lawrence/Delacorte, 1981.
Winter's Tale. San Diego: Harcourt Brace Jovanovich, 1983.
(Adaptor) *Swan Lake*. Illus. Chris Van Allsburg. Boston: Houghton Mifflin, 1989.
A Soldier of the Great War. San Diego: Harcourt Brace Jovanovich, 1991.
Memoir from Antproof Case. San Diego: Harcourt, 1995.
For further information about Mark Helprin, see *Contemporary Authors*, New Revision Series, 47. Detroit: Gale, 1995.

CAROLIVIA HERRON (1947–)

Brenna J. Ryan

BIOGRAPHY

Carolivia (born Carol Olivia) Herron was born on July 22, 1947, in Washington, D.C. She received her B.A. in English literature from Eastern Baptist College in 1969, her M.A. in English from Villanova University in 1973, and her Ph.D. in comparative literature and literary theory from the University of Pennsylvania in 1985. She also received a second master's degree in English literature and creative writing from the University of Pennsylvania in 1985, and she has held faculty appointments at both Mount Holyoke College and Harvard University. She lives presently in Brighton, Massachusetts, where she is a visiting professor in the Divinity School at Harvard University.

As a child, Herron suffered severe and ritualized sexual abuse; she describes herself as sold into childhood "prostitution" at age three by her aunt, and she was forced to serve in a brothel until the age of eleven. However, Herron likens her experience more to that of a slave because, she posits, prostitution insinuates an awareness of economics, and as she experienced this sexual abuse as a child, she had no awareness of the "economics" of her situation. As a result of this sexual "slavery," she has suffered for more than forty years from multiple-personality disorder; at one point, she reports, she had nine personalities that she knew of. Now "integrated," Herron is dealing with a new illness—temporal-lobe epilepsy—that adversely affects her vision but leaves her otherwise unencumbered to teach, read, and write.

A precocious child, Herron read *Beowulf* and Herodotus before she was ten; she devoured *Paradise Lost* by age eleven. Since then, she has developed a passion for the "classical epic," and this early influence informs both her fictional and her scholarly works. She is also interested in the epics of the Third

World, Africa in particular, and has spent much time abroad studying African epics and their relationship to epics of the Western world. During her time studying abroad, she has lived and taught in Zaire and Congo-Brazzaville.

Since the age of twenty-three, Herron has been interested in Judaism, but it was not until 1991, when she was teaching at Mount Holyoke College, that she made the decision to convert. As a black woman, she describes herself as used to the proselytizing behavior of the Baptists and an unusual candidate for conversion; but because of her disdain for religions featuring human figureheads, her love for the literary and narrative art of the Hebrew Bible, her distrust of the democratic facade of the New Testament, and her attraction to and understanding of the experiences and hardships of "otherness," she practices and embraces the religion as if she were born into it. She made her bat mitzvah at the Harvard Hillel on January 27, 1996.

In addition, Herron states that "Judaism asserts that this life and this world are good and much to be preferred over the next life. It seems to me that Christians as a whole think the world is bad, and that on one day a year (Christmas) there is a special dispensation that allows for life to be good. But in Judaism every day of the year is good." She posits that envy for the love of this life is the source of many of the tensions between Jews and others, and she delights in the freedom Judaism affords her.

MAJOR WORKS AND THEMES

Because Herron is a scholar of the epic (her dissertation, "The Vacillating Epic: The Dialectic of Opposing World Views in the Expansion of the Epic Literary Genre," highlights her position that epic works have no "innate correlation with a unified world view"), her fiction reflects her years of study. The structure of her novel *Thereafter Johnnie*, in particular, is likened by reviewers to that of the *Odyssey*, even though Herron says that her text has more in common with the *Iliad*. However, she compares *Thereafter Johnnie* even more with Milton's *Paradise Lost*, asserting that its twenty-four chapters mirror Milton's twelve books—even though Milton fashioned his text after Homer's.

Like many epic texts, Herron's feature an apocalyptic vision; many of her characters find themselves plagued by a historical dilemma or "argument" that they must solve in order to achieve inner peace. However, the historical dilemma Herron offers is that of slavery; her African-American female characters experience difficulties reconciling themselves with the fact that "slavery happened." Because slavery facilitated miscegenation and incest, white slavemasters sleeping with their daughters and sisters, the modern African-American female characters must accept her origins in rape and violation, and this is the cause of her present trauma as seen in the aforementioned novel and Herron's short story "That Place."

However, Herron's multiple-personality disorder also informs her fiction and her worldview. Her characters are fragmented and, arguably, also suffer from multiple-personality disorder. But in her fiction, Herron argues that this splitting also and ultimately has its roots in slavery. She blames her characters' fragmentation on the rape and violation against African-American women that persists into the twentieth century from past centuries. She considers it a curse and a legacy that African-American males are murdered by the white males in power, and that African-American females are sexualized and used by the same power source.

Herron's fiction is only slightly differentiated from her autobiography. She admits that one of her own personalities authors her texts; thus the existence of different, ambiguous, and fragmented narrative voices informs this blur between genres. Herron uses certain literary devices to signal the advent of a personality split: usually a character's reflecting into a pool of water or looking out a window heralds her retreat into somnambulistic reverie. One of her personalities, "Jane," appears characterized in her fiction; thus Herron herself can be seen hiding in her words, daring the reader to catch her if he or she can. The author's phantasmagoric appearance in her own fiction suggests her own disloyalty to confines of genre; moreover, her emulation of epic styles and traditions further indicates this rejection of literary confines and conventions.

Herron calls her forthcoming novel *Asenath* a "comedy" or spoof of the graduate student's dissertation-writing process; however, elements from her "serious" fiction invade this text and arguably detract from the lightheartedness she intends with its writing. Herron appears in this novel in the character of "Carol OH!"; and Carol OH! writes her dissertation in a mirroring of Herron's writing of her own. The novel has its roots in autobiography even though Herron presents it as fiction, and this merging of genres likewise mirrors Herron's belief that the epic, tragedy, comedy, and "storytelling" can all occur simultaneously.

CRITICAL RECEPTION

As yet, except for numerous reviews of *Thereafter Johnnie*, no scholarly writings have appeared on any of Herron's texts; however, forthcoming studies of Herron's work will include Brenna J. Ryan's dissertation "Herron's Magic" and Rosaria Champagne's *The Politics of Survivorship: Incest, Women's Literature, and Popular Culture*. Although she has not specifically contributed any works to Jewish-American scholarship, Herron's experience as an African American converted to Judaism anticipates insights that have proven valuable in the works of Julius Lester, an African-American writer who converted to Judaism in the later 1980s.

BIBLIOGRAPHY

Works by Carolivia Herron

Fiction

"That Place." *Callaloo* 10:3 (1987): 391–413.
Thereafter Johnnie. New York: Random House, 1991.

"The Old Lady." In *Afrekete: An Anthology of Black Lesbian Writing*. New York: Doubleday, 1995, 101–24. Edited: 1st Anchor Book ed.

Selected Nonfiction

"Milton and Afro-American Literature." In *Re-membering Milton: Essays on the Texts and Traditions*, ed. Mary Nyquist and Margaret W. Ferguson. New York: Methuen, 1987, 278–300.

"Philology as Subversion: The Case of Afro-America." In *On Philology*, ed. Jan Ziolkowski. University Park: Pennsylvania State University Press, 1990, 62–65.

Selected Works of Angelina Weld Grimke. Ed. Carolivia Herron. Oxford: Oxford University Press, 1991.

LAURA Z. HOBSON (1900–1986)

Mashey Bernstein

BIOGRAPHY

Laura Z. Hobson was born Laura Kean Zametkin in New York City on June 19, 1900, the daughter of Michael and Adella Kean Zametkin. Her father was a Russian immigrant who was the editor of the *Jewish Daily Forward*, a newspaper published in Yiddish, and a labor organizer. He and his wife were both socialists. While Jewish, Laura once told an interviewer, "I grew up in an agnostic broad-minded family. I think of myself as a plain human being who happens to be an American" (*New York Times*, March 2, 1986).

Hobson and her twin sister Alice, from whom she became estranged till late in life, grew up on Long Island. She attended Hunter College and obtained a bachelor's degree from Cornell University. She married Francis Thayer Hobson, the vice president of a small publishing house, and for several years the couple collaborated under the pen name Peter Field in writing western novels, including *Outlaws Three* (1933) and *Dry Gulch Adams* (1934). At the same time, she worked as an advertising copy writer. The marriage ended in divorce in 1935. Following a brief affair with a person whose name she kept secret, she gave birth at the age of forty-one to a son, Christopher, and adopted a second son, Michael, the following year, quite a daring act for a single woman at that time.

Following her career in advertising, she became a reporter for the *New York Post* and then joined the staff of Luce Publications, responsible for *Time, Life*, and *Fortune*. She wrote her first short story in 1935 and was soon writing for *Collier's, Ladies' Home Journal*, and other magazines. In 1940, she gave up her professional career to devote herself to writing full-time. Her first novel was *The Trespassers* (1943), a critique of fascism that told of the plight of Europe's World War II exiles who were turned away from haven in the United States.

Although the work met with poor reviews, she persevered, and her next work, *Gentleman's Agreement* (1947), which explored the theme of ''genteel antisemitism'' in American upper echelons, proved to be her greatest success. In the early 1960s, she wrote a five-days-a-week news feature column, ''Assignment: America,'' for the International News Service.

In all, Hobson wrote nine novels, including *The Other Father* (1950); *The Celebrity* (1951), about the achievement of success; *The Tenth Month* (1971), about an unwed mother, which was made into a television movie starring Carol Burnett; and her last, *Untold Millions* (1982). Besides *Gentleman's Agreement*, only two other novels, *First Papers* (1964) and *Over and Above* (1979), contain Jewish figures, and only one other novel, *Consenting Adult* (1975), which dealt with a mother coming to terms with her homosexual son, had any of the success of her second novel. Her autobiography, *Laura Z: A Life*, appeared in 1983; a second volume was published posthumously in 1986. Besides the aforementioned works, she also wrote hundreds of short stories, magazine articles, and news features in a career that spanned six decades.

MAJOR WORKS AND THEMES

An assimilated Jew in many respects, Hobson brought to her work those values that were clearly inculcated from a particular Jewish background prevalent in the early years of the twentieth century and that were often translated from a Jewish setting and a Jewish sensibility into a more secular arena. In her work, therefore, Hobson reflects her socialist upbringing and a particular strain of liberal thought. Although she moved in the halls of power and was familiar with some of the prime movers of her generation, she championed the cause of the outsider and members of minority groups who suffered alienation from the mainstream of society. To make a strong impression, she wrote as a member of a privileged class who has to come to terms with—or in some cases even become aware of—the needs of others on whom these rights are not easily bestowed.

No novel brings this point out more clearly than her greatest success, *Gentleman's Agreement*, the work by which she is remembered today. The novel, which sold 100,000 copies in its first day of publication and eventually was translated into a dozen languages, joins those few works of literature, for example, Zola's ''J'Accuse,'' to which it bears a social sensibility, which can be said to have altered the social and moral fabric of a nation. In dealing with the genteel veneer of bigotry that was taken for granted among people who might otherwise be considered enlightened, and the restrictive practices of certain institutions, as well as, among other things, Jewish self-hatred and the need to hide one's ethnic identity, the novel struck a chord in the hearts and minds of the readers of the time. This sensitivity was heightened by the film version, which went on to win the 1947 Academy Award for Best Picture. Since that time, it has passed into Jewish-American folklore.

The novel recounts the efforts of a non-Jewish writer, Philip Green, to report on anti-Semitism in American society for a New York magazine. Since he is new to the magazine, he tells his coworkers and his new acquaintances that he is Jewish and thus is able to gain firsthand experience of the myriad ways that Jews are victimized: they are unable to get into "restricted" hotels, discriminated against in housing and jobs, and vilified in the press and in the halls of power. The real crux of the novel is concerned not with the petty actions of hotel clerks and the like but with the upper-class world of his fiancée. Eventually, Philip learns more than he bargained for. He writes the article and at the risk of personal loss rejects the "gentleman's agreement" by which prejudice and bigotry run rife in society in general.

A contemporary reader may question this roseate solution to prejudice and may even question its appearance just two years after news of the horrors of the Holocaust spread westward. The denial to a Jew of a room in a "restricted" hotel may strike one as inconsequential given the nature of the acts being revealed in Europe. In fact, no mention is made of World War II in the book. Hobson defended her approach by arguing that the Holocaust was "too religious" in thematic material, and she would have greater success in getting her point across if she stuck to the kind of prejudices she had encountered firsthand. Many pro-Nazi groups had support in the United States, she felt, as a result of a "longer" war that people like her were losing, the war against bigotry.

Hobson's argument, though, hints at a deeper problem of the novel. Not only are the conclusions facile, but her presentation of Judaism and Jews lacks depth and dimension. They seem devoid of any "real" life. They are, in fact, just "Jews in Protestant face." It might be easy to buy her argument that Jews are just like "everyone else" because they seem no different from Phil Green himself. They have no social identity. Her Jews want to be accepted because the only "value" being Jewish has is in being hated. Rather than being accepted for their differences, they want to be accepted for their sameness. In an article in 1982, Hobson ironically revealed this weakness, though she seemed to see it as a virtue: "Alas, if I were writing that book this very minute, and merely changed the word Jew to black or Puerto Rican or gay or Mexican-American, I could leave most of the scenes intact" (*Laura Z: A Life*, 313)—hence the work's strength and weakness. The novel is really about "passing," denying one's essential ethnic or personal identity in order to be accepted by society. In an age that has seen the emergence of groups that have asserted their rights to be accepted notwithstanding their religious, ethnic, or sexual differences, this novel has the opposite effect. It denies the very points it could have been glorifying.

Ironically, one of these groups, gays, is the subject of her other most successful novel, *Consenting Adult*, which was made into a critically well-received television movie. Written at the early stages of the emerging gay liberation movement, this novel has the same plea for acceptance as a mother tries to come to terms with the homosexuality of her son. Just as *Gentleman's Agreement* tackled a taboo subject, this later novel too broke new ground and was one of the first novels written by a heterosexual, male or female, to deal sympathetically with a subject that until then had been treated with scorn or ignorance.

Other than *First Papers*, which is more a portrait of liberals than of Jews and close to the upbringing that Hobson herself received, her only remaining work to treat a Jewish subject was her penultimate novel, *Over and Above*, which deals, through examining the lives of three generations of Jewish women, with the question of what it means to be Jewish—and to hide it—in modern American society. She also used the novel to explore her attitudes toward Israel, Palestine, and terrorism. According to her son Christopher, Amy, the "middle" generation, reflected Hobson's own views, which were pro-Israel, antiterrorist, and in the novel, at least, dismissive of the idea of a Palestinian nationality. A daughter of intellectual and agnostic Jews, Amy learns to reidentify with her Jewish past and present. Amy's daughter, Julie, cannot come to terms with her Jewish identity, and the novel ends on an ambiguous note where the mother, while letting her daughter off the hook in terms of her quest, affirms her own need to keep saying that she is Jewish.

CRITICAL RECEPTION

Hobson's critical reception vacillated greatly between acclaim and dismissal. Her first solo novel, *The Trespassers*, received generally poor reviews. Diana Trilling dismissed it as "inept" and "rather tasteless" (454), and the *New York Times* argued that it seemed to have been written in "an emotional vacuum" (9). The reception for *Gentleman's Agreement* could not have been more different, though it too did not escape criticism, especially of its optimistic conclusion. Nonetheless, the *New York Times* called it "honest" and managed with "brilliance" (2). H. S. Hayward in the *Christian Science Monitor* praised the book's "wisdom" (18), and Ann Whitmore in the *Library Journal* called it "courageous, convincing and highly enjoyable" (F15).

One suspects that the attention paid to her next novel, *The Other Father*, a potboiler about a father who has an affair with a younger woman while his daughter has an affair with an older man, was due to the great success of her previous novel. The critics were scathing, ranging in their denunciation from "a weary, inert novel" (Sandrock, 393) to "genuinely depressing" (*New Yorker*, 119) and "told with the primness of a textbook" (*New Republic*, 20). *The Celebrity* fared somewhat better, usually being damned with faint praise: "Will no doubt be a best seller and a good duplicate pay collection item," as C. J. Roth wrote in the *Library Journal* (1563).

Hobson did not write another novel for fourteen years. Most of the reviews of *First Papers* praised Hobson's style, though they felt that the plot was slow-moving and, despite the fact that it was close to her own personal history, uninvolving, "nostalgic as Thornton Wilder's *Our Town*" (Phelps, 9).

Her next novel, *I'm Going to Have a Baby*, about an impending birth in a family told from the point of view of a six-year-old boy, received scant attention in the press, with the *Times Literary Supplement* calling it a work that "will offend no one" (465). *The Tenth Month*, about an unwed mother giving birth, received mixed reviews. Edwin Fadiman saw it in the tradition of *Gentleman's Agreement*, in that it attacked middle-class, neo-Puritan morality, and called it "wise, witty and loving" (34), but he was definitely in the minority. The *New Republic* called it "slick, genteel soap opera" (34). *Consenting Adult*, a novel timely in its subject matter, received a rave review from Martin Duberman in the *New York Times*. He praised Hobson's "courage" and called on her readers to meet the novel's "moral challenge" and "try and understand and respect that which is different" (5). The critical silence that greeted her deeply felt novel *Over and Above* disappointed Hobson. The book was not reviewed in the major press and sold badly, a fate that also befell her final novel, *Untold Millions*.

However, her final published work, her autobiography, was met with great critical interest, though not all of it was favorable. While the critics praised her life, they felt that the work lacked perspective and objectivity. Nora Johnson, for example, felt that the work had no depth (15). Anne Roiphe, however, called the book "fascinating" and praised the writer's "vitality and stubborn decency" (58). The comment by Christopher Portfield seems to sum up much of Hobson's approach to the subject matter of her fiction: "Hobson falls into a modish woman's magazine tone in which even problems sound like boons" (74). Hobson, however, will always be known for her authorship of *Gentleman's Agreement*, a novel that brought into the American consciousness the "dirty, little secrets" of genteel anti-Semitism.

BIBLIOGRAPHY

Works by Laura Z. Hobson

Outlaws Three. Laura Hobson and Thayer Hobson as Peter Field. New York: Morrow, 1933.
Dry Gulch Adams. Laura Hobson and Thayer Hobson as Peter Field. New York: Morrow, 1934.
A Dog of His Own. New York: Viking, 1941.
The Trespassers. New York: Simon and Schuster, 1943.
Gentleman's Agreement. New York: Simon and Schuster, 1947.
The Other Father. New York: Simon and Schuster, 1950.
The Celebrity. New York: Simon and Schuster, 1951.
First Papers. New York: Random House, 1964.
I'm Going to Have a Baby. New York: Day, 1967.
The Tenth Month. New York: Simon and Schuster, 1971.
Consenting Adult. Garden City, NY: Doubleday, 1975.
Over and Above. Garden City, NY: Doubleday, 1979.
Untold Millions. New York: Harper and Row, 1982.

Laura Z: A Life. New York: Arbor House, 1983.
Laura Z: A Life: Years of Fulfillment. New York: Donald I. Fine, 1986.

Works Cited and Studies of Laura Z. Hobson

Du Bois, William. Review of *Gentleman's Agreement*. *New York Times Book Review*, March 2, 1947, 2.

Duberman, Martin. Review of *Consenting Adult*. *New York Times Book Review*, January 6, 1975, 5.

Fadiman, Edwin. Review of *The Tenth Month*. *Saturday Review of Literature*, January 16, 1971, 34.

Farber, Marjorie. Review of *The Trespassers*. *New York Times Book Review*, September 19, 1943, 9.

Hayward, H. S. Review of *Gentlemen's Agreement*. *Christian Science Monitor*, March 21, 1947, 18.

Review of *I'm Going to Have a Baby*. *Times Literary Supplement*, May 25, 1967, 465.

Johnson, Nora. Review of *Laura Z: A Life*. *New York Times Book Review*, October 23, 1983, 15.

Liptzin, Sol. *The Jew in American Literature*. New York: Bloch, 1966, 193–94.

Review of *The Other Father*. *New Republic*, May 29, 1950, 20.

Review of *The Other Father*. *New Yorker*, May 20, 1950, 119.

Phelps, Lyon. Review of *First Papers*. *Christian Science Monitor*, January 9, 1965, 9.

Portfield, Christopher. Review of *Laura Z: A Life*. *Time*, October 10, 1983, 74.

Roiphe, Anne. Review of *Laura Z: A Life*. *Saturday Review*, December 1983, 58.

Roth, C. J. Review of *The Celebrity*. *Library Journal*, October 1, 1951, 1563.

Sandrock. Review of *The Other Father*. *Catholic World*, August 1950, 393.

Review of *The Tenth Month*. *New Republic*, February 6, 1971, 34.

Trilling, Diana. Review of *The Trespassers*. *Nation*, September 16, 1943, 454.

Whitmore, Ann. Review of *Gentlemen's Agreement*. *Library Journal*, February 15, 1947, F15.

JUDITH KATZ   (1951–   )

Ludger Brinker

BIOGRAPHY

Judith Katz was born in Worcester, Massachusetts, on February 7, 1951, the oldest daughter in a family of three children. Her father owned a chain of small supermarkets in central and eastern Massachusetts, while her mother remained a housewife. Raised in a traditional Jewish family, Katz attended Beth Israel Synagogue, a Conservative congregation, and its Hebrew School through her senior year in high school.

After graduating with a bachelor's degree in English from the University of Massachusetts at Amherst in May 1973, Katz became a member of the Omaha Magic Theater in Omaha, Nebraska, from 1975 to 1979. There she worked in various capacities as actor, writer, technician, and producer. After returning to Massachusetts, she received a master's degree in theater with an emphasis in playwriting from Smith College in Northampton, Massachusetts, in May 1980. While her four plays to date include many lesbian characters, none of them is Jewish. In her master's thesis play, "Tribes: A Play of Dreams," the mother character is clearly Jewish, but her daughter has the voice of assimilation. The explanation for this lack of Jewish content is that Katz spent the 1970s and early 1980s concerned mostly about women's and lesbian issues. All this changed during and after a lesbian seder at Smith College, when she realized—was, in fact, pushed to realize by many of her Jewish friends—that she was missing something by trying to erase her Jewish identity. Thus Katz's Jewish lesbian voice did not come to the fore until she stopped writing plays and turned to writing fiction. In her quest to find this voice, Katz was mainly influenced by those Jewish women writers, like Anzia Yezierska and Jo Sinclair, who did not stay at home, but who instead fought Jewish patriarchal culture. In addition, she credits her reading of African-American women writers, in particular Toni Morrison and Alice Walker, in helping her understand how to construct an effective literary voice.

From the early 1980s until 1985 Katz worked as an administrator at At the Foot of the Mountain Theater in Minneapolis, but also found time to do some acting and playwriting. Since 1983 she has been an adjunct faculty member in the Women's Studies Department at the University of Minnesota. In addition, she is on the faculty at Hamline University in the M.A.L.S./M.F.A. program.

Katz's first novel, *Running Fiercely toward a High Thin Sound*, the completion of which was supported by several grants, including one from the National Endowment for the Arts, was published in 1992 to great acclaim and was awarded that year's Lambda Literary Award for Best Lesbian Fiction, a prestigious honor in the gay and lesbian writing community. Currently Katz is putting finishing touches on her second novel, *The Escape Artist*, and has started a third novel, tentatively entitled *Queer Summer*.

MAJOR WORKS AND THEMES

Judith Katz belongs to that generation of emerging writers whose creativity and range of subject matter once again prove premature the dour predictions of the imminent demise of American Jewish literature so often pronounced by literary critics and writers alike. Katz and other Jewish gay and lesbian writers give a voice to heretofore excluded or marginalized groups within Judaism. In fact, in the introduction to the recent collection of short fiction, *Writing Our Way Home*, Nessa Rapoport, without mentioning Katz by name, acknowledges the significance of such efforts by looking toward "children and grandchildren of Holocaust survivors, converts to Judaism, Sephardim, descendants of *conversos* in the American Southwest, lesbians, and gay men" (xviii) to keep American Jewish literature dynamic and vital.

Historically, American Jewish gay and lesbian writers have tended to be secularists; for them, "Jewish" is not necessarily an indicator of a particular religious position or sensibility but an affirmation of ethnic and cultural identity. Probably the major reason for this lack of religious content in much of American Jewish gay and lesbian writing is the Mosaic code as expressed in Leviticus. Conservative and Orthodox Jewish circles argue that the Torah explicitly forbids and condemns homosexuality, while the Reform and Reconstructionist branches argue for a new reading of Leviticus. The latter also argue for a complete acceptance of gays and lesbians into their ranks based on the history of Jewish liberal thought. The Reform and Reconstructionist branches of Judaism have been among the first religious groups in any of the major faiths in America to accept gays as part of their synagogues, ordaining gay clergy and, more recently, permitting gay commitment ceremonies. The Conservative and Orthodox branches have been less forthcoming, as was evident by the argument over whether members of the New York gay synagogue Beth Simchat Torah, affiliated with the Reform movement, were to be allowed to march in the 1993 New York Salute to Israel parade.

Not surprisingly, most openly gay and lesbian American Jewish writing has appeared in the post-Stonewall era. The sheer number of fiction writers, poets, and playwrights who have come to be recognized is astounding, and these writers are not known only to a small number of readers; David Leavitt, Irena Klepfisz, Larry Kramer, Tony Kushner, Adrienne Rich, and Sarah Schulman, to name just a very few, are, if not household names, certainly well known in most literary circles. One of the discernible trends in the literature of the past twenty-five years is that gay male writers most often tend to treat Jewishness as an ethnic and cultural identity, while lesbian authors also attempt to explore the religious dimensions of Judaism. Along with those American Jewish gay and lesbian writers who, on the basis of common religious and cultural traditions, have attempted to be welcomed back into the Jewish community in which they were raised, Katz wants to win acceptance, find a home, and end the status of gays and lesbians as marginal outsiders. That is, these writers want to overcome and actually abolish the border that has kept them outside the mainstream of Judaism. They also stress a wish to retain and deepen their affiliation with Judaism because they see it as having long been the preserve and refuge of outsiders.

In her one novel to date, *Running Fiercely toward a High Thin Sound*, Katz clearly intends to give a voice to women who have been traditionally excluded from much of Judaism. This novel, fusing magic realism with tales of survival, is the most powerful example so far in American Jewish lesbian writing of what Katz herself has described as ''pushing on the boundaries of what it means to be queer and Jewish.''

Jewish male writers can write with an authority that Jewish women writers have struggled to achieve over the past two decades or so. Thus the drive to rewrite, retranslate, or redeem traditional Jewish sources for the benefit of women has proven the most powerful impulse behind the feminist drive to make Judaism more relevant for modern Jews. While Jewish women's writing is now widely acknowledged as a vital force in American Jewish writing, Jewish lesbian writers still struggle for similar recognition and acceptance of their spiritual search. Since there are so few Jewish or lesbian literary models to emulate, Jewish lesbian writers, aided by the example of other contemporary Jewish women writers, are now, by necessity, in the process of establishing a new tradition from the ground up.

Thus Judith Katz and other contemporary American Jewish lesbian writers aim to transcend the androcentric and heterocentric Jewish tradition insofar as they create, through a reinterpretation of Jewish history and textual tradition, a countermythos that attempts to reconcile traditional Judaism with an equally strong and valid emerging lesbian feminist tradition. Women, traditionally marginalized in Jewish culture, are recast as the narrative center. Katz, for example, accomplishes this feat in the mythic dream sequences of *Running Fiercely to-*

ward a High Thin Sound by providing a historical framework into which she injects her faith in the creative and healing powers of Jewish women.

But Katz goes beyond the attempt to construct new Jewish feminist ceremonies and rituals, as many Jewish women writers did during the 1970s and 1980s—Esther Broner's *A Weave of Women* and *The Telling*, for example, come to mind. Rather, she relies more on Jewish mysticism by creating a dream netherworld that several of her characters enter, in which strong Jewish women of the past and present work together as healers in a nightmarish universe. Through the injection of this subterranean dream world, made up of sedimentary layers of cultural and religious memory, into an otherwise realistic narrative, Katz reinterprets Jewish culture and identity by connecting the contemporary world of American Jews with that of the European past, particularly that of the Eastern European ghettos during the Holocaust. Katz seems to suggest that if Jewish women had had a greater role in Eastern European Jewish affairs, much suffering could have been prevented. Of course, she describes hypothetical situations in which her desire to give power to women rubs against historical reality. While such bending of historical events is not unproblematic, Katz's goal is to empower Nadine and Rose, who have entered this dream world. The vital tasks that these two women must perform there have a lasting effect on their lives. Once they leave the netherworld, their daily lives become more purposeful.

These scenes serve to enlarge both the Jewish and the lesbian consciousness of the characters who participate in them. Here the role of women as healers, as cultural saviors, forms the all-important background. Lesbians and heterosexual women work and worship together, creating a new vision of sisterhood. Katz thus creates a rich synthesis between religious and lesbian mythmaking, a synthesis that stretches, almost to the breaking point, the boundaries of what it means to be lesbian and Jewish. In this she echoes Irena Klepfisz's assertion that ''lesbians have been fighting Jewish battles wherever they need to be fought.'' Katz and Klepfisz share the view that being Jewish and being lesbian are positive values that cannot be separated from one another.

The novel's plot is propelled forward by the first-person accounts of four characters, Fay Morningstar, the mother of Jane and Nadine, who both also tell their versions of the same story, and Rose Shapiro, a lesbian *luftmensh*, who becomes Nadine's lover. Since this novel solely concerns itself with relationships among women—mother and daughter, daughter and daughter, lover and lover—men are relegated to the sidelines. Nadine, the middle daughter of the Morningstar family, is mentally troubled from the very beginning. Often she is compared to a wolf. Her mother calls her ''*Vildeh chei-eh!* Wild animal,'' and the image of Nadine being less than human—or Jewish—is consistently employed. Even Nadine refers to herself as a wolf; she is an outcast, caught between the desire to return to her Jewish home and the knowledge that she will never be welcome there. She even changes her name—from Nadine Morningstar to Nadine Pagan—to reflect this condition. Her mother's troubled relationship with her stems from envy and jealousy; it is Nadine who is taught to play her grandfather's violin and not Fay, who had always wished to learn but was discouraged by her own mother. To Fay, Nadine represents everything she was not allowed to do as a Jewish woman. Her dreams of self-fulfillment—"How I longed to study *Talmud* and *Torah*, pronounce justice, and learn to play the violin as well"—were sacrificed to Jewish traditions that locked women out of serious participation in many spiritual aspects of Judaism.

The fact that Jane and Nadine are lesbians is disparagingly acknowledged by their mother, who cannot understand them, but is taken as a given by her daughters. While Jane is portrayed as a mentally healthy, well-adjusted lesbian, who becomes socially and politically active in college, it is the mentally disturbed Nadine around whom many of the novel's religious symbols are created and who becomes a prophet of sorts. When Electa, the oldest daughter, is married, Nadine, who had run away from home over five years before, returns secretly and hides among the Torah scrolls in the Ark of the temple to watch the wedding ceremony. In a scene that does not lack sardonic humor, she acts, in the words of her sister Jane, "like a jack-in-the-box and jumps out of the Ark—the Holy Ark for God's sake!—and lands on the rabbi." While here Nadine's connection to the Torah scrolls is tenuous and used for dark comedy, she later, after entering the dream netherworld, in one of the pivotal scenes of the novel, is triumphantly carried around on women's shoulders high over the heads of the participants during an enormous lesbian wedding ceremony as a living Torah in the same way that Torah scrolls are carried by observant Jews on Simchat Torah. In scenes like this, Nadine, despite, or maybe because of, her mental illness, becomes the new and living embodiment of the spirit of Judaism, fighting injustice and speaking out for righteousness. The incorporation of ancient biblical language and metaphor into this otherwise modern tale transforms Katz's netherworld into a utopian borderland encompassing her vision for a new and all-inclusive tolerant Judaism.

Evocations of Jewish religious tradition are not limited to such a passage. After the wedding debacle, Nadine goes to a river on Rosh Hashanah, where she performs, in analogy to *tashlich*, the traditional ritual of throwing away one's sins, an act of cleansing by flinging all of her clothing into the water. She then goes one step further: believing that she can never be reconciled with her family, she throws herself into the river in a final act of desperation. But instead of drowning, she enters a Jewish netherworld, a mythical place, in which she is healed—as far as that is possible—through the act of healing and helping others. Reemerging from this world on Passover, Nadine decides to make peace with her family and to ask for mutual forgiveness. She arrives just in time to enter the house during that part of the seder when the door is opened to welcome the prophet Elijah. In the chapter "The *Tsimmes* at *Pesach*" Jane describes that still no real communication between family members is possible because of the accumulation of old griefs. Nadine is not forgiven and instead departs with Rose, not to be seen again. But in the final chapter, significantly entitled "*Tikkun*," Jane dreams that she is on a mountaintop with Nadine; surrounded by other women, the sisters wrestle with each other and keep asking one another for forgiveness. Only in dreams, Katz seems to suggest, can this dysfunctional Jewish family find reconciliation and the courage to forgive.

While the main action of the novel remains consistently serious, Katz does not hesitate to employ humor and comedy as well. The influences of the godfathers of the novel's humor, Sholom Aleichem and Isaac Bashevis Singer, are particularly discernible in the figure of Rose Shapiro, Nadine's lover, a marijuana-smoking Jewish lesbian who works at a lesbian restaurant, Lechem V'Shalom, run by a lesbian collective. Rose is the *luftmensh* of Yiddish literature, an undisciplined, apolitical character, for whom radical means "smoking a joint on the New Chelm town commons." It is through her experiences in the netherworld, parodically also run by a Jewish women's collective, that Rose emerges as a wiser and more compassionate character, now finally ready to become Nadine's understanding lover.

Katz's powerful novel of Jewish lesbian spiritual search through revisioning Jewish texts and rituals points toward potential future directions in American Jewish literature. Other contemporary Jewish gay and lesbian writers share her attraction to the sacred, her spiritual search for a meaningful Judaism. Katz refuses to engage in cultural mediation for a perceived mainstream reader, something many minority writers still feel compelled to do to reach the largest potential audience. Her novel is unapologetically Jewish: there are no translations of Hebrew or Yiddish terms, no glossary, and no special explanation of religious rituals. Katz makes no attempt to make the reading smoother for non-Jewish or heterosexual audiences. The text is a proud declaration of literary, religious, and cultural independence. While Jewishness can be bleached into universality and has been by many American Jewish writers, Judaism cannot. Thus it is no coincidence that both Katz's novel and Sarah Schulman's recent novel *Empathy* end with the Passover seder. If Jewish texts are the mediating devices in an ongoing discussion of what it means to be a Jew in America, then these conscious evocations of the ending of Jo Sinclair's novel *Wasteland*, in their intertextuality, indicate that these writers want to show, both by referring to and revising the Jewish lesbian textual past, how far American Jewish gay and lesbian writing has progressed since 1946, when Sinclair's groundbreaking Jewish lesbian novel was first published. Minding the Torah's injunction, "The stranger in your midst shall be as the native. For remember, once you were a stranger in the land of Egypt," which forms a central part of every Passover seder, Katz and other gay and lesbian writers have managed to become, through their spiritual search, full participants in the discussion of what it means to be Jewish and a Jewish writer in the late twentieth century in America.

CRITICAL RECEPTION

Running Fiercely toward a High Thin Sound received numerous reviews, in particular in feminist and lesbian publications. Most reviews were very positive and praised Katz's achievement, which was also honored with the 1992 Lambda

Literary Award for Best Lesbian Fiction. Irena Klepfisz, for example, praised the novel for its truthfulness, its flawlessness in rendering women's voices, and its refusal to romanticize lesbians or Jews.

In her review of several lesbian works, Karla Jay focused less on the novel's artistic merits but instead, and rightfully so, bemoaned the lack of mainstream publishing opportunities for lesbian writers of experimental fiction. She also broached the touchy subject of Jewish lesbian writers and lesbian writers of color being relegated to small publishing houses because of the claim that the subject matter of these writers who constitute a minority within a minority is not broad enough to warrant publication by a mainstream press. This complaint was echoed by Victoria Brownworth, who also analyzed Katz's novel in the context of the Diaspora. Brownworth was emphatic to establish the significance of minority writing in the lesbian community by stating that Jewish lesbian writing "has deep resonance for all Lesbians, because forcing visibility means breaking silence" (48).

Ludger Brinker and Daniel Schiffrin concentrated on the Jewish aspects of the novel. Schiffrin's highly laudatory review, appearing in the *Baltimore Jewish Times*, a mainstream Jewish publication, focused in particular on the novel's religious aspects. Brinker's two essays, published in *Studies in American Jewish Literature* and *The Gay and Lesbian Literary Heritage*, treated contemporary Jewish lesbian writers in the context of the history of Jewish gay and lesbian writing in the United States. Brinker read Katz's novel as one of the best contemporary efforts to reconcile religious, ethnic, and sexual-orientation issues.

BIBLIOGRAPHY

Works by Judith Katz

Running Fiercely toward a High Thin Sound. Ithaca, NY: Firebrand, 1992.
"The Escape Artist." In *Tasting Life Twice: Literary Lesbian Fiction by New American Writers*, ed. E. J. Levy. New York: Avon, 1995, 65–77.

Studies of Judith Katz

Brinker, Ludger. "The Bat Mitzvah of American-Jewish Lesbian Fiction: Newman, Katz, and Felman." *Studies in American Jewish Literature* 13 (1994): 72–84.
———. "Jewish-American Literature." In *The Gay and Lesbian Literary Heritage*, ed. Claude J. Summers. New York: Holt, 1995, 408–13.
Brownworth, Victoria A. "Jewish Lesbians Fight to Be Heard: Writers Confront Publishers Afraid of Books That Seem Too 'Jewish.' " *Washington Blade*, December 4, 1993, 48, 51.
Jay, Karla. "Is Lesbian Literature Going Mainstream?" *Ms.*, July/August 1993, 70–73.
Klepfisz, Irena. "Reconstructed Selves." *Ms.*, March/April 1993, 63–64.
Schiffrin, Daniel. "A Stranger among Us: The Protagonist in Judith Katz's First Novel

Is a Lesbian Searching for a Place within Judaism.'' *Baltimore Jewish Times*, April 30, 1993, 14–16.

Solotaroff, Ted and Nessa Rapoport, eds. *Writing Our Way Home*. New York: Schocken Books, 1992.

JULIUS LESTER (1939–)

Joel Shatzky and Michael Taub

BIOGRAPHY

Julius Lester was born on January 27, 1939, the son of W. D. and Julia Smith Lester. As he later discovered, his great-grandfather was a Jew. He received a B.A. from Fisk University in 1960. In 1962 he married Joan Steinau; they were divorced in 1970, and in 1979 he married Alida Carolyn Fechner. He has two children by his first marriage, Jody Simone and Malcolm Coltrane, and a step-daughter, Elena Milad, and a son, David Julius, by his second.

Lester has had a varied career as a professional musician, radio-show host and producer, novelist, writer of children's books, and academic. His book *Look Out Whitey! Black Power's Gon' Get Your Mama!* (1968) was one of the more well-known expressions of the black power movement of the 1960s. In the 1980s Julius Lester converted to Judaism, and his writings of particular interest to readers of Jewish literature are on relations between African Americans and the Jewish community.

Lester has made recordings of songs with Pete Seeger, has performed at the Newport Folk Festival, and was a talk-show host on WBAI in New York City as well as of "Free Time," a live television program on WNET. He was Professor of Afro-American Studies at the University of Massachusetts, Amherst, from 1971 to 1988 and has been Professor of Near Eastern and Judaic Studies there since 1982. He has also held posts at the Institute for Advanced Studies in Humanities, the New School for Social Research, and Vanderbilt University.

Among his many honors are a Newbery Honor Book citation and several Lewis Carroll Shelf Awards, a National Book Award finalist (1973), and numerous awards for outstanding teaching. The bulk of his writings are children's books, the best-known among them being *To Be a Slave* (1969), for which he received the Newbery citation, *The Tales of Uncle Remus* in three volumes (1987, 1988, 1990), and studies on African-American history.

MAJOR WORKS AND THEMES

Lester has been a particularly prolific writer in the area of children's literature with African-American content. In addition to *To Be a Slave* and the *Uncle Remus* tales, he has compiled *The Knee-High Man and Other Tales* (1972), six black folktales, and has also written a number of studies of the African-American experience in *Long Journey Home* (1972), which was a finalist for the National Book Award, *Two Love Stories* (1972), and *This Strange New Feeling* (1982).

The work that Lester has done in the area of the troubled relationship between the African-American and Jewish communities, however, makes him unique in Jewish-American literature. Lester's second autobiography, *Lovesong: Becoming a Jew* (1988), about his conversion to Judaism, provides a valuable insight into the views of a sensitive and highly knowledgeable writer who has seen both sides of the issues between blacks and Jews, for Lester's personal life seems to be the embodiment of his view of literature: a series of controversies.

In 1968, as host to a talk show on WBAI in New York City during the controversial teachers' strike concerning community control in Ocean Hill/Brownsville in Brooklyn, Lester permitted some of the black students and an involved teacher to read anti-Semitic poetry over the air. His earlier career as a civil rights activist and associate of Stokely Carmichael in the Student Nonviolent Coordinating Committee (SNCC) was controversial as well, particularly with the publication of *Look Out Whitey!* During his academic career at Amherst, he has also been embroiled in controversy, being criticized by black faculty members of the Afro-American Studies Department for his stand on the dismissal of Andrew Young as U.N. ambassador after he spoke to the PLO and his position criticizing guest instructor James Baldwin for "anti-semitic" [*sic*] remarks. As a result of these and other issues, Lester left the Department of Afro-American Studies while retaining his position in Near Eastern and Judaic Studies. In a collection of essays, *Falling Pieces of a Broken Sky* (1990), Lester asserts, according to Leigh Donaldson, "that ethnicity is insufficient for uniting people. [Lester]'s still interested in that 'universal ground' so many of us have trouble finding in either ourselves or others" (25).

CRITICAL RECEPTION

Of particular interest to readers of this volume would be the reception of *Lovesong: Becoming a Jew*. In her review in *Jewish Currents*, Cheryl Greenberg considered it "an extraordinary book" (12) and wondered, considering the many turns of Lester's life that are apparently contradictory, "Perhaps his passionate commitment to Judaism is an attempt to grapple with the contradictions that make him up'' (14). Most of his earlier work speaks for itself in terms of both recognition and controversy. In his review of *Black Folktales*, John A. Williams wrote in the *New York Times Book Review*: ''It is a tribute to the universality of these tales—and Lester's ability to see it—that we are thus presented with old truths dressed for today'' (quoted in *Something about the Author*, 161).

Perhaps it is just this capacity of Lester to see the universality in contradictions that makes his view of the contradictions of his own life comprehensible to him by developing a unified vision. As he himself said in an address he delivered at a meeting of the National Executive Committee of the Anti-Defamation League of B'nai B'rith in 1992, ''Perhaps it is time we stopped speaking of a Black problem and began talking about an American problem'' (''A Report on Black Anti-Semitism,'' 8).

BIBLIOGRAPHY

Works by Julius Lester

The Angry Children of Malcolm X. Southern Student Organizing Committee, 1966.
The Mud of Vietnam: Photographs and Poems. Berkeley, CA: Folklore Press, 1967.
Look Out Whitey! Black Power's Gon' Get Your Mama! New York: Dial, 1968.
Black Folktales. Illus. by Tom Feelings. New York: R.W. Baron, 1969.
Revolutionary Notes. New York: Grove Press, 1969.
Search for the New Land: History as Subjective Experience. New York: Dial, 1969.
To Be a Slave. Illus. by Tom Feelings. New York: Dial, 1968.
(Editor) *The Seventh Son: The Thoughts and Writings of W.E.B. Du Bois*. 2 vols. New
     York: Random House, 1971.
The Knee-high Man and Other Tales. Illus. Ralph Pinto. New York: Dial, 1972.
Long Journey Home: Stories from Black History. New York: Dial, 1972.
Two Love Stories. New York: Dial, 1972.
(Editor) Crouch, Stanley. *Ain't No Ambulances for No Nigguhs Tonight* (poems). Laguna
     Beach, CA: Baron, 1972.
All Is Well: An Autobiography. New York: Morrow, 1976.
This Strange New Feeling, (short stories). New York: Dial, 1982.
Do Lord Remember Me. New York: Holt, Rinehart and Winston, 1984.
The Tales of Uncle Remus. 4 vols. Illus. Jerry Pinkney. New York: Dial Books, 1987.
Lovesong: Becoming a Jew. New York: Holt, 1988.
Falling Pieces of a Broken Sky. New York: Arcade, 1990.
''The Outsiders: Blacks and Jews and the Soul of America.'' *Transition* 68 (Dec. 1995):
     66–86.

Works Cited and Studies of Julius Lester

Donaldson, Leigh. ''To Be Black and Jewish: The Conversion of Julius Lester.'' *Mid-
     stream* 39 (November 1993): 23–25.

Greenberg, Cheryl. Review of *Lovesong: Becoming a Jew. Jewish Currents*, February 1989, 12–15.

Lester, Julius. "A Report on Black Anti-Semitism." *Jewish Currents*, May 1992, 5–9.

For further information about Julius Lester, consult *Something About the Author* 74. Detroit: Gale, 1994.

MEYER LEVIN (1905–1981)

Mashey Bernstein

BIOGRAPHY

Meyer Levin, the child of Eastern European parents, Joseph and Goldie Batiste Levin, was born on October 5, 1905, in Chicago, where he was raised. He began his career as a reporter for the *Chicago Daily News* in 1923 while he was still a student at the University of Chicago. He graduated in 1924. A trip through Europe and Palestine the following year helped forge many of the ideas and concepts that were to stay with him all his life. In Europe he met the artists Marek Szwarc and his daughter Tereska, who would later become his second wife. In the Szwarc circle he began to change his ideas about his religion. Hitherto he had felt that religion would be a negative factor in his chosen career, but now he began to realize that it had much to offer him. He began to explore his Jewish roots and to look for a way by which to fuse its lessons with his art meaningfully. This newfound feeling was cemented further by his visit to Palestine, where he covered the opening of the Hebrew University and worked for the Jewish Telegraphic Agency. He returned to the United States but decided to try and settle in Palestine. In 1929 he joined Kibbutz Yagar near Haifa. About this time, his first novel, *Reporter*, based on his experiences as a journalist in Chicago, was published; however, it was withdrawn shortly after publication under threat of a libel suit by a newspaperwoman who believed that Levin had used her as a model for one of the characters. Nonetheless, Levin now returned to the United States to concentrate on a literary career. After two more novels, he published *The Golden Mountain* (1932), a retelling of the legendary tales of the founder of the Hasidic movement, the Baal Shem Tov. In this collection he gave expression to another of his primary interests, the mystical elements of Hasidism, which heightened his already-growing sense of positive identification with Jews as a people. Thus the die was cast for his future career, in which he vacillated between his home in Israel and frequent visits to America. He finally settled permanently in Israel in 1958. If physically Levin constantly journeyed between America and Palestine/Israel, spiritually he also moved back and forth from the gritty realism of Chicago to the magical aspirations of the Hasidic movement. His subsequent career was punctuated by controversy and success.

Among the most critical times for Levin, on the personal as well as the universal fronts, was the period of the 1940s and 1950s. With the outbreak of World War II, Levin joined the Office of War Information, worked on films in the United States and England, and also served with the Psychological War Division in France. He accompanied American forces in their liberation of Europe and the concentration camps, visiting Buchenwald, Dachau, and Theresienstadt. After the war, he covered the plight of the Jewish illegals who attempted to enter Palestine in the face of British opposition and witnessed Israel's War of Independence.

The decade of the 1950s produced a major event in Levin's personal life and one that would haunt him for years: the trial over his dramatization of *The Diary of Anne Frank*. Levin's wife, Tereska, discovered a French edition of the diary and showed it to her husband, who arranged to have it published in America. His review of it in the *New York Times Book Review* played a large part in its gaining attention and acclaim. Levin had plans to turn the book into a play and wrote a draft that was accepted by the Broadway producer Cheryl Crawford. Crawford showed Levin's version to the playwright Lillian Hellman, who felt that the play was "unactable." She suggested that the husband-and-wife writing team of Frances Goodrich and Albert Hackett could produce a better version. Crawford followed her advice, and Goodrich and Hackett wrote a version that went on to become a great success.

Levin, bitter at the way he had been treated, sued the successful playwrights, along with Anne's father Otto and Broadway producer Kermit Bloomgarden. He felt that the Broadway version had appropriated much of his material and was not faithful to the Jewish ideas and feelings in the original. After years of litigation, he won a pyrrhic victory. He was awarded a sum in damages and agreed not to have his version produced. Levin never got over his sense of having been wronged and never reconciled himself to this defeat. (In more recent years, his version has been produced in Israel and elsewhere.) Levin went on to describe the events and the characters involved in his novel *The Fanatic* (1964) and more openly in his autobiography *The Obsession* (1976). A more objective accounting of the case can be found in Lawrence Graver's recent work on Levin.

The defeat occurred at the same time that Levin was to achieve his greatest success, the publication of *Compulsion* (1956). He published more than a dozen novels and numerous other works, including film documentaries. He died in Israel in 1981.

MAJOR WORKS AND THEMES

Although Levin was a writer on the American Jewish scene for over fifty years, he never received the kind of critical or popular acclaim bestowed on many of his contemporaries. Despite this fact, Levin was a consistent writer who produced a wide variety of works touching on almost every aspect of Jewish and American Jewish life in the twentieth century. He examined everything from ancient Hasidic tales to the creation of the State of Israel. He was also one of the first writers to deal with the Holocaust. He did not write as an outsider or as a voyeur, but as one who had fully absorbed the history and experiences of the Jewish people.

Nonetheless, his novels failed to capture the imagination of the public or the approval of the critics. One reason for the public's lack of interest may have been that stylistically Levin never escaped his days as a newspaper reporter, and his prose style has a certain Dreiseresque flooding of detail and verisimilitude that lacks the spark of real imagination. Overall, he wrote in a realistic quasi-documentary style with a highly moralistic frame of reference. Thus his characters, especially his Jewish characters, are presented in affirmative and optimistic tones and lack the more universal implications that Saul Bellow, Bernard Malamud, and others of their ilk were able to elicit from their Jewish backgrounds.

This departure from the popular image was deliberate on Levin's part. He eschewed the portrait of the Jew popularized by Yiddish writers of earlier generations and again by his contemporaries, the concept of the schlemiel, the pathetic underdog of the ghetto, or the idea of the Jew as some kind of universal existential man. Instead, he created a Jew who paralleled the type of Jew that the State of Israel was in the process of creating when he visited there in 1925. He found in Israel a Jew free from the shackles of the past, able to escape negativity and even shame, and affirming his Jewishness in positive and inspiring ways. He chose, therefore, Ari Ben Canaan over Moses Herzog. In his autobiography *In Search* (1950), Levin stated as his credo that he could accept the messianic idea so long as he could embody it ''in the people'' instead of an individual Messiah. For Levin, the creation of the State of Israel and ''the example of Jewish history . . . can give courage to all humanity.'' This thesis permeated his entire oeuvre.

Following *Reporter* (1929), Levin wrote a love story, *Frankie and Johnnie* (1930), also based in Chicago, which was unsuccessful. He then, as was to be his pattern, turned to Palestine for his inspiration and wrote *Yehuda* (1931). Based on his intimate knowledge and understanding of kibbutz life, this work, one of the first to deal with this way of life, examines the struggle a violinist faces when he feels torn between an artistic career and working for his kibbutz.

Levin's next novel, following a pattern now evolving, concerns life in a big city in America, in this case, New York: *The New Bridge* (1933). This story, divided into two parts, takes place over a twenty-four-hour period and deals with the eviction of a family from a building. In resisting the eviction, a boy is killed. In the second part, the tenants capture and try the police and marshal to fix responsibility for the killing.

After reporting from the Loyalist side in the Spanish Civil War, Levin produced a work that must be considered among his most significant, the novel *The Old Bunch* (1937). Levin returned to the Chicago slums of his childhood in a broad and comprehensive novel that has its roots in Dos Passos and the proletarian novels of the era. It depicts the lives of a dozen Jewish boys and girls from 1921 until the Century of Progress World's Fair in 1934. Each of these youths, different from one another in emotional makeup, ultimately meets diverse career goals, but none are able to escape their Jewishness and their Americanness. Levin's next novel, *Citizens* (1940), a fictionalized account of the slaying of ten steel-mill strikers in Chicago on Memorial Day 1937, when the police prevented the striking workers from establishing a picket line in front of the plant, shows Levin at his forte as a reporter in full command of his faculties. His novel *My Father's House* (1947) covers both the Holocaust and the efforts of Jews to enter Palestine.

In 1957 came Levin's greatest triumph, *Compulsion*, a roman à clef based on the 1924 Leopold and Loeb abduction and murder of Bobby Franks, a case that rocked not only Chicago and America but Jews worldwide since the perpetrators and victim were Jews from one of Chicago's richest neighborhoods. Levin divided the book into two main sections: the first part probes deeply into the psychological aspects of the crime, while the second is devoted to the trial. The novel was turned into an acclaimed motion picture.

Levin's next novel, *Eva* (1959), told the story of a young girl living through the horrors of World War II and the concentration camps. The similarity to the plight of Anne Frank was all too obvious, and the novel pales in comparison. He returned to the topic in *The Stronghold* (1965).

Levin's last works concentrated on life in Israel. The comic novel *Gore and Igor* (1968) details the story of a Californian, Gore, and a Russian, Igor, who end up fighting in Israel during the Six-Day War. *The Settlers* (1972) and its sequel *The Harvest* (1978) deal with the early settlement in Israel, the first book interweaves the adventures of a large Russian immigrant family, the Chaimovitches, with the events of the era that saw the triumph of the first agricultural settlements, while the second continues the history up to Israel's independence.

Levin's final novel, *The Architect* (1981), reveals a complete change in subject matter and style. Once again, Levin returns to his native Chicago and recounts the rise to fame of one Andrew Lane (a thinly disguised Frank Lloyd Wright) to the point where personal scandal and tragedy mark an end to the early phase of his career. The novel is free of the moralizing and turgid prose style that marred so much of his work, appears devoid of anger and spite, and is so ripe in imagination that it makes a perfect swan song to a life devoted to writing and creativity.

CRITICAL RECEPTION

In his review of *Citizens*, James T. Farrell summed up the strengths and weaknesses of Levin as a novelist in criticism that remained valid for most of his career: "In his general narrative, Mr. Levin writes in a manner similar to Sinclair Lewis, except that he lacks Lewis' pungency when Lewis is at his best. Mr. Levin sees details with a reportorial eye: he seems to have that dictator's view of characters and moments which is characteristic of the reporter. His style is that of a competent journalist. At times, however, one feels as if one were reading the warmed-over headlines of yesterday's 'extra' rather than the vivid recreation of characters and events which one expects to find in the pages of an admittedly realistic novel" (11). For these reasons, few of Levin's works escaped the critics' scalpels.

Frankie and Johnnie was reviewed by Theodore Purdy in the *Saturday Review of Literature* as a "bleak and uncomfortably fleshy tale, unleavened by pity or tenderness. . . . [It] succeeds rather in disgusting the reader than in moving him to pity" (992). *Yehuda* was received well by the critics, including Lionel Trilling in the *Nation*, who praised Levin's ironic realism (684).

Critics of *The New Bridge* praised the first section but were less pleased with the second. One critic noted that it reminded him of "a play rather than a novel" (*Boston Transcript*, 1). While *The Old Bunch* received high praise, the novel was not without its detractors who felt that it was cumbersome and without dramatic conflict. As Philip Rahv commented in the *Nation*, "Though written with complete sincerity and in a language whose color and association keep pace with the movement of events, the novel's comprehensiveness and fidelity of social observation do not wholly make up for its lack of tension" (384).

Even though reviewers took exception to the sexual and scatological content of *Compulsion*, as well as its graphic language, the acclaim was universal. Rose Feld in the *New York Herald Tribune* compared it to Dreiser's *An American Tragedy* (5), while E. S. Gardner in the *New York Times* called it a "masterly achievement in literary craftsmanship" (7). Levin was not to receive such unqualified praise again.

Rose Feld in the *New York Herald Tribune* called *Eva* a "thin ersatz" of the actual material contained in the Nuremberg trials and other documentary works that appeared contemporaneously, such as Leon Uris's *Exodus* (10). Others were even less kind, calling it "propaganda rather than literature" (Laski, 13) and "drab" (Burkham, 4). Feld summed up the problem succinctly: "The survival of individuals masks the multitudes who perish. Survival is a happy ending but I am not sure that the final response to it is a satisfactory one. Tragedy so massive is better expressed by an Anne Frank than an Eva, finally a happy mother in Israel" (10).

Levin's next work on the Holocaust, *The Stronghold*, fared slightly better, with one reviewer calling it a "passionately moral book" (*Saturday Review of Literature*, 33). *The Settlers* and its sequel *The Harvest* met with generally poor reviews. Irving Halperin in *Studies in American-Jewish Literature* noted, "It may be that [the novels] will retain some value as historical documents. But, despite Mr. Levin's energy and ambitiousness, their pretense as fiction is thin and uninteresting" (97). Levin's attempts, however, at expressing the reactions of Jewish Americans to such events as the Holocaust and the creation of the State of Israel, and, of course, his popular success, *Compulsion*, have given him a place in the canon of Jewish-American literature.

BIBLIOGRAPHY

Works by Meyer Levin

Novels

Reporter. New York: Day, 1929.
Frankie and Johnnie: A Love Story. New York: Day, 1930. Revised as *The Young Lovers*. New York: New American Library, 1952.
Yehudah. New York: Cape and Smith, 1931.
The New Bridge. New York: Covici Friede, 1933.
The Old Bunch. New York: Viking, 1937.
Citizens. New York: Viking, 1940.
My Father's House. New York: Viking, 1947.
Compulsion. New York: Simon and Schuster, 1956.
Eva. New York: Simon and Schuster, 1959.
The Fanatic. New York: Simon and Schuster, 1964.
The Stronghold. New York: Simon and Schuster, 1965.
Gore and Igor: An Extravaganza. New York: Simon and Schuster, 1968.
The Settlers. New York: Simon and Schuster, 1972.
The Harvest. New York: Simon and Schuster, 1978.
The Architect. New York: Simon and Schuster, 1981.

Other Works

The Golden Mountain. New York: Cape and Ballou, 1932. Reprinted as *Classic Hassidic Tales*. New York: Citadel, 1966.
In Search: An Autobiography. New York: Horizon, 1950.
The Story of Israel. New York: Putnam's, 1966.
The Obsession. New York: Simon and Schuster, 1973.

Works Cited and Studies of Meyer Levin

Burkham, John. Review of *Eva*. *New York Times Book Review*, August 23, 1959, 4.
Farrell, James T. Review of *Citizens*. *Saturday Review of Literature*, March 30, 1940, 11.
Feld, Rose. Review of *Compulsion*. *New York Herald Tribune Book Review*, October 28, 1956, 5.
———. Review of *Eva*. *New York Herald Tribune*, August 30, 1959, 10.

Gardner, E. S. Review of *Compulsion*. *New York Times Book Review*, October 28, 1956, 7.

Graver, Lawrence. *An Obsession with Anne Frank: Meyer Levin and the Diary*. Berkeley: University of California Press, 1995.

Halperin, Irving. *Studies in American Jewish Literature* 2 (1982): 197.

Laski, Marghanita. Review of *Eva*. *Saturday Review of Literature*, August 29, 1959, 13–14.

Liptzin, Sol. *The Jew in American Literature*. New York: Bloch, 1966, 218–21.

Review of *The New Bridge*. *Boston Transcript*, March 1, 1933, 1.

Purdy, Theodore. Review of *Frankie and Johnnie*. *Saturday Review of Literature*, April 26, 1930, 992.

Rahv, Philip. Review of *The Old Bunch*. *Nation*, April 3, 1937, 384.

Review of *The Stronghold*. *Saturday Review of Literature*, November 6, 1965, 33.

Trilling, Lionel. Review of *Yehuda*. *Nation*, January 24, 1931, 684.

Varon, Benno Weiser. "The Haunting of Meyer Levin." *Midstream* 22 (1976): 7–23.

PHILLIP LOPATE

(1943–   )

Diane Stevenson

BIOGRAPHY

Phillip Lopate was born on November 16, 1943, in Brooklyn, New York. In 1964 he graduated from Columbia College. Between 1971 and 1980 he was Project Director of Teachers and Writers Collaborative in New York City. *Being with Children* was published in 1975; *Journal of a Living Experiment* was published in 1979. The first is a pedagogic memoir; the second is a documentary history. Both came out of his experience as an early and influential member of the writer-in-the-schools movement. Later he moved from teaching elementary-school children to teaching college students. He was Associate Professor of English at the University of Houston from 1980 to 1988. At present he is Adams Chair Professor at Hofstra University.

Lopate has published two collections of poetry: *The Eyes Don't Always Want to Stay Open* (1972) and *The Daily Round* (1976). These poems are confessional, but not in the way one usually thinks of confessional poetry, as almost involuntary public utterances, propelled by deep psychic need, agitated and even shrill—Sylvia Plath or the more courtly, though no less agitated, John Berryman come to mind. The poems of Phillip Lopate are confessional in another way. His revelations are casual, mundane, and rendered in an ordinary speaking voice. Their effect is comic rather than tragic, petty rather than grand, and the pleasure we take in them is the same pleasure we take in good gossip, epiphanies, if you will, that leave us sturdier on our feet. The poet appeals to our recognition of common ethical raggedness. In Kenneth Burke's sense, Phillip Lopate is a debunker.

What is true of Lopate's poetry is also true of his two novels. His first novel, *Confessions of Summer* (1979), bears witness in its title to just such a continuity.

His second, *The Rug Merchant* (1987), drops the first-person narrator of *Confessions* but keeps the same emotional revelation. In fact, this second novel can be seen as a companion novel to the first. Its protagonist, Cyrus, is the other side of *Confession*'s narrator, Eric: he is meditative rather than manic, outward rather than inward.

But it is above all the essays that take the voice of the poems and run with its possibilities. What was casual and at the same time confessional reaches full fruition there. *The Art of the Personal Essay*, an anthology edited and introduced by Lopate, was an unexpected success in 1994—unexpected, that is, by those who believed the essay to be a dead and buried literary genre. With its publication Lopate became firmly established as a champion of the personal essay. Two collections of his own essays had already appeared: *Bachelorhood* in 1981 and *Against Joie de Vivre* in 1989. A third collection, *Portrait of My Body*, appeared in 1996, and beginning in 1997 he will edit for Doubleday/Anchor an annual volume, *Best Essays of the Year*.

In 1978 Phillip Lopate received a National Endowment for the Arts grant for critical writing; in 1985 a National Endowment for the Arts grant for fiction; and in 1988 a Guggenheim Foundation Fellowship. He has been a member of the Pulitzer Prize committee in poetry (1984–1985); the National Book Award panel in fiction (1990); and a member of the New York Film Festival selection committee (1988–1991).

MAJOR WORKS AND THEMES

Phillip Lopate grew up in a working-class neighborhood. He went off to college in the 1960s, and this meant a move from Brooklyn to Manhattan, from one class into the precincts of another. Privilege at Columbia College may not be stamped in the same way as it is at Princeton or Yale or Harvard; the energies of the great port city include the energies of its immigrants, and these are not to be denied even within the precincts of an Ivy League institution. Yet at Columbia privilege is nonetheless inescapable; the confidence and complacency of a ruling class leave an indelible mark on the place, a mark the outsider feels. This was a difficult time for Phillip Lopate, but a time of triumphs, too—the merit boy makes good. With graduation, however, the triumphs came to an end. A bigger and less rarefied, less immediately rewarding world beckoned (where paychecks and not grades mattered). This fall from grace and the immediate aftermath is the moment that opens *Confessions of Summer*. The book's narrator, Eric, like its author, is working-class and a graduate of an elite school. Graduation has left him in limbo, experiencing a kind of down, a slump, a depression. The novel begins:

It was a period of my life I am not particularly proud of. It happened before the era of accomplishment. I had not yet become the hero of my life, nor was I even its villain. I was twenty-six, a graduate of a prestige college, believing that I was meant to lead and not take orders—a belief which in no way was shared by those who employed me. Powerlessness gave life a peculiarly iodized taste, like mercurochrome: it seemed to me that before I could enjoy to the full a sunset, a love affair, drunken nights, the so-called pleasures of youth, I would have to get this taste of powerlessness out of my mouth.

Eric's best friend at college had been Jack. Jack's transition into the adult world of careers is going more smoothly than Eric's. He lives on Park Avenue; he travels in a circle of success that takes his own for granted. He is up-and-coming, but not exactly on his own momentum. Eric is the one Jack's girlfriend Marie considers manly and decisive, the one she pictures in the driver's seat. This is the story of a triangle. Marie is caught between Jack and Eric, between the two poles of outward success and inward drive, or, more bluntly, between the privileged classes and the working classes as represented by the two men. She has in common with Eric that both are Jewish; she shares with Jack that both have money.

She is Jack's girl, but Jack drives a hard bargain. When he goes to California to track down a story he is writing for a magazine, he shacks up with a woman out there, as is his wont. He even gets a venereal disease he uses as an excuse to extend his stay: he's taking the cure; he won't be up for sex; Marie will have to wait. Marie is supposed to put up with this. She is supposed to accept who he is and what he does: like a mainstay or like a mother doling out unconditional love? Marie isn't quite up to it. Underneath her precocious sophistication, she is truly naive. So, when Jack fails her, Eric rushes in, again and again. Each time Marie drops him, he wonders why it is that she inevitably chooses Jack over him. Marie's dilemma, her recurrent indecision, is not cynical or made-up. If it were, perhaps the signals would be clearer and Eric would cease to be haunted by her. But she responds authentically to the two different men and to their real differences. What Marie has to offer Eric is the "magic" of their compatibility and the uncanny grace of their communication. This keeps him hooked.

At one point in *Confessions of Summer* Marie reproaches Eric for always bringing up class when they're together. She senses resentment or reproach. What place does that resentment have in their relationship? she seems to be asking. Class counts when you don't have it, his rejoinder goes; money means when it's not yours. But Marie is right: Eric is enacting a social configuration as well as a sexual one, and he doesn't quite recognize what he is doing. The Oedipal configuration is the one he thinks he may be enacting with Marie— killing the father, killing Jack—or maybe he's involved in that other Freudian paradigm: two men sharing a woman who represents their homosexual desires. He speculates about both motives but significantly not about the class motive. He doesn't want to see Marie as a social validation he seeks, as his way of taking on his best friend's social terms; he prefers to disguise his social ambitions in sexual terms. Something over and above romantic desire is at work, and Marie tentatively associates whatever this is with embarrassments of class. Eric is right to bring up class, but because he doesn't get the added weight that class is carrying for him, he can't adequately take into account Marie's concern. Still, class cannot be brushed aside or made to disappear simply by waving the magic wand of intimacy.

In *The Rug Merchant* class difference is embodied in the very concrete of the city itself. A neighborhood is changing. Its older middle-class tenants and the businesses they patronize are being supplanted by a newer Yuppie constituency, a change the rug merchant Cyrus must face and can't. He was content with an older, more casual way of doing business, but now he is being forced to up his profits by a new landlord who wants to up his and who raises Cyrus's rent, so that, in a kind of imposed trickle-down economics, Cyrus can no longer be satisfied with the income that he had been satisfied with before. He is the opposite of Eric in the energies he can muster. He is meditative, reticent, and withdrawing. A graduate, too, of an elite college, he gives up graduate studies because he anticipates that his scholarly endeavors will never rank with the best. He remains an amateur, scribbling away in his shop, which he uses as a shield against the world. Few customers distract him. His store is his retreat.

The gentrification of his neighborhood means an accelerated pace Cyrus does not wish to gear up to. Eventually, he abandons his business and joins his brother's. He loses his own shop and he loses the Zoroastrian girl his mother had wanted for him in an attempt to bring him back safely into the ethnic fold. Both losses are the result of his lack of momentum. Meanwhile, he remembers an old girlfriend whose sleepy lovemaking reminded him of death—another passivity—and he fantasizes a woman he met at a sex club. This encounter, too, had echoes of retreat and surrender. Cyrus is something of a scholar and a hermit. He has tried to make solitude the place of identity and wholeness.

This brings us back to *Confessions of Summer*. Eric is the opposite of passive. His affair with Marie was a matter of assertion from the outset. If anything, he fears stasis. The only abeyance he appears to countenance is the abeyance of intimacy—that empathy that he establishes with Marie, the "magic" they share. In a way, Eric has sacrificed the singular communion he shared with Jack for communion with Jack's girl.

Confessions of Summer is the story of a triangle, the story of class humiliations experienced as sexual humiliations. The coincidence of the two is not new to fiction. The adulteries of Julien Sorel and Jay Gatsby and of Anna Karenina and Emma Bovary are fraught with the tensions of class. Their sexual transgressions are bound up with social ambitions, and each pays for the sexual and social mobility he or she asserts. There is an ambiguity at the center of these stories: is the transgression primarily social or sexual? Whatever the answer, Lopate's novel stands in this tradition, one in which the pressures and embarrassments of class are a central theme.

The rise of the novel as a literary form is bound up with the rise of the bourgeoisie as a social class. The bourgeoisie likes to represent its own rise as the individual's rise in life. That is the story the novel so often tells: the story of the parvenu, the social climber, Julien Sorel or Jay Gatsby or Martin Eden in Jack London's novel of that title. Eric in *Confessions of Summer* gives a new twist to the novelistic tradition of the parvenu protagonist: he is the parvenu who has lost confidence in what he is seeking.

In America the story of the parvenu has been recast as the American Dream. It is the American Dream to rise, and those at the top at one time or another had a family member wildly successful at the game of social mobility. America is a nation of parvenus. But what happens when status appears to make the man rather than the man his status? What happens when the idea of excellence is viewed more cynically, when we lose the kind of confidence in his own genius that sent Jack London's Martin Eden on his rise from working-class origins to the top of the world, sure that the top was made for men like him? What happens, in short, when something like an upper-middle-class ethic replaces a middle-class one? What happens when a working-class boy smacks up against the complacencies of the rich without the romantic's rock, his genius, to stand on? For all that Eric appears to stand there, that rock is turning to sand. He has become the superfluous man of Russian fiction.

Cyrus, the rug merchant, doesn't believe in his own genius and gives up his studies. Eric does believe in his own genius, but he doesn't quite believe in success, certainly not commercial success—the very trap he finds his once-brilliant friend Jack falling into. For isn't Jack's commercial success dependent on how much brilliance he's willing to squander? What if "genius" is the thing merit boys stack up against the gentlemen's Cs of the privileged class, and it doesn't really even out the playing field? Is genius, then, just a democratic mirage?

Unlike Jack London's Martin Eden, Eric doesn't finally believe in where he is going. He is a social climber who no longer believes that there is a place to climb to that means anything. Julien Sorel was the social climber punished for his transgression and put to death by society. Martin Eden dies by his own hand: he is a social climber who gets to the top and finds that it's not what he expected. Eric is the social climber who has lost faith in the top before he even gets there, the social climber with no great expectations.

Unlike Martin Eden, Eric will not end up a suicide. Death is too old-fashioned a fate. He may even end up a success. Whatever the outcome, Eric's road to success, like Cyrus's path to failure, manifests class tensions seething under the surface of American society, class tensions that are implicit in the American Dream but that Americans almost never face straight on, and Phillip Lopate's novels do this at a moment when it is unfashionable even to invoke that dream at all.

CRITICAL RECEPTION

In describing Lopate's book of poetry *The Daily Round*, Hayden Carruth said, "The daily round is exactly what he writes about, and a damned, dull, dreadful, despairing round it is too, most of the time. Oh, occasionally, a tentative cheer for the sunset in the park, a dry exclamation at the sight of a girl with her jeans off; sometimes there's even a gasp of refreshing radical anger. But the prevailing tone is melancholy: specifically, the melancholy of New York'' (15). What is true of the poetry is as true of the novels, and as his reviewers have many times pointed out, Lopate's subject is as much the city as the self. ''The Self is the unit upon which it all rests, an accepting, humane, realistic self,'' wrote Aram Saroyan about the same book of poetry (27). Saroyan continued, ''The life in it need not be extravagant in display. It's on-going, a fact, and this is Lopate's real celebration, the life that he is simply given.'' Again this statement applies as well to the novels.

Lopate's attention to the daily—the way that dailiness is inscribed on an urban landscape or on an urban dweller—and the very detail with which that dailiness is reported has impressed his reviewers. The mere fact that his characters have jobs and go to work, and that this work is an important fact of their lives, not something cordoned off from the rest of emotional existence, is an aspect of his portrayal of ordinariness that is often remarked on. The details count in his work. As Carruth said, ''He can pin down quantities of metaphysical horror in one observed fragment'' (15). To filter the ordinary through the consciousness of a character in order to reveal sensibility is common practice in novels. What is special about Lopate's novels is the way they have the ordinary shade into the strange, the way their observations of the everyday, transformed by the sensibility of the character into surprising epiphanies of recognition, bring home to us the very strangeness of the city—the strangeness we take for granted, our own and other people's. It is this dual subject, the city and the self, that has attracted the most comment from Lopate's critics.

BIBLIOGRAPHY

Works by Phillip Lopate

Poetry

The Eyes Don't Always Want to Stay Open. Kissimmee, FL: Sun Press, 1972.
The Daily Round. Kissimmee, FL: Sun Press, 1976.
Bachelorhood (essays, stories, and poems). Boston: Little, Brown, 1981.

Novels

Confessions of Summer. Garden City, NY: Doubleday, 1979.
The Rug Merchant. New York: Viking Press, 1987.

Other Works

Being with Children. Garden City, NY: Doubleday, 1975.
Journal of a Living Experiment. New York: Virgil Press, 1979.
Against Joie de Vivre. New York: Poseidon/Simon and Schuster, 1989.

(Editor) *The Art of the Personal Essay.* New York: Doubleday/Anchor, 1994.
Portrait of My Body. New York: Doubleday/Anchor, 1996.

Works Cited and Studies of Phillip Lopate

Carruth, Hayden. Review of *The Daily Round. New York Times Book Review*, August 7, 1977, 15.
Saroyan, Aram. Review of *The Daily Round. Village Voice*, January 24, 1977, 27.

NORMAN MAILER

(1923–)

Eberhard Alsen

BIOGRAPHY

Norman Mailer was born on January 31, 1923, in Long Branch, New Jersey. His parents were Isaac Barnet Mailer and Fanny Schneider. His father worked sporadically as an accountant, and his mother ran Sunlight Oil, a small business purveying oil to bakeries and food-processing companies. The family moved to Brooklyn in 1927, where Norman turned out to be one of the best students at Boys' High School. He began to write fiction at the age of seven and even wrote a science-fiction novel while still in high school. He was bar mitzvahed at the Shaare Tzaddik temple on Eastern Parkway, and on that occasion he demonstrated his precociousness by giving not only the standard speech but also a second one on the philosopher Spinoza.

Entering Harvard University at the age of sixteen, Norman was determined to become a professional writer, but he majored in engineering, not in English, and he was never tempted to make the switch. As he later explained, "If I stayed with engineering I'd have more time to write" (Manso, 61). Nevertheless, he took some advanced writing courses, one of them from the poet Robert Hillyer, for whom he wrote a novella, "A Calculus at Heaven," about American soldiers fighting in the Pacific. Mailer later published part of "Calculus" in *Advertisements for Myself*. Mailer wrote constantly while at Harvard, and he published a number of short stories in one of the three student magazines, the *Harvard Advocate*. At the suggestion of one of his writing instructors, he submitted a story called "The Greatest Thing in the World" to the annual short-story contest of *Story* magazine and won first prize. That story is also reprinted in *Advertisements for Myself*.

Mailer's gentile classmates at Harvard remembered that he was "blatantly and abrasively Jewish'' (Mills, 64), and that he insisted on presenting himself as ''a poor Jewish boy from Brooklyn'' (Manso, 62). However, some of his Jewish classmates, who made up about one-fifth of the student population at Harvard, remembered that he had no interest in Judaism and did not observe Jewish holidays. As his Harvard roommate Harold Katz put it, ''Norman was not then an assimilationist, but neither was he a hard-core Jew'' (Mills, 64).

In 1943, Mailer graduated from Harvard cum laude with a B.S. degree in engineering. At that time he conceived of the plan to write the Great American War Novel—for which ''A Calculus at Heaven'' had been an exercise—and he decided that it would be better for him to experience the war in the Pacific than in Europe. He got his wish the next year, shortly after he married Beatrice Silverman, for he was drafted and sent to the Philippines. His experiences as an infantryman on the island of Luzon provided him with the material for what most critics believe to be the best novel to come out of World War II, *The Naked and the Dead* (1948). Mailer was in Paris, taking advantage of the GI Bill to study at the Sorbonne, when he learned of the enthusiastic reception that book reviewers had given that novel. Instantly translated into French, German, and several other languages, *The Naked and the Dead* became a huge financial success both in Europe and in America.

Following the publication of *The Naked and the Dead*, Mailer's career stalled for over a decade. After devoting much time and energy to support the abortive presidential campaign of Henry Wallace, the Progressive Party's candidate, Mailer tried his hand unsuccessfully as a screenwriter for Metro-Goldwyn-Mayer. Back in New York, Mailer published his second novel, begun in Paris. However, *Barbary Shore* (1951) was panned by most reviewers. Then he embarked on the project of writing an eight-part epic about the life of an existential hero, Sergius O'Shaugnessy. He did not complete that project, but out of it came a notorious short story, ''The Time of Her Time,'' not published until 1959, as well as his third novel, *The Deer Park* (1955). Set in a milieu that combines the worst of Hollywood and Las Vegas, *The Deer Park* is a tale about an aspiring novelist and his interaction with movie producers, screenwriters, actresses, prostitutes, and Mafiosi. It received mostly negative reviews.

Mailer restarted his career in 1959, and the 1960s and 1970s became his most productive years. The turning point in Mailer's career was the publication of *Advertisements for Myself* (1959), a collection that included some previously published and unpublished short fiction but consisted mostly of highly opinionated nonfiction. *Advertisements* shows Mailer helping invent what has come to be called ''the New Journalism,'' a kind of writing on the borderline between fiction and reporting in which the writer abandons the journalist's traditional claim of objectivity and concentrates on his own subjective interpretation of events. Mailer published two more novels in the 1960s. Both received mixed reviews, but some critics now consider one of them, *An American Dream* (1965), to be Mailer's best work. Its protagonist is a psychology professor and television personality who struggles to free himself from the clutches of a satanic multimillionaire whose daughter he had married in order to rise to the pinnacle of political power. The other and lesser novel is *Why Are We in Vietnam?* (1967), a rambling first-person narrative by a foul-mouthed young man who, on a hunting trip with his best friend and his millionaire father, discovers his propensities for homosexual rape and murder and decides to indulge these propensities by volunteering for military service in the Vietnam War.

After Mailer published three more volumes of political essays and cultural criticism (*Deaths for the Ladies*, 1962; *The Presidential Papers*, 1963; and *Cannibals and Christians*, 1966), his career hit its second peak with *The Armies of the Night* (1968), a fictionalized account of the October 1967 march on the Pentagon in protest of the Vietnam War. Subtitled *History as a Novel/The Novel as History*, the book defined a new genre and won Mailer his first Pulitzer Prize. When he tried to repeat this success with *Miami and the Siege of Chicago* (1968), an account of the 1968 Republican and Democratic conventions, he did not receive the same positive critical response. In the next decade, Mailer produced a number of additional collections of essays, including one on the American space program, *Of a Fire on the Moon* (1970), as well as a biography of Marilyn Monroe (1973) and a tribute to the fiction of Henry Miller (1976). Moreover, he also wrote a mystery novel, *Maidstone* (1971), and made three films, *Wild 90* (1968), *Beyond the Law* (1970), and *Maidstone* (1971). But it was not until 1979 that he had another great success, the painstakingly researched "true life novel" *The Executioner's Song*, an account of the life and death of convicted murderer Gary Gilmore. For that book, Mailer received his second Pulitzer Prize.

Mailer continued to be productive into the 1980s and 1990s, most of his work being in forms that combine fiction and biography. His collection of essays *Pieces and Pontifications* (1982) is less remarkable than *Of Women and Their Elegance* (1980), a monologue by a fictionalized Marilyn Monroe, written to accompany the photographs of Milton Green. In that monologue, Mailer has Monroe ramble on about topics as diverse as her sex life, her discussions of Plato with her husband Arthur Miller, and her opinions of other Hollywood stars. The book received chiefly negative reviews; so did his very derivative biography *Portrait of Picasso as a Young Man* (1995). However, Mailer had more success with his most recent book, *Oswald's Tale: An American Mystery* (1995). A fictionalized biography of Lee Harvey Oswald, it is as painstakingly researched as *The Executioner's Song* and draws on recently released KGB files and on interviews with Marina Oswald and many others who knew both Marina and Harvey. The book tries to lay to rest the various conspiracy theories concerning the assassination of John F. Kennedy and to explain Oswald's motivation in terms of his desire to have an impact on history. This book has received the best reviews of any of Mailer's works since *The Executioner's Song*.

During the 1980s and 1990s, Mailer also wrote three more novels. The most ambitious of the three is *Ancient Evenings* (1983), which covers four consecutive incarnations of an ancient Egyptian, Menenhetet. The novel develops Mailer's vision of what people's lives and beliefs were like before the dawn of Judaeo-Christian civilization. The second novel is *Tough Guys Don't Dance* (1984), based on a series of unsolved murders in Provincetown, Massachusetts. Mailer later turned it into a movie that he himself directed. Mailer's most recent novel is *Harlot's Ghost* (1991). Dealing with the way in which the CIA has been shaping American foreign policy, *Harlot's Ghost* stands out because of its great length (1310 pages). It is the incomplete life story of the CIA spy master Hugh Tremont Montague, code named Harlot, incomplete because the last words of the novel are "to be continued."

A closing note on Mailer's personal life is in order. Due to his early success, his calculated self-promotion, and the fact that he loves to analyze himself in print, his turbulent personal life has always been public. The most remarkable thing about that life is not his macho posturing—which includes a knife attack that put his second wife in the hospital with multiple stab wounds—nor his sparring, both figurative and literal, with those he disagrees with, but his having turned into a *paterfamilias* who manages to be on mostly good terms with five ex-wives and eight children. Moreover, his twenty-year marriage to Barbara Norris has been happier than any of his five previous ones. Aside from his penthouse apartment in Brooklyn Heights, Norman Mailer maintains homes in Provincetown, Massachusetts, and on Mount Desert Island, Maine.

MAJOR WORKS AND THEMES

The major themes in all nine of Mailer's novels have been those of the quest for power, of violence and sex as therapy, of the battle of the sexes, of the nature of Evil, and of the corruption of American culture and government. From the mid-1960s on, Mailer's fiction became increasingly romantic and mystical, and new themes emerged, such as those of the struggle between God and the Devil, of magic and the supernatural, and of karma and reincarnation.

Over the years, Mailer's worldview has changed more than his themes. Mailer has labeled himself an existentialist, but he has taken care to point out that his brand of "American Existentialism" is radically different from the European variety of such thinkers as Jean-Paul Sartre and Martin Heidegger because it includes a belief in God and in the ability of the human soul "to migrate from body to body, from existence to existence" (*Cannibals and Christians*, 287). Robert Solotaroff has labeled this outlook "romantic existentialism" (98), but most critics dismiss the existentialist label and point out that Mailer's typical outlook is actually a highly idiosyncratic form of Manicheanism laced with doses of the philosophy of Friedrich Nietzsche and the psychology of Wilhelm Reich. As Mailer's preoccupation with metaphysics has become stronger, an increasing number of critics have linked Mailer's vision of life to that of the nineteenth-century romantics. For instance, J. Michael Lennon and Joseph Wenke saw similarities between Mailer's ideas and the transcendentalism of

Ralph Waldo Emerson, while Samuel Coale saw Mailer as indebted to the Manichean outlook of Nathaniel Hawthorne.

Mailer's first novel, *The Naked and the Dead* (1948), does not yet develop his characteristic vision of life, for when he wrote it, his outlook was essentially nihilistic. This nihilism comes out best in the scene in which two soldiers, Goldstein and Ridges, a Jew and a Christian, both lose their belief in God. The two are trying to carry a wounded comrade to safety, but on the third day, the man dies, and on the following day, the men lose his body as they try to cross a torrential stream. Weak with fatigue and hunger, the two come to similar conclusions about the futility of human life. Ridges thinks, "What kind of God could there be who always tricked you in the end? . . . he wept from exhaustion and failure and the shattering naked conviction that nothing mattered." Goldstein's thoughts also turn toward nothingness: "There was nothing in him at the moment, nothing but a vague anger, a deep resentment, and the origins of a vast hopelessness" (531).

However, *The Naked and the Dead* already develops one of Mailer's perennial themes, that of the quest for power. This quest is illustrated in the stories of two Nietzschean characters, General Cummings and Sergeant Croft, who assert their superiority by walking over the corpses of weaker individuals, figuratively and literally. However, in keeping with Mailer's nihilist outlook, both quests come to nothing. General Cummings hopes to distinguish himself in the war so that he may have a shot at the presidency afterwards. When his efforts to take the island of Luzon from the Japanese stall, Cummings leaves the island trying to get navy support for a major attack. During his absence, a random American artillery barrage happens to hit both the headquarters of the Japanese and their major ammunition dump. Thus, under the leadership of the fumbling Major Dalleson, Cummings's second-in-command, the American forces overrun the Japanese and secure the island.

Pure chance also frustrates Sergeant Croft's quest for power. Sent on a reconnaissance mission behind the Japanese lines, Croft faces two challenges to his leadership. One is his superior, Lieutenant Hearn, whom he disposes of by letting him walk into a Japanese ambush. The other challenge is the island's highest mountain, Mount Anaka, which Croft decides to cross because the terrain is so difficult that it is unlikely that there will be any Japanese outposts. The sheer mass of the mountain "inflames" and "taunts" Sergeant Croft, much as Moby Dick had taunted Captain Ahab. But while Croft and his platoon are scaling the mountain, they disturb a hornets' nest. Attacked by the hornets, the men panic, toss away their weapons and equipment, and flee down the jungle-covered mountain. By failing to conquer Mount Anaka and to complete the reconnaissance mission, Croft fails to assert his power over his men and over nature. But as it turns out, the mission was pointless anyway, because while Croft and his platoon were trying to get behind the Japanese lines, the Japanese had been defeated.

In later novels, Mailer develops the theme of the quest for power quite differently because his vision of life was no longer a nihilist one. The shift in Mailer's vision of life occurred sometime in the middle 1950s when evidence of a belief in transcendence began to appear in his writings. We can see the first indications of that shift in his third novel, *The Deer Park* (1955), where Mailer begins to explore the metaphysical dimensions of the twin desires for power and sex. He creates a satanic character named Marion Faye, a gangster whom the narrator describes as "a religious man turned inside out" (147). Because Faye does not believe in the existence of a benevolent God, he wants to prove the existence of an evil one, of the Devil. He thinks he can prove the supreme power of the Devil if he can act out his most vicious power fantasies without being held to account. A pusher of hard drugs and a pimp, Faye claims to find delight in destroying people's lives. At one point, for instance, he talks a girl into committing suicide. But Faye cannot find pleasure in what he is doing, and at one point he prays, "Make me cold, Devil, and I will run the world for you" (331). Faye is not granted his wish. He often feels close to bursting with despair, for he recognizes that "there was no pressure in all the world like the effort to beat off compassion" (154). It is Faye's unsuccessful struggle to free himself from goodness and from God that makes the narrator and protagonist, the aspiring novelist Sergius O'Shaugnessy, question his own atheism.

Looking back on his experiences, particularly on his sexual ones, Sergius O'Shaugnessy concludes the novel by trying to reconcile hedonism and idealism, sex and religion. He says, "If there is a God, and sometimes I believe there is one, I'm sure He says, 'Go on, my boy. I don't know that I can help you, but we wouldn't want all those people to tell you what to do.' There are hours when I would have the arrogance to reply to the Lord Himself, and so I ask, 'Would You agree that sex is where philosophy begins?' " (374–75). These ideas are the germs of the worldview that Mailer developed in his later novels.

Mailer's most representative novel is *An American Dream* (1965). It contains the most explicit expression of his Manichean vision of life and interweaves his major themes better than any of his other novels. The protagonist of the novel is the ex-congressman, university professor, and television personality Stephen Rojack, who describes himself as "half-Jewish." On one of his television shows, Rojack succinctly spells out Mailer's cosmology when he says that "God's engaged in a war with the Devil, and God may lose" (221).

The two major themes of the novel are the interrelated ones of the quest for power and the corruption of American politics. The quest for power is central to the novel, because the protagonist, Rojack, once had the ambition to become President of the United States. This ambition led him to marry Deborah Kelly, the daughter of multimillionaire Barney Oswald Kelly, who has connections to the highest circles of political power. But as the novel begins, Rojack has come to hate Deborah with a passion because she has "occupied [his] center" and dried up all his creative impulses, and he has begun to realize that by marrying Deborah he has made a "devil's contract" (24). The plot of the novel traces Rojack's struggle to extricate himself from this contract. Rojack's feeling that his quest for power has aligned him with the forces of Evil is confirmed in the novel's climactic scene when Barney Oswald Kelly calls himself a "solicitor for the Devil" and tells Rojack that "God and the Devil are very attentive to people at the summit. I don't know if they stir much in the average man's stew ... but do you expect God and the Devil left Lenin and Hitler and Churchill alone?" (230).

Another typical Mailer theme, that of the redemptive nature of violence, is illustrated early in *An American Dream* when Rojack takes the first step in freeing himself from his Devil's contract by strangling Deborah. Just before he snaps Deborah's neck, Rojack has a beatific vision: "Heaven was there, some quiver of jeweled cities shining in the glow of a tropical dusk" (35). After Deborah is dead, Rojack feels "weary with a most honorable fatigue." He even says, "I had not felt so nice since I was twelve" (36). Rojack not only feels purged of his corrosive hate for Deborah, but also realizes that he has now aligned himself against Barney Oswald Kelly and the forces of Evil.

The most notorious scene in *An American Dream* is one that develops another theme that recurs in Mailer's fiction, that of sex as a means of aligning oneself either with the forces of Good or of Evil. In this scene Rojack has sex with Deborah's German maid, Fräulein Ruta, switching back and forth between anal and vaginal penetration, or, as he puts it, "a minute for one, a minute for the other, a raid on the Devil and a trip back to the Lord" (48). Rojack stresses that his anal assault on Ruta is triggered by hate, by his desire to impose his will on Ruta and to "plug a Nazi." As Mailer has explained in various interviews and essays, he sees procreative sex as a means of putting oneself in touch with God and all sexual activity that does not allow for the chance of conception as a way of enhancing the power of the Devil, and in Mailer's view the most evil of all sexual activities is anal sex, particularly when one person forces it upon another in order to assert his power (this is illustrated abundantly in *Ancient Evenings*).

The scene between Rojack and Ruta also foreshadows another recurring theme that Mailer develops later in the novel, that of the corruption of American culture and of the American Dream. That theme is hinted at when Rojack has another vision, an inversion of the heavenly city he saw when he killed Deborah. Just after he ejaculates into Ruta's anus, Rojack sees "a huge city in the desert [where] the colors had the unreal pastel of a plastic and the main street was flaming with light at five A.M." (49). As we find out in the last chapter, this city is Las Vegas, a symbol of what has gone wrong with America. The terms "pastel" and "plastic" are code words for all that is tawdry and unnatural in American culture. In a 1968 interview with Paul Carroll, Mailer defined "plastic" as "a second principle of evil" and "a pervasive substance in the technological world which comes from artificial synthesis rather than from nature" (74). Las Vegas is an unnatural city stamped out of the desert by the Mafia for the exclusive purposes of entertainment and exploitation. It is a plastic place where people go because they think they can achieve the American Dream not with perseverance and hard work but instantly with a roll of the dice. To Rojack it seems that every year America is becoming more like Las Vegas. This is why, at the end of the novel, Rojack leaves the United States and goes to Central America.

None of Mailer's subsequent five novels develops his major themes as clearly as does *An American Dream*. However, *Ancient Evenings* (1983) is notable because it presents in fictionalized form a relatively recent part of Mailer's vision of life, his belief in karma and reincarnation, which he had been mentioning in his essays since the 1970s. Moreover, while in *An American Dream* we can explain away the supernatural elements, in *Ancient Evenings* we have to suspend our disbelief because the plot traces four successive incarnations of the protagonist, and the book abounds with scenes that do not make sense unless we entertain a belief in magic and witchcraft, ghosts and spirits, ESP and clairvoyance.

Jewish characters and Jewish ideas in Mailer's writings became fewer as his career progressed. In *The Naked and the Dead*, he develops two Jewish characters, Roth and Goldstein, an atheist and a believer. The portrait of the unbeliever, Roth, is an unflattering one, and Roth eventually becomes the victim of his own sense of insecurity and falls to his death during the climb up Mount Anaka. Goldstein, however, becomes the spokesman for Mailer's outlook when he loses his belief in God but gains a belief in human solidarity.

Two short stories of the 1950s, "The Man Who Studied Yoga" and "The Time of Her Time" (both in *Advertisements for Myself*), also contain Jewish characters; however, they are all as unlikeable as Roth in *The Naked and the Dead*. In "The Man Who Studied Yoga," we encounter three Jewish couples who are watching a pornographic movie together, and the protagonist Sam Slovoda, though only one-quarter Jewish, exhibits the kind of negative attitude toward his own Jewishness that many critics have attributed to Mailer himself. In "The Time of Her Time," the Irish-American protagonist Sergius O'Shaugnessy plays a sexual power game with a Jewish graduate student named Denise Gondelman who has never had a vaginal orgasm. O'Shaugnessy manages to give her that experience by alternating between anal and vaginal intercourse and by calling her "You dirty little Jew" (*Advertisements*, 450).

Aside from Goldstein in *The Naked and the Dead*, the only fully drawn Jewish character Mailer ever developed is the screenwriter Charles Eitel in *The Deer Park*. Eitel's personality stands out because he is torn not only between his aspirations as a serious artist and the commercialism of his work for Hollywood studios, but also between his loyalty to his friends and the pressure that the Communist hunters of the HUAC put on him. Compared to stock villains such as the cigar-chomping Jewish movie producer Herman Teppis, Eitel remains a sympathetic character even though he winds up betraying some old friends in order to keep his job. Thus, like most of Mailer's Jewish characters, he is more notable for his weaknesses than for his strengths.

The lack of Jewish ideas in Mailer's fiction is not surprising in the light of statements that Mailer has made about his own Jewishness. In *The Armies of the Night* (1968) Mailer said that he considered his residual Jewishness ''a fatal taint, a last remaining speck of the one personality which [I] found absolutely unsupportable—the nice Jewish boy from Brooklyn'' (153). However, this statement should not be taken as a total disavowal of everything Jewish, for in a later chapter of *Armies of the Night* Mailer acknowledged his Jewishness and got into a shouting match with a neo-Nazi. Moreover, during the early 1960s he wrote a series of five columns for *Commentary* magazine in which he used Martin Buber's *Tales of the Hasidim* as springboards for meditations on the Holocaust and what it means for the relationship between God and the Jews. Three of these columns are reprinted in *The Presidential Papers* (1963) and a fourth in *Cannibals and Christians* (1966).

CRITICAL RECEPTION

Normal Mailer has generally fared better with gentiles than with his Jewish critics because many Jewish critics, like Sanford Pinsker, feel that ''Mailer's fictional landscape has little to do with Jewish-American characters, and nothing whatsoever with Jewish-American ideas'' (106). Pinsker conceded that Mailer has written ''a certain number of valuable books'' but then qualified that statement by saying that none of them ''add one jot to the story of Jewish-American fiction, except as an aberration, and perhaps as a cautionary tale'' (109). In the same vein, Louis Harap called Mailer a ''Jew manqué'' who has allowed his Jewishness ''to influence him only as a component of the insecurity in his personality which has all too often led him into speculative flights difficult to decipher'' (160). Mark Shechner offered a different explanation for Mailer's failure to produce work that is equal to his talent. He believed that it is ''Mailer's fascination with success and the refusal to give credit to failure that sets Mailer apart from other Jewish writers (making him presumably more 'American') and has prevented him from realizing some of his own best intuitions about the deeper ironies of the American dream'' (229).

More positive are the views of Allen Guttmann and Helen Weinberg. Guttmann considered Mailer to be ''unquestionably among the most gifted'' of the generation of writers who came into prominence since 1945. Guttmann understood that Mailer considers himself as a ''non-Jewish Jew, that is, as a secular Jew for whom the customs of conventional Jews are of little importance'' (154). Considering Mailer less important as a novelist than as a political journalist, Guttmann concluded that Mailer is ''the secular Jew as revolutionary . . . the personification of a mood shared by many intellectuals in this present crisis of our civilization . . . a modern prophet who demands attention even when he cannot command fealty'' (172). Helen Weinberg is one of the few critics who sees a connection between Mailer's ideas and Jewish tradition. She commented on Mailer's hope of changing the consciousness of his generation through his writing, and she considered this ambition ''peculiarly Jewish.'' Moreover, Weinberg presented evidence that Mailer's vision of life, his special brand of Manichalanism, might be rooted in Hasidic mysticism, and she suggested that Mailer's activism should be ''seen against the prophetic tradition and Hasidic impulses'' (96). Weinberg concluded that Mailer's ''life reverberates with the messianic urgency of Jewish willfulness and this fact of his life is known and recognized in his work, his writing'' (97).

Non-Jewish critics have been less interested in the question of Mailer's relation to Judaism than in the question of his place in American literature and his ultimate merit as a writer. On this question opinions have also diverged radically. On the one hand, there are those who think that posterity will remember Mailer only for his first novel, *The Naked and the Dead*. On the other hand, there are those who consider him a protean genius who has not only produced outstanding fiction and outstanding journalism but has also created hybrid forms such as the nonfiction novel and the fictionalized autobiography. Most critics, however, take a more balanced view of Mailer's uneven output and point to half a dozen unquestionable successes that assure Mailer an important place in literary history. The works most often singled out for such praise are *The Naked and the Dead* (1948), *Advertisements for Myself* (1959), *An American Dream* (1965), *The Armies of the Night* (1968), *The Executioner's Song* (1979), and *Oswald's Tale* (1995). It is notable that only two of these six titles are conventional novels. Thus it is likely that Mailer will ultimately be remembered more as a journalist than as a novelist. This is a possibility he himself is not too sanguine about, for in *The Armies of the Night*, he recorded a conversation in which the poet Robert Lowell irritated him with the backhanded compliment, ''Norman, I really think you are the best journalist in America'' (32).

BIBLIOGRAPHY

Works by Norman Mailer

Fiction

The Naked and the Dead. New York: Rinehart, 1948.
Barbary Shore. New York: Rinehart, 1951.
The Deer Park. New York: Putnam, 1955.
An American Dream. New York: Dial, 1965.
The Short Fiction of Norman Mailer. New York: Dell, 1967.
Why Are We in Vietnam? New York: Putnam, 1967.
Maidstone: A Mystery. New York: New American Library, 1971.
The Executioner's Song. Boston: Little, Brown, 1979.
Of Women and Their Elegance. New York: Simon and Schuster, 1980.
Ancient Evenings. Boston: Little, Brown, 1983.
Tough Guys Don't Dance. New York: Random House, 1984.
Harlot's Ghost. New York: Random House, 1991.
Oswald's Tale: An American Mystery. New York: Random House, 1995.

Nonfiction

The White Negro: Superficial Reflections on the Hipster. San Francisco: City Lights, 1957.

Advertisements for Myself. New York: Putnam, 1959.

Deaths for the Ladies and Other Disasters. New York: Putnam, 1962.

The Presidential Papers. New York: Putnam, 1963.

Cannibals and Christians. New York: Dial, 1966.

The Armies of the Night: History as a Novel/The Novel as History. New York: New American Library, 1968.

The Idol and the Octopus. New York: Dell, 1968.

Miami and the Siege of Chicago. New York: New American Library, 1968.

Of a Fire on the Moon. Boston: Little, Brown, 1970.

The Prisoner of Sex. Boston: Little, Brown, 1971.

Existential Errands. Boston: Little, Brown, 1972.

St. George and the Godfather. New York: New American Library, 1972.

Marilyn: A Biography. New York: Grosset and Dunlap, 1973.

The Faith of Graffiti. New York: Praeger, 1974.

The Fight. Boston: Little, Brown, 1975.

Genius and Lust: A Journey through the Major Writings of Henry Miller. New York: Grove, 1976.

Some Honorable Men: Political Conventions, 1960–1972. Boston: Little, Brown, 1976.

Pieces and Pontifications. Boston: Little, Brown, 1982.

Portrait of Picasso as a Young Man. New York: Atlantic Monthly Press, 1995.

Works Cited and Studies of Norman Mailer

Carroll, Paul. "Playboy Interview: Norman Mailer." *Playboy* 15 (January 1968): 69–84.

Coale, Samuel. *In Hawthorne's Shadow: American Romance from Melville to Mailer.* Lexington: University Press of Kentucky, 1985.

Gerson, Jessica. "Sex, Creativity, and God." In *Modern Critical Views: Norman Mailer*, ed. Harold Bloom. New York: Chelsea House, 1986.

Gordon, Andrew. "Norman Mailer." *Twentieth-Century American-Jewish Fiction Writers.* vol. 28 of *Dictionary of Literary Biography*, ed. Daniel Walden. New York: Garland, 1984.

Guttmann, Allen. *The Jewish Writer in America: Assimilation and the Crisis of Identity.* New York: Oxford University Press, 1971.

Harap, Louis. *In the Mainstream: The Jewish Presence in Twentieth-Century American Literature, 1950s–1980s.* New York: Greenwood, 1987.

Lennon, J. Michael. "Mailer's Cosmology." In *Critical Essays on Norman Mailer*, ed. J. Michael Lennon. Boston: G. K. Hall, 1986.

Manso, Peter. *Mailer: His Life and Times.* New York: Simon and Schuster, 1985.

Mills, Hilary. *Mailer: A Biography.* New York: Empire Books, 1982.

Pinsker, Sanford. *Jewish-American Fiction, 1917–1987.* New York: Twayne, 1992.

Shechner, Mark. "Jewish Writers." In *The Harvard Guide to Contemporary American Writing*, ed. Daniel Hoffman. Cambridge: Harvard University Press, 1979.

Solotaroff, Robert. "The Formulation Expanded: Mailer's Existentialism." In *Down Mailer's Way.* Urbana: University of Illinois Press, 1974.

Weinberg, Helen. ''The Activist Norman Mailer.'' In *Contemporary American-Jewish Literature: Critical Essays*, ed. Irving Malin. Bloomington: Indiana University Press, 1973.

Wenke, Joseph. *Mailer's America*. Hanover, NH: University Press of New England, 1987.

BERNARD MALAMUD   (1914–1986)

Sanford Pinsker

BIOGRAPHY

Bernard Malamud was born in Brooklyn, New York, on April 24, 1914, to Max and Bertha Fidelman Malamud. His parents were Russian-Jewish immigrants who ran a small grocery store in Brooklyn, a mom-and-pop operation of the sort Malamud used as the setting for *The Assistant* (1957), his tale of suffering and spiritual redemption in Depression-era America. Indeed, the ambiance of Malamud's early life in Brooklyn provided the essential backdrop for his most characteristic stories, as well as the mannerisms, speech patterns, and essential values of his most distinctive characters.

From 1928 to 1932, Malamud was a student at Brooklyn's Erasmus Hall High School, where his earliest stories were published in the literary magazine, the *Erasmian*. In 1936, Malamud received his B.A. from the City College of New York; and in 1942, he earned an M.A. (with a thesis on Thomas Hardy's *The Dynasts*) from Columbia University.

Initially, Malamud had planned on a career as a teacher of English in the New York public schools, but a poor job market forced him to take a job in Washington, D.C., with the Bureau of the Census. He soon returned to his native Brooklyn, however, where he wrote during the day and taught classes in English at Erasmus Hall High's night-school division. On November 6, 1945, he married Ann De Chiara, an Italian American, and thus began a lifelong interest in Italian culture, as well as increasingly frequent trips to Italy itself. The result can be seen in those of Malamud's stories that feature Italian-American characters or Italian locales.

In the early years of his marriage, Malamud worked at a wide variety of teaching and nonteaching jobs. His last New York teaching position of this period was in 1948–1949, for the evening school of Harlem High School. Not surprisingly, the stories he wrote between grading papers and preparing his classes reflect the experiences of New York City's ethnic minorities: Italians, blacks, Jews, and others. His son, Paul, was born in 1947.

In 1949, Malamud accepted an instructorship in the English Department at Oregon State University in Corvallis. Eventually he was promoted to associate professor and stayed at Oregon State until 1961. During this period, a daughter, Janna, was born in 1952, and Malamud continued writing despite an onerous load of composition courses taught in a university more widely known for its commitment to agricultural and technical arts programs. *A New Life* (1961) reflects Malamud's ambivalent feelings about the West in general and Oregon State University in particular.

Nineteen sixty-one was also the year in which Malamud left Oregon to accept a position in the Division of Language and Literature at Bennington College in Vermont. If Oregon State University was devoted to the pragmatic, Bennington has a deserved reputation of quite a different sort: looser, more experimental, and absolutely devoted to the arts. Malamud taught one creative-writing course a year (quite a change from his regimen at Oregon State) and divided his time between a residence in rural Vermont and an apartment in New York City. A novel such as *Dubin's Lives* (1979) reflects the lushness of Vermont's pastoral setting, although even that work is filled with the moral suffering and transcendence that identifies Malamud's work like a thumbprint.

Malamud died on March 20, 1986, at the age of seventy-one. His fiction was much honored during his lifetime (two National Book Awards, for *The Magic Barrel* and *The Fixer*; a Pulitzer Prize for *The Fixer*), and his reputation as one of Jewish-American literature's most impressive talents seems secure.

MAJOR WORKS AND THEMES

Malamud was always uneasy about being identified as an American Jewish writer. He found the label inadequate: "I have interests beyond that," he insisted, stressing, instead, that he felt that he wrote "for all men" (*New York Times*, D-26). However, before one can write about, and for, "all men," one must learn how to write about a particular person anchored in a particular time, place, and situation. Malamud himself insisted as much in the foreword to his justly famous *The Stories of Bernard Malamud* (1983): "Writing the short story is a good way to begin writing seriously." In Malamud's case, the beginning was a short story entitled "The Cost of Living" that he published in *Harper's Bazaar* and later refashioned into the novel *The Assistant*. In either form, the tale of immigrant Jewish poverty looks, sounds, and, most important, feels like nobody else's. Indeed, much the same thing could be said of the other twenty-four stories he chose. In his work, the rhythms of immigrant speech are so constricted that sorrow and joy, comic wonder and tragic recognition, fight for space in the same sparse paragraph:

He was talking to me how bitter was his life, and he touched me on the sleeve to say something else, but the next minute his face got small and he fell down dead, the wife screaming, the little girls crying that it made in my heart pain. I am myself a sick man and when I saw him lying on the floor, I said to myself, "Rosen, say goodbye, this guy is finished." So I said it. ("Take Pity," 88)

Although he soon fell asleep he could not sleep her out of his mind. He worked, beating his breast. Though he prayed to be rid of her, his prayers went unanswered. Through days of torment he endlessly struggled not to love her, fearing success, he escaped it. He then concluded to convert her to goodness, himself to God. The idea alternately nauseated him and exalted him. ("The Magic Barrel," 212–13)

To reread *The Stories of Bernard Malamud* is to be reminded of those days when craft meant discipline, and austerity. It is also to feel in the grim circumstances of his fictions—the failing mom-and-pop stores, the entrapments of mind and body, the lash of necessity—Malamud's largeness of heart. For the consummate storyteller, a few pages can, in Malamud's own phrase, "predicate a lifetime"; his best fictions do precisely that.

Malamud's first novel, *The Natural* (1952), centers on baseball and a protagonist (Roy Hobbes) who yearns to be the best only to discover that ambition has cost him his humanity. In this sense, the tale, filled as it is with elements of Arthurian legend and Jungian archetypes, is not as far from the immigrant Jewish world of subsequent stories as one might imagine, for Roy Hobbes is akin to the antiheroes and bumbling schlemiels who will populate Malamud's later fiction. He too struggles to make his life better in a world of bad luck, however much the novel's mythic machinery shapes the outlines of his moral fable.

The Natural continues to enjoy a deserved reputation as one of America's finest novels about baseball, and had Malamud continued to write such overtly "American" books, he would have been assured a successful career, but not as the Malamud honored as a looming presence in the American Jewish renaissance. The stories of *The Magic Barrel* (1958) were responsible for that, and for good reason. These early stories—partly moral fable, partly parable—pushed plot action into new configurations that had not been either the concern or the province of previous Jewish-American fiction. One thinks, for example, of Pinye Salzman in "The Magic Barrel," chanting the words of the *Kaddish* (prayer for the dead) as his wayward daughter awaits the desperate, love-smitten rabbi rushing toward her; of the characters in "The Mourners," each sitting *shivah* for the other and himself; or of the white feather wafting gently downward from the heavens in "The Jewbird." Quick brush strokes set the typical Malamud story into motion, simultaneously evoking a familiar landscape and moving us past it. Moreover, this sense of "motion" not only operates in stories where, say, a Pinye Salzman flits about his business as matchmaker with a mercurial speed (and, one might add, a general disregard for the laws of physics and realistic probability), but also in a novel such as *The Fixer* (1966), where Yakov Bok spends much of his time in the cramped quarters of a czarist jail.

In much of Malamud's early fiction, secret sharers slip out of their skins and become their antagonists. One thinks, for example, of Manishevitz and the "Angel Levine"; of Lieb the baker and Kobotsky ("The Loan"); and of George Stoyonovich and Mr. Cattanzara ("A Summer's Reading"). In Malamud's best stories, the gritty surfaces of realistic detail give way to astonishing imaginative bursts, almost as if the essential features of the folktale had been filtered through quite another sensibility. The result makes for a daring experimentation that has not yet received its full due, for what is most thoroughly modern about Malamud's best writing—the conflation of landscape and psychological condition, the wrenching of expectation and outcome, and the alternating currents of social realism and imaginative fancy—can be found less in the Yiddishized rhythms of his characters than in how he foregrounds the world in which they speak.

In this sense, *The Assistant* (1957) is at once an extended example of cityscape as psychological condition (the backroom of Bober's failing grocery store is an appropriate setting for sighs that seem to have their genesis in the destruction of the Temple) and a moral fable about saintly transference. Like the social realism that Malamud renders in shorthand, Bober's patient suffering merely is; and it is the task of Frank Alpine, his assistant—and the novel's particular burden—to learn what such suffering means and how it might be applied.

Bober suffers the slings and arrows of bad timing. In the prison of his grocery store there are no jailers, only prisoners. What Rosen, the protagonist of "Take Pity," says of his recently departed friend, Axel Kalish, could, with a snip here, a tuck there, be said equally of Bober:

He worked like a blind horse when he got to America, and saved maybe two–three thousand dollars that he bought with the money this pisher grocery in a dead neighborhood where he didn't have a chance. He called my company up for credit and they sent me I should see. . . . So right away I told him, without tricks, "Kiddo, this is a mistake. This place is a grave. Here they will bury you if you don't get out quick." (*Magic Barrel*, 87)

Only Frank Alpine, ex-criminal and Jewish sufferer-in-training, keeps faith with Bober's complicated arithmetic of what it means to be fully human: "If you live, you suffer. Some people suffer more, but not because they want. But I think if a Jew don't suffer for the Law, he will suffer for nothing" (*Assistant*, 125). But Frank's stylized graduation from assistant to master is fraught with peril and riddled with ambivalence. His fate as Bober's psychological replacement reminds us of the fears Feld projects for his daughter in "The First Seven Years":

Then he realized that what he had called ugly was not Sobel but Miriam's life if she married him. He felt for his daughter a strange and gripping sorrow, as if she were already Sobel's bride, the wife, after all, of a shoemaker, and had in her life no more than her mother had had. And all his dreams for her—why he had slaved and destroyed his heart with anxiety and labor—all these dreams of a better life were dead. (*Magic Barrel*, 15)

Thus Frank will replace Bober by becoming him: he will now slice a daily roll for the spiteful, vaguely anti-Semitic customer; he will share a morning cup of tea with Breitbart, the ironically named light-bulb peddler, whose leitmotif is a long, soulful sigh; and most of all, he will surely marry Helen in a future Malamud intimates but does not record.

In *The Assistant*, then, visions of the "future" are inextricably linked to aspects of the past, to ghosts of the heart that cling to us stubbornly and without our full understanding. By contrast, Malamud grounded *The Fixer* (1966) in the nearly forgotten story of Mendele Beiliss and the spectacular blood libel trial of 1911 that swirled around him in the Russia of peasant superstition and czarist persecution. This, in short, was Jewish history of a decidedly different order than Morris Bober's makeshift Jewish theology. At the same time, however, Malamud so orchestrated the events of his "retelling" that they were simultaneously reinscribed on the contemporary sociopolitical landscape with the force of moral fable.

Yakov Bok, the novel's protagonist, is the quintessential flop. Cuckolded and then deserted by his wife, he seems to have come from a long line of those who were the innocent victims of absurd accident: "His own father had been killed in an accident not more than a year after Yakov's birth—something less than a pogrom and less than useless: two drunken soldiers shot the first three Jews in their path, his father had been the second" (*Fixer*, 4). Yet neither his father's death nor his own impoverished condition is enough to turn Yakov into a conventional handwringer. Rather, he brings to shtetl poverty the same conflation of *kvetch* (complaint) and sigh that Morris Bober unpacked in his grocery store. About Morris we learn that "the world suffers. He felt every schmerz" (*Assistant*, 10); about Yakov that he drank his tea unsweetened ("It tasted bitter and he blamed existence" [*Fixer*, 5]).

Opportunity, in short, is as dead in the shtetl as it proved to be in Morris's mom-and-pop grocery store. But that said, Yakov, unlike Morris, tries to change his luck by setting off to Kiev. Perhaps things will go better there. Unfortunately (but hardly surprisingly), Yakov finds himself beleaguered by the accidents that befall him along the way, none of which (ironically enough) he is able to "fix." Moreover, it is his penchant for doing good deeds that contributes to his misfortune and that ultimately seals his kinship with similar bunglers in Malamud's canon.

Yakov makes much of his insistence that he is not a "political person," but the novel insists otherwise—first by embroiling him in accusations of ritual murder and then by forcing him to wait in jail for his trial. The long, agonizing prison scenes in *The Fixer* must surely have given pause to those critics who complained that Malamud was longer on vaguely spiritual metaphors than on dramatically convincing detail (e.g., metaphorical Jews, metaphorical tenements, metaphorical suffering), for whatever else a Yakov might be, his chains and the inhuman treatment are very real indeed. Furthermore, Yakov earns his rights as an Everyman. Caught in a web of bureaucratic absurdity, he suggests that "somebody has made a serious mistake," only to find that the case against him is growing stronger every day.

Yakov's learning comes slowly, interspersed by scenes in which momentary bits of self-deprecation are offset by his systematic torture. One by one, former friends betray him—victims of bribery for the most part—until Yakov is left totally alone. Even his one Russian ally, Bibikov (a Russian version of Eugene Debs who spouts lines such as "if the law doesn't protect you, it will not, in the end, protect me") is murdered or, what seems more likely, is forced to commit suicide. Yakov, on the other hand, wears his prayer shawl under his suit ("to keep warm"), employing strategies of pragmatism to stay alive. The novel illuminates Yakov's realization that he "was the accidental choice for the sacrifice. He would be tried because the accusation had been made, there didn't have to be any other reason. Being born a Jew meant being vulnerable to history, including its worst errors" (*Fixer*, 143).

With *The Tenants* (1971), Malamud places Harry Lesser, his writerly Jew, in an apartment building that, like Lesser himself, has seen better days. Lesser's very name is a directional arrow of his writerly curve, one that threatens to go from lesser to least. His third book, now some ten years in the unmaking, may have started its life in the temple of Lesser's Art, but now it quite literally stands for Lesser's life. Both are on the line and, as it were, in doubt.

For Levenspiel, the building's owner and the novel's one-man Greek chorus, the rickety steps and faulty plumbing, the erratic furnace and the broken windows, represent an opportunity—that is, if only the fiercely stubborn Lesser would accept his generous offers to relocate and make it possible for a new, more profitable apartment building to rise, phoenixlike, from the ashes of the old. After all, Lesser is not the only man lugging his bundle of grief through the world. He, Levenspiel, has *tzuris* too: a crazy mother, a sick wife, and a knocked-up teenaged daughter. Not surprisingly, Lesser won't budge because the building, wretched though it may be, has become his triggering town, his sorrow-riddled doppelgänger. As he puts it, "Home is where my book is."

Enter Willie Spearmint, an angry young black writer who stakes out a squatter's spot in Lesser's building. The morris dance that results as each writer simultaneously becomes the other—and the Other—is what Malamud's dark fable of deteriorating black-Jewish relations means to explore.

Dubin's Lives (1979) is a novel that also focuses on a writer (this time, a successful biographer) who finds it increasingly difficult to maintain a necessary aesthetic distance between himself and the subject of his next book, D. H.

Lawrence. The result is that Life and Art spill over into one another, often with comic consequences, but also with the same steady insistence on man's capacity to elevate himself beyond his suffering that characterizes Malamud's most representative work.

God's Grace (1982), the last novel published during Malamud's lifetime, represents both a continuation (it achieves the condition of pure fable) and a departure because of its apocalyptic, end-of-human-history ruminations. The result is possibly Malamud's darkest vision as well as his funniest.

The People and Uncollected Fiction (1989) is a posthumous gathering that includes sixteen chapters of an uncompleted novel and fourteen previously uncollected short stories, five published now for the first time. The uncompleted novel *The People* represents an effort to, in Malamud's words, "prime the pump" by seeking new material. As he put it, writing in the 1970s: "I may have done as much as I can with the sort of short story I have been writing so long—the somewhat mythological, biblically oriented tales. . . . What I see as possible is another variation of the comic-mythological—possibly working out the Chief Joseph of the Nez Perce idea—in other words, the Jewish Indian." The notion, long a favorite of Leslie Fiedler, the literary critic, and the Mel Brooks of *Blazing Saddles*, seems merely strained in the sketchy chapters we have. However, given what we know about Malamud's meticulous craftsmanship, there is every reason to believe that *The People* would have become a credible novel had Malamud lived long enough to complete it.

CRITICAL RECEPTION

From the start of his career, Bernard Malamud enjoyed both a wide readership and the serious attention of reviewers, critics, and scholars. Reviewing *The Magic Barrel* on the front page of the *New York Times Book Review*, Irving Howe not only proclaimed Malamud "one of the very few American writers about whom it makes sense to say that his work has a distinctly 'Jewish' tone," but also noted that Malamud's work takes full possession of a distinctly Yiddish imagination: "Malamud can grind a character to the earth, but there is always a hard ironic pity, a wry affection better than wet gestures of love, which makes him seem a grandson of the Yiddish writers" (*Celebrations and Attacks*, 34).

Howe's words struck at the very core of what subsequent scholars would explore in an ever-mounting series of critical articles and books. Among the earliest full-length studies—and still perhaps the best in terms of enunciating Malamud's thematic concerns—is Sidney Richman's *Bernard Malamud* (1966). Richman's book was followed by anthologies that collected the best articles by scholar-critics who went about the business of detailing Malamud's use of mythic sources, literary influences, and patterns of imagery. In this regard, Leslie and Joyce Field were tireless workers, first publishing *Bernard Malamud and the Critics* in 1970 and then *Bernard Malamud: A Collection of Critical Essays* in 1975.

Because many critics linked Malamud's work to that of Saul Bellow and Philip Roth, it is hardly surprising that all three felt an obligation to point out that they were individual American writers rather than dues-paying members of an (imaginary) American Jewish triumvirate. Philip Roth went even farther, insisting that he imagined Jews quite differently than either Malamud or Bellow: Malamud's characters, for example, "live in a timeless depression and a placeless Lower East Side; their society is not affluent, their predicament is not cultural" (Roth, 184). At the same time, however, those who equated Malamud with the portrait of E. I. Lonoff, the quintessential Jewish writer of Roth's *The Ghost Writer* (1979), were not entirely wrong, for Lonoff's fastidious attention to the details of his craft is not unlike Malamud's, and the reverence with which a young Nathan Zuckerman held Lonoff was duplicated in the high regard Roth had for Malamud.

Bernard Malamud was a major writer and surely one of the figures who contributed to a renewed interest in the imaginative possibilities of Jewish-American fiction. That he received an extensive obituary notice in the *New York Times* is further evidence of his stature. In that obituary, Robert Alter, one of Malamud's most insightful critics, put it this way: A handful of Malamud's best short stories will be read "as long as anyone continues to care about American fiction written in the twentieth century" (*New York Times*, D-26). There is every reason to believe that Alter's prediction will prove true, and that Malamud's work will remain as both a presence and an abiding influence for subsequent American Jewish writers.

BIBLIOGRAPHY

Works by Bernard Malamud

The Natural. New York: Harcourt, Brace, 1952; London: Eyre and Spottiswood, 1963.
The Assistant. New York: Farrar, Straus and Cudahy, 1957.
The Magic Barrel. New York: Farrar, Straus and Cudahy, 1958; London: Eyre and Spottiswood, 1959.
A New Life. New York: Farrar, Straus and Cudahy, 1961; London: Eyre and Spottiswood, 1962.
The Fixer. New York: Farrar, Straus and Giroux, 1966; London: Eyre and Spottiswood, 1967.
The Tenants. New York: Farrar, Straus and Giroux, 1971; London: Eyre Methuen, 1972.
Dubin's Lives. New York: Farrar, Straus and Giroux, 1979; London: Chatto and Windus, 1979.
God's Grace. New York: Farrar, Straus and Giroux, 1982; London: Chatto and Windus, 1982.
The Stories of Bernard Malamud. New York: Farrar, Straus and Giroux, 1983; London: Chatto and Windus, 1984.
The People and Uncollected Fiction. New York: Farrar, Straus and Giroux, 1989; London: Chatto and Windus, 1990.

Works Cited and Studies of Bernard Malamud

Bibliographies

Grau, Joseph A. "Bernard Malamud: A Bibliographical Addendum." *Bulletin of Bibliography* 37 (October–December 1980): 157–66, 184.

Habich, Robert D. "Bernard Malamud: A Bibliographic Survey." *Studies in American Jewish Literature* 4 (Spring 1978): 78–84.

Kosofsky, Nathalie. *Bernard Malamud: An Annotated Checklist*. Kent, OH: Kent State University Press, 1969.

Kosofsky, Rita N. *Bernard Malamud: A Descriptive Bibliography*. New York: Greenwood Press, 1991.

O'Keefe, Richard R. "Bibliographical Essay: Bernard Malamud." *Studies in American Jewish Literature* 7 (Fall 1988): 240–50.

Salzberg, Joel. *Bernard Malamud: A Reference Guide*. Boston: G. K. Hall, 1985.

Other Works

Abramson, Edward A. *Bernard Malamud Revisited*. New York: Twayne, 1993.

Ahokas, Pirjo. *Forging a New Self: The Adamic Protagonist and the Emergence of a Jewish-American Author as Revealed through the Novels of Bernard Malamud*. Turku: Turun Yliopisto, 1991.

Alter, Iska. *The Good Man's Dilemma: Social Criticism in the Fiction of Bernard Malamud*. New York: AMS, 1981.

Alter, Robert. "Malamud as Jewish Writer." *Commentary* 42 (September 1966): 71–76.

Astro, Richard, and Jackson J. Benson, eds. *The Fiction of Bernard Malamud*. Corvallis: Oregon State University Press, 1977.

Baris, Sharon Deykin. "Intertextuality and Reader Responsibility: Living On in Malamud's 'The Mourners.' " *Studies in American Jewish Literature* 11 (Spring 1992): 45–61.

Baumbach, Jonathan. "All Men Are Jews: *The Assistant* by Bernard Malamud." In *The Landscape of Nightmare*. New York: New York University Press, 1965, 101–22.

———. "The Economy of Life: The Novels of Bernard Malamud." *Kenyon Review* 25 (Summer 1963): 438–57.

Bellman, Samuel Irving. "Women, Children, and Idiots First: The Transformation Psychology of Bernard Malamud." *Critique* 7 (Winter 1964–1965): 123–38.

"Bernard Malamud" (obituary). *New York Times*, March 20, 1986, D-26.

Bilik, Dorothy Seidman. "Malamud's Secular Saints and Comic Jobs." In *Immigrant-Survivors: Post-Holocaust Consciousness in Recent Jewish American Fiction*. Middletown, CT: Wesleyan University Press, 1981, 53–80.

Burrows, David, Lewis M. Dubney, Milne Holton, and Grosoenor E. Powell. "The American Past in Malamud's *A New Life*." In *Private Dealings*, ed. David Burrows. Stockholm: Almqvist & Wiksell, 1970, 86–94.

Cancel-Ortiz, Rafael. "The Passion of William Dubin: D. H. Lawrence's Themes in Bernard Malamud's *Dubin's Lives*." *D. H. Lawrence Review* 16 (Spring 1983): 83–99.

Cohen, Sandy. *Bernard Malamud and the Trial by Love*. Amsterdam: Rodopi, 1974.

Dessner, Lawrence Jay. "The Playfulness of Bernard Malamud's 'The Magic Barrel.' " *Essays in Literature* 15 (Spring 1988): 87–101.

Ducharme, Robert. *Art and Idea in the Novels of Bernard Malamud: Toward The Fixer.* The Hague: Mouton, 1974.

Eigner, Edwin M. "Malamud's Use of the Quest Romance." *Genre* 1 (January 1968): 55–75.

Field, Leslie A., and Joyce W. Field, eds. *Bernard Malamud: A Collection of Critical Essays.* Englewood Cliffs, NJ: Prentice-Hall, 1975.

———, eds. *Bernard Malamud and the Critics.* New York: New York University Press, 1970.

Fisch, Harold. "Biblical Archetypes in *The Fixer.*" *Studies in American Jewish Literature* 7 (Fall 1988): 162–76.

Fuchs, Daniel. "Malamud's Dubin's Lives: A Jewish Writer and the Sexual Ethic." *Studies in American Jewish Literature* 7 (Fall 1988): 205–12.

Gealy, Marcia. "Malamud's Short Stories: A Reshaping of Hasidic Tradition." *Judaism* 28 (Winter 1979): 51–61.

Gollin, Rita K. "Malamud's Dubin and the Morality of Desire." *Papers on Language and Literature* 18 (Spring 1982): 198–207.

Gunn, Giles B. "Bernard Malamud and the High Cost of Living." In *Adversity and Grace,* ed. Nathan A. Scott, Jr. Chicago: University of Chicago Press, 1968, 59–85.

Hays, Peter L. "The Complex Pattern of Redemption in *The Assistant.*" *Centennial Review* 13 (Spring 1969): 200–214.

Helterman, Jeffrey. *Understanding Bernard Malamud.* Columbia: University of South Carolina Press, 1985.

Hershinow, Sheldon J. *Bernard Malamud.* New York: Ungar, 1980.

Hoag, Gerald. "Malamud's Trial: *The Fixer* and the Critics." *Western Humanities Review* 24 (Winter 1970): 1–12.

Howe, Irving. "The Stories of Bernard Malamud." In *Celebrations and Attacks.* New York: Horizon, 1979.

Klein, Marcus. "Bernard Malamud: The Sadness of Goodness." In *After Alienation.* Cleveland: World Publishing, 1964, 247–93.

Kumar, P. Shiv. "Marionettes in Taleysim: Yiddish Folkfigures in Two Malamud Stories." *Indian Journal of American Studies* 8 (July 1977): 18–24.

Leer, Norman. "The Double Theme in Malamud's *Assistant*: Dostoevsky with Irony." *Mosaic* 4:3 (1971): 89–102.

Lindberg-Seyersted, Brita. "A Reading of Bernard Malamud's *The Tenants.*" *Journal of American Studies* 9 (April 1975): 85–102.

Malin, Irving. "*The Fixer*: An Overview." *Studies in American Jewish Literature* 4 (Spring 1978): 40–50.

Ozick, Cynthia. "Literary Blacks and Jews." *Midstream* 18 (June–July 1972): 10–24.

Pinsker, Sanford. "The Schlemiel as Moral Bungler: Bernard Malamud's Ironic Heroes." In *The Schlemiel as Metaphor.* Carbondale: Southern Illinois University Press, 1971, 87–124.

Quart, Barbara Koenig. "Women in Bernard Malamud's Fiction." *Studies in American Jewish Literature* 3 (1983): 138–50.

Ratner, Marc L. "Style and Humanity in Malamud's Fiction." *Massachusetts Review* 5 (Summer 1964): 663–83.

Richman, Sidney. *Bernard Malamud.* New York: Twayne, 1966.

Roth, Philip. "Imagining Jews." In *Reading Myself and Others*. New York: Farrar, Straus and Giroux, 1975.

Rovit, Earl H. "Bernard Malamud and the Jewish Literary Tradition." *Critique* 3:2 (1960): 3–10.

Salzberg, Joel. *Critical Essays on Bernard Malamud*. Boston: G. K. Hall, 1987.

Schulz, Max F. "Bernard Malamud's Mythic Proletarians." In *Radical Sophistication*. Athens: Ohio University Press, 1969, 56–68.

Schwartz, Helen J. "Malamud's Turning Point: The End of Redemption in *Pictures of Fidelman*." *Studies in American Jewish Literature* 2 (Winter 1976): 26–37.

Shear, Walter. "Culture Conflict in 'The Assistant.' " *Midwest Quarterly* 7 (July 1966): 367–80.

Sheres, Ita. "The Alienated Sufferer: Malamud's Novels from the Perspective of Old Testament and Jewish Mystical Thought." *Studies in American Jewish Literature* 4 (Spring 1978): 68–76.

Solotaroff, Robert. *Bernard Malamud: A Study of the Short Fiction*. Boston: Twayne, 1989.

Standley, Fred L. "Bernard Malamud: The Novel of Redemption." *Southern Humanities Review* 5 (Fall 1971): 309–18.

Tanner, Tony. "A New Life." In *City of Words*. New York: Harper and Row, 1971, 322–43.

Wisse, Ruth R. "Requiem in Several Voices." In *The Schlemiel as Modern Hero*. Chicago: University of Chicago Press, 1971, 108–24.

Witherington, Paul. "Malamud's Allusive Design in *A New Life*." *Western American Literature* 10 (Summer 1975): 115–23.

Wohlgelernter, Maurice. "Blood Libel—Fact and Fiction." *Tradition* 8 (Fall 1966): 62–72.

Zlotnick, Joan. "Malamud's *The Assistant*: Of Morris, Frank, and St. Francis." *Studies in American Jewish Literature* 1 (Winter 1975): 20–23.

WALLACE MARKFIELD   (1926–   )

Joel Shatzky and Michael Taub

BIOGRAPHY

Wallace Markfield was born in Brooklyn, New York, on August 12, 1926. He attended *cheder* (Jewish day school) and Abraham Lincoln High School, the same school attended by Daniel Fuchs and Joseph Heller, among other distinguished Jewish-American novelists, and graduated from Brooklyn College in 1947. He also did graduate work at New York University.

Markfield began his literary career while still in college when he wrote film reviews for the *New Leader* in the late 1940s and supported himself and his family as a publicist for Jewish agencies. He has been writer-in-residence at San Francisco State College, Queens College, and Columbia University. He was the recipient of a Guggenheim Fellowship in 1965 and an award from the National Council on the Arts in 1966. He married Anna May Goodman in 1949; they have one daughter.

MAJOR WORKS AND THEMES

Like Bernard Malamud in his earlier works, Markfield focuses on working-class and lower-middle-class characters from the period of his formative years from the Depression to the early 1950s, and like Philip Roth, he maintains a satirical stance in his work. He began publishing short stories in his late teens and reflects a Jewish secular milieu in those works that were first published in *Partisan Review*. It was more than a decade later, however, that Markfield wrote his first novel, *To An Early Grave* (1964), a satirical journey of four friends to the funeral of a recently deceased literary journalist. Made into a hilarious movie, *Bye, Bye Braverman* (1968), directed by Sidney Lumet, it records the adventures of the four friends of Leslie Braverman, who end up at the right cemetary after attending the wrong funeral. Some critics believe that Braverman is a caricature of the mercurial Delmore Schwartz, and relations between Markfield and the staff of *Commentary*, who believed that they were the targets of his humor, considerably cooled after the novel was published.

Markfield's second novel, *Teitlebaum's Window* (1970), is a brilliant evocation of the working-class Brighton Beach Jewish community as well as a *Bildungsroman* of Simon Sloan, growing up in the 1930s. This novel was followed by *You Could Live If They Let You* (1974), a portrait of a Jewish "insult" comic that, critics to the contrary, is not a fictionalized version of Lenny Bruce but more of a "Jerry Lewis comedian." After a number of abortive attempts at another novel and the space of seventeen years, Markfield published *Radical Surgery* in 1991, a departure in his work: a political thriller.

In all of his work, Markfield finds in the confusions and difficulties of Jewish life in America a remarkable resilience in the humor and wit that has preserved their sanity or heightened their insanity to almost epic proportions. It is in his collection of what might be mistakenly dismissed as "types" that he has created a world that celebrates the enduring qualities of Jewish-American values and that finds its greatest consolations through *sechel* (intelligence) and laughter.

CRITICAL RECEPTION

To an Early Grave received highly favorable reviews from such eminent critics as Stanley Edgar Hyman and praise on the book jacket from Joseph Heller and Harold Rosenberg. It was even linked with the Hades episode from James Joyce's *Ulysses*, while Markfield himself regarded Italo Svevo's novel *The Confessions of Zeno* as his inspiration (*DLB*, 177). *Teitelbaum's Window* has been regarded as a better novel, but it was not as well received, Alfred Kazin calling it "a warehouse of Jewish folklore" rather than an original work (*DLB*, 179). But despite the mixed reception, Wallace Markfield's portrait of characters who experience the "pleasure and pain of Jewishness, the clash between thought and feeling" (*DLB*, 179) has added a valued dimension to Jewish-American literature.

SELECTED BIBLIOGRAPHY

Novels

To an Early Grave. New York: Simon and Schuster, 1964.
Teitlebaum's Window. New York: Knopf, 1970.
You Could Live If They Let You. New York: Knopf, 1974.
Radical Surgery. New York: Bantam, 1991.

Stories and Other Periodical Publications

"Ph.D." *Partisan Review* 14 (September–October 1947): 466–71.

"A Season of Change." *Midstream* 4 (Autumn 1958): 25–48.

"Eulogy for an American Boy." *Commentary* 31 (March 1961): 513–18.

"Yiddishization of American Humor." *Esquire* 64 (October 1965): 114–15.

"Under the Marquee." *New York Herald Tribune*, February 13, 1966.

For further information on Wallace Markfield, see *Twentieth-Century American-Jewish Fiction Writers*, ed. Daniel Walden. Vol. 28 of *Dictionary of Literary Biography*. Detroit: Gale Research, 1984, 175–81.

DAPHNE MERKIN   (1954–   )

Carolyn Ariella Sofia

BIOGRAPHY

"Perfect sex is like some Platonic essence," notes Daphne Merkin in "The Woman in the Balcony," her reading of the biblical Song of Songs, because it takes "place only in our heads, safe from the incursions of an always-blemished reality." This notion of an ideal experience shadowing the real-life experience and a self-consciousness about the painful chasm separating the two seems embedded in Merkin's earliest experiences of life.

Born the fourth of six closely spaced children to a well-to-do German-Jewish Orthodox couple who had emigrated to the United States, Merkin was raised in Manhattan and sent to Jewish day schools. Spiritual impulses at home were sometimes "buried under layers of German formality and propriety" (telephone interview), and the young Merkin resented her perceived marginality based on gender. Sent to study Talmud-Torah like her three brothers, she recalled that while they got the chance to showcase their knowledge publicly at the time of their bar mitzvahs, her twelfth-year rite of passage consisted simply of a family outing to a local kosher restaurant. "I have never been a true believer," she writes in "The Woman in the Balcony," and gives her reason as not understanding her "role in the religiously ordained hierarchy" of synagogue life "other than to mutely observe and admire . . . the men's club going great guns downstairs."

An emotionally sensitive child, Merkin chafed under the authoritarian character of her parents and developed a tendency toward depression at an early age. Hospitalized for two weeks of psychiatric observation at age eight because of a belief that she was being "hounded" by family and friends, she was sent home and continued individual therapy on an outpatient basis.

In 1975 Merkin graduated magna cum laude from Barnard College and was awarded departmental honors in English as well as the school's prize for poetry. During the following year she worked briefly as an assistant at both the *New York Review of Books* and the *New Yorker*. Deciding to return to school in 1976, she enrolled in a graduate program at Columbia University to study literature. She remained there until 1978, but left before being awarded a degree. During her time at Columbia, Merkin published her first literary criticism in *Commentary* and the *New Leader*, as well as her first fiction in *Mademoiselle* and *Encounter*. Named the *New Leader*'s lead fiction critic in 1978, she left several years later to join the editorial staff at *McCall's* and to work on her own fiction.

Asked in a telephone interview which author she considered the most influential on her development, Merkin readily cited V. S. Pritchett because of a "certain kind of limpidness" in his writing and because, like her, he has combined careers as a fiction writer and a literary critic. Running a close second was Walker Percy, whose 1961 novel *The Moviegoer* is one Merkin wishes she "had written herself," both for its use of language and for its inclusion of her twin obsessions, fiction and movies.

Enchantment (1986), her debut novel, aroused more fanfare than the typical first novel, in part because of the wealth of literary friends Merkin had accumulated as she moved in and around the publishing world. Her fiction-writing abilities were brought to the attention of publisher William Jovanovich by critic Diana Trilling, who showed him one of Merkin's short stories. Jovanovich invited Merkin to lunch and ended up offering her a $20,000 advance to complete a manuscript that would become a semiautobiographical novel about a girl growing up in a wealthy, modern Orthodox German-Jewish family in Manhattan. Subsequently, he hired Merkin as a senior editor.

Using the events of her personal life as a springboard to matters of cultural criticism, Merkin often writes personal essays for the *New York Times* and other publications. A new novel called *The Discovery of Sex* has been under way for several years. The story's narrator is Hannah Lehmann, the protagonist of *Enchantment*, who relates the tale of a woman in publishing who is sexually obsessed with a lawyer.

MAJOR WORKS AND THEMES

Thwarted love, not for a man, but for a mother, lies at the heart of *Enchantment*, and the nexus of memory and identity forms another persistent trope. Hannah Lehmann, the twenty-six-year-old narrator, shares her recollections of growing up in a family remarkably similar to Merkin's own: the well-off Lehmann clan is German-Jewish Orthodox, lives on Manhattan's Upper East Side, includes six closely spaced children, and has one daughter apparently more sensitive than the others.

Written in the tone of a memoir, the novel traces no distinct plot. It relies instead on the vagaries of memory to order its scenes. Linked vignettes shape it into a series of prose snapshots highlighting the Lehmann family's emotional history. The ordering and meaning of the scenes belong to Hannah, but she realizes by the novel's end that family histories may be more constructed than factual: "Even my brother's memories don't match mine," she thinks, recalling that he cites a different litany of facts and perceptions concerning remembered childhood events.

What Hannah therefore wants, and cannot seem to find, is someone to agree with her vision of the past, someone to share her recollections completely: "I would love to find someone whose memories matched mine, little hurt for little hurt." The reader is positioned to be the active, sympathetic listener, and what Hannah especially wants confirmed is the part her mother played (and continues to play) in her emotional life.

Love is not a strong enough word to describe the attachment Hannah feels for her mother. It is an implacable need, a driving force: "It is a mystery to me, the waves of emotion I keep breaking against her," she says. "I am a Woodpecker, and my mother is a tree. Love. Hate. Emotions keep slipping off the end of my mind, to be followed by wholly different ones. Hate. Love. Which will do to wear her bark away? And who is torturing whom?" At its center Hannah's problem is that she cannot accept her psychiatrist's interpretation that the solution to her obsession lies within herself, that her mother has no real power over her anymore, other than what Hannah grants her. Unable to give up the desire to be totally, unconditionally loved, she relives scenes of desperate longing. Close to the novel's end, she is still recalling a time when, trying repeatedly to attract her mother's attention and to succeed in getting her to confess her failings as a mother, Hannah drove herself as far as self-mutilation, marking her wrists with a pair of her mother's nail scissors and deliberately pointing out the cuts in case they should escape detection.

The father is virtually absent in this book; Mr. Lehmann is reduced to a kind of stranger who just happened to marry Hannah's mother. The relationship between mother and child remains the preeminent dyad, especially for its ability to serve as a paradigm for future relationships. Thus the troubling aspect of Hannah's relationship with her mother broadens and becomes sexualized by the novel's close when she forms a masochistic attachment to a man determined, alternately, to love and humiliate her.

Merkin's novel-in-progress, *The Discovery of Sex*, will focus on similar themes of love and obsession. According to Merkin, however, questions about Jewish identity may be explored more fully since one of the book's male characters will undergo a spiritual conversion and consider significantly increasing his level of Jewish ritual observance.

Certainly, in the years since the publication of her first novel, Merkin herself has sought a higher profile in Jewish intellectual circles through her essays. In "After the Massacre" (1994), she explores the possibility of emigrating to Israel despite its entrenched problems between Jews and Arabs. Recent essays in *Tikkun* include two later collected in anthologies. The journal's self-assigned role as cultural gadfly offers Merkin an ideal venue for her own ideas. "A Closet of One's Own: On Not Becoming a Lesbian" (1995) caused, according to *Tikkun*'s editor, Michael Lerner, "a furor of upset, hurt and anger among lesbians" (letter). According to him, "The inner conflicts in Merkin's soul often seem to get resolved by writing provocative essays designed to offend many whose love she may unconsciously crave."

CRITICAL RECEPTION

Enchantment was well received by reviewers, all of whom appeared sensitive to the tangle and intensity of childhood emotions portrayed in the story. For Janet Hadda, it was a "deeply female" work because of the way Merkin portrays the "doubt and frustration of dawning womanhood" (2). The obsessive quality of the attachment Hannah Lehmann has for her mother caused Patricia Hampl to redefine Hannah's enchantment for her female parent as a kind of thralldom, a state of emotional bondage from which the twenty-six-year-old protagonist is unable to free herself or her reader. Katherine Bucknell likewise saw a coerced role for the reader, this time as someone who is expected to join Hannah in finger-pointing accusation of her family.

Unlike Hampl or Bucknell, John Gross did not find the closed world that Hannah inhabits claustrophobic, and where Mrs. Lehmann was portrayed by Hampl as a woman who "seems not unfeeling, but possessed of a peasant faith, an airy confidence in life's habit of righting itself" (7), and not as a woman arbitrarily cruel enough to merit the position of villain in her daughter's mind, Gross concentrated on what he considered an accurate perception by Hannah of her mother's "coolly punitive approach" to child raising, so much so that the daughter, as a child, fantasized that her mother had once been an officer in a concentration camp. Like Gross, Rochelle Ratner also found that the buildup of minute details, the television trivia that resurrects the zeitgeist of the 1950s, for instance, helps intensify the portrait of Hannah's family life.

BIBLIOGRAPHY

Works by Daphne Merkin

"Why Potok Is Popular." *Commentary*, February 1976, 73–75.
"Looking Back." *Commentary*, July 1977, 63–65.
"The Plight of Reading: In Search of the New Fiction." *Partisan Review*, 1984–1985, 739–50.
"All about Mommie Damnedest." *Film Comment*, November–December 1985, 38–40.
Enchantment. San Diego: Harcourt Brace Jovanovich, 1986. An excerpt from the novel-in-progress appeared originally in the *New Yorker*, April 2, 1984, 42–46; reprinted in *Writing Our Way Home: Contemporary Stories by American Jewish Writers*, ed. Ted Solotaroff and Nessa Rapoport. New York: Schocken Books, 1992.
"Ecclesiastes: A Reading Out-of-Season." In *Congregation: Contemporary Writers*

Read the Jewish Bible, ed. David Rosenberg. San Diego: Harcourt Brace Jova-
    novich, 1987, 393–405.

"Ready, Willing, and Wary." *New York Times Magazine*, July 16, 1989, 12–14.

"Dreaming of Hitler: From the Postwar Generation, a Memoir of Self-Hatred." *Esquire*,
    August 1989, 75–83. Reprinted in *Testimony: Contemporary Writers Make the
    Holocaust Personal*, ed. David Rosenberg. New York: Random House, 1989.

"Prince Charming Comes Back." *New York Times Magazine*, July 15, 1990, 18–20.

"Now Voyeur." *Premier*, Winter 1991, 108.

"Are These Women Bullies?" *New York Times Magazine*, July 21, 1991, 17.

"Count Your Losses." *New York Times Magazine*, May 5, 1991, 22–24.

"Name That Decade." *New York Times*, May 25, 1992, 14.

"Philip Roth's Diasporism: A Symposium." *Tikkun*, May–June 1993, 41–46.

"Notes of a Lonely White Woman." *Partisan Review*, Fall 1993, 654–60.

"After the Massacre: Life under a Low Sky." *Partisan Review*, Spring 1994, 220–32.

"The Woman in the Balcony: On Reading the *Song of Songs*." *Tikkun*, May–June 1994,
    59–64. Reprinted in *Out of the Garden: Women Writers on the Bible*, ed. Christina
    Buchmann and Celina Spiegel. New York: Fawcett Columbine, 1994.

"The Curse of Eros." Review of *Secret Life*, an autobiography of poet Michael Ryan.
    New York Times Book Review, July 9, 1995, sec. 7, 3ff.

"A Closet of One's Own: On Not Becoming a Lesbian." *Tikkun*, November–December
    1995, 21–24ff. Reprinted in *Surface Tension: Love, Sex, and Politics between
    Lesbians and Straight Women*, ed. Meg Daly. New York: Simon and Schuster,
    1996.

Studies of Daphne Merkin

"Between Issues." *New Leader*, September 8, 1986, 2.

Bucknell, Katherine. *Times Literary Supplement*, August 14, 1987, 873.

Cieri, Carol des Lauriers. Review of *Enchantment*. *Christian Science Monitor* (Eastern
    edition), September 29, 1986, 22.

Gross, John. Review of *Enchantment*. *New York Times*, September 8, 1986, C19.

Hadda, Janet. Review of *Enchantment*. *Los Angeles Times Book Review*, September 14,
    1986, 2ff.

Hampl, Patricia. Review of *Enchantment*. *New York Times Book Review*, October 5,
    1986, 7.

Ratner, Rochelle. Review of *Enchantment*. *Library Journal*, August 1986, 171.

Sofia, Carolyn Ariella. "Daphne Merkin." In *Jewish American Women Writers: A Bio-
    Bibliographical and Critical Sourcebook*, ed. Ann R. Shapiro. Westport, CT:
    Greenwood Press, 1994, 227–31.

Tyre, Peg. "By the Books." *New York*, September 22, 1986, 38.

FAYE STOLLMAN MOSKOWITZ (1930–)

Myrna Goldenberg

BIOGRAPHY

The eldest child and only daughter of Aaron Stollman and Sophie Eisenberg, Faye Moskowitz recollects her childhood experiences in her books and essays from two perspectives, the Great Depression and Yiddishkeit. She and her two younger brothers, Hyman and Reuben, were raised in a Jewish neighborhood in Detroit until 1935, when their father moved the family to nearby Jackson, where he found work in a relative's junk business, which later evolved into a scrap business. About a decade later, the Stollmans returned to Detroit and the Jewish neighborhood of friends, family, and familiarity.

The years in Jackson impressed Moskowitz. Where her Jewishness had been "seamless" in Detroit, simply and fully an element of her life, it was, in Jackson, a characteristic that differentiated her sharply from classmates and neighbors. Rather than being motivated to assimilate, she accepted her outsider status, becoming a sharp observer of her surroundings. As a teenager who returned to Detroit, she relished her reimmersion in *Yiddishkeit* and joined Habonim, the Labor Zionism youth movement. In 1948, she married Jack Moskowitz.

By 1950, the Moskowitzes followed the ex-urban trend and moved to a tract house in the Detroit suburbs. Jack Moskowitz finished law school during these years and began a challenging career. The Moskowitzes have four children: Shoshana, born in 1950; Frank, 1952; Seth, 1955; and Elizabeth, 1959. Moskowitz's liberal values, however, were born much earlier—"mitzvah training"—inculcated, she says, as part of her Jewish upbringing.

In 1962, her husband's political activities led to a new job that entailed a move to Washington, D.C., and he continued his liberal activism professionally. Among other projects, he was one of the founders of Common Cause. Faye

Moskowitz enrolled in George Washington University, where she met her mentor, creative-writing instructor Louis Schaffer. He recognized her talent as a writer, a talent she had nurtured as a diarist from the age of twelve. Soon after finishing his class, she began publishing in the *George Washington Forum*, the *Chronicle of Higher Education*, the *Washington Post*, where an op-ed piece was reprinted and syndicated, *Lilith, Belles Lettres, Modern Maturity*, the *Jewish Journal*, and others.

In 1980, following Marilyn Hacker's suggestion, she applied for and received a three-month residency at a writers' colony in Vence, France, where she stayed two and one-half months. Some of her experiences were chronicled in *A Leak in the Heart*. While she was there, the *New York Times* published one piece. Writing opportunities opened fast after that: she was invited to submit four pieces for the popular column "Hers." Reception to her work was so positive that she was asked to write a total of eight pieces.

She became a commentator on National Public Radio and wrote for *Woman's Day*. Even more significant, she was offered her first paying job as Director of the Middle School at the Edmund Burke School in Washington, D.C., and as an instructor in the George Washington University Adult Education Program. Recent honors include a fellowship and scholarship to the Bread Loaf Writers Conference (1983, 1985); the Ed Press Special Merit Award (1987); First Prize for Poetry by Arts Project Renaissance (1992); and the PEN Syndicated Fiction Award (1993, 1994).

In 1985, she published her first book, *A Leak in the Heart*, a collection of autobiographical essays. Three years later, *Whoever Finds This: I Love You*, a collection of short stories drawn largely from her years in Michigan, garnered very positive reviews, as had *Leak. And the Bridge is Love*, a collection of essays, was published in 1991. Her most recent work, *Her Face in the Mirror* (1994), is an edited collection of writings by Jewish women on their experiences as mothers and daughters and received a Jewish Book Award nomination.

MAJOR WORKS AND THEMES

Moskowitz writes about Jewishness, family, childhood, adolescence, relationships, love, and the pains and joys of connecting all the obligations of living honestly and morally. Although she is unaware of it, her stories have an oral quality to them in the tradition of Sholom Aleichem, I. L. Peretz, and Tillie Olsen. She had not even read Tillie Olsen until her creative-writing teacher commented on her resemblance of tone and idiom. Like Olsen, "her personal mentor," she is a very careful writer, revising intensively by weighing each word. The finished piece is spare, vivid, and extraordinarily tight. Each work, whether observation or story or a combination of both, is replete with smells, tastes, textures, and shades of light and dark, evoking a place and a mood. The essays are epiphanies, narratives that are laced with truths, common sense, warmth, and sometimes sadness or laughter. In the nature of epiphanies, they change the reader, enlarging her or his life by reviving memories of lived or regretted unlived moments. Like all epiphanies, they resonate and reveal a truth that the reader knew at some subconscious level.

A "Hers" column (*New York Times*, October 22, 1981) relates the struggle to reconcile living with her mother-in-law and defending her own privacy and position in the family: "Roles were not merely reversing . . . ; they were doing backflips." Another column (*New York Times*, November 19, 1981) recalls the anguish of silencing her dying mother: "Something terrible happens when we stop the mouths of the dying before they are dead. A silence grows up between us then, profounder than the grave. If we force the dying to go speechless, the stone dropped into the well will fall forever before the answering splash is heard."

The autobiographical essay, a form that Moskowitz has perfected, comprises her first and third books. Short stories, thinly disguised snapshots of revelatory moments in a girl's or woman's life, fill *Whoever Finds This: I Love You*. Other women's autobiographical short works comprise the fourth book, *Her Face in the Mirror*. In *A Leak in the Heart* (1985), Moskowitz takes us from Jackson, Michigan, and her childhood years of discovery to Washington, D.C., where her daily experiences as mother, student, teacher, and daughter-in-law are juxtaposed with the Jackson and Detroit of her childhood and adolescence: the death of a baby sister whose affliction was labeled a "leak in the heart"; denial of the poverty of the Depression—"Only people who have no hope are poor"; permanent outsider status as a Jew in a non-Jewish small town: "English came on cereal boxes and Bon Ami cans," a foil for the Yiddish of the *Jewish Daily Forward* that arrived in the mail each morning; travel to a writers' colony in southern France, the first time she was "alone" in her life; reconciliation of her obligations to her mother-in-law, who lived with the Moskowitzes from the postwar housing shortage in 1948 until her death in 1984.

Whoever Finds This: I Love You brims with both irony and recognition of self. She controls the sorrow, as in the stories of a child's death from a heart defect and a woman's (her mother's) isolation and pain after a mastectomy, and the hilarity embedded in "Presents," a virtual script of a bridal shower, excessive in its trappings, hypocrisy, and ritual. In the latter story, the very pregnant and uncomfortable narrator knows that she is outclassed: "Now it's pretty clear that if one-upmanship is a parachute to survival here, I'm the kid without a rip cord."

A strong first-person voice dominates the essays in *And the Bridge Is Love*, moving easily between Detroit, Jackson, Washington, and the farm country of Virginia. The breadth of this volume is the breadth of life, encompassing four generations and almost two thousand miles between its covers. Nurturing the terminally sick with cancer and AIDS, clinging to Jewish wedding ritual in the face of assimilation, negotiating the *goyishe* world of rural Virginia and the Yiddish world of "by us, we do," and partaking in the elaborate food rituals that mark life's events fill these pages. The limitations of both the non-Jewish and Jewish worlds are evident, the major difference being the passport one holds. Besides the anthropological treasures the book holds (which is true of the other books as well), *Bridge* contains wisdom that transcends ethnic boundaries: "To deny students exposure to classics for fear they are not ready for them is to consign them to books that may entertain but never challenge"; "One of the guests that day was my elderly aunt, who set aside her religious convictions against intermarriage to honor an even more basic tenet of universal faith: the love and preservation of family."

In her fourth book, Moskowitz included "strong and beautiful writing by Jewish women whether their names were readily recognizable or not . . . new voices . . . a gathering that might feel fresh." This is a dazzling collection in its honesty and breadth, unified by sentiments of tenderness, regretted moments, recollected pain, intergenerational ritual, conflicted but connected feelings, unfulfilled desires between mothers and daughters, difficult natural separations, and growing up, from the full range of Jewish identification to assimilation. Although the pages of *Her Face in the Mirror* share well-known names, such as Anne Roiphe, Vivian Gornick, Kim Chernin, Maxine Kumin, Linda Pastan, Irena Klepfisz, Barbara Goldberg, Grace Paley, and Alicia S. Ostriker, Moskowitz also includes lesser-known writers, such as Jody Bolz, and Judith Steinbergh.

CRITICAL RECEPTION

Frequently reviewed in the Jewish and feminist presses, Moskowitz has been favorably received, universally so in the former and slightly less enthusiastically so in the latter. Criticism centers on her omission of stories of domestic violence in Jewish families: Writing in the *Women's Review of Books*, Eunice Lipton harshly reproached Moskowitz for excluding works that reflect a daughter's anger against her mother or a mother's rage at her daughter. *Her Face in the Mirror*, Lipton charged, presents fairy tales (6–7). Much more representative are the comments by Merrill Joan Gerber, which are true for all four books. As she read, Gerber found it "necessary . . . to stop reading and connect with some imperative in [her] own history and track the parallel story in [her] own life." Each time she resumed reading, she "had the sensation that [she] was bodily lifted into a scene" (7). Moskowitz, as writer and editor, provides her readers with stories that resonate, experiences they recognize because they are familiar and true.

BIBLIOGRAPHY

Works by Faye Stollman Moskowitz

A Leak in the Heart. Boston: Godine, 1985.
Whoever Finds This: I Love You. Boston: Godine, 1988.
And the Bridge Is Love. Boston: Beacon, 1991.

(Editor) *Her Face in the Mirror: Jewish Women on Mothers and Daughters*. Boston: Beacon, 1994.

Works Cited and Studies of Faye Stollman Moskowitz

Gerber, Merrill Joan. Review of *Her Face in the Mirror*. *Belles Letters*, Fall 1994, 7.
Lipton, Eunice. Review of *Her Face in the Mirror*. *Women's Review of Books*, February 1995, 6–7.

JAY NEUGEBOREN (1938–)

Steven Goldleaf

BIOGRAPHY

Jay Neugeboren was born Jacob Mordecai Neugeboren in Brooklyn, New York, on May 30, 1938, to David and Anne Nassofer Neugeboren. His first and middle names were changed to Jay Michael because of his father's desire for his sons to be "Americans." Neugeboren was educated in racially integrated schools and received a B.A. from Columbia University in 1959 and an M.A. from Indiana University in 1963. He has been married twice, first to Betsy Bendorf in 1964, with whom he had three children; they were divorced in 1983. In 1985 he married Judy Krasnik, they were divorced in 1987. Before establishing himself as a writer, Neugeboren was an English teacher in New York City area schools from 1961 to 1966. Since then, he has taught at Columbia and the State University of New York at Old Westbury and in 1971 became writer-in-residence at the University of Massachusetts at Amherst. Among his awards, Neugeboren has received a Bread Loaf Conference De Voto Fellowship (1966); a *Transatlantic Review* novella award (1969); a National Endowment for the Arts grant (1973); a Guggenheim Fellowship (1975); six PEN syndicated fiction prizes (1982–1988); and a National Endowment for the Arts fellowship (1989).

MAJOR WORKS AND THEMES

Jay Neugeboren presents the time and place he grew up in—the middle-class, largely Jewish Flatbush section of Brooklyn in the intensely patriotic years during and just after World War II—with a far more complex, disturbing vision than it usually receives. "I want to turn my readers' expectations on their heads," Neugeboren explains in a conversation with this chapter's author. Resisting being labeled—or mislabeled—a "Jewish writer," he continues to describe Judaism's religious, cultural, political, moral, and personal concerns. Though his subject matter—postwar Brooklyn, family life, and sports, among other things—is often shown in nostalgic accounts, Neugeboren focuses instead on its subtle conflicts. He is fond of citing Flannery O'Connor's response to the idea that writers need to live exciting lives: "Her answer was that anyone who survived childhood should have enough material to last a lifetime. If you can't make fiction out of a little material, you're not going to make it out of a lot."

His family, far from the traditional tight-knit, loving Jewish family, was full of characters, some of them strange and violent: his grandparents, for example, lived apart but still managed to fight constantly. "My grandmother, an aunt, and an uncle would not come to my Bar Mitzvah," Neugeboren recalled thirty-five years after that event, "*because* my grandfather came." He describes his mother's family as "a crazy, warring Russian brood" whose mysterious, seemingly unmotivated behavior puzzled and sometimes frightened him. Although he had written fiction as early as age eight, it was only when he left his parents' apartment in 1955 to attend Columbia that he considered becoming a fiction writer.

Exposed during college to a broader range of literature than the Steinbeck and Farrell he had read voraciously as a boy—to say nothing of the worldly professors, his ambitious fellow students, and the ideas they generated—Neugeboren became a prodigious writer. He completed his first novel in his sophomore year. "It was almost as if I had done something heroic," Neugeboren recalls. "That I at the age of—what was it, eighteen or nineteen?—had done such a thing, had written a novel." By his senior year, he had written another one, and five others by the age of twenty-seven. All these early works remain unpublished, though through no lack of Neugeboren's effort. Several Columbia professors encouraged him to submit them to publishers; later editors, agents, and fellow writers would also urge him to keep writing fiction. Neugeboren collected literally thousands of rejection letters and had had only a few stories accepted when he caught his big break. "The Application," a story rejected dozens of times, was taken by the *Transatlantic Review* and then reprinted in Martha Foley's anthology *Best American Short Stories of 1965*. Soon after, *Big Man* became Neugeboren's first published novel (1966).

Neugeboren's published work (now totalling a dozen volumes) increasingly reveals more about his life. "Not a lot of my fiction is autobiographical," he observed recently; his earliest published work is devotedly antiautobiographical. "I never thought of myself as having imagination," he confessed in 1981, "even though I had written, published and unpublished, maybe sixteen books of fiction—which are, of course, works of the imagination." He attributed his storytelling ability to his stubbornness, to his will, and to his hard work, but only after years of analysis was he able to see that his love of storytelling and his imagination were not such different qualities.

Neugeboren's early books contain no characters who stand in for himself: the title characters of his first two novels are a black athlete and a Puerto Rican teenager. His first collection of short fiction, *Corky's Brother* (1969), is partly narrated by voices close to Neugeboren's own—the title novella and the story "Luther" most memorably—but other stories, such as "The Application," are related in his more impersonal early style. Even his first nonfiction book, *Parentheses: An Autobiographical Journey* (1970), concerns his political perspectives more than his personal history.

"I've had intensely happy periods in my life—two separate periods, in fact, of a wonderful family life—and some wildly horrible times," Neugeboren says, and the 1970s were a joyous period. By now the father of three children, Neugeboren grew more and more interested in exploring Judaism. He led his synagogue's youth group and eventually served as synagogue president. "In my own life," he told an interviewer in 1979, "the fact of Judaism is central. I put on *tfillim* in the morning and when sabbath comes I stop my work." His 1974 novel *Sam's Legacy* had a Jewish title character, but it was his next two novels, *An Orphan's Tale* (1976) and *The Stolen Jew* (1981) that explored in depth the issues sparked by his new interest in Judaism.

The wildly horrible times for Neugeboren erupted in the early 1980s. In chapters of *The Stolen Jew*, he had described a severely strained marriage; shortly after that novel was published, his own marriage broke up. After a traumatic divorce, in which he got custody of his three children, he discovered his second period of close family life as a single father. In 1985, he published the novel *Before My Life Began*, his ninth published book in twenty years, but in the following period of over a decade he published one book, *Poli* (1989), a novel for young adults. However, Neugeboren remained active and successful, even prolific, in other genres: he wrote several award-winning plays, including a 1991 PBS adaptation of Hortense Calisher's *The Hollow Boy* (about a friendship between a Jew and a German at the start of World War II), and he has continued to publish short fiction in many of the best periodicals. His second collection of short stories, *Don't Worry about the Kids*, is being published in 1997, and he has completed another novel about what he terms "the new American Diaspora" in a style more intensely surrealistic than his previous work; he is now completing a novel set in the years 1915 through 1930, before (as his last published novel's title put it) his life began.

Neugeboren's major theme has been one of identity. Like Shakespeare's Antipholus, his characters, from his first novel through his most recent, question "if that I am I." What qualities, Neugeboren asks, determine people's essence? Are their identities determined by what they do, or who they love, or which moral values they choose? Like Antipholus, too, his protagonists' identities are entwined with the identities of their brothers. Mack Davis, Neugeboren's "Big Man," is a basketball star cut off from his only source of joy by his participation in a point-shaving scandal. (Though reviewers have noted Davis's similarity to athletes such as Connie Hawkins, a real-life Brooklyn ghetto basketball star whose career was blighted by point shaving, none has noted the parallel between

Mack Davis and Neugeboren's college mentor Charles Van Doren, whose literary career was destroyed in the other great crisis of personal integrity of the 1950s, the television quiz-show scandal.) The relationship between Davis and his younger brother, whose sense of self is shaken by his big brother's larger crisis, presages many other disappointing relationships between brothers in Neugeboren's work: the novella "Corky's Brother" concerns a younger brother learning who he is now that his revered older brother has died; in the novel *The Stolen Jew*, the identity of the younger, more fragile brother becomes subsumed in his surviving brother's identity—after his death on page one, the younger brother's vivid presence continues to be felt, both in the older brother's mind, where they continue to converse, and in his life, where the older brother romances his younger brother's widow. In *Before My Life Began* (1985), the protagonist astonishingly falls out of the novel halfway through the book; when the story resumes after a fifteen-year hiatus, Neugeboren mentions neither the protagonist's name, wife, child, nor personal history. Even the narration shifts in the book's second half, and the protagonist's new identity must be pieced together. Finally, the reader senses the protagonist's presence through his absence, a paradox consistent with Neugeboren's often touching irony. "I understand loss," one of his characters proclaims, and it is through loss that his characters acquire their essence. That question of his characters' identity joins with the question of their cultural identity: "What are the sources of survival, both in an individual and in a people?" Neugeboren asked an interviewer. "The question of who is to live and who to die . . . comes up again and again in [*The Stolen Jew*]. . . . These things interest me profoundly, historically . . . and emotionally" (Basel, 326). Yet the whole subject of Jewish writing does not interest Neugeboren much:

It comes out of what I would call a sociological imagination. It tends to treat literature as sociology, and that's not literature's strength. It tends to put writers into very small and dull boxes: a Jewish writer, a black writer, a native-American writer, a feminist writer, et cetera. Readers or potential readers then approach these writers, or think of them, only in these terms and therefore are not open to the incredible pleasures the writers can give—pleasures that exist apart from the sociological or ethnic background of fiction. (Basel, 328).

CRITICAL RECEPTION

Despite Neugeboren's objections, critics have often put him into such "small and dull boxes." Pearl K. Bell wrote of *An Orphan's Tale* that "the literary theme of the devout orphan's search for a Jewish family and home, a sense of belonging, was developed with a learned abundance of Jewish lore, and placed Neugeboren within a new generation of writers committed in varying ways to Jewish tradition, if not religion" (quoted in Basel, 326). Marilyn K. Basel, in her *Contemporary Authors* sketch on Neugeboren, contrasted that perspective with John Leonard's *New York Times* dismissal of Judaism as the primary "source of energy . . . for the extraordinary power of *An Orphan's Tale*," (Basel, 326). In *MELUS*, Cordelia Candelaria noted that while Neugeboren's self-referential playfulness might be attributed to midrashic or talmudic style, it could as well derive from the self-referentialness of postmodernist metafiction, which also uses the motif of a text commenting on an inner text. Neugeboren has received adulating reviews in the *New York Times Book Review* (for *Big Man*), in *Commonweal* (for *Listen Ruben Fontanez*), in *Partisan Review* (for *The Stolen Jew*), and numerous other prestigious critical venues, yet overall his work has not earned the critical attention it has deserved. *The Stolen Jew* won the American Jewish Committee's award for best novel of 1981, and *Before My Life Began* was awarded the Edward Lewis Wallant Prize in 1985.

"God created man because he loves stories," a character in *The Stolen Jew* observes, and Neugeboren's excellence has been recognized by his fellow storytellers (ranging from James Michener to Anne Tyler), who often award literary honors such as Neugeboren's six consecutive PEN syndicated fiction prizes, a Guggenheim Fellowship, and a pair of NEA grants. But to date his fellow writers have voiced more nearly unanimously than the critics a warmer recognition of the quality of his work.

BIBLIOGRAPHY

Works by Jay Neugeboren

Novels

Big Man. Boston: Houghton Mifflin, 1966.
Listen Ruben Fontanez. Boston: Houghton Mifflin, 1968.
Sam's Legacy. New York: Holt, Rinehart and Winston, 1974.
An Orphan's Tale. New York: Holt, Rinehart and Winston, 1976.
The Stolen Jew. New York: Holt, Rinehart and Winston, 1981.
Before My Life Began. New York: Simon and Schuster, 1985.

Short Stories

Corky's Brother and Other Stories. New York: Farrar, Straus, and Giroux, 1969.
Penguin Modern Stories, 3. With others. London: Penguin, 1970.

Selected Periodical Publications

"My Son, the Freedom Rider." *Colorado Quarterly* 13 (Summer 1964): 71–76.
"The Application." *Transatlantic Review* 17 (Autumn 1964): 52–58.
"Something Is Rotten in the Borough of Brooklyn." *Ararat* 8 (Autumn 1967), 27–35.
"Connorsville, Virginia." *Transatlantic Review* 31 (Winter 1969): 11–23.
"The Place Kicking Specialist." *Transatlantic Review* 50 (Fall/Winter 1974), 111–26.
"His Violin." *Atlantic Monthly* 242 (November 1978): 48–50.
"Star of David." *TriQuarterly* 45: (Spring 1979): 5–15.
"The St. Dominick's Game." *Atlantic Monthly* 244 (December 1979): 54–58.

"Visiting Hour." *Shenandoah* 31 (March 1980): 23–29.
"Poppa's Books." *Atlantic Monthly* 246 (May 1980): 59–63.
"Bonus Baby." *John O'Hara Journal* 3 (Fall/Winter 1980): 10–21.
"Stairs." *Present Tense* 12 (Fall 1985).
"Don't Worry about the Kids." *Georgia Review*. Spring 1987, 121–39.
"Your Child Has Been Towed." *Gettysburg Review*, Autumn 1988.
"Overseas." *Michigan Quarterly Review*, Summer 1990, 695–721.

Plays

The Edict. Produced, New York, 1981.
The Hollow Bay (television play). 1991.

Other Works

Parentheses: An Autobiographical Journey. New York: Dutton, 1970.
Poli: A Mexican Boy in Early Texas. San Antonio: Corona, 1989.

Studies of Jay Neugeboren

Basel, Marilyn. "Jay Neugeboren." In *Contemporary Authors* 21. Detroit: Gale, 1987, 324–29.
Candelaria, Cordelia. "A Decade of the Ethnic Fiction of Jay Neugeboren." *MELUS*, Winter 1978, 71–78.
———. "Jay Neugeboren." In *Twentieth-Century American-Jewish Fiction Writers*, ed. Daniel Walden. vol. 28 of *Dictionary of Literary Biography*. Detroit: Gale, 1978.
Goldleaf, Steven. "A Jew without Portfolio." *Partisan Review*, Summer 1983, 444–46.
Moran, Charles. "Parentheses." *Massachusetts Review*, Summer 1970. 613–16

HUGH NISSENSON (1933–)

Andrew Furman

BIOGRAPHY

In broad strokes, the story of Hugh Nissenson's childhood is the story of countless other Jews of his generation. He was born on March 10, 1933, in Brooklyn,
New York. His father, Charles Nissenson, immigrated to the United States from
Warsaw as a youth in 1910 and settled on the Lower East Side of New York,
where he worked in a sweatshop sweater factory. Charles Nissenson thus lived
in the world that Abraham Cahan first brought to national attention in *The Rise
of David Levinsky* (1917), and the world that Hugh Nissenson would later depict
in *My Own Ground* (1976). Fortunately, Charles Nissenson eventually procured
a better job as a salesman. Hugh Nissenson's mother, Harriette Dolch, was born
in Brooklyn after her parents immigrated from Lvov, Poland.

Charles and Harriette Nissenson embraced the secular world of America and
saw no reason why their son should acquire traditional religious training. Instead, they enrolled Hugh Nissenson in prestigious secular schools. Nissenson
graduated from New York's Fieldston School and Phi Beta Kappa from Swarth-
more College in 1955. Many of the world's mythologies—Jewish, Greek,
Hindu, and Christian—intrigued Nissenson, and as was the case for several other
secular Jews, his consciousness as he matured became increasingly absorbed by
the two central Jewish events of the twentieth century: the Holocaust and the
creation of Israel. These essential elements—mysticism, Israel, and the Holocaust—inspired Nissenson's literary imagination from the start.

The years 1959 through the 1960s were watershed years for Hugh Nissenson.
The stories that were later collected in his first book, *A Pile of Stones* (1965),
began to appear in prestigious magazines like *Harper's, Commentary,* and *Esquire.* In 1961, he received a coveted Wallace Stegner Fellowship at Stanford

and traveled to Israel to report on the Adolf Eichmann trial for *Commentary*. In the summers of 1965 and 1967, Hugh Nissenson returned to Israel and lived on the Kibbutz Mayan Baruch, situated perilously on the Syrian border near the Golan Heights. These, of course, were volatile years leading up to Israel's climactic Six-Day War, and Nissenson documented his experiences living on the kibbutz in his nonfiction work, *Notes from the Frontier* (1968). Nissenson and his wife, Marilyn Claster Nissenson, have since visited Israel on countless occasions.

Nissenson and his wife have lived on New York's Upper West Side for several years and have two daughters, Kate and Kore. Nissenson has held visiting positions teaching English and religion at Manhattanville College, Yale, Ohio Wesleyan, Denison, and the Universities of Milan and Pavia. He is presently writing and illustrating a new novel, *Song of the Earth*, which takes place in Nebraska during the first decades of the twenty-first century. The novel, Nissenson tells me, complements his two earlier novels to complete the trilogy, but at the same time it represents a total departure aesthetically. The possibilities of the novel as an art form fascinate Nissenson. He puts it tersely: "I am a modernist. My goal is to make it new."

MAJOR WORKS AND THEMES

In the wake of Hugh Nissenson's first collection of stories, *A Pile of Stones*, Robert Alter lauded Nissenson as a "genuinely religious writer" (75). *A Pile of Stones* and Nissenson's subsequent work bear out Alter's contention. What unifies the stories collected in *A Pile of Stones* is Nissenson's persistent exploration of the role of covenantal belief amid environments seemingly devoid of redemptive possibilities. In the two stories set in Poland before the Holocaust, the covenanted status of the Jew, with all its burdens, emerges as an inescapable element of Jewish life in the European Diaspora. In "The Prisoner," for example, a Jewish prisoner in a czarist jail recalls witnessing a vicious pogrom that has shaken his religious faith. The prisoner ostensibly rejects the covenant and embraces socialism, seeing the imminent workers' revolution as a secular alternative to an illusory faith in the Messiah. However, the more the prisoner attempts to extricate himself from a covenantal existence, the more covenanted burdens him. A recurring nightmare plagues him in which he sees order and meaning in both the sordid conditions in his prison cell and in the evil of the pogrom he witnessed as a child.

In the three stories in *A Pile of Stones* set in a secular and materialistic America, Nissenson illustrates the waning of traditional religious observance. Still, a precious few maintain their beliefs and fulfill their religious duties. In "The Law," a disaffected narrator reflects upon his younger cousin's determination at his bar mitzvah to recite his Haftorah (a portion of the Torah) in front of the synagogue congregation despite his severe stammer. The boy, who listens attentively to his father's concentration-camp memories, follows his father's example as he embraces the covenant at the bar mitzvah. Ultimately, then, in the stories set in both Europe and America, Nissenson depicts covenantal existence as a burden, but a burden that must be met. In two stories, "The Blessing" and "The Well," it does not seem that covenantal faith will survive in Israel. In "The Blessing," for example, the protagonist, Yitzhak, whose young son has just died of cancer, cannot attend his son's religious funeral since he knows that he cannot pray over his son's grave. Yitzhak laments his inability to affirm the covenant and clings to the possibility that he might regain his faith, but Nissenson provides no indication that this will happen. In "The Well," Jewish militarism threatens the redemptive possibilities in the Middle East as Nissenson depicts the insurmountable tensions between a Jewish kibbutz and a neighboring Bedouin village.

In Nissenson's second collection of stories, *In the Reign of Peace* (1972), he returns to the problem of Israeli militarism and explores the viability of Israeli socialism as a substitute for religion as well. In the title story, a young Orthodox Jew shows a socialist kibbutznik a mouse being eaten alive by ants to help him visualize what the Messiah will redeem in the "reign of peace"; he thereby exposes the paltriness of the socialist alternative to religion. A Jewish doctor in Palestine during the British occupation wonders in "The Throne of Good" whether any good can come from the violent tactics of his boyhood friend's nationalist gang, and in "Forcing the End," we are forced to consider the moral implications when members of a different militant nationalist group murder an Orthodox rabbi who espouses passivism. In "Crazy Old Man," an elderly Orthodox Jew shoots an Arab prisoner during the 1948 War of Independence—he commits a sin of violence—to prevent two native Israeli soldiers from tainting themselves with the sin. Finally, another religious Israeli laments Israel's adoption of a militaristic code in "Going Up" after he "goes up" to the Golan Heights just after the Six-Day War and sees the Arab carnage. He also finds it difficult to celebrate Jerusalem's liberation when he considers the story of the Israeli paratrooper who cries at the Western Wall because he does not know how to pray.

"Lamentations" possibly represents the best in the collection. In it, Nissenson confronts the problems both of Israeli militarism and of secularism. In the opening scene, Nissenson dramatizes what militarism has wrought upon Israel. A young pregnant woman whose boyfriend was just killed in a battle against the Egyptians tells her friend Yigal that she plans to marry the boyfriend over his grave so that her child will have his name. The story revolves primarily around Yigal, who has shunned religion and harbors bitter feelings for Israel's religious passivists. He sees no reason to affirm the covenant since secular Jewish soldiers and not the Messiah created Israel. However, Yigal finds that he cannot turn a deaf ear to the spiritual component of his identity. As he walks his pregnant friend home, he peers into a small synagogue and stands transfixed by the sight of the Ark (which holds the Torah), the *bima* (a synagogue pulpit), and, especially, the nasal-sounding prayers. Yigal knows that he can never share the faith of the synagogue men, and tears well up in his eyes. Religion seems irretrievably lost to the modern Israeli in Nissenson's first two story collections, and this loss is particularly tragic since no other viable mythic or spiritual component replaces traditional Judaism.

Nissenson's two novels that followed *In the Reign of Peace* represent, in varying degrees, departures from his earlier work. In *My Own Ground* (1976), Nissenson turns his attention from Jewish existence in the European shtetl and Israel and focuses exclusively upon the experiences of Jacob Brody on New York's Lower East Side. Brody, looking back over fifty years later upon one tumultuous summer in 1912, tells his story as a memoir. Borrowing from his father's and grandfather's stories of the Lower East Side, Nissenson creates a realistic, thoroughly unromanticized portrait of Jewish immigrant assimilation along New York's gritty streets. Indeed, the world that greets Brody, a street-smart orphan, is a world replete with rape, murder, sexual barbarity, drug abuse, slave labor, prostitution, and suicide.

Though Nissenson's portrait of Hester Street contrasts sharply with his earlier depictions of, say, life on a kibbutz, his overarching concern remains the same: can religion survive the modern pressures that challenge the Jews' covenantal belief? It appears that the boot of American materialism and secularism has squashed the religious life altogether. A pious rabbi, Isaacs, cannot adopt the materialistic code of his American congregation, and so he quits and withers away before our eyes; his daughter, Hannah, who had been pious in Europe, loses her faith, resorts to a life of prostitution, and ultimately kills herself; her sadistic pimp, Schlifka, maintains that he lived an observant life in Europe, but to survive in America he adopts a code of brutality. What is more, Brody's friends who resist the American creed of avaricious capitalism seek secular Marxist and Zionist alternatives.

In a striking parallel to a running theme in *In the Reign of Peace*, a rabbi toward the end of *My Own Ground* sees no alternative but to bring on the Messiah, to "force the end," through encouraging humankind's continued descent to the lowest levels of humanity. Here, Nissenson alludes eerily to the forthcoming Holocaust. While the prospect of redemption appears bleak in the novel, Liela Goldman is correct to recognize a glimmer of hope in the conclusion, which culminates in a birth. America will simply have to suffice as a spiritual locus. When the crazy Rabbi Isaacs informs Brody in a dream sequence that "everything" is holy ground, we believe him.

While Nissenson breaks some "new ground" in *My Own Ground*, his second novel, *The Tree of Life* (1985), represents his most striking artistic departure. The novel consists entirely of a series of journal entries by Thomas Keene, a Harvard-educated minister living on the Ohio frontier. In scrupulous detail, Keene documents approximately a year of his life between 1811 and 1812. As one reads Keene's accounts of his efforts to learn how to throw a tomahawk and reload his rifle while galloping on his horse, one realizes that Nissenson has indeed ventured onto new terrain. In style, plotting, setting, and its specific theme (the Christian protagonist's loss of faith), the novel stands firmly on its own. Still, though Nissenson substitutes the Ohio frontier for the Golan Heights and the United States' War of 1812 for Israel's War of 1967, his essential concerns remain the same. For Keene, like Nissenson's Jewish protagonists, struggles to regain his faith in a brutish and apparently godless world (he must cope with his wife's untimely death and the horrific acts of savagery inflicted by and upon both the American settlers and the Native American Indians). It should be noted that Keene's very act of writing his diary and handing it down to his son represents a triumph against nihilism.

Throughout his career as a fiction writer, Nissenson returns again and again to the quandary: can faith and religious duty survive the exigencies bearing down upon his protagonists? "What happens when people lose faith," Nissenson tells me, "has been the ongoing drama of the twentieth century. I try to give a portrait of people who have lost faith." Nissenson's work remains fresh and inventive as he creates portraits of such distinctive characters and persistently varies his settings, historical periods, and circumstances. He thus constantly shifts the frame of reference through which he addresses his enduring artistic concern. Synthesizing the breadth of Nissenson's work, Alan Berger aptly noted that "Nissenson's struggle to seek redemption in spite of a world without God, and his insistence on pursuing the religious impulse in the face of rampant evil, mark him an exemplar of the Jewish theological imagination" ("American Jewish Fiction," 233).

CRITICAL RECEPTION

Though Hugh Nissenson has yet to garner a widespread popular readership, critics have consistently lauded his work. His first collection of stories, *A Pile of Stones*, earned Nissenson the Edward Lewis Wallant Prize—the award recognizing the year's most significant book on a Jewish-American subject. The collection convinced several eminent scholars and critics that Nissenson, a writer wholly immersed in Jewish themes and spiritual introspection, was something special to hit the Jewish-American literary scene. Robert Alter, for example, praised Nissenson's "imaginative integrity" and observed that "while other Jewish writers haul in our forefathers by their pious beards to provide scenic effect or symbolic suggestiveness, the introduction of such figures in Nissenson's work is an act of serious self-examination: can the God of the kaftaned grandfather still be the God of the buttoned-down grandson, especially with the terrible shadow of the Holocaust intervening between then and now?" (75).

Alan Berger, like Alter, recognized the theological concerns at the center of Nissenson's first collection. "*A Pile of Stones*," Berger observed, "focuses on the religious ambiguity of post-Holocaust covenant faith asking if redemption is possible in a world of diminished deity" ("Judaism," 59). Berger and several other critics like Lawrence Berkove, Cynthia Ozick, and Ruth Wisse went so far as to characterize Nissenson's early stories as midrashim, revelatory commentaries on religious texts.

The publication of Nissenson's second collection of stories, *In the Reign of Peace*, solidified his status as a "religious" writer. In her review of the collection, Cynthia Ozick drew a sharp contrast between Nissenson's theological imagination and the largely secular vision of his most notable predecessors, Bellow, Roth, and Malamud. "He means to sink into Godhood itself," Ozick asserted (4). She continued later, "He is the first American Jewish writer to step beyond social observation, beyond communal experience, into the listening places of the voice of the Lord of History" (4). Reflecting upon Nissenson's first two story collections, Ruth Wisse noted that he "feel[s] the historic, moral, and religious weight of Judaism, and want[s] to represent it in literature" (45).

While critics generally praise Nissenson's theological imagination, some have taken him to task for the overtness of his allegorical content. Ruth Wisse argued that he ungracefully imposes his "moral design upon his characters" (43), while Alter put it a bit more colorfully, claiming that Nissenson's stories tend to "read like neatly arranged laboratory situations for testing out a series of problems of faith and theodicy" (75). Perhaps the most incisive critique of *In the Reign of Peace* came from Harold Fisch, who questioned the validity of Nissenson's neat secular/militaristic, religious/passivist dichotomy. Nissenson, Fisch asserted, insists upon presenting a consistent religious antipathy toward militarism, though it "doesn't always work that way in Israel" (72). Still, Fisch gave credit where credit was due and praised Nissenson for "seriously hand[ling] the religious problem of the modern Jew" (72).

To be sure, Hugh Nissenson has distinguished himself primarily as a short-story writer; the republication of several of Nissenson's early stories in *The Elephant and My Jewish Problem: Selected Stories and Journals* (1988) illustrates their enduring relevance and power. Moreover, these early stories continue to garner most of the scholarly attention afforded to Nissenson. However, his two novels, *My Own Ground* and *The Tree of Life*, received mostly favorable reviews; the latter novel was nominated for the American Book Award and the PEN/Faulkner Award and won the Ohioana Book Award for fiction in 1986.

Several reviewers applauded the gritty realism of Nissenson's *My Own Ground*. In her review of the novel in the *New Leader*, Pearl Bell commended it for its "unwavering command of its place and time—the redolent immediacy of the streets and the houses" (19). Peter Shaw also praised the novel for its realism, noting that Nissenson makes a "positive assault" on the immigrant myth (29). Finally, Alvin Rosenfeld viewed *My Own Ground* as a progression in Nissenson's fiction insofar as New York's Lower East Side represents more debased and thus more "fertile ground" on which Nissenson explores his central artistic concern, the redemptive possibilities in the modern world: "The question this time . . . becomes not whether it is possible to create a humane civilization without God but, given man's inclination for degrading and inhumane action,

what needs to be done to bring the creature down before he can be raised up?''
(56).

Most reviewers praised Nissenson's terse novel *The Tree of Life* for its realism, as well, but they also appreciated its emotional intensity and inventiveness. Eliot Fremont-Smith observed that ''it's a tale more moving and haunting
than one thinks it can possibly be. The ruse of authenticity really works'' (45).
Christopher Lehmann-Haupt called it a "*tour de force* of realism'' (C20). While
reviewers emphasized the distinctiveness of *The Tree of Life*, those who had
followed Nissenson's career from the start were quick to draw parallels to Nissenson's earlier work. Diane Cole contended that ''though their religions differ,
the characters in all his books suffer similar crises of faith. . . . In the Lower
East Side tenements of 'My Own Ground,' and in the makeshift cabins on the
Ohio frontier of 'The Tree of Life,' Nissenson depicts tormented souls who
renounce all belief in God, or declare themselves followers of the god of pure
chance'' (57–58).

Nissenson's oeuvre is relatively small but nonetheless dazzling. His name
invariably crops up when scholars of Jewish-American literature reflect upon
the most exciting Jewish-American voices in contemporary literature. All told,
Lawrence Berkove echoed popular consensus as he considered Nissenson's stories: ''In these stories of the Jewish spirit, no doubt some of the best ever written
by an American Jew, Hugh Nissenson has achieved a rare blending of beauty
and power. Successful first as literary portraits of human beings, they are also
movingly affirmative of Jewish tradition. In the best tradition of Judaism, they
illustrate how much being Jewish has to say about being human'' (81).

BIBLIOGRAPHY

Works by Hugh Nissenson

A Pile of Stones: Short Stories. New York: Scribner, 1965.
Notes from the Frontier. New York: Dial, 1968.
In the Reign of Peace. New York: Farrar, Straus and Giroux, 1972.
My Own Ground. New York: Farrar, Straus and Giroux, 1976.
The Tree of Life. New York: Harper and Row, 1985.
The Elephant Journals, 1957–1987. New York: Harper and Row, 1988.

Works Cited and Studies of Hugh Nissenson

Alter, Robert. ''Sentimentalizing the Jews.'' *Commentary*, September 1965, 71–75.
Aronson, Steven M. L. ''Frontier Obsession: Realizing History through Tomahawks,
        Blunderbusses, Buckskins, Powder Horns, Drums, and a Hudson's Bay Coat.''
        House and Garden, November 1985, 70, 76, 80, 84.
Bell, Pearl. ''Idylls of the Tribe.'' Review of *My Own Ground. New Leader*, April 12,
        1976, 19.
Berger, Alan L. ''American Jewish Fiction.'' *Modern Judaism* 10 (1990): 221–41.

————. "Judaism as a Religious Value System." In *Crisis and Covenant: The Holocaust in American Jewish Fiction*, Ed. Alan L. Berger. Albany: State University of New York Press, 1985, 59–65.

————. "Pre-Holocaust America: Jewish Existence and Covenant Diminishment." In *Crisis and Covenant: The Holocaust in American Jewish Fiction*. Albany: State University of New York Press, 1985, 137–44.

Berkove, Lawrence I. "American Midrashim: Hugh Nissenson's Stories." *Critique* 20 (1978): 75–82.

Cole, Diane. Review of *The Tree of Life*. *Present Tense* 13 (1985): 57–58.

Fisch, Harold. "High Adventure and Spiritual Quest." Review of *In the Reign of Peace*. *Midstream*, January 1973, 71–72.

Fremont-Smith, Eliot. "Ohio Death Trip." Review of *The Tree of Life*. *Village Voice*, October 22, 1985, 45.

Furman, Andrew. "Hugh Nissenson's Israel: In Search of a Viable Israeli Ethos." *Studies in American Jewish Literature* 13 (1994): 59–71.

Goldman, Liela H. "Hugh Nissenson." In *Twentieth-Century American-Jewish Fiction Writers*, ed. Daniel Walden. Vol. 28 of *Dictionary of Literary Biography*. Detroit: Gale, 1984. 189–195.

Lehmann-Haupt, Christopher. Review of *The Tree of Life*. *New York Times*, October 14, 1985, C20.

Ozick, Cynthia. Review of *In the Reign of Peace*. *New York Times Book Review*, March 19, 1972, 4, 22.

Rosenfeld, Alvin H. "Israel and the Idea of Redemption in the Fiction of Hugh Nissenson." *Midstream*, April 1980, 54–56.

Shaw, Peter. Review of *My Own Ground*. *New Republic*, April 10, 1976, 29.

Wisse, Ruth R. "American Jewish Writing, Act II." *Commentary*, June 1976, 40–45.

TILLIE OLSEN   (1912 or 1913–   )

Karen L. Polster

BIOGRAPHY

Fiction writer, essayist, educator, and inspiration to women writers in America, Tillie Olsen was born Tillie Lerner on January 14, 1912 or 1913, the second child in a large family. Her birth was not recorded, and Olsen herself has never been sure of the exact year. Her parents were Jewish socialists who fled Russia after the 1905 rebellion and settled in Nebraska, where her family continued the political activism that would influence her life and work. Her father was State Secretary of the Nebraska Socialist Party and ran as the Socialist candidate for state representative. Olsen left high school to help support her large family with a variety of jobs, including slaughterhouse trimmer, power-press operator, hash slinger, mayonnaise-jar capper, and checker in a warehouse. She continued her interrupted education on her own by reading voraciously at the Omaha public library, boasting that she had read all the fiction there almost through the M's (Rosenfelt, 371–406). As Deborah Rosenfelt has noted, Olsen's reading was "remarkably eclectic"; however, it was predisposed to American populists like Walt Whitman, realists such as Elizabeth Madox Roberts and Willa Cather, and proletarian writers like Upton Sinclair, Mike Gold, and Henry Roth (218–19).

In 1933, Olsen moved to San Francisco and for the next several years worked as a political activist for the Young Communist League while beginning her writing career. She published several polemical essays, including "The Strike" and "Thousand-Dollar Vagrant," which chronicled her involvement in the 1934 maritime strike in San Francisco. At the time, she was arrested and briefly jailed. She also wrote two poems during this period. "There Is a Lesson" (1934) concerns the murder of Austrian socialists by the fascist Dollfuss government. "I Want You Women up North to Know" (1934) is a powerful indictment of the abuses suffered by garment workers in Mexico. In 1932, she began *Yonnondio*, a novel about a working-class family of the 1920s. One chapter, "The Iron Throat," was published in 1934. However, Olsen never completed the project, and the work was forgotten until four decades later.

The single mother of a daughter, Karla, she began a lifelong relationship with Jack Olsen, a printer who shared her union concerns, in 1936. They married in 1944. Tillie and Jack had three more daughters, Julie, Kathie, and Laurie, and she again put aside her writing for a series of jobs to help support her family. It was twenty years before she published again. The short story "Help Her to Believe" (later renamed "I Stand Here Ironing") appeared in 1956. A Stanford University Creative Writing Center Fellowship and a Ford Foundation Grant in Literature in 1959 allowed her to continue writing. Though her short stories are still concerned with the lives of the working class, they are less didactic than her earlier, more political works. The fiction is characterized by an evocative, imagistic style. In 1960, the story "Tell Me a Riddle" won the O. Henry Award for Best Story of the Year.

Her first book was not published until 1961, when Olsen was nearly fifty. It was a collection of her short stories titled *Tell Me a Riddle*. With a two-year fellowship for independent study at Radcliffe Institute and a 1967 National Endowment for the Arts Grant in Literature, she was able to complete the short story "Requa," publishing it in 1970. Meanwhile, her husband had found fragments of the unfinished novel *Yonnondio* among her papers, and Olsen reassembled them and published the work as *Yonnondio: From the Thirties* in 1974.

Both her activist early writing and her highly polished short fiction centered on the lives of women. Because of this feminist vision, Olsen has become more well known for her inspiration to other women writers than for her own fiction. In 1971 she took a position as Visiting Lecturer at Stanford University Writing Center Seminar and gave a course on women and literature, constructing the first reading list for women's studies. She continued to lecture on feminist concerns on campuses throughout the United States, including the Massachusetts Institute of Technology, the University of Massachusetts at Boston, and the University of California campuses at Los Angeles, San Diego, and Santa Cruz. She received a Guggenheim Fellowship in 1975 and was cited for her distinguished contribution to American literature by the American Academy and National Institute of Arts and Letters.

Through her own experience, Olsen became interested in the constraints motherhood places on women's writing careers. In 1978 she published *Silences*, a collection of essays and other nonfiction that delineated the pressures of being a woman, a mother, and an artist. Her concern with the demands and rewards of motherhood is evident in two collections she edited: a daybook entitled *Mother to Daughter, Daughter to Mother* (1984) and a book of photographs called *Mothers and Daughters* (1987).

Olsen continues to influence feminist studies and encourage writers throughout the world. In 1980, she traveled as the International Visiting Scholar for

Norwegian Universities. Her reading lists are used nationwide to develop women's studies courses, and she still works to reclaim women's "lost" texts. Rebecca Harding Davis's *Life in the Iron Mills*, Agnes Smedley's *Daughters of Earth*, and Charlotte Perkins Gilman's *The Yellow Wallpaper* were all reprinted at her suggestion (Barr). Olsen foregrounds the lives of women in her work and places their domestic struggles at the center of political action.

MAJOR WORKS AND THEMES

Olsen's small but distinguished body of work is characterized by her insistence that the lives of the working class, particularly working-class mothers, are appropriate subjects for literature. Her work is dedicated to giving a voice to marginalized people silenced by class and/or gender. Realistic dialogue, evocative interior monologues, emotionally charged imagery, and lyrical passages are hallmarks of her writing. Olsen's work falls roughly into three periods: the polemic activist publications of the 1930s and 1940s; the highly praised short fiction of the 1950s and 1960s; and the feminist-humanist nonfiction writing, teaching, and public speaking from the 1970s to the present.

While her work does not center specifically on the Jewish experience, Olsen claims that her Jewish socialist upbringing, her "Yiddishkeit," backgrounds all her work. In an unpublished interview in 1983, she noted that it provided her with two important insights: the knowledge and experience of injustice, and an absolute belief in the potentiality of human beings (quoted in Lyons, 91). Joyce Antler noted that Olsen came of age in the 1930s, and like other Jewish women writers of this time, for example, Tess Slesinger, Leane Zugsmith, Hortense Calisher, and Jo Sinclair, she did not write predominantly of Jewish characters or milieus. Rather, they identified with the poor and joined the progressive writers—many of them Jewish—producing proletarian fiction. "These writers," Antler explained, "resolved the traditional Jewish American novelist's concerns of assimilation through their characters' identification with political ideas and movements" (8).

Olsen began writing in the 1930s as a socialist voice for the working class. The novel *Yonnondio* is the story of the desperate life of the Holbrooks struggling to survive in the 1920s. The novel is named after Walt Whitman's lament for the Native Americans who have been silenced: "Yonnondio! Yonnondio!—unlimned they disappear; / . . . A muffled sonorous sound, a wailing word . . . / Then blank and gone and still, and utterly lost."

While her husband toils in a Wyoming mine, Anna dreams of a small family farm and a better life for her children. However, they are trapped within their poverty. They fail miserably at farming and end up in a squalid, overcrowded slaughterhouse town in Omaha. The novel is clearly a call for social and political action. Olsen writes graphic descriptions of workers as they enter the suffocating darkness of "The Iron Throat," or mineshaft, and portrays the horrific scalding of packinghouse workers as a steam pipe breaks.

However, *Yonnondio* is more than a polemical diatribe. Olsen planned the novel as the story of young Mazie Holbrook's development as a woman and an artist. Mazie has an imaginative gift, loves books, and does well in school—when she is able to attend. However, both her class and her gender stunt her creative development. There is never enough money to buy her books, and it is Mazie, not her brother Will, who is expected to help her mother in the drudgery of domestic chores.

In its unfinished state, the novel highlights the plight of Anna rather than her daughter. The double weight of her poverty and her role as caregiver "loomed gigantic beyond her, impossible ever to achieve, beyond any effort of doing of hers: that task of making a better life for her children to which her being was bound" (127). Motherhood confines Anna and liberates her as well. While stroking her daughter's hair, she goes into "a kind of languor, a swoon." Mazie feels the "strange happiness in her mother's body . . . happiness . . . and self-ness" (145–46). In an interview with Constance Coiner, Olsen has said that children and art "are different aspects of your being. There is . . . no separation. A life combining meaningful work and motherhood could and should be possible for women" (Coiner, 147). Olsen consistently considers the paradox of motherhood in her fiction and nonfiction works.

Anna's dreams for a better life for her children are stifled; however, the human drive to create remains. The novel ends with the youngest child, Bess, discovering her powers. As she bangs a jar lid on the table, there is a "[l]ightning in her brain. She releases, grabs, releases, grabs. I can do. Bang! . . . I achieve, I use my powers; I! I!" (190–91). Olsen's work attests that the potential for individual assertion and artistic self-expression is born within everyone. Though still didactic in tone, *Yonnondio* is also an early example of the rich imagery and skillful use of dialogue that characterize Olsen's later works. The landscape itself reflects the stifling economic and social environment the Holbrooks face.

In the 1950s and 1960s, Olsen entered her greatest period of fiction writing. The short stories "I Stand Here Ironing" (1956), "Hey Sailor, What Ship?" (1957), and the enormously successful "Tell Me a Riddle" (1961) were all published to critical acclaim. All three stories were republished in 1962 in Olsen's first book, a collection of short stories titled *Tell Me a Riddle*. Throughout the stories, her imagistic style delineates separations of race, gender, and class and foregrounds the relationships between mothers and daughters.

"Tell Me a Riddle" concerns a Jewish immigrant couple whose revolutionary zeal has faded with assimilation. Olsen focuses on the wife, Eva, who looks back on her life with regret for the sacrifice of her own identity to her family's demands. Housework and child rearing have drained her energy and left her no time to pursue her own interests. Olsen suggests that when women live only through their families, they are denied their own individuality and connection to humankind (Antler, 12). On her deathbed, Eva dreams of "[n] ever again to be forced to move to the rhythms of others" (68).

Through Olsen's skillful reproduction of the locutions of Yiddish speech, we know that Eva is Jewish, but like Olsen herself, she is not religious (Antler, 12). Eva has no nostalgia for religion or heritage. "Tell them to write: Race, human; Religion, none," Eva demands as she is admitted to the hospital (80). As Elaine Orr has noted, religion was an instrument for maintaining things as they were, the acceptance of suffering and of the subordinate role of women in Judaism (106–7).

In "I Stand Here Ironing," Olsen re-creates the interior monologue of a mother trying to reason why the school counselor believes that her daughter "needs help" (1). As a single parent, the necessity of earning a living prevented her from spending sufficient time with her first child, Emily. Now married and with other children, the mother recalls how her difficult early circumstances shaped the personality of her daughter, who has showed promise as an actress and a writer. Emily shines in the school play and invents words to comfort the younger children.

Despite the school's claims that there is a "problem" with Emily, her mother hopes that she can still be an artist and not be stunted by economic circumstances. She has had little control over her own life and hopes that her daughter will be able to determine her own future despite the disadvantages of her background. "So all that is in her will not bloom," the mother laments, "but in how many does it? There is still enough left to live by. Only help her to know . . . that she is more than this dress on the ironing board, helpless before the iron" (12).

"Tell Me a Riddle" and "I Stand Here Ironing" demonstrate the manner in which the demands of the family restrict the individual. "Hey Sailor, What Ship?" explores the waste of human potential without the family structure. Whitey, an aging sailor, had struggled in early union battles with his friend, Lennie. Now loneliness and alcoholism have impaired him, while Lennie has married and is raising children. Without a family, all of Whitey's relationships are empty. His only companionship is bought at the bar or Marie's Hospitality House. He seeks solace in the house of his old friend, but his rough seaman's language is censured in the home and he is silenced. In Olsen's work, silencing is the evidence of estrangement and alienation.

The uneasy relations between the social constructions of race are chronicled in "O Yes." Two best friends, one black, one white, are separated as cultural pressures divide them into different worlds. The story includes Olsen's evocative imagery of the sights and sounds of an African-American revival meeting. As in all Olsen's work, there is a final hope that despite the differences of race and class, there is a chance that the girls will resume their friendship as their mothers have. As Barr noted, "Individuals *can* circumvent social rules and economic differences" (200).

Silences (1978) is Olsen's renowned commentary on the circumstances that silence writers and her explanation for the relatively small number of acknowledged women authors. A collection of essays, autobiographical notes, historical retrospectives, and poetic fragments, the work mourns the loss to literature when potentially great writers are stifled by the situations of their class and gender. It reclaims the work of women excluded from traditional literary canons. Her own experience lends credence to her argument:

In the twenty years I bore and reared my children, usually had to work on the job as well, the simplest circumstances for creation did not exist. . . . Time on the bus, even when I had to stand, was enough; the stolen moments at work, enough; the deep night hours for as long as I could stay awake, after the kids were in bed, after the household tasks were done, sometimes during. It is no accident that the first work I considered publishable began: "I stand here ironing." (38–39)

For women, their desire to nurture and the expectations placed upon them to care for others' needs rather than their own are particularly damaging to their creative output. "The habits of a lifetime," Olsen explains, "are not easily broken." "[R]esponse to others, distractibility, responsibility for daily matters— stay with you, mark you. . . . I speak of myself here . . . for it need not, must not continue to be . . . and to remind us of those (I so nearly was one) who never come to writing at all" (39). Olsen maintains that the oppression of women is different than that of class and race. "It is an oppression," she writes, "entangled through with human love, human need . . . AND YET THE TREE DID— DOES—BEAR FRUIT" (258). Again, the human drive for creativity survives.

Silences also recovers the work of Rebecca Harding Davis, a neglected writer whose novel *Life in the Iron Mills; or, The Korl Woman* inspired *Yonnandio*. Davis's work is the story of a poor iron worker who sculpts the beautiful image of a woman out of the korl, or waste, from the smelting of ore. Olsen reviews the author's life and reproduces most of the novel.

In her latest fiction, Olsen shifts her focus from the mother-daughter bond to a "father and son" relationship. Included in the *Best American Short Stories of 1971*, "Requa" is the story of an orphaned boy who is taken in by his uncle. Stevie spends his days sleeping, withdrawing from life after his mother dies. His Uncle Wes, who salvages usable items in a junkyard, restores his nephew's will to live. As she did in *Silences*, Olsen experiments with traditional narrative form in "Requa." Lists of nouns are placed in vertical rows on the page. Isolated word images and fragmented sentences serve as entire paragraphs. Olsen's fragmented style reflects the lack of wholeness in her characters and encourages the reader to participate in the creative act of the writing process.

Olsen's work celebrates human potential. By giving voice to those members of society considered lost, she reflects her hope for a whole, unfragmented, balanced community in which human capacities are never wasted.

CRITICAL RECEPTION

The critical reaction to *Yonnondio* has been overwhelmingly positive. Robert Cantwell called "The Iron Throat," a short story that would later become a chapter of *Yonnondio*, "a work of early genius" (297). Immediately after the article appeared, the editors of two publishing houses wired him to locate the author. Peter Ackroyd called the reclaimed work a "romantic novel" because of the connection between "Nature" and the characters. Scott Turow noted that "without apology, this is a proletarian novel, didactic in intent. . . . The greatness of *Yonnandio* rests on its portrayal of the relationship between poverty and the acts of an embattled spirit, evoking it as a true human process" (2).

Joyce Carol Oates deemed "Tell Me a Riddle" "supremely beautiful in its nuances" (32). Irving Howe's review praised Olsen's perception of the traditional Jewish-American theme of "loss and forgetting," but considered her subject matter limited in scope: "Mrs. Olson's [*sic*] stories depend heavily on her own experience, and that experience seems to be narrow. But to judge from the stories, it is also one that she has felt very deeply and pondered and imaginatively absorbed. The one remarkable story in her book, 'Tell Me a Riddle' is a tour de force which pits aging and dying immigrant Jews against their native born children" (22).

Richard M. Elman's 1961 review claimed that Olsen's work is not limited and reaches beyond the scope of typical proletarian fiction. "Some critics will persist in finding analogies to Mrs. Olson's [*sic*] work in the socially conscious literature of the thirties, but [she] has been more daring. Sometimes she is able to compress within the space of a single sentence or brief paragraph the peculiar density of a . . . lifetime in the manner of lyric poetry" (251).

As her short stories gained popularity, many critics began to place Olsen within a Jewish socialist-feminist literary tradition. In her seminal study "From the Thirties: Tillie Olsen and the Radical Tradition," Deborah Rosenfelt identified this tradition with writers who share "a certain kind of consciousness . . . an involvement in a progressive political and cultural movement" (371). According to Rosenfelt, Olsen is in a line of women writers associated with the American Left who unite a class consciousness with feminism, including Edna St. Vincent Millay, Katherine Anne Porter, Dorothy Parker, and Adrienne Rich.

In 1986 Bonnie Lyons noted that the two principal sources of Olsen's vision derive from her experience as a Jew and a woman in her important study, "Tillie Olsen: The Writer as a Jewish Woman." According to Lyons, "What is most deeply Jewish in Olsen is the secular messianic utopianism she inherited from her immigrant parents" (89). One can add to this Olsen's continuation of Anzia Yezierska's work in giving voice to the silenced. "As one of the dumb, voiceless ones, I speak," Yezierska's protagonist claims in her 1922 short story "America and I" (reprinted in Antler, 72).

While all critics recognize the importance of Olsen's message in *Silences*, some are critical of her experimental narrative form. Margaret Atwood's review defined the format as "a scrapbook, a patchwork quilt. [B]its and pieces joined to form a powerful whole. And, despite the condensed and fragmentary quality of this book, the whole is powerful. . . . The tone is right" (27).

Joyce Carol Oates, on the other hand, was critical of what she considered inconsistent writing and inadequate editing. She also believed that the work lacks balance. "[T]here is little or no mention of successful women writers of our time," she wrote, and produced her own list of examples. "[T]he thinking that underlies *Silences* is simply glib and superficial," she continued, "set in contrast to the imagination that created *Tell Me a Riddle* and *Yonnondio*" (34).

Silences continues to inspire feminist theory. As Linda Wagner-Martin commented, "It would be hard to find a feminist critic . . . who was not influenced in key ways by" the work (Hedges and Fishkin, 31). A large number of minority writers and critics, including Alice Walker, Gloria Naylor, Sandra Cisneros, Hortense Spillers, and Maxine Hong Kingston cite *Silences* as centrally important for them (Hedges and Fishkin, 34). As recently as 1994, a collection of essays in feminist criticism, *Listening to Silences*, edited by Elaine Hedges and Shelley Fisher Fishkin, gave homage to Olsen's work. While Olsen will always be connected to feminist and class issues, her art ultimately reflects themes common in Jewish-American literature: the pull between conflicting identities, the condition of marginality, and the commitment to social reform.

BIBLIOGRAPHY

Works by Tillie Olsen

"The Iron Throat." *Partisan Review* 1.2 (1934): 3–9. Reprinted in *Yonnondio: From the Thirties*. New York: Delacorte, 1974; Dell, 1975.

"I Want You Women up North to Know." *Partisan Review* 1 (March 1934): 4.

"There Is a Lesson." *Partisan Review* 1 (April–May 1934): 4.

"Thousand-Dollar Vagrant." *New Republic* 80 (August 1934): 67–69.

"The Strike." *Partisan Review* 1 (September–October 1934): 3–9.

"Help Her to Believe." *Pacific Spectator* 10:1 (1956): 55–63. Reprinted as "I Stand Here Ironing."

"Baptism." *Prairie Schooner* 31:1 (1957): 70–80.

"Hey Sailor, What Ship?" In *New Campus Writing*, no. 2, ed. Noland Miller. New York: Putnam, 1957, 199–213.

Tell Me a Riddle. New York: Dell, 1961. Contains "I Stand Here Ironing"; "Hey Sailor, What Ship?"; "O Yes"; "Tell Me a Riddle."

"Requa." *Iowa Review* 1 (Summer 1970): 54–74. Reprinted as "Requa I" in *The Best American Short Stories, 1971*, ed. Martha Foley and David Burnett. Boston: Houghton Mifflin, 1971.

"A Biographical Interpretation." In *Life in the Iron Mills*, by Rebecca Harding Davis. New York: Feminist Press, 1972.

Yonnondio: From the Thirties. New York: Delacorte, 1974; Dell, 1975.

Silences. New York: Delacorte, 1978.

"Dream-Vision." In *Mother to Daughter, Daughter to Mother*, ed. Tillie Olsen. New York: Feminist Press, 1984.

"Foreword." In *Black Women Writers at Work*, ed. Claudia Tate. New York: Continuum, 1983.

"Mothers and Daughters." With Julie Olsen Edwards. In *Mothers and Daughters: That*

Special Quality: Photographs, ed. Tillie Olsen, Julie Olsen Edwards, and Estelle Jussim. New York: Aperture, 1987.

Works Cited and Studies of Tillie Olsen

Ackroyd, Peter. Review of *Yonnondio. Spectator*, December 14, 1974. 767.

Antler, Joyce. "Introduction." In *America and I: Short Stories by American Jewish Women Writers*, ed. Joyce Antler. Boston: Beacon, 1990.

Atwood, Margaret. Review of *Silences. New York Times Book Review*, July 30, 1978, 27.

Barr, Marleen. "Tillie Olsen." *Twentieth-Century American-Jewish Fiction Writers*, ed. Daniel Walden. Vol. 28 of *Dictionary of Literary Biography*. Detroit: Gale, 1984.

Burkom, Selma, and Margaret Williams. "De-Riddling Tillie Olsen's Writings." *San Jose Studies* 2:1 (1976): 65–83.

Cantwell, Robert. Review of "Iron Throat." *New Republic*, July 25, 1937, 297.

Clayton, John. "Grace Paley and Tillie Olsen: Radical Jewish Humanists." *Response* 14 (Spring 1984): 37–52.

Coiner, Constance. *Better Red: The Writing and Resistance of Tillie Olsen and Meridel Le Sueur*. New York: Oxford University Press, 1995.

Elman, Richard M. Review of "Tell Me a Riddle." *Commonweal*, December 8, 1961, 251.

Faulkner, Mara. *Protest and Possibility in the Writing of Tillie Olsen*. Charlottesville; University Press of Virginia, 1993.

Fishkin, Shelley Fisher. "The Borderlands of Culture: Writing by W.E.B. Du Bois, James Agee, Tillie Olsen, and Gloria Anzaldua." In *Literary Journalism in the Twentieth Century*, ed. Norman Sims. New York: Oxford University Press, 1990, 133–82.

Frye, Joanne S. " 'I Stand Here Ironing': Motherhood as Experience and Metaphor." *Studies in Short Fiction* 18:3 (1981): 287–92.

Gelfant, Blanche H. "After Long Silence: Tillie Olsen's 'Requa.' " *Studies in American Fiction* 12:1 (1984): 61–69.

Hedges, Elaine, and Shelley Fisher Fishkin, eds. *Listening to Silences: New Essays in Feminist Criticism*. New York: Oxford University Press, 1994.

Howe, Irving. Review of "Tell Me a Riddle." *New Republic*, November 13, 1961, 22.

Kamel, Rose Yalow. "Riddles and Silences: Tillie Olsen's Autobiographical Fiction." In *Aggravating the Conscience: Jewish-American Literary Mothers in the Promised Land*. New York: Peter Lang, 1988, 81–114.

Lester, Elenore. "The Riddle of Tillie Olsen." *Midstream*, January 1975, 75–79.

Lyons, Bonnie. "Tillie Olsen: The Writer as a Jewish Woman." *Studies in American Jewish Literature* 5 (1986): 89–102.

Oates, Joyce Carol. Review of "Tell Me a Riddle." *New Republic*, July 29, 1978, 32–34.

Orr, Miriam. "Tillie Olsen's Vision: A Different Way of Keeping Faith." Dissertation, December 1985. Emory University.

Pearlman, Mickey, and Abby H. P. Werlock. *Tillie Olsen*. Boston: Twayne, 1991.

Rosenfelt, Deborah. "From the Thirties: Tillie Olsen and the Radical Tradition." *Fem-

inist Studies 7 (Fall 1981): 371–406. Reprinted in *Feminist Criticism and Social Change: Sex, Class, and Race in Literature and Culture*, ed. Judith Newton and Deborah Rosenfelt. New York: Methuen, 1985.

Turow, Scott. Review of *Yonnondio*. *Ploughshares* 2 (1974): 2.

CYNTHIA OZICK (1928–　)

Suzanne Klingenstein

BIOGRAPHY

Cynthia Ozick was born in New York City on April 17, 1928. Her father, William (Velvl) Ozick, arrived in America from Hlusk, near Minsk in White Russia, at the age of twenty-one. Her mother, Celia (Shiphra) Regelson, the fifth of eight children, was smuggled across the Russian border with four of her siblings when her mother decided to join her husband and three older children in America. Celia arrived in New York City in 1906 as a ten-year-old child. Although William Ozick had graduated from a Russian gymnasium (high school), where he had studied Latin and German, and Celia Regelson had attended American schools, where she became an avid reader, the family language was Yiddish, at least until the death of Ozick's maternal grandmother in 1939. Thereafter Yiddish declined into the speech of reminiscence for her parents, and English, which Ozick had always spoken to her older brother, began to dominate the home. The Depression years were hard for Ozick's parents, who ran the Parkview Pharmacy and its soda fountain in the Pelham Bay section of the Bronx. Their daughter, however, who had fallen in love with literature and knew at the age of ten that she wanted to become a writer, was immune to hardship.

Ozick attended P.S. 71, where she felt "friendless and forlorn." She was "publicly shamed in Assembly because I am caught not singing Christmas carols" and "repeatedly accused of deicide" (*Art and Ardor*, 302). Simultaneously she received a traditional Jewish elementary education, on which her maternal grandmother had insisted—not vis-à-vis Ozick's parents, but vis-à-vis the rabbi, who did not want to admit girls to his *heder*. Ozick's Jewish learning, however, which is evident in her fictional and essayistic work, was the result of years of intensive reading on her own. Ozick went on to Hunter High School in Manhattan (1941–1946), where her Bronx speech was excised, her intellect sharpened, and her passion for literature stoked by the study of Latin and the classic writers. In the spring of 1946 Ozick entered New York University. She discovered there the brilliant world of the New York Intellectuals who displayed their sharp-creased minds in the pages of countless literary magazines. Graduating cum laude and Phi Beta Kappa in 1949, she transferred to Ohio State University, where she received her M.A. in 1951 for a thesis on "Parable in the Late Novels of Henry James."

She returned to New York City and under the pretense of pursuing a doctoral degree enrolled at Columbia University so that she could study with Lionel Trilling, whose recent book *The Liberal Imagination* (1950) had made him one of the preeminent literary and cultural critics in America and the first whose home was entirely in academe. Ozick did not want to pursue a doctorate because the culture of the time perceived academic scholarship and creative writing as diametric opposites. Fiction writers were free spirits, whereas literature professors were custodians of a museum. By 1951 Ozick had embarked on a philosophical novel with the Blakean title *Mercy, Pity, Peace, and Love*. She married Bernard Hallote, an attorney, in 1952. Their daughter, Rachel, was born in 1965.

Ozick is recognized as one of America's outstanding stylists and has received many honors and awards for her essayistic and fictional work. Among them are a National Endowment for the Arts fellowship (1968), the Wallant award (1972), the B'nai B'rith award (1972), the Jewish Book Council award (1972, 1977), the American Academy award (1973), the Hadassah Myrtle Wreath award (1974), the Lampart prize (1980), a Guggenheim Fellowship (1982), the Strauss Living award (1983), and the Rea award for short story (1986). She holds honorary doctorates from Yeshiva University (1984), Hebrew Union College (1984), Williams College (1986), Hunter College of the City University of New York (1987), Jewish Theological Seminary (1988), Boston Hebrew College (1988), Adelphi University (1988), the State University of New York (1989), Brandeis University (1990), Bard College (1991), Spertus College (1991), and Skidmore College (1992). She has taught at New York University as instructor in English (1964–1965) and as distinguished artist-in-residence (1982). She was Stolnitz Lecturer at Indiana University at Bloomington (1972) and delivered the Phi Beta Kappa Oration at Harvard University in 1985. In 1988 she was elected to the American Academy of Arts and Letters.

MAJOR WORKS AND THEMES

When Ozick finished her novel *Trust* on November 22, 1963, the day John F. Kennedy was shot, she had actually completed her third novel. The first, *Mercy, Pity, Peace, and Love*, a philosophical work pitting the "Liberal-Modernists against the Neo-Thomists" (Kauvar, *Cynthia Ozick's Fiction*, 1), she had abandoned after 300,000 words and six years of labor. The second, *The Conversion of John Andersmall*, she had written within six weeks, but never published. *Trust* (1966) was a satirical and symbolistic work about postwar America in the form of a growing-up novel. The narrator and nameless central character, a precocious, sharp-witted girl, is suspended between her amnesic, socialite mother, Allegra, and three father figures. Allegra's first husband, William, a Protestant Wall Street lawyer, represents Calvinist probity and American capitalism. Allegra's current husband, Enoch, a Jew, whose task as American envoy to Europe in 1945 is to record the names of those killed in the Holocaust, represents the intellectual and moral forces of Judaism originating not in faith but in an intense awareness of history. The girl's biological father, finally, Gustave Nicholas, an incarnation of pagan Greece, a worshipper of pleasure and beauty, plays Pan to Enoch's Moses and William's Christ. Chronicling the narrator's journey toward the discovery of her true father, the 600-page novel is an exhaustive probe into the nature of creativity. Although the author acknowledges the Dionysian force of Pan as progenitor of the creative drive, she also illuminates brilliantly Pan's brutal, orgiastic self-destructiveness when his Dionysian side is not reined in by Apollonian self-discipline, or, more to the point in *Trust*, by submission to the God of History, and hence to the principles of moral seriousness and social justice.

The central theme of *Trust*, the artist's suspension between Pan and Moses, dominated Ozick's work for the next two decades. Having toiled on *Trust* for six years, she vowed not to engage again in something so long. "After such an extended immolation," she said in a 1983 interview, "I needed frequent spurts of immediacy—that is, short stories which could get published right away (Rainwater 258)." In the mid-1960s, her fiction began to appear in America's leading literary magazines, among them *Commentary, Esquire, Partisan Review, Salmagundi*, and the *New Yorker*. It has been gathered into three collections to date.

The Pagan Rabbi and Other Stories (1971) contains several of Ozick's best-known fictions. The title story, first published in 1966, begins with a rabbi's suicide in a public park. When a former classmate at the rabbinic seminary visits the rabbi's widow, a concentration-camp survivor, he learns from her that his pious friend had fallen in love with nature, more particularly, with a dyad sporting eggplantlike skin. From the rabbi's diary he gathers that the Talmud scholar had, contrary to Jewish belief, come to think of nature as suffused with divinity ("Great Pan lives") and craved to liberate his soul from the burden of history. Sharpening the central theme of *Trust*, Ozick presents Pan and Moses, pantheism and monotheism, nature and history, poetry and ethics, and self-indulgence and social responsibility as irreconcilable opposites. Her story forces the reader to choose between justice (the widow's anger) and pleasure (the rabbi's beautiful poetry).

In "The Dock Witch" (1971), Ozick dramatizes the destructiveness of the unbridled Dionysian drive, while in "Virility" (1971), the usurper of that force, a literary fraud, goes mad. In "The Suitcase" (1971), Ozick links for the first time the Apollonian aspect of creativity, aesthetic perfection, to the Nazis' insane drive to create pure beauty in a master race. "The German Final Solution,"

Ozick wrote in 1970, "was an aesthetic solution: it was a job of editing, it was the artist's finger removing a smudge, it simply annihilated what was considered not harmonious" (*Art and Ardor*, 165). The most celebrated story in *The Pagan Rabbi*, however, is the marvelously funny "Envy; or, Yiddish in America." It depicts the plight of two Yiddish poets, Edelshtein and Baumzweig, who have no audience because no one reads Yiddish anymore. They envy their colleague Ostrover, a prose writer, whom Edelshtein calls "a pantheist, a pagan, a goy," because Ostrover's virile creativity appeals to the younger generation, who sees in him "a Freudian, a Jungian, a sensibility. No little love stories. A contemporary. He speaks for everybody" (95). Ostrover's stories are translated into English and become a huge success, while Edelshtein and Baumzweig, who write in the language of the Jews, languish in oblivion. At the time of its publication, "Envy" created a firestorm of rage and mortification in the Yiddish community because it was read as a *raconte à clef*. Ostrover was identified as Isaac Bashevis Singer and Edelshtein as the Yiddish poet Jacob Glatstein, who was deeply wounded by the story. Ozick admitted to the first, but denied the second identification. She explained that she had modeled Edelshtein on her uncle Abraham Regelson, a Hebrew poet, who had eked out a minimal subsistence as a journalist in New York during the 1930s and 1940s.

In Ozick's second collection, *Bloodshed and Three Novellas* (1976), the focus shifted from the nature of the creative drive to the nature of fiction. The title story and the long novella "Usurpation (Other People's Stories)" (1974) are probably Ozick's most difficult poetological fictions. "Bloodshed" revolves around the dynamics of "instead of," that is, around the function of metaphor. The story illustrates how mistaking the image for the thing, that is, confusing fiction and reality, can lead to crimes as horrendous as the Holocaust, engineered by a people who recast human beings as vermin and exterminated them as such. "Usurpation," too, is a story written against the creation of fiction, "The point being," Ozick wrote in her preface to *Bloodshed*, "that the storymaking faculty itself can be a corridor to the corruptions and abominations of idol-worship, of the adoration of magical event." Yet "Usurpation" is also a story about the writer's mind, so usurped and haunted by "other people's stories" as to become unfree to make up its own. This prompted the critic Harold Bloom to consider "Usurpation" a fictional commentary on his book *The Anxiety of Influence* (1973). The theory of poetry Bloom unfolded there claimed that the belated poet finds himself locked into a perpetual struggle with his precursors. Originality was not possible since all good poetry was an anxious revision of a strong precursor's work. "To beget here means to usurp," wrote Bloom (*Anxiety*, 37). But Ozick's story goes beyond Bloom and back into the world of rabbinic learning by establishing a connection between the usurper and the idolator.

The remaining stories in *Bloodshed* are no less complex. They present different aspects of the themes developed in "Usurpation." Haunted by Jerzy Kosinski's novel *The Painted Bird*, "A Mercenary" (1975) explores the reasons for impersonation and its consequences. "An Education" (1964), the first story

Ozick ever wrote, betrays in plot, tone, and narrative perspective the profound influence of Henry James on the maturing Ozick. It chronicles in the manner of James's story "The Pupil" the infatuation of a serious, sophisticated, but unworldly young woman with a couple of accomplished cultural fakes.

In 1982, Ozick's third collection, *Levitation: Five Fictions*, appeared. The critic Elaine Kauvar called the volume an "imaginary gallery, [hung with] portraits of artists in the act of imaginative creation" (Kauvar, *Cynthia Ozick's Fiction*, 111). The title story (1979) about "a pair of novelists," Feingold and his non-Jewish wife Lucy, compares two kinds of sensibilities. Mired in mediocrity because they are out of touch with the core of their different selves, "they fancied themselves in love with what they called 'imagination.' It was not true. What they were addicted to was counterfeit pity, and this was because they were absorbed by power and were powerless" (*Levitation*, 7). The appearance of a Holocaust survivor at the Feingolds' literary party acts as a catalyst, separating Lucy and Feingold from each other and propelling each on an idiosyncratic flight of fancy, designed to illuminate their true identity and to illustrate once more the difference between Pan and Moses. While Feingold is riveted to the survivor's historical narrative, Lucy experiences a pagan epiphany. She envisions a Dionysian celebration in Central Park, complete with satyrs, music, dance, and all-male sex. Lucy comprehends her true cultural identity. The dancers "celebrate the Madonna, giver of fertility and fecundity. Lucy is glorified. She is exalted. . . . Lucy sees how she abandoned nature, how she has lost true religion on account of the God of the Jews" (8). Because Ozick comes down so strongly on the side of history and moral seriousness, it has often been overlooked that she does not judge Lucy, who gives in to her natural impulse. She simply writes her off as irrelevant to the moral and intellectual life.

Ozick is much tougher on a new character, Ruth Puttermesser, who makes her appearance in two of *Levitation*'s five fictions. The reader first meets her as a thirty-four-year-old single lawyer in "Puttermesser: Her Work History, Her Ancestry, Her Afterlife" (1977), which is a funny study in contrast between Puttermesser's current WASP work environment and her New York Jewish family life as a child. When we meet brainy Puttermesser again in "Puttermesser and Xanthippe" (1982), she is forty-six, still unmarried, and employed by New York City's Department of Receipts and Disbursements. In an act of frenzied worry about corruption in New York City, the rationalist Puttermesser creates a female golem, an animated human figure made of clay. This creature, self-named Xanthippe, helps Puttermesser to become mayor of New York and to clean up and reform the city. But soon thereafter the golem's libidinal drives run amok, and Xanthippe destroys the paradise she had helped to build. Like Rabbi Loew in seventeenth-century Prague, the most famous creator of a golem in Jewish lore, Puttermesser is forced to undo her own creation in order to regain control over it. During a talk at the Jewish Museum in New York in 1988, Ozick called Xanthippe a "metaphor for art." Art, her story claims, unfolds its destructive potential as soon as it leaves the realm of the imagination and enters the real world.

In Ozick's most recent Puttermesser story to date, "Puttermesser Paired" (*New Yorker*, October 8, 1990), the perilous boundary crossing between life and art is explored from another angle. The still-unmarried Puttermesser is now "fifty plus" and madly in love with George Eliot. She becomes the half-willing victim of a copyist, Rupert Rabeeno, who is obsessed with the idea of "reenacting the masters." He seduces Puttermesser into reliving the life of George Eliot. After an imaginary honeymoon in the writer's tracks, Puttermesser is abruptly deserted by her new husband Rupert. She discovers that he had not been playing Eliot's cherished companion George Lewes, but the young Johnny Cross, whom Eliot married at the age of sixty-one. During the couple's honeymoon in Venice, Johnny went temporarily mad and jumped from the hotel balcony into the Grand Canal. Rupert, however, is sane enough to leave Puttermesser through her apartment door. "Hey! Puttermesser's biographer! What will you do with her now?" (*Levitation*, 38), read the final sentences of the first Puttermesser story. Only this much is known: Ozick is planning to write one more Puttermesser story before assembling her tales in one volume.

In 1983 Ozick published her second novel, *The Cannibal Galaxy*, a first version of which had appeared as a novella titled "The Laughter of Akiva" in the *New Yorker* (November 10, 1980). It told the story of an intellectually ambitious Jewish boy, Joseph Brill, who survives the Nazi occupation of France in the cellar of a convent. After the war Brill comes to America and founds a school with a Dual Curriculum: "Chumash, Gemara, Social Studies, French: the waters of Shiloh springing from the head of Western Civilization!" (36). It was to be a "fusion of scholarly Europe and burnished Jerusalem" (27). In fact, it was a reflection of Brill's "two minds" (26). Ozick's Pan-Moses dichotomy gets interesting and Brill's intellectual seriousness is severely tested when a well-known "imagistic linguistic logician" (47) wants to enroll her daughter in Brill's school. He accepts the child, who fails the interview, on account of her famous mother. In love with his own cultural sophistication, Brill is blind to the girl's hidden talents and fails miserably as a teacher. He does not recognize his error until years later, when the girl emerges as a celebrated artist. The novel develops from a reflection on the tension between artistic imagination and moral responsibility to a relentlessly satiric analysis of intellectual mediocrity.

In 1983 Ozick published *Art and Ardor*, a collection of essays, which was followed by a second volume, *Metaphor and Memory* in 1989, and a third, *Fame and Folly*, in 1996. Her essays never comment on her own work and rarely on her life as a writer. Instead, they present shrewd analyses of other writers (from Henry James and Virginia Woolf to Sholom Aleichem and Harold Bloom) as well as assessments of the writer's task and the moral responsibilities of the public intellectual.

In 1987 Ozick's third novel, *The Messiah of Stockholm*, appeared. It tells the story of a Swedish book reviewer, Lars Andemening, who, deeply in love with literary art, imagines himself the son of the Polish-Jewish writer Bruno Schulz. Schulz was shot by an SS man in Nazi-occupied Poland in 1942, and the manuscript of his unpublished novel *The Messiah* disappeared in the chaos of the war. Ozick's plot revolves around its reappearance in the possession of a woman claiming to be Schulz's daughter. Lars is introduced to her by a German exile, the mysterious owner of his favorite bookstore. It is home to a wonderfully Jamesian family of con artists who try to convince Lars to announce the resurrection of *The Messiah* in his book-review column. Infatuated with Schulz, Lars very much wants the manuscript to be authentic, but in the end he escapes the snare and declares it to be a fake. The con artists disband. Despite its many hilarious scenes depicting the narrow, inbred world of book reviewers, *The Messiah of Stockholm* is a tightly constructed novel of ideas in which Ozick spells out her theory of Western aesthetics. Through the concept of idolatry she links paganism, Christianity, romanticism, and Nazism as ideologies that indulge Western aesthetic sensibilities at the expense of historic perspicacity and moral commitment.

Although in many of Ozick's fictions the Holocaust had served as the touchstone for a character's moral reliability, the destruction of the European Jews had not figured directly in her work. The exception to this rule was the short story "The Shawl," which appeared in the *New Yorker* on May 26, 1980. In 1989 Ozick combined it with the novella "Rosa," first published in the *New Yorker* on March 21, 1983, in a slender volume called *The Shawl*. The short story depicts the murder of Rosa's infant daughter Magda in a German concentration camp. The novella, set thirty-five years later, shows Rosa still tormented by the event. The novella's intense focus on Rosa's vivid recollections and on her fierce imagination, which revives her daughter and invents for her different lives, unfolds before the reader the complex emotions and psychology of an ordinary woman who lived through extraordinary hell.

In the late 1980s, Ozick started to work on a play for which she borrowed the plot line and some characters from *The Shawl*. When *Blue Light* (directed by Sidney Lumet) opened in Sag Harbor, New York, in August 1994, it became obvious that the play had developed its own focus. As Ozick explained at Harvard University in February 1995, "My play is about a new phenomenon, called Holocaust denial." Its central character is a clever young man who in the guise of a psychologist descends on Rosa, wins her confidence by feigning interest in her story, and in the end tries to make her sign papers testifying that her recollections are all fantasies. "The play," Ozick expanded at Harvard, "is about the devil and his seductions. It is pessimistic. The devil, though he is ultimately confronted by passionate opposition, nevertheless walks out and goes freely into the world, where the devil can always be found, peddling his wares and snatching souls." The New York City premiere of *Blue Light*, which at the insistence of its producers has been retitled *The Shawl*, was staged in the spring of 1996.

CRITICAL RECEPTION

Almost from the start Ozick's work was reviewed by top-tier literary critics in American newspapers and literary magazines. Serious academic criticism set in belatedly in the mid-1970s and swelled to a flood of articles during the 1980s. Monographs on her work started to appear in the late 1980s, but like the early critical articles, they tended to be superficial and to see Ozick's fiction only in the context of American Jewish literature. More substantial and thorough studies were published during the 1990s placing her work in the larger context of English and American literature. The best analysis to date is a critical study by Elaine Kauvar (1993), which traces the literary and cultural sources (Jewish and Gentile) of Ozick's fictions and interprets the novels and stories in the light of Ozick's literary essays. Ozick intrigues academics because her work is satiric, tightly constructed, and at times difficult because it is full of literary allusions. These features have limited appeal to the general reading public. While Ozick's work was widely—and, for the most part, positively—reviewed, it was not as widely read, with the exception, perhaps, of *The Shawl*, which made the *New York Times* best-seller list.

Overall, reviewers at large have done Ozick's fiction justice. They recognized, for example, the scope of literary influences that shaped it. About *Trust*, Eugene Goodheart wrote, "The baroque idiosyncratic rhetoric of writers as different from one another as James, Melville, Carlyle, Whitman and Dickens suggests the places where Mrs. Ozick has sought her artistic freedom" (100). Yet Goodheart was unhappy with the result. "One might say," he concluded his review, "that the general condition of the novel is a discontinuity between language and reality or between expression and feeling. The language expands . . . like . . . a wild growth that quickly conceals its roots in feeling" (102).

Reviews of *The Pagan Rabbi* were positive throughout. Thomas Lask wrote in the *New York Times* that Ozick had lost none of the skills "she exhibited in her novel *Trust*. But they seem better harnessed in these tales." He called Ozick "a writer who refuses to play games with her art. She treats it with an uncontemporary seriousness and brings to it that order, stability and balance that the life she is mirroring obviously lacks" (17).

Bloodshed, which contained some difficult stories, received more mixed reviews. Rosellen Brown, who called Ozick "a unique and challenging writer whose intellect is vivified by all the lively juices of a reveller in language," thought that the stories suffered from "overthink" but suggested that "Ozick's failures are infinitely more interesting than most writers' successes." Responding to the rise of feminist criticism at the time, Brown concluded that "Ozick's stories make discussions of 'female' *v.* 'male' experiences seem puerile and irrelevant. Half of these are told from 'male' perspectives. They turn out to be works conceived at a [philosophic] level . . . that makes these distinctions too arbitrary to be indulged" (30–31).

By the time *Levitation* appeared, critics perceived that something not seen since Saul Bellow's early novels was happening in Ozick's prose. A. Alvarez wrote about the author of *Levitation*, "Cynthia Ozick is a carver, a stylist in the best and most complete sense: in language, in wit, in her apprehension of reality and her curious, crooked flight of imagination. She once described an early work [*Trust*] as 'both "mandarin" and "lapidary," every paragraph a poem.' Although there is nothing stiff or overcompacted about her writing now, she still has the poet's perfectionist habit of mind and obsession with language, as though one word out of place would undo the whole fabric." Reading Ozick entirely within the context of a newly invigorated American Jewish literature, Alvarez concluded his review by saying, "Certainly she is too authentic an artist to go running after immigrant rhythms or Hester Street kitsch. The English she writes is pure and controlled and, in a wholly twentieth century way, classical. Yet she seems, nevertheless, to hanker after Bashevis Singer's shtetl. . . . Miss Ozick bends her subtle, beautifully controlled prose and strange imagination to the service of folk magic. It is, in the end—despite the brilliance, despite the humour—an odd and uneasy displacement, like the Chagalls in Lincoln Center" (22–23).

With the publication of *The Cannibal Galaxy*, Ozick was firmly established in the firmament of American writers. Reviewing the novel for the *New York Times Book Review*, E. B. White remarked, "Like [Henry] James, Miss Ozick is a moralist—not a purveyor of slogans, of dark or optimistic lessons, but someone who is always submitting experience to an ethical inquiry. The design of the novel, certainly its strength, derives from her moral phrasing of questions about idolatry. Although there is a great deal of melody in the supple, caressing, inexhaustible language, the large structures of her fiction—plot, suspense, character development, ideas—are never musical. I mean to say that Miss Ozick never commits herself to a predetermined form. Rather, the shape of her tales succumbs to the sinuosity of thought, the wholly natural but not very tidy motions of a mind at work" (3). White concluded his review with lavish praise: "Precisely on account of her style, Miss Ozick strikes me as the best American writer to have emerged in recent years. Her artistic strength derives from her moral energy, for Miss Ozick is not an esthete. Judaism has given her what Catholicism gave to Flannery O'Connor—authority, penetration and imagination" (47).

The sharp, polemical quality of Ozick's literary essays evoked some equally sharp responses from reviewers. About the author of *Art and Ardor* Anatole Broyard wrote, "Miss Ozick polices modern literature and tries to arrest what she sees as self indulgence. She seems to be morally insatiable, to want every author to wrestle with his book, like Jacob wrestling with the angel, until it blesses him, or us. She is the antidote to all the soft reviews, the easy forgiveness. As she points out, sympathy can be an offense against truth." Broyard was not happy with this stance. "There is something relentless, something humorless, in 'Art and Ardor,' " he complained. "She appears to have chosen for herself, in literary criticism, the role of the anxious mother who wants only the best for her children, who expects them to be serious'' (23). Barbara Koenig Quart, writing for the *Nation*, felt similarly coerced. ''Here [in Ozick's nonfeminist essays on Virginia Woolf and Edith Wharton], and frequently elsewhere, one feels that buried under the literary sophistication, high intelligence and stylish prose are the values of one's Brooklyn aunt . . . —the kinds of parental injunctions that Philip Roth's heroes do intense though ambivalent battle against'' (88).

Four years later, when *Metaphor and Memory* appeared and academic criticism was moving toward its highest polemic pitch on issues of multiculturalism, critics no longer saw Ozick's literary essays as pushing a specific moral agenda. ''Neither separately nor collectively can those essays be confined to the narrowness of a credo,'' wrote Elaine Kauvar in her review. ''Rather they belong to that capacious term *belles lettres*, which once reflected the exhilaration and nobility of a literary culture. Against the countervailing forces of postmodernist rupture and scission, stands the humane and inclusive vision of Cynthia Ozick'' (18).

Critical unison shattered as soon as *The Messiah of Stockholm* arrived on the scene. Two of America's preeminent literary critics, Harold Bloom and Robert Alter, differed sharply in their assessment of Ozick's third novel. Bloom called it ''brilliant'' and its protagonist Lars ''the most persuasive and poignant figure in a fiction by Ms. Ozick. . . . The difference between Lars and her previous protagonists resides in the subtle internalization, in this book, of the author's preoccupations. Beyond question, and yet with superb, almost Jamesian, indirection, Lars is Ms. Ozick's surrogate, an emblem for her own maturation as an artist as she becomes a true daughter of Schulz, whose Jewishness, like Kafka's, is fascinatingly implicit in his writing'' (36). To Robert Alter, however, ''the novel never seems fully convincing, for all the interest of its informing idea, because, like a good deal of Miss Ozick's fiction, it is finally too cerebral.'' Echoing Goodheart's complaint about *Trust* twenty years earlier, Alter argued that ''the novel is notable in its rendering of sensations but lacks the resonance of real experience beneath the level of sensation. . . . The result is a prose that is often mannered, overwritten, oddly violent in excess of the objects of representation. . . . [T]he violent extravagance of the metaphors . . . betrays an attempt to substitute rhetorical intensity for experiential depth'' (53).

With the publication of *The Shawl*, complaints about Ozick's mannered prose subsided. ''The story's tone,'' wrote Francine Prose, ''is a departure from the more cerebral, ironic voice of much of Ozick's fiction; its rhythms grow almost incantatory as Rosa witnesses her daughter's death'' (38). Robert Taylor, however, commented on the risks of Ozick's style, which might ''intervene by calling attention to itself. Yet Ozick brings off the narrative triumphantly and succeeds in giving voice to the unspeakable losses of the Holocaust's victims'' (41). In the end Michiko Kakutani's description endures: ''Fierce, concentrated, and brutal, *The Shawl* burns itself into the reader's imagination with almost surreal power'' (C17).

BIBLIOGRAPHY

Works by Cynthia Ozick

Trust. New York: New American Library, 1966.
The Pagan Rabbi and Other Stories. New York: Knopf, 1971.
Bloodshed and Three Novellas. New York: Knopf, 1976.
Levitation: Five Fictions. New York: Knopf, 1982.
Art and Ardor. New York: Knopf, 1983.
The Cannibal Galaxy. New York: Knopf, 1983.
The Messiah of Stockholm. New York: Knopf, 1987.
Metaphor and Memory. New York: Knopf, 1989.
The Shawl. New York: Knopf, 1989.
Blue Light (play). Premiere: Bay Street Theater, Sag Harbor, NY, August 12, 1994. New York City production under the title *The Shawl* (Spring 1996).
Fame and Folly. New York: Knopf, 1996.

Interviews with Cynthia Ozick

Kauvar, Elaine M. ''An Interview with Cynthia Ozick.'' *Contemporary Literature* 26 (Winter 1985): 375–401.
———. ''An Interview with Cynthia Ozick.'' *Contemporary Literature* 34 (Fall 1993): 358–94.
Ottenberg, Eve. ''The Rich Visions of Cynthia Ozick.'' *New York Times Magazine,* April 10, 1983, 46, 62–66.
Rainwater, Catherine, and William J. Scheick. ''An Interview with Cynthia Ozick (Summer 1982).'' *Texas Studies in Literature and Language* 25 (Summer 1983): 255–65.
Teicholz, Toni. ''The Art of Fiction XCV: Cynthia Ozick.'' *Paris Review* 29 (Spring 1987): 154–90.

Works Cited and Studies of Cynthia Ozick

Alter, Robert. Review of *The Messiah of Stockholm. Commentary* 84 (July 1987): 53.
Alvarez, A. Review of *Levitation. New York Review of Books,* May 13, 1982, 22–23.
Bloom, Harold, ed. *Modern Critical Views: Cynthia Ozick.* New York: Chelsea House, 1986.
———. Review of *The Messiah of Stockholm. New York Times Book Review,* March 22, 1987, 1, 36.
Bloom, Harold. *The Anxiety of Influence.* London: Oxford University Press, 1975.
Brown, Rosellen. Review of *Bloodshed. New Republic* 174 (June 5, 1976): 30–31.
Broyard, Anatole. Review of *Art and Ardor. New York Times,* April 27, 1983, 23.
Cohen, Sarah Blacher. *Cynthia Ozick's Comic Art: From Levity to Liturgy.* Bloomington: Indiana University Press, 1994.

Finkelstein, Norman. ''The Struggle for Historicity in the Fiction of Cynthia Ozick.'' *LIT: Literature Interpretation Theory* 1 (1990): 291–302.

Friedman, Lawrence S. *Understanding Cynthia Ozick.* Columbia: University of South Carolina Press, 1991.

Goodheart, Eugene. Review of *Trust. Critique* 9 (1967): 100–102.

Kakutani, Michiko. Review of *The Shawl. New York Times*, September 5, 1989, C17.

Kauvar, Elaine M. *Cynthia Ozick's Fiction: Tradition and Invention.* Bloomington: Indiana University Press, 1993.

———. Review of *Metaphor and Memory. Congress Monthly* 56 (November/December 1989): 18.

Kielsky, Vera Emuna. *Inevitable Exiles: Cynthia Ozick's View of the Precariousness of Jewish Existence in a Gentile Society.* Frankfurt: Peter Lang, 1989.

Klingenstein, Susanne. '' 'In Life, I Am Not Free': The Writer Cynthia Ozick and Her Jewish Obligations.'' In *Daughters of Valor: Jewish American Women Writers from 1950 to the Present*, ed. Jay L. Halio and Benjamin Siegel. Newark: University of Delaware Press, 1997.

Lask, Thomas. Review of *The Pagan Rabbi. New York Times*, July 5, 1971, 17.

Lowin, Joseph. *Cynthia Ozick.* Boston: Twayne, 1988.

Pinsker, Sanford. *The Uncompromising Fictions of Cynthia Ozick.* Columbia: University of Missouri Press, 1987.

Prose, Francine. Review of *The Shawl. New York Times Book Review*, September 10, 1989, 38.

Quart, Barbara Koenig. Review of *Art and Ardor. Nation*, July 23–30, 1983, 88.

Rzadtki, Beate. *Judische Tradition in der amerikanischen Diaspora: Das Erzählwerk Cynthia Ozicks.* Frankfurt: Peter Lang, 1991.

Sokoloff, Naomi. ''Interpretation: Cynthia Ozick's Cannibal Galaxy.'' *Prooftexts* 6 (September 1986): 239–57.

Strandberg, Victor. *Greek Mind, Jewish Soul: The Conflicted Art of Cynthia Ozick.* Madison: University of Wisconsin Press, 1994.

Taylor, Robert. Review of *The Shawl. Boston Globe*, September 13, 1989, 41.

Walden, Daniel, ed. *The World of Cynthia Ozick. Studies in American Jewish Literature* 6 (Fall 1987).

White, E. B. Review of *The Cannibal Galaxy. New York Times Book Review*, September 11, 1983, 3, 47.

GRACE PALEY   (1922–)

Thomas Frank

BIOGRAPHY

Speaking of her work, Grace Paley has said that "the form comes from literature, but language and the subject matter really come from the neighbor and the
street and my family" (interview with Merchant and Ingersoll, 614). Paley's
stories are virtual neighborhoods of storytelling families—fathers, mothers,
aunts, cousins, husbands, children, lovers—and their various counterparts encountered in the apartments, parks, and protests of New York City from the
1930s to the 1980s.

Paley's background provides the context for understanding how she emerged
as a "storytelling story hearer" (Isaacs, xi). The youngest child of Isaac and
Manya Goodside, Grace Paley was born in the Bronx, New York, on December
11, 1922. Her parents, Jewish socialists who had been exiled for political reasons
in Russia, had emigrated from the Ukraine to the Lower East Side of New York
City in 1906 (Arcana, 9–10). By 1918, Isaac Goodside had become a physician
and, by the time of Paley's birth, had established a solid medical practice amidst
the upwardly mobile Jewish communities of the Bronx. The Bronx of Paley's
youth was a storied world of "Russian Jewry, . . . pogroms, revolution, Zionism,
Socialism, immigration, and upward mobility" (Aarons, "Grace Paley," 279).
Paley's eventual transcription into literature of her primary themes—family,
politics, and writing—began in the Bronx of her youth.

Growing up as "the beloved little one in a family of grown-ups," Paley wrote
her first poems at the age of five and as an adolescent thought of herself as a
"young poet . . . a blooming anarchist and a confirmed romantic" (Arcana, 19,
27). Encouraged by her older brother and sister in her literary efforts, Paley
grew up in an intellectual environment not atypical in Jewish America: one that

stressed learning and had strong ties to familial traditions of storytelling and even stronger ones to the American traditions of upward mobility.

Paley's world was a secular one. Paley later described herself as "coming from a long line of anti-religionists" (interview with Hulley, 20). The secularism of Paley's youth not only accounts for the Yiddishist sense of justice in her stories, but the backgrounding of what is arguably the great theme of second-generation American Jewish writers. As a child of immigrants, Paley belongs to what historians call the "lost generation," American Jews "torn between the Jewish world of their parents and the American world of the streets" (Shapiro, 14). As a result, Paley's focus in her stories is not on the tensions generated by the problems of assimilation and acculturation, but on the inequities of American society associated with gender. Paley relentlessly depicts in her fiction the problems women, children, and men face living in a patriarchal world structurally prejudiced against women and their children.

Out of the Bronx stories of her youth and the Jewish secularism of her family, Paley's literary biography developed through three major phases. The first involved her life in the Bronx, through her marriage to Jess Paley in 1942 (they were divorced in 1971), the birth of her two children Nora (born in 1949) and Danny (born in 1951), and her subsequent life on the playgrounds of Greenwich Village of the 1950s. During this phase, Paley began to bring together her love of poetry, her experiences as a mother, and a growing political consciousness that contributed to her emergence as a literary storyteller. By the time of the publication of her first collection in 1959, Paley's three demanding "pulls" of family, politics, and writing were firmly established.

The second phase, occurring roughly between the publication of *The Little Disturbances of Man* (1959) and the publication of *Enormous Changes at the Last Minute* (1974), involved Paley's political activism. In the 1950s, Paley's politics had been primarily local, but in the 1960s, Paley increasingly became involved in national politics, primarily in the anti–Vietnam War movement. In 1961, she helped found the Greenwich Village Peace Center. In 1966, she spent six days in jail for participating in a demonstration opposing Armed Forces Day. In 1969, she went to Hanoi to "arrange for the return of three prisoners of war" (Sorkin, 228). In the early 1970s, her pacifist politics took her to Chile and, as a member of the War Resisters' League, to the World Peace Congress in Moscow in 1973. During this time, Paley's activism greatly expanded to protesting against war, nuclear energy, sexual discrimination, against "anything . . . that hampers the discourse of difference," as Kathleen Hulley put it ("Grace Paley's Resistant Form," 5).

During this phase, her literature began to focus more on storytelling and the ethics of writing. It was at this time that Paley began to be recognized for her stories, receiving a Guggenheim award in 1961, a National Endowment for the Arts grant in 1969, and an American Academy and Institute of Arts and Letters award in 1970. Further recognition came in the form of teaching positions at

Syracuse University and Columbia University in the early 1960s. In 1966, Paley joined the faculty of Sarah Lawrence College, from which she retired in 1987.

The third phase began after the publication of *Enormous Changes at the Last Minute* and was marked by Paley's increasing recognition as a major American short-story writer, central to postmodern, women's, and American Jewish literature. Paley's political activities continued from earlier decades and expanded to environmental issues, the literary politics of PEN, and feminist issues. Inducted into the American Institute of Arts and Letters in 1980, Paley published her third collection of stories, *Later the Same Day*, in 1985, in which she continued to explore narrative techniques, voice, and the ethics of the writer as a political activist.

Since the mid-1980s, Paley has published three volumes of poetry—*Leaning Forward* (1985), *Long Walks and Intimate Talks* (1991), and *New and Collected Poems* (1992)—that reflect her move to Vermont, where she now lives with her second husband, the poet Robert Nichols. Often quite different in subject matter from the streets of Greenwich Village and New York City that inform her stories, Paley's published poetry also includes an increasingly direct engagement with the Jewish tradition and the history it suggests. Thus in her most recent work, Paley, in a sense, returns to her origins in the Bronx. Together, Paley's stories and poems suggest that a world of justice is a world that remembers.

MAJOR WORKS AND THEMES

Paley's work has a distinct social purpose to it, which Janet Burstein described as the "rebuilding of community" (21). Making literature that works toward community building is a feature that Paley shares with other contemporary women writers as diverse as Tillie Olsen, Toni Morrison, and Louise Erdrich. Deeply influenced by the example of Tillie Olsen, Paley likewise works out of a commitment to the words and the people who speak them in the form of "telling stories" in order to create a literature that will, as Paley's signal character Faith Darwin puts it, "save a few lives" (*CS*, 133).[1] As a writer whose work reflects the aims of her political activism, Paley aims to help bring about a world where "[p]eople . . . live in mutual aid and concern, listening to one another's stories" ("A Symposium on Fiction," 31).

Writing stories that work to build a community of storytellers and storyhearers reveals the ethics informing Paley's work. It is a measure of the moral complexity of her stories that they include an often quite critical examination of those who choose to write in ways that have distinct political aims. This latter theme of the writer's responsibility is tracked through Faith Darwin, also a politically engaged writer. As Paley became more and more well known as both a writer and an activist in the 1960s and 1970s, the ethics of writing as a theme became more pronounced. Paley's most often discussed story, "A Conversation with my Father," exemplifies this theme in that it is a story about an intergenerational conflict over what stories should be in terms of form and what lessons such forms should convey. The conflict occurs between Faith Darwin, who writes open-ended stories (much like Grace Paley), and Faith's father, who desires a more closed, determined story, "a simple story . . . the kind Maupassant wrote." For Faith, however, such stories take "all hope away" (*CS*, 232). To write such a story would violate her ethical code as a writer. "A Conversation with My Father" not only points to the ethics of storytelling, but also shows that attitudes regarding writing and reading stories are influenced by different sensibilities rooted in different generations and genders.

A distinct thematic progression can be traced through Paley's stories. The first, *The Little Disturbances of Man: Stories of Women and Men at Love*, grows out of Paley's experiences observing and listening to women tell their stories about suffering the consequences of embattled love. The second collection, *Enormous Changes at the Last Minute*, chronicles a shift into a more politically engaged form of life and a more reflexive attitude toward the writing of stories in order to show how the three—suffering, politics, and storytelling—are intertwined. Like a braid, tracing any one thematic strand involves tracing the other two. The third collection, *Later the Same Day*, continues these three themes but expands their concerns to the international scene and reflects a growing sense of holism on Paley's part that stresses the interconnected nature of the world. Paley's most recent published work, her poetry, stresses such interconnectedness in poems about the Vermont countryside and Jewish identity as it connects to memory.

The themes of any particular story are directly related to the circumstances that generate a story's "telling." As Paley puts it in the introduction to her *Collected Stories*, she only began to write short stories because she was "suffering the storyteller's pain: 'Listen! I have to tell you something' " (ix). For Paley, a story emerges out of a knowledge-induced pressure, sometimes "just to the right of the heart," that generates the action of her writing a story out of the voices to whom she has listened. In "Wants," the unnamed narrator ends the story with a wry observation about herself: "That when a person or event comes along to jolt me or appraise me, I can take some appropriate action" (*CS*, 131). For Paley, writing a story is the "appropriate action" taken when something "jolts" her to the degree that she has to tell somebody something. Her story, in turn, retains the possibility of "jolting" a reader, and thus the possibility of another "pressured" telling can result from her story. Because Paley designs her stories to reveal what "has been hidden" (Gibbons, 234) in literature and politics, such "tellings" can provide information. In so doing, Paley can contribute to the possibility of social change—enormous changes at the last minute. As Faith Darwin implores the reader in "Faith in the Afternoon": "As for you, fellow independent thinker of the Western Bloc, if you have anything sensible to say, don't wait. Shout it out loud right this minute" (*CS*, 146). Shouting out loud "sensible things" is a hallmark of the kind of political action Paley has participated in since the early 1960s.

Faith Darwin's self-confidence to implore readers to shout sensibly is a consequence of breaking out of her suffering in the urban world depicted in *The Little Disturbances of Man: Stories of Women and Men at Love*. The title contains much of Paley's distinctive approach in subject matter and literary style. The replacement of the world ''in'' by ''at'' turns a cliché into a complex observation regarding sometimes cruel, yet often comic, struggles among women and men. Both are contained in the irony of what constitutes ''the little disturbances of man.'' The collection's title derives from ''An Interest in Life,'' a story in which a neighbor of Faith Darwin's, Virginia, is cruelly abandoned by her husband, whose world has been disturbed by the presence of their three little children and Virginia's physical appearance in her pregnancy.

Commiserating with an old friend, ex-neighbor, and soon-to-be lover, John Raftery, Virginia explains that she wants to write to *Strike It Rich*, a game show that specializes in suffering, in the hope that her ''list of troubles . . . [that] could have brought tears to the eyes of God'' will bring her just rewards. John laughs it off, explaining that ''they'd laugh you out of the studio. Those people really suffer . . . tornadoes, . . . floods—catastrophes of God.'' According to John, what Virginia suffers are merely ''the little disturbances of man'' (*CS*, 64, 65). The absurdity of John's interpretation is painfully clear, but what Paley brings to the surface is the importance of attending to a society where women can only truly suffer according to the categories established by men. Paley's stories of women and men at love reveal the dehumanizing nature of a world that denies people their own sense of legitimate suffering while simultaneously commercializing it for profitable entertainment.

Paley's attending to the suffering of women and children that results from being ''at love'' reveals fiction performing one of the traditional roles of poetry—that of witness. If the urge to write comes from an irrepressible urge to tell, then it gains an urgency as a written work to force a demand on the reader to pay attention to what this story is telling—people needlessly suffer because of the misguided values that create a world in which men cannot recognize women's suffering as legitimate. The anger that permeates Paley's work derives from this inability to see injustice. Saving a few lives, then, is possible when stories help people see other people's suffering. Reducing suffering depends on helping people recognize such pain. Such recognition is an important step toward changing the political contexts that not only contribute to the suffering but reinforce our collective inability to see it as suffering. Any political activism that aims at social justice is going to have a strong connection to understanding not only those ''little disturbances'' in and of themselves, but the social structures that determine what and whose disturbances are ''real.''

''An Interest in Life'' shows how an unintentional callousness toward suffering can permeate the most intimate circumstances when the ''everyday'' problems of poverty and male/female relationships gone bad are determined ''little'' from within a simple-minded male discourse. As more than one critic has noted, however, Paley's stories do not blame the characters, but work to point the reader toward the larger social and cultural factors that determine or influence the world views of men and women that are largely responsible for the pain they mutually cause in the course of their lives together. What holds for interpersonal relationships depicted in *Little Disturbances*, Paley extends outward toward the larger, political world in her second collection, *Enormous Changes at the Last Minute*. Any hope for the relief of interpersonal suffering lies with political action, even if it is at the last minute.

One of the notable features of Paley's work in following out these conflicts, misunderstandings, and comic failures at mutual comprehension between women and men is the destructive nature such adult irresponsibility has on children. The world is bleak for the children in Paley's fiction. Children die, are abandoned, go insane, and are raped, murdered, neglected, and abused, even if they are loved by those embattled women, such as Virginia. Paley celebrates such love without losing sight of the fact that our militaristic world is destructive to children and their parents. Rare among contemporary literature, Paley's fiction, such as "In Time Which Made a Monkey of Us All," shows how destructive this world is to men by revealing how it destroys male dignity when it teaches boys to solve problems through violence and to treat girls as their "natural" inferiors. Through such beginnings the stage is set for adult suffering, which in turn affects their children. Paley breaks this vicious circle by showing that when Faith Darwin turns to politics, she does so as a result of watching her son, Richard, react to her own passivity in the face of political repression.

Faith turns to political activism, and to the wider public sphere, often being chastised by her young son for failing to resist an absurd law that prevents political speech protesting the killing of children. Paley's story "Faith in a Tree" contains all the elements of Paley's fiction: an innovative narrative technique that results from the urge to tell a story of the little disturbance of erotic loneliness against the backdrop of the great disturbance of the Vietnam War. The story ends with Faith's transformation in a moment of *t'shuva*—a moral turning. Watching Richard, in tears, write "in letters fifteen feet high, so the entire world could see—WOULD YOU BURN A CHILD? . . . WHEN NEC-ESSARY" is an appraising event, one that "jolts" Faith into changing her life. As Faith recalls it: "That is exactly when events turned me around, changing my hairdo, my job uptown, my style of living and telling . . . and directed out of that sexy playground by my children's heartfelt brains, I thought more and more and everyday about the world" (*CS*, 194). "Faith in a Tree" is the centerpiece of Paley's three collections—the fulcrum on which the other two balance. Faith's *t'shuva*, itself central to the Jewish tradition, epitomizes moral action through commitment to community and signifies the potential of the enormous changes that can happen at the last minute of any day.

In *Later the Same Day*, Paley extends the possibility of enormous change toward national and international situations and toward her own identity as a "poet-citizen." The politics of writing becomes a subject side by side with Paley's two other principal subjects—family and politics. All three are linked by Paley's commitment to antioppression, to antimonolithism, whether in terms of the threat of nuclear war, patriarchy, racism, the silencing of individual and group voices, or the tyranny of narrative designs that "end" with resounding finality. Stories in *Later the Same Day* stress the consequences attending earlier actions, events, statements and stories. Everything, and everyone, is connected to something, and she must attend to the consequences, whether they are children, lovers, neighbors, or friends. Through Faith Darwin, Paley extends this sense of attending consequences to literary subject matter in "Listening" when Faith is confronted with her own inattention, such as the excluding from her literature the experiences of people she professes politically to care about and on whose behalf she is writing.

"Listening" concludes Paley's *Collected Stories* and *Later the Same Day* by ending with a blistering critique of Faith for failing to live up to her professed ethics as a writer, for failing to listen, in the broad sense that informs Paley's work as a whole. In the story, Faith recounts giving her lesbian friend Cassie a ride. Listening to Faith's comment about an attractive man, Cassie hones in on the absence of her life, her stories, in Faith's work, speaking in a language that recalls Paley's first story collection: "Listen, Faith, why don't you tell my story? You've told everybody's story but mine. . . . Where is my life? It's been women and men, women and men. . . . where the hell is my woman and woman, woman-loving life in all this? . . . it's really strange, why have you left me out of everybody's life?" Stunned by Cassie's reading of her work against her ethos as a writer committed to social justice, Faith acknowledges the absence of Cassie's stories in her work and asks Cassie for forgiveness, to which Cassie replies with the line that ends the book: "I do not forgive you" (*CS*, 385, 386). By ending her collected stories this way, Paley applies her own ethics against her work and finds it flawed. At the same time, she instructs the reader to be like Cassie, vigilantly reading writers against their own professed ethos. In this way, there can be a joint working on the part of readers and writers toward a more just world rooted in a pervasive, ongoing, mutual celebration of human dignity.

CRITICAL RECEPTION

On the whole, Grace Paley's short fiction has been uniformly praised. Outside of Carol Iannone's "A Dissent on Grace Paley," it is difficult to find criticism that does not exude admiration for both Grace Paley and her literature. Central to Paley's work is the presentation to the reading world of those voices previously unavailable in literature. If, as Kathleen Hulley noted in "Grace Paley's Resistant Form," critics in the early 1980s had difficulty finding methods with which to write about the complexity of Paley's work, the multitude of critical approaches—critical voices—emerging since enables readers to make even better sense of a politically engaged, ethically concerned writer who celebrates and defends the variety of voices that we encounter in our daily lives. As a result, Paley's work dovetails well with the concerns in recent literary criticism and theory over the past decade. Consequently, Paley's work has received some excellent critical analysis. The overall social depth, moral complexity, and linguistic richness of her literature as a whole come to the fore in the work of such Paley scholars as Judith Arcana, Victoria Aarons, Jacqueline Taylor, and Neil Isaacs.

Judith Arcana's excellent *Grace Paley's Life Stories: A Literary Biography* (1993) provides a detailed overview of the biographical relationship between Grace Paley's life and her stories and poems, as well as her uncollected poems, prose, and journalism. Anyone interested in Paley's work from a biographical approach should consult Arcana's book. Other good overviews of Paley's life can be found in Aarons (1994) and Isaacs's (1990) innovative use of the many interviews that Paley has given over the past twenty-five years. Good bibliographies of Paley's writings and criticism can be found in Halfmann and Gerlach (1989); Aarons (1994); Isaacs (1990); and Arcana (1993).

Throughout Paley's career, critics have consistently singled out her voice and her virtuosity in creating such complex, multifaceted, peopled worlds within the confines of the short story. *Little Disturbances of Man* generated criticism that also focused on her descriptions of New York City life. With *Enormous Changes at the Last Minute* and *Later the Same Day*, Paley's work began to gain more sustained attention of scholars, especially those who were attuned to postmodernist writers and who looked with favor on those writers who were exploring metafiction and alternative narrative techniques to traditional fiction making. Alan Wilde's chapter on Paley in his *Middle Grounds: Studies in Contemporary American Fiction* (1987) located Paley in the development of American postmodernist fiction. Shorter works, such as those by Humy (1982) and Taylor ("Tracing Connections," 1990), focused on Paley's narrative technique. Feminist approaches such as those by Schleifer (1985) and Cronin (1992) detailed how Paley's innovative narrative techniques work politically to undermine a social order that has historically denied women a participatory voice. Paley's work has also benefited from the renewed critical sense of the varieties and complexities of American Jewish literature. Bonnie Lyons, Jeanne Criswell, Murray Baumgarten, Janet Burstein, and Dena Mandel are only a few of the scholars who have produced valuable readings of Paley's stories by showing the various ways they fit within and are constitutive of American Jewish literature as it has developed since World War II.

If any one thing links all the Paley criticism, it is language. Nearly all the critics and scholars who write about Paley give her language, and the voices embedded therein, its due. The criticism illuminates how each of Paley's storied worlds carries its own language. Because Paley's conception of language is inseparable from the people who speak it, critical attention to her language works toward attending to these people. By doing so, Paley criticism parallels the stories in that both orient readers toward the world evoked by the language and thereby contribute toward recognizing the dignity of the "hidden" people in Grace Paley's storytelling worlds.

NOTE

1. All references to Grace Paley's stories are from *The Collected Stories* (1994), cited as *CS*.

BIBLIOGRAPHY

Works by Grace Paley

Fiction

The Little Disturbances of Man: Stories of Women and Men at Love. Garden City, NY: Doubleday, 1959.
Enormous Changes at the Last Minute. New York: Farrar, Straus and Giroux, 1974.
Later the Same Day. New York: Farrar, Straus and Giroux, 1985.
The Collected Stories. New York: Farrar, Straus and Giroux, 1994.

Poetry

Leaning Forward. Afterword by Jane Cooper. Penobscot, ME: Granite Press, 1985.
Long Walks and Intimate Talks. Paintings by Vera Williams. New York: Feminist Press, 1991.
New and Collected Poems. Gardiner, ME: Tilbury House, 1992.

Interviews

Chamberlain, Mary, ed. *Writing Lives: Conversations between Women Writers*. London: Virago, 1988.
Dee, Jonathan, Barbara Jones, and Larissa MacFarquhar. "Grace Paley: The Art of Fiction CXXXI." *Paris Review* 34 (Fall 1992): 180–209.
"Grace Paley." *Contemporary Authors*, New Revision Series, 14 (1984): 532–33.
Hulley, Kathleen. "Interview with Grace Paley." *Delta* 14 (May 1982): 19–40.
Earl Ingersoll, and Marchant, Peter. "A Conversation with Grace Paley." *Massachusetts Review* 25 (1985): 606–14.

Symposie

Gibbons, Reginald, ed. *The Writer in Our World: A Symposium Sponsored by Tri-Quarterly Magazine*. Boston: Atlantic Monthly Press, 1986.
"A Symposium on Fiction." *Shenandoah* 27 (Winter 1976): 3–31.

Works Cited and Studies of Grace Paley

Aarons, Victoria. "Grace Paley." In *Jewish American Women Writers: A Bio-Critical Sourcebook*, ed. Ann R. Shapiro. Westport, CT: Greenwood Press, 1994.
———. "The Outsider Within: Women in Contemporary Jewish-American Fiction." *Contemporary Literature* 28:3 (1987): 378–93.
———. "A Perfect Marginality: Public and Private Telling in the Stories of Grace Paley." *Studies in Short Fiction* 27 (Winter 1990): 35–43.

————. "Talking Lives: Storytelling and Renewal in Grace Paley's Short Fiction." *Studies in American Jewish Literature* 9:1 (1990): 20–35.

Arcana, Judith. *Grace Paley's Life Stories: A Literary Biography*. Urbana: University of Illinois Press, 1993.

Ascher, Carol, Louise DeSalvo, and Sara Ruddick. *Between Women: Biographers, Novelists, Critics, Teachers, and Artists Write about Their Work on Women*. Boston: Beacon, 1984.

Baba, Minako. "Faith Darwin as Writer-Heroine: A Study of Grace Paley's Short Stories." *Studies in American Jewish Literature* 7 (Spring 1988): 40–54.

Baumgarten, Murray. "Urban Rites and Civic Premises in the Fiction of Saul Bellow, Grace Paley, and Sandra Schor." *Contemporary Literature* 34 (Fall 1993): 395–424.

Blake, Henry. "Grace Paley, a Plea for English Writing." *Delta* 14 (May 1982): 73–80.

Bruce, Melissa. *"Enormous Changes at the Last Minute*: A Subversive Song Book." *Delta* 14 (May 1982): 97–114.

Burstein, Janet. "Jewish-American Women's Literature: The Long Quarrel with God." *Studies in American Jewish Literature* 8 (Spring 1989): 9–25.

Clayton, John. "Grace Paley and Tillie Olsen: Radical Jewish Humanists." *Response* 14 (1984): 37–52.

Coppula, Kathleen A. "Not for Literary Reasons: The Fiction of Grace Paley." *Mid-American Review* 7:1 (1986): 63–72.

Cousineau, Diane. "The Desires of Women, the Presence of Men." *Delta* 14 (May 1982): 55–66.

Crawford, John. "Archetypal Patterns in Grace Paley's 'Runner.' " *Notes on Contemporary Literature* 11 (September 1981): 10–12.

Criswell, Jeanne Sallade. "Cynthia Ozick and Grace Paley: Diverse Visions in Jewish and Women's Literature." In *Since Flannery O'Connor: Essays on the Contemporary American Short Story*, ed. Loren Logsdon and Charles W. Mayer. Macomb: Western Illinois University Press, 1987.

Cronin, Gloria L. "Melodramas of Beset Womanhood: Resistance, Subversion, and Survival in the Fiction of Grace Paley." *Studies in American Jewish Literature* 11: 2 (1992): 140–49.

Eckstein, Barbara. "Grace Paley's Community: Gradual Epiphanies in the Meantime." In *Politics and the Muse: Studies in the Politics of Recent American Literature*, ed. Adam J. Sorkin. Bowling Green: Popular Press, 1989, 124–41.

Fredericksen, Brooke. "Home Is Where the Text Is: Exile, Homeland, and Jewish American Writing." *Studies in American Jewish Literature* 11:1 (1992): 36–43.

Halfmann, Ulrich, and Phillip Gerlach. "Grace Paley: A Bibliography." *Tulsa Studies in Women's Literature* 8 (Fall 1989): 339–54.

Hulley, Kathleen, ed. "Grace Paley." Special Issue of *Delta: Revue du Centre d'Etudes et de Rechercher sur les Ecrivains du Sud aux Etats-Unis* 14 (May 1982).

————. "Grace Paley's Resistant Form." *Delta* 14 (May 1982): 3–18.

Humy, Nicholas Peter. "A Different Responsibility: Form and Technique in Grace Paley's 'Conversation with My Father.' " *Delta* 14 (May 1982): 96–97.

Iannone, Carol. "A Dissent on Grace Paley." *Commentary*, August 1985, 54–58.

Isaacs, Neil D. *Grace Paley: A Study of the Short Fiction*. Boston: G. K. Hall/Twayne Series, 1990.

Kamel, Rose. "To Aggravate the Conscience: Grace Paley's Loud Voice." *Journal of Ethnic Studies* 11 (Fall 1983): 29–49.

Lyons, Bonnie K. "American Jewish Fiction since 1945." In *Handbook of American-Jewish Literature: An Analytical Guide to Topics, Themes, and Sources*, ed. Lewis Fried. Westport, CT: Greenwood Press, 1988.

———. "Grace Paley's Jewish Miniatures." *Studies in American Jewish Literature* 8 (Spring 1989): 26–33.

Mandel, Dena. "Keeping Up with Faith: Grace Paley's Sturdy American Jewess." *Studies in American Jewish Literature* 3 (Spring 1983): 85–98.

Olendorf, Donna. "Grace Paley." *Contemporary Authors*, New Revision Series, 13. Detroit: Gale Research, 1984. 397–401.

Pinsker, Sanford. Review of *"The Collected Stories* by Grace Paley." *Studies in Short Fiction* 31:4 (1994): 689–690.

Schleifer, Ronald. "Grace Paley: Chaste Compactness." In *Contemporary. American Women Writers: Narrative Strategies*, ed. Catherine Rainwater and William J. Scheick. Lexington: University Press of Kentucky, 1985.

Seltzer, Robert M. *Jewish People, Jewish Thought: The Jewish Experience in History*. New York: Macmillan, 1980.

Shapiro, Edward S. *A Time for Healing: American Jewry since World War II*. Vol. 5 in *The Jewish People in America*, ed. Henry L. Feingold. Baltimore: Johns Hopkins University Press, 1992.

Sorkin, Adam J. "Grace Paley." In Twentieth-Century American-Jewish Fiction Writers, ed. Daniel Walden. Vol. 28 of *Dictionary of Literary Biography*. Detroit: Gale Research, 1984, 225–31.

Taylor, Jacqueline. *Grace Paley: Illuminating the Dark Lives*. Austin: University of Texas Press, 1990.

———. "Tracing Connections between Women's Personal Narratives and the Short Stories of Grace Paley." *Text and Performance Quarterly* 10 (January 1990): 20–33.

Wilde, Alan. *Middle Grounds: Studies in Contemporary American Fiction*. Philadelphia: University of Pennsylvania Press, 1987.

MARGE PIERCY (1936–   )

Holli Levitsky

BIOGRAPHY

Marge Piercy was born on March 31, 1936, in Detroit, Michigan. Raised Jewish and poor in a predominantly black working-class neighborhood in Detroit, she regularly experienced racism, classism, and anti-Semitism. Piercy's mother, Bert Bernice Bunnin (family name Badonya), the eldest daughter of nine children, was not a practicing Jew. Because of the pervasive anti-Semitism of the time, she urged Marge to lie about her religion, which Piercy refused to do. Her father, Robert Douglas Piercy, was a nonreligious man (born a Presbyterian) of Welsh and English heritage.

Piercy was always much closer to her mother's family. She was particularly fond of her Grandmother Hannah, a Yiddish-speaking immigrant, who gave Piercy her Hebrew name, Marah. Her grandmother's father had been a *shtetl* rabbi in Lithuania; consequently, her grandmother Hannah was pious and a great storyteller. Her mother's father, Russian-born, was a union organizer murdered while organizing bakery workers. Piercy claims that "my mother made me a poet," but the great storytelling skill of her maternal grandmother and the left-wing activist politics of her maternal grandfather are clearly evident in the skill with which she narrates the deeply felt lives of her many socially conscious fictional characters.

In the summer of 1941, Piercy's family took a road trip from Detroit to south Florida, a place where hurricanes were known to unleash their fury. At the water's edge, dodging the dying, poison-filled Portuguese men-of-war, Piercy listened while her mother pointed across the ocean, raging that "over there" Jews just like them were being killed. The combined images of rage-filled hurricanes, deadly men-of-war, and the murder of Jews became inextricably bound together in the young Marge Piercy's memory.

Growing up during World War II, Piercy was given the impression that being Jewish was a "dangerous dramatic destiny, an ancient and hazardous treasure being handed on to me" (Rosenberg, 173). Her grandmother, visiting the Piercy home every summer and sharing Piercy's room, brought into her granddaughter's life delicious kosher food and a deeply religious lifestyle as well as stories about the Lithuanian people from her childhood. But more significantly, her mother and grandmother would discuss the atrocities of the war. It was well known among American Jews that European Jews were being rounded up, placed in camps, and murdered. Jewish papers were full of stories and smuggled photographs. Seeing these two women whom she loved deeply filled with grief only added to the deep-seated effect Judaism would have on her work: a constant sense of longing for a return.

Piercy was reasonably happy in early childhood, although that changed when she began school and was one of only two Jews there. For this, she was regularly beaten up. Moreover, halfway through grade school she became dangerously ill with German measles and rheumatic fever. She went from being a healthy and tomboyish little girl to being somewhat of an invalid, during which time she learned to take refuge in books. She had an extraordinary IQ and read voraciously, but remained sickly until about the eighth grade.

At seventeen Piercy won a scholarship to the University of Michigan, becoming the first person in her family to go to college. Until that time, Piercy considered her Jewishness mostly cultural, but thanks to her grandmother's influence she felt it deeply and permanently. In college she began to explore what it meant to be a Jew. She won various Hopwood (writing) awards for her fiction and poetry and received her bachelor of arts degree in 1957. One year later, after a fellowship at Northwestern University, she received her M.A.

She married her first husband, Michel Schiff, in 1957. He was a particle physicist and French Jew whom she met in Ann Arbor and with whom she eventually moved to Paris. After that marriage failed, she moved to Chicago, working part-time and training herself as a writer. She was already interested in subjects that later became central to feminist culture, but in which no one else at the time seemed interested. She was also involved in the civil rights movement. The Chicago years were perhaps the hardest of her life; she was a divorcée at twenty-three, poor, and writing novels she could not get published because they were too feminist and too political for the time.

In 1962 she married Robert Shapiro, a computer scientist. They lived around Boston and in New York. The second marriage was an open relationship and for the most part proved more satisfying to Piercy, although it too eventually ended in divorce. Still, during the marriage she was heavily involved in such New Left organizations as the Students for a Democratic Society (SDS), starting an MDS (off-campus) chapter of the SDS when she lived in Brooklyn. In 1967 she left the infighting of the SDS organization to work only with women's causes. In 1969 she became very ill with chronic bronchitis and a serious back injury and was confined to bed for several months. During her recovery the following year she and Robert Shapiro moved to Cape Cod; for Piercy this was a significant and permanent change of environment. She is currently married to her third husband, the novelist and playwright Ira Wood.

Although Piercy chose early to make her career as a full-time writer, she has held many different positions in academic circles and has been involved politically in numerous organizations. She has taught, lectured, and/or given workshops at Indiana University, the University of Kansas, College of the Holy Cross, Purdue University, the State University of New York at Buffalo, Ohio State University, the University of Cincinnati, the University of Michigan, and others. Her political activities are numerous and include work on arts councils, women's centers, public policy boards, advisory boards, the Israeli Center for the Arts and Literature, the Israeli Center for the Creative Arts (HILAI), and the National Endowment for the Arts, all since 1989. She has been a member of the International Board of the Israeli Center for Creative Arts (1986–1988) and ALEPH (1993); an advisor of the Siddur Project, P'nai Or (1986–); and a member of the artistic advisory board of Am-Ha-Yam (1988–).

Piercy has won wide public recognition for her literary output, including a National Endowment for the Arts award (1978); Sheaffer Eaton–PEN New England Award for Literary Excellence (1989); Brit ha-Darot Award, Shalom Center (1992); and the Arthur C. Clarke Award for best science-fiction novel in the United Kingdom (1992). She has been named the James B. Angell and Lucinda Goodrich Downs Scholar and has received the Orion Scott Award in Humanities and an honorary Litt.D. from Bridgewater State College.

MAJOR WORKS AND THEMES

The Hasidic authority, the Baal Shem Tov, said these words, which are also carved above the entrance to the memorial hall at Yad Vashem in Israel: "Forgetting lengthens the period of exile. In remembrance lies the secret of deliverance." These words not only describe the novelist in Marge Piercy, but also define her worldview, which is highly political, deeply empathetic, and yet tightly bound to certain sacred traditions.

Piercy's stories are character-driven. The novel progresses as the character or characters develop, as they struggle against internal (and sometimes external) resistance in order to be "delivered" from the pain of exile, of lost identity and desperation. These characters are and are not like ordinary people; they certainly are or become political. Like Piercy, they are often from working-class, Jewish backgrounds. In fact, while Piercy's earlier characters are often political mouthpieces, her later works, such as *Gone to Soldiers* (1987), reveal characters who undergo a process of personal change in a graphically detailed historical or sociological context. As Dorothy Allison remarked in her review of *Gone to Soldiers*, "History books and sociological studies . . . never have the impact of fiction, in which the lives of individual people take on the weight of generations, of all who lived through those times and were changed by them—all our parents and grandparents. Piercy has brought . . . into *Gone to Soldiers*, the sweep of change, loss, and growth, the feel of life going on—the lives that will eventually become our own'' (45).

While Piercy continues to write books of poetry and has written one play, she has made a major contribution to contemporary fiction with twelve novels. Like her poetry, her fictional work is considered strongly feminist and often autobiographical. Almost all of her major novels have some Jewish characters and themes, beginning with her first published novel, *Going Down Fast* (1969).

Perhaps Piercy best expresses her feelings as a novelist whose work is shaped both by internal forces and a desire to recognize common experience. Her need to share her life with others even as she incorporates others' lives into her own reflects Piercy's determination to write into her stories both her Judaism and her feminism. In an essay on the Holocaust, she wrote: ''I don't remember a time I did not imagine I would have to confront World War Two in my writing. I cannot remember back past the intention to write such a novel'' (Rosenberg, 183).

In *Going Down Fast*, Piercy begins to explore the multiple points of view she will later develop more fully in her World War II novel *Gone to Soldiers*. The story takes place within an academic community in Chicago. It follows the interconnected lives of two young female teachers (one Jewish, one black), as well as a blues singer, a welfare caseworker, and an underground filmmaker, set against the background of ''urban renewal.'' While Piercy gets under the skin of both her black and white (Jewish) characters, the young Jewish Anna's passivity, albeit well defined, is an especially visible contrast to later Piercy feminist academics who become agents of change.

Going Down Fast refers both to the people living in buildings recently condemned and the buildings themselves. In *Small Changes* (1973), an explicitly feminist novel, the phrase ''small change'' is used not to refer to something cheap and petty but, as Catherine R. Stimpson claimed, to mean ''the way in which a New Woman, a New Man, will be generated: one halting step after another'' (565). *Small Changes* does in fact reflect Piercy's active involvement in the women's movement while maintaining a persistent sympathy with working-class ethnic and racial minorities with much greater explicitness than in *Going Down Fast*. The character of Miriam, a New York Jewish middle-class woman, is, like Piercy, a product of a family with political commitments. Miriam tries to balance her personal life with her growing desire (and need) to articulate her intellectual and feminist vision.

In *The High Cost of Living* (1978) Piercy takes a closer look at women's personal lives, exploring the repressive sexual and social nature of the time. Like *Braided Lives* (1982), the later novel that most resembles it in theme and focus, *The High Cost of Living* focuses almost exclusively on women's point of view. While *Braided Lives* takes place mostly in Ann Arbor, the earlier novel takes place within the academic setting of Wayne State University in Detroit. The major theme of this novel is the compromise of values and principles when faced with the pressures of succeeding as either a writer or a professional within an academic community.

Piercy returns to the Left with her fugitive heroine of the eponymous novel *Vida* (1979). However, Davida (Vida) Asch is a self-consciously Jewish political fugitive who will not give up the cause. Still on the run for her participation in a ten-year-old bombing, Vida is torn between her old loyalties to the radical group within which she still operates and a recurring desire to slip back into society and resume a normal life. In her loneliness and desolation, Vida ruminates often on her prior life, including what it means to be a Jew in hiding. Born of a Jewish mother and a gentile father, she considers herself Jewish even though her brother, born of the same lineage, considers himself gentile. Most of the men in her life have been Jewish, including her husband and her current lover.

Braided Lives is the most autobiographical of Piercy's novels. In it she chronicles the life of Jill Stuart, a high-school senior at the novel's beginning (in the 1950s), who longs to be a writer. Like Piercy, Jill is dark, born of a Jewish mother and a gentile father. Again, like Piercy, Jill wins a scholarship to the University of Michigan and becomes the first person in her family to attend college. We witness the emerging personality of this young woman as she discovers the obstacles in her way to becoming the recognized, published author she longs to be. At the same time, we get a view of what life was like for a young Jewish woman on the streets of Detroit's working-class neighborhoods, witnessing the decay, the anti-Semitism, and the sharp class divisions much as Piercy herself must have.

In *Gone to Soldiers* we are back in a novel with multiple points of view. It is also the only Piercy novel that deals directly with the Holocaust, and with Jews inside and outside its direct perils. Piercy writes, ''Working on *Gone to Soldiers* and the death of my mother, a year saying Kaddish for her, engaged me actively with Judaism again, made me want to create and experience a religion I could give myself to without turning off any part of my mind or my experience'' (Rosenberg, 189). Piercy narrates the lives of ten characters who experience different forms of grief and loss during World War II. Told from the viewpoint of one character at a time, the novel is structured so that each separate set of chapters could be read as a separate book. While Piercy's emphasis—as in most of her novels—is primarily on women, she also documents here what life was like for men in a more personal way than war novels usually do. She details the life of Jacqueline, living as an underground soldier in France, and that of her young sister Naomi, living with relatives in Detroit, but also their cousin Duvey's (short) life. There is a Jewish woman journalist and her Jewish ex-husband professor, among others, Jewish and non-Jewish, all of whom are attempting to live under the impact of loss and turmoil.

Piercy narrates the story of a Jewish musician, Dinah, in *Summer People*

(1989). The narrative begins with Dinah in a long-term ménage à trois with her neighbors, but by the end she longs for a more stable and exclusive relationship with a single man and finds it with another Jewish musician. Along with Piercy's last novel, *The Longings of Women* (1994), *Summer People* is primarily a feminist novel, a story of politically committed, independent women, some of whom happen to be Jewish.

The Piercy novel that analyzes a Jewish theme most closely is her science-fiction/utopian *He, She, and It* (1991). The theme is that of the necessity for shared communal practice as a means for transformation of the world. A twenty-first-century cyborg (Yod) is being programmed by the scientist Malkah in the communal town of Tikva. Malkah weaves a narrative for Yod about his ancestor, the seventeenth-century golem, and his creator within the ghetto of Prague. Yod's beginnings, social interactions, and ultimate destruction parallel that of the golem. However, his story is bound up with that of Malkah's granddaughter (and scientist) Shira, whom she raised, and who has returned to the free town of Tikva after living (and losing custody of her son) in the brutal (and huge) corporate enclaves. Yod turns out to be the perfect companion and lover for Shira, but sacrifices himself and the laboratory that bore him in order to protect the town and disallow any more creations like himself.

Piercy's latest novel, *The Longings of Women*, weaves together the narratives of three women, one of whom is Jewish. Leila is committed to her work and her family, but longs for more and discovers within herself reservoirs of strength after her husband leaves her in midlife. Piercy also provides interesting commentary on a "modern Jewish family." Leila's family includes a lesbian grandmother, a cowgirl, a philandering dramatist, and a sensitive son. Her new lover, also Jewish, is a woodsy veterinarian.

CRITICAL RECEPTION

Going Down Fast, Piercy's first novel, was given a very positive critical reception. Even in her earliest fiction, her talent for strong characterizations and plausible political scenarios was noted. John Leonard, in the *New York Times*, observed, "That her characters should derive from their experience madness or death or radical commitment flows convincingly from the logic of the 'fat' nation she examines" (45). Martin Levin focused even more on her ability to create well-defined characters of many types, noting that Piercy "gets beneath the skin of her dramatis personae, black and white" (70).

Widely reviewed by established magazines and newspapers, *Small Changes* received qualified praise. The objections to it were for the most part concerned with Piercy's rhetoric, which was believed by some to be too polemical. However, no critics dismissed the novel as unimportant. In fact, Catherine R. Stimpson of the *Nation* saw in Piercy's characters "the creation of a new sexuality and a new psychology, which will permeate and bind a broad genuine equality" (565).

For *Vida*, Piercy again received mixed critical reviews. However, much of the criticism was leveled at Piercy's politics. She was seen as too much the insider; context was left unexplained, and critics contended that this affected the novel. Noted Elinor Langer in the *New York Times Book Review*, "There is no perspective, there are not even any explanations. Why we are against the war, who the enemy is, what measures are justified against the state—all these are simply taken for granted." Yet Langer later praised *Vida* as "a fully controlled, tightly structured dramatic narrative of such artful intensity that it leads the reader on at almost every page" (1).

Piercy's next major work, *Braided Lives*, seemed to bring out extremes of feelings in its reviewers. Renee Gold wrote that the book was "Piercy's best novel to date" (582). However, Roger Scruton, in the *Times Literary Supplement*, characterized the book's style as "too reminiscent of a woman's magazine to sustain the feminist ideology of the text" (807). While most critics agreed that the book was interesting, they asserted that Piercy wrote too much. Katha Pollitt summed it up in her comment that "*Braided Lives* won't win any literary prizes, but it will make its readers pay more attention to . . . the imperiled gains of the women's movement" (7).

That Piercy's work is unquestionably literary was finally proven with the publication of her 703-page opus *Gone to Soldiers*. Many critics found the writing smoother and the numerous perspectives fascinating rather than annoying. In her review of the book, Dorothy Allison saw Piercy as "as much a poet as a novelist, with a poet's gift for language and capturing the moment in essential details" (45).

Although the reviews for *He, She, and It* were mixed overall, many critics found the book exciting and innovative. The distinguishing feature of the novel for the *London Times Literary Supplement*'s Anne-Marie Conway "is the way Marge Piercy combines the story of Shira and Yod with the Yiddish myth of the Golem" (21). Diana O'Hehir revealed that she "was amazed at the fertility of Piercy's imaginings" (25). In his review for *Tikkun*, Arthur Waskow declared that Piercy's characters "are recognizably human. . . . [She] lets her readers see people like themselves, who can make change happen, so her readers can come to see themselves as agents of change" (72).

Finally, in her review of Piercy's most recent work of fiction, *The Longings of Women*, Elayne Rapping supplied a reason for Piercy's staying power as a novelist. She wrote that Piercy imagines, "from a feminist and class perspective, all the heartbreaking truths that go into the making of so many commonplace tragedies in the lives of commonplace, mostly invisible and anonymous, women" (46).

If Piercy's ongoing moralistic stance in her novels has alienated some readers, it is because her writing is distinguished by its honesty and commitment to personal and social justice. Piercy has come to maturity in her writing; while she has always revealed a high degree of emotional engagement with her characters, her later novels suggest more satisfaction and hopefulness. Piercy's long detachment from Judaism and her frank distaste for its patriarchal origins and traditions would seem to be replaced by her renewed belief in Reconstructionism. However, what has always made Piercy special as a contemporary writer has been her political angle of vision. When she ably connects her feminist spiritual awakening to her political and social feminism, her writing is deeply felt.

BIBLIOGRAPHY

Works by Marge Piercy

Going Down Fast. New York: Trident, 1969.
Dance the Eagle to Sleep. Garden City, NY: Doubleday, 1970.
Small Changes. Garden City, NY: Doubleday, 1973.
Woman on the Edge of Time. New York: Knopf, 1976.
The High Cost of Living. New York: Harper and Row, 1978.
Vida. New York: Fawcett Crest, 1979.
Braided Lives. New York: Summit, 1982.
Fly Away Home. New York: Fawcett Crest, 1984.
Gone to Soldiers. New York: Fawcett Crest, 1987.
Summer People. New York: Summit, 1989.
He, She, and It. New York: Knopf, 1991.
The Longings of Women. New York: Fawcett Columbine, 1994.
Piercy, Marge. *Parti-colored Blocks for a Quilt.* Poets on Poetry. Ann Arbor: University of Michigan Press, 1982.
———. "The Repair of the World." Review of *On Being a Jewish Feminist: A Reader*, ed. Suzanne Heschel. *Women's Review of Books*, February 1994, 5–6.

Studies of Marge Piercy

Allison, Dorothy. "Marge Piercy Makes War." Review of *Gone to Soldiers. Village Voice*, May 19, 1987, 45.
Conway, Anne-Marie. Review of *He, She, and It. London Times Literary Supplement*, May 29, 1992, 21.
Gold, Renee. Review of *Braided Lives. Wilson Library Bulletin* 56:7 (March 1982): 582.
Langer, Elinor. Review of *Vida. New York Times*, February 24, 1980, 1.
Leonard, John. Review of *Going Down Fast. New York Times*, October 21, 1969, 45.
Levin, Martin. Review of *Going Down Fast. New York Times Book Review*, November 9, 1969, 70.
O'Hehir, Diana. Review of *He, She, and It. Belles Lettres*, Spring 1992, 25.
Pollitt, Katha. "A Complete Catalog of Female Suffering." Review of *Braided Lives. New York Times Book Review*, February 7, 1982, 7, 30–31.
Rapping, Elayne. "Vintage Piercy." Review of *The Longings of Women. Women's Review of Books* 11:10–11 (1994), 46.
Rosenberg, David, ed. *Testimony: Contemporary Writers Make the Holocaust Personal.* New York: Random House, 1989.

Scruton, Roger. "Bodily Tracts." Review of *Braided Lives. Times Literary Supplement* 4138, (July 23, 1982): 807.

Stimpson, Catherine R. Review of *Small Changes. Nation*, November 30, 1974, 565.

Walker, Sue, and Eugenie Hamner, eds. *Ways of Knowing: Essays on Marge Piercy.* Mobile, AL: Negative Capability Press, 1991.

Waskow, Arthur. "Androgyny and Beyond." Review of *He, She, and It.* Tikkun 7:6 (November 1992): 72–74.

CHAIM POTOK

(1929–)

S. Lillian Kremer

BIOGRAPHY

Chaim Potok was born on February 17, 1929, to Polish-Jewish immigrants Mollie Friedman and Benjamin Max Potok, who reared him in a traditional Jewish home and provided him an orthodox Jewish education. He was religiously and secularly educated at Yeshiva University, where he earned the B.A. summa cum laude in 1950; at the Jewish Theological Seminary of America, where he received the Hebrew Literature Prize, Homiletics Prize, Bible Prize, M.H.L., and rabbinic ordination in 1954; and at the University of Pennsylvania, where he earned a Ph.D. in philosophy in 1965. When Potok became enamored of literature, he determined that fiction would be his vehicle to engage Jewish civilization. Following service as a U.S. Army chaplain in Korea (1955–1957), Potok has had a distinguished teaching and publication career in Jewish studies and American literature. He taught at the University of Judaism in Los Angeles (1957–1959), served as scholar-in-residence at Har Zion Temple in Philadelphia (1959–1963), taught at the Jewish Theological Seminary Teachers' Institute (1963–1964), and currently teaches at the University of Pennsylvania. His publishing career has included positions as editor of *Conservative Judaism* (1964–1965) and editor for the Jewish Publication Society (1965–1975), where he collaborated on the new authorized Bible translation. *Wanderings: Chaim Potok's History of the Jews* (1978) is a compendium of scholarship about cultural encounters between Jewish civilization and the myriad cultures with which Judaism has come into contact.

MAJOR WORKS AND THEMES

Commitment to Judaism and the literary influences of Evelyn Waugh, James Joyce, and Flannery O'Connor are evident in Potok's efforts to show characters in relation to God and to dramatize the importance of religion in a secular age and society. His characters, like Waugh's and Joyce's, display a strong sense of continuity with national history and are often presented against a backdrop of the demands of family, community, and religion. The genesis and substance of every Potok novel until *I Am the Clay* is Jewish religious, historic, and cultural experience in a non-Judaic world. The novelist's affirmative vision, veneration of life, positive assessment of human nature, and pervasive striving for meaning in the midst of chaos, for good in the face of evil, derive from Judaism. He joins other Jewish-American novelists in advocating the Jewish view of a sanctified world and enduring and noble humanity, revealing a vital philosophy to counter twentieth-century alienation and despair. His characters are conversant with Jewish theology, liturgy, and rabbinic commentaries, and it is through these texts and historic memory that they strive to comprehend the human condition. His characters are frequently presented in the context of synagogue, yeshiva, and observant Jewish homes, occupied in prayer, study, and communal service. Even when his Jews enter secular professions, they maintain orthodox private lives. In place of the recalcitrant Hebraically illiterate students and abusive teachers who have become a cliché in postwar American fiction, Potok's students and teachers remind the reader of brilliant minds and ardent scholars common in Yiddish literature. Judaic scholarship is exciting drama in the Potokian universe. Through analysis of talmudic tractate and textual emendation, whether in public forum or private tutorial sessions, Potok's delineation of Hebrew higher education is superb.

The recurrent theme of Potok's fictional universe is "the interplay of the Jewish tradition with the secular twentieth-century" (Kremer, "Interview," 85). He writes of Jews "who are at the very heart of their Judaism and at the same time . . . encountering elements that are at the very heart of the umbrella civilization" (85). In *The Chosen* and *The Promise* two sets of core-to-core confrontations evolve: first within the context of Orthodox Judaism between traditionalists and Hasidim and then between religious orthodoxy and Western secular humanism. In *My Name Is Asher Lev* and *The Gift of Asher Lev* the confrontation is with Western art; in *In the Beginning* with scientific biblical criticism and modern Western anti-Semitism; in *The Book of Lights* with the Orient and the destructive implications of atomic physics; and in *Davita's Harp* with communism. Each of the novels considers whether American Jewry has succumbed to secularism or has used its freedom to reeducate itself and create a new Jewish civilization in the post-Holocaust era.

The dramatic tension of *The Chosen* (1967) stems from encounters between Hasidim, known for their mystical interpretation of Judaic sources and intense devotion to their spiritual leaders, and Orthodox Jews, who emphasize a rational, intellectual approach to Judaic law and theology. Representative of Potok's recurrent use of paired foil characters, the fathers and sons of the novel express antithetical religious and political positions. Danny Saunders, son of the Hasidic charismatic leader, and Reuven Malter, son of a modern scholar who applies textual explication to talmudic studies, reflect or reject the training they experience as sons of men passionately devoted to Jewish tradition and history while living in a predominantly secular age and society. Just as Malter fuses the best in Judaic scholarship with the best in secular culture, his son combines intellectual excellence in sacred and secular studies, complementing talmudic studies with forays into symbolic logic, mathematics, and secular philosophy. In marked contrast to the Malters' communicative relationship is the strained silence between Reb Saunders and Danny, who is being prepared for Hasidic leadership. Convinced that it is dangerous to relegate the soul to the dominance of the mind, Saunders uses silence to teach his brilliant son the value of heart and soul. When they are not engaged in talmudic study, Reb Saunders builds a wall of silence between them in an effort to strengthen Danny's soul through suffering and thereby help ready him to assume the burdens of his followers. Reb Saunders fails. Although Danny remains an observant Jew, he rejects the traditional role of spiritual guide and becomes instead its secular counterpart, a clinical psychologist, while Reuven Malter follows his father's scholarly course.

The Promise (1969) continues the careers of the two friends, the influence or lack thereof of their fathers, and their conflicts with their teachers. Reuven is preparing for rabbinical ordination at an Orthodox seminary, while Danny is adjusting to secular life in pursuit of a psychology degree at Columbia University. Shorn of beard, earlocks, and Hasidic garb, Danny nevertheless remains a Hasid in spirit. Paralleling his separation from his traditional Hasidic role is his departure from orthodox psychiatric practice. Although Reuven is dedicated to Judaic studies, he opposes his traditional instructor's insistence that he remain true to classic talmudic scholarship and refrain from using modern textual criticism. Both adopt their fathers' teaching. Danny adapts Reb Saunders's technique for creative suffering through silence to clinical psychology, and Reuven incorporates Malter's critical method to elucidate the Talmud. Just as the fathers defined themselves within the Jewish context, the sons find their elemental and existential purpose in Judaism, despite the incursion of secular interests in their lives. As in the first novel, the dramatic conflict and thematic emphasis are in the arena of Judaic scholarship, a conflict between those who read Scripture as divine revelation and those who insist on human attribution. Using a structural scheme reminiscent of medieval morality drama, the novelist casts his rabbinical student at the center of discord between hermeneutic rivals, between a fundamentalist who fears and resents critical emendation and a practitioner of the method.

Potok's third novel, *My Name Is Asher Lev* (1972), a traditional initiation novel, delineates the coming of age of an artist living in a Hasidic society inherently hostile to his endeavor. The first-person narrative is cast as a retrospective of the artist's conflict with his Hasidic detractors who hold him guilty of betraying his religious heritage and encroaching upon a tradition sacred to Christianity. Asher persistently defies his father's demand that he sacrifice art to religion and community service as a Hasidic emissary. Paradoxically, while most members of the community associate the artist's gift with the demonic, the *rebbe* regards his ability as a divine gift. The *rebbe* engages a mentor under whose tutelage Asher undergoes a program of expansion and discovery that introduces him to the subjects and modes of Western art and transports him from the religious to the secular world. The artist's torment, resulting from conflict between critical and public acclaim offset by family and Hasidic denunciation, is expressed in the "Brooklyn Crucifixion," describing, not religious martyrdom, but anguish and torment stemming from the tragic division he has imposed upon his family. Informed by the *rebbe* that he must leave the community to which he has brought much pain, Asher experiences an epiphany of the divine and demonic possibilities of the creative impulse. Potok, like Joyce, treats the artist's isolation and alienation from family, school, and religious community, culminating in exile, as a progressive step that will lead to reconciliation of the artist's spiritual and aesthetic natures.

Potok's portrait of an artist as young Hasid reveals a powerful Joycean influence of subject, structure, and mythic patterning. His use of interior monologue, stream-of-consciousness techniques, and epiphany clearly reveals his indebtedness to the Joycean model. Corresponding to Joyce's fusion of the religionational perspective through Catholic Irish history and Greek mythology is Potok's incorporation of Jewish history and biblical and Joycean allusion and analogy. Not only does Potok satisfy the anticipated Daedalus-Icarus parallel with the analogous Kahn-Lev and mythic ancestor–Lev relationships, he further enriches the novel's symbolic implications by casting the biological father-son relationship in the Abraham-Isaac mold. Lev, like Stephen, is shaped by the religious and political beliefs of his community, yet resists total absorption by the forces and values that define his community and expresses his reservation as artist quester-in-exile.

In *The Gift of Asher Lev* (1990), the reader meets the artist during a midlife and midcareer crisis. By the beginning of the novel he has achieved a balance between his religious beliefs and the imperatives of art during his twenty-year exile in France. During this time he has been an observant member of a French Hasidic community and a painter of international renown. Despite decades of critical acclaim, he has arrived at an artistic impasse, and reviewers are now faulting his work as repetitious. Returning to Brooklyn for his uncle's funeral, Lev is once again plunged into communal and familial conflict. His "gift" is his son, whom the *rebbe* claims for the Hasidic community. The childless *rebbe* will appoint Lev's father as his successor, but only if he is assured that a dynastic line will follow to avoid internecine rancor upon the elder Lev's demise. Reconciliation with self, family, and community is achieved through Lev's capitulation to the *rebbe*'s wisdom. After much agonizing, he grasps the parallel between his own artistic anointment by his artistic mentor and the *rebbe*'s need for continuity. Asher hands the child to his father and the *rebbe* during a joyous holiday celebrating Torah learning. Just as the holiday signifies the continuation of Jewish devotion to the Torah, so Asher's "gift" to the *rebbe* signifies the harmonious continuation of the Hasidim.

The Book of Lights (1981) continues the Potokian pattern of exploring ideas through the juxtaposition of scholarly males. Two young rabbis, Gershon Loran and Arthur Leiden, are followed from their seminary studies through their search for meaning in the Judaic tradition while living in a secular society. The narrative is presented from the point of view of Gershon Loran, who started rabbinic study in the traditional talmudic fashion and was drawn to Jewish mysticism by a brilliant teacher modeled on the famous scholar Gershom Scholem and his readings in the Zohar (The Book of Radiance). Arthur Leiden travels the road to the rabbinate indirectly, by way of penance for what he perceives to be his father's sins as an atomic physicist. Through Arthur's plight Potok grapples with the terrible truths of our time, the reality of a promising technological age that delivered devastation. In his search for the meaning of human experience, Potok has, in this novel, moved outward spatially, thematically, and technically from his traditional Orthodox environments of New York to the Orient, from the talmudic intellectual core of traditional Judaism to the mystical sphere of Kabbalah. Although he employs the traditional literary convention of the spiritual quest, he situates the quest in new territory, having his protagonist experience the grandeur of God's creation in the "pagan" Orient before furthering his quest in Jerusalem. Departing from his successful delineation of the dynamics of studying a page of the Talmud, he here undertakes the aesthetic challenge of rendering the dynamics of a page of Kabbalah, of creating visions and the interplay of people in the visions.

A significant departure from the Potokian male-dominated world of Judaic scholarship appears in *Davita's Harp* (1985). Although female scholars have appeared in Potok's fictional world before, it is not until *Davita's Harp* that Potok focuses on female characters and develops an intellectually gifted young woman's point of view. His protagonist, Ilana Davita Chandal, is influenced by the contradictory philosophies of her father, a gentile Yankee committed to the Communist Party and killed in the Spanish Civil War at Guernica, and her mother, an apostate Jew who embraced Marxism until the Hitler-Stalin nonaggression pact, Stalin's trials and purges, and her daughter's interest provoked her return to Judaism. The novel focuses on Davita's intellectual and spiritual journey through her encounter with communism during the Spanish Civil War, the war against fascism, and her subsequent adoption of and confrontation with patriarchal Orthodox Judaism.

Potok engages the encounter of feminism and Judaism in *Davita's Harp* as two generations counter discrimination against women in Orthodox Jewish practice that excuses or excludes women from obligatory prayer, ritual, and study that observant men must perform. Illustrative of the discrimination women experience is prohibition against women reciting the Kaddish, the mourner's prayer, an obligatory duty for men. This humiliation, paradoxically, accounts for a mature woman's return to Judaism and awakens her daughter to limitations for women in Orthodox Judaism. While they defy one prohibition in the synagogue, Davita to recite the prayer for her father and Channah to recite it for her friend, they suffer defeat in the yeshiva. Davita's pivotal disillusionment with orthodoxy occurs at the novel's climax. Davita is deprived of the Akiva Award for academic excellence on the grounds that girls cannot be seen to be more capable of academic performance in the yeshiva than are boys. Through this experience, Potok approaches a central theme of Jewish feminist writing, the struggle of Orthodox women for equality in religious practice. Through sympathetic rendition of the aggrieved woman's point of view and female characters who choose to remain religious despite sexist discrimination, Potok suggests that the rights of Jewish women must be accommodated from within the context of Judaism.

Potok's favored dramatic strategy is to parallel his protagonists' spiritual quests with collective Jewish memory and history. Illustrative is his focus on the two orienting events of twentieth-century Jewish history, the Holocaust and the founding of the modern Jewish state in Israel. Potok is one of a select group of American novelists who have treated the Holocaust in relation to the revitalization of Judaism. Two major aspects of this phenomenon, American Judaic scholarship and support for Israel as a Jewish nation, have been among Potok's recurring themes.

Although the Holocaust remains a muted topic in Potok's first novel, it is presented as a hovering pestilence in the larger context of America at war. Here, Potok links the Holocaust and the creation of the State of Israel, a theme to which he will return in later works. The final third of *The Chosen* is narrated in the context of the Zionist struggle, and the experiences of the characters are intimately bound with that of Israel. Out of the ashes, Malter insists, new life must emerge. The only meaning to be derived from the destruction of one-third of world Jewry is the renaissance of the nation in its ancient territory. Beyond its thematic import, Zionism is integrated into the novel's dramatic conflict between the Malters and the Saunders. Predictably, Reb Saunders supports a post-messianic Israel and bitterly denounces secular Zionism, while the Malters support secular Zionist goals.

The autobiographical fourth novel *In the Beginning* (1975) confronts twentieth-century persecution of world Jewry, reflecting the writer's conviction, expressed in *Wanderings*, that ''the Jew sees all his contemporary history through the ocean of blood that is the Holocaust'' (398). Alternately bitter and melancholic in tone, *In the Beginning* reflects Jewish despair in the wake of Depression- and Holocaust-era anti-Semitism. The corresponding pathologies of Christian and Nazi anti-Semitic evils emerge in the consciousness of the young protagonist David Lurie, a studious, thoughtful child whose status as the son of immigrants sensitizes him to European influences on American life and policy. David is the object of Polish-American anti-Semitic outbursts that correspond, in a diminutive form, to the abuse his father suffered in Poland following World War I. Through the microcosm of the Polish boy's persecution of David that begins with boorish harassment and progresses to repeated attempts to push him into oncoming traffic, Potok suggests a parallel writ small to European anti-

Semitic escalations from encroachment on civil rights to denial of human rights, culminating in Russian pogrom and Nazi genocide. The Holocaust is introduced in the context of Jewish martyrology and the Yom Kippur memorial prayer in which David mourns the death of a Nazi victim as he chants the ancient lament for the martyrdom of Roman-era Torah sages. Finally, Potok evokes the impact of the Holocaust through reference to newspaper photographs of Bergen-Belsen. Only when he writes of the photographs of "hills of corpses, pits of bones, the naked rubble of the dead, and the staring eyes and hollow faces of the survivors" (400) and when David imagines the trains that crossed Europe, behind whose sealed doors he sees "a multitude of writhing human beings packed together riding in filth and terror" (412), does the American novelist treat Holocaust atrocities graphically. From Holocaust despair, the novel shifts to postwar re-juvenation of Judaism and Jewry exemplified in the son's dedication to biblical scholarship and the father's active support of a vibrant and secure Israel.

The impact of the Holocaust on the nonwitnessing Jew emerges again in *The Gift of Asher Lev*. Lev has learned something of anguish from his wife, a sur-vivor, who shares with him her Holocaust-wrought pain of years in a sealed apartment after her parents' arrest in the July 1942 roundup of Parisian Jews. In contrast to his earlier work, mirroring the psychological pain of his family tensions, Lev's exilic paintings and drawings depict suffering produced by the century's political and social outrages, and his artistic block is resolved when he begins work on the Holocaust, a new subject and a new mode of expression for him. Although the sequel falls short of Potok's original intention of showing the artist wrestling with the aesthetic problem of Holocaust interpretation, in the final paragraph we learn that Lev is painting "strange images in sealed rooms," and the work now flows. By bequeathing his son to the mission of Jewish regeneration Asher Lev is freed to interpret the century's Jewish calamity and thereby fulfill his mythic ancestor's injunction that he paint the suffering of humanity. Lev's decision will lead to redemption for the pain he has caused his Hasidic community and to his own immortality as the son and father of Hasidic spiritual leaders.

Although the Holocaust has been thematically and metaphorically present since the earliest fiction of Potok, it comes to the forefront in *The Trope Teacher* (1992) and *The Canal* (1993). The works, which have appeared in Dutch trans-lation but have not yet been published in America, show the destructive after-effects of the Holocaust experience on their protagonists, neither of whom is any longer an observant Jew. Benjamin Walter, the central character of *The Trope Teacher*, enters a strange liaison with a renowned writer living next door who extracts stories from his past that revive memories of his childhood years, including stories about his trope teacher, an eccentric who taught him a sacred melody echoing the terrors of World War I. The stories also revive his memories of World War II and the death camp his unit liberated. *The Canal* deals with an Auschwitz survivor, Amos Brickman, who has become a wealthy and famous American architect. Commissioned to design a church, Brickman returns to Warsaw, Krakow, Auschwitz, forests, and canal in a journey that operates as a descent into the past to confront the terrifying memory.

CRITICAL RECEPTION

Critics have responded to Potok's work with denunciation and acclaim. The detractors fault his prose and find his affirmative philosophy unconvincing. They charge him with composing banal or bookish speeches, employing a pompous tone, predictability and lack of complexity in character construction, and a reluctance to dramatize. The champions laud his descriptions of Jewish religious life, his delineation of the tensions inherent in living in two cultures simultaneously, his explication of and commentary on Judaic texts, his use of historical background, and his concern for writing fiction that engages serious ideas and issues. Representative of these polar positions are Curt Leviant's characterization of the dialogue between the adolescents of *The Chosen* as "more like a mature man's bookish presumption of what their talk should sound like than authentic speech itself" (80) and Judah Stampfer's objection to presentation of humorless and joyless Hasidim coupled with commendation of Potok's yeshiva scenes. Criticism of the subsequent fiction has thus far followed similar diametrical lines. James Murray faulted Potok as being "concerned far more with matter than with form" (274) in *The Promise* and for "reluctance to dramatize" (274), while novelist Hugh Nissenson found the book to be "a brilliantly and intricately conceived thematic elaboration of the quote from Pascal" (5). *My Name Is Asher Lev* garnered more consistent praise. Guy Davenport described it as "a tragedy of terrifying dimensions" (5). Leonard Cheever commended *In the Beginning* as an important novel, one of richness and complexity, while Ruth Wisse attacked *The Book of Lights* for Judaizing the atomic bomb and indulging in a "drama of Jewish self-accusation and expiation" (48) and lamented Potok's departure from his original authentic representation of Jewish life, "validating traditional Judaism [to take] his cues from the culture at large" (48). Marius Buning, who defended Potok's minimalist style, cited the increasing narrative complexity evidenced in the "more distinct free-indirect speech patterns approaching a stream of consciousness presentation of inner thought and emotions, as in the case of *I Am the Clay* and especially in *The Canal*" (15).

Most readers would probably agree with Sanford Marovitz's judgment of Potok as a "highly learned and intellectual writer, a novelist of ideas" ("Freedom, Faith, and Fanaticism," 130) whose books merit careful reading and Sheldon Grebstein's citation of "moral fervor, strong emotions experienced by sensitive characters, the portrayal of ancient and deeply felt traditions, the depiction of intimate family life, and an essentially affirmative view of human nature" (25) as explanations for Potok's popularity. Potok has created an enduring fiction that is centrally Jewish, erudite in its presentation of Jewish values and liturgy, establishing him as a significant voice in Jewish-American writing for moving religion and culture from the periphery to the center.

BIBLIOGRAPHY

Works by Chaim Potok

Fiction

The Chosen. New York: Simon and Schuster, 1967.
The Promise. New York: Alfred A. Knopf, 1969.
My Name Is Asher Lev. New York: Alfred A. Knopf, 1972.
In the Beginning. New York: Alfred A. Knopf, 1975.
The Book of Lights. New York: Alfred A. Knopf, 1981.
Davita's Harp. New York: Alfred A. Knopf, 1985.
The Gift of Asher Lev. New York: Alfred A. Knopf, 1990.
I Am the Clay. New York: Alfred A. Knopf, 1992.
The Tree of Here. A Children's Book. Illustrations by Tony Auth. New York: Alfred A. Knopf, 1993.
The Sky of Now. A Children's Book. Illustrations by Tony Auth. New York: Alfred A. Knopf, 1995.

Nonfiction

The Jew Confronts Himself in American Literature. Hales Corners, WI: Sacred Heart School of Theology, 1975.
Wanderings: Chaim Potok's History of the Jews. New York: Alfred A. Knopf, 1978.
Ethical Living for a Modern World: Jewish Insights. New York: Jewish Theological Seminary of America, 1985.
Theo Tobiasse: Artist in Exile. New York: Rizzoli, 1986.
The Gates of November—Chronicles of the Slepak Family. New York: Alfred A. Knopf, 1996.

Interviews

Abrams, Alan. "When Cultures Collide." *Jewish News*, June 22, 1984, 13ff.
Bookspan, Martin. "A Conversation with Chaim Potok." *Eternal Light*, no. 1453. Transcript of NBC Radio Network broadcast, November 22, 1981. New York: Jewish Theological Seminary of America, 1981.
Forbes, Cheryl. "Judaism Under the Secular Umbrella." *Christianity Today* 22 (September 8, 1978): 14–21.
Herstein, Wendy. "An Interview with Chaim Potok." *The World and I*, August 1992, 309–13.
Kauvar, Elaine. "An Interview with Chaim Potok." *Contemporary Literature* 27:3 (Fall 1986): 291–317.
Kipen, Aviva. "The Odyssey of Asher Lev." *Jewish Quarterly*, Spring 1993, 1–5.
Kremer, S. Lillian. "A Conversation with Chaim Potok." In *Dictionary of Literary Biography Yearbook 1984*, ed. Jean W. Ross. Detroit: Gale Research, 1985, 83–87.
———. "Interview with Chaim Potok." *Studies in American Jewish Literature* 4 (1984): 84–99.
Ribalow, Harold. "Chaim Potok." In *The Tie That Binds: Conversations with Jewish Writers.* New York: A. S. Barnes, 1980.

Works Cited and Studies of Chaim Potok

Abramson, Edward A. *Chaim Potok*. Boston: Twayne, 1986.

Bluefarb, Sam. "The Head, the Heart, and the Conflict of Generations in Chaim Potok's *The Chosen*." *College Language Association Journal* 14 (June 1971): 402–9.

Buning, Marius. *Chaim Potok*. Post-war Literatures in English. Amsterdam: Free University Amsterdam, 1995.

Cheever, Leonard. "Rectangles of Frozen Memory: Potok's *In the Beginning*." *Publications of the Arkansas Philological Association* 4 (1978): 8–12.

Davenport, Guy. "*My Name Is Asher Lev*." *New York Times Book Review*, April 16, 1972, 5, 18.

Del Fattore, Joan. "Women as Scholars in Chaim Potok's Novels." *Studies in American Jewish Literature* 4 (1984): 52–61.

Fagerheim, Cynthia. "A Bibliographic Essay." *Studies in American Jewish Literature* 4 (1985): 107–20.

Field, Leslie. "Chaim Potok and the Critics: Sampler from a Consistent Spectrum." *Studies in American Jewish Literature* 4 (1984): 3–12.

Gilmore, Michael T. "A Fading Promise." *Midstream* 16 (January 1970): 76–80.

Grebstein, Sheldon. "Phenomenon of the Really Jewish Best-Seller: Potok's *The Chosen*." *Studies in American Jewish Literature* 1 (1975): 23–31.

Guttmann, Allen. *The Jewish Writer in America: Assimilation and the Crisis of Identity*. New York: Oxford University Press, 1971.

Halio, Jay. "American Dreams." *Southern Review* 13 (1977): 837–44.

Holman, J. Martin. "A Voice from the Earth." *The World and I*, August 1992, 303–8.

Kremer, S. Lillian. "Chaim Potok." In *Twentieth-Century American-Jewish Fiction Writers*, ed. Daniel Walden. Vol. 28 of *Dictionary of Literary Biography*. Detroit: Gale Research, 1984, 232–43.

———. "Chaim Potok." In *Dictionary of Literary Biography: American Novelists since World War II*, Fourth Series, eds. James R. Giles and Wanda H. Giles. Detroit: Bruccoli Clark Layman, 1995.

———. "Dedalus in Brooklyn: Influences of *A Portrait of the Artist as a Young Man* on *My Name Is Asher Lev*." *Studies in American Jewish Literature* 4 (1984): 26–38.

———. "Encountering the Other." *The World and I*, August 1992, 315–325.

———. "Eternal Light: The Holocaust and the Revival of Judaism and Jewish Civilization in the Fiction of Chaim Potok." In *Witness through the Imagination: Jewish American Holocaust Literature*. Detroit: Wayne State University Press, 1989, 300–323.

Leviant, Curt. "The Hasid as American Hero." *Midstream* 13 (November 1967): 76–80.

Margolies, Edward. "Chaim Potok's *Book of Lights* and the Jewish American Novel." *Yiddish* 6:4 (1987): 93–98.

Marovitz, Sanford. "*The Book of Lights*: Jewish Mysticism in the Shadow of the Bomb." *Studies in American Jewish Literature* 4 (1984): 62–83.

———. "Freedom, Faith, and Fanaticism: Cultural Conflict in the Novels of Chaim Potok." *Studies in American Jewish Literature* 5 (1986): 129–40.

Milch, Robert J. "My Name Is Asher Lev." *Saturday Review*, April 15, 1972, 65.

Murray, James. Review of *The Promise*. *America*. October 4, 1969, 74.

Nissenson, Hugh. "The Promise." *New York Times Book Review*, September 14, 1969, 5, 21.

Pinsker, Sanford. "The Crucifixion of Chaim Potok/The Excommunication of Asher Lev: Art and the Hasidic World." *Studies in American Jewish Literature* 4 (1984): 39–51.

Purcell, William F. "Potok's Fathers and Sons." *Studies in American Literature* 26 (1989): 75–92.

Rabinowitz, Dorothy. "Sequels." *Commentary* 50 (May 1970): 104–8.

Regenbaum, Shelly. "Art, Gender, and the Jewish Tradition in Yezierska's *Red Ribbon on a White Horse* and Potok's *My Name Is Asher Lev*." *Studies in American Jewish Literature* 7 (1988): 55–66.

Schiff, Ellen. "To Be Young, Gifted, and Oppressed: The Plight of the Ethnic Artist." *MELUS* 6 (1979): 73–80.

Soll, Will. "Chaim Potok's *Book of Lights*: Reappropriating Kabbalah in the Nuclear Age." *Religion and Literature* 21:1 (1989): 111–35.

Stampfer, Judah. "The Tension of Piety." *Judaism* 16 (Fall 1967): 494–98.

Stern, David. "Two Worlds." *Commentary* (October 1972): 102, 104.

Stiller, Nikki. "*The Gift of Asher Lev*." *New York Times Book Review*, May 13, 1990, 29.

Sutherland, Sam. "Asher Lev's Visions of His Mythic Ancestor." *Re: Artes Liberales* 3 (1977): 51–54.

True, Warren. "Potok and Joyce: The Artist and His Culture." *Studies in American Jewish Literature* 2 (1982): 181–90.

Uffen, Ellen. "*My Name Is Asher Lev*: Chaim Potok's Portrait of the Young Hasid as Artist." *Studies in American Jewish Literature* 2 (1982): 174–80.

Walden, Daniel. "Chaim Potok: A *Zwischenmensch* Adrift in the Cultures." *Studies in American Jewish Literature* 4 (1984): 19–25.

Wisse, Ruth R. "Jewish Dreams." *Commentary* 73 (March 1982): 45–48.

Zlotnick, Joan. "The Chosen Borough: Chaim Potok's Brooklyn." *Studies in American Jewish Literature* 4 (1984): 13–18.

LEV RAPHAEL   (1954–)

Ludger Brinker

BIOGRAPHY

Born Reuben Steinberg on May 19, 1954, in New York, Lev Raphael grew up
in the Upper Manhattan neighborhood of Washington Heights, the younger of
two brothers. His parents, Alex and Helen Steinberg, are Holocaust survivors
who, like many others, kept a resolute silence about what had happened to them
as slave laborers and in the camps. In his essays and fiction Raphael has movingly articulated the psychological toll that such silence took on him, since
details about their preimmigration lives emerged only piecemeal. His religious
upbringing as a Jew was minimal, limited to the observation of some holidays
without, however, marking their spiritual content. Like the sons of many immigrants, Raphael was also deeply aware of the cultural differences separating
him from his parents, to the point of being ashamed of their accents when they
spoke English.

Raphael received a B.A. in English from Fordham University at Lincoln Center in 1975. He had chosen to attend this largely Catholic institution not to deny
his Jewishness, but to hide from it as much as possible. Ironically, the opposite
happened. As one of the few Jewish students at Fordham, Raphael stood out,
and because he dated a Christian woman for some time and even considered
marriage, he felt for the first time seriously compelled to examine what being
Jewish meant to him. The slow process of that examination was further exac-
erbated by the publication of his first short story, "War Stories," in *Redbook*
in March 1976, while he was an M.F.A. student in creative writing at the University of Massachusetts at Amherst. This partially autobiographical story about
the child of Holocaust survivors, which won first prize in the university's Harvey
Swados Fiction Contest, brought about a furious reaction from his parents, who

felt betrayed by their son's invasion of their privacy, but it helped Raphael—individually and artistically—to come to terms with his alienation from Judaism and Jewish culture.

This healing process was aided by a trip to Israel, from which Raphael returned determined to change his given name to one that reflected a more Jewish identity. He took the name Lev from his mother's older brother, who had been killed in the Battle of Stalingrad. Several years later, after a mystical experience, he changed his last name to Raphael, meaning "God will heal," to underscore symbolically his connection with Judaism. For Raphael, the name change marked not only a new beginning as a Jew but also the rejection of an identity imposed on Jews by eighteenth-century German and Austrian laws, forcing them to adopt German names. In a manner reminiscent of the name changes that some African Americans have undertaken, Raphael cast off remnants of linguistic colonialism. As a final proclamation of his faith, Raphael was bar mitzvah at the age of thirty, thus entering into and completing what Irving Greenberg has termed "voluntary covenant"—a reaffirmation of Judaism in the wake of the Holocaust characterized by inclusiveness and pluralism.

Having received an M.F.A. in creative writing and English from the University of Massachusetts at Amherst in 1978, Raphael taught for two years as an adjunct instructor in English at Fordham University, strengthening his ties to Judaism through preparing and teaching a course in Holocaust literature. However, it was not until his years as a Ph.D. candidate in American studies at Michigan State University that Raphael successfully started to integrate his religious and cultural beliefs as a Jew and his emerging gay sensibility. His sense of disconnection from Judaism was supplanted by one of connection through full participation in the services of an Orthodox congregation, and his uncertainty about being gay was superseded by joyous affirmation when he fell in love with Gershen Kaufman, a Jewish professor in the Counseling Center at Michigan State, who has become his life partner.

Since receiving his Ph.D. in American studies in 1986 and teaching as an assistant professor in the Department of American Thought and Language at Michigan State from 1986 to 1988, Raphael has devoted his life to a full-time writing career, publishing fiction and essays in journals and magazines from *Christopher Street* and *Lambda Book Report* to the *Forward* and the *Baltimore Jewish Times*. As a consequence, he has received considerable recognition and acclaim in both the gay and Jewish communities. His first book of short stories, *Dancing on Tisha B'Av*, won the 1990 Lambda Literary Award for Best Gay Male Debut, a prestigious honor in the gay and lesbian writing community. More recently, Raphael was the recipient of the Crossing Boundaries Award, awarded by *International Quarterly*, for his powerful essay "Losing My Mother: Scenes from a Memoir" (contained in *Journeys and Arrivals*). While further establishing himself as a versatile fiction writer with *Winter Eyes* and *Let's Get Criminal* and as an engaged essayist with the publication of *Journeys and Arrivals: On Being Gay and Jewish*, Raphael has continued to publish academic works as well, particularly *Edith Wharton's Prisoners of Shame* and most recently, together with Gershen Kaufman, *Coming out of Shame: Transforming Gay and Lesbian Lives*. For over ten years, Raphael and Kaufman have made their home in Okemos, Michigan.

Concerning his identity as a Jewish and gay writer, Raphael has written:

I have seen that my work is helping other Jewish gay writers to combine both sides of their life in their writing. There's a rich body of work by Jewish lesbians; hopefully my work can contribute to the growth of the men's literature. This sense of mission is what I felt in the late seventies when I contemplated teaching and writing about the Holocaust. But the present mission is based on a deeper and calmer vision. It's truly social action in the Jewish sense of *tikkun olam*, repairing the world. ("To Be a Jew," *Journeys and Arrivals*, 30)

MAJOR WORKS AND THEMES

Unlike most American Jewish gay and lesbian writers, Lev Raphael has achieved what even a decade ago many people would have claimed impossible to accomplish: to bridge the Jewish and gay communities, writing essays and fiction for both gay and Jewish magazines and journals and publishing his books with major mainstream publishers. The success of Raphael's work bears eloquent testimony to an increased willingness and sensitivity on the part of his readers—Jewish and gay—to confront otherness and to perceive significant commonalities in Raphael's treatment of the themes of inclusion and exclusion—whether on the basis of religious belief or sexual orientation. While other gay and lesbian Jews have attempted to reconcile their different roles and identities as Jews and gays and lesbians, Raphael's writing so far offers the single most articulate, sustained vision of how to enrich and balance the often opposing demands of the different aspects of one's personality.

Among the several recurrent themes that dominate Raphael's writing, the Holocaust—especially the indelible influence it has on the lives and psyches of the children of survivors—forms the background for many characters' discovery and acceptance of Jewish identity. Raphael frequently focuses in particular on the often serious repercussions of what it means to be Jewish and gay, coming out to one's family, and dealing with antigay or anti-Semitic verbal harassment or physical violence. In addition, some of his fiction (not surprisingly, considering Raphael's background and career) features an academic setting that is, depending on the subject, either lampooned or treated seriously. Yet even if Raphael's gay protagonists agonize about their role within the Jewish community, his writing is informed by a post-Stonewall sensibility in his characters' refusal to deny or camouflage that vital part of their being. Raphael's aim is, for the most part, to create a meaningful and fruitful bond between Judaism and the gayness of his characters.

The crippling psychological impact of the Holocaust on the lives of all the members in survivor families is one of the themes Raphael explores in several of the stories in *Dancing on Tisha B'Av*. Clearly drawing on his own experiences, Raphael gives a voice to the children of survivors who, through the act of slowly learning to understand their parents' pain and unrelieved suffering, become witnesses themselves. Since they are the last ones to have intimate contact with those saved from the destruction of European Jews, these children break the silence and, willingly or not, start to testify on their parents' behalf. Yet the act of testifying by these American children is often fraught with serious potential for misunderstanding and further suffering. In ''The Tanteh,'' for example, an observant family lives with a great aunt who is their only surviving European relative. Aunt Rose, grand in manner and ridiculing all faith—''They prayed,'' she says, ''And still they died'' (17)—considers her American relatives naive and intellectually her inferiors. Apart from such cryptic remarks, she shrouds herself in silence. But when the narrator utilizes her experiences and his sense of being crushed by them for a writing assignment, her defenses break down, and after an impassioned outburst during which she tells him that her life is not a writing assignment, she flees from the family to travel and die in Europe. Only then, too late, does the narrator begin to sense his aunt's unbearable pain and the omnipresence of the Holocaust in the lives of all Jews. As a result, his acknowledgment of guilt on Yom Kippur, his attempt to atone, seems too little, too late. Yet the story itself bears witness. As a text, it links one Jewish generation to the other, it forges a connection between European and American Jews, and it thus mediates between Jewish generations, becoming part of the Jewish textual tradition.

Raphael's best tales link Jewish and gay experiences, drawing connections between both, particularly in his insistence that anti-Semitism and homophobia stem from the same source, and that both are evils that must be overcome. Together with Judith Katz, Raphael is at the forefront of exploring the boundaries of what it means to be Jewish and queer. If earlier generations of Jewish gay and lesbian writers were intensely secular in their outlook, Katz and Raphael respond again to the attraction of the sacred. Thus their texts take part in a very Jewish dynamic—the constantly alternating pull of the sacred and the secular. Raphael pointedly articulates this dynamic in three interrelated stories in *Dancing on Tisha B'Av* that explore the relationships between three characters, Nat, Mark, and Nat's sister Brenda. In the title story, Nat and Mark, devout Orthodox Jews, fall in love, establishing an ideal relationship as they share the same devotion to both Judaism and their gay selves. The sacred texts move Nat so profoundly that he has switched from the Reform synagogue of which his parents are members to an Orthodox shul. It is Brenda, Nat's far more secular sister, who cannot understand the transformation taking place in her brother. Since this story is told from Brenda's perspective, the reader participates both in her doubts about Nat's religious choices and in her uneasiness, despite her avowed tolerance, of his sexual orientation. The choice to make Brenda the narrator serves two purposes: it allows Raphael to ease a nongay reader into the story's conflicts through the eyes of a concerned family member; in addition, the slow changes in Brenda's attitude are psychologically sound and thus encourage the reader to undergo a similar transformation. The story convincingly conveys the paradox for the observant Jew: the devotion to a faith that will deny him a place in its sanctuary. When their relationship is discovered by other members of their *minyan*, Nat and Mark, in a powerfully emotional scene, are banished from worshipping at the Orthodox synagogue they attend. It is remarkable that in the chaos that ensues Nat still manages to kiss the *mezuzah* on his way out; his faith, despite the ugly scene that has just occurred, has not been shaken. Yet Nat goes out dancing at a gay club on Tisha B'Av to vent his frustrations and to take revenge on a faith he feels profoundly betrayed by. For Nat, as Brenda comes to understand at the end of the story, dancing is both an act of rebellion and also an affirmation of the dignity of his self.

"Another Life" retells almost the same events from Nat's perspective, poignantly focusing on his dilemma as a gay Jewish male. Having initially joined the Orthodox *minyan* on the campus of Michigan State University as a remedy to deny and escape from his attraction to men, Nat learns how to combine his search for spirituality and intimate human contact in his relationship with Mark. He comes to see faith and sexual orientation not as mutually exclusive but as mutually enhancing. In a series of searching conversations with Mark, Nat overcomes, with the help of the older man who has experienced similar questions, his internalized homophobia.

In the last of these stories, "Abominations," Brenda, again the narrator, is forced to make choices about her future relationship with her brother. Outraged by antigay graffiti sprayed on the campus, Brenda unintentionally outs her brother in an interview with a reporter. Reaction on this middle-American campus is swift: Nat's dorm room is torched. The story ends with Brenda, Nat, and Mark on their way to face the parents, thus completing Nat's coming-out process. In a gesture that underscores the extent of Brenda's growth and her rejection of all forms of injustice and intolerance, she pins a gay liberation pink triangle button, the only object to survive the fire in Nat's room, on her dress to signal her active support for her brother. It is for Brenda, the historian and sister of a gay Jewish man, to make the connection between persecution of Jews and that of gays when she thinks of the Nazis' burning of synagogues, homes, and human beings.

In this trilogy of stories Raphael universalizes the meaning of the Holocaust. His fiction is a call to action to his readers who may have doubts, similar to those expressed by Brenda in the first story, about the compatibility of religious beliefs and homosexuality. Certainly Raphael is a writer who believes that the act of writing and publishing can transform ideas, prejudices, and lives. While the title "Abominations" constitutes a direct reference to the condemnation of homosexuality in Leviticus, it becomes clear that for Raphael the real abomination is the persecution and victimization of any human being on the basis of religious or secular prejudices. The sense of justice so strongly evident in stories like "Abominations" and in his essays places Raphael firmly in the Jewish prophetic tradition.

Winter Eyes, Raphael's first novel, explores, in the person of Stefan Borowski, the lives of Holocaust survivors and their children and the question of sexual orientation. Stefan is the child of Polish survivors who keep that fact hidden from him well into adolescence and raise him as a Polish Catholic in the mistaken belief that they can shield their son from the unspeakable traumas of the past. The depiction of Stefan's hermetically sealed childhood becomes an overwhelming case study of the psychological effects that the distant parents' silence has on their son. The entire family, including his Uncle Sasha, who teaches Stefan how to play the piano, and whom the child prefers over his parents, is engaged in this act of deception. All involuntary references to the Holocaust and the past in general end in unfinished sentences and denials that leave the child baffled, resentful, and withdrawn. Despite claiming to be Catholic, both parents deride any expressions of religious belief in the world around them because they hold such beliefs responsible for the deaths of millions of people. But Stefan's parents are also contradictory in their statements about Europe; normally emphasizing European civilization's superiority over what they consider to be vulgar and uncivilized American customs, they at other times also seem to hate anything relating to Poland and Polish traditions. The first part of the novel is a masterful evocation of an emotionally stifling atmosphere that denies the child any connection with his ethnic and religious heritage; Raphael movingly delineates the consequences of living in the vacuum that the denial of one's past creates.

Stefan's only solace is the music he studies with his kind and melancholy Uncle Sasha, who also becomes his guardian when his parents divorce and Stefan refuses to live with either of them. The middle part of the novel, "Separate Lives," deals with Stefan's inability to create human connections. The one passionate sexual relationship he forms with Louie, a neighbor's son, also becomes a secretive affair because Louie refuses to acknowledge any deeper emotions for Stefan apart from those of quick sexual release. Attracted by Louie's family's strong sense of the past, their apartment overflowing with mementos of family and religion, Stefan feels further isolated because he instinctively realizes that he cannot discuss his nascent physical and romantic relationship with Louie with anyone. Adding on to the secrets of his parents, Stefan creates his own world of secrets, making his isolation almost claustrophobically complete. When Stefan finally learns the truth about his parents' history from his ill father, he responds with rage and hatred. He does not want to have anything to do with a religion he considers weak.

In the third part of the novel, significantly entitled "Connections," Stefan learns slowly how to integrate and accept the different aspects of his parents' past experiences, their current lives, and his own emotional needs and desires. At Syracuse University he meets Marsha, a slightly older Jewish woman who draws him out of his cocoon and helps him to discover his religious and ethnic heritage. The emotional and romantic bond they form promises potential fulfillment, not least because Marsha understands Stefan's attraction to men since she herself has had sexual relationships with women.

The various elements of this post-Holocaust Jewish *Bildungsroman*—religion, ethnicity, and sexual identity—are intricately interwoven, particularly in the final section. For the first time in his life Stefan gives a complete account of his psychological ordeals after he declares that he hates being Jewish. He shares his family's history, his parents' attempt at erasing anything Jewish about them, his first grade's No-Jew Club, and Louie's anti-Semitic statements. Marsha is familiar with such self-hatred since, as an adolescent, she had felt that Judaism excluded women from its rituals. Consequently, she stopped attending services when she left home. But despite such feelings, Marsha is exuberantly Jewish, reading Jewish books, including volumes on the Holocaust. Like many contemporary Jewish women, she is in the process of creating her own identity as a Jew. She is instrumental in helping Stefan to accept his own identity as a Jew and his sexual orientation, for the acceptance of one is based on the acceptance of the other. As a first public acknowledgment of his Jewishness, Stefan and Marsha visit his remarried mother and her husband, who, in the past, had always seemed too Jewish to Stefan. The final pages of the novel again broach the issue of Stefan's sexual identity, but he is now content not to ask for absolute answers any longer. Instead, he finally begins to integrate into a coherent shape the hitherto disparate elements of his identity.

While Raphael seems to leave the territory of his short stories and his first novel with *Let's Get Criminal*, closer inspection reveals that the previous interrelated topics of Jewish identity in a post-Holocaust world and sexual identity are still present. However, they have been successfully integrated into an academic mystery novel. Set at the fictitious State University of Michigan, the novel reintroduces Stefan Borowski, now a successful novelist and writer-in-residence at the university. For ten years, we learn, he has shared his life with Nick Hoffman, an assistant professor of English at the same institution. While Stefan was the absolute narrative center in *Winter Eyes*, it is Nick who is the narrator of this novel. Unlike the still-brooding and sharply observant Stefan, Nick is not averse to sharing academic gossip, making rash judgments, and displaying his love for Stefan through at times petty, jealous behavior. Making Nick the narrator enables Raphael to bring up events from Stefan's past and subject them to a different interpretation. For example, the fact that Stefan and his father are still not fully reconciled bothers Nick, who has not shared similar experiences and who finally manages to bring about a reconciliation between father and estranged son.

The plot revolves around the mystery created by the murder of Perry Cross, a new tenure-track assistant professor of Canadian studies, who was hired quickly over several more qualified candidates and in whom Stefan had a romantic interest before he met Nick. During the murder investigation both Nick and Stefan come under suspicion because they were the last people to have seen

Perry Cross alive. Nick's attempt to play private sleuth, in the manner of Hercule Poirot and other literary detectives, enables Raphael to paint a wonderfully satiric picture of much of today's academic world—from sexual harassment of graduate students to exploitation of the fears of tenure-track faculty members. While much of this material has been covered in other academic mysteries, Raphael offers a wonderfully fresh take on this environment through the eyes of a gay couple. In addition, Raphael's satire is propelled forward by an intriguing complement of unsavory issues: academic dishonesty and intellectual theft, the role of former Nazi sympathizers (à la Paul de Man) in the American academic establishment, and academic blackmail.

While the novel follows some of the same formulas of literary detective fiction that Nick claims to dislike, Raphael manages to offer here a lighthearted approach to serious issues that he has explored in his earlier work. Perhaps the greatest achievement of this novel lies in its depiction of the domesticity of the ordinary Jewish home that these two gay men have created and maintained for ten years. They are no different from their neighbors in the time and care they expend on their garden, lawn, and the general appearance of their home. Stefan has lost much of his Jewish self-hatred, so insightfully depicted in *Winter Eyes*. Yet his past is never fully forgotten. As Nick observes, "Stefan could join me in the blessings, and a mild bit of Jewish observance, but he was still haunted by all those years his parents and uncle pretended they weren't Jewish" (124). With Nick, unambiguously Jewish and gay, Raphael has created a likable character who, despite his proneness to gossip and potential overreaction to situations, is delightfully normal, unburdened by any guilt and secure in his relationship.

Lev Raphael's essays, collected in *Journeys and Arrivals*, show him as an engaged thinker, deeply pondering the issues of identity and religion. His essays and fiction, despite the obvious differences in tone and approach, complement each other. While the fiction works out questions of identity, religious observance, and the role of the children of Holocaust survivors in the context of invented lives, the essays provide a philosophical basis for the lives depicted in the stories and novels. Central to both are the questions of Jewish and gay identity, themes to which Raphael devotes abundant attention. What he points out time and again is the fact that these identities are not mutually exclusive, but that, ideally, they form part of one single consciousness that is enriched by the different aspects of which it is made up. Often emanating from an autobiographical impulse, these essays transcend the merely personal and are important reflections on the state of affairs in contemporary gay America. The fact that Raphael emphasizes the inevitable connection (in his view) with Judaism sets him apart from many other contemporary gay Jewish writers whose identities seem to be shaped more by their gayness than by their Jewishness. Raphael's ardent desire to find connections between Jewish and gay experiences puts him into the forefront of writers who refuse to be identified by one convenient and simplistic label. Writing as the gay son of Holocaust survivors, Raphael is always aware of issues of oppression, ready to expose anti-Semitic or antigay acts or remarks.

CRITICAL RECEPTION

So far, Raphael is an almost singular phenomenon in the publishing world. Belonging to two minority groups, he has nevertheless been published by major commercial publishers and has been reviewed widely and approvingly in a diverse assortment of publications. He is one of the few writers to bridge successfully the Jewish and gay markets and to have earned continued mainstream approval.

Reviews of Raphael's short-story collection *Dancing on Tisha B'Av* were numerous and positive throughout. The impact of the stories on the gay literary community was best expressed by their winning a Lambda Literary Award, a prestigious honor. Since many of the stories had originally been published in a variety of Jewish publications, among them *Midstream, Commentary, Jewish Currents*, and *Agada*, it is no wonder that a significant number of reviews appeared in Jewish newspapers and magazines. Most Jewish reviewers are in agreement with Rabbi Allen Bennett, who stated that Raphael's subject matter is quintessentially Jewish, "dealing with the existential pain in our lives, with questions about relationships within families (both religious and sexual) and with the Holocaust" (27). Haviva Krasner-Davidson, writing one of the most insightful reviews, dealt admirably with Raphael's double vision as Jew and gay man. She was one of the few writers to discuss Jewish homophobia, pleading for a Judaism that is neither oppressive nor repressive. Finally, comparing Raphael to other gay Jewish writers like David Leavitt and David Feinberg, she wrote, "At least Raphael's vision includes God—a concept beyond the macabre reality of a world that can sometimes seem unbearably grim" (22). In her review for the *Los Angeles Times*, Faye Kellerman also paid tribute to the religious and gay themes of Raphael's stories but universalized them as tales of outsiders looking in.

Winter Eyes was also warmly received by critics. Focusing on the novel's theme of the effect of the Holocaust on the children of survivors, Garth Wolkoff praised the work's ultimate optimism because "honesty about the self can break the artificial lens of falsehood, a distorted vision caused by the kind of suffering we all know the *Shoah* produced for its survivors" (41).

Probably the most comprehensive evaluation of Raphael's work in the context of second-generation witnesses so far has been produced by Alan Berger. His two scholarly essays systematically placed Raphael into a Jewish tradition that also encompasses writers with as diverse subject matter as Elie Wiesel and Art Spiegelman. For Berger, Raphael's "writing is both an act of protest and a means of stopping Holocaust modes of thought. Consequently, the secular act of writing may have a profoundly sacred impact" ("The Holocaust," 42).

Perhaps the greatest compliment Raphael has received came from fellow Jewish gay writer Doug Sadownick in his review of *Winter Eyes* in *Lambda Book Report*: "Raphael has cracked a nut no one else has fully tackled in the Jewish gay writing scene. . . . To the list of Cynthia Ozick, Vivian Gornick, and Saul Bellow we ought to add the list of gay and lesbian authors whose hearts burn with a Jewish heritage, one rich with conflicts and ancestors. To be sure, Lev Raphael is an important contender'' (16).

BIBLIOGRAPHY

Works by Lev Raphael

Dancing on Tisha B'Av. New York: St. Martin's, 1990.
Stick up for Yourself! Every Kid's Guide to Personal Power and Positive Self-Esteem.
  With Gershen Kaufman. Minneapolis: Free Spirit, 1990.
Dynamics of Power: Fighting Shame and Building Self-Esteem. With Gershen Kaufman.
  Rev. 2nd ed. Rochester, VT: Schenkman, 1991.
Edith Wharton's Prisoners of Shame: A New Perspective on Her Neglected Fiction. New
  York: St. Martin's, 1991.
Winter Eyes. New York: St. Martin's, 1992.
Coming out of Shame: Transforming Gay and Lesbian Lives. With Gershen Kaufman.
  New York: Doubleday, 1996.
Journeys and Arrivals: On Being Gay and Jewish. Boston: Faber, 1996.
Let's Get Criminal. New York: St. Martin's, 1996.

Studies of Lev Raphael

Bennett, Allen. "Powerful Stories Speak to Jews about 'Pain of Our Lives.' " Review
  of *Dancing on Tisha B'Av*. *Northern California Jewish Bulletin*, July 19, 1991,
  27.
Berger, Alan L. "Bearing Witness: Second Generation Literature of the *Shoah*." *Modern
  Judaism* 10:1 (February 1990): 43–63.
———. "The Holocaust, Second-Generation Witness, and the Voluntary Covenant in
  American Judaism." *Religion and American Culture* 5:1 (Winter 1995): 23–47.
Brinker, Ludger. "Jewish-American Literature." In *The Gay and Lesbian Literary Her-
  itage*, ed. Claude J. Summers. New York: Holt, 1995, 408–13.
Kellerman, Faye. "Pariahs on Parade." Review of *Dancing on Tisha B'Av*. *Los Angeles
  Times Book Review*, November 11, 1990, 8.
Krasner-Davidson, Haviva. "Coming Out Twice: Writing about Being Jewish and Gay."
  Jewish Journal July 31–August 6, 1992, 22.
Sadownick, Doug. "A Jewish Heart and Heritage: Conflicts and Ancestors in Lev Raph-
  ael's Eyes." Review of *Winter Eyes*. *Lambda Book Report*, January 1993, 16.
Wolkoff, Garth. "Survivors 'Come out of Closet' in Lev Raphael's 1st Novel." Review
  of *Winter Eyes*. *Jewish Bulletin* (San Francisco), February 5, 1993, 41.

TOVA REICH   (1942–   )

Blossom S. Kirschenbaum

BIOGRAPHY

Tova Rachel Reich was born December 24, 1942, in Liberty, New York, to
Moshe and Miriam Weiss, each descended from a long line of rabbis. Her father
spent his early years in the town of Oscwiecim, Poland (later known as Auschwitz); he arrived in the United States just before World War II. An Orthodox
rabbi, he now lives in Israel. Tova Reich's three brothers are also rabbis. The
family spoke English, Hebrew, and Yiddish at home and also read in all three
languages. Through high school Reich studied at yeshivot. She continues to
study, and use for her writing, Jewish books old and new. By age eleven she
had already decided that she was a writer.

Reich attended Brooklyn College of City University of New York (B.A.,
1964) and New York University (M.A., 1965). On June 10, 1965, she married
Walter Reich, psychiatrist and Senior Scholar at the Woodrow Wilson Center
and author of books and articles on Soviet psychiatry, Middle East issues, and
other topics. Their children are Daniel Salo, David Emil, and Rebecca Zohar;
to them she dedicated her third novel, *The Jewish War*. The family's home is
in Chevy Chase, Maryland.

Tova Reich has taught at Southern Connecticut State College in New Haven
(1972–1973), American University in Washington, D.C. (1974–1977), and as
Visiting Writer at the University of Maryland (1991–1992, 1994). A National
Endowment for the Arts Creative Writing Fellowship supported her writing during 1984–1985. Her second novel, *Master of the Return*, received the Edward
Lewis Wallant Award. She has traveled extensively throughout Europe and has
been to Israel many times.

MAJOR WORKS AND THEMES

Tova Reich's novels and still-uncollected stories point up tensions between American criteria of success and Judaic morality, between American hedonistic materialism and Hebraic consecration of the corporeal world with hope of redemption. Yet she can also show the obverse, zealous American Zionists refusing to cede land for peace and hence passionately defying not only Arab neighbors but also the secular Israeli state, the operative antagonism being between messianic religiosity and political pragmatism. In both Israeli and U.S. contexts, she shows Jews compelled to recognize fellow Jews as "Other," while gentiles and even anti-Semites offer to make common cause. Echoes of the Holocaust pervade her writing. Characters adapt to changing times, different cultures, and new opportunities; whether or not they change names, identity for all its persistence is resilient and mutable. Sometimes the brave and clever devise preposterous successes, sometimes they go down to defeat, while children and fools accidentally survive—or not, for reasons that human reason may never fathom; hence the need to grieve, wonder, and give thanks.

In Reich's sardonic views of what Gertrude Stein called "the making of Americans," child-rearing practices are often bizarre. Parents with the highest motives and the wackiest foibles blunder to control their young, who must mature through painful experiences that both they and their parents may fail to understand. Hazards abound, violence hovers, vice and inanity flourish, and life goes on. The narrative voice variously sports with, challenges, resists, withdraws from, or aligns itself with an ancient and comprehensive history, teasing a reader into reexaminations.

Thus Reich's first novel, *Mara* (1978), presents a rabbi who has sent his nubile daughter to Israel as to a finishing school. When she inevitably strays, he tries with the full weight of institutional power, connections, and dubiously acquired money to compel her behavior; but she is as willful and elusive as he, and he fails. Mara herself, poorly educated and both over- and underprivileged, must follow her own soul path. At the book's conclusion she is solitary, battered, and still in love.

In *Master of the Return* (1988), devoted mothers in Israel care for children and each other independently of men, while fathers are busy with pilgrimages, prayer, computers, numerology, fighting, and other affairs. Crippled Ivriya, who once performed naked like Lady Godiva, gives three-year-old Akiva bread and honey and milk, while her husband, converted from hippie to Bratslaver Hasid, has found no better way to support them than to go off on abortive pilgrimages to Uman. Like other families in Reich's fiction, this family appears dysfunctional; but children find love, escape disaster, and usually survive misguided parental neglect or zeal.

More ominous is *The Jewish War* (1995), where Israel, "just another Jewish neighborhood, like Flatbush, or Brighton Beach, or Borough Park," has become the new frontier for American Jews. Yehudi HaGoel (formerly Jerry Goldberg) and his right-hand man and best buddy Hoshea HaLevi (formerly Herbie Levy) are determined to restore the Kingdom of David and build the Third Temple. To keep Judea and Samaria, they first declare secession and attempt subversion; then in more embattled resistance they "cut off all negotiations, all communication with the State of Israel." With the cooperation of their women and children, they maintain "active waiting" underground in the Machpelah during the days before Yom Kippur, defying the besieging army's "state-of-the-art equipment" through dreadful silence and invisibility. General Lapidot, watching from a hilltop overlooking Hebron, reads Josephus's account of what happened inside Masada but considers Josephus "a notorious opportunist and self-server, a writer of fiction." High ideals that loving parents adduce in indoctrinating children here come in for critical review. If *Mara* shows the ineffectuality of parental remoteness, the counterproductivity of bombast, bribery, and threat, and the lack of true guidance, and if *Master of the Return* shows excessive maternal complaisance vis-à-vis paternal excess, *The Jewish War* illuminates the dark side of religious faith that renders parents willing to make severe demands on beloved children.

Destructive zeal and the perversion in a mother's trying to live through her child are displayed with gleeful horror in "Gifted and Talented" (1985). This story shows a middle-class American child deprived and threatened precisely because he is advantaged and supervised. The narrator, the wife of an American podiatrist, living near the nation's capital, is determined to guarantee her only child's future by giving him the best possible education. She has his intelligence tested while he is still in diapers. Programmed through special schools, he is given every "enrichment." Systematically the process ruins his childhood. At the story's end, the child is poised for a fall from which his mother will not be able to save him.

Various spiritual journeys and strivings for redemption figure in Reich's fiction. To decline the quest or cheat in it proves self-defeating. Thus in *Mara* Rabbi Leib professes piety but flounders hypocritically between righteousness and greed. His wife gorges on food and hungers for more, insatiable because she cannot find spiritual sustenance or love. Amoral Sudah, when he becomes a celibate Buddhist, abandons his wife, his people, and his ancestral faith, but ironically fulfills Rabbi Leib's pronouncement that the ideal life is devoted to religious study.

Master of the Return, set in an Israel that has become at once more secular and more devout, makes fun of the yearning for redemption while taking it seriously and celebrates the triumph of life over absolutism. Its protagonist, an ex-hippie American Bratslaver, craves holiness for his three-year-old Akiva but cannot stay to care for him because he is driven by a frenzy to reach Uman, there to recite psalms and be relieved of nocturnal emissions.

In *The Jewish War*, the war games of Yehudi HaGoel and his cohorts reflect the actual battle between the Israeli government and Jewish settlers in disputed territories. Dispute over land is also ideological confrontation. Civil disobedience, an accepted strategy in such circumstances, is Yehudi's way throughout most of *The Jewish War*. Dedication is matched with patient perseverance. Beyond heroics (his advisors reconnoiter, "all of them with Uzis strapped on their shoulders and knives and pistol concealed under their clothing") and his own relish of kingship and its privileges (including three wives), he is canny in building his movement and eloquent in self-defense against charges of attempted murder, membership in a terrorist organization, and illicit possession and transport of explosives.

The most bizarre spiritual journeys, however, occur in the eerie "Mengele in Jerusalem" (1986). The narrator, a Holocaust survivor who has prospered in America, feels emotionally dead. He learns of a "spiritual spa" at the table of Reb Mendele in Jerusalem. There he witnesses the ritual drinking of the prune juice to the greater glory of the bowels, rendered with homely exegetical detail in a characteristic Reichian parody of Hasidic ritual that concludes, "Ya ba ba, ya ba ba, ya ba bum." Among the converts in an alley, the narrator recognizes Reb Mengele, the sadistic concentration-camp doctor. The reader, following the story as it is told to "smug" and unsurprised Krystina, the narrator's consort, is left to ponder the encounter between anti-Semitic Jew and Jew-obsessed persecutor turned Hasid. The deracinated, unhappy narrator of this story, trumped by his torturer, refuses the redemption he cannot buy. As for the unpunished Mengele figure, his conversion remains suspect since there is no evidence that he has confessed or tried to make reparation, and it is not clear for what purpose he has returned.

Reich's fiction explores the meaning of Israel for American Jews. In *Mara*, Israel functions as a conveniently remote campus that allows the parents to avoid dealing directly with the active sexuality of their daughter. She is consigned for further course work and finding a Jewish spouse. As Reich shows, however, there are no guarantees, not even when Mara's conventional sister is sent as an ambassador to save Mara from herself. Israel is also where American Jews are surprised and even outmaneuvered by other Jews whose Old World is not Europe.

In *Master of the Return*, Israel is the terrain where a Jew's mythos, history, ideals, and daily life may fuse, perilously and sometimes ludicrously. For refugees, including now American refugees, Israel provides haven and alternative. As Ivriya watches her son at breakfast, the authorial voice comments, "For the sake of this milk and this honey, you must speak no ill of the land, and of its inhabitants say no unkind word." The Jewish War shows Israel as the meeting place of the three great monotheistic faiths. That makes it a place for territorial struggle—of a kind by no means peculiar to the Middle East. Such struggle occurs even in America, in the "acknowledged Jewish territory" of the Catskills, which one character claims as "God-given birthright."

Like the United States, Israel is a nation of immigrants and hence a multiethnic society, a laboratory for working out national and ethnic bigotries. Both nations are involved in the story "Solidarity," where Rabbi Ozer, an American who has visited Israel and whose own wife is Middle Eastern, proves too ready to trust another Middle Eastern Jew. Overcompensating for possible bias, Ozer misses clues and fails to heed advice, and an innocent widow suffers. Even in its diversity, Israel complicates the Diaspora, however, as is illustrated in "Moscow Night in New York" (1979), where Kagan, twice hospitalized as crazy in Russia and now feted "like some prize Russian bear" in the United States, would rather be in Israel—but his wife is Gentile.

"Gertrude Stein" (1982), though not about the eponymous author of *The Making of Americans* and *The Geographical History of America*, shares her preoccupation with the American character as shaped by American history and institutions—that is, with the making of Americans. Reich's story probes hostility between desperate whites and vengeful blacks, simultaneously needling and disdaining each other, and simultaneously breeding.

The "making of Americans" as an updating of the immigrant experience with its attendant dislocations occurs in "Moscow Night in New York." Here a dinner party brings together an "émigre élite," eight persons "among whom there must already be ten books in various stages, . . . three about the Gulag alone." The "Moscow night" of borscht, high culture, and soul baring that Irina, the hostess, has arranged is soon undercut when the next course is hot dogs and hamburgers. Afterwards, Irina's husband finds her weeping at the kitchen sink because New York cannot provide the "true Russian night" she had wanted.

Cohesion of Jews in the Diaspora is the problem in "Solidarity." An Orthodox American congregation, guided by its rabbi, Rabbi Ozer, rallies to a Middle Eastern Jew named Saadia Rachamim, who has been accused of a crime but protests his innocence. Several conflicts converge: the Orthodox defensiveness against Conservative and Reform factions as well as against Gentiles; national and ethnic bigotry among Jews and overcompensation for it; the presence of criminal elements among a people enjoined to be a beacon unto others; and the urge to give the benefit of the doubt without denying the real evidence on which stereotypes are based—that is, the impulse to trust while fearing betrayal. Rabbi Ozer's misplaced trust results from high-minded failure to imagine evil and from insufficient heed to his wife's cautions. He confounds "solidarity" with "uniformity," as though the oneness of a people implied identical individual purpose, interest, and feeling. When his myopic idealism has brought trauma to someone already bereaved, he is forced to violate the Sabbath and call for help from local police.

"The Hostage" further explores the theme of the naive American abroad introduced in *Mara*. Its protagonist, accountant Herbie Mitnick, is any Jew, a modest struggling mensch at risk just by being alive. At the same time, he is an ordinary good-hearted American, taken hostage when he gets in the way of a terrorist raid. So innocent and amiable that his captors think him a superspy, he is first mauled and indoctrinated and later released as irrelevant to their plans.

His wife says, when he telephones, "Oh, go on, Herbie. You're a hostage like I'm a hostage." In effect, the story points out, we are all hostages.

A common thread in all the fiction is that things are not what they seem. Nazi-like behavior occurs in Reich's stories where it is least expected, for instance, in a mother's ruthless determination to make a child "succeed," in the brutal tactics of the rescue squad that tackles Leah Levavi, or in the barbarities of arranging a secret abortion. In "Gertrude Stein," the motherless daughter at the mercy of a masked and clinically detached white doctor is a frightening image, not rendered more reassuring because the doctor is her father. Love blooms unexpectedly, however, between a crippled woman and a desperate Hasid, or between two women in a madhouse, or between boyhood buddies who remain loyal to an ideal and to each other even unto death. Identity is putative and metamorphic, unreliable, but in its malleability it offers possibilities for new growth. Thus in *Master of the Return*, Sora Katz of Mea Shearim was formerly Pam Buck of Macon, Georgia, and Rebbetzin Bruriah Lurie of Uman House was Barbara Horowitz of Brooklyn. Life teems with duplicity and chicanery, but also with hope of salvation.

CRITICAL RECEPTION

Mara was called "a bitter, black comedy" by A. C. Kempf, who noted that in Hebrew the name "Mara" means "bitter." Kempf stated that the novel "explores the emptiness of ritual divorced from ethics" (1937). Jerome Charyn termed *Mara* "startling, playful and irreverent," adding, "It has none of the pieties one would expect in a book cluttered with wedding canopies, crocheted skullcaps, ritual baths, and the Hebrew bill of divorcement called the get. . . . 'Mara' is a fine, poignant first novel, but if Tova Reich had given us more of Leon and less of Sudah and his friends, 'Mara' would have been an extraordinary book" (12). J. N. Baker admired "a series of splendidly crafted set pieces," but felt that the novel did not quite jell, though "Reich's voice is nonetheless a striking one: she has a gift for outrageous, hard-edged comedy that Evelyn Waugh might have appreciated" (71).

Molly Abramowitz highly recommended *Master of the Return*: "Described with affection and great insight, the riotous adventures of these sincere but sometimes misguided penitents easily mix the supernatural with human events. Reich pinpoints absurdity and self-righteousness beautifully. . . . An arresting contemporary treatment of Jewish spirituality and renewal" (96). Benjamin DeMott called the novel "an ambush—a wildly funny story that becomes mysteriously touching and ponderable before the end." Noting the farcical situations, he added, "The steadying presence of history in the story also counts for something. . . . And so, too, does the recurrence of feelings that, although extreme in their expression, are normative at their core." He lauded Reich's "astringent" manner and "cool, unillusioned eye," concluding, "Tova Reich is a marvelously enigmatic original, and there are effects in her book that are beyond casual summoning, secrets reason can't reach'' (94).

Hugh Nissenson praised the way the author "dramatizes her complex theme: that the immemorial Jewish quest for absolute purity is crazy." As he said, "Almost everyone in 'Master of the Return' is a fanatic of one kind or another. Jews, Arabs, Moslems, Christians, even agnostics and atheists, are possessed by their respective beliefs, which emanate from the land itself. . . . Israel is a state of mind. . . . The past is the present among the wadis, on the sacred mountains, and in the holy city of Jerusalem. It drives everyone nuts." He saw life triumphant over demands of the absolute: "In the end, Tova Reich's comic vision gives the last word to life, not death; her novel becomes a rapturous celebration of the maternal principle" (10).

Elie Wiesel saw Rabbi Nachman in *Master of the Return* as "the celebration of the Hasidic imagination" (8), focusing on his gift for storytelling, his oscillating between despair and ecstasy. Like Sanford Pinsker, Wiesel noted that an understanding of this great-grandson of the Baal Shem Tov is prerequisite to savoring Reich's novel: "She has found here a subject worthy of her talent. The language is rich and poetic, and often penetrated with humor . . . The scatterbrained, bizarre characters, disgusted by earthly life, search for a way to make it pure." Wiesel continued, "The most incredible events unfold completely naturally," and "we are taken by the rhythm of the language and by the imagination of the storyteller." He concluded, "Tova Reich has given us a gift smiling: How can we not thank her for it?" (8). Pinsker added that the Bratslav Rabbi also made a difficult pilgrimage, to Israel, and that the novel "refers to specific Nachman tales" and "reduplicates their essential rhythms" (12). Reich is "pouring old obsessions into new technological bottles," thereby not only calling attention to their vitality, but also reinvigorating Jewish-American fiction. Ellen Serlen Uffen, making a similar point, noted the figure of "Ivriya's mother, Dr. Frieda Mendelssohn, a huge comic character who storms in and out of the book and her daughter's marriage, resenting the Chassidic life" (162–63)—a comment that links Reich's perspectives on religion with those on family relations in fiction that is "actually *about* Jewishness and Judaism" (162).

"With *The Jewish War*," said Sanford Pinsker, "Reich is at the top of her game: inventive, wickedly funny and, perhaps most of all, able to give an exasperating subject—one as timely as tomorrow's headlines—the compassionate, humane treatment it deserves." Since the setting is Hebron, "one cannot turn Reich's pages without being reminded of Baruch Goldstein who, in February 1994, opened fire on the worshippers in a Hebron mosque''; yet "Reich's fiction becomes so mesmerizing, so powerful and, yes, so scary, that the acts of a solitary, deranged gunman pale by comparison" (35). He and others pointed out that the title deliberately echoes Josephus's account of mass martyrdom at Masada.

Rosellen Brown advised that "readers will be either delighted or scandalized, depending on the particulars of their piety and their political perspective."

Reich's view of the "politics of peace" has "West Bank settlers eager to finish once and for all this nasty business of sharing space with the Arabs" while overhead "helicopters of the Israel Defense Forces hover intrusively," and Brown relished "these Borscht Belt boychiks" and the summer girlfriends who marry them." She admired Reich's "skewering of cliché" and the "many deliciously deranged moments when Reich lets her characters walk over the edge." Finally, she wondered where the satire leaves off and whether at the end "the author was trumping us with a statement of faith herself, snuck in at the last to take us by surprise." She called the book "lively, intelligent, disturbing and irreverent," conceding that "an alternation of effects is only appropriate for a book about Israel" (25–27). Molly Abramowitz noted that "Reich once again shows empathy for her less-than-balanced characters, who are caught between their hopes for peace and the cruel facts of Middle East realities" (97). She highly recommended the book for all readers. Troy Graham called the novel a "scathing, sobering look at extremist theology and a trenchant, witty work of political satire . . . alternately chilling and hysterical" and, if predictable, also inevitable (8). Sybil Steinberg agreed, "calling the book outrageously funny, wickedly irreverent" (67–68). Patrick McGrath concurred that this is "political and religious satire of the highest order. It is also a vigorous and at times moving story peopled with fallible, complicated, entirely credible characters. And, perhaps most impressive, it displays an unerring control of tone, moving from the high comedy of a summer camp in the Catskills in the early 1960s to a grand, dramatic conclusion in the ancient city of Hebron in the late 1990s." He correctly noted that "this is a story as much about [the women] as about the men they support," and "depiction of the women's activities—and especially their discussions with one another—is what sustains the novel's delicate balance of poignancy, irony, compassion and black comedy. Here we see the domestic and the grandiose coexisting in odd but plausible harmony." He concluded, "With its merciless skewering of all that is ridiculous in religious fanaticism, and at the same time its sympathy for those burning with a holy vision of their land, 'The Jewish War' succeeds marvelously in depicting some of the many complexities of Israel today. It brings this off in great style, with relentless humor and broad humanity—and also, one suspects, with no little prescience" (10).

BIBLIOGRAPHY

Works by Tova Reich

Novels

Mara. New York: Farrar, Straus, Giroux, 1978.
Master of the Return. San Diego: Harcourt Brace Jovanovich, 1988.
The Jewish War. New York: Pantheon Books, 1995.
Birth Wish. Unpublished.

Uncollected Stories

"Moscow Night in New York." *Commentary*, December 1979, 67–71.
"The Hostage." *Harper's*, April 1980, 81–84.
"Gertrude Stein." *Harper's*, August 1982, 46–53.
"Solidarity." *Atlantic Monthly*, January 1984, 70–80.
"The Death of Leah Levavi." *Moment*, December 1984, 52–55.
"Gifted and Talented." *Commentary*, July 1985, 56–61.
"Bring Us to Uman." *Moment*, July/August 1985, 35–46.
"Mengele in Jerusalem." *Harper's*, June 1986, 64–68.
"The Siege of Hebron: Scenes from a Novel." *New York Times*, April 3, 1994, 11.

Studies of Tova Reich

Abramowitz, Molly. Review of *The Jewish War*. *Library Journal*, May 15, 1995, 97.
———. Review of *Master of the Return*. *Library Journal*, April 15, 1988, 96.
Baker, J. N. Review of *Mara*. *Newsweek*, August 21, 1978, 71.
Bell, P. K. Review of *Mara*. *Commentary*, September 1978, 70.
Berman, Paul. Review of *Mara*. *Harper's*, August 1978, 89.
Brown, Rosellen. Review of *The Jewish War*. *New Leader*, June 5, 1995, 25–27.
Charyn, Jerome. Review of *Mara*. *New York Times Book Review*, June 11, 1978, 12.
DeMott, Benjamin. Review of *Master of the Return*. *Atlantic*, May 1988, 92–94.
Graham, Troy. Review of *The Jewish War*. *Washington Post*, November 19, 1995, 8.
Jonas, Gerald. Review of *Master of the Return*. *Present Tense*, November/December 1988, 59.
Kempf, A. C. Review of *Mara*. *Library Journal*, July 1978, 1437.
Kirschenbaum, Blossom S. "So Who's Crazy?—Two Stories by Tova Reich." *Modern Jewish Studies*, in press.
Lyons, Bonnie. Review of *Mara*. *Congress Monthly*, January 1979, 18–19.
McGrath, Patrick. Review of *The Jewish War*. *New York Times Book Review*, July 23, 1995, 10.
Nissenson, Hugh. Review of *Master of the Return*. *New York Times Book Review*, May 29, 1988, 10.
Pinsker, Sanford. Review of *The Jewish War*. *Metrowest Jewish News*, September 28, 1995, 35.
———. "New Voices and the Contemporary Jewish-American Novel." In *Jewish Book Annual*, ed. Jacob Kabakoff. New York: Jewish Book Council, 1991, 6–20.
Pollack, Eileen. Review of *The Jewish War*. *Boston Globe*, July 16, 1995, 34.
Steinberg, Sybil. Review of *The Jewish War*. *Publishers Weekly*, May 29, 1995, 67–68.
———. Review of *Master of the Return*. *Publishers Weekly*, February 26, 1988, 182.
Uffen, Ellen Serlen. *Strands of the Cable: The Place of the Past in Jewish American Women's Writing*. New York: Peter Lang, 1992, 162–63.
Wiesel, Elie. Review of *Master of the Return*. *New Leader*, May 16, 1988, 7–8.

MORDECAI RICHLER (1931–)

Esther Frank and Joel Shatzky

BIOGRAPHY

Mordecai Richler was born on January 27, 1931, in Montreal, Quebec. In 1931, out of a population of about 1 million, 58 thousand were Jews. He grew up in a predominantly Jewish working-class neighborhood about which he writes in many of his works. Richler's forebears immigrated to Canada from Russia and Poland early in the century. One of his grandfathers was a Hasid who wrote religious texts and translated the Zohar into modern Hebrew. In Montreal he became a peddler.

One of Richler's uncles managed a Yiddish theater in New York and was a playwright. Although the family sprang from generations of rabbis, this tradition was not continued in Canada. Richler's father was a junk dealer, and Mordecai Richler himself moved away from orthodoxy by the time he was thirteen. Little is known about Richler's mother. After the parents were divorced in the 1940s, she supported the family by renting rooms and cooking for her neighbors. Growing up in the Jewish quarter of Montreal, Richler attended Talmud Torah, a private primary school then associated with acquiring a traditional Jewish education. He studied English and French subjects and also received instruction in Hebrew in the Talmud and in the Torah. He also went to cheder (Hebrew grade school) at night and continued his studies in Talmud and in modern Hebrew. By the age of thirteen, however, Richler broke away from his orthodox background and stopped obeying all the rules and rituals associated with it. He went on to Baron Byng High School, a high school run by the Protestant School Board of Greater Montreal, and then to Sir George Williams College, now Concordia University. It was there that Richler discovered that he wanted to be a writer.

In 1950 Richler's formal education ended. At the age of nineteen he left for

Europe, where he spent two years, living periodically in Paris, London, and on the Spanish Isle of Ibiza and enjoying his stay with literary companions including Herbert Gold, Allen Ginsberg, James Baldwin, Mavis Gallant, Mason Hoffenberg, Allen Temko, and Terry Southern. Soon after Richler's arrival, his first pieces were published in a Paris literary magazine, but he could not yet sustain himself as a writer in Europe. At the same time as Richler began to make plans to return to Montreal, he submitted his writing for publication. With an offer from a London publisher he returned to Canada in 1952.

Once in Canada, after working on all sorts of odd jobs, he became a news editor for the Canadian Broadcasting Corporation (CBC) and began revising his first novel, *The Acrobats* (1954). Richler remained in Canada for only two years. He returned to London in 1954 and lived there for the next eighteen years, marrying Florence Wood in 1959. They had four children during the 1960s. Richler wrote and published many novels, stories, essays, and all sorts of other pieces while he was living in London. It is this body of writing that established Richler as an important writer in Canada and abroad and gave him a reputation as an *enfant terrible* of Canadian letters.

In the years before his return to his homeland, Richler wrote six novels, including the one for which he will probably be best remembered, *The Apprenticeship of Duddy Kravitz* (1959), which has many autobiographical elements in it, as does *Son of a Smaller Hero* (1955). Richler also wrote *A Choice of Enemies* (1957), *The Incomparable Atuk* (1963), about an Eskimo who becomes a celebrity in Canada, *Cocksure* (1968), a satire on the entertainment industry, *The Street* (1969), a collection of short stories, and *St. Urbain's Horseman* (1971), a novel set in the same Jewish neighborhood that was home to Duddy Kravitz.

In 1972 Richler returned to Canada and settled in Montreal with his wife and family. Since then he has produced two more novels, *Joshua Then and Now* (1980) and *Solomon Gursky Was Here* (1989), as well as a number of collections of essays.

Richler is one of Canada's best-known contemporary writers and one of the country's most distinguished authors. He has won many honors and awards. These include a Guggenheim Fellowship in creative writing, a Canada Council senior arts fellowship, a Governor General's Award for fiction and essays (1968), and the 1971 Governor General's Award for fiction. He also won the Writers' Guild Award (1974) for the film version of his novel *The Apprenticeship of Duddy Kravitz*. In 1976 Richler was appointed to the editorial board of the Book-of-the-Month Club. He has also been writer-in-residence at Concordia and Carlton Universities. Richler continues to maintain a high profile as a novelist and as a recorder of culture and to sustain wide recognition for his works.

MAJOR WORKS AND THEMES

In articles and interviews over the years Richler has talked about the informing concerns of his fiction, and one of the features he stresses is his rootedness in Montreal. For Richler, the particulars that he remembers, and that find their way into his writings, are those of the so-called ghetto streets, the moods and the experiences of his childhood and youth. These are associated with St. Urbain Street, where Jews once lived and where they built a neighborhood, where they established their own institutions and their own way of life. In his stories these aspects of Jewish life are both a source of value and a focus of his criticism. Richler himself has said that he is interested in criticizing the "things I believe in or am attached to"—liberal values, Jews, and Canada. Even at the beginning of his career, Richler spoke in an interview with Nathan Cohen in 1956 (later published in Sheps) about his need to "say what I feel about values and about people living in a time when to my mind there is no agreement on values" (29).

A major element in Richler's work is his satire, and its direction suggests that his works have a moral basis, but that this is also a force that counters his constructive concerns. The extent to which Richler has combined these two forces and made them work to complement each other and the energy this combination has released have become a focus in some of the studies of his writings.

The relationship between Richler and his readers has been an ambiguous one. While he is respected as one of Canada's finest writers at home and abroad, he has not enjoyed the stature or fame accorded to his American counterparts with whom he is compared. It seems as if he has received publicity for his writing on political or cultural issues in Canada that has had delimiting consequences on how he is viewed as a writer. While over the past decade revisions in critical theory have expanded the scope and focus of Richler criticism, many of the old questions still persist: Is Richler a constructive or a destructive writer? What tradition is more prominent for this Jewish Canadian—the Jewish or the Canadian? To this and other questions have been added historicist, feminist, and gender approaches and the author's own responses, which, when directed to questions about his writing, are designed to disdain categorizations and to mock the attempt. Thus Richler has been seen since the 1950s as an engaged writer, eager to exchange ideas with his readers on social, political, and ethical concerns, and on a personal level as a self-protective writer who has his characters speak his mind.

Of the novels Richler has written, of most interest to readers of Jewish literature are *Son of a Smaller Hero, The Apprenticeship of Duddy Kravitz, St. Urbain's Horseman*, and *Joshua Then and Now*. In the first of these, *Son of a Smaller Hero*, Noah Adler, the central figure, growing up in the Jewish neighborhood that is the setting for a number of Richler's novels, tries to escape from the restrictions of his religious and family background and chooses to leave his home for Europe and a quest to discover his own identity. A typical *Bildungsroman* with a Jewish-Canadian milieu, *Son of a Smaller Hero* anticipates a number of themes that Richler later develops in *Duddy Kravitz* and *St. Urbain's Horseman*: alienation from one's roots, a sense of exile, and Richler's own highly critical view of both his Jewish and his Canadian culture.

The Apprenticeship of Duddy Kravitz brought Richler to the attention of

American audiences when it was made into a very successful film starring Richard Dreyfus and established the young actor's reputation. It was given an Oscar nomination and garnered Richler recognition as a screenwriter with an award from the Writers' Guild. In this "making-it" novel in the tradition of *What Makes Sammy Run?* Duddy begins life as the product of the Jewish ghetto of Montreal, which Richler records with such pitiless observations as to invite the accusation that he, like Philip Roth, is a "self-hating Jew." In the course of the novel, Duddy attempts a number of schemes to become a success and eventually own land, but in the course of his "apprenticeship," which includes a hilarious project to market bar mitzvah documentaries to wealthy parents, wonderfully portrayed in the movie, he betrays the two people who have really been most important in his young life: his mistress, Yvette, and Virgil, the epileptic whom he befriends only to exploit.

Richler's next-best-known novel, *St. Urbain's Horseman*, takes place along St. Urbain Street, the heart of the old Jewish district of Montreal. The central figure, Jake Hersh, a successful man, creates a fantasy about his cousin, Joey, an almost mythical figure, "the Horseman" who represents the old Jewish heroes who championed and defended their people against their enemies.

Joshua Then and Now centers on Joshua Shapiro, a successful author who is married to the gentile daughter of a prominent politician. Joshua is in the same mold as Duddy Kravitz and Jake Hersh, a man on the make who is not particularly pleasant and finds himself in a moral crisis considering his humble origins and the affluence of his marriage to a WASP. His present situation is contrasted with memories of his childhood with his father, Reuben, a small-time operator who would take him on his various trips.

Solomon Gursky Was Here, Richler's most recent work, written in 1989, has not gotten much attention in comparison to his earlier novels. It is about a Jewish family of bootleggers and con men who become wealthy businessmen and also paints an unflattering picture of upper-crust Canadian and English society.

CRITICAL RECEPTION

With the rapid growth of the study of Canadian literature in universities in the 1970s, Richler's novels and other writings became the subject of academic literary criticism. Some studies concentrate on the Jewish themes in Richler's novels. These offer a corrective to the many attacks made by some readers on his depiction of Jewish traits or characters, complaints that have often greeted Richler's work over the years. Attention has also been paid to the varying ways in which his writings represent Canadian concerns. The publication of two books on Richler in the early 1970s marked the moment when he came into prominence as a Canadian writer. G. David Sheps's *Mordecai Richler* in the Critical Views on Canadian Writers Series is a collection of previously published critical pieces; George Woodcock's *Mordecai Richler: A Critical Study of His Writings*, offers an analysis of his fiction by a leading Canadian man of letters.

It is first and foremost Richler's characters that capture the attention of critics. As G. David Sheps observed: "Characteristically, Richler's protagonists are those romantic, adolescent (of whatever age) 'rebels without a cause' popularized by James Dean in the 1950's. This hero has no particular notions about the reconstruction of society or about the reconstruction of himself. His individualism is a matter of posture, a stance without content he adopts in opposition to his society. Hence, it is often expressed as a generational conflict between father (or grandfathers) and sons" (xviii).

Of Richler's first novel with clearly Jewish characters and milieu, *Son of a Smaller Hero*, David Evanier observed, "[It has] some fine things despite an awkwardness that gives it the feeling of being a first novel (it was Richler's second). It has a rich feel of the Jewish neighborhood of Montreal that Richler grew up in, although its characters frequently seem like caricatures" (28).

The Apprenticeship of Duddy Kravitz, however, has probably received more critical comment than any of Richler's other works. John Ower said, "As a 'Jewish' novel, *The Apprenticeship* has both a pungent ethnic flavor and the convincingness that arises when a writer deals with a milieu with which he is completely familiar. At the same time, Richler treats the ambivalent relationships of the Montreal ghetto to both English and French-Canadian cultures" (413). But Ower also observed, "[A] central dilemma in Richler's novel, which is never fully resolved, is how to reconcile the hard necessities of a wicked world with ethics" (428). The French critic Naim Kattan also warned, "In this novel, which is without doubt its author's most accomplished work, one can measure his talent against his limitations. Stirred by a demanding passion, he is led to destroy his characters through caricature. Facing a society which he wishes to conquer, he has not time to look at it, to understand it, to perceive its complete ambiguity" (97). But David Myers noted, "The great variety of moods in this novel suggests that Richler's forte as a writer is satiric farce with a tragic undertone. The satiric point of view prevents him from lapsing into bathos, and a potentially tragic perspective obviates the emergence of merely trivial farce. In this respect, *Duddy Kravitz* clearly anticipates *St. Urbain's Horseman*" (51). Of the later work, Kerry McSweeney stated:

The center of the novel is a crisis point in the life of Jake Hersh, a successful thirty-seven year old "alienated Jew. Modishly ugly" with a "gorgeous wife" and three children. . . . There are two generic components of Jake's crisis: (a) the advent of the mid-life crunch . . . which is triggered by a sense of professional unfulfillment and intimations of mortality; (b) the cumulative malaise of Jake's " 'American generation'—'Always the wrong age. Ever observers, never participants. The Whirlwind elsewhere.' " (127)

McSweeney noted, however, "The thematic skeleton of *St. Urbain's Horseman* is, then, solid and substantial; it is in its incarnation that the weakness of the novel lies. Everything depends on the presentation of Jake. . . . Unfortunately

Jake is characterized too superficially'' (127). Another critic, David Evanier, observed, ''Long stretches of the novel strike the reader as a prolonged kvetch, a recital of the anxieties stalking a character approaching affluent middle-age'' (33). But Robert Fulford saw that in this novel ''Richler has pushed far beyond anecdote and opinion into the denser, more rewarding world of fantasy rooted in experience. His book conveys memorably the physical and personal world of Jake's observable life, but more importantly it moves into his inner world'' (26). Of *Joshua Then and Now*, John Lahr declared, ''Richler writes funny. Laughter, not chicken soup, is the real Jewish penicillin, doing shtick while waiting for the coronary. . . . The narrative gusto of *Joshua Then and Now* rushes the reader past its longueurs and turns it into a kind of *A la Recherche du Temps Perdu* for the Ritz Brothers'' (79).

Solomon Gursky Was Here, Richler's most recent novel, unfortunately, has not been so well treated. Carol Iannone noted, ''Richler ranges, rudderless, from farce to fabulism to mythology to satire to romanticism to realism to naturalism to whatever. It is often difficult to know what is going on'' (51).

Still, Leslie Fiedler, in assessing Richler's work, observed, ''Richler himself belongs to the world of mass culture . . . so that he seems ultimately—seems, I think, rather than is . . . harmless. . . . It is quite another aspect of his work which makes Richler more dangerous than he seems perhaps even to himself: his concern with exile, his compulsion to define all predicaments in terms of that hopelessly Jewish concept, and his implicit suggestion that, after all, we are—everyone of us—Jews'' (105).

BIBLIOGRAPHY

Works by Mordecai Richler

Fiction

The Acrobats. New York: Putnam, 1954.
Son of a Smaller Hero. Toronto: Collins, 1955.
A Choice of Enemies. Toronto: Collins, 1957.
The Apprenticeship of Duddy Kravitz. Boston: Little, Brown, 1959.
The Incomparable Atuk. New York: Simon and Schuster, 1963.
Cocksure. New York: Simon and Schuster, 1968.
The Street: Stories. Toronto: McClelland and Stewart, 1969.
St. Urbain's Horseman. New York: Knopf, 1971.
Joshua Then and Now. New York: Knopf, 1980.
Solomon Gursky Was Here. New York: Viking, 1989.

Juvenile Fiction

Jacob Two-Two Meets the Hooded Fang. New York: Knopf, 1975.
Jacob Two-Two and the Dinosaur. New York: Knopf, 1987.

Nonfiction

Hunting Tigers under Glass: Essays and Reports. Toronto: McClelland and Stewart, 1968.

Shoveling Trouble (essays). Toronto: McClelland and Stewart, 1973.

Notes on an Endangered Species and Others (essays). New York: Knopf, 1974.

Images of Spain. Photographs by Peter Christopher. New York: Norton, 1977.

The Great Comic Book Heroes and Other Essays. Toronto: McClelland and Stewart, 1978.

Home Sweet Home: My Canadian Album (nonfiction). New York: Knopf, 1984.

Major Screenplays

The Apprenticeship of Duddy Kravitz (adapted from his novel). Paramount, 1974.

Fun with Dick and Jane. With David Giler and Jerry Belson. Bart/Palevsky, 1977.

Joshua Then and Now (adapted from his novel). Twentieth-Century Fox, 1985.

Works Cited and Studies of Mordecai Richler

Brenner, Rachel Feldhay. *Assimilation and Assertion: The Response to the Holocaust in Mordecai Richler's Writings.* New York: Peter Lang, 1989.

Darling, Michael. *Perspectives on Mordecai Richler.* Toronto: ECW Press, 1986.

Evanier, David. "The Jewish Mordecai Richler." *Midstream,* December 1974, 24–37.

Fiedler, Leslie. "Some Notes on the Jewish Novel in English; or, Looking Backward from Exile." *Running Man* 1 (July–August 1968). Reprinted in *Mordecai Richler,* ed. G. David Sheps. Toronto: McGraw-Hill, Ryerson, 1971, 99–105.

Fulford, Robert. "All the Mordecais, Together at Last." *Saturday Night,* June 1971, 25–26.

Greenstein, Michael. "Mordecai Richler and Jewish-Canadian Humor." In *Jewish Wry: Essays on Jewish Humor,* ed. Sarah Blacher Cohen. Bloomington: Indiana University Press, 1987.

Iannone, Carol. Review of *Solomon Gursky Was Here. Commentary* 89 (June 1990): 51.

Kattan, Naim. "Mordecai Richler: Craftsman or Artist." Trans. George Woodcock. *Canadian Literature,* Summer 1964. Reprinted in Mordecai Richler, ed. G. David Sheps. Toronto: McGraw-Hill, Ryerson, 1971, 92–98.

Lahr, John. "Shrieks and Kvetches: 'Joshua Then and Now.'" *New York Magazine,* June 16, 1980, 79.

McNaught, Kenneth. "Mordecai Richler Was Here." *Journal of Canadian Studies,* Winter 1992, 141–43.

McSweeney, Kerry. "Revaluing Mordecai Richler." *Studies in Canadian Literature* 4 (Summer 1979): 120–31.

Myers, David. "Mordecai Richler as Satirist." *Ariel* 4 (January 1973): 47–61.

Northey, Margot. *The Haunted Wilderness: The Gothic and Grotesque in Canadian Fiction.* Toronto: University of Toronto Press, 1976.

Ower, John. "Sociology, Psychology, and Satire in 'The Apprenticeship of Duddy Kravitz.'" *Modern Fiction Studies,* Autumn 1976, 413–28.

Ramraj, Victor J. *Mordecai Richler.* Boston: Twayne, 1983.

Sheps, G. David, ed. *Mordecai Richler.* Toronto: McGraw-Hill, Ryerson, 1971.

Woodcock, George. *Mordecai Richler: A Critical Study of His Writings.* Toronto: McClelland and Stewart, 1970.

LUCY (GABRIELLE) ROSENTHAL (1933–)

Diane Stevenson

BIOGRAPHY

Lucy Rosenthal was born on January 3, 1933, in New York City. She attended the University of Michigan, Columbia Graduate School of Journalism, Yale Drama School, and the University of Iowa Writers Workshop.

She has had a varied career in writing and publishing. She is the author of an important novel, *The Ticket Out* (1983), the writer of stories and plays and articles, and the editor of anthologies, as well as a member of the editorial board of judges for Book-of-the-Month Club from 1965 to 1968. Her time there was a time when feminism was revving up, and as its third female member in fifty years, the first in twenty years, Rosenthal added a voice to its deliberations that was new and compelling. During her tenure, Susan Brownmiller's *Against Our Will* was selected as a Book-of-the-Month offering, and so too were Susan Fromberg Schaeffer's *Time in Its Flight* and Susan Isaacs's *Compromising Positions*. She has written in praise of Marge Piercy, Norma Klein, Judith Rossner, Gail Godwin, and Alix Kates Shulman. Her career in publishing coincided with an important stage in literary feminism that she played an influential role both in bringing about and promoting.

In 1968 Lucy Rosenthal was awarded a Pulitzer Fellowship in Critical Writing; she was a member of the Pulitzer Prize biography jury in 1980 and the American Book Awards board in 1981–1982. She presently teaches fiction writing at Sarah Lawrence College.

MAJOR WORKS AND THEMES

At Columbia University in the 1920s Lucy Rosenthal's father, Henry Rosenthal, was a great friend of Lionel Trilling. Both published stories about their friendship in the *Menorah Journal*. In these portraits—fictional but based on fact—Henry comes across as passionate in intellect and in Jewishness, satirical about others and about himself. Lionel Trilling is gentler and less aggressive as an individual and in his ethnic identity. They represent, perhaps, two poles on a continuum: the ways in which precocious, literary young men, among the first Jews to attend Columbia University, responded to their secular status. Rosenthal held to his religious identity. He graduated from Columbia, attended seminary, and became a rabbi. Being an intellectual was for him inextricably connected with being Jewish. One was not subordinate to the other. Trilling was to take his stand in a different tradition, the cultural tradition represented by Matthew Arnold. His commitment to the *Menorah Journal* did not outlast his years at Columbia; and later, when he was asked to serve on the editorial board of *Commentary* by his friend Eliot Cohen, he refused. He rejected "American Jewish culture as appropriate ground for the development of an intellectual life" (Grumet, 170).

Whatever one makes of the responses of these two young men, they were compelled by the times. That Jewish intellectuals were beginning to matter, not only among themselves, but to the American community at large, was a simple fact. They were called upon to come to terms with this fact. Each of the two friends took his stand. They argued with each other and, in doing so, generated a passionate debate about culture and the role individuals play in culture. It is tempting to call one position—Rosenthal's—more authentic, more Jewish, than the other; it is particularly tempting to do so now, in retrospect, at a time when identity politics is so much a given in national life, and it was, no doubt, just such a judgment that Trilling was, in part, defending himself against when, in his book *Sincerity and Authenticity*, he set himself on the side of "sincerity." "Sincerity" in Trilling's sense means accepting the standards of the polity. "Authenticity," in his sense, means to hold to a more individual standard. But it is imperative to put things in context and call both responses, Rosenthal's and Trilling's, responses of an emerging literary elite to a host elite—at once hospitable *and* hostile. Both men, indisputably, were engaging in survivor tactics.

What is one to make, then, of the fact that Lucy Rosenthal, while heir to this passionate cultural debate, appears to opt out of it, choosing as the first-person narrator for her wonderful and wonderfully written novel *The Ticket Out* not only a man—a striking choice for a woman writer—but a man who is a Christian? Was she repudiating the identity her father felt crucial to the life of the mind as well as to the life of the heart? One must remember the changes that had taken place. Her fiction had hanging over it something those two young men, Henry Rosenthal and Lionel Trilling, did not yet have hanging over theirs. The Holocaust had taken place. Feminism had come to the fore. The American otherness she was to explore, Christian and male, carried more sinister connotations for her than it had had for the earlier generation. The imperative of the earlier debate—What does Jewishness mean?—becomes for her an imperative about the other. What does it mean to be the other? What does that meaning have to do with my Jewishness, or my womanness?

What Lucy Rosenthal uncovers in her foray into the enemy camp is the complacency of power and authority, its easy decline into manipulation, and the petulances and resentments that result when manipulation turns out to have failed. Jack Church, her character, is forthright about how he feels, but his feelings are circumscribed by a selfishness he misperceives as self-respect. His struggle with personal power—most of all in his ill-fated marriage—mirrors struggles with power on a larger canvas and the way in which those on top become intrusive and bullying, simply because they have power. Jack Church will not see himself for who he really is—his own actions appear to him enlightened, compassionate, and sacrificing—and therefore the people most vulnerable to him, his wife and his brother, cannot see themselves either. Jack experiences a mental breakdown, almost taking his wife with him. His brother dies.

Lucy Rosenthal has said about her novel that it explored, in part, what it meant to her father to have a brother die.

I didn't realize where the idea for the novel came from until I was closing my mother's apartment and came across family papers. I had always known that my father had a brother who died young. But I did not know when. Finally I was able to date it, after the novel was essentially completed. I was six when it happened, and I had no memory of it, or of the impact on the family. I remember very clearly my sister's second birthday some weeks before, and remember a great deal after that, but I do not remember my uncle's death, only that I have always had a preoccupation with the death of a brother. The deaths of brothers later in my life had incredible impact—including the deaths of the Kennedy brothers. I put the novel aside when Bobby Kennedy was killed. I put it aside for a lot of reasons, but I remember thinking, history is overtaking my theme, I can't deal with it.

I frankly think I couldn't finish the novel until I was strong enough, which for me meant when I knew something about grief first-hand. I was simply very frightened of what I was writing about. I began to work on the novel again almost immediately after my father died. I think that I had become stronger to sustain the invention over a period of time, to be alone with those characters in a room, and get it on paper. A trip to Israel was important for me, sort of a mid-point in the evolution of the novel. If you're going to write from the point of view of a man, and put him through experiences you've never had in a literal sense, you have to have a quite strong sense of yourself. And I think what this trip to Israel did was restore a sense of self on some important level. I had never been ashamed to be Jewish, but I think I have been *afraid* of being Jewish. Because I grew up during the war and saw film clips of concentration camps in 1945, I was stunned I think. There was something about being in Israel in the museum which is a memorial to the victims of the Holocaust. I forced myself, standing on Israeli soil, to look at those exhibits, and walk through and face into that history. It was healing for me, made me strong enough to write about rootlessness. It is interesting to me that the one contribution I made to the jacket copy was the word ''transplanted,'' Jack Church, ''a transplanted mid-Westerner.'' (Parke, 165–66)

In this passage Lucy Rosenthal speaks of her father and the death of her father's brother; she speaks of the Kennedy brothers. She speaks of the Holocaust, and she speaks of displacement. Her mother was from Europe; her father was from Louisville, Kentucky. Both were transplanted to New York City. The complex biographical and historical particulars and the way they are woven—inextricably—into a texture of disruption and loss are very much relevant to *The Ticket Out*: something from the past is lost forever to the present.

There are several movements in the book. First, Jack moves away from work and, in a sense, away from a character who is a father figure, an alcoholic who has burned all his bridges and is being fired from his job. He is Jack's boss and mentor, and in a gesture of solidarity, Jack, too, leaves the job. Ironically, this brings him no closer to his old friend, who now isolates himself and refuses Jack's consolation. Jack is strikingly at bay, not only financially and in terms of his career, but emotionally. Next, he enters into a rather hasty marriage with a very young woman who can neither cook nor, as it turns out, satisfy Jack sexually. To be fair, he does not satisfy her either; and it is she who holds the steady job. His marriage fails on the two fronts of food and sex: it is no haven, and it is no home. He leaves his wife, and now he is doubly homeless, for the apartment the couple had moved into was his.

Before Jack's marriage, his brother had come to him to ask for money for an abortion. He had gotten a girl pregnant, and now he was letting her down. She wanted to have the money. Jack intervenes and gets them to marry. They have the child. In a parallel development, Jack, in what amounts to a one-night stand, impregnates a friend whose husband is sterile. She has the baby, so Jack, too, is a father, but a father who cannot claim his offspring. There is in the novel an assortment of false beginnings, false solaces, and false homecomings.

Finally, Jack Church, a wreck after his separation from his wife and after the death of his brother, returns to the Midwest to his family and to the promise of that home. In his despair he goes so far as to attempt to place his head in his mother's lap. He is rebuffed. This, he is told, is the act of a child, and he is a man. Soon after his symbolic attempt to return to the womb, he gets himself committed to a mental ward. Eventually he recovers enough to return to his wife, who, not much more than a child herself, recovering a bit from the nastiness of their marriage, agrees to take Jack in. She tells him that she wants a child this time. The novel ends here.

If we think of the young Lionel Trilling and the young Henry Rosenthal as taking part in a timely and significant debate about the meaning of a double identity, Jewish and American, then it might be claimed that Lucy Rosenthal's

The Ticket Out takes up their debate where they leave off, going on to explore its other half—the half of the other and the way things look from that side. In her novel she takes up the project of her father: to imagine or to try to imagine the territory of Jewish loss and reclamation, but by looking through the eyes of the culturally other. Like her father, she is solidly situated in a Jewishness strong enough to allow her this exploration outside herself, a solidity he has vouchsafed for her and that her trip to Israel also vouchsafed. Like Lionel Trilling, she wears the mask of a culture and tradition different from her own with ease and grace and uncanny self-possession. Lucy Rosenthal's novel is an act of reconnaissance. She enters an alien camp with the subversive sensitivities of an artist to find out and help formulate exactly what cultural identity is, what being Jewish is, what being Christian is, and what being American is—that people from its inception a nation of displaced persons.

CRITICAL RECEPTION

The Ticket Out has been praised for its wonderful writing, for its sensitivity and intelligence, for its wit and humor, and for its portrait of Jack Church, "so remarkably full and true that time and again I found it almost impossible to believe that a woman had written this book, so thoroughly does Rosenthal enter into the male psyche" (15). Thus did Susan Fromberg Schaeffer judge Rosenthal's ability to decipher male psychology as almost uncanny, and her *Chicago Tribune Book World* review continued to express her astonishment: "*The Ticket Out* is much more than a work of mental transvestitism. Its author has taken an imaginative leap so prodigious that she seems to have once been, in some previous incarnation, the man of whom she writes. It is as if male territory had been silently invaded, surveyed, reported on and judged" (15). Though the male is judged with proper toughness, the judgment is tempered with "rare intelligence, wit and high humor." Another reviewer, Josephine Hendlin in the *Nation*, put the matter in this way: "Lucy Rosenthal's first novel, *The Ticket Out*, is a love story that avoids ideological clichés about sexual liberation, female oppression and male tyranny" (167).

BIBLIOGRAPHY

Works by Lucy Rosenthal

The Ticket Out. New York: Harcourt Brace Jovanovich, 1983.
Great American Love Stories, ed. Boston: Little, Brown, 1988.
The World Treasury of Love Stories, ed. New York: Oxford University Press, 1995.

Works Cited and Studies of Lucy Rosenthal

Grumet, Elinor. "The Apprenticeship of Lionel Trilling." *Prooftexts* 4 (1984): 153–73.
Hendlin, Josephine. Review of *The Ticket Out*. *Nation*, February 22, 1984, 167.

Parke, Catherine. "An Interview with Lucy Rosenthal." *Missouri Review* 8:1 (1984): 159–75.

Schaeffer, Susan Fromberg. Review of *The Ticket Out*. *Chicago Tribune Book World*, November 27, 1983, 15.

Stern, Dan. Review of *The Ticket Out*. *New York Times Book Review*, January 1, 1984, 20.

Trilling, Lionel. *Sincerity and Authenticity*. New York: Harcourt Brace Jovanovich, 1980.

HENRY ROTH   (1906–1995)

Hana Wirth-Nesher

BIOGRAPHY

Henry Roth was born in 1906 in Tysmenitz, a small town in Austro-Hungarian Galicia. He arrived in New York in 1909 with his mother after his father had emigrated the previous year. This was the first of several journeys in his life, all of which shaped his literary odyssey. Up to the age of eight he lived in Yiddish-speaking Brownsville and the Lower East Side until his parents made the move uptown to Harlem, which was predominantly Irish and Italian. In Roth's accounts of his life, this was a watershed event, as it removed him from a sense of home that he was never able to recover. It was in Harlem that he encountered street gangs and violence, that he first felt like an outsider in America, and that he was exposed to anti-Semitism. After attending Stuyvesant and De Witt Clinton High School, he was admitted to City College. In 1927 he met Eda Lou Walton, New York University lecturer, poet, critic, and scholar who both supported him and encouraged him to write *Call It Sleep*, which first appeared in 1934 and which he dedicated to her. During the years in which he lived with Walton at her Greenwich Village home, Roth became part of a literary and intellectual circle that included Hart Crane, Louise Bogan, Margaret Mead, and Kenneth Burke. Through Walton he also discovered Joyce.

After his marriage to the composer Muriel Parker in 1939 and the birth of their two sons, he moved to Maine, where he tried many occupations, such as precision-tool grinder, substitute Latin teacher, attendant at a hospital for the mentally ill, and poultry farmer. Although he made several attempts at writing another novel, he finally destroyed the manuscript. Four years after the reissuance of *Call It Sleep* in 1964, the Roths moved to Albuquerque, New Mexico, where Muriel died in 1990. During the last five years of his life Roth edited the

3200-page manuscript that was planned as a series of six novels entitled *Mercy of a Rude Stream. A Star Shines over Mt. Morris Park*, the first of these, was published in 1994, *A Diving Rock on the Hudson* in 1995, and *From Bondage* (posthumously) in 1996.

MAJOR WORKS AND THEMES

The paradox of the great writer's art is that it is indisputably representative and at the same time unique. James Joyce is without doubt an Irish writer, an exilic writer, a European writer, and a modernist writer. His construction in language of the relationship among these various identities is his signature, is what makes him Joyce. Henry Roth is without doubt a Jewish writer, an immigrant writer, an American writer, and a modernist writer (and a Joycean). How he maintains these identities in tension in his multilingual works is his signature. While the sixty-year silence between the publication of his first brilliant novel, *Call It Sleep*, and his recent comeback made him a legend, it is the writing itself that defines his place in Jewish-American literature.

Despite the success of his first novel both in reviews and sales, Roth's growing commitment to communism made him acutely sensitive to the rebuke he received from the anonymous *New Masses* reviewer who bemoaned the fact that "so many young writers drawn from the proletariat can make no better use of their working class experience than as material for introspective, febrile novels" (quoted in Allen, 443). In a futile attempt to integrate his moral and political commitments with his artistic ambitions, he embarked on a novel commissioned by Maxwell Perkins at Scribner's about a midwestern factory worker that he abandoned despite Perkins's encouragement. What followed was Roth's legendary writer's block, a sixty-year spell of silence broken only in 1994 with the publication of the first volume of *Mercy of a Rude Stream*. Speculation about this block has yielded many theories, from his having exhausted all of his materials as a deracinated Jew in *Call It Sleep*, a classic of disinheritance, to his beating at the hands of longshoremen while trying to obtain material for his second work. In later years, Roth admitted to reaching an impasse stylistically as he strove to exorcise Joyce from his writings and to invent a form more appropriate to his Jewish sensibility, and he attributed his renewed writing powers to his renewed Jewish identity brought about by his identification with Israel during the 1967 war.

Call It Sleep is the story of David Schearl's quest for the divine in the industrial and alienating New York to which his parents immigrated when he was only two. Narrated almost entirely from his point of view as a small child, the book maps David's movement outward, away from home both psychologically, as he experiences his Oedipal phase, and sociologically, as he moves out of his Yiddish environment toward American culture. The book's theme of the irrevocable move away from home, both socially and psychologically, and the irretrievable losses necessitated by that move is evident in the artistic strategies as well. The reader experiences the actions at a linguistic remove, as if the text were a translation with a missing original, or from a forgotten language.

Call It Sleep is a Jewish-American version of the portrait of the artist as a young boy, but because the boy is the child of immigrants, he must be absorbed into a society entirely "Other," not part of the collective memory of his family. As a result, *Call It Sleep* is the urban odyssey of a young man who must find his identity in the city of a strange country, who must leave his mother and finally assimilate the Statue of Liberty into his cultural repertoire so that it will be "home."

Through David's naive piecing together of information, we learn that his mother Genya had an unhappy romance in her native Poland with a Gentile who abandoned her for an aristocratic Polish woman. Despite her lover's betrayal, Genya cherishes the memory of that first love, symbolized for her by a picture of cornflowers purchased from a peddler and wistfully hung on the wall of her spare tenement flat. Although Genya regards it as a nosegay of early romance, the picture is also a moral rebuke for her having sinned against her people in her affair with a Gentile. Her tyrannical and overbearing husband Albert is also haunted by his past, for he witnessed his father gored to death by a bull without coming to his aid. He relives his guilt also by bringing a tormenting reminder of his sin into his home: a set of bull's horns. They signify not only his crime of patricide, but also his strength and virility before he came to be bullied by others in the New World. Moreover, the horns also indicate his obsessive distrust of his wife and his suspicion that he has been cuckolded, and that David is not his child. While eventually Albert affirms his paternity, the child's literal parentage in this book is far less significant than the shifting definitions of patrimony in the cultural migration of immigrant children.

The literal patricide that has made Albert Schearl a bitter and paranoid man sets the stage for the book's dominant theme, the cultural patricide inherent in the story of successful immigration and assimilation. The child David, whose given name means "beloved" in Hebrew and who is bound to his loving mother as, in Freud's family romance, only a five-year-old can be, must also carry out the meaning of his surname Schearl, which means "scissors" in Yiddish and which refers to the severing of the bond with the parent culture in order to assimilate into his new home. What the power of the mother's love restores for the child is rent again and again by the power of mind, and what the inheritance of generations provides, the act of immigration sunders.

Call It Sleep is a multilingual book that inscribes Yiddish, Hebrew, and Aramaic onto its pages as well as English that ranges from medieval romance to folk rhymes and jingles. Yiddish is literally the language of David's childhood; it acts as the mother tongue for which he, just like his author, retains an emotional attachment. As a counterpoint to this mother tongue looms Hebrew, the liturgical language that is the Law of the Father, the paternal legacy of Judaism. The rival to both of these is English, which exacts the child's allegiance in all its varied forms, but which also exacts a loss of Jewish identity, an abrupt disinheritance. Roth makes uses of religious texts such as the Book of Isaiah and the Passover Haggadah to invoke both Jewish and Christian hermeneutics as competing forces for the child's soul.

Roth's silence between the publication of *Call It Sleep* and *Mercy of a Rude Stream* was broken only by a collection of several of his shorter pieces in *Shifting Landscape* edited by Mario Materassi in 1987. Interviews with Roth are interspersed between the few short stories and sketches, which include his first published work, a short story entitled "Impressions of a Plumber" written for an English course assignment at City College, and his remarks on the occasion of the award of the 1987 Premio Ninino for the translation of *Call It Sleep* into Italian by Materassi ("The Eternal Plebeian and Other Matters"). Also recorded in the collection is Roth's response to the 1967 Arab-Israeli War, a turning point for the author, who felt "as if I were personally under attack" and who found himself "heading back to being a Jew." His awakening desire to write again produced "Nature's First Green," also reprinted in *Shifting Landscape*. The most remarkable story in this collection, "The Surveyor," revolves around collective memory: a Jewish-American tourist to Spain surveys one of the main intersections in Seville in order to lay a wreath at the exact spot where, during the Inquisition, his ancestors were burned to death as heretics.

Mercy of a Rude Stream, the first volume of which was published in 1994, picks up where *Call It Sleep* leaves off in that the protagonist, whose family has just moved from the Lower East Side to Harlem (as Roth's family had done), is eight years old, and the year is 1914. It is a fictionalized autobiography with Ira Stigman as the young Roth encountering the vulgarity of the streets, on the one hand, and the wonders of language and the joys of playing with words, on the other. "How do you say it? Before the pale blue twilight left your eyes you had to say it, use words that said it: blue, indigo, blue, indigo. Words that matched, matched that swimming star above the hill and tower; what words matched it?" Whereas *Call It Sleep* is Joycean and high modernist in its use of stream-of-consciousness and experimental narrative techniques, *Mercy of a Rude Stream* is more consistently naturalistic, aiming for an evocation of the period, its preoccupation with the war, and its many voices both inside and outside home. Its only departure from this realistic narration is a metanarrative in which the aging author reflects on his own selective memory and artistic choices as he composes on his computer who is also his confidant, and whom he names Ecclesias.

Mercy of a Rude Stream continues Roth's experimentation with multilingualism in that it contains an even greater proportion of non-English words than did *Call It Sleep*. Whereas in the earlier book the non-English references were explained to the reader in a variety of artistic strategies within the narrative, in *Mercy of a Rude Stream* an appended Yiddish glossary provides definitions of single words, idioms, and religious terms. The book charts Ira's Americanization, from his embarrassment at being overheard speaking Yiddish on the train to his great appetite for American literature and folklore: "He was a Christian when he read." The character is filled with self-hatred at times, acutely aware of his outsider status in American culture.

The dialogue between the author and his younger self is repeated in the dialogue between cultures as exemplified in the epigram, an excerpt from Shakespeare's *Henry VIII* (from which the title *Mercy of a Rude Stream* is derived) and a commentary on that excerpt. In a talmudic spirit, Henry Roth criticizes and interprets Shakespeare's lines, and his taking issue with the Bard is characteristic of his overall stance regarding the English language and culture: reverence and dissent. "Not to dare quibble with peerless Will, I still question," begins Henry Roth's commentary on Shakespeare's Henry.

The second volume of *Mercy of a Rude Stream*, entitled *A Diving Rock on the Hudson*, begins with Ira being expelled from high school for stealing a fountain pen and ends with his vindication as a promising young writer who has just won a literary prize at his university. During the years as adolescent and young adult, Ira is obsessed with two subjects, sexuality and Jewishness. Both are sources of self-loathing. He romanticizes the Gentile world, currying favor with Gentile classmates. His Jewish domestic world is portrayed as a claustrophobic and provincial one in which his father is abusive toward both him and his mother. His rebellion against this tyrannical father is linked with his sexual exploits, namely, an incestuous relationship with his sister that lasts many years and that is depicted as a mutual compulsion devoid of all emotion. Intensifying his self-hatred, the incest may account for the stigma in Stigman, for the octogenarian narrator accuses his younger self of committing abominations. "But he had broken through that barrier, broken through religion or taboo, or whatever it was. Before he knew it, he had broken through it. And paid, and paid."

As the autobiographical fiction moves forward to the long silence of Henry Roth, it also offers a new explanation for that silence. The most recent volume, published posthumously, *From Bondage*, recounts Ira's relationship with a university lecturer named Edith (clearly Eda Lou Walton) and complicates the retrospective style in that the author judges not only the young Ira but also the octogenarian writer's attitude toward the youthful character as evident in the manuscript written only five years earlier.

All of Roth's work has focused on border crossings as acts of betrayal and of liberation, whether the borders are of nation, religion, language, or, as in *A Diving Rock on the Hudson*, kinship taboos. Caught in a double bind, Roth's central protagonist as both child and adult can choose either to leave home for a Christian world to which he remains an outsider or to remain tied to his family, a choice that is ultimately represented as incestuous. Cast in their extremity, the choices inevitably lead to contamination of one sort or another, to abomination, and to guilt. The only haven for a brilliant mind so caught between worlds is to trace the linguistic and cultural contours of the space carved out by the writer. Having mythologized his own life in his fictions, Roth tells the story of a tragic banishment from an unlikely Eden, a homogeneous Jewish neighborhood in

Manhattan. "Instead of the Muse," wrote Roth, "I turn for inspiration and a sense of renewal to the Lower East Side."

CRITICAL RECEPTION

When *Call It Sleep* was originally published, it received some mixed reviews, but those who saw its talent were unequivocal in their praise. Writing in the *Nation*, Horace Gregory said, "Henry Roth has written a novel of extraordinary character." Alfred Hayes observed, "There has appeared in America no novel to rival the veracity of this childhood. It is as honest as Dreiser's *Dawn*, but far more sensitive. . . . It is as brilliant as Joyce's *Portrait of the Artist*, but with a wider scope, a richer emotion, a deeper realism." In the Sunday *New York Herald Tribune Books*, Fred T. Marsh claimed that *Call It Sleep* was "the most compelling and moving, the most accurate and profound study of an American slum childhood that has yet appeared in this day. . . . I should like to see *Call It Sleep* win the Pulitzer Prize" (6).

The story of the novel's comeback is unique in the history of American letters. For the twenty-fifth anniversary of the Phi Beta Kappa journal, the *American Scholar*, the editors ran a special feature entitled "The Most Neglected Books of the Past 25 Years." The only title to be mentioned more than once was *Call It Sleep*, cited by both Alfred Kazin and Leslie Fiedler. In Kazin's words, "If you imagine the patient sensibility of Wordsworth and the unselfconscious honesty of Dreiser brought to the shock of his [Roth's] environment upon the senses, you may have some inkling of the slowness, the patience and the strange inner serenity of this book—as of something won, very far deep within, against the conventional cruelties of modern city life" ("The Most Neglected," 478). Fiedler was as lavish with his praise: "For sheer virtuosity, *Call It Sleep* is hard to best; no one has ever distilled such poetry and wit from the counterpoint between the maimed English and the subtle Yiddish of the immigrant. No one has reproduced so sensitively the terror of family life in the imagination of a child caught between two cultures" ("The Most Neglected," 478).

In 1964 Avon reissued the book; it sold a million copies and has since then never been out of print. Irving Howe called it "one of the few genuinely distinguished novels written by a 20th-century American" (jacket cover). A book that had become inaccessible except to a coterie of admirers was transformed overnight into more than a best-seller—"*Call It Sleep* has become a classic," observed the novelist William Styron; "it's embedded, a landmark in our literature." (Allen, 443)

In subsequent reviews, the first two volumes of Roth's six-volume project, *Mercy of a Rude Stream*, have not received nearly the attention nor the adulation of his first work when it was rediscovered. Whatever the assessments of these works that have appeared only recently, it is undoubtedly for *Call It Sleep* that Henry Roth will be remembered as the author of, as some critics have suggested, the great Jewish-American novel.

BIBLIOGRAPHY

Works by Henry Roth

Call It Sleep. 1934. New York: Farrar, Straus and Giroux, 1991.

Shifting Landscape. Philadelphia: Jewish Publication Society, 1987.

Mercy of a Rude Stream I: A Star Shines over Mt. Morris Park. New York: St. Martin's Press, 1994.

A Diving Rock on the Hudson. New York: St. Martin's Press, 1995.

From Bondage. New York: St. Martin's Press, 1996.

Works Cited and Studies of Henry Roth

Allen, Walter. Afterword to *Call It Sleep*. New York: Avon Books, 1964.

Adams, Stephen J. "The Noisiest Novel Ever Written: The Soundscape of Henry Roth's *Call It Sleep*." *Twentieth Century Literature* 35 (Spring 1989): 43–64.

Altenbernd, Lynn. "An American Messiah: Myth in Henry Roth's *Call It Sleep*." *Modern Fiction Studies* 35:4 (Winter 1989): 673–87.

Alter, Robert. *After the Tradition: Essays on Modern Jewish Writing*. New York: Dutton, 1969.

Baumgarten, Murray. *City Scriptures: Modern Jewish Writing*. Cambridge: Harvard University Press, 1982.

Diamant, Naomi. "Linguistic Universes in Henry Roth's *Call It Sleep*." *Contemporary Literature* 27:3 (1986): 336–55.

Epstein, Gary. "Auto-Obituary: The Death of the Artist in Henry Roth's *Call It Sleep*." *Studies in American Jewish Literature* 5:1 (1979): 37–45.

Ferraro, Thomas J. *Ethnic Passages: Literary Immigrants in Twentieth-Century America*. Chicago: University of Chicago Press, 1993.

Fiedler, Leslie. "The Jew in the American Novel." In *To The Gentiles*. New York: Stein and Day, 1971.

———. "The Many Myths of Henry Roth." In *New Essays on Call It Sleep*, ed. Hana Wirth-Nesher. Cambridge: Cambridge University Press, 1996.

———. "The Most Neglected Books of the Past 25 Years." *The American Scholar* 25: 4 (Autumn 1956): 478.

Freedman, William. "Mystical Initiation and Experience in *Call It Sleep*." *Studies in American Jewish Literature* 5.1 (1979): 27–37.

Girgus, Sam. *The New Covenant: Jewish Writers and the American Idea*. Chapel Hill: University of North Carolina Press, 1984.

Gregory, Horace. Review of *Call It Sleep*. *Nation*, February 27, 1935, 235.

Guttmann, Allen. *The Jewish Writer in America: Assimilation and the Crisis of Identity*. New York: Oxford University Press, 1971.

Hayes, Alfred. Review of *Call It Sleep*. *Daily Worker*, March 5, 1935.

Howe, Irving. *World of Our Fathers: The Journey of the East European Jews to America and the Life They Found and Made*. New York: Harcourt Brace Jovanovich, 1976.

Kazin, Alfred. "The Art of 'Call It Sleep.'" *New York Review of Books*, October 10, 1991, 15–18.

———. "The Most Neglected Books of the Last 25 Years." *The American Scholar* 25: 4 Autumn 1956: 478.

Lawrence, Karen. "Roth's *Call It Sleep*: Modernism on the Lower East Side." In *New Essays on Call It Sleep*, ed. Hana Wirth-Nesher. Cambridge: Cambridge University Press, 1996.

Ledbetter, Kenneth. "Henry Roth's *Call It Sleep*: The Revival of a Proletarian Novel." *Twentieth Century Literature* 12 (October 1966): 123–30.

Lesser, Wayne. "A Narrative's Revolutionary Energy: The Example of Henry Roth's *Call It Sleep*." *Criticism* 23:2 (1981): 155–76.

Lyons, Bonnie. *Henry Roth: The Man and His Work*. New York: Cooper Square Publishers, 1976.

Marsh, Fred T. "A Great Novel about Manhattan Boyhood." *New York Herald Tribune Books*, February 17, 1935, 6.

Materassi, Mario. "Shifting Urbanscape: Roth's 'Private' New York City." In *New Essays on Call It Sleep*, ed. Hana Wirth-Nesher. Cambridge: Cambridge University Press, 1996.

McHale, Brian. "Henry Roth in Nighttown, or, Containing *Ulysses*." In *New Essays on Call It Sleep*, ed. Hana Wirth-Nesher. Cambridge: Cambridge University Press, 1996.

Pinsker, Sanford. "The Re-Awakening of Henry Roth's *Call It Sleep*." *Jewish Social Studies* 28:3 (July 1966): 148–58.

Rideout, Walter. *The Radical Novel in the United States, 1900–1954*. Cambridge, MA: Harvard University Press, 1956.

Robbins, Bruce. "Modernism in History, Modernism in Power." In *Modernism Reconsidered*, ed. Robert Kiely. Cambridge, MA: Harvard University Press, 1983.

Samet, Tom. "Henry Roth's Bull Story: Guilt and Betrayal in *Call It Sleep*." *Studies in the Novel* 7:4 (Winter 1975): 569–83.

Sollors, Werner. "A World Somewhere, Somewhere Else: Language, Nostalgic Mournfulness, and Immigrant Family Romance in *Call It Sleep*." In *New Essays on Call It Sleep*, ed. Hana Wirth-Nesher. Cambridge: Cambridge University Press, 1996.

Walden, Daniel. "Henry Roth's *Call It Sleep*: Ethnicity, 'The Sign,' and the Power." *Modern Fiction Studies* 25:2 (Summer 1979): 268–72.

Wirth-Nesher, Hana. "Between Mother Tongue and Native Language: Multilingualism in Henry Roth's *Call It Sleep*." *Prooftexts: A Journal of Jewish Literary History* 10 (1990): 297–312. Reprinted as the Afterword to the Farrar, Straus and Giroux edition of *Call It Sleep*, 1991.

———. "The Modern Jewish Novel: Franz Kafka, Henry Roth, and Amos Oz." *Modern Fiction Studies* 24 (Spring 1978): 91–111.

Wisse, Ruth. "The Classic of Disinheritance." In *New Essays on Call It Sleep*, ed. Hana Wirth-Nesher. Cambridge: Cambridge University Press, 1996.

PHILIP ROTH

(1933–)

Mark Shechner

BIOGRAPHY

Philip Roth was born in Beth Israel Hospital in Newark, New Jersey, on March 9, 1933, to Herman and Bess (Finkel) Roth. Of his mother we know little, and tempted though we might be to take the mothers of his novels—the ego-deflating Sophie Portnoy of *Portnoy's Complaint* and the indulgent Selma Zuckerman of *Zuckerman Unbound*—as approximations of her, we should be cautioned to read them as only fictions and schematic counterlives, shrewish yin and doting yang. Roth's father, however, looms large in his son's writing: in both fiction and memoir he is a *paterfamilias* of operatic dimensions. Owner at one time of a family shoe store that went bankrupt, he became an insurance salesman for Metropolitan Life and was a devoted employee who went door-to-door in the poor black neighborhoods of Newark, extracting from his policyholders premiums they had scarcely the means to pay. Through persistence and devotion to a gentile-run firm that hired few Jews and promoted even fewer, Herman Roth eventually rose to an executive rank and managed an office staff of fifty-two people. *Patrimony*, Roth's portrait of his father's last year of life as he was dying of brain cancer, portrays Herman Roth as a willful man and a practitioner of "tough love" decades before that concept became a mantra of Parent Effectiveness Training.

Herman Roth was not always easy to love in return, and in portraying his father, Philip Roth does not soften all that was spiky and stiff-necked in him. A man of stern judgment and granite will, "He would have told you that you can lead a horse to water and you *can* make him drink—you just hock him and hock him and hock him until he comes to his senses and does it" (*Patrimony*). He was also the great teacher of the plain vision and the plain style: "He taught me the vernacular. He *was* the vernacular, unpoetic and expressive and point-blank, with all the vernacular's glaring limitations and all its durable force" (*Patrimony*).

From 1946 to 1950, Roth attended Weequahic High School in a largely Jewish section of Newark, at a time when, for most Americans, a booming economy and rising expectations did much to soothe the tensions of the emerging Cold War. For Jews, however, the recent slaughter of their European cousins and the subsequent founding of the State of Israel in a condition of peril were still vivid in memory, and in America anti-Semitism was still both an institution and a sport. In his memoir *The Facts*, Roth recalls vividly how gangs from other neighborhoods known as "Down Neck" and "The Ironbound," places as ominous and legendary as the Russian steppes, would swoop down on the placid Jewish community like marauding Cossacks, with baseball bats in their hands and dreams of pogrom in their hearts, especially if Weequahic's football team had had the audacity to defeat its traditional rival, Barringer High. Newark's Weequahic section was a sheltered enclave unaccustomed to rumbling, where young people cultivated all the qualities that were opposed to hardness of heart and fist.

After high school, Roth attended Bucknell University, where he received his B.A., and the University of Chicago, where he completed his M.A. and taught English. It was at Bucknell that Roth did his apprenticeship in scandal when, as editor of the literary magazine, he wrote a satiric sendup of the school's weekly newspaper, whose editor-in-chief was also a captain of the cheerleading squad. The satire occasioned an admonition from the Dean of Men, a censure from the Board of Publications, and a threatening visit by a chivalrous friend of the aggrieved editor. The outline of what would become a pivot of Roth's career, to offend by some act of satire and parody, was already sketched in before graduation from college. Higher registers of literary solemnity were also under cultivation, and Roth published his story "The Day It Snowed" in the *Chicago Review* in 1954, while he was still an undergraduate.

Following a stint in the army, from which Roth received a medical discharge—an early short story, "Novotny's Pain" (1962), is about a soldier with psychosomatic lower-back trouble—Roth enrolled in a Ph.D. program in English at the University of Chicago, where he began to work at his career as a writer. His march toward success was unusually swift; his story "The Contest for Aaron Gold" was published in *Epoch* in 1955 and chosen for *Martha Foley's Best American Short Stories of 1956*.

Roth's marriage in 1959 to Margaret Martinson Williams, a divorcée with a daughter, proved to be a major watershed in his life, a calamity that diverted him from the lockstep progress toward higher attainments he had enjoyed until then, but that also supplied him with the intractable material of problem fiction that his reading in the great classics of modernism had taught him to revere. The street-smart daughter of an alcoholic father, Margaret was a formidable adversary, tricking Roth into marriage by faking her pregnancy with a urine sample bought from a pregnant woman. Though she and Roth were legally separated in 1963, Margaret refused Roth a divorce, and the marriage was only dissolved by Margaret's death in a car crash in 1968. The marriage and Roth's vexation over his vulnerability to a cunning and determined woman left a lasting mark on him, and he would mine and smelt the ore of that marriage for every microgram of pity and terror in it, even comb through the slag, in a host of novels, from *Letting Go* and *When She Was Good* to *My Life as a Man*, that *Encyclopaedia Judaica* of conjugal catastrophe, and down to *Sabbath's Theater*. Indeed, if there is any subject into which Roth's corrosive sense of humor has never fully penetrated, it is that marriage, which calls up no less fear and loathing in *Sabbath's Theater* than it did twenty-one years earlier in *My Life as a Man*.

Roth married again only in 1990, to British actress Claire Bloom, with whom he had already been sharing a life, and that relationship broke up in 1995. Since Roth guards his private life carefully, we know little about that marriage or its dissolution, unless one is to take the novella *Deception*, published in 1990, about a wife's discovery of her writer-husband's journal of adultery, as a window onto the trouble behind that relationship. But Roth is a writer of great cunning, and though we may be certain of this bare minimum—that his art is always nourished by his life—we are on soft ground otherwise in drawing inferences more particular and certain than that.

What we can say with confidence is that Roth's life as a writer has been a full one and that the events that bulk large in his career will, in the long run, be central to his life as well. The privacy he guards is that of a writer whose life has been bound to words, his own and the words of others, and has been far more cloistered than those of his reckless and careening characters. His friendships with other writers, such as Chicago novelist Richard Stern, Israeli writer Aharon Appelfeld, and the Czech novelist Milan Kundera; his championship of writers from Eastern Europe during the bleakest hours of the Communist dictatorships; his editing of the series Writers from the Other Europe for Viking/Penguin Books; his steady production of books at the almost metronomic rate of one every two years, despite distractions and crushing bouts of bad health, including open-heart surgery in 1989; the theatrical playfulness of his later work; and his daring reinventions of other writers, most spectacularly Franz Kafka and Anne Frank, all mark Roth as the most resolutely bookish of our major contemporary writers, the writer for whom the major arena of risk and reward is the written word. "As for living, our servants can that do for us" goes a famous line from the play *Axel* by Villiers de l'Isle-Adam. Rephrase that for Roth and you get, "As for living, our characters can do that for us." That is a significant half-truth, and while Roth has not been as stubborn an anchorite of the sentence as Henry James or Marcel Proust or Roth's own novelist-ascetic, E. I. Lonoff of *The Ghost Writer*, he did put enough of himself into Lonoff to keep us mindful that he is to be numbered among those who, in the phrase of W. B. Yeats, has made his art his life. In the thirty-seven years between 1959 and 1996, Roth has published twenty-one books and much writing that has yet to be collected. This is a capacious and abundant career whose full meaning will take generations of patient scholars to fully interpret and assess.

MAJOR WORKS AND THEMES

The Basic Conflict

Roth's writing through twenty-one books is rich with the experiments and surprises and the detours and reversals that we expect of a major writer, and yet for all its variety, it returns insistently to a single master conflict. It is a theme, moreover, that declares Roth to be a typical product of the Jewish-American synthesis: the struggle to negotiate the competing claims of the individual imperative—the American theme—with the group imperative—the Jewish theme. The former is the optimistic triad of individual happiness, personal freedom, and self-reliance that personifies America's official myth of itself. The other is the belief among Jews at large, a belief both naive and profound, that Jewish writers are "their" writers: heirs to the common history, partners in the common destiny, and therefore spokesmen for the common will. They are agents of the Jewish folk spirit and therefore, like the early masters of secular Yiddish fiction, Mendele Moykher Sforim (S. Y. Abramovitch), I. L. Peretz, and Sholom Aleichem, inseparable from the people about whom they write. The claim is naive for being founded upon an expectation that any modern writer would reject as an infringement upon the absolute right of self-expression. It is naive also in its assumption that the classic Yiddish writers always wrote from firmly within the confines of community sentiment, as if, in effect, Sholom Aleichem waited for a poll before putting pen to paper. They too took critical stances toward the Jewish community and worked at one remove from their subjects. (Of course, Roth can work at up to ten removes from his Jewish subjects. Sholom Aleichem he is not.) There is the added problem that among Jews the common will is notoriously hard to find. Yet the belief that "our" writers are OUR writers is also profound in that the dream of an ideal collectivity based on common destinies and shared responsibilities is lodged in the heart of very many Jews, even the most unyielding of its rebels, of whom Roth is usually accounted one. In wrestling with his or her community, the renegade artist of the high modernist tradition, flying by the nets of nationality, language, and religion, is also wrestling with himself or herself.

Though this tension is only fitfully present in Roth's first three books, *Goodbye, Columbus and Five Short Stories* (1959), *Letting Go* (1962), and *When She Was Good* (1967), for which reason, among others, they have now receded to the status of minor writing, some of the stories in the *Goodbye, Columbus* collection, especially "Eli the Fanatic," "The Defender of the Faith," and "Epstein," do prefigure the struggle that would later erupt with fury in and around Roth's major cause célèbre, *Portnoy's Complaint*, in 1969. It was over his defense of his right to express himself free of community pressures and even to openly face them down that Roth's career and the public perception of it took its initial shape.

Love and Sex

That conflict is not enough to constitute a full and complex body of work, and Roth's writing is sufficiently thick with overlays, abundant with detours and epiphanies, and florid with closely observed particulars of contemporary life to give it the density of a major literature. The thickest of those overlays is the romantic/erotic, which, from *Goodbye, Columbus* in 1959 to *Sabbath's Theater* in 1995, remains remarkably constant: epics of hopeless longing punctuated by bursts of pleasure and then pratfalls and collapses. From Neil Klugman's shattered romance with Brenda Patimkin in *Goodbye, Columbus* to Mickey Sabbath's reckless mourning for Drenka Balich in *Sabbath's Theater*, thirty-six years later, the drama of love and loss and the pressure of pent-up sexuality that drives it remains constant in Roth's writing, expressing itself as ever more demanding, ever more uncontrollable, ever more anarchic and dangerous as the years go on.

Though there is always the bustle of coming and going in Roth's writing, much of its meaning clusters where the loyalty/independence tug-of-war and the romantic/erotic roughhousing intersect. Roth's imagination catches fire at that crossroads, and it is there that most of the more inspired fictions originate: *Portnoy's Complaint, The Ghost Writer, The Anatomy Lesson, The Counterlife, Operation Shylock*, and *Sabbath's Theater*. There it is too that some of Roth's most vivid characters can be found: not only Alex Portnoy, Mickey Sabbath, and the many versions of Nathan Zuckerman who pop out of the Zuckerman dressing room like rabbits out of a magician's hat, but also their inevitable consort, the Shiksa, in all her variety: the Pilgrim, the Pumpkin, and the Monkey of *Portnoy*; man-eating wives named Lydia and Maureen in *My Life as a Man;* the Maria of the many flavors in *The Counterlife*; the Jenny, the Diana, and the Jaga who queue up to minister to an afflicted Nathan Zuckerman in *The Anatomy Lesson*; the beguiling Amy Bellette of *The Ghost Writer*; the treacherous Jinx Possesski of *Operation Shylock*; and the polymorphously perverse Drenka Balich of *Sabbath's Theater*. She is the one and the many, the great carnal cupcake and the poisoned apple all in one. Yet there too, at that intersection of identity and appetite, we find her countertype, who may be the most inspired and risky of all Roth's female inventions: the Anne Frank of *The Ghost Writer*, whom a young Nathan Zuckerman dreams Amy Bellette might be.

The Ego, the Id, and the Superego

Third, there is the anguish of being oneself and the intense concentration on the afflicted ego that has occasioned the charges of narcissism and self-indulgence that have been leveled at Roth. Roth's central male characters are more unremittingly introspective and more persistently tormented than any others in American literature. If this is to be accounted a shortcoming in Roth's writing, it is one in which an entire literary culture is complicit, insofar as the main avenue of Jewish fiction writing in America, from Abraham Cahan to the present, has dedicated itself to the project of creating a Jewish persona that could detach itself from the shackles of Old World tradition and submit itself to the self-reliance, the uncertainty, the desublimation, and the commercialism of American life, but would also distinguish itself from the Jewish middle class by the obstacles of conscience it set in its own path to self-realization. To disaffiliate from both cultures while exercising one's right to the pursuit of happiness was the intricate and Sisyphean enterprise to which these writers applied themselves. A composite Jewish persona that evolved in American fiction, from David Levinsky in Abraham Cahan's novel through Sara Smolinsky in Anzia Yezierska's *The Bread Givers*, David Schearl in Henry Roth's *Call It Sleep*, the personae created in fiction and poetry by Delmore Schwartz and Isaac Rosenfeld, and the assorted troubled heroes of Saul Bellow's novels, to virtually every "comedian of alienation" (Irving Howe's slashing phrase) Roth ever created, expressed a consistency of anxiety, self-absorption, and neurosis that identified it as a typical product of the Jewish-American synthesis. In America, this countertradition of alienation developed its own tradition, for which Roth is the last champion and Mickey Sabbath of *Sabbath's Theater*, the character who finally crosses the line from naughtiness to criminality, is the final, dazzling incarnation.

If Roth exploits the ceremonies of alienation that a prior literature had handed to him, however, he does push them to a febrile pitch of panic, creating characters who invent themselves by dismantling themselves, enduring such grievous self-affliction at times that their dramas of transgression and atonement assume ludicrous and surrealistic proportions. Thus the gruesome ending of *The Anatomy Lesson*, in which Nathan Zuckerman lies speechless in a hospital room, his jaw broken and his wagging tongue silenced by an intoxicated fall against a tombstone at the end of a flight of rage and misbehavior; thus too the end of *Sabbath's Theater*, in which a roguish and depressed Mickey Sabbath steps back from his intended suicide, uttering this marvelous last line: "How could he leave? How could he go? Everything he hated was here." Thus all the books in which Alex Portnoy, Peter Tarnopol, David Alan Kepesh, Nathan Zuckerman, and characters named Philip Roth wind up in hospitals, on analysts' couches, in their brothers' apartments, blubbering like infants, in divorce courts, inside the skin of a gigantic female breast, in the grave, loveless and alone in Newark.

Some of these dramas are mediated by psychoanalysis, and analysts named Spielvogel and Klinger do cameo appearances in some books (*Portnoy's Complaint, The Breast, My Life as a Man*), where, as reality instructors, they are also guides to the psychopathology of everyday life. In other novels and stories, the upwellings of the hallucinatory and wildly improbable are sponsored by Franz Kafka (in the story "Imagining Kafka, or, 'I Always Wanted You to

Admire My Fasting' '' and the novel *The Professor of Desire*) or stoked by drugs and alcohol, as in *The Anatomy Lesson*, where a killer combination of marijuana, Percodan, and vodka propels Nathan Zuckerman from mere indignation over hostile reviews into a death spiral of rage.

Why take an interest in any of this, since in summary it sounds claustral and dreary and substantially lacking in sharable, public meaning? To that question there is a five-word answer that sums up Roth's value to us as a writer: because it is utterly brilliant.

The Voice

Roth's severest critics never fail to concede the qualities that send us back to his books time and again, no matter how distressed we may have been with the last performance. Roth is a master stylist whose ear for speech is the most finely calibrated of any living American writer and who shows a composer's ability to modulate between timbres and registers of the speaking voice. In *The Ghost Writer*, E. I. Lonoff, the master to whom the young Nathan Zuckerman retreats for solace and instruction, speaks admiringly of Nathan's own voice, "the most compelling voice I've encountered in years, certainly for somebody starting out." In a memorable phrase, he distinguishes voice from style: "I mean voice, something that begins at around the back of the knees and reaches well above the head." In a recent article on Jewish stylistics, Robert Alter noted how Roth gets "some of his liveliest effects by playing one linguistic register against another" and observed that the strength and weakness in much of Roth's writing are in "the energy of its verbal improvisations; so that instead of character, event, and moral or conceptual development, we get a series of shtiklach, the best of them displaying stylistic and attitudinal fireworks, many bearing the signs of self-indulgence" ("The Jewish Voice," 39).

Archetype and Mask

As a creator of character, Roth works comfortably with a dual conception of character as both archetype and mask, drawing upon the one or the other according to his needs. From the one he derives what is lasting in human relations, like the son's feelings for the father, out of which he gets the touching, sometimes grueling encounters of fathers and sons, like those between himself and his father in *Patrimony* or between Nathan Zuckerman and his dying father in *Zuckerman Unbound* or David Kepesh and his father in *The Professor of Desire*. Each relationship draws upon a depth of emotion, a legacy of recollection, and a heartstring stretched to the breaking point. *Patrimony* stands out among Roth's fictions of life in crisis and the world in flux as a testament to the piece of his own heart that is as durable and tough-minded as his father was.

From the conception of character as mask Roth gets the brisk theatrical effects of *The Counterlife*. A novel in five freestanding episodes, it plays variations on a pas de deux of two brothers, Nathan and Henry Zuckerman, as they wrestle with their heart problems (amorous and medical), their Jewish identities and beliefs, and their brotherhood in the company of Henry's wife Carol, a troupe of mad Israelis—including a militant rabbi, a terrorist wannabe, and members of Israel's Shin Bet or internal-security force—and the usual chorus line of delectable shiksas. Characters refuse to stay fixed in this floating world, as Henry and Nathan trade lives and predicaments, even heart surgeries and deaths, as easily as actors change wardrobes, and Nathan even submits to an interview from the grave. An elegant performance, *The Counterlife* traces an elaborate counterpoint between the inertia of history and the agility of the imagination and would appear to be evidence that a novel may contradict itself repeatedly without losing its unity of purpose, and that by keeping its fragments in suspension it can keep its readers in suspense.

That side of Roth too is responsible for the subsequent novel *Deception: A Novel* (1990). A spare and meticulous performance, *Deception* features a novelist named "Philip," whose wife has discovered a notebook in which her novelist-husband had detailed his clandestine affair with another woman. Don't be deceived, protests "Philip." I have imagined the woman and this relationship; you're confusing my art with my life, and my life is humdrum so that my art can live more daringly than I do. He even claims to have invented the "I" of his journal. "It is *far* from myself—it's play, it's a game, it is an *impersonation* of myself! Me ventriloquizing myself."

Raw Nerve and Raw Nerves

The voice by which we now know Roth did not come easily, and when it came, it proved to be irreverent, desperate, satirical, libidinous, and unsociable. Even when it was charming, it could be provoking. The book in which it made its debut was Roth's fourth, *Portnoy's Complaint* (1969), an exhibition so spectacular that it remains, twenty-seven years since publication, Roth's signature book. *Portnoy's Complaint* paraded itself as a "breakthrough" novel in which psychoanalysis operated as both couch and culture, setting and viewpoint. It was the opposite of everything *Letting Go* (1962) and *When She Was Good* (1967) had aspired to be: unbuttoned where they were contained, raunchy where they were sober, low-minded where they were high-minded. It was an excited confession of masturbation, filial impiety, sexual obsession, and sexual failure, performed as a brand of Freudian slapstick, with ego, id, and superego going after each other with wooden sticks. Its blend of cultural rebellion, comic mayhem, and psychoanalysis brought Roth a mass audience and a movie contract, though not the universal approbation of literary critics or Jewish parents, who peered uneasily past the laughter toward the sharp teeth below.

Portnoy's Complaint was also Roth's wager that he would strike pay dirt and redeem his energies, his time, and his reputation from the nightmare that haunts all writers: the slide into being just another face in the crowd. It succeeded so brilliantly that volumes could be written about its literary reception alone, and it is not accidental that Roth himself has remained obsessed by the subject. From the moment of its debut, *Portnoy's Complaint* became a red flag, and virtually everything Roth would write for the next twenty-seven years would bear some relation to it: as footnote, midrash, expiation, or challenge to go beyond. *Portnoy's Complaint* became the touchstone of Roth's career, a show-piece as well as an exorcism gone awry, which in turn would need to be ex-orcised or, now and then, one-upped.

The Breast (1972) is a footnote. A parable of an English professor who is transformed overnight into a man-sized female breast, it reads like a dream that a patient such as Alex Portnoy might produce for an analyst such as Dr. Spiel-vogel. It is a performance for the left hand, a midsummer night's wet dream that disappointed those readers hoping for a rollicking Portnoyan encore. Poten-tially hilarious though the situation was, Roth kept the humor in check and told the story as a case history, though a case history written up by the case. The novel did signal the arrival of a new patron saint, who would soon displace Freud as the source of parables and paradoxes in Roth's writing: Franz Kafka.

Roth did not, however, jettison his comic gift in subsequent novels, he just depersonalized it and projected it outward: satirically toward President Richard Nixon in *Our Gang* (1971), a satiric monologue on one President Trick E. Dixon, friend to the unborn, and lovingly toward baseball in a *vaudeville noir* about a team without a home field, *The Great American Novel* (1973). The former book is scattershot, and Richard Nixon was always a sitting duck, while the latter book is a harum-scarum in which the baseball evolves into a metaphor for Jewry and the wandering team becomes the Diaspora. That the team comes to grief is the inevitable end to the parable, though along the way, before the Jewish parallels grow clear, there is much of the madcap comedy that was Roth's trademark in the 1970s.

The Breast, Our Gang, and *The Great American Novel* were diversions from the main axis of Roth's writing, the pseudoautobiographical: autobiographical because Roth's own life has provided its basic scripts and pseudo because they are so overwrought with dreamwork that the most intimate therapeutic purges are likely to be the most hyperbolic inventions. In other words, one cannot read Roth's fiction for the "life" behind it any more than one can ignore the personal premise. The mystery of their connection, which changes from book to book, keeps the reader in suspense.

No book better displayed the Roth shell game than *My Life as a Man* (1973), whose counterpoint of life and art is hard-wired into the book's structure. A novel about the marital misadventures of the novelist Peter Tarnopol, it is di-vided into three sections: two "useful fictions," Tarnopol's own efforts to turn his marriage into fiction, "Salad Days" and "Courting Disaster (or Serious in the Fifties)," and a long coda entitled "My True Story." Personal experience and grief are turned into theme and variations, in which "My True Story" need be no truer to the life of the writer within the book than the useful fictions; it is merely framed to give a sturdier illusion of verisimilitude. *My Life as a Man* was a major production that survives rereading. Its prose is pungent and aquiver with the asperities of a sour marriage, the jargon of the clinic, and the argot of the street. It is this sensitivity to language that explains the final assessment of psychoanalysis in this book, for it is language at last that drives a wedge between Peter Tarnopol and his analyst, Dr. Spielvogel, and sends the former back to his writers' colony and his typewriter for a session of autotherapy that may produce, if not the glow of release, at least a manuscript for his agent.

If we concede that the next novel, *The Professor of Desire* (1977), is an interregnum, a *reculer pour mieux sauter*, then the next major work of Roth's career might be the trilogy of novels that appeared in rapid succession over a period of four years: *The Ghost Writer* (1979), *Zuckerman Unbound* (1981), and *The Anatomy Lesson* (1983), to which the novella *The Prague Orgy* (1985) would serve as an epilogue in a bound volume titled *Zuckerman Bound* in 1985. Though there is no continuous narrative that requires us to read them in sequence, they are discrete windows on the life of the novelist Nathan Zuckerman, whose adventures at times parallel Roth's own. All are fables of martyrdom: *The Ghost Writer* a fable of the artist as a martyr to language, *Zuckerman Unbound* a fable of the artist as a martyr to his fame, and *The Anatomy Lesson* a fable of the artist as a martyr to his critics.

The martyred artist in *The Ghost Writer* is a Zuckerman who has outraged his family with the short story "Higher Education," which hung family laundry out for public inspection. In his flight from censure in Newark, Zuckerman finds respite in the New England home of one E. I. Lonoff, a Chekhov-like writer who refuses to be martyred except by sentences, over which he labors obsessively, turning them around and around and around. In Lonoff's home, Zuckerman meets a young woman whom he fancies to be Anne Frank and about her he dreams up a story of her escape and flight to America under an assumed name. He aspires to marry her on the spot as a way of outflanking his critics and acquiring a Jewish identity as one might acquire a tattoo. This tinkering with Anne Frank was a gambit that most critics deemed successful, prompting some to proclaim *The Ghost Writer* Roth's most consummately crafted novel. It is certainly a daring invention in which Roth demonstrated that he could spin elaborate fables around an autobiographical base and strike notes of wonder, mystery, and delicate irony while not neglecting to remind critics and adversaries that he had not forgotten them.

The two other novels in the Zuckerman series also exist in the backwash of *Portnoy's Complaint*, as Zuckerman finds himself having to deal with the aftershocks of his own *succès de scandale*, a novel titled *Carnovsky*, which had bedeviled him with crazed admirers and indignant detractors. One turns to these books less for their plots and characters than for the exhibition of mastery, as Roth pulls rabbits out of hats, cards out of sleeves, coins out of ears, and phrases out of a word hoard that seems as dense as the *Oxford English Dictionary*. Even in moments of high agitation, the reader is aware of the maestro at work, jotting off his *Sturm* and his *Drang* as coolly as he lays down his *allegro* and his *penseroso*. While in the book the waters may be roiled, this Prospero is in full command of earth, wind, fire, and water. Not that character is neglected: indeed, *Zuckerman Unbound* features a splendid grotesque named Alvin Pepler, an ex-marine, a muttering yenta, and an idiot savant of pop arcana, whose past as a game-show fall guy is based on the life of Herbert Stempel, who took a fall for Charles Van Doren on "Twenty-One" in 1956 and was betrayed by the show's producers afterwards.

The Anatomy Lesson is a belated rejoinder to an attack leveled by Irving Howe in 1972, discussed in the section "Critical Reception." Howe's strident indictments festered until Roth went ballistic over them in *The Anatomy Lesson*, a brawling, splenetic farce in which Howe and *Commentary* editor Norman Podhoretz are cast as villainous clowns, and Nathan Zuckerman himself is a blowtop who spews his rage on everyone, including himself. A more rancorous book than the later *Sabbath's Theater* and lacking the latter's polymorphous perversity and tender reminiscence, *The Anatomy Lesson* was Roth baying on the heath like a Jewish King Lear, his Zuckerman mad on grievances and pharmaceuticals, as an object lesson in what happens when the return of the repressed meets the rock of reality: a shattered ego and a shattered jaw.

Published together as *Zuckerman Bound* in 1985, these novels were provided with an epilogue, *The Prague Orgy*, in which Zuckerman's ordeal of personal martyrdom is dissolved in the greater martyrdom of a nation, Czechoslovakia, where Zuckerman has gone on a mission to smuggle out Yiddish manuscripts, only to run afoul of the Czech police, who exercise a brand of literary criticism far more crushing than anything Zuckerman had encountered in Newark or *Commentary*. In the 1970s, Roth became involved with Eastern Europe and its writers, not only as a champion of exiled writers, like Milan Kundera, but as the editor of a series for Penguin Books, Writers from the Other Europe, that introduced many important writers to Western readers for the first time, among them Kundera, Tadeusz Borowski, Tadeusz Konwicki, Ludvík Vaculík, Bruno Schulz, and George Konrád. Any comprehensive assessment of Roth's career as a writer and a public intellectual will have to include this episode and his contribution to the international cause of intellectual freedom.

The last of the Zuckerman novels is *The Counterlife* (1986), which brought the Zuckerman variations to a rousing conclusion with a Zuckerman fugue all its own. Already discussed under the heading of "Archetype and Mask" as one of Roth's premier demonstrations of Oscar Wilde's "freedom of masks," it is a tale told in five movements, like a Shakespeare play or perhaps the Five Books of Moses. The freestanding acts, "Basel," "Judea," "Aloft," "Gloucestershire," and "Christendom," form something of an open circuit, insofar as the end of "Christendom" represents no particular resolution of the problems posed in "Basel." Each one restates in different terms the book's central problem: what is a Jew and how is he (and it is always he) to live? What is the relation of Diaspora Jewry to Israel, or Israel to the Diaspora, or the "I" of Western individualism to the "we" of Middle Eastern communitarianism? True to Roth's sense of Jewish history as open-ended, fixed points turn out to be floating decimals, and even the Star of David is a black hole. The novel was evidence of Roth's fascination with theater during the 1980s, due perhaps to his life with Claire Bloom, or possibly as a sign of the performative side of his talent wanting to break out into actual theater, at least by imitating it in prose.

This flirtation with the masquerade of identity, the "me ventriloquizing myself," spilled over into Roth's short memoir of his youth in Newark and early manhood, *The Facts* (1988), which plays off against *The Counterlife* by having Roth submit a draft manuscript of the book to Nathan Zuckerman, asking his advice on whether the book should be published. Zuckerman fires off this reply: don't publish it. "You are far better off writing about me than 'accurately' reporting on your own life."

Zuckerman's case against *The Facts* is that it is only one slant on the facts among many, designed in particular to cast a halo over a childhood that appears to be far more tense and dramatic in Roth's fiction. It casts Roth himself in the unlikely role of a man without will or force, someone to whom things happen, like a disastrous marriage. "You try to pass off here as frankness what looks to me like the dance of the seven veils—what's on the page is like a code for something missing." "Are you not aware yourself of [*The Facts'*] fiction-making tricks? Think of the exclusions, the selective nature of it, the very pose of fact-facer. Is all this manipulation truly unconscious or is it pretending to be unconscious?" By this time, however, the counterlife gambit has grown shopworn, and *The Facts* lacks the vitality and force of Roth's later memoir of his father, *Patrimony*, in which the weight of the actual seems to have more traction and thrust than the blatantly invented.

Odds and Ends

The roster of post-*Counterlife* books presents more surprises than continuities: *Deception: A Novel* (1990); *Patrimony: A True Story* (1991); *Operation Shylock: A Confession* (1993); and *Sabbath's Theater* (1995). As always, there are balletic phrases, darkside encounters, riffs of wacky humor, and drop-dead epiphanies that seize the heart, and *Sabbath's Theater* won the National Book Award for 1995, Roth's first since *Goodbye, Columbus* in 1959. However, Roth himself slips out of focus, and in *Operation Shylock*, he gives in to windiness and scatter, as the scalded heart shrivels to a mere poisoned pen. Even the doubling, in which a character named Philip Roth encounters in Israel another Philip Roth, a Dostoyevskian doppelgänger and nemesis, appears to flow mechanically from modern-fiction formula rather than organically from the issues of Zionism and the Holocaust, which are presumably what the book is about. Few things Roth has written have come off as less convincing than the face-off between the two Philip Roths: Roth the writer and the double whom the first Roth refers to as Moishe Pipik—even though it may in fact have happened that way, as Roth has claimed in interviews. A reckless, overstated, improvident, and paranoid book about reckless, overstated, improvident, and paranoid Israeli politics, *Operation Shylock* is woven with the intricacies of Israel's Palestinian dilemma and teeming with characters out of standard moral allegory: the evil twins—a good Roth and a bad Roth—one Wanda Jane "Jinx" Possesski, the Jew-hating (except in bed) consort of Roth-Pipik, George Ziad, an American-educated Palestinian who has become a PLO operative, and Louis Smilesburger, a Mossad agent, who recruits "Roth" for a secret mission. The plot is dense, but the history, the politics, the intrigue, the menace, the scheming, the charlatanry, the paranoia, and the tirades, "the whole pungent ideological mulch of overstatement and lucidity," as "Roth" puts it, have the air of simple reportage with the normal sensory filters turned off.

Which brings us in the end to *Sabbath's Theater*, the book whose naked psychic spillage and free-ranging venery—its scenes of sodomy, fetishism, voyeurism, water sports, and all-purpose whoopie—won a National Book Award that had to be footnoted with embarrassed disclaimers by members of the awards committee. The crucial difference between Mickey Sabbath of *Sabbath's Theater* and previous Roth heroes who have found themselves either overstimulated or overwrought or overcome is that the former all wanted to be relieved of their illnesses, while Sabbath wants only to be perfected in his: to be totally perverse, totally humiliated, totally defeated. At sixty-four, so crippled by arthritis that he can no longer perform the Indecent Theater that used only fingers for puppets, Sabbath has made his illness his art in order to plumb the secrets of shame: to learn how it feels to be thoroughly isolated, alienated, and without justification.

Yet the power of *Sabbath's Theater* is inseparable from its abrasiveness: soften the tone and you sap its energy. Abrasiveness and power come right out of Roth's myth of himself as the renegade Jew, forever outside the legion of decency, the society of good taste, and the entire world, Jewish and American, of the Normal. *Sabbath's Theater* is an antinormality screed in the middle of a career that has featured flirtations with various definitions of the healthy and the normal. If one can "explain" this at all, risky business at best, one might say that it is the latest and most extreme elaboration of Roth's abiding myth of himself as the renegade and unassimilable Jew, defiantly estranged from his community, after certain preceding books had raised expectations that Roth was poised to relent and join the congregation. Here is our author, sixty-something, quadruple bypassed, and separated from his companion of twenty years, actress Claire Bloom, and just as red in cock and claw as he was twenty-six years ago in *Portnoy's Complaint* (1969).

CRITICAL RECEPTION

The sheer magnitude of the critical writing about Roth stupefies. If by the mid-1970s we might have spoken of a Roth critical industry, what about the 1990s? A Roth multinational corporation? The effort to list it, let alone read and make sense of it, is likely to knock the most patient scholar senseless. To cite a simple example, the best monitoring posts for book reviews of any American writer are the Gale Research series *Contemporary Authors* (*CA*) and *Contemporary Literary Criticism* (*CLC*) and a recent check shows synoptic essays on Roth in *CA* 1–4, *CANR* 1, and *CA* 46, as well as *CLC*, volumes 1, 2, 3, 4, 6, 9, 15, 22, 31, 47, 66, and 86. Some of these entries are long, including one in *CLC* 66 that runs to thirty-nine pages on *Portnoy's Complaint* alone. If the magnitude of the Roth critical canon alone tells us anything, even before we read any of it, it is that Roth possesses a sizable readership of people to whom he matters, and that to read him is to have an opinion about him. There are approximately fifteen books on Roth alone and perhaps three times that many with long chapters devoted to him. Almost all of this writing belongs to one of two categories: disinterested scholarship, in which Roth is studied and dissected as entomologists might study and dissect butterflies or *drosophilae*, and raging debate, in which Roth is studied and dissected as prosecutors and defense attorneys might study and dissect a serial killer on trial. The trial transcripts are more engaging than the scholarly monographs, reflecting as they do the schismatic cultural environment into which his books were published and in which they have had their most telling impact.

It is not true, however, that Roth has had merely an adversarial relationship with his reviewers and critics. That is the myth that he himself has disseminated, and while Roth has in fact felt the lash with uncommon frequency, he has received an equal amount—nay, an overabundance—of extravagant praise that should buffer the blows and cauterize the wounds. How else to account for these prizes alone: the National Book Award for Fiction in 1960 for *Goodbye, Columbus*; the National Book Critics Circle Award in 1987 for *The Counterlife*; the National Book Critics Circle Award in 1992 for *Patrimony*; the PEN/Faulkner Award for Fiction in 1993 for *Operation Shylock; Time* magazine's Best American Novel of 1993 award for *Operation Shylock*; and the National Book Award for Fiction in 1995 for *Sabbath's Theater*? Add to these a Guggenheim Fellowship, a Ford Foundation grant, something called the Aga Khan Award, and a run of toasts and celebrations that should stroke the ego and swell the head, not to say the purse, of any ambitious writer. Toss in a crate of critical books, commercially successful films made of *Goodbye, Columbus* and *Portnoy's Complaint*, a PBS television play made of *The Ghost Writer*, and stage productions of some early stories by director Larry Arrick.

Still, devastating condemnation did come Roth's way in sharp blows, leaving a mark on his writing and on his equilibrium. Roth took none of this lightly, recorded some of it bitterly, and even in some books and essays stood toe-to-toe with his detractors—see Roth's own *Reading Myself and Others*, most particularly essays titled "Writing and the Powers That Be," "On Portnoy's Complaint," "Document Dated July 27, 1969," and "Writing about Jews." There was a certain panic and wariness in the response to Roth's writing by

Jewish readers that extended back to the *Goodbye, Columbus* stories. Roth laid out this history in "Writing about Jews," and if the indignant and menacing tone of some of the hostile letters quoted by Roth brings to mind the case of Indian novelist Salman Rushdie, who is under *fatwa* from Iranian Islamic authorities and lives in hiding, there is good reason why it should. For Roth's sin of suggesting in public that a Jew might commit adultery, as he did in the story "Epstein," the Anti-Defamation League received a letter demanding, "What is being done to silence this Man? Medieval Jews would have known what to do with him." And that was only for "Epstein."

The storm that broke over Roth with the publication of *Portnoy's Complaint* in 1969 was so violent that Roth had to leave the country while waiting for it to blow over, which it did not for many years. Typical of the smart bombs dropped on Roth during this period was Bruno Bettelheim's putting Alex Portnoy and his creator on the couch and declaring them both self-hating Jews living in exile. Just as Roth thought that reason might be restored, he was blindsided by a one-two punch in the December 1972 issue of *Commentary*, a brief screed titled "Laureate of the New Class" by *Commentary* editor Norman Podhoretz and a long diatribe, "Philip Roth Reconsidered," by Irving Howe. The details of the Podhoretz-Howe thesis have been amply dealt with elsewhere (see especially Mark Shechner, "Philip Roth: The Road of Excess" in *After the Revolution*). Sidestepping the vulgar issue that Roth was an informer to the Gentiles—the general thesis of the earlier attacks—Podhoretz assailed Roth as the novelist laureate of "the New Class," a social class of lightweight arrivistes that set the new cultural agendas—radical chic—and political ones—anti-Communist—that were seen as corrosive to American security and moral resoluteness. Howe's agenda came down to a few points: that Roth was a "willful" writer who imposed himself on his characters and denied them fullness, contour, or surprise; that he lacked patience for uncertainties, mysteries, and doubts; that he was vulgar; and that he was hampered by a "thin personal culture." Fuel was added to this fire a few months later by Marie Syrkin, who, in a letter to *Commentary* (March 1973), suggested that Podhoretz and Howe had let Roth off rather too lightly.

Roth had his defenders, Wilfred Sheed's response in the *New York Times Book Review* the following year being both vigorous and sensible. Roth too not only leaped to his own defense but struck back hard in essays and novels. *The Ghost Writer* finds Nathan Zuckerman riding out a storm of family indignation over a story much like "Epstein" in the countryside retreat of the writer E. I. Lonoff, and *The Anatomy Lesson*, which deals directly with the attacks in *Commentary*, casts Podhoretz and Howe as hypocrites and lurid clowns named Morton Horowitz and Milton Appel, about whom Nathan Zuckerman, stoned out of his mind on a plane ride, tells ribald and riotously funny stories.

This *Kulturkampf* is the framework into which much later commentary would fall, censure and justification, and it has tended to drown out the "value-neutral" scholarship, since reviewers and scholars still feel constrained, by Roth's writing as well as by his history, to stake out positions. Roth will always occasion polemics: the disdain of the righteous is a confirmation he courts, the eye of a storm is a command post he cherishes, and it must strike him as ironic that he should win the National Book Award in 1995 with his most abrasive book to date, *Sabbath's Theater*. Yet it is also evident from the reviews of *Sabbath's Theater*, which were predictably mixed, that the charged atmosphere of cultural crisis that enveloped the earlier polemics has lifted, and nothing vital seems to be at stake in Roth's literary high crimes and misdemeanors. He has become just another major writer, a Jewish John Updike with a tad more egotism and performative energy and verbal fireworks in him. It is as if his famous aphorism about the difference between literature under communism and under democracy has turned out to be prophetic for his own career: under the former, nothing goes and everything matters; under the latter, everything goes and nothing matters. How ironic indeed! You set out to be a scandal, and you wind up being the toast of New York, an irony that Roth more than anyone else should be able to savor.

BIBLIOGRAPHY

Works by Philip Roth

This list of works by Roth is limited to books and collections. There is enough uncollected writing to fill another three or four sizable volumes.

Fiction

Goodbye, Columbus and Five Short Stories. Boston: Houghton Mifflin, 1959.
Letting Go. New York: Random House, 1962.
When She Was Good. New York: Random House, 1967.
Portnoy's Complaint. New York: Random House, 1969.
Our Gang (Starring Tricky and His Friends). New York: Random House, 1971.
The Breast. New York: Holt, Rinehart and Winston, 1972.
The Great American Novel. New York: Holt, Rinehart and Winston, 1973.
My Life as a Man. New York: Holt, Rinehart and Winston, 1974.
The Professor of Desire. New York: Farrar, Straus and Giroux, 1977.
The Ghost Writer. New York: Farrar, Straus and Giroux, 1979.
A Philip Roth Reader. New York: Farrar, Straus and Giroux, 1980.
Zuckerman Unbound. New York: Farrar, Straus and Giroux, 1981.
The Anatomy Lesson. New York: Farrar, Straus and Giroux, 1983.
Zuckerman Bound: A Trilogy and Epilogue. New York: Farrar, Straus and Giroux, 1985.
The Counterlife. New York: Farrar, Straus and Giroux, 1986.
Deception: A Novel. New York: Simon and Schuster, 1990.
Operation Shylock: A Confession. New York: Simon and Schuster, 1993.
Sabbath's Theater. Boston: Houghton Mifflin, 1995.

Nonfiction

Reading Myself and Others. New York: Farrar, Straus and Giroux, 1975.
The Facts: A Novelist's Autobiography. New York: Farrar, Straus and Giroux, 1988.
Patrimony: A True Story. New York: Simon and Schuster, 1991.

Works Cited and Studies of Philip Roth

Books, Including Collections, Bibliographies, and Book-Length Critical Studies

Appelfeld, Aharon. *Beyond Despair: Three Lectures and a Conversation with Philip Roth.* Trans. Jeffrey Green. New York: Fromm International, 1994.
Baumgarten, Murray, and Barbara Gottfried. *Understanding Philip Roth.* Columbia: University of South Carolina Press, 1990.
Bloom, Harold, ed. *Philip Roth.* New York: Chelsea House, 1986.
Cooper, Alan. *Philip Roth and the Jews.* Albany: State University of New York Press, 1996.
Halio, Jay L. *Philip Roth Revisited.* New York: Twayne, 1992.
Jones, Judith Paterson, and Guinevera A. Nance. *Philip Roth.* New York: Ungar, 1981.
Lee, Hermione. *Philip Roth.* New York: Methuen, 1982.
McDaniel, John N. *The Fiction of Philip Roth.* Haddonfield, NJ: Haddonfield House, 1974.
Milbauer, Asher Z., and Donald G. Watson, eds. *Reading Philip Roth.* New York: St. Martin's Press, 1988.
Pinsker, Sanford. *The Comedy That "Hoits": An Essay on the Fiction of Philip Roth.* Columbia: University of Missouri Press, 1975.
———, ed. *Critical Essays on Philip Roth.* Boston: G. K. Hall, 1982.
Rodgers, Bernard F., Jr. *Philip Roth.* Boston: Twayne, 1978.
———. *Philip Roth: A Bibliography.* Metuchen, NJ: Scarecrow Press, 1974 and 1984.
Searles, George J., ed. *Conversations with Philip Roth.* Jackson: University Press of Mississippi, 1992.
———. *The Fiction of Philip Roth and John Updike.* Carbondale: Southern Illinois University Press, 1985.
Walden, Daniel, ed. *The Changing Mosaic: From Cahan to Malamud, Roth, and Ozick.* Albany: State University of New York Press, 1993.

Articles or Parts of Books

This section is so vast that all one can do is draw a circle, cast out whole categories, and then throw darts at the remaining items and hope to hit a few important ones. Omitted are most book reviews from metropolitan newspapers and popular weeklies, though a good deal of this writing is as acute and penetrating as anything to be found in the scholarly journals. For the rest, one takes informed guesses based on intuition and already-existing collections of citations, like those in *Contemporary Authors* or *Contemporary Literary Criticism*, to which I refer readers desiring more material. There is a bias here toward recent material, from the late 1980s and 1990s, on the principle that it is likely to contain citations to earlier essays and studies, thus leading scholars and students back through a chain of references to the earlier commentary. I am indebted to

Derek Royal, whose Philip Roth home page on the World Wide Web is the source of many of these citations.

Alter, Robert. "Defenders of the Faith." *Commentary* 84 (July 1987): 52–55.

———. "The Jewish Voice: Jewish Intellectual Life." *Commentary* 100:4 (October 1995): 39ff.

———. "The Spritzer." *New Republic* 208:14 (April 5, 1993): 31–34.

Atlas, James. "The Laureates of Lewd: P. Roth, G. Vidal, and J. Updike." *Gentlemen's Quarterly* 63 (April 1993): 202–7.

Bailey, Peter J. " 'Why Not Tell the Truth?': The Autobiographies of Three Fiction Writers." *Critique* 32 (1991): 211–23.

Berryman, Charles. "Philip Roth and Nathan Zuckerman: A Portrait of the Artist as a Young Prometheus." *Contemporary Literature* 31 (1990): 177–90.

Bertens, J. W. " 'The Measured Self' vs. 'the Insatiable Self': Some Notes on Philip Roth." In *From Cooper to Philip Roth: Essays on American Literature*, ed. J. Bakker and D.R.M. Wilkinson. Amsterdam: Rodopi, 1980, 93–107.

Bettelheim, Bruno. "Portnoy Psychoanalyzed." *Midstream* 15 (1969): 3–10.

Birnbaum, Milton. "Philip Roth: The Artist in Search of Self." *Modern Age* 36 (Fall 1993): 82.

Brent, Jonathan. "What Facts? A Talk with Roth." *New York Times Book Review*, September 25, 1988, 3.

Brown, Russell E. "Philip Roth and Bruno Schulz." *ANQ* 6 (1993): 211–14.

Cohen, Joseph. "Paradise Lost, Paradise Regained: Reflections on Philip Roth's Recent Fiction." *Studies in American Jewish Literature* 8 (1989): 196–204.

Crews, Frederick. "Uplift." *New York Review of Books*, November 16, 1972, 18–20.

Dickstein, Morris. "Black Humor and History: The Early Sixties." In *Gates of Eden: American Culture in the Sixties*. New York: Basic Books, 1977, 91–127.

Epstein, Joseph. "Fiction: What Does Philip Roth Want?" *Commentary* 77 (January 1984): 62–67.

Ezrahi, Sidra DeKoven, Daniel Lazare, Daphne Merkin, Morris Dickstein, and Anita Norich. "Philip Roth's Diasporism: A Symposium." *Tikkun* 8:3 (May 1993): 41–45.

Finney, Brian. "Roth's Counterlife: Destabilizing the Facts." *Biography* 16 (1993): 370–87.

Fredericksen, Brooke. "Home Is Where the Text Is: Exile, Homeland, and Jewish American Writing." *Studies in American Jewish Literature* 11 (1992): 36–44.

Furman, Andrew. "The Ineluctable Holocaust in the Fiction of Philip Roth." *Studies in American Jewish Literature* 12 (1993): 109–22.

———. "A New 'Other' Emerges in American Jewish Literature: Philip Roth's Israel Fiction." *Contemporary Literature* 36 (1995): 633–53.

Girgus, Sam. " 'The New Covenant' and the Dilemma of Dissensus: Bercovitch, Roth, and Doctorow." In *Summoning: Ideas of the Covenant and Interpretive Theory*, ed. Ellen Spolsky. Albany: State University of New York Press, 1993.

Goodheart, Eugene. " 'Postmodern' Meditations on the Self: The Work of Philip Roth and Don DeLillo." In *Desire and Its Discontents*. New York: Columbia University Press, 1991.

———. "Writing and the Unmaking of the Self." *Contemporary Literature* 29 (1988): 438–53.

Green, Geoffrey. "Metamorphosing Kafka: The Example of Philip Roth." In *The Dove and the Mole: Kafka's Journey into Darkness and Creativity*, ed. Ronald Gottesman and Moshe Lazar. Malibu: Undena, 1987, 35–46.

Halkin, Hillel. "How to Read Philip Roth." *Commentary* 97 (February 1994): 43–48.

Howe, Irving. "Philip Roth Reconsidered." *Commentary*, December 1972, 69–77.

Kamenetz, Roger. " 'The Hocker, Misnomer . . . Love/Dad': Philip Roth's *Patrimony*." *Southern Review* 27 (1991): 937–45.

Kauvar, Elaine M. "This Doubly Reflected Communication: Philip Roth's Autobiographies." *Contemporary Literature* 36 (1995): 412–46.

Kazin, Alfred. "The Earthly City of Jews." In *Bright Book of Life*. Boston: Atlantic, Little, Brown and Co., 1973, 144–49.

Kellman, Steven G. "Philip Roth's Ghost Writer." *Comparative Literature Studies* 21 (1984): 175–85.

Leavey, Ann. "Philip Roth: A Bibliographic Essay (1984–1988)." *Studies in American Jewish Literature* 8 (1989): 212–18.

Lee, Hermione. "The Art of Fiction LXXXIV: Philip Roth" (interview). *Paris Review* 26 (Fall 1984): 215–47.

O'Donnell, Patrick. "The Disappearing Text: Philip Roth's The Ghost Writer." *Contemporary Literature* 24 (1983): 365–78.

Pinsker, Sanford. "Deconstruction as Apology: The Counterfictions of Philip Roth." In *Bearing the Bad News*. Iowa City: University of Iowa Press, 1990.

———. "The Facts, the 'Unvarnished Truth,' and the Fictions of Philip Roth." *Studies in American Jewish Literature* 11 (1992): 108–17.

———. "Imagination on the Ropes." *Georgia Review* 37 (1983): 880–88.

———. "Imagining American Reality." *Southern Review* 29 (1993): 767–81.

———. "Jewish-American Literature's Lost-and-Found Department: How Philip Roth and Cynthia Ozick Reimagine Their Significant Dead." *Modern Fiction Studies* 35 (1989): 223–35.

Podhoretz, Norman. "Laureate of the New Class." *Commentary*, December 1972, 4.

Ravvin, Norman. "Strange Presences on the Family Tree: The Unacknowledged Literary Father in Philip Roth's 'The Prague Orgy.' " *English Studies in Canada* 17 (1991): 197–207.

Rubin-Dorsky, Jeffrey. "Honor Thy Father." *Raritan* 11 (1992): 137–45.

———. "Philip Roth's The Ghost Writer: Literary Heritage and Jewish Irreverence." *Studies in American Jewish Literature* 8 (1989): 168–85.

Shechner, Mark. "Philip Roth." *Partisan Review* 41 (1974): 410–27.

———. "Philip Roth: The Road of Excess." *After the Revolution: Studies in the Contemporary Jewish-American Imagination*. Bloomington: Indiana University Press, 1987, 196–238.

———. "Zuckerman's Travels." *American Literary History* 1 (1989): 219–30. Reprinted in Mark Shechner, *The Conversion of the Jews and Other Essays*. New York: St. Martin's, 1990, 91–103.

Sheed, Wilfred. "Howe's Complaint." *New York Times Book Review*, May 6, 1973, 2.

Sokoloff, Naomi. "Imagining Israel in American Jewish Fiction: Anne Roiphe's Lovingkindness and Philip Roth's The Counterlife." *Studies in American Jewish Literature* 10 (1991): 65–80.

Solotaroff, Theodore. "The Journey of Philip Roth." *Atlantic*, April 1969, 64–72.

Syrkin, Marie. Letter on *Portnoy's Complaint*. *Commentary*, March 1973, 8, 10.

Trachtenberg, Stanley. "In the Egosphere: Philip Roth's Anti-Bildungsroman." *Papers on Language and Literature* 25 (1989): 326–41.

Updike, John. "Recruiting Raw Nerves." *New Yorker* 69:4 (March 15, 1993): 109–12.

Wallace, James D. " 'This Nation of Narrators': Transgression, Revenge, and Desire in *Zuckerman Bound*." *Modern Language Studies* 21 (1991): 17–34.

Whitfield, Stephen J. "Comic Echoes of Kafka." *American Humor* 9 (1982): 1–5.

———. "Laughter in the Dark: Notes on American-Jewish Humor." *Midstream*, February 1978, 48–58.

Wilson, Matthew. "Fathers and Sons in History: Philip Roth's The Counterlife." *Prooftexts* 11 (1991): 41–56.

———. "The Ghost Writer: Kafka, Het Achterhuis, and History." *Studies in American Jewish Literature* 10 (1991): 44–53.

Wirth-Nesher, Hana. "The Artist Tales of Philip Roth." *Prooftexts* 3 (1983): 263–72.

BUDD SCHULBERG   (1914–)

Seth Barron

BIOGRAPHY

Budd Schulberg, the son and grandson of poor Jewish immigrants, was born in New York City on March 27, 1914, but was raised, as his memoir's subtitle puts it, a "Hollywood prince." His father, B. P. Schulberg, a first-generation American, was one of the early motion-picture industry's first "scenaricists," devising the story lines of hundreds of movies; his mother, Adeline Jaffe Schulberg, was born in Russia and came to the United States as an infant. Schulberg grew up in prosperous circumstances and as a small child moved to California with his parents to become part of the new, largely Jewish aristocracy that dominated Hollywood and the early cinema.

Schulberg's youth and adolescence were spent surrounded by great wealth and luxury, and his early playmates included the sons and daughters of the Hollywood elite: his autobiography, *Moving Pictures* (1981), includes a photograph of Schulberg as a guest at Jackie Coogan's tenth birthday party. But growing up amidst the glamour of studio culture had a deglamorizing effect on young Budd: "For me the magic was stripped away when I was still struggling in the early grades at the Wilton Place public school. I saw Hollywood as a company town" (*Moving Pictures*, 125). Schulberg was exposed at a very early age to the radical ambiguity of a city whose primary industry was the production of fantasy, but that was driven by fierce competition and greed: it is precisely this dichotomy and the intellectual influence of Budd's politically left-leaning mother that inform a great deal of his work.

Schulberg returned to the East to attend prep school at the Deerfield Academy in Connecticut and then went to Dartmouth for his undergraduate work. He graduated in 1936 and in the late 1930s traveled to the Soviet Union, where he attended the First Writers' Congress and met or heard such luminaries as Gorky, Babel, Bukharin, and many other Soviet writers who were later imprisoned or killed by the Stalinist regime. But Schulberg upon visiting was struck and inspired by what at that point still seemed to be the possibility for a living and potent social realism that worked to promote the revolutionary ethos. Upon returning to the United States, Schulberg joined the Communist Party, of which he remained a member until 1940, when he became disillusioned both by Stalinist excesses and what he perceived to be undue demands by the Party for control over the content of his own artistic work.

Schulberg's Party membership eventually resulted in his being called before the House Committee on Un-American Activities (commonly known as HUAC) in 1952 to testify on his knowledge of subversive activity in the Hollywood community. HUAC had begun investigation of Hollywood Communists in the late 1940s and had initiated a "blacklist" of known members. Because the entire entertainment industry respected the list, being on it meant that one could not work. It was possible to have oneself removed from the blacklist by betraying others to the committee in a supposed show of good faith: "naming names," as the act of testifying came to be known, became an ethical test that many members of the industry had to face. Many, including Dalton Trumbo and Lilliam Hellman, refused to testify; others, including Budd Schulberg, agreed to do so. Though Schulberg discounts the ultimate importance of his testimony to his later career, his involvement in what came to be known as the "Hollywood witchhunts" was in many ways both traumatic and crucial.

However, it is not fair to depict Schulberg as an opportunist. Arguably, he had principled objections to the American Communist Party's hard line on what constituted acceptable revolutionary art, and he claims to have recoiled strongly from its apologies for Stalin's own treatment of artists. In any case, he has remained committed to progressive social causes. In 1965, after the Watts riots, which destroyed large portions of South Central Los Angeles, Schulberg established the Watts Writers Workshop, a center aimed at helping talented poor, mostly black, ghetto youth develop their skill as writers. A selective anthology of the work that emerged from the workshop, entitled *From the Ashes*, was edited by Schulberg in 1967.

Budd Schulberg's own literary career began in 1941 when he published his first and most famous novel, *What Makes Sammy Run?* For the past fifty-five years Schulberg has continued to write novels, short stories, plays, screenplays, and journalistic essays, some of which have been collected and published, including his most recent work, *Sparring with Hemingway*, a collection of essays on boxing, one of Schulberg's major interests. He has won a variety of awards, including an Academy Award for the screenplay of *On the Waterfront* and the German Film Critics award for his screenplay *A Face in the Crowd*, as well as honorary degrees and service awards for his work with underprivileged ghetto writers.

Budd Schulberg has been married four times, most recently to Betsy Anne Langman, and has sired five children. He lives today in Brookside, New York.

MAJOR WORKS AND THEMES

Though Budd Schulberg is a Jew, his literary work evinces little central concern with the question of Jewish identity; the majority of his books, in fact, have nothing to do with Jews at all. However, befitting his upbringing in the midst of an industry that was largely run by Jews and whose ultimate product was a fantasy of gentile "Americanness," when Schulberg does treat Jewish issues, he does so in a manner that is fruitfully ambiguous.

In *What Makes Sammy Run?* we witness the rise of Sammy Glick, a ferociously competitive go-getter and the novel's eponymous antihero. The novel's title comes from its narrator's persistent musing on the source of Glick's drive to succeed, a drive that is presented as something almost primal. Glick is in fact so strongly driven that he has come to represent a cultural type: people who have never read the novel may be familiar with the character or the title, and it is Schulberg's best-known work.

The novel deals basically with the relationship between Glick and the narrator: two Jews, each of whom can be seen to represent a different type of prewar American Jew. The narrator, Al Manheim, is college educated, was raised in bucolic central Connecticut, and though the son of a rabbi, is relatively well assimilated. Sammy Glick, on the other hand, was raised by extremely religious Jews who live in squalid poverty on the Lower East Side of New York. Where Manheim is intellectual, sensitive, and throughout the novel becomes progressively socially conscious, Sammy Glick is represented as an extreme case of an anti-Semitic stereotype: he is materialistic, selfish, vulgar, and sexually crass. One way in which the novel is particularly interesting is in its representation of the conflict between these two characters, which at times is formulated in expressions of Jewish self-hatred, rare for a prewar American novel. At one point, Manheim attempts to convince Sammy Glick, who has in less than one hundred pages of text risen from newspaper copyboy to successful Hollywood screenwriter, to give some credit to the starving writer who wrote a script for which Glick has claimed full credit:

I tried everything I could to break him down, flattery, nostalgia, the brotherhood of man, the camaraderie of the newspaper game and even, as a last resort, the need of Jews to help each other in self-defense.

"Don't pull that Jewish crapola on me," Sammy said. "What the hell did the Jews ever do for me?—except maybe get my head cracked open for me when I was a kid."

What makes Sammy run? The childhood, Kit had said, look into the childhood. . . .

"Jews," he said bitterly and absently.
"Jews," he said, like a storm-trooper. (133–34)

Glick, an emblem of a classic kind of escape from the poverty of ghetto existence, is seen to be running, at least in part, away from his Jewish identity, which he presumably associates with the passivity and weakness we later see to have defined his family. Glick, paradoxically, embodies a particular aspect of the Jewish-American experience—the common view of Jews as successful, enterprising, "self-starting"—even as he scorns Jews generally.

But Al Manheim, the more enlightened, humanistic Jew, is not exempt from a certain unease with his own Jewish roots. Though he thinks sentimentally about his rabbi father, he oddly characterizes him as a man who had "led a life of community service and true Christ-like gentility that had won him Middletown's approval and genuine respect" (27). Assimilation, obviously enough, bears the price of meeting the normative demands of Protestant American society: failure to meet those norms by remaining "too Jewish" thus becomes a fear of social failure. Al's fascination with and repulsion from Glick, his alternating admiration and disgust, speak to an ambivalence about his own Jewishness and a sense of his own marginal status in American culture: he resides ultimately on the outskirts of "Middletown."

What Makes Sammy Run? thus presents a dialectic of Jewishness that resolves in Schulberg's rather anticlimactic assertion that what makes Sammy run is, finally, general social pressures like poverty and an exploitative economic structure. Glick is put forth, in a move not surprising for a Communist who was attempting to develop his own version of social realism, as a product of his economic environment.

Schulberg's later work touches on Jewish issues only sporadically, but a recently published short story of his treats the question in a puzzling manner. "Passport to Nowhere," collected in *Love, Action, Laughter* (1989), is the story of painter Nathan Solomon, a Jew in prewar Poland who escapes a pogrom, wanders through Germany, settles briefly in Paris, finally decides to move to Palestine, only to be denied entrance because he has no money, and so is left on the dock in Cyprus. Nathan is a sort of wandering Jew, and his journey is meant to represent the instability of Jewish identity and its rootlessness. The story is not especially remarkable, but it too presents an oddly Christological register of imagery. Nathan is continually referred to explicitly as Christ, "making his way through a German railway station, the holes in his feet trailing blood" (76). Schulberg is of course not the only Jewish-American author to blend Christian and Jewish symbologies—Bernard Malamud, for example, makes effective use of them—but Schulberg's use of the blend here winds up intriguingly confused, especially when his character, blond and muscular, is called "Nazi" in a Jewish ghetto. Schulberg seems to be suggesting that his character is alienated even from the Jews; but if this is the case, why endow him with the iconology of the dominant culture? The story is significant ultimately in how it bespeaks an ambivalence on Schulberg's part about his role as a Jewish-American writer treating Jewish themes.

Schulberg's later work, however, deals mainly with the larger socioeconomic issues raised at the end of *What Makes Sammy Run?* It is actually fair to say that he is in many ways a political novelist, always concerned with questions of power and power's corrosive influence. He is particularly interested in the possibility for collective action, especially in the labor movement. A subplot of *Sammy* deals with the formation of the Screenwriters' Guild, but Schulberg's most interesting treatment of the individual's role in the collective occurs in his script for *On the Waterfront*, the 1954 film directed by Elia Kazan and starring Marlon Brando.

On the Waterfront is the story of Terry, a small-time ex-prizefighter who works as a longshoreman on the mob-controlled docks of New York harbor. He is asked to testify in front of the Waterfront Crime Commission against the organized-crime syndicate that controls the docks, and of which Terry's brother Charlie is an important member. Terry at first refuses, but under the influence of a conscientious priest and the beautiful sister of a ''stoolie'' whose murder was partially Terry's fault, he eventually does testify against the mob, heroically making it again possible for honest work to take place on the docks, now free from corruption.

The film has been read, most notably by Peter Biskind, as an allegory of Schulberg and Kazan's involvement in the HUAC hearings, where both agreed to testify against their former fellow members of the Communist Party. The movie works elaborately to demonstrate that Terry's choice to testify, despite community condemnation and the threat of personal harm, is a deep act of courage: perhaps, offered Biskind, Schulberg and Kazan were presenting their own testimony as a similarly courageous act. Biskind demonstrated how the film engages in a Christological representation of Terry, who, like the Passion Christ, is jeered and mocked even as he fulfills his redemptive mission.

It seems hard to escape the idea that the film, following Schulberg's HUAC appearance by two years, must bear in some way upon his testimony, which alienated him from segments of the entertainment world that cast him as a variety of stool pigeon: pigeons, incidentally, are a major image in *On the Waterfront*. If Biskind's thesis is even partially correct, then the film becomes an exercise in self-justification, for it is rather overdetermined in its message that, as its title states, ''self-appointed tyrants can be fought and defeated by right-thinking men in a vital democracy'' (Biskind, 28.) Terry testifies against vicious criminals who murder for their own profit, while Schulberg testified against associates who, however misguidedly, held political beliefs. The film's politics are therefore somewhat complicated by its makers' own historical position, but for this very reason it is deeply interesting as a symptom of a true crisis in mid-1950s American political thought.

Schulberg deals with the question of the individual's role in political action elsewhere as well. In *Sanctuary V* (1969), the protagonist is the ineffectual figurehead president of a small revolutionary Latin American nation modeled on Castroist Cuba. About to be arrested and purged by the country's real leader, a charismatic dictator, the President seeks asylum within the embassy of a neutral country. What follows is an at times phantasmagoric prison narrative in which the former President undergoes a physical denigration that results in total spiritual confusion. Haunted by blistering sexual fantasies and the prospect of an indefinite, pathetic stay within the extraterritorial compound, the President betrays himself for the promise of an adulterous affair and winds up in an actual prison for political dissidents. The novel is bleak and offers little hope for the emergence of a successful, moderate liberalism in the face of ideological dogmatism.

Everything That Moves (1980), Budd Schulberg's last novel, depicts the rise of a fictional labor union, modeled loosely on the Teamsters. The union movement begins as a grass-roots effort to impose effective safety standards on a niggardly corporate structure, but, somewhat predictably, itself becomes bloated and corrupt, coming to resemble nothing less than the corporate structure it initially opposed. This book is by no means a great novel in terms of structure, detail, or characterization, but the story it tells is in some sense the ultimate Schulbergian one: the lure of power and its corrosive influence on ideals.

But despite his career-long preoccupation with the problem of effective progressive political action, Budd Schulberg is best known for his literary contribution to the mythicization and demythicization of Hollywood in the American imagination. *What Makes Sammy Run?* and his third and possibly best novel, *The Disenchanted* (1950), are two significant monuments in a tradition of writing about Hollywood that stretches from F. Scott Fitzgerald and Nathanael West on the one side to Norman Mailer and Joan Didion on the other and even through to contemporary works such as the Coen Brothers' film *Barton Fink*. Each of the novels in this tradition focuses on the role of the writer in Hollywood and thereby addresses the greater question of the function of the artist in modern American society generally. *The Disenchanted* tells the story of two screenwriters, Shep Stearns and Manley Halliday, who are generally accepted to have been based loosely on Schulberg himself and F. Scott Fitzgerald. Stearns is a young and inexperienced writer who finds himself paired to collaborate with Halliday, his literary hero, who has become washed-up. A story of double disenchantment, the novel ends with Halliday's drunken, diabetic death and ultimately suggests that there is no room for the artist in Hollywood.

CRITICAL RECEPTION

Considering the length and depth of Budd Schulberg's career, there has been comparatively little scholarship done on his work. Most Schulberg criticism focuses on his depictions of Hollywood: Walter Wells's *Tycoons and Locusts* and Jonas Spatz's *Hollywood in Fiction* are studies in the "Hollywood novel" that treat *What Makes Sammy Run?* and *The Disenchanted* in some detail.

Wells's essay is particularly valuable in its examination of Schulberg's exploitation of cliché, and he suggests rather articulately that Schulberg himself sometimes lapses unintentionally into a clichéd representation of Hollywood. Leslie Fiedler referred to Schulberg several times in essays about Hollywood and Jewish writers and made insightful points both about Schulberg's "liberaloid" politics and his confusing and often confused formulation of Jewish identity. The Bibliography lists works that deal with Schulberg's work in a significant way or that, in passing, say interesting things about it.

BIBLIOGRAPHY

Works by Budd Schulberg

Fiction

What Makes Sammy Run? New York: Random House, 1941.
The Harder They Fall. New York: Random House, 1947.
The Disenchanted. New York: Random House, 1950.
Some Faces in the Crowd. New York: Random House, 1953.
Waterfront. New York: Random House, 1955.
A Face in the Crowd: A Play for the Screen. New York: Random House, 1957.
Across the Everglades: A Play for the Screen. New York: Random House, 1958.
The Disenchanted: A Play. With Harvey Breit. New York: Random House, 1959.
What Makes Sammy Run? A New Musical. With Stuart Schulberg. New York: Random House, 1964.
Sanctuary V. New York: New American Library, 1969.
Everything That Moves. Garden City, NY: Doubleday, 1980.
On the Waterfront: A Screenplay. Carbondale: Southern Illinois University Press, 1980.
Love, Action, Laughter. New York: Random House, 1989.

Nonfiction

From the Ashes: Voices of Watts, ed. New York: New American Library, 1967.
The Four Seasons of Success. Garden City, NY: Doubleday, 1972.
Loser and Still Champion: Muhammed Ali. Garden City, NY: Doubleday, 1972.
Swan Watch. With Geraldine Brooks. New York: Delacorte, 1975.
Moving Pictures: Memories of a Hollywood Prince. New York: Stein and Day, 1981.
Sparring with Hemingway. Chicago: I. R. Dee, 1995.

Screenplays

Little Orphan Annie. With Samuel Ornitz. Paramount, 1938.
Winter Carnival. With Maurice Rapf and Lester Cole. United Artists, 1939.
On the Waterfront. Columbia, 1954.
A Face in the Crowd. Warner Bros., 1957.
Wind Across the Everglades. Warner Bros., 1958.

Works Cited and Studies of Budd Schulberg

Biskind, Peter. "The Politics of Power in On the Waterfront." *Film Quarterly*, Fall 1975, 25–38.

Eisinger, Chester. *Fiction of the Forties*. Chicago: University of Chicago Press, 1963.
Fiedler, Leslie. "The Jew in the American Novel." In *The Collected Essays of Leslie Fiedler*, vol. 2. New York: Stein and Day, 1971.
Freedman, Morris. "New England and Hollywood." *Commentary*, October 1953, 389–92.
Georgakas, Dan. "The Screen Playwright as Author: An Interview with Budd Schulberg." *Cineaste* 11:4 (1982): 6–15.
Navasky, Victor. *Naming Names*. New York: Viking Press, 1980.
Scholnick, Sylvia Huberman. "Money versus Mitzvot." *Yiddish* 6:4 (1987): 48–55.
Spatz, Jonas. *Hollywood in Fiction*. The Hague: Mouton, 1969.
Wells, Walter. *Tycoons and Locusts*. Carbondale: Southern Illinois University Press, 1973.
Winchell, Mark Royden. "Fantasy Seen: Hollywood Fiction since West." In *Los Angeles in Fiction*, ed. David Fine. Albuquerque: University of New Mexico Press, 1984.

ALIX KATES SHULMAN   (1932–   )

Frances Flannery-Dailey

BIOGRAPHY

The works of Alix Kates Shulman reveal a woman who has embraced her life as a series of lives lived anew: as the vibrant feminist, ardent political activist, passionate mother, writer visionary, and, finally, the joyous solitaire. Alix Kates Shulman was born in a suburb of Cleveland, Ohio, on August 17, 1932. Her father, Samuel Simon Kates, was a labor arbitrator, a just, principled, and gentle man. Her mother, Dorothy Davis Kates, was also engaged in politics and for a time was president of the Federation of Jewish Women's Organizations in Cleveland. Though her parents' influence seems evident in Shulman's later political activism, it was her aunt, Celia Davis Hymes, who opened up cultural possibilities to her beyond the confines of her childhood community, feeding the young Alix on great literature and music.

Shulman's Reformed parents, though themselves secular Jews, saw to it that she and her brother Robert attended Hebrew school to preserve some solidarity with their Jewish heritage, especially in light of the Jewish pain of World War II. However, like Sasha, the heroine of her celebrated first novel, *Memoirs of an Ex-Prom Queen* (1972), Shulman met her religious tradition with a skeptical eye. Socially, moreover, she experienced her Jewishness mainly as a restrictive force that kept the Jewish and Gentile halves of her high school from associating with one another, leading to separate sororities and fraternities, hangout spots, and even proms. The divisions ran so deep as to separate the two groups at their thirty-fifth high-school reunion, of which Shulman has written in her article "Gentiles and Jews at the Hop."

By the end of high school, Shulman wanted to escape the domestic destiny of the girls in her conventional neighborhood, so she plunged into her intellectual life with ferocity. After receiving her bachelor's degree in English and history at the age of twenty from Case Western Reserve University, she fled the Midwest for the freedom and stimulation of New York City. There she studied philosophy at the Graduate School of Columbia University and then mathematics at New York University, where she earned a master's degree in humanities. She was driven by an insatiable desire to know everything possible and saw these varied disciplines as different ways of grasping and ordering the vastness of human thought. It was this same hunger for the new that led her to the beatnik life of Greenwich Village in the 1950s, an experience echoed in her novel *Burning Questions* (1978).

Amidst her schooling, Shulman married young, divorced young, and shortly thereafter married again. Though that marriage would also eventually end in divorce, her life was forever changed by the birth of her son Teddy in 1961 and her daughter Polly in 1963. Shulman was passionate about her parenting, and her novels and memoir all clearly portray children as the fixed center around which the life of a mother spins.

It was in the late 1960s in New York City that Alix Kates Shulman, then in her thirties and raising a family, became part of the feminist movement. She was one of the earliest members of New York Radical Women and Redstockings, radical feminist groups that through consciousness-raising actively waged a war against the establishment in New York. Acting out of the basic understanding that women deserve equal consideration and rights in all respects to men, and that sexism, like racism and imperialism, is unjust, they organized women from all walks of life, waging protests and demonstrations against institutions that denigrated women. They found strength and indeed made changes by "marching down Fifth Avenue, telling the world about our orgasms and abortions, tossing out our brooms and girdles, bringing suits to overturn laws" (*Drinking the Rain*, 89). They integrated exclusively male clubs, schools, and professions. In addition, they staged some attention-grabbing events that provoked thought about the issues of equality, dignity, and fairness, including a "Whistle-In on Wall Street," in which they pinched brokers on the sidewalk at lunchtime, and an event where they crowned a live sheep Miss America. With the outstanding success of her first novel, *Memoirs of an Ex-Prom Queen*, Shulman became a voice and even an icon for many in the feminist movement. Her subsequent works, including three additional novels, a memoir, two collections of Emma Goldman's essays, a biography of Goldman, and over fifty published articles have each, in some way, grown out of her feminist perspective.

Shulman has enjoyed considerable popular and critical success and has been honored with numerous academic appointments, awards, grants, and fellowships. Moreover, her work has been included in over thirty-five edited collections and continues to be reviewed in academic publications and studied at colleges and universities. She has led writing workshops in programs across the country and has given over a hundred keynote addresses, university and public lectures, symposia, and academic conferences, as well as many readings of her work and radio and television interviews. She currently divides her time between New York City and an island off the coast of Maine and is working on a memoir of her family.

Shulman's academic appointments have included ones at the University of Arizona, the University of Hawaii, Ohio State University, the University of Colorado, New York University, Yale, and the New School for Social Research. Literary awards include finalist in the *Los Angeles Times* Book Prize (1995) and the Body Mind Spirit Award of Excellence (1996) for *Drinking the Rain*; Outstanding Book of 1981 for *On the Stroll* by the *New York Times Book Review*; final selection for a National Book Award (1972) for *Memoirs of an Ex-Prom Queen*; Outstanding Book of 1971 for *To the Barricades* by the *New York Times Book Review* and *Library Journal*; She received a National Endowment for the Arts fiction grant (1983) and has been a visiting writer at the American Academy in Rome, a DeWitt Wallace Fellow (1979), a MacDowell Colony for the Arts Fellow (1975–1977, 1979, 1981), and a Millay Colony for the Arts Fellow (1978).

MAJOR WORKS AND THEMES

Shulman has never ceased to write and rewrite her own character. Her recently released memoir, *Drinking the Rain* (1995), chronicles a transformation that has marked the last decade or so of the author's life, catalyzed by the soulful experience at age fifty of spending a summer alone on an island off the coast of Maine. In her island cottage she led a simplified existence, with no running water, phone, or electricity, dependent upon the local plants and sea life for food and upon the rain for water. To her surprise, she found that as she adapted the rhythms of her formerly hectic life to the rhythms of life on the island, she was met by new, luminous thoughts and pleasures. With a freedom won by age, she found that solitude is a treasure, that certain choice relationships are to be savored, and that an awareness of grace and peace is possible. The revelations of that first summer on the island returned with her as she traveled back to New York and integrated the lessons that she had learned into old and new relationships and places.

It was in this period that Shulman became reengaged with her Judaism while embarking upon a new, broadened spiritual path. In *Drinking the Rain* she recounts a transcendental vision of unity that she had experienced earlier, despite considering herself an agnostic with atheistic tendencies (55). Even though she found no way to explain, relate, or process the experience at the time, Shulman nevertheless was unable to deny its validity and transformative power. Years later, on her island in Maine, she gained a renewed understanding of her vision. Slowly, the former skeptic found a new spirituality unfolding for her, one that at times resonated with Judaism. Thus in *Drinking the Rain* she likens her inability to describe the silence of her vision to "why the name of God cannot be spoken," feels the calm of her island return while listening to lectures given by a kabbalistic rabbi, and quotes Philo and Rabbi Tarfon for inspiration (96, 166).

This new regard for her tradition contrasts with a suspicion of Judaism attested in her earlier fiction. Sasha, the heroine of *Memoirs of an Ex-Prom Queen* (1972), is highly skeptical about the teachings of her Hebrew school, and this grows into a general scorn for religion. Sasha says of the God of Abraham, "If He existed at all, He was chicken shit—certainly not worthy of worship," and turns to philosophy for her answers (*Memoirs*, 138–39). Sasha is likewise displeased with the cultural restrictions that her heritage brings, experiencing the same social segregation as Shulman herself: "Just as the Cortney kids wouldn't play with me because I was a Jew, the boys wouldn't play with me because I was a girl" (*Memoirs*, 20).

Despite the fact that two of Shulman's main heroines are Jewish (Sasha of *Memoirs of an Ex-Prom Queen* and Zane of *Burning Questions*), and that Shulman is the biographer of the Jewish Emma Goldman, these themes are not the most prevalent in her works. Her most steady concern is the importance of women sharing their experiences.

Shulman's celebrated first novel, *Memoirs of an Ex-Prom Queen*, was dubbed by the publishers and by many critics as the first feminist novel of the current feminist movement. It is the tale of Sasha, a pretty, all-American girl, who, although she is able to attain the ideals that her sex role mandates—dashing and gainfully employed husband, clean, well-fed children, beautiful home—remains dissatisfied. Her ever-widening quests for unconventional happiness leave her just as disappointed, for Sasha's problem is that she is so often defined by the men who attach themselves to her: whose girlfriend is she, whose wife, whose mistress, whose lover?

There is another Sasha, however, who pursues her own interests and concerns, regardless of male validation. She is unflinchingly devoted to philosophy, though her intelligence is seen as merely an asset to her beauty; she is a perfectionist in her mothering, though her husband laments the loss of his carefree bride. As Sasha winds her way through society's expectations, she sometimes adopts the path already charted for her. Yet in certain precious moments she becomes her own trailblazer and, slowly, her own whole person.

While *Memoirs of an Ex-Prom Queen* traces the life of a woman before the feminist movement, *Burning Questions* (1978) is the fictional memoir of a feminist rebel. Many of Shulman's own experiences appear to be mirrored in the character of Zane, an unusual young woman who, partially under the inspiration of an unconventional, leftist aunt, trades the suburban life of the Midwest for the bohemian life of Greenwich Village. Finally exhausted by conforming to nonconformity, she eventually settles for marriage, but one that she hopes will have some beatnik overtones. Instead, she is rather quickly transformed by the births of her three children into "something else entirely . . . A unit; a schedule; a family" (*Burning Questions*, 143).

As in Shulman's own life, it is precisely in this period that Zane stumbles upon the feminist movement and finds her life infused with a new energy and purpose. She is liberated by the shared recognition of sexism, which she had encountered in both her conventional and nonconformist incarnations, and becomes an enthusiastic political activist who draws inspiration from the women rebels in history who have gone before her.

On the Stroll (1981), Shulman's third novel, departs from the first-person accounts of her earlier fiction. This compassionate tale of life on the streets for a young prostitute, Robin, and an old bag lady, Owl, grew out of Shulman's experiences as a volunteer for several years at a New York City shelter for homeless women. Through these characters Shulman examines the plight of women deprived of conventional means of support, who thus end up on the outskirts of society. Her well-researched portrayals are convincing, with a complexity that belies any simple stereotyping of prostitute, bag lady, and even pimp.

Shulman's fourth novel, *In Every Woman's Life* . . . (1987), explores the question of marriage as it arises in the lives of a variety of strong women: Nora, independent and career minded, involved with a married man and contemptuous of marriage herself; Rosemary, torn between career and family, between the duties of a mother and wife and her extramarital love affair; and young Daisy, Rosemary's unconventional daughter, dedicated to new experiences and freedoms. Shulman resists forcing any single character's view as the favored one, suggesting that neither feminism nor marriage is monolithic; rather, both are as varied as are women's experiences.

The feminist movement of the 1960s recognized the need to resurrect the memory of early feminists who were absent from too many history books. Shulman aided the revival of women's history with three works on Emma Goldman: *Red Emma Speaks: Selected Writings and Speeches by Emma Goldman* (1972), rereleased in 1983 and 1996 with additional material, *The Traffic in Women and Other Essays on Feminism* (1970), and a biography aimed at young adults, *To the Barricades: The Anarchist Life of Emma Goldman* (1971). In the latter Shulman describes Goldman as rising from the four "curses" with which she was born, being "Russian, Jewish, female, and unloved," to become perhaps the most outspoken and notorious political activist of her time (*To the Barricades*, 1). Shulman has also written numerous articles and three children's books: *Bosley on the Number Line*, a mathematical fantasy about a young boy and living numbers, *Awake or Asleep*, a philosophical questioning of reality on a level accessible to young children, and *Finders Keepers*, a hidden-picture book.

CRITICAL RECEPTION

The work that has enjoyed the widest popular and critical success continues to be Shulman's first novel, *Memoirs of an Ex-Prom Queen* (1972). Shulman's perceptive articulation of the heroine's experiences struck such a sympathetic chord with the all-female secretaries of the paperback houses to which it was sent that it became a sensational underground success before it was ever published. Consequently, the novel sold for the highest price to date for a first novel and since then has been continuously reprinted.

Nevertheless, *Memoirs* has not been free of negative criticism. Marilyn Bender labeled the heroine as "The girl who couldn't say no" and "too much of a pushover" and the work itself as "the familiar, bouncy voyage from mattress to mattress" (36). Frank Lipsius viewed the matter differently, accusing the heroine of "exaggerated hangups" and calling for the feminist movement to "abandon the sentimental chestbeating" (77). Yet while Lipsius dubbed the work "half-novel and half-diatribe in the cause of Women's Lib" (77), Sally Helgeson saw it as "totally lacking in the politicized dogmatism that characterizes so many books dealing with female liberation today" (32).

Overall, the reception of *Memoirs* has been mostly positive. Eric Mahon called the novel "both witty and compelling" and maintained that Shulman's descriptions of high school were "chilling in the extreme" (560). Laurie Muchnik is one recent reviewer who has proclaimed that this work is "if anything more pertinent" twenty-five years later, as "there's always a new generation of women growing up, encountering discrimination for the first time" (21).

Burning Questions (1978) contains the clearest emphasis on feminism and politics of all of Shulman's works and therefore sparks controversy in both of these arenas. Pearl Bell said that Shulman "spares her rebel girl not ONE of the fashionable lib-rad-fem simplicities and platitudes about politics and history, men and women" (12). Other critics, however, not only praised the novel, but saw it as a landmark for the feminist movement. Elizabeth Fox-Genovese saw Shulman as breaking new ground, "trying to find a new heritage for female literary culture by wedding the American domestic tradition to a female revolutionary tradition" (216). Angela Carter said that *Burning Questions* "sets the women's liberation movement crisply in its socio-historic context" and is "never guilty of anything less than the broadest perspective" in its historic task (726).

On the Stroll (1981) has received mostly praise from reviewers. Though the novel is a departure in topic and form from Shulman's earlier fiction, her skill at sketching vivid characters seems to carry over. Thus Mary Cantwell, though viewing the plot as only "sufficient," praised the portrait of the bag lady Owl, calling her "a genuine creation" in literature (12).

In Every Woman's Life . . . (1987) met with mixed reviews. Sarah Schulman considered the characters too upper class and successful to be interesting, stating that "their love problems never go beyond their insular, privileged caste" (19). But Grace Lichtenstein applauded the character of Rosemary, "a liberated mom with warmth and sensuality," yet found Shulman's premise of staying married for the sake of the children "an old-fashioned and somewhat cynical attitude for a feminist author" (7).

For Shulman's recently released memoir, *Drinking the Rain* (1995), there has been little negative criticism. Claire Messud called the work "an inspiring journey," but worried over its naivete, in that "behind Shulman's gleeful experiments in natural living rests a base of financial security." Messud noted that "Russian peasants," for example, "might have little sympathy for Shulman's spiritual quest and might hanker for flush toilets," although she thought that the work was saved by Shulman's "self-recognition and humility" (36).

A quiet peace infuses *Drinking the Rain*, but this does not mean that Shulman has forgotten the injustices that are the focus of her earlier works. Rather, this is a portrait of a deeply feeling, thinking woman who has embraced both the pains and the joys of living. As she herself affirms: "Here I am when the tide goes out—speeder slowing down, fighter finding harmony . . . communard become solitaire, rationalist grown spiritual, teacher turned student, desirer dissolving in contentment" (*Drinking the Rain*, 65).

BIBLIOGRAPHY

Works by Alix Kates Shulman

Fiction

The Traffic in Women and Other Essays on Feminism, ed. New York: Times Change Press, 1970.
To the Barricades: The Anarchist Life of Emma Goldman. New York: Crowell, 1971.
Memoirs of an Ex-Prom Queen. New York: Alfred A. Knopf, 1972.
Red Emma Speaks: Selected Writings and Speeches by Emma Goldman, ed. New York: Random House, 1972.
Burning Questions. New York: Alfred A. Knopf, 1978.
On the Stroll. New York: Alfred A. Knopf, 1981.
In Every Woman's Life . . . New York: Alfred A. Knopf, 1987.
"Gentiles and Jews at the Hop: A Reunion Retrospective." *Lilith* 18 (Spring 1993): 12–15.
Drinking the Rain. New York: Farrar, Straus and Giroux, 1995.

Fiction for Children

Bosley on the Number Line. New York: McKay, 1970.
Awake or Asleep. Reading, MA: Young Scott Books, 1971.
Finders Keepers. Scarsdale, NY: Bradbury Press, 1971.

Works Cited and Studies of Alix Kates Shulman

Bell, Pearl. Review of *Burning Questions*. *New York Times Book Review*, March 26, 1978, 12.
Bender, Marilyn. Review of *Memoirs of an Ex-Prom Queen*. *New York Times Book Review*, April 23, 1972, 36.
Breines, Wini. *Young, White, and Miserable: Growing Up Female in the Fifties*. Boston: Beacon Press, 1992.

Brown, Cheryl, L., and Karen Olson, eds. *Feminist Criticism: Essays on Theory, Poetry, and Prose.* Metuchen, NJ: Scarecrow Press, 1978.

Cantwell, Mary. Review of *On the Stroll. New York Times Book Review*, September 27, 1981, 12.

Carter, Angela. Review of *Burning Questions. New Society*, June 21, 1979, 726.

Fox-Genovese, Elizabeth. "The New Female Literary Culture." *Antioch Review* 38 (Spring 1980): 193–217.

Helgeson, Sally. Review of *Memoirs of an Ex-Prom Queen. Village Voice*, September 21, 1972, 32.

Hendin, Josephine. *Vulnerable People: A View of American Fiction since 1945.* New York: Oxford University Press, 1978.

Hiatt, Mary. *The Way Women Write.* New York: Teachers College Press, 1977.

Lichtenstein, Grace. Review of *In Every Woman's Life. Book World, Washington Post*, May 31, 1987, 7.

Lipsius, Frank. Review of *Memoirs of an Ex-Prom Queen. Books and Bookmen* 18 (August 1973): 77.

Mahon, Eric. Review of *Memoirs of an Ex-Prom Queen. Listener*, April 26, 1973, 560.

Messud, Claire. Review of *Drinking the Rain. Times Literary Supplement*, June 30, 1995, 36.

Michelson, Peter. *Speaking the Unspeakable: A Poetics of Obscenity.* Albany: State University of New York Press, 1993.

Morgan, Ellen. "Human-becoming: Form and Focus in the Neo-Feminist Novel." In *Images of Women in Fiction: Feminist Perspectives*, Susan Koppelman Cornillon, ed. Bowling Green, OH: Bowling Green University Popular Press, 1972: 183–205.

Muchnik, Laurie. Review of *Memoirs of an Ex-Prom Queen. Voice Literary Supplement*, October 1993, 21.

Schulman, Sarah. Review of *In Every Woman's Life. American Book Review* 9 (November 1987): 19.

Stimpson, Catharine R. *Where the Meanings Are.* New York: Methuen, 1988.

ROBERTA SILMAN   (1934–   )

Judy Epstein

BIOGRAPHY

Roberta Silman was born Roberta Karpel on December 29, 1934, in Brooklyn, New York. Her family moved to the Long Island suburb of Cedarhurst in 1942. After high school, she attended Cornell University in upstate Ithaca, New York, graduating in 1956 with honors in English literature and Phi Beta Kappa. The following month, she married Robert Silman. They moved for a year to Petersburg, Virginia, where he served in the army and she worked as a secretary. They then moved to Queens, New York, and Roberta Silman went to work for the *Saturday Review*, first as secretary to the associate publisher and then as assistant to the science editor.

The Silmans moved to Ardsley, New York, in Westchester County, in 1961, where they still live. Their first child, Miriam, was born the same year. Their son Joshua was born in 1966, and their daughter Ruth was born in 1968.

Silman continued her formal education in 1972 when she entered the M.F.A. program in writing at Sarah Lawrence College in nearby Bronxville, New York. There she worked with Grace Paley and Jane Cooper, graduating in 1975. She commented in *Contemporary Authors*: "I started to write fiction when my children were still young and began, as many women do, with stories. As the children got older there was more uninterrupted time to write, so I made the longer commitment to the novel" (*Contemporary Authors*, 467). Silman was awarded a Guggenheim Memorial Foundation Fellowship for fiction in 1979 and a National Endowment for the Arts Fellowship for fiction in 1983.

MAJOR WORKS AND THEMES

The dominant theme in Silman's works seems to be the intensity and complexity of human relationships, predominantly family ties. Many of her narratives revolve around the death of close family members: husband, mother, or child. There is also a recurring undercurrent of the impact of Hitler's rise in Germany on life in America and on the life of American Jews.

The author's first published book, *Somebody Else's Child*, is a children's novel that is somewhat of an exception, although this story of an adopted boy certainly deals with the intensity of family relationships. Published in 1976, it won the Child Study Association Award for the Best Children's Book in 1977.

In 1977 *Blood Relations* was published—a collection of sixteen short stories, several of which had appeared in the *Atlantic Monthly* and the *New Yorker*. As the title implies, these stories deal with "the intimate languages and ritual silences of Family—parents and children, brothers and sisters—and the investments of love and governance made in each other's lives" (*Kirkus Reviews*). The book received Honorable Mention for the PEN Hemingway Prize for the best book of first fiction in 1978, as well as Honorable Mention for the Janet Heidinger Kafka Prize for the best novel by an American woman in 1978.

Silman's first novel, *Boundaries*, appeared in 1979. It centers around Mady Glazer, a Jewish upper-middle-class mother of three who loses her adored husband in an airplane accident. The book follows the development of her evolving relationship with Hans, a German potter and sculptor struggling with his own inner demons from his Nazi upbringing. It won an Honorable Mention for the Janet Heidinger Kafka Prize for the best novel by an American woman in 1980. Silman commented in *Contemporary Authors*, "For me, fiction is the history of the world. I think it is my job as a serious fiction writer to tell the truth about what I know or what I have the imagination to invent. The writing itself becomes a way of understanding something I have been unable to fathom or untangle— certain kinds of family relationships in *Blood Relations*, what an adopted child feels in *Somebody Else's Child*, and the modern relationship between Jews and Germans in *Boundaries*" (467).

Silman's next novel, *The Dream Dredger*, published in 1986, again deals with a Jewish family in the suburbs of New York City and with the complexities of the relationships within the family. The patriarch in this story is the narrator's grandfather, a Viennese Jew who had the foresight to move to America in 1931, but the main character is the narrator's mother, who must struggle with her own torment when her first child dies from polio at the age of eight.

The writer's most recently published novel is *Beginning the World Again* (1990). This fictionalized account of the lives of the families at Los Alamos, New Mexico, during the Manhattan Project allows Silman a new approach to many of her underlying concerns. She is still exploring the intimate lives of Jews in America and has created a new context of connectedness to Nazi Germany.

CRITICAL RECEPTION

David Guy, in a review in the *New York Times Book Review*, commented that Silman "writes in an elegantly simple prose that appears to be telling a story it does not quite know, one it has partly heard, perhaps, partly researched'' (12). Reviews of her book of short stories, *Blood Relations*, focused on her characters. Although Julia O'Faolain, in the *New York Times Book Review*, found Silman's characters too alike and ''mild and mournful,'' she noted a Russian-Jewish grandfather who stood out as an exception. ''He turns up in three stories and has a character honed into high relief by a tough, tight society'' (15).

Silman's first novel, *Boundaries* (1979), is perhaps her most widely reviewed book. Again, the reviews tended to focus on character. In the *New York Times Book Review*, Nora Johnson called this ''a warm and gentle tale of the return of a widow to wholeness . . . the pleasant story of some sane, attractive and intelligent people'' (14).

Her next novel, *The Dream Dredger*, was called ''a courageous novel of imaginative reconstruction'' by David Guy in the *New York Times Book Review*. He noted that while everything in the first half seemed too easy, ''The narrative becomes most problematic in the middle of the book, when Lise marries and the first nine years of the marriage elapse in three pages'' (12). He also noted that ''the most successful part of this novel by far is its extraordinary conclusion. . . . Here Ms. Silman's elegant prose works very much in her favor, as it stands in stark contrast to what she is describing'' (12).

Reviewing Silman's most recent novel, *Beginning the World Again*, Jonathan Penner in the *New York Times Book Review* referred to it as ''an earnest and well-intentioned novel,'' but one that ''demonstrates many of the problems with telling true stories'' (29).

Silman's writing is apparently most successful when she remains centered close to home. Her consciousness seems steeped in the traditions of the American Jewish experience, and this, coupled with her keen intuition, drives her best writing.

BIBLIOGRAPHY

Works by Roberta Silman

Somebody Else's Child. New York: Warne, 1976.
Blood Relations. Boston: Atlantic–Little, Brown, 1977.
Boundaries. Boston: Atlantic–Little, Brown, 1979.
The Dream Dredger. New York: Persea Books, 1986.
Beginning the World Again. New York: Viking, 1990.

Studies of Roberta Silman

Contemporary Authors 101. Detroit: Gale Research, 1981.
Guy, David. ''A Death in the Fairy-Tale Family.'' *New York Times Book Review*, January 4, 1987, 12.
Johnson, Nora. ''Two Down, One Up.'' *New York Times Book Review*, May 20, 1979, 14.

O'Faolain, Julia. "Small Goods in Small Packages." *New York Times Book Review*, July
    31, 1977, 15.
Penner, Jonathan. "All's Fair in Love and Physics." *New York Times Book Review*,
    November 4, 1990, 29.

JO SINCLAIR, Pseudonym for Ruth Seid (1913–1995)

Elisabeth Sandberg

BIOGRAPHY

Ruth Seid's family history is marked by displacement, which started when her paternal grandmother ordered her family in 1895 to move to Argentina, where Maurice de Hirsch, founder of the Jewish Colonization Association, had bought land for Russian Jews to escape pogroms. Seid's parents were newly married when they moved to Argentina, where their first child was born. Since it was difficult to reach a rabbi and maintain koshrith on the large Argentinean tract, Grandmother Seid ordered her family back to Russia after a year, where the second child was born, and then, in 1907, to Brooklyn, where the last three children were born. Ruth Seid was born on July 1, 1913, the youngest child. Three years after her birth, the Seids moved to Cleveland, which they made their permanent home in a then primarily Jewish but increasingly multiethnic and finally black neighborhood.

The Seids were displaced in several ways, and the immediate cause for their transitions was the family matriarch whose presence permeates the female-centered texts of "Jo Sinclair." She appears in the autobiographically true scenes in *Wasteland* and *The Changelings* as the protagonist's grandmother. In *Wasteland*, she is the stern emasculating woman who, by merely pointing a finger, makes her children move with their families to three continents in little more than a decade to find a safe home as Jews (165–73). In *The Changelings*, the matriarch is the uncompromising Jew who is outraged that her great-grandson has an Irish Catholic father and who atones for the assimilation of her family by returning to Palestine to die (172–81). In *Anna Teller*, the paternal grandmother reappears as a fictional character, "the General," a Hungarian Freedom Fighter in her seventies who survives war and refugee camps before being brought safely to the United States by her son. "The General" appears in a number of stories, including "I Trade You Tomatoes" (*Reader's Digest*, May 1956), in which an elderly immigrant learns the names of presidents for her naturalization test in exchange for teaching an embittered one-armed war veteran how to tie tomatoes to a stake with his teeth.

The displacement stemming from Ruth's indomitable grandmother informed the lives of the Seids. For one thing, they remained uncomfortable with English, which, combined with the Eastern European Jewish heritage she instilled in them, impeded their assimilation in America at a time of growing anti-Semitism. Like their *landsleit*, the Seids were poor. Ruth's father, who had become an ineffectual carpenter, took refuge from his alienation by reading Yiddish dailies. Ruth herself was clearly the outsider by her "deviant" masculine traits. Her refuge was in writing. She published four novels, a memoir, and approximately fifty stories. She had various radio plays aired and one play performed. In addition, there are some two hundred unpublished stories and sketches, an unpublished completed novel called *Approach to the Meaning*, and a novel-in-progress tentatively entitled *Mainland*. The Ruth Seid collection is at Boston University.

Ruth Seid attended John Hay, a commercial high school, from 1926 to 1930. She loved English and composition and excelled in her classes. The school paper, school plays, and track and field gave her the intellectual and physical outlets she needed. However, this involvement and popularity were not enough to hide Ruth's anger and frustration from herself. In her early teens, she felt trapped in physical and spiritual ghettoes: "With me, *ghetto*, takes in emotions, family, creativity, sex, religion. It is prison, double-locked gates on Self" (*Seasons*, 46). She lived with the fear of being sexually different in a homophobic society. She suffered from the sense of not having received acceptance, art, and a language of love from her family, whom she called "illiterates of the soul" (*Seasons*, 34) for their inability to express love and for their lack of culture. She thought somehow to give others what she had not received.

Although she was class valedictorian and yearned for higher education, she was a child of the Depression. College was financially out of the question. The day after graduation, out of a sense of loyalty to her parents, Ruth started work in the advertising department of Higbee. For the next four years, she had a tedious job ranging from reading proof for telephone directories to making boxes. However, two interrelated activities helped her during these difficult years: reading and writing. The Cleveland Public Library became her alma mater, and the habit of writing sustained her throughout her life.

When *New Masses* published her first story, "Noon Lynching," in 1936, the credit helped her get a job on the Foreign Language Newspaper Digest of the Works Progress Administration (WPA). She also felt like an author because the story was published under her pseudonym, a name that was deliberately ambiguous in terms of gender and deliberately anglicized in accordance with the assimilationist mood of the country. "Jo Sinclair" highlights the simplicity of the choice of her name: "Esquire Magazine was buying stories from only men. I came up with 'Jo'—a name I figured was used by men and women. The 'Sinclair' sounded right as a tail. I did sell to Esquire (twice), and to the same publisher's other two magazines: Ken and Coronet. . . . So my pseudonym is that simple" (Sinclair, letter to Sandberg). The choice is probably more complex. She says the name 'Jo' "sounded like an anonymous writer's name and she liked Upton Sinclair." She also admired Sinclair Lewis' (*Seasons*, 5), so her name identifies her with famous authors. Even though her work has been greatly appreciated by American Jews, who have bestowed many honors on her, the pseudonym does hide her heritage. The introduction to the memoir evades this issue but does emphasize the significance of the ambiguous "Jo": "Yes, she would hang on to that pseudonym she had made up as one more 'being different' for that Ruth trapped in a ghetto. She would keep using that shining pen name, but add the right credits to this first grubby one—and smash open her trap!" (*Seasons*, 3).

The pseudonym was important to her because it seemed to promise a recreated self. The writer "Jo" would move "ghetto-Ruth" into the "garden of the world" (*Seasons*, 2). The 1940 collage based on her experience on the WPA called *They Gave Us a Job* shows her preoccupation with the key concepts "attitude" and "morale." Though she revered Roosevelt, her characters in the story "I Was on Relief" (*Harper's*, January 1942) and in three of her novels worry about the stigma of working on his relief program. Their worry sounds historically plausible, but it certainly reflects Ruth Seid's joylessness, her "messed-up soul . . . [which] was a ghastly confusion of anger, shame, longing to live and die" (*Seasons*, 85). Her memoir, *The Seasons: Death and Transfiguration*, is a tragic account of her roller-coaster emotional life with bouts of drinking and despair punctuated by her fear of rejection. Writing gave meaning to her life. When her manuscripts were rejected, she felt dead—and she deadened herself.

While Ruth Seid was on the WPA, she won a couple of grants at Cleveland College to attend evening classes in playwriting. She became a publicity writer for the Red Cross, and many of her plays were aired on the radio. Her writing for the Red Cross gave her national exposure, and her work was upbeat because her purpose was to boost public morale by showing how everybody could contribute to winning the fight for democracy. She also met Helen Buchman, her first significant other.

Helen Buchman and Ruth Seid met on May 25, 1938, at the Contemporary Theatre that Buchman had founded. Two years later, Buchman invited Ruth Seid to move in with her, her husband, and their two children. Seid lived in an upstairs suite, separate from the family. She most commonly referred to the Buchmans as her "adopted" family to downplay any possible sexuality between Helen and herself. Accordingly, "adoption" is the central theme in "I Choose You" (*Collier's*, July 23, 1954), and it reappears in *Sing at My Wake*, *Anna Teller*, and the unpublished *Approach to the Meaning*. Instead of focusing on a chosen people, Sinclair focuses on chosen individuals.

Helen Buchman recognized and released the writer in Ruth Seid, first with informal "therapy" sessions (*Seasons*, 85–86) and with constant love, help, and affirmation. The Buchmans always had a garden where she could release her physical energy and also contribute to the family household. "Gardening" is a central metaphor in Sinclair's canon: her purpose is to plant the seed of love while weeding out prejudice. Aided by Helen Buchman's constant love and support (the Seid collection at Boston University is the result of manuscripts that Helen Buchman salvaged from the trash bin and stored in the attic), Sinclair wrote *Wasteland*, a novel about the successful psychotherapy of a Jewish man and his lesbian sister who have internalized anti-Semitism and homophobia, respectively. The novel, which took less than a year to draft by hand and originally contained names of real places and people (including her own), is dedicated to Helen, "who hates any kind of waste." From her multiple displacements, Jo Sinclair made a place for herself in the literary canon by giving a voice to American Jews during a peak year of anti-Semitism. She was thrilled when Richard Wright wrote her a letter for having "said about the Jewish family what I've been trying to say about Negro families. And you say it well, poetically" (quoted in *Seasons*, 140).

The times would not tolerate applauding the lesbian theme, but Sinclair received much fan mail from grateful women. Some of those letters came from Joan Mandell, a teenager confused by her attraction to girls, but who listened when Jo Sinclair told her to be open to all kinds of people. She kept the author apprised of her life, letting her know that she married a Samuel Soffer in 1949 and was raising two sons. That correspondence led to a lifelong friendship. In 1973, ten years after Helen's death, Joan asked Ruth to move in with her in her house in Jenkintown, Pennsylvania, where there was a huge garden that Ruth/ "Jo" could continue to till. In the meantime, the spectacular success of *Wasteland* and the $10,000 Harper prize it won gave Sinclair the means and faith to quit her publicity work for the Red Cross and become a freelance writer.

In 1951, *The Long Moment*, a play about "passing," was rejected by Karamu House, a "social settlement in Cleveland that had become nationally famous for its theater and arts" (*Seasons*, 67). However, Helen Buchman arranged to have it performed with an interracial cast at the experimental stage of the Cleveland Play House for an eight-week run, followed by a couple of performances in Harlem. In 1951, Sinclair's second novel, *Sing at My Wake*, was published and became the second-novel disaster that Sinclair had feared. Although it is about seeking fulfillment, it is also about messing up the lives of our children, a theme that Sinclair called "repeat of generations" and that she returned to often. (*The Changelings* is an explicit challenge to the idea that we are preprogrammed to continue the mistakes of our parents.) Still, Catherine Huffman's transformation from a fragile unwed mother to a sexually active and attractive mature woman is not credible enough to sustain this theme as the central focus of *Sing at My Wake*.

If 1951 encapsulates the ups and downs of Sinclair's emotions, then the period

1952–1953 stands out in stark contrast despite the financial problems of the Buchman household and the daughter's escape from it through marriage. Sinclair considered the year her "annus mirabilis" because *The Changelings* was "exploding" in her head. She had started the novel as an eighteen-year-old, and it went through four major revisions and three titles (*Now Comes the Black* and *The Long Moment* before the final published title). There are many overlaps in titles and characters in Sinclair's works that emphasize how focused she is on her central theme of "de-ghettoization." The protagonist Vincent of the third novel is the adolescent Deborah Brown of *Wasteland*, both of whom are fictionalized portraits of the author. *The Changelings* marks the fruition of the Jewish soul searching in *Wasteland*, for in *The Changelings* the focus is not on the inner struggle for ethnic identity in a second-generation Jew; rather, it is on the struggle of immigrant children who break away from the ignorance and prejudice of their parents. The children are rooted in their ethnic backgrounds, yet the mark of a changeling is being a bona fide American, recognizing and appreciating the distinctiveness of all Americans.

In 1957, while Sinclair was struggling with her fourth novel, *Anna Teller*, her dear editor from Harper, Ed Aswell, died. Along with Helen Buchman, he had been her most sensitive critic, and he was one of the few men for whom Ruth Seid genuinely cared. Another friend, Oscar Ban, whom she had met and idolized on the WPA project, became estranged from her because *Anna Teller* was based on him. He had appeared in the WPA texts, *Sing at My Wake*, and various short stories, but he could focus only on her portrayal of his marital infidelity and emasculation by his mother, "the General," and Sinclair dedicated the novel to Edward Aswell.

The decade between 1960 and 1970 was a heartbreaking blur for Ruth Seid, starting with her mother's death in 1960. Three years later, Helen Buchman died. Ruth Seid was devastated. Years later, Helen's daughter claimed that her father was so angry at Ruth, presumably from jealousy, that his health might fail him were he to be interviewed. The daughter's own strained and sometimes severed relations with Ruth are indicative of tension in the ménage à trois of her childhood home. Yet Mort Buchman and Ruth Seid mourned the same woman from opposite parts of the house for the next seven years, during which she wrote five drafts of the novel originally entitled *Jenny* and then *Three Women*. It was completed as *Approach to the Meaning* and dedicated to her sister Fannie, a cocktail waitress, who had always loved and supported Ruth. The central themes include Jewishness in America, the repetition of generations, and adoption.

A bright spot in the decade occurred in 1964, when Howard Gotlieb contacted Sinclair about making her collection the cornerstone of the newly funded Special Collections at Boston University. They completed their negotiations in 1970, although she needed to ask his assistance to pay the taxes on the purchase. She often referred, both sardonically and gratefully, to her "morgue" (a pun based on terminology her news-photographer brother taught her) near Kennedy's birthplace.

In 1968, Sinclair was the first recipient of Cleveland's Jewish Community Center Play Writing Grant and was commissioned to write a play commemorating the center's twentieth anniversary. She never received the second $1,000 because the play was never performed for being too "Jew-Jew-Jew" (Sinclair, letter to Johnson) and too long-winded. *The Survivors* is a dramatic fusion of the search for and acceptance of Jewish identity in *Wasteland* and the guilt of the Americanized Jew in *Anna Teller*. The theme of *The Survivors* is defining Jewishness in the United States at the time of the Six-Day War and the impact of renewed Jewish consciousness on an America already bored with the subject. The grant committee's response to the play is analogous to Alfred Kazin's observation that the nation was too saturated with the Depression to be entertained by Depression literature. The play is unrealistic in that the issues of Jewishness and Zionism are exaggerated. Neither assimilated American Jews nor Americans bored with Jewish suffering were receptive to a play so relentlessly concentrated on Judaism.

As a way of trying to transform Helen's death into creative life for herself—the rejections were "proof" her creativity had died—Ruth started her memoir *The Seasons: Death and Transfiguration*, the title inspired by the symphonic poem by Richard Strauss. She also wanted the memoir to be a source of inspiration for people who had not experienced the transforming power of love, a family history, a lyrical ode to the shifting seasons in Ohio, and a depiction of publishing in the United States over a twenty-year span. She felt that the book was a phony, that she was not transfigured, but writing it and leaving Mort to move into her own place were signs that she was a survivor. The ultimate lifesaving grace happened when Joan Soffer asked her to move to Jenkintown, where Ruth Seid died on April 4, 1995. For twenty years, she had been working on a new novel that she was calling *Mainland*, her name for "straightland" (Sinclair to Sandberg, phone call).

MAJOR WORKS AND THEMES

It is impossible to separate the life of Ruth Seid from the writings of Jo Sinclair. Writing was her life. Her central theme of spiritual de-ghettoization is thus a recurring treatment and is therefore emphasized in the biography section of this entry. Identity is the strongest recurring motif. In *Wasteland*, the two crucial identities to be recaptured are those of the self-affirming Jew in Jake Braunowitz and the self-affirming lesbian in Debby Brown. They reclaim their identities with the help of therapy, by talking openly with each other and their family members, and finally with the help of art. Debby is an aspiring writer, while Jake is a news photographer who keeps a separate file drawer for his art photographs. When they discuss their artistic credos, they are clearly the mouthpiece of Jo Sinclair: "I write about unfortunates, the people who have wandered off into odd alleys. . . . The strange people, the ones who are despised, or condemned, or lost. [Jake responds] . . . that's just like me with my camera! . . . I always called them—Jewish pictures . . . [t]here was something queer about every picture I took. Like—well, like it had some of our family in it" (*Wasteland*, 207–9). Both characters come to terms with themselves in the great melting pot of America, symbolized in their donating blood to the war effort.

Donating blood had been one of Sinclair's major motifs in her Red Cross publicity pieces. "We were born in Spain" is also a recurring motif in stories and in *Anna Teller*, emphasizing how global her vision became when she started working for the WPA. Adoption, sex (always hetero), art, talking, love, mother, family, gardening, and roots are all themes that constantly reappear. Sinclair took plots, characters, and titles from herself and reworked them again and again because her theme is always the same: labels kill people and "minority" is a dirty word. Her characters seek and affirm their identities: some as Jews, some as homosexuals, some as artists—and one, Debby Brown in *Wasteland*, as all three. America is the best country in the world, but it must become a land where people can be free.

CRITICAL RECEPTION

There were favorable reviews of Sinclair's novels in the national press. *Wasteland* was on the best-seller lists for months, and *The Changelings* restored her fame. Despite the positive reviews, Sinclair's novels were criticized for their length. Helen told her once that "you're afraid your readers won't get the point" (*Seasons*, 68).

The republished novels all contain interesting and thought-provoking introductions and afterwords. Johnnetta Cole and Elizabeth Oakes ask at the end of *The Changelings* why Sinclair focuses on an "individual's unique action, in isolation from his or her social context" (346). Sinclair felt personally singled out for her mannish looks, and society at large did everything it could to suppress gay and lesbian solidarity, so it seems natural for her to look to the strength of the individual. Also, her "Biographical Notes" to *The Seasons* says that even though her first story was published in *New Masses*, "she did not want to be part of anonymous, shabby, huddling masses of people; she wanted to be free and independent" (3). She opposed communism and fervently wanted to achieve the American Dream for herself. Anne Halley's focus on the family is a sensible approach to the sprawling story in *Anna Teller* and will probably inspire further examination of the role of the mother in Sinclair's works.

The articles by Ellen Surlen Uffen and Gay Wilentz heralded problems future critics will have with Sinclair. Uffen questioned Jake's "cure" in *Wasteland*: "Is it right to believe that a man who despised himself and his family for being foreigners and Jews, is 'cured' when he is able to see himself as an anonymous Everyman?" ("John Brown," 49). Wilentz asked a similar question, "What vision does the work present to readers if the only true way to affirm both lesbian and Jewish otherness is to somehow subsume difference?'' ''(Re)Constructing Identity,'' 100). These questions reflect our current emphasis on acculturation, on identifying and celebrating differences. Sinclair's most important texts were written when assimilation was highly valued, but she seems to say that you cannot be a good American or a whole person until you know and accept yourself and your roots. Jake can donate blood and enlist only because he affirms his heritage; otherwise, the anonymity would still be a way for him to deny his Jewishness.

Wilentz also had trouble with Sandberg's reading of Sinclair, which seemed to downplay the Jewish content. This seems strange since Sandberg quoted Sinclair as telling her how much she has always felt very much a Jew. Like most American Jews, Sinclair redefined her Jewishness as she learned about the atrocities committed against Jews during World War II, when Israel was declared a nation in 1948, and when the Six-Day War erupted in June 1967. She did reject the patriarchal aspect of Judaism because ''the Jewish God and prayers (Orthodox) belonged to my father, to men and sons, and neither Pa nor the Hebrew made strength for me—or warmth. . . . [Still,] I've always been glad to be a Jew. That's one ghetto I didn't have to smash'' (*Seasons*, 116–17). Even though she maintained that she did not seek out Jewish themes, her texts depict Jewish environments because she knew them the best.

Jan Clausen and Vivian Gornick both intimated the primary issues that future critics will have with Sinclair. Clausen wanted to smack a ''sweet baby butch'' in her class who complained that *The Changelings* is not sufficiently queer-positive (8). In fact, the 1942 draft has strong lesbian undertones, not publishable in the family-oriented 1950s, and was called *The Long Moment*. Gornick located Jewish-American novels of the 1940s as being in a long moment because they are thoughtful novels that probe the period of transition for American Jews. Sinclair was an old-fashioned writer who harked back to Anzia Yezierska and immigration literature rather than to modern Jewish lesbians like Jyl Lynn Felman, although her novels anticipate books like *Nice Jewish Girls: A Lesbian Anthology* and *Twice Blessed: On Being Lesbian, Gay, and Jewish*. Through writing, Jo Sinclair explored the meaning of being a lesbian Jewish American as she tried to free her readers from their private ''ghettoes'' and ''Nazis.''

BIBLIOGRAPHY

Works by Jo Sinclair

Wasteland. 1946. Philadelphia: Jewish Publication Society, 1987.
The Long Moment. Agent, Audrey Wood. Brooks Theater of the Cleveland Play House. April 5–end of May 1950. May 22–25, 1951 at St. Martin's Lttle Theatre, Harlem. November 14, 1951 at Fellowship House, Cleveland.
Sing at My Wake. New York: McGraw-Hill, 1951.
The Changelings. 1955. Old Westbury, NY: Feminist Press, 1985.

"Mama Bufano's." "The Jane Wyman Show." Cleveland, channel 3, April 9, 1957.
Anna Teller. 1960. New York: Feminist Press, 1992.
The Survivors. Play commissioned by the Cleveland Jewish Community Center, 1968.
　　Never performed.
Approach to the Meaning. 1969. Unpublished.
The Seasons: Death and Transfiguration. New York: Feminist Press, 1993.
Mainland. Work in progress since the 1970s.

Works Cited and Studies of Jo Sinclair

Clausen, Jan. "Testament of Friendship." Review of *The Seasons: Death and Transfig-
　　uration. Women's Review of Books*, December 1992, 7–8.
Cole, Johnnetta B., and Elizabeth H. Oakes. "On Racism and Ethnocentrism." In *The
　　Changelings*, 339–47.
Gitenstein, R. Barbara. "Jo Sinclair (Ruth Seid)." In *Twentieth-Century American Jewish
　　Fiction Writers*, ed. Daniel Walden. Vol. 28. of *Dictionary of Literary Biography*.
　　Detroit: Gale, 1984, 295–97.
Gornick, Vivian. "Introduction." In *Wasteland*, 1987, no page numbers.
Halley, Anne. "Afterword: The Family in *Anna Teller*." In *Anna Teller*, 597–610.
Harte, Barbara, and Carolyn Riley, eds. "Seid, Ruth." *Contemporary Authors: A Bio-
　　Bibliographical Guide to Current Authors and Their Works*. Vol. 5–8. Detroit:
　　Gale, 1969.
Hutchens, John K. "People Who Read and Write." *New York Times Book Review*,
　　January 6, 1946, 18.
"Jo Sinclair Shuns Gotham: Ohio's a Tremendous Joint." *Cleveland Plain Dealer*, No-
　　vember 27, 1960, B1.
Kunitz, Stanley J., ed. "Sinclair, Jo." *Twentieth Century Authors: A Biographical
　　Dictionary of Modern Literature*. 1st supplement. New York: Wilson, 1955, 916–
　　17.
McKay, Nellie. "Afterword." In *The Changelings*, 323–37.
Sandberg, Elisabeth. "A Biographical Note." In *The Changelings*, 349–52.
———. "Jo Sinclair." *American Women Writers*, Supplement, ed. Carol Hurd Green
　　and Mary G. Mason. New York: Crossroad/Continuum, 1994, 411–13.
———. "Jo Sinclair: A Gardener of Souls." *Studies in American Jewish Literature* 12
　　(1993): 72–78.
———. "Jo Sinclair: Toward a Critical Biography." Ph.D. diss., University of Massa-
　　chusetts, 1985.
"Seid, Ruth (Jo Sinclair, pseud.)." *Book Review Digest*, 1946, 1951, 1955, 1961.
"Seid, Ruth (Jo Sinclair, Pseudonym)." *Who's Who in America*. 42nd ed. Vol. 2. 1982–
　　83.
Sinclair, Jo. Letter to Margot Johnson. November 12, 1968. Boston University, Ruth
　　Seid ("Jo Sinclair") Collection, box 44.
———. Letter to Elisabeth Sandberg. October 18, 1983.
———. Phone call to Elisabeth Sandberg. Jenkintown, PA, to Boston, evening, August
　　10, 1984.
Uffen, Ellen Serlen. "John Brown (Né Jake Braunowitz) of the [*sic*] *Wasteland* of Jo
　　Sinclair (Née Ruth Seid)." *Midwestern Miscellany* 16, ed. David D. Anderson.
　　East Lansing, MI: Midwestern Press, 1988.

————. *Strands of the Cable: The Place of the Past in Jewish American Women's Writing.* Twentieth Century American Jewish Writers' Series. New York: Peter Lang, 1992, chap. 3.

Warfel, Harry R., ed. "Jo Sinclair." *American Novelists of Today.* New York: American Book, 1951, 388.

Weigel, John A. "Sinclair, Jo." *Contemporary Novelists,* ed. James Vinson. 2nd ed. New York: St. Martin's Press, 1976, 1246–48.

Wilentz, Gay. "Jo Sinclair (Ruth Seid) (1913–)." In *Jewish American Women Writers: A Bio-Bibliographical and Critical Sourcebook,* ed. Ann R. Shapiro. Westport, CT: Greenwood, 1994.

————. "(Re)Constructing Identity: 'Angled' Presentation in Sinclair/Seid's *Wasteland.*" In *Multicultural Literatures through Feminist/poststructuralist Lenses,* ed. by Barbara Fay Waxman Knoxville: University of Tennessee Press, 1993, 84–103.

Yezierska, Anzia. "Landlords of the City." *New York Times Book Review,* September 25, 1955, 33.

DAVID SLAVITT (1935–)

Joel Shatzky and Michael Taub

BIOGRAPHY

David Slavitt was born in White Plains, New York, on March 33, 1935, the son of Samuel Saul and Adele Beatrice Rytman Slavitt. He was educated at Phillips Academy in Andover, Massachusetts, where he became influenced by the great classicist, Dudley Fitts, one of the most important translators, with Robert Fitzgerald, of classic Greek drama. In 1952 Slavitt entered Yale and graduated magna cum laude four years later. He received an M.A. from Columbia in 1957. After a year of teaching at Georgia Tech, he worked at *Newsweek* from 1958 to 1965, becoming a movie critic and occasional book reviewer. Slavitt has been twice married: to Lynn Nita Meyer in 1956 (divorced in 1977) and in 1978 to Janet Lee Abrahm. He has three children by his first marriage: Evan, Sarah, and Joshua.

He has taught, lectured, and given poetry readings at Yale, Harvard, Bennington, Hollins College, the University of Texas, the Folger Library, and the Library of Congress. He has also been a visiting lecturer and professor at the University of Maryland, Drexel, Temple, Columbia, Rutgers/Camden Campus, Princeton, and the University of Pennsylvania, where he is presently a lecturer in English.

Slavitt has received both a Pennsylvania Council on the Arts Individual Artist Fellowship in fiction and poetry and a National Endowment for the Arts Fellowship in translation. He has also received a National Academy and Institute of Arts and Letters Award in Literature, a Rockefeller Foundation Residency award, and a number of citations for his work from the PEN Book-of-the-Month Club and the Book-of-the-Month Club.

MAJOR WORKS AND THEMES

Slavitt is remarkably prolific and his work amazingly varied. He has a significant reputation as a translator of classical Greek and Latin poets and playwrights, including Aeschylus, Seneca, Ovid, and Virgil. His mastery of subjects ranges from social psychology to Virgil; he has edited two series of volumes on classical drama, *The Complete Greek Drama* and *The Complete Roman Drama* with Palmer Bovie; he has had several plays produced in New York City and Philadelphia; and he has written fifteen books of poetry, eleven books of translations from Latin literature, seventeen novels under his own name, and nine other pseudonymous novels. In the area of Jewish literature, as he put it in a letter to Joel Shatzky, "[t]he Jewish thread runs through the whole tapestry."

Slavitt's own view of his place as a Jewish-American writer is in part defined by his feelings concerning Holocaust writing, a subject many American Jews with no firsthand experience have been writing about with increasing frequency since the 1960s. He does not feel comfortable with the subject and has reservations about his right to talk about it. Yet he also recognizes that through the last few centuries, the Jew has been the one to "speak about the unspeakable," not only through a Marx and a Freud, but also through the darkly comic shtick of Lenny Bruce, the earlier farce of Jack Benny and Milton Berle, or today's fin de siècle versions: Roseanne and Howard Stern.

To Slavitt, "comedy is to the Jews what the blues are to African Americans," and his fondness and addiction to it is evident in conversation when he finds the opportunity to try out a "new one." Perhaps for Slavitt the answer to the haunting questions of this abattoir we call the twentieth century is not silence but laughter.

Among those works in which there are specific Jewish characters, several stories in the collection *Short Stories Are Not Real Life* (1991) are about the rituals of family life: a bris, a wedding, the birthday of the family patriarch. But there is a touch of bitterness as well as detachment about both the losses and gains of assimilation. Hearing a klezmer band on WEVD, the Jewish-language radio station in New York, the narrator observes: "It was funny, schmaltzy, ridiculous music to which we responded with both laughter and sadness, laughter for its excesses and its naiveté, and sadness for what we miss, what has leached out of our lives" ("Conflations," *Short Stories*, 40). There are some jokes in this series of stories; one particular favorite—it is used again in *Turkish Delights*—is about a woman who asks someone on a subway platform to identify the Long Island train for her so she *won't* take it; but even much of the humor has a certain black irony about it.

The most interesting work of the fiction that has a Jewish theme is one that, on the surface, seems to have little to do with Jews. *Lives of the Saints* (1989) is about a Nathanael Westian narrator who works for a schlock journal on the order of the *National Observer* and is assigned a sensational story in which he is to interview the family of the victims of a senseless mass murder, one of those random massacres in a shopping center. In the course of his interviews he tries to deal with the deeper senselessness of the losses in his own life: the death of his wife and only child at the hands of a drunken driver. Throughout the novel the narrator sees in the pointless lives of the others who have been bereft a distorted mirror of his own suffering. But while the dominant symbol of the novel is the lives of saints that the narrator records to illustrate the illusory rewards of suffering, and the premise of the seventeenth-century theologian Nicholas Malebranche that there is no such thing as cause and effect—except through the will of God—there is a profoundly Jewish twist to the story. The narrator observes, "There is a slip of paper on my desk, a note I made for myself and then tucked away and forgot about, with interesting information about the Cabalists' belief that each person has his own Torah" (99). Thus the narrator tries to find his Torah, his own moral center.

Like a Bellovian figure who probes through the wisdom of both Eastern and Western culture—he is interested in the Chinese poet Yuan Chen as well as the Christian fathers—the narrator attempts to find some meaning in his suffering, cynical as he pretends to be. Near the end of the novel he faces the man who was responsible for his loved ones' deaths, at a hearing, and realizes the "banality of evil," the evil he had been trying to understand, when he asks the man about his dead victims: "Do you think about them? Are you sorry?" "W-w-w-whatever you w-w-w-want" is the stuttered answer (194). The novel ends on a hopeful note when the one interesting woman he meets among the family members of the victims seems willing to make a life with him.

Yet, as he also admits, "I cannot believe. I am a Jew, but also a humanist. A secularist. A skeptic. A rationalist. . . . All those things those rabid preachers inveigh against. And the rabid rabbis used to inveigh against—think of Spinoza!" (204). As he quotes Augustine, "Credebant quia absurdum" (They believed because it is absurd), the narrator cannot forsake hope, despite all of the reasons he can find for surrendering to that darkness within him.

Where Slavitt's Jewish roots are most clearly found, however, is in his poetry. In his collection *Big Nose* (1983), the splendid poem "Jacob" expresses in the wrestlings of the patriarch with the angel the poet's own wrestlings of the spirit: "knowing that there's no help, that all alone / we wrestle with our angels on our own" (14). In another poem, *Villanelle*, the dreams of the dead father "unravel in my head," but despite their disturbing nature, "I am proud. Those dreams are what he bred / in me; they are the heritage I keep" (33). Even if this heritage is sometimes expressed through silence or denial, the poet must let it speak through his heart if not his head.

CRITICAL RECEPTION

Although Slavitt's work has often been undeservedly scanted—his most well-known fiction is *The Exhibitionist*, which was written under the pseudonym

Henry Sutton—George Garrett has correctly described him as "one of the most adroitly versatile and productive writers in America . . . "a poet of almost brutally ironic contradictions" (quoted in *Contemporary Authors*, 413). *Lives of the Saints* met with very positive reviews in which Slavitt was recognized for his originality and ingenuity as a writer who deserves to be better known. Although this novel may have flaws in its too-easily earned optimistic ending, perhaps Slavitt's fate will have earned its own optimism. When the success of *The Exhibitionist* led a publisher to suggest that Slavitt might become wealthy through the writing of best-sellers, "I replied . . . thanking him for his interest but letting him know that he had the wrong fellow. I was a high-brow low-revenue kind of author" (quoted in *Contemporary Authors*, 414). This is where Slavitt seems most comfortable, despite his prolific output, and it is in keeping with that knowledge of himself that he does his work.

BIBLIOGRAPHY

For a complete bibliography, see *Contemporary Authors*, NR 41, 411.

Works by David Slavitt

Fiction

The Exhibitionist. As Henry Sutton. New York: Bernard Geis Associates, 1967.
Rochelle; or, Virtue Rewarded. New York: Delacorte, 1967.
Feel Free. New York: Delacorte, 1968.
Anagrams. Garden City, NY: Doubleday, 1971.
The Killing of the King. Garden City, NY: Doubleday, 1974.
Alice at 80. Garden City, NY: Doubleday, 1984.
The Hussar. Baton Rouge: Louisiana State University Press, 1987.
Lives of the Saints. New York: Atheneum, 1989.
Short Stories Are Not Real Life. Baton Rouge: Louisiana State University Press, 1991.
Turkish Delights. Baton Rouge: Louisiana State University Press, 1993.

Poetry

Suits for the Dead. New York: Scribners, 1961.
Rounding the Horn. Baton Rouge: Louisiana State University Press, 1978.
Big Nose. Baton Rouge: Louisiana State University Press, 1983.
Quotes are cited from *Contemporary Authors*, New Revision Series, 41. Detroit: Gale Research, 1994.

SUSAN SONTAG   (1933–   )

Evan J. Nisonson

BIOGRAPHY

Born in New York City on January 16, 1933, Susan Sontag spent her early years apart from her parents, who managed an export business in China. Her grandparents raised her and her sister Judith, who was born in 1936, while the parents worked abroad. This absence of parents would prove to be instrumental in developing Sontag's cultural and literary aesthetic in later years. After her father succumbed to tuberculosis in China in 1938, Sontag's mother returned to New York, and in 1939, the family relocated to Tucson, Arizona, where it was hoped that the environment would prove beneficial to Sontag's asthma.

The family later moved to California, where Sontag enrolled at the University of California at Berkeley at the age of fifteen. Soon thereafter, she transferred to the University of Chicago, where she met Professor Philip Rieff while auditing a course on Freud. They were married ten days later. Upon completing her B.A. in 1951, she and her husband moved to Boston, where Sontag continued her studies at Harvard University while he taught at Brandeis University. She earned her M.A. in English in 1954 and her M.A. in philosophy a year later. Shortly after entering the Ph.D. program in philosophy at Harvard, Sontag gave birth to a son, David (who would be her only child). In 1957, as part of a scholarship to study abroad, Sontag traveled to St. Anne's College, in Oxford, and then to the University of Paris, where she was to be further influenced by such European intellectuals as Claude Lévi-Strauss, Roland Barthes, and Jacques Lacan, such writers as Alain Robbe-Grillet, Nathalie Sarraute, and Jean Genet, and such filmmakers as Alain Resnais, François Truffaut, and Jean-Luc Godard. Upon returning to the United States, Sontag divorced Rieff in 1959.

Living in New York City with her son, Sontag lectured at Sarah Lawrence

College and the City College of New York while editing for a short time on the staff of *Commentary*. She also lectured in the Department of Religion at Columbia University. During the period 1962–1965, Sontag's literary production intensified: she published twenty-six essays, book reviews, theater reviews, and film reviews that marked her as an astute critic of American culture. She published her first novel, *The Benefactor*, in 1963, receiving favorable critical reception as a fiction writer. She continued her critique of art and culture in the highly influential collection of essays *Against Interpretation* (1966). She followed this work with her second novel, *Death Kit*, in 1967, an account of her experiences in Vietnam in 1968 entitled *Trip to Hanoi*, which continued her assault on the war abroad, and another collection of essays, *Styles of Radical Will* (1969), drawn from her works in *Esquire, Rolling Stone*, and *Partisan Review*.

Her early interest in the film medium came to fruition in the late 1960s with her first work as a screenwriter and director on *Duet for Cannibals* (1969). She continued to work in the film medium, completing *Brother Carl* (1971) and a documentary entitled *Promised Lands* (1974), a response to the Yom Kippur War. This documentary is her only work to date that directly engages Jewish issues. Her interest in the visual medium continued, resulting in *On Photography* (1977), which earned her the National Book Critics Circle Award.

Sontag was diagnosed with breast cancer in 1975. Her subsequent mastectomy and chemotherapy led her to examine the theme of illness in her work *Illness as Metaphor* (1978), a discussion of disease and its place in Western culture. In the 1980s she exhibited an acute sensitivity to the AIDS epidemic, publishing two works that further explored the theme of illness, *AIDS and Its Metaphors* (1989) and *The Way We Live Now* (1991), a fictionalized account of the death of her friend, photographer Robert Mapplethorpe.

Subsequent to her bout with cancer, she continued to work in a variety of media, publishing a short-story collection entitled *I, Etcetera* (1978) and, most recently, a historical novel, *The Volcano Lover* (1992), which received the warmest critical reception of all her works of fiction. Her passion for film and theater continued in 1983 with *Unguided Tour* and in 1985, when she directed the premiere production of Milan Kundera's play *Jacques and His Master*. Her play *Alice in Bed* had its premiere in Bonn in the autumn of 1991. She continues to make her biggest mark in the area of cultural criticism, having published a second collection of essays in 1980, *Under the Sign of Saturn*, and *A Susan Sontag Reader* two years later. She has been honored professionally for her active role in cultural and literary criticism, having been elected to the American Academy of Arts and Letters in 1976 and having been named president of PEN International in 1987. She resides in New York City, where she continues to write for the *New Yorker* and other magazines.

MAJOR WORKS AND THEMES

In both content and form, Susan Sontag is most definitely a modernist writer. Central to her fictional works is an anxiety concerning the place of the self within the world—a modernist preoccupation that manifests itself in the themes of negation, alienation, "disburdenment," and death that pervade her works.

The Benefactor exemplifies negation through the efforts of the protagonist, Hippolyte, a young Paris intellectual, to realize his nocturnal dreams. In this way, Hippolyte's dreams problematize the reality of his waking life as he envisions and revisions his past and possible future fate within the dream state. Thus Sontag questions the nature of experience through Hippolyte's narrative, which involves his attempt to dissolve his relationship with his mistress, Frau Anders. Juxtaposed with the dream state, the world, for Sontag, becomes "entirely plastic" (Kazin, 181).

Death Kit intensifies this exploration of reality and dreams as the protagonist, Dalton Harron, known as Diddy, questions whether or not he has killed a man or has merely dreamed the incident (Diddy can be read as Did he?). Indeed, Diddy continues Hippolyte's task and learns that thinking self-deletion does not necessarily purge one of oneself (Sayres, *Susan Sontag*, 73). Sontag again interweaves dream and referential narrative as she follows the relationship of Diddy and his blind lover, Hester, in their search for the truth behind the murder of a train worker, making her work an example of "how the head gets rid of the world" (Tanner, 446). The novel also reveals Sontag's modernist fascination with alienation and death, as the conclusion exemplifies: Diddy and Hester return to the scene of the crime, the train tunnel—clearly symbolic of that corridor between life and death, reality and dream—and reenact the moment of the murder. Through her protagonist, Diddy, Sontag questions the nature of experience and examines the exercise of perceiving and interpreting—a prime consideration within her criticism.

I, Etcetera, a collection of eight short stories, centers around the theme of exploring the various states of human consciousness and their relationship to art. Sontag utilizes a variety of literary genres to accomplish this task. "The Dummy," for example, draws upon the literary tradition of the uncanny as it develops Sontag's previous themes: the desire to escape from one's role in life and to continue to function as an observer. "Doctor Jekyll" further exemplifies Sontag's reliance upon the tradition of the uncanny as she revisions Stevenson's Jekyll as envious of Hyde's freedom—again, Sontag plays with the binary oppositions of reality and dream, life and death. "Project for a Trip to China" and "Unguided Tour" modify the travelogue tradition while employing modernist form with their sketchlike, epigrammatic bits to present ideas on art and life. Sontag later developed a script and directed a film based on "Unguided Tour." Her 1968 work *Trip to Hanoi* also utilizes this travelogue form to further expound upon culture and aesthetics. Indeed, travel serves as an apt metaphor for Sontag's modernist *Kunstwöllen*, as it allows her to function as a voyager with a sense of detachment.

Her most recent work of fiction, *The Volcano Lover*, exemplifies a prominent theme in Sontag's work: the questioning of experience and reality. A historical romance, the work follows the relationships of Sir William Hamilton, his wife, Lady Emma Hamilton, and her lover, Horatio Nelson. *The Volcano Lover* evidences Sontag's attempt to "connect a bygone time with the present," certainly a modernist yearning or frustration. Much of the novel relies upon the discourses of the narrator—who has a twentieth-century sensibility—upon the routines and characteristics of Hamilton, Emma, and Nelson, who are referred to as the Cavaliere, the Cavaliere's wife, and the Hero, respectively. Most notable of these discourses is the Cavaliere's passion for collecting, which extends to his treatment of Emma, whom he attempts to transform, Pygmalion-like, from a lower-class mistress into a sophisticated dame of society. In so doing, the Cavaliere introduces her to a world in which she can equally create desire in other men. She becomes a consummate work of art for the collector, the Cavaliere, for she functions like a commodity, gaining in value in the eyes of the Cavaliere as her affair with the Hero develops. Collecting mirrors Sontag's own critical sensibility in that the collector and the critic both desire to possess and re-create that object anew (Linkon, 417). The juxtaposition of past and present vis-à-vis the twentieth-century perspective of the narrator and the juxtaposition of historical reality and the fictional re-creation of the lives of the characters underscores the tension between experience and reality—a familiar modernist leitmotif heard in Sontag's earlier works vis-à-vis the tension between the world of dreams and reality. Indeed, her references within *The Volcano Lover* concerning the unreliability of art and the use of literature as a means of escape further this tension while problematizing the nature of aesthetic experience itself (Bawer, 37).

Even Sontag's works that concern illness examine the nature of experience. In *Illness as Metaphor*, Sontag discusses the ways in which society conceptualizes disease. She deconstructs the single-cause theory of disease, advocating divorcing agency from the affliction or the afflicted. *AIDS and Its Metaphors* and *The Way We Live Now* continue her examination of disease along these lines, with the former work focusing on the tension between the imaginary and the real vis-à-vis perceptions of the disease versus the reality and how the one distorts the other. The latter work originally appeared as a short story in the *New Yorker* and describes the reactions of a group of New Yorkers to their friend's affliction with AIDS.

It is often difficult to differentiate Sontag the fiction writer from Sontag the cultural critic. Even she herself readily admits that everything she writes is a fiction of sorts. Yet it is for her cultural criticism that Susan Sontag is most well known and most well regarded. Her essays on aesthetics and cultural criticism, beginning with *Against Interpretation*, in which she favors experience over interpretation, continue to comment upon culture and art as much as they influence the two. "Against Interpretation," the title essay in her first collection of criticism, offers a modernist aesthetic sensibility positing that art must be responded to with the sensory, not the intellectual, faculties, emphasizing form rather than content. Sontag also targets art form in the controversial essay "Notes on Camp," in which she asserts that "camp" is a legitimate art form that is "serious about the frivolous, frivolous about the serious," a critical position that seems in accordance with the artistic school of pop art, prevalent at that time. Her later collection, *Styles of Radical Will*, contains the equally provocative essays "The Pornographic Imagination," in which she defends pornography as a valid literary genre, and "The Aesthetics of Silence," in which she analyzes the noncommunicative elements in the musical works of John Cage and the drama of Samuel Beckett. Sontag's emphasis upon a new sensibility in evaluating art and culture blends the formal considerations of modernist aesthetics with an emerging understanding of postmodern tenets of deconstruction.

Sontag's only work that draws directly on Jewish themes is her documentary, *Promised Lands*. Yet even in this film she continues her detached critical method as she observes and chronicles. What distinguishes her, her criticism, and her fiction as being part of an American Jewish literary tradition manifests itself in three interrelated ways. Her seemingly "un-Jewish" essays betray a strong connection with the European Jewish intellectual tradition. She embraced such European Jewish critics as Walter Benjamin and Georg Lukács early in her discourse, lauding their ideas before they had gained full acceptance in academic circles in America. Indeed, she locates herself very definitely in that tradition, liberally introducing the ideas of these critics and others into her own essays as foundation and support. At the same time, she also aligns herself with the New York intelligentsia of mostly Jewish writers associated with *Partisan Review, Commentary, Politic*, and *Dissent*. While it was in this milieu that Sontag honed her modernist craft, one might also recognize that she carried with her a sense of cultural displacement, a result of her early experiences, her relocating to and from California and New York and her European aesthetics transplanted in American soil. In this regard, many, if not the same, stylistics that define her as a modernist equally define her as an American Jewish writer of diaspora. The term "diaspora" has recently come into vogue in academic criticism to describe such transnational movements and cultural transplantations as the African-American literary and artistic movements. The literary critic qua historian, however, cannot forget the original historical significance of that term—from the Greek *diasporein*, "the scattering of seeds"—as it related first to Jews of the eighth century B.C.E., then to Jews of the sixth century B.C.E., and much later to European Jews who emigrated to America in the mid-to-late nineteenth century. Aside from the obvious sense of European cultural displacement prevalent in her work, Sontag evidences this diasporism with her emphasis upon alienation and otherness through the aesthetic of "disburdenment."

Frank Kermode found that underlying Sontag's critical voice is a distinct notion of difference. She concerns herself in her role as critic with tracing the sensuous contours of culture in order to make "her sensitive to the cultural difference of the alien sage'' (42). Indeed, Sontag has borrowed Elias Canetti's observation that ''the world has always been a world of exiles''—a distinction that could readily apply to this sense of diasporism as a literary style vis-à-vis her ability to simultaneously share in and maintain a distance from the human condition (Roudiez, 223). Her biography evidences this sense of alienation and exile. Her parents' living abroad for the majority of Sontag's childhood and her first encounter with a synagogue, which occurred on European soil at the age of twenty-four while she was visiting Florence, are significant examples of this diasporism as forming an integral part of her American Jewish identity. To recognize alienation, negation, and exile as significant aspects of both modernism and diasporism is perhaps to revision modernism itself as an aesthetical movement of exile and diaspora, with Susan Sontag (among others) as a linchpin to this reinterpretation.

CRITICAL RECEPTION

While many critics recognize a prevailing consistency in Sontag's literary style—a unity of form and content—literary scholars have given Sontag's fiction mixed reviews. Some critics laud her ideas, but they likewise critique the stylistic weaknesses of her works. Alfred Kazin admired both *The Benefactor* and *Death Kit* because they evidence Sontag's aesthetic belief that ''fiction is a trying-out, an hypothesis which you carry out, not prove'' (181). Theodore Solotaroff more boldly condemned *The Benefactor* for its lack of ''vitality,'' claiming that ''it could have been taken for a parody of the post-expressionist novel of moral exhaustion and exquisite nerves were it not so exhausted and nervous itself'' (265). Bruce Bawer dismissed Sontag's fiction as being wholly derivative. He regarded *The Benefactor* as a recapitulation of Albert Camus and Canetti and *Death Kit* as a ''labored'' and ''humorless'' attempt at ''the New Novel of Nathalie Sarraute and Alain Robbe-Grillet'' (31). He recognized in Sontag's writing an air of cultural elitism that deliberately alienates rather than engages the reader. Others, such as Anne Tyler, however, recognized both the shortcomings and the intellectual effusiveness and chutzpah of Sontag's literary style. Tyler remarked that *I, Etcetera* ''is not always an easy book to read; it's not always a rewarding book, even. But it does possess its own kind of spirit and nerve, and it takes some magnificent chances . . . [it] reflect[s] a vital and restless imagination cooking away in several directions'' (29–30). Sontag's most recent novel, *The Volcano Lover*, has received both critical and commercial acclaim, gaining best-seller status. Michiko Kakutani saw the work as a ''passionate and often radical novel of ideas that afford all the old-fashioned pleasures of a traditional historical novel'' (quoted in Linkon, 418). Bawer contended that *The Volcano Lover* is a work marred by the author's chief purpose, ''to serve as a framework for [her] cerebrations; it is an act of will rather than of visionary compulsion, a work crowded with ideas rather than with life'' (34).

Still other critics have difficulty in locating her critical voice. As stated, Sontag most clearly situates herself in a European, especially a French, literary tradition evidencing the influences of Barthes, Camus, Gide, Artaud, and Duras, among others. But John Breslin situated Sontag the critic in the tradition of Matthew Arnold, stating that in her critiques of culture and art, Sontag "bears a resemblance to Matthew Arnold whose love affair with Europe gave to his literary and cultural criticism a breadth of reference otherwise lacking in early Victorian England" (E3). Walter Kendrick concurred, seeing these European influences as "red herrings, excrescences on a body of work that belongs squarely in the mainstream of the Anglo-American tradition of the essay" ("Eminent Victorian," 46).

Sontag's political stances have also generated conflict. Her political essays regarding Hanoi and Cuba problematized the relationship between aesthetics and foreign policy. Feminist critics are equally ambivalent about embracing Sontag, chastising her for her detachment from the women's movement and for adopting a male perspective in much of her fiction (Roudiez, 220). Indeed, her perspective on feminism seems more in line with an androgynous utopian vision à la Virginia Woolf than with a vision that attempts to question the process of gender identification à la Judith Butler or attempts to posit an essential feminine "self" à la Hélène Cixous. Sontag's brand of feminism emerges in the statement "If I'm going to play chess, I don't think I should play it differently because I'm a woman. . . . It would be nice if men could be more feminine and women more masculine. To me, that would be a more attractive world" (*Rolling Stone*, October 4, 1979).

Sontag, then, emerges as a multifaceted figure of controversy. Critics contend that it is her critical method rather than her subject of criticism that takes precedence for Sontag. Critic Cary Nelson argued that "Sontag is less concerned with exploring specific questions than with examining the nature of criticism itself by recording her own critical processes" (quoted in Linkon, 419). Jay Parini diagnosed what he believed to be the problem with Sontag: "She wants everything all ways: a 'radical' stance . . . with the cool amoral impartiality of Wildean aestheticism" (418). With her fragmentary style of discourse, Sontag has been accused of critical dilettantism, with claims that "her aesthetic comes down to a celebration of novelty" (Phillips, 394). William Phillips regarded these claims as unfair, arguing that Sontag "can't be held responsible for a dilemma all modern criticism has failed to resolve: the dilemma of how to judge—or relate—new works that defy the old criteria" (394). In this regard, critics such as Phillips view Sontag's cultural reactions as a measure of Sontag's consistency in "keeping up" with culture. What remains undisputed is her political perspective and her contribution to contemporary critical discourse. Sontag is influenced by as much as she influences the American cultural scene. She is a cultural critic who writes "contrapuntally," to borrow a phrase from Edward Said, not just reading against the cultural and ideological grain, but writing against it as well. Above all, Susan Sontag is a critic who has situated herself in the contemporary academic school of cultural studies, which she, in turn, has helped to erect. She concerns herself with both recognizing tradition and then deconstructing it to rebuild anew. As Sontag contended in a symposium in 1982: "Either you're abolishing a tradition ... or you're founding a new one ... you're starting a new tradition, which often calls itself an anti-tradition" (*Shenandoah*, 29).

BIBLIOGRAPHY

Works by Susan Sontag

Fiction

The Benefactor. New York: Farrar, Straus and Giroux, 1963; London: Eyre and Spottiswoode, 1964.
"Man with a Pain." *Harper's*, April 1964, 72–75.
"The Will and the Way." *Partisan Review* 33 (Summer 1965): 373–96.
Death Kit. New York: Farrar, Straus and Giroux, 1967; London: Secker and Warburg, 1968.
"The Letter Scene." *New Yorker*, August 18, 1968, 24–32.
I, Etcetera. New York: Farrar, Straus and Giroux, 1978.
The Way We Live Now. New York: Noonday Press, Farrar, Straus and Giroux, 1991.
The Volcano Lover: A Romance. New York: Farrar, Straus and Giroux, 1992.
Misrach, Richard. *Violent Legacies: Three Cantos.* Fiction by Susan Sontag. New York: Aperture, 1992.

Selected Criticism

Against Interpretation. New York: Farrar, Straus and Giroux, 1966; London: Eyre and Spottiswoode, 1967.
Trip to Hanoi. New York: Farrar, Straus and Giroux, 1968; London: Panther, 1969.
"Some Thoughts on the Right Way (for Us) to Love the Cuban Revolution." *Ramparts* 7 (April 1969): 6, 10, 14, 16, 18–19.
Styles of Radical Will. New York: Farrar, Straus and Giroux, 1969; London: Secker and Warburg, 1969.
"The Third World of Women." *Partisan Review* 40 (Summer 1973): 180–206.
On Photography. New York: Farrar, Straus and Giroux, 1977.
Illness as Metaphor. New York: Farrar, Straus and Giroux, 1978.
Under the Sign of Saturn. New York: Farrar, Straus and Giroux, 1980.
A Susan Sontag Reader. Intro. by Elizabeth Hardwick. New York: Farrar, Straus and Giroux, 1982.
"Sontag on Mapplethorpe." *Vanity Fair*, July 1985, 69–73.
"The Pleasure of the Image." *Art in America*, November 1987, 122–31.
"This Man, The Country." Collected in *For Nelson Mandela*, eds. Jacques Derrida, Mustapha Teiei. New York: Seaver Books, 1987, 47–52.
AIDS and Its Metaphors. New York: Farrar, Straus and Giroux, 1989.
Cage-Cunningham-Johns: Dancers on a Plane: In Memory of Their Feelings. Susan Sontag [with] Richard Francis. New York: A. A. Knopf in association with A. d'Offay Gallery, 1990.

Films

Duet for Cannibals. Written and directed by Sontag. Prod. Goran Lindgren for Sandrew
    Film and Theater (AB) Sweden, 1969 (distributed by Evergreen Films, USA). In
    Swedish; subtitles by Sontag. Black and white, 105 min.
Brother Carl. Written and directed by Sontag. Prod. Goran Lindgren for Sandrew Film
    and Theater (AB) and Svenska Filminstitutet, 1971 (distributed by New Yorker
    Films). In Swedish, with English soundtrack. Black and white, 97 min.
Promised Lands (a documentary on Israel). Written and directed by Sontag, 1974 (dis-
    tributed by New Yorker Films). Color, 87 min.
Unguided Tour (from the short story). Written and directed by Sontag, 1983. Prod.
    Giovannella Zannoni for Lunga Gittata Cooperative, RAI rete 3. Color, 72 min.

Plays

"A Parsifal." *Antaeus* 67 (Fall 1991): 180–85.
Alice in Bed: A Play in Eight Scenes. New York: Farrar, Straus and Giroux, 1993.

Introductions/Prefaces

Roland Barthes. *Writing Degree Zero and Elements of Semiology.* Preface copyrighted
    1968 by Susan Sontag. Boston: Beacon, 1970. "Preface" xi–xxv.
E.M. Cioran. *The Temptation to Exist.* Trans. Richard Howard. Introduction by Susan
    Sontag, copyright 1968. Chicago: Quadrangle Paperback, 1970. "Introduction,"
    9–29.
Dugald Stermer. *The Art of Revolution: 96 Posters from Cuba.* Introduction by Susan
    Sontag. "Posters: advertisements, art, political artifact, commodity," vii–xxiii.
    New York: McGraw Hill, 1970.
Antonin Artaud. *Selected Writings.* Ed. with intro. by Susan Sontag. Trans. Helen Wea-
    ver: notes by Sontag and Don Eric Levine. New York: Farrar, Straus & Giroux,
    1976.
Roland Barthes. *A Roland Barthes Reader.* Ed. with intro. by Susan Sontag. New York:
    Hill & Wang, 1981.
Maria Irene Fornes. *Plays.* Preface by Susan Sontag, copyright 1985. "Preface" 7–10.
    New York: PAJ, 1986.
Vera Lehndorff, Holger Trulzsch. *Verushka: Transfigurations.* Introduction by Susan
    Sontag, copyright 1986. "Fragments of an Aesthetic of Melancholy," 6–12. New
    York: A New York Graphic Society Book, Little, Brown & Company, 1986.

Selected Interviews

Toback, James. "Whatever You'd Like Susan Sontag to Think, She Doesn't." *Esquire*,
    (July 1968): 59–61, 114.
Bellamy, Joe David. "Susan Sontag." *The New Fiction: Interviews with Innovative
    American Writers.* Urbana: Univ. of Illinois Press, 1974: 113–29.
Boyers, Robert and Maxine Bernstein. "Women, The Arts & The Politics of Culture.
    An Interview with Susan Sontag." *Salmagundi*, No. 31–31 (Fall 1975–Winter
    1976): 29–48.
Copeland, Roger. "The Habits of Consciousness." *Commonweal*, 13 Feb. 1981: 83–87.
Russ, Charles. "Susan Sontag: Past, Present and Future." *NYTBR*, 24 Oct. 1982: 11, 39.

Manion/Simon. "An Interview with Susan Sontag." *Canadian Journal of Political and Social Theory*, 9:1 (Winter 1985): 7–15.

Works Cited and Studies of Susan Sontag

Aronowitz, Stanley. "Sontag versus Barthes for Barthes' Sake." *Village Voice Literary Supplement*, November 1982, 1, 24.

Banville, John. "By Lava Possessed." *New York Times Book Review*, August 9, 1992, 1, 26–27.

Bassoff, Bruce. "Private Revolution: Susan Sontag's *The Benefactor.*" *enclitic* 3 (1979): 59–73.

Bawer, Bruce. "That Sontag Woman." *New Criterion* 11:1 (September 1992): 30–37.

Branham, Robert J. "Speaking Itself: Susan Sontag's Town Hall Address." *Quarterly Journal of Speech*, August 1989, 259–77.

Breslin, John B. "Complexities of Consciousness." *Book World*, December 17, 1978, E3.

Brooks, Cleanth. "The Primacy of the Reader." *Mississippi Review* 6:2 (1983): 189–201.

Brooks, Peter. "Death of/as Metaphor." *Missouri Review* 46 (Summer 1979): 438–44.

Cott, Jonathon. "Susan Sontag: The Rolling Stone Interview." *Rolling Stone*, 4 Oct. 1979: 46–53.

Finkelstein, Joanne L. "Sociology and Susan Sontag: Reshaping the Discipline." *Women's Studies International Quarterly* 4 (1981): 179–90.

Gates, Davis. "There Is No Crater Love." *Newsweek*, August 24, 1992, 63.

Grenier, Richard. "Conversations with Susan Sontag." *New Republic* 186 (April 14, 1982): 5–19.

Jenkyns, Richard. "Eruptions." *New Republic*, September 7, 1992: 46–49.

Johnson, Alexandra. "Romance as Metaphor." *Nation*, October 5, 1992, 365–68.

Kael, Pauline. "Private World." *New Yorker*, November 1, 1969, 141–42.

Kakutani, Michiko. "Historical Novel Flavored with Passion and Ideas." *New York Times*, August 4, 1992, B2.

Kazin, Alfred. *Bright Book of Life: American Novelists and Storytellers from Hemingway to Mailer*. Boston: Little, Brown, 1973, 180–84.

Kendrick, Walter. "Eminent Victorian." *Village Voice* 25:42 (October 15–21, 1980): 44–46.

———. "In a Gulf of Her Own." *Nation*, October 23, 1982, 404.

Kennedy, Liam. "Precocious Archaeology: Susan Sontag and the Criticism of Culture." *Journal of American Studies* 24 (April 1990): 23–39.

Kermode, Frank. "Alien Sages." *New York Review of Books* 27:17 (November 6, 1980): 42–43.

Kher, P. R. "Susan Sontag's Aesthetic: A Moral Point of View." *Osmania Journal of English Studies* 15 (1979): 55–64.

Kipnis, Laura. "Aesthetics and Foreign Policy." *Social Text* 15 (Fall 1986): 89–98.

Kramer, Hilton. "Anti-Communism and the Sontag Circle." *New Criterion* 5:1 (September 1986): 1–7.

———. "The Pasionaria of Style." *Atlantic* 250:3 (September 1982): 88–93.

Laing, Jeffrey M. "John Hawkes's Aesthetic: The William Gass–Susan Sontag Connection." *Notes on Contemporary Literature* 15 (November 1985): 9.

Larner, James. "Susan Sontag into the Fray." *Washington Post*, March 16, 1982: C1–C9.

Light, Steve. "The Noise of Decomposition: Response to Susan Sontag." *Substance* 26 (1980): 85–94.

Linkon, Sherry Lee. "Susan Sontag." In *Jewish American Women Writers: A Bio-Bibliographical and Critical Sourcebook*, ed. Ann R. Shapiro. Westport, CT: Greenwood Press, 1994, 415–22.

Louvre, Alf. "The Reluctant Historians: Sontag, Mailer, and American Culture. Critics in the 1960's." *Prose Studies* 9 (May 1986): 47–61.

McCaffery, Larry. "*Death Kit*: Susan Sontag's Dream Narrative." *Contemporary Literature* 20 (Autumn 1979): 484–99.

McRobbie, Angela. "The Modernist Style of Susan Sontag." *Feminist Review* 38 (Summer 1991): 1–9.

Nelson, Cary. "Reading Criticism." *PMLA* 91 (1976): 801–15.

———. "Soliciting Self-Knowledge: The Rhetoric of Susan Sontag's Criticism." *Critical Inquiry* (Summer 1980): 707–62.

"On Literary Tradition: A Symposium." *Shenandoah*, 32:3 (1982): 3–46.

Parini, Jay. "Reading the Readers: Barthes and Sontag." *Hudson Review* 36:2 (Summer 1983): 411–19.

Phillips, William. "Radical Styles." *Partisan Review* 36:3 (1969): 388–400.

Roudiez, Leon S. "Susan Sontag: Against the Ideological Grain." *World Literature Today* 57 (Spring 1983): 219–23.

Sayres, Sohnya. "Susan Sontag and the Practice of Modernism." *American Literary History* 1 (Fall 1989): 593–611.

———. *Susan Sontag: The Elegaic Modernist*. New York: Routledge, 1990.

Sheppard, R. Z. "Lava Soap." *Time*, August 17, 1992, 66–67.

Simon, John. "The Light that Never Failed." *New York Times Book Review*, December 24, 1984, 1.

———. "The Valkyrie of Lava." *National Review*, August 31, 1992, 63–65.

Solotaroff, Theodore. "Interpreting Susan Sontag" (1967). In *The Red Hot Vacuum and Other Pieces on the Writing of the Sixties*. New York: Atheneum, 1970, 261–68.

Tanner, Tony. "Space Odyssey." *Partisan Review* 35 (Summer 1968): 446–51.

Taylor, Benjamin. "A Centered Voice: Susan Sontag's Short Fiction." *Georgia Review* 34 (Winter 1980): 907–16.

Timmerman, Jacobo. "Moral Symmetry." *Nation*, March 6, 1982, 261.

———. "Setting the Record Straight." *Nation*, March 13, 1982, 292.

Tyler, Anne. "*I, Etcetera*." *New Republic*, November 25, 1978, 29–30.

Vidal, Gore. "Miss Sontag's New Novel." In *Reflections upon a Sinking Ship*. Boston: Little, Brown, 1969, 41–47.

Wineapple, Brenda. "Damn Them All." *Belles Lettres* 8 (Spring 1993); 2–3, 60–61.

ART SPIEGELMAN (1948–)

Sara R. Horowitz

BIOGRAPHY

For Art Spiegelman, "Any decade before my birth has a strong nostalgic pull on me. In fact, I suppose that the world before genocide is about the easiest place to move to let the pleasure principle operate" (quoted in Maginda). Any biographical or critical treatment of Art Spiegelman must begin before his birth—not before, however, but during the years of the Nazi genocide. The catastrophic events of those years—for Spiegelman's family, as for all the Jews of Europe—indelibly marked Spiegelman's life and work.

Spiegelman was born on February 15, 1948, in Stockholm, Sweden, to Vladek and Anja (Zylberberg) Spiegelman, both Polish Jews who survived the Nazi genocide. Vladek was from a religious Czestochowa family, while Anja's was a wealthy, more secular family. After suffering the daily degradations and hardships that constituted the lives of European Jews under Hitler, disguising themselves as Aryans, hiding out in a series of locations to escape transport, and witnessing the disappearance of friends and family, Vladek and Anja were taken finally to Auschwitz; Vladek was later taken to Dachau. Although the couple were reunited after the war, Richieu—their young son and Art's brother—perished, as did most of their relatives and friends. Having lost all of their property and possessions, and with Jews unwelcome in postwar Poland, Vladek and Anja traveled to Sweden, hoping to obtain permission to immigrate to the United States. In 1951, when Art was three years old, the family finally arrived in the United States and settled in the Rego Park section of Queens in New York City. Vladek worked first in New York's flourishing garment trade and later in the diamond business.

In many ways, Art Spiegelman experienced aspects of family relationships particular to children of Holocaust survivors: an experiential gulf between parent and child, a sense of being haunted by memories and losses not one's own, and a feeling of diminishment in the face of the parents' extraordinary fact of survival. Spiegelman lived with the presence of his "ghost brother," Richieu, and with parents emotionally marked by atrocity. The Holocaust past informed his childhood in Rego Park, New York, in ways he only began to recognize and account for later on. He recollects, "It's only when I left home that I got some sense that not everyone had parents who woke up screaming in the night" (Van Biema, 98).

From an early age, Spiegelman loved to draw. He liked to imitate the styles of his favorite comic books, especially the comic-strip satire magazine *Mad*. By the time he was in high school, he was earning money as a freelance cartoonist and illustrator, selling cartoons, for example, to the *Long Island Press*. An honors student at Russell Sage Junior High, he produced *Blasé*, a magazine modeled on *Mad*. His work caught the eye of an editor for United Features Syndicate who offered to help him develop a syndicated comic strip. But already in high school Spiegelman's interests lay more in the direction of the experimental and self-expressive, rather than the commercial. This serious commitment to art rather than financial success remained with him even as he attained wide recognition.

His parents, on the other hand, urged him to choose a profession that offered financial security, such as dentistry. Instead, after graduating from high school in 1965, Spiegelman enrolled in Harpur College in Binghamton, New York, and studied art and philosophy. While in college Spiegelman also began working as a freelance artist, writer, and designer for Topps Chewing Gum in Brooklyn, an association that was to continue for over two decades. Over the years, Spiegelman drew bubble-gum cartoons, cards, stickers, and other novelty items, including the satirical "Garbage Pail Kids," a sendup of the faddish toy the Cabbage Patch Dolls.

During the turbulent 1960s at Harpur, Spiegelman published comic strips and cartoons in the college newspaper and in underground tabloids. At the same time, Spiegelman was grappling with his own inner turbulence. In 1968, he underwent what he refers to as a "psychotic breakdown" (Wechsler, 103). Withdrawing from Harpur, he entered a mental health hospital in upstate New York. He recollects that while there, he engaged in behavior reminiscent of his father's stories of survival during the Holocaust—habits that his father retained long after the war years and that Spiegelman captures in his portrait of Vladek in *Maus*, such as hoarding useless bits of junk (Gross). After a month, Spiegelman was released to live in his parents' home in Queens.

Several months after Spiegelman's return to Rego Park, however, his mother committed suicide, suffering from a depression set off by the death of her only surviving brother. Spiegelman captured her suicide and his resultant feelings of guilt, anger, and bereavement in a comic strip titled "Prisoner in Hell," published in 1972 in the underground publication *Short Order Comix*.

Soon after Anja's suicide, Spiegelman moved to San Francisco and became part of the burgeoning underground comics movement, which produced avant-garde, stylistically innovative, and politically radical cartoons and comic strips, or "comix" (or, as Spiegelman sometimes spells it, "commix"). "Rather than comics, I prefer the word commix, to mix together, because to talk about comics is to talk about mixing together words and pictures to tell a story" ("Commix," 61).

As comix gained recognition as an art form and medium of social critique, Spiegelman found more avenues to pursue his work. In 1974–1975, he taught a studio class in cartoon strips at the San Francisco Academy of Art. Together with cartoon artist Bill Griffith, Spiegelman edited *Arcade*, an important anthology of comix art.

During the San Francisco years, Spiegelman also published an early, three-page version of *Maus*, which he refers to as the "Ur Maus." Invited to contribute a cartoon strip to an underground comic magazine based on animals, called *Funny Animals*, Spiegelman was struck by the realization that the cat-and-mouse animated cartoons he watched on television were "just a metaphor for some kind of oppression" (quoted in *Contemporary Authors*, 421). He had learned in film class that the rodents in early cartoons represented African Americans and considered making the metaphor more explicit in a cat-and-mouse cartoon about slavery.

Realizing that he knew little about the black experience in America and could not do it justice, Spiegelman saw the cat-and-mouse motif as an apt symbol for the Jews of Europe during the Holocaust. In 1972, he published a cartoon featuring Die Katzen who persecuted mice and sent them to Mauschwitz. Spiegelman based the comic strip on stories heard as a child—stories told not in order to educate Spiegelman about the Holocaust, but as part of the daily negotiations of intimate life. For example, when looking for a bathroom during shopping trips, his mother would speak of the humiliation and danger of limited access to latrines in concentration camps.

During the 1970s, Spiegelman published several full-length comix, or graphic novels, including *The Complete Mr. Infinity* (1970), *The Viper Vicar of Vice, Villainy, and Vickedness* (1972), *Ace Hole, Midge Detective* (1974), and *Every Day Has Its Dog* (1979). He also published with Bob Schneider the nongraphic *Whole Grains: A Book of Quotations* (1973), a trenchant social and cultural satire consisting of a montage of quotations from such diverse sources as philosophy, popular culture, poetry, film, and journalism. Eventually, Spiegelman's enthusiasm for the world of underground comics diminished, in part because of the lack of public acceptance of comix as an art form and in part because of the decline of the movement itself.

Spiegelman returned to New York, where he met Francoise Mouly, a French art student who did not look at comics condescendingly. The couple married on July 12, 1977. During a 1977 trip to Europe with Mouly, Spiegelman was introduced to the European tradition of comic books—"comics on a myriad of

subjects, in a myriad of styles, in hardcover, on good paper, in every bookstore''
(Spiegelman, *Read Yourself Raw*, 7). Spiegelman collected the best examples
of European cartoon art. Inspired by these works, in 1980 Spiegelman and
Mouly founded the annual comic anthology *Raw*, a self-consciously avant-garde
publication with roots in the American comix of the 1950s and the European
adult comic-book tradition. Initially, *Raw* was produced as an oversize book, in
part as a marketing strategy. Shelved and marketed with other, more commercially viable books with an ''aura of new-wave hipness'' and a ''lack of content,'' *Raw*, it was hoped, might gain the wider readership that had eluded
Spiegelman's previous publishing ventures. In a relatively short time, *Raw* did
win the more mainstream audience that Spiegelman and Mouly had hoped to
interest; currently the anthology is published by Penguin in a conventionally
sized volume.

In 1978, at the age of thirty, Spiegelman began work on his most acclaimed
work, *Maus*, which depicts in unsentimentalized terms the double story of Vladek and Anja's experiences during the Holocaust and Art Spiegelman's troubled
relationship with his father. Completed over the course of thirteen years, *Maus*
reflects over forty hours of interviews with Vladek, discussions with other survivors and their families, extensive research, and visits to Auschwitz, Dachau,
and Sosnowiec, where his parents had lived.

Although widely regarded as a masterwork, *Maus* was initially rejected—
albeit ''lovingly,'' Spiegelman notes—by many publishers. However, it quickly
became a commercial and critical success, garnering the Joel M. Cavior Award
for Jewish writing in 1986 and 1992, the National Book Critics Circle nomination in 1986, the *Los Angeles Times* book prize in 1992, and a special Pulitzer
Prize in 1992. *Maus* has been translated into more than fifteen languages. Spiegelman was also awarded a Guggenheim Fellowship. Because its unusual format
makes the Holocaust accessible to that segment of the public intimidated by
more conventional modes of representing Nazi atrocity, *Maus* has educated
many readers about the Holocaust. At the same time, Spiegelman's successful
use of the comic-strip format has gained legitimacy for that genre in the eyes
of a large audience as a serious art form.

However, Spiegelman regards the success of *Maus* with ambivalence. ''The
scary part to me is that *Maus* may also have given people an easy way to deal
with the Holocaust, to feel that they've 'wrapped it up,' that reading *Maus* now
makes it possible for them to feel that they understand it, and that's that. And
since that isn't true for me, it's peculiar if it's true for people reading my book''
(''Saying Goodbye to Maus,'' 45). Spiegelman has turned down countless offers
to produce a film version of *Maus*. However, a 1994 CD-ROM version of *Maus*
includes not only the two-volume work, but also two hours of audio interviews
with Vladek, a more extensive transcript of Spiegelman's sessions with his father, and preliminary sketches of *Maus*, along with family and archival photographs. The CD-ROM (Voyager, 1994) compilation reveals the layers of
Spiegelman's work.

Since November 1992, Spiegelman has served as contributing editor and artist at the *New Yorker* magazine. On February 15, 1993, the magazine published Spiegelman's controversial Valentine's Day cover depicting a Hasidic male Jew kissing a black woman. Intended as a "love letter" to the Jewish and African-American communities of New York, whose relations were marked by tension, the cover drew fire from both communities, who found it offensive.

In addition, Spiegelman published an illustrated volume of Joseph Moncure March's 1928 narrative poem *The Wild Party*. Depicting an evening in the life of a flapper, the poem captures the character of the jazz age. The poem appealed to Spiegelman both because it reflects a pre-Holocaust innocence, and because its values underlie our own era: "that Lost Generation between the wars, of that kind of unsentimental world view that's now become our basic set of glasses, from MTV to 'Pulp Fiction' to 'Sesame Street.' That attitude is the late 20th century's attitude, and this is the birth of it" (quoted in Mitchell, 7).

Spiegelman sees his major artistic influences—the writers and artists who "stayed with me"—in Kafka, Faulkner, Nabokov, Gertrude Stein, and *Mad* magazine along with the comics of the 1940s, which Vladek bought in the 1950s because he was too cheap to buy new comic books. While Spiegelman does not intend to become known exclusively as a Holocaust author, his parents' jagged legacy continues to inform his life. Ultimately, he takes from it a moral imperative. In a 1992 column for the *Los Angeles Times* about the "ethnic cleansing" in Bosnia, Spiegelman asserted, "The haunted hollow eyes are my parents' eyes 50 years ago, when they were in the death camps and the rest of the world sat complicitously by, and they are the eyes of all our children if we fail to act" (7).

In addition, working on *Maus* has caused Spiegelman to reflect on his own identity as a Jewish-American child of survivors. Although Vladek came from an Orthodox family, Spiegelman himself is not religiously observant. He remarks, "The Holocaust made [Vladek] an atheist, which is to say, Conservative. ... Around the age of 14, I ducked out of Yom Kippur services and had a sausage pizza. When lightning didn't strike, my days as a theologian were numbered" (quoted in Maginda). Instead, Art Spiegelman sees himself "more interested in Jewishness than in Judaism. I relish the position of being a ruthless cosmopolitan, in being a Diaspora Jew" (quoted in Maginda). Spiegelman and Mouly live in New York City with their children, Nadja Rachel and Dashiell Alan.

MAJOR WORKS AND THEMES

Any discussion of Art Spiegelman as a Jewish-American novelist must address the issue of genre. Do the sequential cartoons that comprise most of Spiegelman's output fit the category of novel? More pointedly, how does one categorize *Maus*, recognized as Spiegelman's masterwork, which is based on his father's Holocaust experiences and his own relationship with his father, but is transposed metaphorically onto humanoid mice, cats, pigs, and other animals?

Neither completely text nor completely drawing, the formal elements of the comic strip include narrative, the graphic design of the individual panel, and the relationship of sequential panels. The underground comix of the 1950s and 1960s generated the serious, full-length avant-garde comix of the 1980s and 1990s, referred to as "graphic novels," "comic novels," "sequential art," "graphic narratives," "adult-oriented graphic storytelling," and "narrative cartoons," producing what Spiegelman calls a "self-referential literary tradition" with formal and intertextual links with the conventional novel and cinema. According to Spiegelman, comix work by means of "symphonic effects"—that is, a layering of drawings, works, symbols, and allusions in a compact space, all taken in simultaneously by the reader. Both language and graphics move the narrative through time and space; indeed, Spiegelman observes, "comics are time made visible as space" (quoted in "Mitchell," 7). As an emergent art form, comix embody the "REAL political, sexual, and formal energy" that museum art has lost, "not daring the risks that come with a 'risky' topic" (Spiegelman, "A Project for Artforum," 115). This sense of daring, political radicalism, and cultural critique informs Spiegelman's earlier graphic novels, such as *The Viper of Vice, Villainy, and Vickedness* (1972) and *Ace Hole, Midge Detective* (1974). Replete with visual and verbal puns and gaming, Spiegelman's comix are at once intellectual and visceral.

The almost universal critical acclaim for *Maus* is particularly striking given the popular perception of the comic strip as a juvenile or low art form. When Spiegelman published the first volume, critics and reviewers expressed astonishment that this degenerate vehicle could deal with the Holocaust in a serious and complex manner. Yet the questions of genre and category emerge most urgently with regard to *Maus*. Spiegelman drew a sharp distinction between invention—what he called "a novelist's license"—and artistry—what he called "a novelistic structure."

Spiegelman correctly perceived that the iconographic device of depicting Jews as mice, Germans as cats, Poles as pigs, and Americans as dogs accounts for the *New York Times* initially relegating *Maus* to the fiction list, and he wryly suggested the creation of a new category, "mice." Following an editorial meeting to decide the status of *Maus*—where one editor reportedly advised, "Let's ring Spiegelman's doorbell. If a giant mouse answers, we'll put *Maus* in nonfiction" (Blume)—the *Times* shifted *Maus* to the nonfiction best-seller list, thereby according with its Library of Congress classification.

Although critics have pointed to the uncanny appropriateness of the animal metaphor—Nazi propaganda depicting Jews as vermin, the German word *mauschel* as a derogatory term for Jew (Halkin, 55), the relationship between cats and mice in the natural world—Spiegelman sees the symbolism as "absolutely flawed," but no more so than any representation of the Holocaust. "As far as I'm concerned the entire metaphor is problematic. Dealing with the Holocaust is problematic. . . . The idea is to work against the metaphor as often as I work with it'' (quoted in Cantor, 39).

In *Maus* and in subsequent cartoon strips, Spiegelman also explores his own identity as a Jewish American, an identity bound up in an ethical imperative. Inevitably, his Jewishness is linked to the Holocaust. The legacy of Vladek and Anja's Holocaust experience marks Art, separating him from other American children whose parents do not cry out each night from nightmarish revisitations of the concentration-camp universe. At the same time, Spiegelman acknowledges the boundaries and parallels between past and present. In *Maus*, Francoise chastises Vladek for his irrational dislike of ''shvartsers''—''How can you of all people be such a racist! You talk about blacks the way the Nazis talked about the Jews!'' (99). The tense relationship between contemporary Jewish-American and African-American communities in New York underlies Spiegelman's controversial Valentine's Day cover for the *New Yorker*, intended as a vision of less antagonistic possibilities.

Spiegelman's works prior to *Maus* gained him recognition among aficionados of comix and other avant-garde art forms. With the growing popularity of *Raw* and the increased appreciation for the comic strip in academic cultural studies, his reputation has grown. Not until *Maus*, however, did Spiegelman gain a large following outside of counterculture, art, and scholarly circles.

CRITICAL RECEPTION

Reviews of both volumes of *Maus* have been, for the most part, glowing. Lawrence Langer called *Maus* a ''serious form of pictorial art . . . an original and authentic form to draw us closer to [the] bleak heart [of the Holocaust]'' (1). Critics also praised the maturity and sophistication of Spiegelman's vision. But few readers discussed the work without reference to genre. Several reviewers and critics expressed admiration for what the comic-strip format could contribute to an exploration of Holocaust memory and saw the genre as instrumental to the work's achievement. ''[M]asterful use of frame, continuity, dialogue, detail, and page layout'' enabled Spiegelman ''to condense his story without simplifying it,'' and the comix's ''schematic devices . . . convey the ambiguities of memory and help Spiegelman begin to tell an untellable story'' (Zurier, 103). For some readers, Spiegelman's achievement in creating a serious comix vehicle for a complex and weighty subject has remade the genre, opening up for it the possibility of new and significant subject matter and winning for it a more mainstream acceptance as an art form. One reviewer commented that Spiegelman has ''vastly expanded the potential of a genre of American cultural expression that most intellectuals have found difficult to take seriously'' (Gerber, 175).

The rare negative review faulted the animal artifice and the cartoon-strip genre as an inherently diminished form, one incapable, in the final analysis, of bearing the weight of Holocaust testimony. ''But what is the point of such imagery? Is there really much to be gained in our understanding of how human beings behaved in the Holocaust by imagining them as various kinds of mammals? I rather think there is more to be lost. . . . [Spiegelman] has not gotten to the heart of anything, nor can he with the tools of his trade'' (Halkin, 55–56). Even admirers of Spiegelman's accomplishment saw *Maus* as an exception, calling it ''no mere comic book that succeeds only in trivializing and sensationalizing its subject'' (Gerber, 159).

A masterwork that exceeds the capacities of the genre, Spiegelman's Holocaust comix reveals ''a level of complexity and ambiguity traditionally beyond the comics'' (La Brecque, 22). Such praise for the message but not for the medium implies that Spiegelman's attainment notwithstanding, the genre in which he works remains outside the pale of art. Spiegelman himself is surprised at such reluctance to view comix seriously, noting the birth of all art in the avant-garde of its era.

BIBLIOGRAPHY

Works by Art Spiegelman

The Complete Mr. Infinity. San Francisco: S. F. Book Co., 1970.
The Viper Vicar of Vice, Villainy, and Vickedness. Private printing, 1972.
Zip-a-Tune and More Melodies. San Francisco: S. F. Book Co., 1972.
Whole Grains: A Book of Quotations. Ed. with Bob Schneider. San Francisco: New York: Quick Fox, 1973.
Ace Hole, Midge Detective. New York: Apex Novelties, 1974.
Breakdowns: From Maus to Now: An Anthology of Strips. New York: Belier Press, 1977.
Every Day Has Its Dog. New York: Raw Books, 1979.
Two-fisted Painters Action Adventure. New York: Raw Books, 1980.
Work and Turn. New York: Raw Books, 1980.
Maus: A Survivor's Tale. New York: Pantheon, 1986.
Read Yourself Raw, ed., with Francoise Mouly. New York: Pantheon, 1987.
''Commix: An Idiosyncratic Historical and Aesthetic Overview.'' *Print* 42 (November/ December 1988): 61–73ff.
Maus II. New York: Pantheon, 1991.
''A Jew in Rostock.'' *New Yorker*, December 7, 1992, 119–21.
The Wild Party (illustrator) by Joseph Moncure March. New York: Pantheon, 1995.
Spiegelman, Art. Column. *Los Angeles Times*, November 23, 1992, 7.
———. ''A Project for Artforum: High at Lowdown Reproduction.'' *Artforum International*, December 1990, 115.
———. ''Saying Goodbye to Maus.'' *Tikkun*, September–October 1992, 45.
Contributing editor, with Bill Griffith. *Arcade, the Comics Revue.* 1975–76.
Founding editor, with Francoise Mouly. *Raw*, 1980–.

Works Cited and Studies of Art Spiegelman

Blume, Harvey. ''Art Spiegelman: Lips.'' *Boston Book Review*, Internet, 1995.
Cantor, Jay. ''Kat and Maus.'' *Yale Review*, December 1987, 39–40.

Contemporary Authors. New Revision Series, 41. Detroit: Gale Research, 1994, 420–23.

Gerber, David A. "Of Mice and Jews: Cartoons, Metaphors, and Children of Holocaust Survivors in Recent Jewish Experience: A Review Essay." *American Jewish History*, September 1987, 159–75.

Gross, Terry. Interview. "Fresh Air," National Public Radio, January 23, 1987.

Halkin, Hillel. "Inhuman Comedy." *Commentary*, February 1992, 55–56.

Hirsch, Marianne. "Family Pictures: Maus, Mourning, and Post-Memory." *Discourse* 15:2 (Winter 1992–1993): 3–29.

Horowitz, Sara R. "Auto/Biography and Fiction after Auschwitz: Probing the Boundaries of Second Generation Aesthetics." In *Breaking the Crystal: Writing and Memory After Auschwitz*, ed. E. Sicher. Bloomington: Indiana University Press, 1997.

———. "The Idea of Fiction." In *Voicing the Void: Muteness and Memory in Holocaust Fiction*. Albany: State University of New York Press, 1996.

Kaplan, Alice Yaeger. "Theweleit and Spiegelman: Of Men and Mice." In *Remaking History*, ed. Barbara Kruger and Phil Mariani. Discussions in Contemporary Culture 4. Seattle: Bay, 1989, 151–72.

La Brecque, Eric. "In Search of the Graphic Novel." *Print*, January/February 1993, 22.

Langer, Lawrence. Review of *Maus II*. *New York Times Book Review*, November 3, 1991, 1.

Leventhal, Robert S. "Art Spiegelman's *Maus*: Working-Through the Trauma of the Holocaust." Internet, 1995.

Maginda, Arthur. "Out of the 'Maus' Trap." *Baltimore Jewish Times*, January 29, 1995.

Mitchell, Sean. "Now for a Little Hedonism." *Los Angeles Times*, December 18, 1994, 7.

Rothberg, Michael. " 'We Were Talking Jewish': Art Spiegelman's *Maus* as 'Holocaust' Production." *Contemporary Literature* 35:4 (Winter, 1994): 661–87.

Rozenszweig, Roy. "So, What's Next for Clio? CD-ROM and Historians." *Journal of American History* 81:4 (March 1995): 1621–40.

Van Biema, David. "Art Spiegelman Battles Holocaust's Demons and His Own in the Epic Cat-and-Mouse Comic Book." *People*, October 27, 1986, 98.

Wechsler, Lawrence. Interview. *Rolling Stone*, November 20, 1986, 103–4.

Witek, Joseph. *Comic Books as History: The Narrative Art of Jack Jackson, Art Spiegelman, and Harvey Pekar*. Jackson: University Press of Mississippi, 1989.

Zurier, Rebecca. Review of *Raw*. *Art Journal* 50 (Fall 1991): 103.

GERTRUDE STEIN (1874–1946)

Richard Kostelanetz

BIOGRAPHY

Gertrude Stein was born on February 3, 1874 of a wealthy German-Jewish family near Pittsburgh. In the 1880s her family lived in California. After her parents' death, Stein returned to the East Coast to study philosophy and psychology at Radcliffe College. After a brief stint at Johns Hopkins, Stein moved to Paris with her brother Leo Stein, himself likewise a writer. In Paris Stein lived with her companion Alica Toklas who survived her after Stein's death in 1946. There she started one of Europe's most celebrated salons, quickly becoming a patron of such painters as Picasso, Matisse, Braque, and Cézanne. Among the literary figures visiting her house were Hemingway, Sherwood Anderson, and F. Scott Fitzgerald. During the Nazi occupation, she chose to stay in France. She died there in 1946.

MAJOR WORKS AND THEMES

Though Gertrude Stein died half a century ago, her books have survived her, so that even those published at her own expense, such as *The Making of Americans* (1924) or *Geography and Plays* (1922) are being reprinted in the 1990s, just as they were offset in the 1960s. Though she has never been a popular writer in the tradition of her sometime protégé Ernest Hemingway, she is customarily ranked among the greatest literary inventors, and her best writings still seem very contemporary. Indeed, it is hard for a reader today to believe that Stein, born near Pittsburgh in 1874, belongs by birth to the generation of Theodore Dreiser (born 1871), Stephen Crane (born 1871), and H. L. Mencken (born 1880).

In 1926, Stein wrote, in her inimitable style, ''For a very long time everybody refuses and then almost without a pause almost everybody accepts. In the history of the refused in arts and literature the rapidity of change is always startling. Now the only difficulty with the *volte face* concerning the arts is this: When the acceptance comes, by that acceptance the thing created becomes a classic.'' She continued, ''And what is the characteristic quality of a classic. The characteristic quality of a classic is that it is beautiful. . . . Of course it is beautiful but first all beauty in it is denied and then all the beauty of it is accepted.'' In her familiarity with the career of avant-garde art, Stein implicitly predicted that her own much-scorned scribblings would eventually be regarded as beautiful and, yes, classic.

It is common to divide Stein's books into two classes, the simple ones and the more difficult ones, although these terms are too simplistic to provide much critical insight. The ''simple'' ones are those enjoyed by moderately sophisticated readers of realistic fiction—not only *Three Lives* (1909) and *Q.E.D.* (1950, but written nearly half a century earlier), but such memoirs as *The Autobiography of Alice B. Toklas* (1933), *Everybody's Autobiography* (1937), *Paris, France* (1941), and *Wars I Have Seen* (1945). Quite simply, nearly everything written between *Three Lives* and *Toklas* can be considered difficult. Indicatively, her work was self-published during her lifetime and then, after her death, published by Yale University Press with a subsidy from the Stein estate (a selection from the latter is my own *The Yale Gertrude Stein* [1980]).

Early in her career, Stein assimilated a primary strategy of experimental art: doing the opposite of convention. If most writers strive for variety in expression, she repeated certain words and phrases in numerous slightly differing clauses. (''It is not all repetition,'' she once told a reporter. ''I always change the words a little.'') If literate writers customarily strive to display a rich vocabulary, along with allusions and other literary connotations, she confined herself to common words and their immediate meanings. She avoided myth and most kinds of metaphor. In lieu of balanced sentences, she decided to explore imbalance. Instead of instilling emotion through rhetoric and flowery language, she kept her prose generally free of adjectives and adverbs. Typically, she eschewed not only the naturalism then fashionable in fiction writing but the symbolism favored by French poets. As an American individualist, she was neither a Surrealist nor a Dadaist, neither a Futurist nor a Constructivist, to cite several European terms that are erroneously applied to her work. Always, Gertrude Stein was something else.

Essentially, she was a literary inventor who reworked many dimensions of creative literature. She was continually shifting the order of words so that the syntactical parts of a sentence fell in unusual places. Adverbs that conventionally came after their verbs now appeared before; likewise with prepositional phrases. The object of a clause became the subject (e.g., ''the ink write it down''), and both adjectives and prepositions had ambiguous references. Some parts of speech were omitted, while others were duplicated. Some of her sentences are unusually short, while others are alarmingly long. From sentences of every length she customarily removed all internal punctuation, thus increasing the possibility of ambiguous comprehension; and she favored participles as well, in part to create a sense of interminable continuity.

Texts often have no apparent relation to their titles or subtitles, even though the rhythm of the words or their taste (especially if read aloud) relates to the experience of that subject. "Custard," for instance, never mentions food but evokes a sensual experience that "has mellow, real mellow." Stein wrote prose in which adjacent words have minimal syntactic or semantic relation to each other: "Lily wet lily wet while. This is so pink so pink so pink in stammer, a long bean which shows bows is collected by a single curly shady, shady get, get set wet bet." Especially if this passage is read aloud, one can hear unities in diction, rhythm, and alliteration, as well as coherences in more subtle qualities like timbre, density, and other nonsyntactic kinds of relatedness.

What Stein was approaching was scrupulously nonrepresentational prose—language that is intended to be appreciated simply as language, apart from anything else. One principle to remember is that reading Stein is the best preparation for reading more Stein, for nobody teaches readers how to read Stein better than Stein herself. Thanks to her experimental attitude toward the mechanics of prose, she created not one original style but a succession of styles, all of which are highly personal and thus eventually inimitable. What all her departures ultimately accomplish is a reinvention of English.

What she also did was recapitulate in language the history of modernist painting. Her initial scrambling of syntax could be considered an appropriate literary analogy for painterly cubism, which likewise scrambled the viewer's perspective upon an identifiable subject. As in painting, such techniques not only distort the representation of worldly reality but also flatten the work's form (by diffusing the traditional ways of focusing its space and time). As cubism brought the reorganization of visual space, so Stein reorganized the frame of literature. Another analogy is the history of atonal music, as composers who avoided the tonics and dominants of classical harmony found other ways of organizing musical sound. All these developments gave mediumistic qualities more prominence than they had before. Just as cubist painting forces the viewer to pay closer attention to two-dimensional composition, so Stein's sentences always call attention to themselves as language. Like the modernist painters, Stein was interested not in new ideas and new subjects but in new perspectives, new perceptions, and new formal possibilities. What you read is most of what there is.

CRITICAL RECEPTION

Perhaps because Gertrude Stein did not proclaim her Jewishness, she is rarely mentioned in most histories of Jewish-American writers and never included in the anthologies parading that epithet. The publicists for Jewish-American writing scarcely acknowledge her, perhaps because, unlike their favorites, her origins were old German, rather than Eastern European; she was educated at Harvard and Hopkins, rather than, say, Chicago, Columbia, or City College; she was homosexual, though "married" for most of her life; and her work remains difficult, rather than sellable to large audiences. Most of her best and most loyal critics have been gentile, beginning with Carl Van Vechten, Sherwood Anderson, and Donald Sutherland. She was also an avid self-publisher, which has always discredited her with "critics" self-consciously beholden only to commercial produce.

However, to my mind she reflects Judaism in her interests in abstraction and in mantric writing (also favored by Allen Ginsberg, who identified the connection in his essay "On Stein's Americans" [1990]). The French, among whom she lived and died, were not deceived. Special arrangements were made to protect her from the occupying Nazis during World War II; and when she died, she was buried where her body still remains, in a section of the famous Père Lachaise (Paris) Cemetery reserved exclusively for Jews.

BIBLIOGRAPHY

Works by Gertrude Stein

Three Lives. New York: Grafton Press, 1909.
Tender Buttons. New York: Claire Marie Press, 1914.
The Making of Americans. New York: Something Else Press, 1966.
The Autobiography of Alice B. Toklas. New York: Random House, 1933.
Four Saints in Three Acts. New York: Random House, 1934.
Everybody's Autobiography. New York: Random House, 1937.
Ida. New York: Random House, 1941.
Wars I Have Seen. New York: Random House, 1945.
Brewsie and Willie. New York: Random House, 1946.
Geography and Plays. 1922. New York: Something Else Press, 1968.
Fernhurst, Q.E.D. and Other Early Writings. New York: Liveright, 1971.
Operas and Plays. 1932. Tarrytown, NY: Station Hill Press, 1987.
Paris, France. 1940. New York: W. W. Norton, 1996.

Studies of Gertrude Stein

Benstock, Shari. *Women of the Left Bank: Paris, 1900–1940*. Austin: University of Texas Press, 1986.
Bridgman, Richard. *Gertrude Stein in Pieces*. New York: Oxford University Press, 1970.
Chessman, Harriet. *The Public Is Invited*. Stanford: Stanford University Press, 1989.
DeKoven, Marianne. *A Different Language: Gertrude Stein's Experimental Writing*. Madison: University of Wisconsin Press, 1983.
Ginsberg, Allen. "On Stein's Americans." In *Gertrude Stein Advanced: An Anthology of Criticism*, ed. Richard Kostelanetz. Jefferson, NC: McFarland Co. Inc. Publishers, 1990.
Hindus, Milton. "Ethnicity and Sexuality in Gertrude Stein." *Midstream* 20 (January 1974): 69–76.

Kellner, Bruce, ed. *A Gertrude Stein Companion*. Westport, CT: Greenwood Press, 1988.

Kostelanetz, Richard. *The Yale Gertrude Stein*. New Haven: Yale University Press, 1980.

Kostelanetz, Richard, ed. *Gertrude Stein Advanced: An Anthology of Criticism*. Jefferson, NC: McFarland Co. Inc. Publishers, 1990.

Mellow, James. *Charmed Circle*. New York: Praeger, 1974.

———. *Hemingway: A Life without Consequences*. Boston: Houghton Mifflin, 1992.

Porter, Katherine Anne. *The Days Before*. New York: Harcourt, Brace, 1952.

Raffel, Gertrude Stein. "There Once Was a Family Called Stein." In *A Primer for the Gradual Understanding of Gertrude Stein*, ed. Robert Bartlett Haas. Los Angeles: Black Sparrow Press, 1971, 127–38.

Simon, Linda, ed. *Gertrude Stein Remembered*. Lincoln: University of Nebraska Press, 1994.

Thomson, Virgil. "Remembering Gertrude Stein." Four essays in *Virgil Thomson: American Composers in Their Own Words*. New York: Schirmer, 1996.

Toklas, Alice B. *What Is Remembered*. New York: Holt, Rinehart and Winston, 1963.

Wilson, Edmund. *Axel's Castle: A Study in the Imaginative Literature of 1870–1930*. New York: Charles Scribner's Sons, 1931, 237–56.

STEVE STERN (1947–   )

Mark Shechner

BIOGRAPHY

Steve Stern was born on December 21, 1947, in Memphis, Tennessee, the son of Sol, a grocer, and Rose Lipman Stern, a homemaker. He married Violet Trosper on October 12, 1983; they were divorced in 1986. Stern received a B.A. from Rhodes College in 1970 and an M.F.A. from the University of Arkansas in 1977. His past employment has been as writer, hog butcher, oral historian, vagabond, and high modernist anchorite of lonely reading. His current employment is creator of magical kingdoms and writer-in-residence at Skidmore College in Saratoga Springs, New York. Stern has taken his own pulse in public on several occasions, usually to confess his lack of qualifications to do what he is doing: write out of an abiding fascination with Jewish folklore, mysticism, and Cabala.

Stern recalls that upon reaching the age to leave Memphis, "I took off, as they say, without a backward glance." There was no reason for anyone to believe that this refugee from Memphis, who had kicked around London, had traveled back and forth on the underground to the British Museum, had immersed himself in the classic texts of literary modernism, and had butchered hogs on the farm when no one else cared to wield the knife, would eventually emerge as the historian/inventor of a lost Jewish world along the Mississippi, peopled by dybbuks and dreidels, the odd wonder rabbi, here a golem, there an everlasting light.

It came about by chance, as the by-product of a run of bad fortune that found Stern, at age thirty-five, without a job, without a literary agent, and without prospects of any kind. Down and out in Memphis, he received a call from a childhood friend, then director of the Center for Southern Folklore, offering him a job chronicling an old Jewish neighborhood along Memphis's North Main Street that had once been known as "the Pinch." Stern's main qualifications for this project, called "Lox and Grits," were that he was local, he was Jewish, and he worked cheap. Interviewing by day and transcribing his tapes by night, Stern uncovered memories of a teeming and abundant life along North Main Street, which by the 1980s was a desolate part of town.

Stern, who knew little of Judaism or of Jewishness, encountered a life that in its energy and effervescence took him by surprise and awoke in him echoes of an existence he felt within himself but had no proper knowledge of. It was all just raw material—ethnography—but to Stern it called for transformation into a great Chagallian frieze, not simply as it would be seen from without, but as, in the mind's eye of Old World Chasidic Jewry, it would look from within. In "The Ghost and Saul Bozoff," a story in the collection *Lazar Malken Enters Heaven*, (1986), a struggling writer named Saul Bozoff, afflicted with writer's block and an absence of vital, living material, is given a glimpse of a visionary North Main Street by a ghost who visits his lonely writer's cell and tells him tales of enchantment in tenements and butcher shops, coin-operated laundries and synagogues. He is being given, he understands, his career, and he wonders "what would happen if he imported the whole cockamamie circus back to his Mississippi River town. How would Second Avenue look resurrected atop bluffs named for Indian tribes? How would the old world visionaries get along with dirt farmers, swamp rats, the high-rolling Negroes around Fourth and Beale? How would they adapt to sitting on liars' benches or pushing their carts across the plank-paved bridge with its creosote aflame in summer?"

What would happen is that Steve Stern's books would be written and the forgotten Jewish land of Memphis would be remembered as the robust little community it really was and the magic kingdom that in its own collective dream life it was poised to become. Starting out with "Lox and Grits" and armed initially only with a tape recorder, Steve Stern has become an inner ethnographer who takes the data of oral history and uses them to reconstruct visionary landscapes of the Jewish dream world.

MAJOR WORKS AND THEMES

Steve Stern is the author of seven books: two novels, *The Moon and Ruben Shein* (1984) and *Harry Kaplan's Adventures Underground* (1991), a collection of novellas, *A Plague of Dreamers* (1994), two collections of stories, *Isaac and the Undertaker's Daughter* (1983) and *Lazar Malkin Enters Heaven* (1986), and two books for children, *Mickey and the Golem* (1986) and *Hershel and the Beast* (1987). Virtually all of this writing is centered in "the Pinch," the prewar Jewish neighborhood of Memphis that adjoined Beale Street and that Stern discovered by chance in the early 1980s while taking part in an oral-history project for the Center for Southern Folklore.

Stern has since taken possession of that world and made it his own, bringing it to life as a fantastic Chasidic shtetl in Eastern Europe, where magic is the norm, incongruity and divine comedy are the daily bread of existence, and revelation is the instrument by which Jews know their relation to the universe. "The solitary custodian of a ghost town," he has said of himself, "I've had personally to assume a number of North Main Street's outmoded professions, such as matchmaker (*shadchan*) to the marriage of present and past. Not to mention the nuptials of life and work, & etc. And strictly as a sideline, understand, though I'd like someday to work it into a regular act, I've attempted to play the jester (*badchan*) at their weddings" (conversation with this chapter's author).

Such writing would seem to have gone out of fashion with the death of Isaac Bashevis Singer, whom Stern resembles with his magical realism, and Bernard Malamud, with whom Stern shares an affinity for a Jewishness on a small scale, flavored with Yiddishkeit and darkened by sadness. So it comes as a surprise to find it vivid and fresh in the writing of Stern, who is in touch not only with the cadences of Yiddish but with the magic and wonder of its worldview. At forty-nine, Stern is old enough to have picked up this lore from his grandparents and yet young enough to have latched onto the latter-day revival of Yiddish culture and Jewish historiography. For if he is the child of Malamud and Singer, he is also one of Gershom Scholem, and, I should add, of Franz Kafka and Bruno Schulz as well, earlier Jewish argonauts of the fabulous and the surreal. His characters are child cabalists and knee-pants wonder rebbes, for whom heaven could be the apartment building next door and God the nebbish down the hall.

The manner of Stern's debut as a miniaturist of Jewish existence with *Lazar Malkin Enters Heaven*, his first book from a major, national publisher, calls to mind Malamud's own with *The Magic Barrel* in 1958. Like Malamud, Stern is a psalmist of life in a minor key, though these small destinies are touched with divinity. The stories in *Lazar Malkin* and in subsequent books, *Harry Kaplan's Adventures Underground* and *A Plague of Dreamers*, are of a piece: stories in which this world collides with "yene velt" (the other world) in the seemingly narrow and unassuming precincts of the Pinch. There, on the banks of Huck Finn's own Mississippi, aging Jewish spinsters marry shabby angels, the angel of death must argue with an old man for the possession of his soul, Morton Gruber, owner of a string of coin-operated laundries, finds himself a ghost writer for the Lord, and a butcher's son soars above the rooftops of Memphis drawn by a flock of inebriated pigeons.

A typical figure in Stern's writing is that of Lazar Malkin in the title story, who, "may he rest in peace, refused to die. This was in keeping with his lifelong stubbornness. Of course there were those who said that he'd passed away already and come back again, as if death were another of his so-called peddling trips, from which he always returned with a sackful of crazy gifts." Everyone is waiting for Malkin to die, especially his son-in-law, the narrator of the story, in whose shed, "propped in a chair in a corner, his burlap sack and a few greasy dishes at his feet," he is camped out. " 'Lazar,' I implored, astonished at my presumption, 'go to heaven already. Your organs and limbs are waiting there for a happy reunion. What do you want to hang around this miserable place for anyway?' " Even the doctor admonishes him, " 'Malkin, this isn't becoming. You can't borrow time the way you borrow gelt.' "

At last, Malkin is visited by a "stoop-shouldered man in his middle years, his face sad and creased like the scat of someone's baggy pants. He was wearing a rumpled blue serge suit, its coat a few sizes large to accommodate the hump on his back. Because it fidgeted and twitched, I thought at first that the hump must be alive; then I understood that it was a hidden pair of wings." It is the Malach-ha-Mavet, the Angel of Death, and the narrator, posted at the door of the barn, overhears a remarkable conversation.

"For the last time, Malkin, are you or aren't you going to give up the ghost? . . . I got my orders to bring you back. And if you don't come dead, I take you alive."

"Take me where?"

"Where else?" said the angel. "To paradise, of course."

There was a tremor on the corner which produced a commotions of moths.

"Don't make me laugh," the old man replied, actually coughing the distant relation of a chortle. "There ain't no such place."

The angel: "I beg your pardon?"

"You heard me," said Lazar, his voice became amazingly clear.

"Okay," said the angel, trying hard not to seem offended. "We're even. In paradise they'll never believe you're for real."

And rising to his feet, shaking off bugs and spider webs, the old man cries, "There ain't no world but this!"

Whereupon the Angel of Death grabs the old man and stuffs him headfirst into one of his own burlap sacks and drags Lazar, still kicking, out the back door of the shed. The son-in-law, watching, gets a glimpse of kingdom come. "It looked exactly like the yard in back of the shop, only—how should I explain it?—sensitive. It was the same brick wall with glass embedded on top, the same ashes and rusty tin cans, but they were tender and ticklish to look at. Intimate like (excuse me) flesh beneath underwear."

This intimation of something pink and tender in the afterlife is vintage Stern, lifting the entire story out of the plane of simple lore and depositing it into modern literature. I quote that story at length for the texture of Stern's language, its casual collapsing of the archaic and the Yiddish-inflected into the breezy and the vernacular. It is a homemade style—"shtetl down home"—but it shares with the tradition of Jewish writing a zest for the spoken word, a disregard of linguistic and cultural boundaries, and a performative energy that identifies it as typical of the Jewish-American literary synthesis.

This irreverent traipsing around in lore and myth has a serious morality, if the preservation of the Jewish way of imagining is its ultimate purpose. More than just skillful storytelling, it is, like Singer's stories, historiography in story form, in which the folk genius of a culture is reincarnated and celebrated. There may not be dybbuks any more than there are angels of death, but there were people whose imaginative life was once inhabited by such beings: they were the ancestors of modern Jews, and the act of entering into their conception of life is an act of solidarity with their world, their life, and the visions that animated and gave purpose to their existence. It is an act of *yizkor* or memory.

The most recent incarnation of this act to date is *A Plague of Dreamers: Three Novellas*, in which the tense compression of the *Lazar Malkin* stories is relaxed in the open form of the novella, producing three fables: "Zelik Rifkin and the Tree of Dreams," "Hyman the Magnificent," and "The Annals of the Kabakoffs." All are variations on the theme of the ineffectual dreamer whose eventual powers grow out of his refusal to stop dreaming: boyish incarnations of Blake's dictum in *The Marriage of Heaven and Hell*, "If the fool would persist in his folly he would become wise."

In "Zelik Rifkin and the Tree of Dreams," the young Zelik Rifkin, scorned by the neighborhood boys for cowardice and hopelessly in love with the brassy Minnie Alabaster, concocts a wild fantasy world in which he is a hero. He reports to his distracted mother, "I killed a man this morning. I robbed the Planters Bank and rubbed out a teller," or "I'm running away to join the circus and ride panthers through hoops of flame." Goaded by the gang to scale an oak tree, Zelik emerges at the top into another North Main Street, this one bathed in a strange moonlight, "as strong as sunlight, if softer, and grainy like a fine yellow mist." He has ascended into the collective dream life of his neighborhood, where he discovers the power to enter and tamper with dreams, to become the benevolent impresario of everyone else's inner theater. Bringing romance to his widowed mother and Mr. Silver, the greengrocer, bringing divine emanations to his decrepit Hebrew teacher, Mr. Notowitz, and bringing adventure to a weary community, Zelik becomes a folk hero, sought after by all and adored by Minnie. But he proves to be a wayward Messiah who, wearying of his exploits, one night gives them up, to become again the pariah of the Pinch. Only at the end, seeing that heroism demands work, does he climb the tree and leave behind "his own outmoded self, fearfully clutching the branches under the ceiling of fog."

These stories are borne along on the amplified vibrato of Stern's voice. At his most excitable he is a riff artist, reeling off fantastic street scenes in brisk arpeggios. Or, if jazz is too remote a metaphor, Stern's writing sometimes imitates Hebrew prayer, a rapid-fire *davenning* that lifts us right out of the congregation and points us toward divinity itself. His voice is lamentation with a kick: funny, haunted, and gleefully perverse, a voice that seems to have come trudging forth from the muddy backwaters of Poland and Galicia, anointed itself with modernity in the salons of Prague and Warsaw, and put down its baggage in the English language, in New York and Hollywood and Memphis. It is Franz

Kafka at the minstrel show, the stand-up dybbuk, ghostly and ironic, oracular and nimble, cracking sardonic jokes in which death is only a punch line.

CRITICAL RECEPTION

The critical reception of Stern's work is positive but scattered; nothing has appeared in a major book. Only in 1987, after *Lazar Malkin Enters Heaven* appeared from a major publisher, Viking, did Stern's work receive national notice at all. Morris Dickstein's review in the *New York Times Book Review* was enthusiastic, setting the tone for what was to come. Heralding Stern as "a prodigiously talented writer, who arrives unheralded like one of the apparitions in his own stories" (11), Dickstein placed Stern firmly in an ancient tradition of Jewish mystical and cabalistic writing:

Mr. Stern's cabalism belongs to the literature of fantasy and horror, not the history of religion. The Jews of medieval Germany, Prague or 17th-century Poland embraced supernatural legends out of their hopes for a world to come, their preference for a numinous world of spirits, even evil spirits, over the mundane miseries of ghetto or shtetl life. Though evidently an unbeliever, Mr. Stern uses his dybbuks and golems in a similar way: to supersede the quotidian, to impose another layer of existence on an otherwise alien city.... Reaching back to a neglected corner of the Jewish psyche, he has taken well-worn materials and turned them alchemically into something rich and strange. (11)

Janet Hadda, reviewing *Lazar Malkin* in the *Los Angeles Times*, called it "a luminous collection" and observed that "Stern's fiction resembles most of all the bursting inventiveness of those artists who found their inspiration in the clash between traditional Eastern European Jewish life and 20th-Century ferment" (6).

Such reviews sounded like auspicious announcements of a major career, as well they might have been, except that shortly after the book's publication, the descendant of a character in one of the stories, claiming to recognize a relative, sued Stern and Viking for more money than Stern could earn in eight or nine incarnations as a successful novelist. The suit lost, but not before the book was removed from the bookstores while litigation was going on.

Stern's subsequent novel, *Harry Kaplan's Adventures Underground*, was not as favorably reviewed, though Francine Prose, writing in the *Washington Post*, did call it "an act of generosity" and took note of its hyped-up, hyperbolic charms and its "inventiveness, playfulness, great narrative energy" (X8). Reviewing the book for the *Los Angeles Times*, Alfred Uhry, author of "Driving Miss Daisy," commended Stern's "rich gift for putting words together and a sharp, ironic sense of humor" but complained that "the higher aspirations of mankind don't get much of an airing in this novel, but that appears to be Stern's intention" (8). Jay Rogoff, writing in *Sewanee Review*, agreed that "this may be a novel at which the good guardians of our social consciences will turn up their bluenoses, but its heart is always and emphatically in the right place. And it is lovingly written, a hymn to our dreams and fallibility, a gift from one of our most talented writers'' (xxxi).

Stern got stronger notices for *A Plague of Dreamers* in 1994, about which Maxine Chernoff wrote in the *New York Times*, "Steve Stern's magical prose is peppered with vivid descriptions of a cast of merchants, rabbis, femmes fatales, golems, angels, butchers, grocers and dybbuks. He allows the reader to partake fully of the excesses of the Pinch, reeking of the Old World where incestuous trysts with phantom relatives and ghostly presences are an everyday occurrence. Gabriel Garcia Marquez might choose to vacation in this timeless place, where magic is as commonplace and pedestrian as the gray-blue glow of a television screen'' (8). In a longer essay in the *Georgia Review*, Daniel Green declared Stern "a worthy successor to these great Jewish writers [Bernard Malamud and Isaac Bashevis Singer], although our interest in his work, as with theirs, should not be restricted to its value as an addition to the multicultural potluck'' (967).

Critical commentary on Stern's writing is still mostly restricted to book reviews in Sunday book supplements and literary journals, with Janet Hadda's essay in *YIVO Annual* 19 being the lone attempt at an overview and assessment of the career as a whole. But all the critics agree that Stern's voice is fresh, his material compelling, and the world he has partially uncovered and partially invented out of his own teeming imagination faithful to the warmth and vitality of the Jewish world it endeavors to resurrect.

BIBLIOGRAPHY

Works by Steve Stern

Fiction

Isaac and the Undertaker's Daughter (stories). San Francisco: Lost Roads, 1983.
The Moon and Ruben Shein. Little Rock, AR: August House, 1984.
Lazar Malkin Enters Heaven (stories). New York: Viking, 1986.
Harry Kaplan's Adventures Underground. New York: Ticknor and Fields, 1991.
A Plague of Dreamers: Three Novellas. New York: Scribner's, 1994.

Fiction for Children

Mickey and the Golem: A Child's Hanukkah in the South. Illus. Jeanne Seagle. Memphis, TN: St. Luke's Press, 1986.
Hershel and the Beast. Illus. K. King Gillis. Memphis, TN: Ion Books, 1987.

Nonfiction

"A Brief Account of a Long Way Home." *YIVO Annual* 19 (1990): 81–91.
"Shtern un Ikh, or Ambushed by Jewishness." *Tikkun* 9:5 (September/October 1994): 51.

Works Cited and Studies of Steve Stern

Chernoff, Maxine. Review of *A Plague of Dreamers*. *New York Times Book Review*, January 2, 1994, 8.

Contemporary Authors, 132. Detroit: Gale Research, 1991, 402–6.

Dickstein, Morris. Review of *Lazar Malkin Enters Heaven*. *New York Times Book Review*, March 1, 1987, 7:11.

Green, Daniel. Review of *A Plague of Dreamers*. *Georgia Review* 49 (Winter 1995): 960–67.

Hadda, Janet. "Ashkenaz on the Mississippi." *YIVO Annual* 19 (1990): 93–103.

———. Review of *Lazar Malkin Enters Heaven*. *Los Angeles Times Book Review*, May 24, 1987, 6.

Kamenetz, Rodger. Review of *A Plague of Dreamers*. *Times-Picayune* (New Orleans), April 3, 1994, E7.

Koeppel, Fredric. Review of *A Plague of Dreamers*. *Commercial Appeal* (Memphis), December 19, 1993, G3.

Levin, Donna. Review of *A Plague of Dreamers*. *San Francisco Chronicle*, May 1, 1994, 4.

Prose, Francine. Review of *Harry Kaplan's Adventures Underground*. *Washington Post Book World*, March 31, 1991, X8.

Rogoff, Jay. Review of *Harry Kaplan's Adventures Underground*. *Sewanee Review* 101 (Winter 1993): xxx–xxxii.

Shechner, Mark. Review of *A Plague of Dreamers*. *Chicago Tribune Book Review*, January 30, 1994, 6.

Uhry, Alfred. Review of *Harry Kaplan's Adventures Underground*. *Los Angeles Times Book Review*, April 21, 1991, 8.

BARRY TARGAN   (1932–   )

Michael Huff

BIOGRAPHY

Barry Targan was born on November 30, 1932, in Atlantic City, the son of Albert, a grocer, and Blanche Simmons Targan. He earned his B.A. in English at Rutgers University in 1954 and his M.A. at the University of Chicago in 1955. After serving in the U.S. Army for two years, on March 9, 1958, he married Arleen Shanken, an artist. They have two children, Anthony and Eric. In 1962 Targan received his Ph.D. from Brandeis University, and later that year he began his teaching career as an assistant professor of English at Syracuse University. He later taught at the State University of New York College at Cortland (1966–1968) and at Skidmore College in Saratoga Springs, New York (1969–1978). He has been teaching at the State University of New York at Binghamton since 1978.

Targan is an extraordinarily eclectic and talented man, a hands-on man. He is or has been a boat builder, sailor, gardener, potter, weaver, violinist, bookbinder, printer, papermaker, photographer, artist, skier, naturalist, bird-watcher, fisherman, editor, and teacher. In addition to his novels, Targan has published two books of poetry, *Let the Wild Rumpus Start* (1971) and *Thoreau Stalks the Land Disguised as a Father* (1975), as well as three collections of short fiction, *Harry Belton and the Mendelssohn Violin Concerto* (1975; winner of the University of Iowa School of Letters Award in Short Fiction), *Surviving Adverse Seasons* (1979; winner of the Saxifrage Prize), and *Falling Free* (1989), which includes winners of the Pushcart Prize and the O. Henry Award.

MAJOR WORKS AND THEMES

Targan's first novel, *Kingdoms* (1980; winner of the AWP Award in the Novel), chronicles the peripatetic adventures of a father and son following the death of their wife and mother, respectively, and the suicide of a close friend of the father. The father rejects all claims the static life has on him, and they embark on a great wandering—"And there were ordinances against us. Against gypsies and vagabonds. Ancient prohibitions against wanderers" (58). The father, a brilliant scholar, self–re-creates himself as a sort of ebullient, liberated Ahasuerus-of-all-trades, and the son orbits dizzily around his father's genius. As they crisscross the United States, sleeping in their pickup truck, stopping to do odd jobs in this town and that, the father educates the son in literature, natural science, astronomy, math, philosophy, and life. They fight enemies. They escape danger. At all stops they see wonders and encounter characters who are vibrant and dull, shallow and deep. The father carries on a perpetual battle with literature, raging at its flatness and patness, its refusal to be like real life. Yet it is the son who engages with other characters in the novel, who steps into the lives of other people and ponders the deep realities of their souls.

Targan dedicated the book to his father, Albert, who died in 1969, and *Kingdoms* is a celebration of Father-and-Son. The book teaches that while we may all be wanderers in this world, we need not be alone, and, indeed, there are obligations and rewards for passing knowledge, beauty, experience, and wisdom on to the next generation. When the novel's father and son go back to Boston, to Widener Library—the site of the father's former life—father shows son the glass-encased Gutenberg Bible and Shakespeare's First Folio: "This is the heart. The left ventricle and the right. This is what keeps it all going. This is where it all comes from" (88). The father explains to the son that the glass case of books is a Delphic Oracle, conduit to the gods,

"The Greco base for all our own present wisdom. . . . Just ask the oracle a question. Anything you want."

"There's no priests," I said. "I can't ask a question because there's no priest. You said you asked the priest to ask the oracle. So let's go."

"I'm a priest," he said. (90)

Knowingly or not, the professedly irreligious father is obeying the God of Israel, who commands, "And ye shall be unto me a kingdom of priests" (Exodus 19.6); and in this sense the father's wandering becomes a *halaka*, a building up of "the kingdom of God" by very pedestrian means.

Kingdoms is also a celebration of knowledge. Yet all the while father is bombarding son with knowledge, the knowledge is not meant for its own sake. At the Widener Library, the father has a heated exchange with a former colleague:

It's lust in action. The waste of shame. . . . You've never learned to trust the words. You've missed the ore for the slag heap, so you hammer your words out of lead instead of gold and turn their dull weight to virtue and wonder why you grow tired and hunchbacked from lugging such a Rood around all your life. Listen, priest, you rip the pulsing heart out of living children and call your act

Divine. But you've got no *glory* in you, Norman Galt. Nothing that matters long or long enough. You've got a small, uncomprehending soul. (98)

Galt has been seduced by the god of knowledge-for-its-own-sake, and as a priest to that god, he is an antifather; he harms the next generation. The father, on the other hand, gives his son knowledge not only for the admitted beauty of knowledge, but for the wisdom that can come with it.

Ultimately, the major lesson the son learns is that the boundaries of kingdoms dissolve and blend into each other, and the most important kingdoms, the son discovers, are people. After years during which the only details that mattered for the son were his father's lessons, he finally begins "to notice people" (179). Eventually, he falls in love and makes love. The boundaries between individuals dissolve.

The climax of this discovery (instinctive at the time) is a pageant, no less—the Miss America Beauty Pageant parade in Atlantic City, at which the son peddles barrels for people to stand on. By the end of the parade, after "the Washington Post March, the flipping acrobats, the mounted police on display, and the stately beauties mounted on display and out of reach," and after the waves of spectators, he is overwhelmed by the humanity: "Vision! Vision! Oh my country! Oh my species! But what I danced to then I think was my own annunciation, some epiphanic call. In the middle of the tumult and the shouting, higher than it all, I heard a trilling in me to be free" (238).

In his second novel, *Tangerine Tango Equation* (1991), Targan pursues the same subjects, but from a different angle. As in *Kingdoms*, the narrator is the son, but this time, it is the son who is the genius, a prodigy, owner of the highest IQ ever measured. At sixteen, his mother and father see him off to college—several years later than he could have begun—ironically, to experience life, since his personal studies have already far exceeded the postgraduate level. This son, Nicky Burden, is burdened with fame, the grotesquely outsized attentions of other students, capitalists, even the tabloids, all looking for a way to leech off of his genius. Most of all, he falls under the tutelage of several academics who can hardly contain their drool at the prospect of studying him. After all of his picaresque adventures, after all of his paradigm-shifting forays in physics, Nicky—like the son of *Kingdoms*—gains an understanding of the real value of knowledge.

Fatherhood is at the center of this novel, as it is with *Kingdoms*. But the paternity question is even more ambiguous here, even more complicated, and by the end, it emerges as the subject of what turns out to be an intense mystery novel. Who will betray Nicky Burden? Who will turn out to be an antifather? As in *Kingdoms*, there are priests who are obligated to help the next generation make the transition from insular adolescence to full-contact, out-in-the-world adulthood. Indeed, there are plenty in academia who pose as such priests for a living, but some of them are like "Nadab and Abihu, the sons of Aaron," who in their office as priests in the temple, "offered strange [incense] before the Lord, which he commanded them not" (Leviticus 10.1). Which of the novel's priests will gaze into a crystal ball and not recognize Nicky's humanity? Which will take pride in baptizing Nicky "in the destructive element" (278)? It is an absorbing ethical mystery.

Unfortunately, God is not monitoring the priests of academia to consume them with fire, as he did Nadab and Abihu. They are free to distort and disjoint and discombobulate their office and obligations to their own self-serving ends. In *Tangerine Tango Equation*, they are more developed, more three-dimensional, more subtle, more attractive, and more sinister than poor Norman Galt in *Kingdoms*.

Since Nicky's knowledge—his accumulation of information—is superior to that of the academics, all they could possibly pass along to him is wisdom and experience concurrent to their knowledge, a currency he could use out in the world, a language. But their equations and sophistry are exposed as plotting, self-centered, crass and mundane, empty and useless. Nicky discovers that the only language of possible use to him, one that still evades him in spite of superior intellect, is one that his biological, unmatriculated father can teach him:

I know or can know mathematical languages. But I do not know this other language, what I heard in the scrape of your shovel in your garden, the click of the rake through the unlimited stones that rose up through the soil through the winter. The frost had pushed them up, you explained; that is why there were always more stones in the spring for you to rake. But now I imagine wildly, you all winter hearing the stones ascending, just as I imagine you listening to the epithelial cells forming on the tips of the root hairs as they thrust down through the grains of the dirt with a force once calculated at an incredible eighty thousand kilograms per millimeter, a force three times greater than the thrust of an oil rig grinding through rock with a diamond bit. Greater than the power of the rockets that lifted the satellites into outer space. (193)

The language Nicky longs to learn is light and color, leaping, unpredictable. After all of his work in physics, where he tried, like Einstein, to imagine how God would imagine the universe, how it would all be ordered, formulated, predicted, he arrives at this conclusion:

In wonder I saw things relate and disappear, come together for a moment in an explosion of energy and then dissipate as quickly. Matter and antimatter colliding and annihilating, but a different matter now, far more marvelous than mere protons and neutrons, electrons, quarks. None of this time could begin or end. Whatever god there could be would have to be an artist. (302)

CRITICAL RECEPTION

In addition to being widely anthologized and receiving many awards for his short fiction, Targan received the Associated Writing Programs Award for the Novel for *Kingdoms*, and *Tangerine Tango Equation* has been optioned to be made into a film. For the time being, however, he eludes the critics. But those who have not been as slow to discover Targan's work have written about it quite warmly.

Eils Lotozo, writing in the *New York Times Book Review*, called Targan's work "passionate arguments with and love songs to a world that offers 'no guarantees, only opportunities. And vicissitudes' " (24). Lotozo also praised Targan's craftsmanship for its formal richness, "dense with luxuriant language and sensuous detail" (24). In the *Antioch Review*, Laurence De Looze said that Targan's fiction is "full of hidden processes, which are seen by and have meaning for only the people who undertake them" (350).

De Looze recognized a major theme in Targan's work, one that Targan himself reveals in his review of Wendy Lesser's *Pictures at an Execution*. Writing in the *Sewanee Review*, Targan explained that "the main flaw in the book is not in her interesting and fascinating individual considerations and explications, but in her unquestioned assumption that we can understand murder and execution from the fictionalized accounts of it" (lxxxi). While murder and execution are not subjects of Targan's work, life is. Real life. As De Looze put it, "the richness is entirely in the experience" (350). Not ironically, the title of Lotozo's review is "Life: Want to Make Something of It?" Targan insists that "literature—*real* literature—is about *life*. A hundred years from now, we'll still be reading *War and Peace* and *Anna Karenina*; but we won't be reading any of today's *theory*" (conversation with this chapter's author). Barry Targan's work reflects his own extraordinary experience, as well as the wisdom and intelligence that have come out of that experience. To read his novels is to come about as close to real life as one can in literature.

BIBLIOGRAPHY

Works by Barry Targan

Let the Wild Rumpus Start. Crete, NE: Best Cellar Press, 1971.
Harry Belton and the Mendelssohn Violin Concerto. Iowa City: University of Iowa Press, 1975.
Thoreau Stalks the Land Disguised as a Father. Greenfield Center, NY: Greenfield Review Press, 1975.
Surviving Adverse Seasons. Urbana: University of Illinois Press, 1979.
Kingdoms. Albany: State University of New York Press, 1980.
Falling Free. Urbana: University of Illinois Press, 1989.
Tangerine Tango Equation. New York: Thunder's Mouth Press, 1990.
"Execution and Its Discontents." *Sewanee Review* 103 (1995): lxxx–lxxxi.

Works Cited

De Looze, Laurence. "Is Gilbert Kaplan to Gustav Mahler as Harry Belton Is to Felix Mendelssohn?" *Antioch Review* 49 (1991): 339–56.

Lotozo, Eils. "Life: Want to Make Something of It?" *New York Times Book Review*, March 4, 1990, 24.

MEREDITH TAX (1942–   )

Joel Shatzky and Michael Taub

BIOGRAPHY

The daughter of Archie H. and Martha Brazy Tax, Meredith Tax was born in Milwaukee on September 18, 1942. She received a B.A. from Brandeis University magna cum laude in 1964 and attended the University of London (1964–1968). She married Jonathan Schwartz in 1968, with whom she had a daughter, Corey Tax-Schwartz. She and Jonathan divorced in 1977. Since 1982 she has been married to Marshall Berman.

Tax has worked as a nurse's aide, legal secretary, assembler and calibrator of magnetic gauges, and wirer and solderer of television sets. She has also been a freelance writer and teacher and has held academic positions at Brandeis University (1968–1969), Hofstra (1978), Rutgers University (1978), and State University of New York, Old Westbury (1979).

She was a cofounder of Bread and Roses, a socialist-feminist organization (1969–1972); a member of the United Farmworker's support committee (1974–1975); and cochair and public spokesperson for (CARASA) the Committee for Abortion Right and against Sterilization Abuse (CARASA) (1977–1980). She has received a Fulbright Scholarship (1964–1966) and a Woodrow Wilson Dissertation Fellowship (1966–1968).

MAJOR WORKS AND THEMES

Tax is best known for her novels *Rivington Street* (1982) and *Union Square* (1988). The first of these is about the history of a Jewish family, the Levys, who emigrate to New York City from Russia in the early 1900s. Unlike many such chronicles by male writers, *Rivington Street* portrays the emigrant experience from a woman's perspective very specifically. It is the story of the community of Eastern European Jewish women, a "class panorama" (quoted in Contemporary Authors, 453). *Union Square* is a sequel to *Rivington Street*, not only in its cast of characters, but in its focus on women's history. The genesis of both books came from Tax's ten years of research for her study of the women's movement, *The Rising of the Women: Feminist Solidarity and Class Conflict, 1880–1917*, published in 1980.

CRITICAL RECEPTION

Both of Tax's novels have been very favorably reviewed. Madelon Bedell in *Ms. Village Voice* regarded *Rivington Street* as "a landmark. . . . There is no false rhetoric, no artificial 'relevances,' no mystic significances . . . no familiar stereotypes." Jane Lazarre stated in the *Nation*, that in *Rivington Street* "The historical sections of the novel are compelling, written with confident knowledge of how contradictory forces can come together in one moment, one event" (quoted in *Contemporary Authors*, 453).

Union Square was regarded as " 'politically correct' but popular fiction" by Eden Ross Lipson in the *New York Times Book Review*, who also added, "The point of Meredith Tax's novels isn't the quality of her prose. She is telling gritty, satisfying stories." But Lillian S. Robinson saw in Tax's work "something different, 'something revolutionary.' She brings women's history to life in the characters and events of her narrative. And she does it through—not despite—the conventions of a popular genre. . . . Tax manages not only to turn her research into creditable historical fiction, but also to encompass a couple of other mass-market genres along the way: the Jewish family saga and the female career novel. She pulls it off" (quoted in *Contemporary Authors*, 453).

BIBLIOGRAPHY

The Rising of the Women: Feminist Solidarity and Class Conflict, 1880–1917. New York: Monthly Review Press, 1980.
Rivington Street. New York: Morrow, 1982.
Union Square. New York: Morrow, 1988.
For further information on Meredith Tax, see *Contemporary Authors* 144. Detroit: Gale Research, 1994, 452–54.

LIONEL TRILLING   (1905–1975)

Hannah Berliner Fischthal

BIOGRAPHY

Lionel Trilling's Jewish background is in itself ambiguous. He was born in New York City on July 4, 1905, where his father had emigrated to from Bialystok at the early age of thirteen; his mother came from London. Thus, while Lionel himself was the child of immigrants, his situation was entirely different from that of other New York Jewish Intellectuals, for Trilling's parents spoke flawless English, not Yiddish, and concomitantly, their problems of acculturation were infinitely simpler. He grew up in a middle-class household, complete with maid. His home was kosher, and his mother lit Sabbath candles. Yet they belonged to no synagogue, and both parents showered Lionel with gifts on Christmas as well as Chanukah. His bar mitzvah was held at the Jewish Theological Seminary; Trilling had been trained by Max Kadushin, a protégé of Mordecai Kaplan.

Lionel's family was in a financial position to send him to Columbia College, from which he graduated in 1925; Jews, in those days, usually attended City College. Even his name (after he dropped his middle name of Mordecai) was not overtly Jewish. In 1929 he married Diana Rubin, who was even less concerned with Judaism than he. In fact, Diana admitted in her fascinating and candid memoirs, *The Beginning of the Journey*, that she was very displeased with her husband's role in the Menorah group, and she spoke disparagingly of his "quest for a Jewish identity, a search in which I refused to share and to which, in fact, I was fully opposed" (44). She also complained about the Jewish wedding she and Lionel had had, performed by Lionel's rabbi friend Henry Rosenthal; and she made telling slips, such as saying that her husband was too good-looking to be recognized as a Jew (322). In short, Lionel evidently would have found little encouragement at home to pursue Jewish interests, had he been so inclined. He and his wife left their roots beneath them as they aspired to more liberal ideology.

Trilling was the first Jew to teach in the English Department at Columbia, yet this position did not come easily. In 1936, he was notified that he was not being reappointed because he was "a Freudian, a Marxist, and a Jew," and thus he would be "more comfortable" elsewhere (Diana Trilling, "Lionel Trilling," 422). Trilling stood up to these complaints and convinced the faculty that Columbia would be making a disastrous mistake to let him go. He was rehired. Soon after, Trilling completed his doctoral dissertation on Matthew Arnold, which was very highly regarded, and he was promoted.

Diana Trilling, in her own highly interesting article and autobiography, took pains to demonstrate that this incident was not entirely, not simply, due to anti-Semitism; nevertheless, it must have affected her husband and, perhaps, made him more hesitant to profess his Jewishness. Indeed, as Diana pointed out, Lionel was specifically told by Emery Neff that his appointment was not made in order to provide "a wedge to open the English department to more Jews" ("Lionel Trilling," 428). On the contrary. Alfred Kazin noted how Clifton Fadiman was refused a position in Columbia's English Department by the chair because "we have room for only one Jew . . . and we have chosen Mr. Trilling" (42–43).

This obviously put some extra psychological pressure on Trilling to submerge whatever Jewish identity he might have felt. Irving Howe surely referred to Trilling when he wrote that Philip Rahv, Delmore Schwartz, and he "held in contempt those Jewish intellectuals and academics who tried to pass themselves off as anything but what they were." "Indeed," Howe added in his memoirs, "we took a malicious delight in poking fun at the handful of Jews who had reached the exalted status of professor, since, we suspected, they had surely had to pay with some unseemly evasions" (252). Howe, of course, became heavily involved with Yiddish literature. "I still recall a remark Lionel Trilling once made to me that he 'suspected' Yiddish literature; I thought there must be something profound behind those words, but later decided there needn't be at all," he added drily (265).

Trilling, however, remained an esteemed member of the faculty at Columbia, eventually earning the distinction of becoming University Professor of Literature from 1970 until his death. He received numerous awards, prizes, and honorary doctorates. His works include one novel, *The Middle of the Journey* (1947), and important nonfiction books, including *Matthew Arnold* (1939), *E. M. Forster* (1943), *The Liberal Imagination* (1950), *The Opposing Self* (1955), *Freud and the Crisis of Our Culture* (1955), *A Gathering of Fugitives* (1956), *Beyond Culture: Essays on Literature and Learning* (1965), *Sincerity and Authenticity* (1972), and *Mind in the Modern World* (1972). Trilling also edited *The Portable Matthew Arnold* (1949), *Selected Letters of John Keats* (1950), *The Life and Work of Sigmund Freud* (1961), *Literary Criticism* (1970), and *The Oxford Anthology of English Literature* (with others, 1973).

None of these works, so central to American literary and cultural history, deals, even remotely, with Judaism. Nowhere is there even a single essay, or a single page of an essay, on the Holocaust. Thus the overtly Jewish pieces Trilling had written as a young man for the *Menorah Journal* are all the more remarkable.

LIONEL TRILLING AS A JEWISH WRITER

Lionel Trilling was a literary and cultural critic, novelist, short-story writer, editor, and educator. His position as a Jewish writer, however, was ambivalent. Early in his career, from 1925 to 1931, he contributed a total of twenty-six stories, articles, translations from the French, and reviews, all with a Jewish interest, for the *Menorah Journal*, edited by Elliot Cohen and Henry Hurwitz. After that date, however, he deliberately dissociated himself from any Jewish movements or groups. With very few exceptions, Trilling made no further explorations, literary or otherwise, into Jewish issues or subject matter after 1931.

The intercollegiate Menorah Association, a forerunner of the Hillel movement, was secular, humanist, and progressive. The aim of the society and its magazine was to stimulate what they termed "positive Judaism," a feeling of ethnic pride that would enforce a sense of identity. Elinor Grumet explained that the *Menorah Journal* writers evoked the terms "self-acceptance," "self-realization," or, sometimes, "authenticity." What was eschewed "went under the name of 'self-hatred' and 'shame' at being a Jew" (159). The *Menorah Journal* paid well (two cents a word) and published such esteemed Jewish authors as Ludwig Lewisohn, Maurice Samuel, Waldo Frank, Mordecai Kaplan, and Israel Zangwill, and non-Jews like Mark Van Doren, Lewis Mumford, and Charles Beard. "For a time," wrote Stephen Tanner, "Trilling was keenly committed to a Jewish cultural renaissance" (13). Mark Krupnick insisted of Trilling that "the idea of himself as a Jew sustained him and gave his writing a focus for some five years" (*Lionel Trilling*, 22). In Trilling's "A Light to the Nations" (1928), he imagines a rabbi repeating over and over again, "What does it mean to be a Jew?" (402). This was a subject he explored in that period of his life.

In 1930 Trilling taught a course on the Jew in fiction at the Menorah Summer School. He also lectured on this theme to the Menorah societies of Hunter and Adelphi. These talks were adapted as "The Changing Myth of the Jew," an article accepted by the *Menorah Journal*, but never published there. Tanner stated that Trilling thought it "inferior and dullish" (14). On the contrary, the essay is a wonderful historical survey from Chaucer to *Daniel Deronda*. *Commentary* did publish it in 1978.

In 1929, while Trilling served as a part-time editorial assistant for the *Menorah Journal*, he promoted the magazine at the Convention of the Menorah Association. Also, at Cohen's request, he wrote a personal endorsement of it. Twelve years later, however, Trilling refused to allow Hurwitz to use the letter publicly. "[T]hose paragraphs were written in a special context which, for me, doesn't exist any longer," Trilling explained (quoted by Tanner, 13).

When Elliot Cohen founded *Commentary* in 1945 and invited his friend Lionel to serve on the advisory board, Trilling declined. In a letter to Cohen, Trilling asserted that he no longer wanted to be associated with a Jewish magazine, for to him it could only be "a posture and a falsehood" (quoted by Tanner, 16). Clement Greenberg, the managing editor, expressed the anger of the staff when he accused Trilling of Jewish self-hatred (Tanner, 16). In retribution, when Trilling's novel *The Middle of the Journey* appeared in 1947, *Commentary* ignored the event, as it did again when *The Liberal Imagination* was published, to much acclaim, in 1950. Not for another half-dozen years was this quarrel mitigated, when Trilling began publishing in *Commentary*. He dedicated *A Gathering of Fugitives* to Cohen in 1956 and even delivered his eulogy three years later.

His literary stance, however, remained rigidly antiethnic. "I do not think of myself as a 'Jewish writer,' " he proclaimed in 1944. "I do not have it in mind to serve by my writing any Jewish purpose. I should regret it if a critic of my work were to discover in it either faults or virtues which he called Jewish" ("Under Forty," 199). He was critical of the years he had spent involved with the Menorah group. "It fostered a willingness to accept exclusion and even to intensify it, a willingness to be provincial and parochial," he complained (201). More harshly, he condemned the "Jewish social group on its middle and wealthy levels—that is, where there is enough leisure to allow a conscious consideration of social and spiritual problems," as being "one of the most self-indulgent and self-admiring groups it is possible to imagine" (201). He concluded this discussion for the *Contemporary Jewish Record* by saying that he knew "of no writer in English who has added a micromillimetre to his stature by 'realizing his Jewishness,' although I know of some who have curtailed their promise by trying to heighten their Jewish consciousness" (201).

Edward Joseph Shoben, Jr., a clinical psychologist, defended Trilling's statements as displaying "firmness of character" (32). Most critics would disagree that this interview was a reflection of moral integrity. Trilling's standpoint, however, was far from being unique. By the 1930s, Jewish intellectuals, especially the New York Intellectuals, generally strove to submerge or even replace their ethnic backgrounds, which they considered to be too parochial, with secularism and internationalism. They idealistically adopted Marxist universalist attitudes, interests, and approaches to life and literature. Mark Krupnick affirmed that most of the other members of the Menorah group shared Trilling's negative attitudes after breaking with the journal in 1931 ("Menorah Journal Group," 61).

But Lionel Trilling parted with Judaism permanently. He consciously avoided contemporary issues of Jewish nationalism. Influential reviewers such as Robert Warshow had criticized his novel *The Middle of the Journey* (1947) for, among other things, failing to recognize the important role Jews had played in the radical politics of the 1930s.

William Chace spoke repeatedly of Trilling's need to "transcend" Judaism;

Mark Shechner wrote more of Trilling's "suppression" of it; Elinor Grumet asserted that Trilling "divorced" his literary career from Jewishness. Whatever the terminology, it is clear that Trilling's attitude toward his own ethnicity became one of deliberate avoidance. His previous comments, after all, were made during the Holocaust, at a time when intellectuals were all too aware of the atrocities being committed abroad, although the full horrific details were not available until after 1945. But Trilling did not budge from his seemingly aloof, purely academic, scholarly stance.

It is true that reactions to the tragedy were generally delayed. Trilling himself wrote in "Art and Fortune" that "the great psychological fact of our time which we all observe with baffled wonder and shame is that there is no possible way of responding to Belsen and Buchenwald. The activity of mind fails before the incommunicability of man's suffering" (256). Nevertheless, sometime during the next twenty-five years of his life, Lionel Trilling, America's leading cultural critic, might have indicated in some fashion a genuine, heartfelt, Jewish cry of grief.

In 1950, Trilling published his last work that was Jewish in subject matter, "Wordsworth and the Rabbis." The author affirmed his knowledge of the *Pirke Avot*, "a collection of maxims and *pensées*, some of them very fine and some of them very dull, which praise the life of study and give advice on how to live it" (124). But he was somewhat apologetic about his having studied this tractate and was quick to point out, "I did not read it out of piety" (124). On the contrary, he read these sayings "when I was supposed to be reading my prayers—very long, and in the Hebrew language, which I never mastered" (124). The hypothesis of his essay, while insightful and provocative, in itself speaks an ambivalence toward his roots. After exploring the possibility that Wordsworth was perhaps too Christian for modern sensibilities, he decided instead that "the quality in Wordsworth that now makes him unacceptable is a Judaic quality" (123). This is scarcely the sort of thesis that fosters Jewish pride. Anyway, the essay is a study of Wordsworth, not of the rabbis.

TRILLING'S "JEWISH" FICTION

Trilling wrote only four short stories for the *Menorah Journal*; they share enough thematic matter and authorial attitude that they can easily be grouped and given a common overview. In "Impediments" (1925), the narrator, a well-dressed college student, rejects the friendship of Hettner, a "scrubby little Jew with shrewd eyes and full, perfect lips that he twisted out of their crisply cut shape." The protagonist admits to "the convenient barrier I was erecting against men who were too much of my own race." He fears that Hettner will protrude into the "tower" or "citadel" he has built around himself. Trilling here reflects the tension between acculturation and unassimilated ethnicity. He equates the former with refinement and elegance, while connecting ethnicity with crudeness. This story is especially interesting in light of the distanced position Trilling himself took from Jewishness within just a few years of publishing this tale. For Lionel Trilling, outward appearance would always be extremely important.

"Chapter for a Fashionable Jewish Novel" (1926) is a more depressing story; the narrator feels totally alienated. Again, as in "Impediments," he submerges his coarser Jewish self, which he imagines as being "lustfully Hebraic, rowling gloriously, drunkenly, madly, in Jewishness, disgusting the inhabitants by the abandon and licentiousness of his Semitic existence." In contrast, his outward mannerisms are anglicized and cosmopolitan.

In Trilling's best, most provocative story, "Funeral at the Club, with Lunch" (1927), a Jewish college instructor (again, a nameless character) feels like an "outlander" among his gentile colleagues. In a moment of epiphany, he realizes the deficiencies of the society of "cultivated men living pleasantly, well-mannered, civilized," for this existence leads to "mediocrity" and dullness. Blatantly declaring his Jewishness, however, would make him "alone, apart, outside," but at the same time, "free." The protagonist eloquently compares pronouncement of his own Jewishness with Huck's confession of smallpox on the raft—a sure way to guarantee being left alone. Trilling repeatedly describes both the attraction to and repulsion against his own heritage.

"Notes on a Departure" (1925) is a more rambling tale, but its themes are similar to those of the earlier three stories. Should the narrator publicly announce his Jewishness? He asks himself here four times, "Jew?" He answers, "Yes. All right. Jew." In all four stories, Trilling presents the problem of Jewish identity in a complex, ambivalent manner.

The stories represent Lionel Trilling's literary and philosophical struggle with his Jewishness. In her Foreword to *Speaking of Literature and Society*, Diana Trilling referred to her husband's "failed search for 'a Jewish identity' in his early writing for *The Menorah Journal*." This can be read in several ways. Did she mean that Trilling had no "Jewish identity" for which to search? Or that he failed to find his "Jewish identity"? In any case, the implication is one of futility.

On the contrary, Lionel Trilling, in these early works, expresses his conflicted feelings. He pits the acculturated Jew against the noticeably ethnic one; he erects barriers and citadels against unwanted intrusions; he contrasts outward appearances with internal realities. Trilling struggles with the negative stereotypes of his race, "the old charges of talkativeness, noisiness, vulgarity, swartness, difference" ("Funeral at the Club"). In each of these stories, his protagonist is an unnamed scholar who can pass for a gentile, who feels ambivalent about his Jewish roots, who tries to live in an ideal world of culture and ideas, but who is unhappily confronted with his background.

"Trilling's constitutional ambivalence," explained Morris Dickstein, "is related to his ordeal of being a Jew in a gentile world, teaching English literature in a gentile university. This problem of identity was a theme in Trilling's early stories, but he turned away from it in his mature fiction, with fateful results"

("Lionel Trilling," 80). The results are mainly a loss of specificity, a vagueness, that mar Trilling's later fiction.

The *Menorah Journal* stories are a clear indication that Trilling deliberately chose, early in his career, to publicly wear what Dickstein called his "Anglophile mask" ("Lionel Trilling," 75). He elected to efface the Jewish Lionel Mordecai and to embrace the more worldly self.

In his psychological study of Trilling, Daniel O'Hara went so far as to speak of Trilling as a clear model of self-loathing, based on Sander Gilman's *Jewish Self-Hatred*, having a resentment "visible in the lives of certain Jewish intellectuals who aspire to assimilate, even partially, to the larger non-Jewish culture" (xii). This is a charge that has been brought against Trilling a number of times. I believe it to be too harsh and too simplistic an assessment.

In any case, Lionel Trilling became a dominant force in mainstream academic culture both in America and abroad. For the most part, however, he remained "a Jew and yet not Jewish," as Kazin remarked (44). The psychological fortress shutting out overt Jewishness, the citadel Lionel Trilling describes in "Impediments," remained virtually impermeable throughout the duration of his illustrious career.

BIBLIOGRAPHY

Works by Lionel Trilling

Selected Criticism

"Impediments." *Menorah Journal*, 1925. In *Of This Time, Of That Place, and Other Stories*, sel. Diana Trilling. Uniform Ed. New York: Harcourt Brace Jovanovich, 1979, 3–10.

"Chapter for a Fashionable Jewish Novel." *Menorah Journal* 12 (June 1926): 275–82.

"Funeral at the Club, with Lunch." *Menorah Journal* 13 (August 1927): 380–90.

"A Light to the Nations." *Menorah Journal* 16 (April 1928): 402–8.

"Another Jewish Problem Novel." Review of *The Disinherited*, by Milton Waldman. *Menorah Journal*, 1929. In *Speaking of Literature and Society*, ed. Diana Trilling. Uniform Ed. New York: Harcourt Brace Jovanovich, 1980, 16–27.

"Notes on a Departure." *Menorah Journal*, 1929. In *Of This Time, Of That Place, and Other Stories*, sel. Diana Trilling. Uniform Ed. New York: Harcourt Brace Jovanovich, 1979, 38–57.

"The Changing Myth of the Jew" (ca. 1930). *Commentary*, 1978. In *Speaking of Literature and Society*, ed. Diana Trilling. Uniform Ed. New York: Harcourt Brace Jovanovich, 1980, 50–77.

"Flawed Instruments." Review of *Adam and Stephen Escott* by Ludwig Lewisohn. *Menorah Journal*, 1930. In *Speaking of Literature and Society*, ed. Diana Trilling. Uniform Ed. New York: Harcourt Brace Jovanovich, 1980, 21–26.

"The Promise of Realism." Review of *Bottom Dogs*, by Edward Dahlberg, *Pay Day*, by Nathan Asch, and *Frankie and Johnnie*, by Meyer Levin. *Menorah Journal*,

1930. In *Speaking of Literature and Society*, ed. Diana Trilling. Uniform Ed. New York: Harcourt Brace Jovanovich, 1980, 27–36.

"Under Forty." *Contemporary Jewish Record*, 1944. In *Speaking of Literature and Society*, ed. Diana Trilling. Uniform Ed. New York: Harcourt Brace Jovanovich, 1980, 197–201.

"Art and Fortune." 1950. In *The Liberal Imagination: Essays on Literature and Society*. Garden City, NY: Doubleday-Anchor, 1979, 247–71.

"Wordsworth and the Rabbis." 1950. In *The Opposing Self: Nine Essays in Criticism*. New York: Viking, 1955, 118–50.

Books by Lionel Trilling

Matthew Arnold. 1939. Uniform Edition. New York: Harcourt Brace Jovanovich, 1977.

E. M. Forster. 1943. Uniform Edition. New York: Harcourt Brace Jovanovich, 1980.

The Middle of the Journey. 1947. Uniform Edition. New York: Harcourt Brace Jovanovich, 1980.

The Liberal Imagination: Essays on Literature and Society. 1950. Uniform Edition: New York: Harcourt Brace Jovanovich, 1979.

Freud and the Crisis of Our Culture. Boston: Beacon, 1955.

The Opposing Self: Nine Essays in Criticism. 1955. Uniform Edition. New York: Harcourt Brace Jovanovich, 1978.

A Gathering of Fugitives. 1956. Uniform Edition. New York: Harcourt Brace Jovanovich, 1977.

Beyond Culture: Essays on Literature and Learning. 1965. Uniform Edition. New York: Harcourt Brace Jovanovich, 1978.

Sincerity and Authenticity. 1972. Uniform Edition. New York: Harcourt Brace Jovanovich, 1980.

Mind in the Modern World: The 1972 Thomas Jefferson Lecture in the Humanities. New York: Viking, 1973.

The Last Decade: 1965–75. Uniform Edition. New York: Harcourt Brace Jovanovich, 1979.

Of This Time, of That Place and Other Stories. Uniform Edition. New York: Harcourt Brace Jovanovich, 1979.

Prefaces to The Experience of Literature. Uniform Edition. New York: Harcourt Brace Jovanovich, 1979.

Speaking of Literature and Society. Ed. Diana Trilling. Uniform Edition. New York: Harcourt Brace Jovanovich, 1980.

Works Cited and Studies of Lionel Trilling

Boyers, Robert. *Lionel Trilling: Negative Capability and the Wisdom of Avoidance*. Columbia: University of Missouri Press, 1977.

Chace, William M. *Lionel Trilling: Criticism and Politics*. Stanford: Stanford University Press, 1980.

Dickstein, Morris. *Gates of Eden*. New York: Basic Books, 1977.

———. *Double Agent: The Critic and Society*. New York: Oxford University Press, 1992.

———. "Lionel Trilling and *The Liberal Imagination*." In *Double Agent: The Critic and Society*. New York: Oxford University Press, 1992. 68–80.

———. "Trilling as a Cultural Critic." In *Double Agent*, 143–50.

French, Philip. *Three Honest Men: Edmund Wilson, F. R. Leavis, Lionel Trilling*. Manchester: Carcanet, 1980.

Grumet, Elinor. "The Apprenticeship of Lionel Trilling." *Prooftexts* 4 (1984): 153–73.

Howe, Irving. *A Margin of Hope: An Intellectual Autobiography*. New York: Harcourt Brace Jovanovich, 1982.

Kazin, Alfred. *New York Jew*. New York: Knopf, 1978.

Krupnick, Mark. *Lionel Trilling and the Fate of Cultural Criticism*. Evanston, IL: Northwestern University Press, 1986.

———. "Lionel Trilling, 'Culture,' and Jewishness." *Denver Quarterly*, Autumn 1983, 106–22.

———. "The Menorah Journal Group and the Origins of Modern Jewish-American Radicalism." *Modern Jewish Studies*, 1979, 55–67.

Leitch, Thomas M. *Lionel Trilling: An Annotated Bibliography*. New York: Garland, 1993.

O'Hara, Daniel T. *Lionel Trilling: The Work of Liberation*. Madison: University of Wisconsin Press, 1988.

Shechner, Mark. "Psychoanalysis and Liberalism: The Case of Lionel Trilling." *Salmagundi* 41 (Spring 1978).

Shoben, Edward Joseph, Jr. *Lionel Trilling: Mind and Character*. New York: Ungar, 1981.

Tanner, Stephen L. *Lionel Trilling*. Boston: Twayne, 1988.

Trilling, Diana. *The Beginning of the Journey: The Marriage of Diana and Lionel Trilling*. New York: Harcourt Brace, 1993.

———. "Foreword." In *Speaking of Literature and Society*, ed. Diana Trilling. Uniform Ed. New York: Harcourt Brace Jovanovich, 1980, n.p.

———. "Lionel Trilling: A Jew at Columbia." *Commentary*, 1979. In *Speaking of Literature and Society*, 411–29.

LEON URIS   (1924–   )

Bennett Lovett-Graff

BIOGRAPHY

Leon Uris was born on August 3, 1924, in Baltimore, Maryland, to shopkeeper Wolf William Uris and his wife, Anna (Blumberg) Uris. Uris attended local Baltimore public schools before entering the U.S. Marine Corps in 1942 for a four-year tour of duty in the Pacific at Guadalcanal and Tarawa. After he returned, he married Betty Katherine Beck, by whom he was to have three children (he would divorce her in 1968). Taking up work as a circulation district manager for the *San Francisco Call-Bulletin* to support his family, Uris began immediately to work on his writing career, collecting rejection after rejection until he sold his first article to *Esquire* for $300. With renewed confidence, Uris started work on his first novel, *Battle Cry* (1953), a laudatory depiction of the Marine Corps that, despite criticism of its undue length, achieved best-seller status. Invigorated by the novel's reception, Uris, now faced with the "awesome problem that many writers of a big first novel never solve" of how to write a successful second novel, "decided to mark time, to branch out to Hollywood and learn screenwriting" ("About Exodus," 125). The result was the screenplay version of *Battle Cry*, which demonstrated Uris's knack for writing for the silver screen. With *The Angry Hills* (1955), a spy tale set in Cyprus, Uris scored another hit, despite criticism this time that the novel was too spare. More important, however, Uris became convinced that it was only "after this second novel that I felt I had acquired the craft to go on and top *Battle Cry*" ("About Exodus," 126).

Top it he did with his dramatic best-seller *Exodus* (1957). Though Uris continued to write for Hollywood, placing in director John Sturges's hand the screenplay for *Gunfight at the O.K. Corral*, he threw himself with extraordinary energy into writing the 600-page novelization of Israel's birth as a nation. The project was clearly new to Uris, who wrote that his "first awakening to a Jewish conscience came . . . during the Arab-Israel War." Because he lacked a formal Jewish education or a speaking knowledge of Hebrew, the obstacles set before him were formidable. But Uris was persistent: "Although I was strange to Jewish life, I wanted to be proud of my people. I wanted to be able to write a book about Jews and be able to face a Jewish audience afterward" ("About Exodus," 126–27). Uris consequently set himself to the task of researching his topic for the next two years, traveling roughly fifty thousand miles (twelve thousand of them in Israel alone), reading over three hundred books, shooting more than a thousand photos, and conducting hundreds of interviews. When *Exodus* was published in 1957, it was an instant success, resulting in, among other things, the 1960 film version directed by Otto Preminger and starring Paul Newman and Eva Marie Saint. Uris then capitalized on his research to produce three years later *Mila 18*, a tale of Warsaw Ghetto fighters. Simultaneously, he worked with photographer Dimitrios Harissiadis to produce a photo-essay, *Exodus Revisited*, the first of three photo-essays he would do (the next two were written with his third wife, photographer Jill Peabody, whom he married in 1970).

In his next two novels, Uris shifted his focus away from Jewish topics, taking as his subject in *Armageddon* (1964) the Berlin airlift, while in *Topaz* (1967) he wrote an iron-curtain spy thriller. But Uris was not to stray far once he decided to return to things Jewish with *QB VII* (1970), the tale of Polish camp survivor turned British citizen Adam Kelno, who sues an American Jewish writer, Abraham Cady, for libel. The case, which revolves around a statement in Cady's novel *The Holocaust* that Kelno had performed "15,000 experimental operations without use of anesthesia," was itself based on a lawsuit filed by Dr. Wladislaw Alexander Dering against Uris, who had written in *Exodus* about a "Dr Dehring" who had "performed seventeen thousand experiments in surgery without anaesthetic" (146). The case, which was tried in April and May 1964, immediately caught the public eye, generating enough interest to provide Mavis M. Hill and L. Norman Williams with material to publish a shortened record of the trial (*Auschwitz in England*) five years before Uris's own novelization of the affair. Following the precedent set by his first three novels and his spy thriller, *Topaz*, all of which had received film treatments (*Topaz* was notably directed by Alfred Hitchcock), *QB VII* was in turn made into a television miniseries that ran to remarkably high ratings in 1974.

After *QB VII*, Uris turned again from Jewish topics to write *Trinity* (1976), a novel about Ireland that attempted to re-create for the Irish the same sense of historical drama *Exodus* had generated for Jews. But Uris's lapse was only temporary, as he returned to Jewish themes in his next two novels, *The Haj* (1984) and *Mitla Pass* (1988). Since *Mitla Pass*, Uris has returned to the question of Ireland in his most recent novel, *Redemption* (1995).

In achieving worldwide recognition as one of America's foremost writers of best-sellers, Uris has won the envy, admiration, and contempt of writers and critics alike. Certainly there is no dearth of official recognition for his achievements. Uris has won a slew of awards, including the California Literature Silver and Gold Medal awards for *Mila 18* and *Armageddon*, respectively, the John F. Kennedy Medal from the Irish/American Society of New York, the Scopus Award from Hebrew University of Jerusalem, and honorary doctorates from the University of Colorado, Santa Clara University, Wittenberg University, and Lincoln College.

MAJOR WORKS AND THEMES

It would be an understatement to suggest that Uris's first foray into Jewish writing created something of a splash. It would be more accurate to describe the appearance of *Exodus* as an explosion. Bursting onto the scene shortly after the 1956 Sinai campaign, *Exodus* performed a considerable amount of work toward winning American hearts and minds to the cause of Israel by dramatizing Israel's national birth. Criticized often for the bias of his historical novels, Uris has been and remains unapologetic about his penchant for transforming history from a series of casual phenomena with no specific end in sight into a dramatic narrative with a morally directed beginning, middle, and end. Despite the broad historical sweep of *Exodus*, for example, which makes ample use of flashbacks (sometimes several generations back) to explain his characters' situations, Uris's version of history is a distinctively teleological one. There are good guys (Jews) and there are bad guys (Nazis, Arabs, British), and while individuals from either camp may cross the line, their roles remain largely determined in Uris's scheme by the exigencies of his version of history.

But Uris's history is more than popular theater. In the case of *Exodus*, it is also religious drama. The opening of book sections with biblical citations and the eternal quoting of the Scripture by the fervid British, pro-Zionist commander, P. P. Malcolm, or the Maccabee terrorists (modeled on the Irgun) under British interrogation, all lend themselves to the sense Uris creates that Israel's birth is nothing less than a working out of the divine will. Consider more closely the case of P. P. Malcolm, who instructs the novel's protagonist, Ari Ben Canaan, and his fellow Palmachniks in the art of reprisal. Cast at first as a "harmless eccentric" (296), Malcolm demonstrates more method than madness in turning to the Bible for important military strategies. At one point, Malcolm cites to his trainees Gideon's use of noise as a diversion to confuse more numerous adversaries (a strategy of clear significance to the outnumbered Jewish population in Palestine) (299); at another, he teaches his troops "the strategic as well as historic value of every wadi and hill and tree by pointing out how the ancient Hebrew generals had used the land and knowledge of it to great military advantage" (300). Not surprisingly, Malcolm's method foreshadows another character's use of Jewish history to point out a little-known Roman road (the "Burma Road") that helps the Haganah break the siege of Jerusalem (563). Even more telling is the use of biblical passages as code for army operations.

"X1416" is Exodus 14.16—"But lift thou up thy rod, and stretch out thine hand over the sea, and divide it; and the children of Israel shall go on dry ground through the midst of the sea" (522)—a signal that orphans from Ben Canaan's home of Gan Dafna have been successfully transported down a cliff and out of harm's way from Arab forces; "I358" is Isaiah 35.8, "And a highway shall be there," a signal that the Burma Road has been readied (566).

For Uris, the history of Israel's birth is the unfolding of a divine history, the surest sign of which comes not from any of the novel's Jewish characters, but from the gentile American nurse, Kitty Fremont. All too human in her passions, Kitty operates primarily as a foil to the warriorlike, superhuman Ben Canaan. Thus when Kitty looks "at the face of Ari Ben Canaan" and his fellow fighters and sees "no army of mortals," but "the ancient Hebrews" themselves, an "army of Israel" that "no force on earth could stop . . . for the power of God was within them" (371), Kitty's sense of the divine, though hyperbolic to us, is cast by Uris as an authentic experience. Ari and his compatriots, in Uris's formulation, are the ancient Hebrews resurrected. But more important than that, whether this is a good thing is not altogether clear (a telling point that has been repeatedly overlooked by critics and reviewers). As Ari Ben Canaan's father, Barak, mournfully notes at the novel's conclusion: "A ghetto? A concentration camp? Extermination ovens? I say anything is worth this. Yet, this freedom of ours . . . the price is so high. We cherish it so fiercely that we have created a race of Jewish Tarzans to defend it," a race, Barak adds, that in mistaking "tenderness for weakness" and "tears for dishonor" (604) may have forgotten how to show as well as feel love.

Notwithstanding the tragedies that beset the characters in *Exodus*, Uris's outlook is largely optimistic. Miracles can happen, as in the case of Israel's birth. But Uris's concerns extend beyond chronicling the miraculousness of Israel's nationhood, inasmuch as he also concerns himself with changing the popular image of Jews from effete, self-tortured *schlemiels* into nationalistic warriors. In substituting one stereotype for another, Uris takes sides in what he sees as a contest of images, a war he wages with renewed vigor in *Mila 18*. Here Uris's subject is the Warsaw Ghetto uprising, in which the fight is less one for survival than for dignity. That the Jewish forces in Warsaw cannot win is obvious. But then again, as Uris makes clear, their fight is less about winning any specific battle than about affecting the texture of modern Jewish history by offering an example of Jewish resistance. Moreover, unlike *Exodus*, in which the Jewish forces, despite differing means, fight for the same ends, *Mila 18* takes up more forcefully the question of Jewish complicity. From the self-hating Piotr Warsinski to black-market kingpin Max Kleperman and the assimilated and vain Paul Bronski, Uris is unforgiving of those who compromise their identities by complying with the Warsaw regime.

A similar theme becomes the central concern of Uris's next foray into the legacy of the Holocaust, *QB VII*, based on his own libel case. Uris inspects, in the case of protagonist Adam Kelno, the Polish doctor accused of performing human sterilizations, Kelno's fateful cooperation with the Nazi regime of doctors who run Jadwiga concentration camp. Despite our suspicions from the novel's very beginning concerning his guilt, Kelno remains one of Uris's most interesting characters because he is offered without irony as a compassionate individual. In the jungles of Sarawak, Borneo, he works hard to relieve the distress of the native Ulans; when he returns to Great Britain to be knighted, he puts social obligation before personal success to work in one of London's poorer districts. Though writer Abraham Cady puts a less-than-generous interpretation on Kelno's moves ("Why did Kelno bring this suit? . . . He feels inferior so he has always gotten himself placed into a position where he could be superior to those around him. In Sarawak, in Jadwiga, in a workingman's clinic in London" [501]), there is no getting around the goodness of the work Kelno in fact does in Sarawak and the clinic. So how to explain his bestial behavior in Jadwiga? According to the novel, three factors contribute to Kelno's undoing: his father's sexual abuse of his mother, his own paternally and nationally inspired anti-Semitism, and finally the strange opportunity presented to him in Jadwiga to express his conscious hatred of Jews and unconscious hatred of his father through Nazi sterilization experiments (501). As much as we are supposed to despise Kelno, Uris wins him some small (albeit very small) sympathy, if only by illustrating how much a victim of historical circumstance Kelno is.

Having treated the psychology of evil in *QB VII*, Uris again tried to demonstrate the weight exerted by history on the individual in his next "Jewish" novel, *The Haj*. Taking up in a sense where *Exodus* leaves off concerning the Arab "problem," Uris presumptuously takes upon himself the task of explaining the Arab hatred of Jews by investigating the Arab mind from the inside. To this end, Uris makes ample use of interior monologue, sometimes in first-person voice, as in the case of his narrator, Ishmael, sometimes in the third-person limited voice of Ishmael's father, Haj Ibrahim. In either case, Uris attempts to demonstrate his thesis by example, so that when Ishmael asserts, "It was me against my brother; me and my brother against our father; my family against my cousins and clan" (15), and so on, we are supposed to accept this rendition of Arab mistrust of everyone else as truth because it is cast as an admission. Irrespective of the tremendous unreality of this image of Arabs, Ishmael's assertion is enough of a confession to provide Uris with the plot elements of a national tragedy as the machinations of Ibrahim and Ishmael, who refuse to trust their Jewish neighbors, backfire upon themselves, destroying them and their families instead of their supposed enemy, the Jews.

In Uris's final foray into Jewish matters, techniques and themes from several of the previous novels reappear in *Mitla Pass*. As the story of protagonist Gideon Zadok's development as a writer and a Jew while in Israel during the Sinai campaign, *Mitla Pass* borrows heavily from Abraham Cady's life story in *QB VII*; as a tale of Israeli toughness, it looks back to *Exodus*; and as a record of Zadok's life told in different voices (sometimes first person, sometimes third) by different individuals, it reuses techniques exploited in *The Haj*. Though cleverly constructed as a double flashback—the first half of the novel cuts back and forth between Gideon Zadok's current residence in Israel and memories of his marriage and early years as a writer, the second half between the time he spends in Sinai and the story of his parents and their immigration to America—*Mitla Pass* remains thematically weak in its attempt to explain how Gideon's evolution as a writer and a Jew leads him to fight with, so he can write about, the Lion's Brigade at Mitla Pass. About the writer's need to understand the importance of coming to terms with his heritage, *Mitla Pass* remains to this date Uris's most intensely autobiographical novel.

CRITICAL RECEPTION

In any discussion of Uris's critical reception, an immediate distinction must be drawn between Uris's readers, on the one hand, and reviewers and literary critics, on the other. That Uris is popular there is no denying. Nearly all of his novels have been best-sellers, a point that continues to stick in the craw of his many critics. The result has consequently been mixed reviews, like those of *Exodus*, which, despite its " 'underground power' " and "capacity to refresh our memory, inform our intelligence and to stir the heart" (Geismar, 30), suffers from the "stultifying conventionality" (Coleman, 44) of its cardboard characterizations. *Mila 18* also received a mixed reception upon its publication. The title of Victor Hass's review speaks for itself: "A Glowing Testament to the Human Spirit." For the reviewer of *Time*, however, Uris not only duplicates John Hersey's achievement, *The Wall*, but, to his detriment, does a far worse job of it ("Back to 'The Wall,' " 94). As for *QB VII*, it fared even less well than its two predecessors. In his tellingly titled "How to Write a Leon Uris," Christopher Lehmann-Haupt charged Uris with the mortal sin of predictability: "Uris need never worry about his characters assuming independent life and taking his story away from him" (45). Martha Duffy considered the novel a "vulgar affront," further marred by Uris's "own wretched writing performance" (80). *The Haj* also came in for considerable criticism, indeed, some of the most incendiary in Uris's writing career. Unlike *Exodus*, which only some faulted for its negative stereotyping of Arabs, *The Haj* was pummeled by nearly all of its reviewers for overplaying the hostility, violence, backwardness, sexism, and anti-Semitism of its Arab characters. *Mitla Pass* fared only marginally better, benefiting from having received even less attention than Uris's earlier novels.

Despite the dearth of significant literary criticism about Uris's novels, the few who have bothered to write about him have been no more gentle than the reviewers. When Jeremy Salt wrote, "I am not concerned in this paper with whether *Exodus* and *The Haj* are good or bad novels" but "whether they are good history" (55), it is not difficult to determine from the article's venue (*Journal of Palestine Studies*) the conclusion Salt drew. Nor do Salt's conclusions differ all that much from those of Elise Salem Manganaro, who coyly used Bakhtin to expose Uris's presumptuous attempt to generate in *The Haj* an "air of authenticity" by "purportedly offer[ing] a multiplicity of points of view" that are, in the end, "shockingly similar" (4). Perhaps the most authoritative essay yet on Uris's fiction is Sharon Downey and Richard Kallan's "Semi-Aesthetic Detachment: The Fusing of Fictional and External Worlds in the Situational Literature of Leon Uris." Drawing on various sources, from Wayne Booth's rhetoric of fiction to an interview with Uris conducted by the authors, Downey and Kallan concluded that Uris's use of various rhetorical tools, including the much-maligned character stereotype, essentially serves the necessary function of creating a semiaesthetic detachment that encourages readers to actually act on their sentiments rather than just indulge them.

Despite the very real weaknesses of Uris's novels, the lack of any in-depth criticism does not seem altogether justified in light of his very real impact. No doubt Paul Breines was right when he wrote of *Exodus* and its nearly sixty paperback printings that the novel's appeal derives largely from its status as a fantasy for American Jewish readers in an age of uncertainty and assimilation (53–55). Nor does this run counter to Uris's own assertion that his stereotypically "tough Jews" are themselves a response to a competing set of stereotypes: "With a great deal of sadness I must say that foremost among the beatnik writers are those Jewish authors who make caricatures of the Jewish people . . . the wily businessman, the brilliant doctor . . . the tortured son . . . the coward" ("About Exodus," 127). Though Uris overstates his case, as Philip Roth made clear in his own telling criticism (137–40), there is no doubt that Uris has achieved an immense task that merits more than, as Joel Carmichael wrote but failed to do, another exercise in "sneering at best-sellers" (86). Aside from Downey and Kallan's and possibly Roth's and Breines's examinations, all other attempts at understanding how such seemingly poor novels have gained such good sales have largely been less informative about than insulting of the intelligence and tastes of popular readers, which leads one to suspect that even if Uris's novels do not demand more criticism on their aesthetic merits, they certainly have earned them in terms of their cultural impact.

BIBLIOGRAPHY

Works by Leon Uris

Fiction

Battle Cry. New York: Putnam, 1953.
The Angry Hills. New York: Random House, 1955.
Exodus. Garden City, NY: Doubleday, 1957.
Mila 18. Garden City, NY: Doubleday, 1961.
Armageddon. Garden City, NY: Doubleday, 1964.
Topaz. New York: McGraw-Hill, 1967.
QB VII. Garden City, NY: Doubleday, 1970.

Trinity. Garden City, NY: Doubleday, 1976.
The Haj. Garden City, NY: Doubleday, 1984.
Mitla Pass. Garden City, NY: Doubleday, 1988.
Redemption: A Novel. New York: HarperCollins, 1995.

Screenplays

Battle Cry. Warner Brothers, 1954.
Gunfight at the O.K. Corral. Paramount, 1957.

Nonfiction

Exodus Revisited. Photographer, Dimitrios Harissiadis. Garden City, NY: Doubleday, 1966. Published in England as *In the Steps of Exodus.* London: Heinemann, 1962.
"What One Writer Likes—and Doesn't." *New York Herald Tribune Book Review*, August 16, 1959, 2, 11.
"About Exodus." In *The Quest for Truth*, ed. Martha Boaz. Metuchen, NJ: Scarecrow, 1967, 123–30.
The Third Temple. (Bound with William Stevenson's *Strike Zion.*) New York: Bantam, 1967.
Ireland: A Terrible Beauty. Photographer, Jill Uris. Garden City, NY: Doubleday, 1975.
Jerusalem, Song of Songs. With Jill Uris. Photographer, Jill Uris. Garden City, NY: Doubleday, 1981.

Studies of Leon Uris

Criticism

Breines, Paul. "The Americanization of Tough Jews." In *Tough Jews: Political Fantasies and the Moral Dilemma of American Jewry.* New York: Basic Books, 1990, 52–56.
Carmichael, Joel. "The Phenomenal Leon Uris." *Midstream* 7 (1961): 86–90.
Decter, Midge. "Popular Jews." In *The Liberated Woman and Other Americans.* New York: Coward, McCann, and Geoghegan, 1971, 117–20.
Delatiner, Barbara. "Leon Uris: Deserting Anonymity." *New York Times* (Long Island edition), July 4, 1993, 10.
Downey, Sharon D., and Richard A. Kallan. "Semi-Aesthetic Detachment: The Fusing of Fictional and External Worlds in the Situational Literature of Leon Uris." *Communication Monographs* 49:3 (1982): 192–204.
Kamins, Mort. "Leon Uris." *Writer's Digest* 67 (August 1987): 38–42.
Manganaro, Elise Salem. "Voicing the Arab: Multivocality and Ideology in Leon Uris' *The Haj.*" *MELUS* 15:4 (1988): 3–13.
Roth, Philip. "Some New Jewish Stereotypes." In *Reading Myself and Others.* New York: Farrar, Straus and Giroux, 1975, 137–47.
Salt, Jeremy. "Fact and Fiction in the Middle Eastern Novels of Leon Uris." *Journal of Palestine Studies* 14:3 (1985): 54–63.

Reviews

Adler, Jerry. "The Unchosen People." Review of *The Haj. Newsweek*, May 21, 1984, 84.

"Back to 'The Wall.' " Review of *Mila 18*. *Time*, June 2, 1961, 94.

Coleman, John. "Proper Study." Review of *Exodus*. *The Spectator*, July 10, 1959, 44.

Duffy, Martha. "Bestseller Revisited." Review of *QB VII*. *Time*, June 28, 1971, 80.

Fitzpatrick, Donovan. Review of *Mitla Pass*. *New York Times Book Review*, January 1, 1989, 14.

Geismar, Maxwell. "Epic of Israel." Review of *Exodus*. *Saturday Review of Literature*, September 27, 1958, 22–23, 30.

Hass, Victor P. "A Glowing Testament to the Human Spirit." Review of *Mila 18*. *Chicago Tribune Magazine of Books*, June 18, 1961, 1.

Hunter, Evan. "Palestine in Black and White." Review of *The Haj*. *New York Times Book Review*, April 22, 1984, 7.

"In Big Things and Small." Review of *Exodus*. *Times Literary Supplement*, July 24, 1959, 433.

Kupferberg, Herbert. "A Novel of Israel's Birth." Review of *Exodus*. *New York Herald Tribune Book Review*, September 28, 1958, 5.

Lehmann-Haupt, Christopher. "How to Write a Leon Uris." Review of *QB VII*. *New York Times*, December 2, 1970, 45.

Michaud, Charles. Review of *Mitla Pass*. *Library Journal*, November 1, 1988, 112.

Spitzer, Jane Stewart. " 'The Haj': Uris's Richly Detailed Palestinian Portrait Lacks Vitality." *Christian Science Monitor*, May 2, 1984, 20.

Steinberg, Sybil. Review of *Mitla Pass*. *Publisher's Weekly*, September 23, 1988, 59.

Wakefield, Dan. Review of *Exodus*. *Nation*, April 11, 1959, 319.

EDWARD LEWIS WALLANT (1926–1962)

Mark Zaitchik and Lisa Jucknath

BIOGRAPHY

Edward Lewis Wallant was born in New Haven on October 19, 1926, the only child of Sol Ellis Wallant and Anna Henrietta Mendel Wallant. His father, a victim of mustard gas while serving in the U.S. Army during World War I, was tubercular, usually hospitalized, and rarely seen by his son. Loving, but absent, he died when Wallant was only six. His mother, a soft-spoken hatmaker and first-generation Russian American, comprised only one voice in a doting matriarchal quartet that oversaw Edward's growing up. Along with her sisters, Edith and Esther, and her mother, Rose Mendel, she groomed Edward in a quiet middle-class home. His uncle Willie and his maternal grandfather were also occupants, but Willie died in 1933, and in any case, aunts Edith and Esther dominated the domestic scene. It is not surprising that virtually all of Wallant's work, published and unpublished, features male protagonists seeking clarification of a father-son relationship or an understanding of their fatherlessness. Nevertheless, grandfather Mendel was a living presence. When he spoke about the old country, Edward was always at his knee: hence the vivid flashbacks of Russia in his first novel, *The Human Season*.

   Though Wallant's adolescence was undramatic in quiet New Haven—a locale he explored with remarkable insight in an as-yet-unpublished novel, *The Odyssey of a Middleman*—he keenly observed the nuances of neighborhood life. His fiction details part-time jobs as plumber's assistant, as brickyard worker, and as delivery boy for a pharmacy across from a Catholic hospital with uncanny accuracy. The portrait of Angelo DeMarco bringing candy bars to the dying in *Children at the Gate* suggests that even as a teenager, Wallant was one on whom nothing was lost.

He was also a young man in love with books. In his essay, "The Artist's Eyesight," Wallant revealed the development of his reading habits. From dime novels he progressed to Dickens, from Tarzan he swung to Twain. He came to understand how literature affects people, how it offers escape from their dull, drab reality, how it touches the imagination and makes them more human. Reading, quite simply, stimulated his desire to be an artist. But growing up in New Haven, he was surrounded by pragmatists whose concessions to art ended where earning a safe living began. When he graduated from high school in 1944, he apparently associated his creativity with the visual. As a commercial artist, he could support himself.

In October 1944, Wallant enlisted in the navy and served as a gunner's mate in the European theater of operations. Outside of a few letters to his family, he seems to have chosen not to discuss his wartime experiences, although *The Odyssey of a Middleman* does include a highly charged, sometimes brilliant description of the Battle of Normandy.

After his discharge in 1946, he returned to New Haven for a year and then moved to New York, where he entered Pratt Art Institute in the fall of 1947. The following year he married Joyce Fromkin, his high-school sweetheart, who worked as a laboratory assistant while he finished his schooling. He graduated in 1950 (without distinction), and the young couple moved to New Rochelle, New York.

While in New Rochelle, he began a successful, if unsatisfying, career in commercial art. His first job was with L. W. Frolich Company, where he served as a "designer of pharmaceutical ethical advertising and direct mail." He also began the formal study of creative writing by enrolling in the New School for Social Research. There he met two major influences on his literary life: Don Wolfe and Harold Glicksburg.

During the next decade he juggled the roles of art director by day and aspiring writer by night and became the father of a son and two daughters. Because he was a man of immense energy, sound duty, and good cheer, according to those who knew him, he slighted none of his obligations. He told friends that he wrote because he had to "work things out." Though his fiction was consistently rejected during the 1950s (with the exception of two short stories, "I Held Back My Hand" [1955] and "The Man Who Made a Nice Appearance" [1958], both published in collections edited by his mentor Don Wolfe), his work had been noticed by Dan Wickenden, trade editor of Harcourt, Brace. They had met on a train to New York City and had quickly become friends. Wickenden at first saw Wallant as an apprentice with much to learn, but he knew immediately that he was "a born writer."

Wallant's apprenticeship ended in 1960 when Harcourt accepted a novel called *A Scattering in the Dark*. It was published in August of that year, retitled as *The Human Season*. The novel was no great commercial success when it appeared, although it was warmly received by the critical world, particularly *Time*. It was honored with the Jewish Book Council Fiction Award, and the following May Wallant won the Daroff Memorial Fiction Prize. With it came a check for $250. That summer, he received a fellowship to attend the Breadloaf Writers Conference. Suddenly he had access to a coterie of literary friends.

In 1961, *The Pawnbroker* appeared. It was well received, and for the first time Wallant consciously entertained notions of giving up his work as an illustrator. Although his wife's father strongly objected, he desired to support the family as a full-time novelist. The following year, with glowing recommendations from John Ciardi and Don Wolfe, he was awarded a Guggenheim Fellowship. He resigned his job at McCann Erickson Advertising Agency.

Before leaving for Europe, he showed two manuscripts to Wickendon, *The Tenants of Moonbloom* and *Children at the Gate*. Both needed significant revision when the Wallant family left for Europe on May 29, 1962. He would make the necessary changes while in Europe. After what his children describe as an idyllic six months in France, Italy, and Spain, Wallant found his European wanderings cut short by the Cuban missile crisis. He returned to America on November 15 and dropped off the promised rewritten version of *Moonbloom*.

Wallant was not feeling well, however. He complained of chronic exhaustion, and Wickendon noticed a significant weight loss. Two physical examinations revealed nothing, and Wallant continued to write. His Guggenheim was renewed for another year. Two days later, he suffered a massive stroke. He died on December 5, 1962. *Children at the Gate*, completed only a day before the fatal aneurysm, reached Wickenden's desk about a week after the funeral.

After Wallant's death, he was awarded a posthumous citation for outstanding literary contributions by the New Haven Festival of Arts. Donations were made to the Brandeis Library and Yale Library in his name. The Edward Lewis Wallant Memorial Book Award was established. Sidney Lumet successfully directed *The Pawnbroker*, featuring Rod Steiger as Sol Nazerman. His last two novels were painstakingly edited by Wickendon. *The Tenants of Moonbloom* was published in May of 1963—it was felt that a comic novel should follow on the heavy heels of *The Pawnbroker*. *Children at the Gate* appeared in 1964.

MAJOR WORKS AND THEMES

A single paradigm dominates theme and structure in Wallant's four published novels: the journey of a solitary self from spiritual numbness to redemptive pain. Each focuses on the pilgrimage of a man who has chosen, for one reason or another—whether the nightmare of history or the barbarism of culture or the simple savagery of human life—to insulate himself from the shared, human world. Wallant allows none of his protagonists to escape joyful, dreadful epiphany, the recognition that paralysis of feeling is a suicide worse than death. His heroes come to know that moral anesthesia is not a state one can suffer in isolation; it is rather a mute crime against humanity.

In *The Human Season*, Joseph Berman withdraws from the world upon the sudden death of his wife. He is, of course, suffering from shock and depression, but Wallant shows no inclination to develop or explain his hero's loss in psychological terms. He is, as we shall see, a religious writer, and the novel is, more than anything, a dirge, a lamentation of the exposed and naked soul brought low for the purpose of resurrection.

Joseph Berman's story, told through the counterpoint of flashback alternating with an ongoing present, begins in Russia in 1907. Berman is a plumber who has courageously, even joyfully, confronted anti-Semitism and physical conflict; he has romped, sometimes with glee, always with zest, in the excrement that is at the heart of his trade; he has accepted the death of his son in World War II with equanimity, without complaint.

Desolation triumphs over hope, however, when his wife dies. He bitterly rejects the consoling rabbi's argument that suffering is a spiritual test. Too hard-boiled to whine, he would rather curse God and die. Existence has become mere burden. He withdraws from his daughter Ruthie and his dear partner Riebold; he evicts boarders who would fill the emptiness of space and provide human company. All the while, the plumber works in shit and hopes to wash away what ails him. He finds, however, that soap and water do not provide the baptism he requires, nor will physical spotlessness cleanse that which he believes the filth of existence has heaped on him.

Awakening arrives with the same suddenness as malaise. Almost electrocuted by a television wire—television, the soporific—Berman is stunned, amazed, shocked to recognition. He prays to emerge from his living death. God, he grasps, is no anthropomorphic Betrayer, no "bearded torturer." He leaves the apartment so filled with memories and, reconnected to love, moves in with his daughter.

In *The Human Season*, Wallant has retold the Job myth, but the myth has not been displaced by the skepticism we find in such secular retellings as Archibald MacLeish's *J.B.* or Robert Frost's *Masque of Reason*. Joseph Berman has no conversation with a personal God, but he comes to understand that there is a "light," that the transcendence of all squalor comes in "little glimmers to your soul" in a universe that is "beyond understanding." Miracle and wonder must provide the faith for human redemption and human love.

In *The Pawnbroker*, Wallant's second novel, the world is packed with infinitely greater squalor. The "glimmers" are decidedly more faint. The voice of complaint is not invective hurled at the heavens, but nihilism compressed to a silent core. Recovery will be more arduous and more painful in the blackness of Harlem than it is in quiet New Haven.

Sol Nazerman, the pawnbroker, has physically survived the concentration camps; his wife and two children have not escaped extermination. Misshapen by the sadistic operations of Nazi doctors, living with a bourgeoise sister and her family who cannot imagine evil, occasionally stopping by the home of fellow survivor Tessie for metallic sex—she whose husband died on the electrified fences of genocide—Nazerman is inured to pain. To feel is to revivify history, and so he exists without emotion for himself or for others. He awaits death, intimate only with the absurd persistence of life, but insulated by the knowledge that "soon enough will come the ax."

The pawnshop is the perfect metaphor for Sol's existence: the randomness of unrelated objects; the tattered fragments of identities, disconnected from what they own and what they are, in various states of disrepair, in advanced stages of decay and disintegration; the neighborhood, mere flotsam, a slum, discarded piece by piece, like the tinny, dying radios that the dying leave for a dollar. Over this hellish realm, Sol, the sun, sits as an indifferent God, unwittingly dispensing the laundered money of Whoremaster Murillo. He is a sun without heat or light. The universe is but a series of transactions. Its only absolute, he tells his assistant, Jesus, is money.

Nazerman's transformation from carrion scrap to wholeness is realized by Wallant with a significant, moral insight. He seems to have grasped that his novel, any novel about the Holocaust, risks the trivialization of the dead: empathy, imagination, and even memory itself are not sufficient for a coming to terms with six million corpses. The past must be left to history. Artifice must withdraw unless its representations serve some purpose beyond the aesthetic recreation of the chambers of death.

The Harlem pawnshop, even with its depravity and sordidness intact, is no mirror of the concentration camps. Nor is it a metaphor for the mass atrocities human beings commit and suffer. Nazerman seeks refuge in the palsied shop, in its stuttering chaos, precisely because money's heartlessness brings control and order. In oxymoron more powerful than irony, Wallant presents Harlem as a Hell of possibility. The awakening to memory of the camps becomes not the mere enumeration of colossal pain, but an American agony of hope.

As the fifteenth anniversary of his family's death approaches, the armor of the pawnbroker's indifference begins to fail him. Nightmares intrude. He experiences, again and again, with fury and clarity, the rape of his wife, the death of his children. He awakens to find himself, alas, alive. Survival itself is his heart of darkness, a darkness that gradually moves him to recognize more than the infliction of the past. Illumination is remorseless: even Holocaust victims cannot evade responsibility for a humane future. He comes to sympathize with his nephew Morton, whose parents have badgered him into isolation, and to empathize with Tessie upon the loss of her father. He refuses, despite threats from racketeer Murillo, to continue as an agent for prostitution. In the novel's dramatic climax, he accepts guilt for the death of Jesus Ortiz. His assistant, in ritual sacrifice, has absorbed a bullet aimed at him.

The death of Jesus Ortiz brings redemptive tears, and, at one level, the allegory is transparently Christian—a selfless crucifixion that redeems the soul. But Nazerman's rebirth also makes possible an understanding of Kaddish. He discovers the joy of mourning, the value of prayers for the dead, who must never be forgotten. He rediscovers also that Kaddish is more than a threnody; it is a song of responsibility to the living. After fifteen years, he is again touched by love. Mired in the dark present, Sol comes to know the plea of do-gooder

Marilyn Birchfield—give me a future endowed with life. He can now inhabit the new land, America.

Wallant continues to explore the awakening of the dead in *The Tenants of Moonbloom*. This time, however, the flight from desolation is rendered as antic comedy. Ironically, Norman Moonbloom, the hero, begins as a model of humorlessness. To gain salvation, he must learn to laugh. Unlike Joseph Berman or Sol Nazerman, he does not require the exorcism of a numbing past to redeem himself. He awaits birth for the first time. The "O's" in MOONBLOOM, refracting from the realty sign on his window, encircle a nullity of feeling, his heart. He is a virgin in every way, unaffected by fracturing human experience, thirty-three, a perpetual student who has hidden behind books, a child whose innocence is hardly virtue.

In the bleak houses owned by his brother, Norman collects rent. At first indifferent to the inhabitants, he moves from apartment to apartment, a collector not only of money but of woe and grotesque idiosyncrasy. Gradually, unwittingly, he becomes the canvas to their thick-stroked deformities. Wallant, the illustrator, never mixed a more extraordinary palette. The images compose a twentieth-century *Pequod*, a cross-section of race, ethnicity, and religion, a catalogue, a microcosm of vibrant, suffering humanity: the anti-Semitic German woman who becomes a Jew, the quixotic, manic candyman who hawks his sweet wares on the daily trains, the whore living with a doting daddy, a black homosexual writing away rage, an immaculate boxer, the 104-year-old alcoholic who reads *Moby Dick* in Yiddish, and Basellecci, the teacher, whose cancerous colon has been projected onto a swollen wall.

At last, Norman accepts the beauty and deformity of his tenants' lives. After a long, feverish sleep, he awakens to responsibility. Since his slumlord brother will not make the needed repairs, Norman decides to fix the run-down apartments with his own hands. He will also reach out to run-down lives. He will no longer shrink from feeling. Lacking skills, lacking funds, risking madness, he begins the impossible task of mending.

The renovations, of course, do not assuage the basic condition of his tenants. Basellecci will still die a horrible death. But as Norman completes the repairs, covered with shit from Basellecci's erupting wall, he understands that there can be no birth without pain, no life without death's communion. At the end of the novel, as Norman awaits firing, the end of his brief career as rent collector, he notices that the final "m" in the painted window has been scraped away: "It thrilled him with his own endlessness . . . almost laughing, he followed its course. Moonblooo-ooo."

With *Children at the Gate*, Wallant concludes his four-volume miracle of human redemption. Angelo DeMarco, like the heroes who precede him, has repressed all feeling. Like Moonbloom, he is very much a child. With the exception of his idiot sister, Theresa, he is a man without connection. He delivers ice cream and candy from the local pharmacy to sick children. They are hospitalized, at the gate of death, in the neighborhood Catholic hospital. But he protects himself from pain, refuses to be violated by emotion, and insists that the only sensible way to live is to "get through things." For Angelo, however, persistence is not a noble, stoic challenge, but a strategy of survival rooted in bitterness and cynicism.

He "gets through things" by distancing himself from his family, divorcing himself from Catholicism, and convincing himself that life is nothing but contingency. When his mother complains about her unhappy life, he tells her that "things happen for no reason." If life is no more than the luck of the draw, the logic is inexorable: moral responsibility is an illusion.

But the logic of naturalism is not acceptable to Wallant. Human beings are responsible for one another. Angelo must be spiritually transformed, and his transformation occurs, as it has for Berman and Nazerman and Moonbloom, through the intercession of some ineffable, irresistible force. Enter Sammy, a drug-addicted, Jewish orderly. Of Wallant's catalysts of redemption, none is more central to plot, better developed, more powerful, than Sammy. He is manic, criminal, saintlike, bizarre, a teller of troubling tales about a troubled past, the personification of the irrational as life force. Understanding the agony of the dying, he administers drugs to alleviate their pain. Understanding human frailty, he seeks forgiveness for Lebedov, a devout man and child molester who must endure the knowledge of his inescapable animality. Both saint and sinner, Sammy forces vulnerability upon the man who would be robot. "It's so lonely not to suffer," he tells Angelo.

When Sammy impales himself on an iron fence—suicide as ritual crucifixion—Angelo cannot escape his nakedness. He has betrayed the agent of his salvation, a Judas informing about Sammy's drug use. As in *The Pawnbroker*, the iconography is Christian, but the epiphany is Jewish. The dead are mourned to serve the living, to remind them of love, of feeling, of social responsibility. At the end of the novel, Angelo DeMarco knows exactly what Joseph Berman's dying father knows in Wallant's first novel: "Yes, yes, so it is sudden. Life is sudden . . . Death . . . you are alive until the moment of death."

CRITICAL RECEPTION

Though he published only four novels, though he carried vast potential to his grave, and though it is unclear what direction his career would have taken had he lived past thirty-six (Diana Trilling, upon reading the first two acts of an uncompleted drama entitled *Lady of Spain*, thought that he would and should become a playwright), the critical response to Wallant suggests that his genius far exceeds the attention paid to his work. Jonathan Baumbach asserted that Wallant's "four haunting, desolating books . . . will survive us all" (138); Earl Rovit, in an essay instructively titled "A Miracle of Moral Animation," saw Wallant as a writer who "in an incontrovertible way . . . enriched our times" (62). Charles Alva Hoyt justified his inclusion of Wallant in a book devoted to minor novelists only on the grounds that Wallant "is almost unknown to the public," adding that he "will not be surprised if future critics award [Wallant] a high place in our literature. . . . No contemporary novelist was more gifted in the sheer grace of constructing a novel" (118); Leo Gurko praised Wallant as "brilliant . . . our ultimate urban novelist" (261).

Frederick Karl, however, was an admirer with a complaint. In *American Fictions, 1940–1980*, he described what he believed to be a central weakness in Wallant's novels of redemption: "His talent is for the bottom, not recovery" (328). Given the theme and structure of Wallant's work, this is a significant criticism, but it was not one shared by Max Schulz, who wrote in *Radical Sophistication* that Wallant "with almost terrifying tenderness was able to sit tearfully mired in the mud of human experience and watch with living joy the stars above" (185).

In *The Rise of American Jewish Literature*, Charles Angoff called Wallant "one of the truly great talents in Jewish-American fiction" (739). Ernst Becker, great philosopher and psychoanalyst, made a compelling argument for this evaluation in his essay, "*The Pawnbroker*: A Study in Basic Human Psychology":

Edward Lewis Wallant was one of those young geniuses—like Kafka—whose emotional and intuitive insight into the human condition was astonishing, and who literally squeezed this insight out of his own living flesh and consumed himself in the effort. Wallant died tragically early—in his middle thirties—but he had already proven himself a rare student of the character of man, and assured himself a place among the select few who can penetrate into the heart of the human condition. Consider the character delineations in such novels as *Children at the Gate*, or *The Pawnbroker*. Here is truly enormous penetration into what we might call "basic psychology": that is, the elemental psychic conditions for living and carrying on as *Homo Sapiens* on this planet. (Becker 75)

Despite a Twayne series study by David Galloway (1978), there has been virtually nothing published about Wallant the man. Recently, little has been written about his work. We can only assume that like that of many a literary genius, his time will come.

BIBLIOGRAPHY

Works by Edward Lewis Wallant

The Human Season. New York: Harcourt, Brace, 1960.
The Pawnbroker. New York: Harcourt, Brace, 1961.
The Tenants of Moonbloom. New York: Harcourt, Brace, 1963.
Children at the Gate. New York: Harcourt, Brace, 1964.
The Artist's Eyesight. New York: Harcourt, Brace, 1963.

Works Cited and Studies of Edward Lewis Wallant

Angoff, Charles, and Meyer Levin. *The Rise of American Jewish Literature*. New York: Simon and Schuster, 1970.

Baumbach, Jonathan. *The Landscape of Nightmare: Studies in the Contemporary American Novel*. New York: New York University Press, 1965.

Becker, Ernst. "*The Pawnbroker*: A Study in Basic Human Psychology." In *Angel in Armor: A Post-Freudian Perspective on the Nature of Man*. New York: George Braziller, 1969.

Galloway, David. *Edward Lewis Wallant*. Boston: Twayne, 1979.

Gurko, Leo. "Edward Lewis Wallant as Urban Novelist." *Twentieth Century Literature*, October. 1974, 252–61.

Hoyt, Charles Alva. "Edward Lewis Wallant." In *Minor American Novelists*. Carbondale: Southern Illinois University Press, 1970.

Karl, Frederick. *American Fictions, 1940–1980*. New York: Harper and Row, 1983.

Rovit, Earl. "A Miracle of Moral Animation." *Shenandoah Review* 16 (1965) 60–68.

Schulz, Max. *Radical Sophistication*. Athens: Ohio University Press, 1969.

Zaitchik, Mark. *Edward Lewis Wallant's The Odyssey of a Middleman: A Critical Introduction*. Ann Arbor, MI: University Microfilms International, 1977.

JEROME WEIDMAN (1913–)

Joel Shatzky and Michael Taub

BIOGRAPHY

Jerome Weidman was born on April 4, 1913, in New York City, to Joseph and Annie Falkovitz Weidman. He was educated at City College, (1931–1933), Washington Square College (1933–1934), and New York University Law School (1934–1937). During the Depression, Weidman worked as a clerk in New York as well as novelist, playwright, and essayist. During World War II he served in the U.S. Office of War Information (1942–1945). In 1943 he married Ann Payne, with whom he has had two sons, Jeffrey and John Whitney.

During a career of over fifty years as a writer, Weidman has produced a number of well-known works, including the novels *I Can Get It for You Wholesale* (1937) and the book for the musical *Fiorello!* (1959), for which he received a Pulitzer Prize, the New York Drama Critics Circle Award, and a Tony in 1960. His last novel, *Praying for Rain*, was published in 1986.

MAJOR WORKS AND THEMES

Weidman is probably best known for his novel *I Can Get It for You Wholesale*, an unflattering picture of the New York garment industry with sharply delineated Jewish characters, and its sequel *What's in It for Me?* (1938), both written by the time Weidman was twenty-five. Other works in which Jewish characters are prominent include *The Enemy Camp* (1958), dealing with Jewish ambivalence toward Christian society, and *The Sound of Bow Bells* (1962), about an unscrupulous Jewish novelist.

Weidman is best known as a popular novelist whose depiction of a Jewish milieu is somewhat in the spirit of Budd Schulberg's Sammy Glick in *What*

Makes Sammy Run? To the post–World War II generation he is better known
as a man of the theater, with such musical hits as *Fiorello!, Tenderloin* (1960),
and the musical version of *I Can Get It for You Wholesale* (1962), as well as
the screenwriter of *The Eddie Cantor Story* (1953). Of his own works, Weidman
has said in an interview with Caroline Heck, ''I am essentially a natural born
storyteller, writing of commonplace rather than heroic events. If you portray
real people, they are entertaining in and of themselves'' (quoted in *Contemporary Authors*, 695).

CRITICAL RECEPTION

The first of Jerome Weidman's novels, *I Can Get It for You Wholesale*, was
very favorably reviewed as ''racy, fresh and continuously interesting'' by
Charles Poore and ''a tough, vigorous, ironic story of an individual poisoned
by ambition,'' according to George Stevens (quoted in *Contemporary Authors*,
695). Other works, however, have not fared as well. One reviewer for *Time*
observed that as a short-story writer, ''Jerome Weidman comes close to being
a really good short story writer; his ear is accurate, and he presents the nubs of
his stories, neatly wrapped, for his readers to carry away. The trouble is that
while there is always something in the package, there is never much'' (quoted
in *Contemporary Authors*, 695). Of another work, *A Family Fortune* (1978), a
New Yorker reviewer noted, ''Mr. Weidman's novel . . . can bear very little scru-
tiny, and it is burdened with annoying anachronisms . . . but this has nothing to
do with its narrative strength and its non-stop flight into high-voltage entertainment'' (quoted in *Contemporary Authors*, 695).

Perhaps Weidman was most comfortable in the milieu of his early years, the
1920s and 1930s, for his most successful work comes from that time. Even
Fiorello! is very much a musical of the 1930s and *Tenderloin* of an even earlier
period. As a Jewish novelist, his contribution is in evoking a period in which
the children of those immigrants who arrived at the turn of the century found
their niche, for good or bad, in mainstream American society. Although Weidman is not as widely recognized as a Jewish-American writer as many others,
his short story ''My Father Sits in the Dark'' has been included in Irving Howe's
Jewish-American Stories collection (1977), one of the most significant postwar
anthologies of Jewish-American literature.

BIBLIOGRAPHY

Works by Jerome Weidman

Novels

I Can Get It for You Wholesale. New York: Simon and Schuster, 1937.
What's in It for Me? New York: Simon and Schuster, 1938.
I'll Never Go There Any More. New York: Simon and Schuster, 1941.

Your Daughter Iris. Garden City, NY: Doubleday, 1955.
The Enemy Camp. New York: Random House, 1958.
The Sound of Bow Bells. Random House, 1962.
Fourth Street East: A Novel of How It Was. New York: Random House, 1970.
A Family Fortune. New York: Simon and Schuster, 1978.
Counselors-at-Law. Garden City, NY: Doubleday, 1980.
Praying for Rain. New York: Harper and Row, 1986.

Short Stories

My Father Sits in the Dark and Other Selected Stories. New York: Random House, 1961.
The Death of Dickie Draper and Nine Other Stories. New York: Random House, 1965.

Broadway Musicals (Book)

Fiorello! With George Abbott. Produced 1959. New York: Random House, 1960.
Tenderloin. Produced 1960. New York: Random House, 1961.
I Can Get It for You Wholesale (based on the novel). Produced 1962. New York: Random House, 1963.
For further information on Jerome Weidman, see *Contemporary Authors*, New Revision Series, 1. Detroit: Gale Research, 1981, 694–95.

HERMAN WOUK   (1915–   )

Laurence W. Mazzeno

BIOGRAPHY

Herman Wouk was born on May 27, 1915, in the Bronx, New York, the oldest child of Russian-Jewish immigrants. The Wouks provided a loving Orthodox home life for the future novelist, his sister, and his brother. His maternal grandfather, Rabbi Mendel Levine, emigrated from Russia in 1928 and took over Herman's talmudic education; in later years, Wouk would cite him as one of the two greatest influences in his life, the other being the U.S. Navy. After attending public elementary schools and the prestigious Townsend Harris High School for gifted adolescents, Wouk matriculated at Columbia in New York. There he became the student and protégé of philosopher and writer Irwin Edman, whose works on practical philosophy reached a wide audience in the years before World War II. Wouk received a degree in comparative literature in 1934.

Rather than going to law school as his parents wished, Wouk went to work in the New York entertainment community. By day he earned his living as a joke writer; at night he composed theatricals that he hoped to see produced on Broadway. The outbreak of World War II changed his career dramatically. In 1941 he went to Washington, D.C., to work for the U.S. Treasury, joining the navy later in the same year. He returned to Columbia for Officer Candidate School; after a short stint in Communications School, he was assigned to U.S.S. *Zane*, a destroyer-minesweeper in the Pacific theater. When the war ended in 1945, he married Betty Sarah Brown, a former navy personnel specialist he had met in California. They were fortunate enough to have three sons, but the eldest died accidentally while the Wouks were vacationing in Mexico City.

Wouk's career as a novelist began during his naval service. At sea, he converted one of his comic dramas into a novel. Assisted by his mentor Edman, he secured a publisher, and in 1947 *Aurora Dawn* appeared on bookshelves and was made a Book-of-the-Month Club selection. He followed that success with *The City Boy* (1948), which was also included in the Book-of-the-Month Club offerings. During this time and until the end of the 1950s, he pursued his ambitions as a playwright; three of his dramas were produced on Broadway. Only *The Caine Mutiny Court-Martial* proved theatrically successful, however, running for more than four hundred performances; it was revived three decades later to similar acclaim.

During the 1950s, while he was enjoying the success generated by the publication of *The Caine Mutiny* (1951) and *Marjorie Morningstar* (1955), Wouk and his family lived in New York, and the novelist found time to teach a course at Yeshiva University. The Wouks moved to St. Thomas, Virgin Islands, in 1958, but returned to the United States in 1964, taking up residence in Washington, D.C., where he began work on *The Winds of War* (1971) and *War and Remembrance* (1978), a two-part fictional account of World War II. Though he continued his relatively secluded life during these years, Wouk traveled to China in 1972, and in the following year he participated in the Aspen Institute in Colorado. During the 1980s and 1990s he divided his time between his Georgetown home and a residence in Palm Springs, California; he and his wife also traveled to Israel on occasion. Turning his attention back to his Jewish roots, he explored the 1972 Arab-Israeli conflict in an imaginative fictional memoir, *Inside, Outside* (1985), and produced a stirring account of the early years of the Israeli state in *The Hope* (1993) and *The Glory* (1994).

During his career Wouk has garnered a number of awards. Most notably, *The Caine Mutiny* won the Pulitzer Prize in 1951 and the Columbia Medal for Literary Excellence the following year. The movie version received a number of Academy Award nominations in 1954. The novelist was awarded an honorary LL.D. by Clark University in 1960 and an honorary Doctor of Literature by American International College in 1979. In 1980 he received the Columbia University Alumni Association's Alexander Hamilton Medal for distinguished service and accomplishment.

MAJOR WORKS AND THEMES

For most of his literary career, Herman Wouk has been motivated by two interests: his Jewish heritage and his experiences in the U.S. Navy. Conservative both politically and religiously, he has used his fiction and drama as a platform for championing an ideology consistent with that outlook. All of his works promote a belief in traditional values, acknowledgment of just authority, and acceptance of restraints on personal freedom in support of a greater social good.

A number of Wouk's novels are based on his personal experiences, some more thinly veiled than others. For example, Wouk's first novel, *Aurora Dawn*, is a gentle satire of the advertising and entertainment industries. Wouk's years as a joke writer in New York provided him both inspiration and materials for the story. His hero, Andrew Reale, a young executive captivated by the lure of easy money and a luxurious if somewhat immoral lifestyle, eventually comes to realize that he can find true happiness only by rejecting that form of living. While the novel is loosely based on details from Wouk's life, it does suggest obliquely the kinds of choices a young Jewish man might face in American society.

The novelist's second work of fiction, *The City Boy*, is more noticeably autobiographical. The boy hero of the novel, Herbie Bookbinder, is the child of immigrant parents who want their son to succeed in their new homeland. Herbie's father, like Wouk's, runs a laundry and uses his earnings to give his children material advantages. One of them is in attendance at summer camp in the Berkshires, and Herbie's adventures there provide many of the laughs that pepper this comic look at growing up in the Jewish community in New York City.

For his third novel, *The Caine Mutiny*, Wouk turned to his experiences in World War II. Setting his tale aboard a rusting destroyer-minesweeper that sees little combat, Wouk describes the impact of war on the cadre of men who made a profession of naval service and the thousands who answered the call of their country when the war broke out. The novel is a *Bildungsroman*, tracing the life of the young reservist Willie Keith from his time as a bumbling officer candidate through his involvement in a mutiny to relieve an incompetent commander to his eventual rise to command of U.S.S. *Caine*. The work explores the conflict between submitting to appointed authority or rebelling against that authority when one judges a commanding officer incompetent.

Four years later, Wouk transformed his experiences of Jewish life in New York into the best-selling *Marjorie Morningstar*. The novel relates the story of Marjorie Morgenstern, the daughter of a Jewish businessman who wants her to succeed in American society without giving up her Orthodox culture. Marjorie has dreams of being an actress and takes an opportunity to work at a summer camp for adults; there she falls in love with Noel Airman, a Jew who has renounced his heritage. Under his influence, the heroine falls away from her faith for a while; in the end, however, she rejects Airman and returns to Orthodox practices. The novel is Wouk's best effort at portraying the struggles of Orthodox Jews faced with the problems of maintaining their lifestyle in a multicultural society.

Wouk followed these popular successes with *Youngblood Hawke* (1962) and *Don't Stop the Carnival* (1965). The former is a penetrating examination of the publishing industry. Its hero wastes his considerable talents as a novelist when he becomes caught up in the lifestyle suddenly open to him once he becomes successful. The latter is a comic portrait of life in the tropics, where Norman Paperman, a disillusioned Jewish New York businessman, retires to find peace, but instead becomes embroiled in a number of mishaps at the hotel he purchases there.

From 1964 until 1978 Wouk spent his time researching and writing *The Winds of War* and *War and Remembrance*, a two-part historical romance about World

War II. In these works Wouk weaves the lives of more than a dozen major fictional characters with real-life participants from among the Allied and Axis powers. These novels allow him to combine his two lifelong preoccupations: his love for the navy and his intense interest in his Jewish heritage. Through the family of navy officer Victor "Pug" Henry, the novelist dramatizes the heroism and sacrifices Americans made in saving the world from the menace of Nazism. Concurrently, Wouk is able to provide a chilling portrait of the Holocaust. With careful detail he outlines the ways Hitler and his henchmen systematically implemented their scheme to eradicate European Jews, relying on the active compliance of frightened Gentiles in conquered nations and the passive acquiescence of key officials in countries such as the United States and Britain who refused to believe reports of atrocities that reached them long before the end of the war. With the possible exception of *Marjorie Morningstar*, nowhere else in his fiction does Wouk present such a comprehensive, sympathetic, and insightful portrait of his people.

In the novels that followed his study of World War II, Wouk turned to the history of the modern State of Israel for inspiration. *Inside, Outside* is a fictional memoir of David Goodkind, an advisor to President Richard Nixon during the crucial period leading up to the 1972 Arab-Israeli War. Wouk intersperses the account of Goodkind's negotiations with Golda Meir's government with reminiscences of the hero's childhood in New York City—a tale even more directly autobiographical than the one Wouk presented in *The City Boy*. This novel was followed by *The Hope* and *The Glory*, both of which focus on the period following World War II when Israel was struggling for independence and acceptance in the Middle East and throughout the world. Like the novels about World War II, these contain a mixture of fictional and historical characters who shaped the Jewish state during its formative years.

CRITICAL RECEPTION

Wouk has aimed his novels at the large reading public, and as a result he has often been the subject of harsh criticism from academics and critics writing for highbrow journals. The division can be seen in the reviews of his very first novel. On the positive side, one critic commended the novelist because Wouk "happily avoids vulgar language and crude love passages" (*Booklist*, 273); another called the work "a delightfully fresh and funny satire" (*New York Herald Tribune*, 3). Among those who wrote disparagingly of the novel, however, was influential academician Diana Trilling, who dismissed the novelist's "affectations" of eighteenth-century techniques as "pretentious and imitative" (636). *The City Boy* was similarly criticized, although many reviewers have found some merit in Wouk's nostalgic portrait of growing up Jewish in New York City. Even Allen Guttmann, not generally a favorable critic of Wouk's writings, praised the novelist for "his ability to tell a story" and his "fine eye for living detail" (120).

Predictably, the novel that has provoked the greatest controversy has been *The Caine Mutiny*. The work is frequently compared with Norman Mailer's *The Naked and the Dead*, James Jones's *From Here to Eternity*, and James Gould Cozzens's *Guard of Honor*. Like its predecessors, the novel was a Book-of-the-Month Club selection and was also offered to subscribers of the Literary Guild, the People's Book Club, and the Doubleday Dollar Book Club. It was condensed in *Reader's Digest*. It ranked first on the *New York Times* and *New York Herald Tribune* best-seller lists for over a year. F. I. Carpenter predicted in 1956 that the work "may well become the most successful novel published in the twentieth century" (212).

The popularity of the novel did not spare it from particularly vitriolic criticism; Wouk's defense of conservative values—and especially his apparent vindication of Captain Queeg at the end of the story—was attacked by a number of writers who agreed with James Browne's assessment that a "moral flaw" lurked at the center of a work that purported to attack authority for nearly five hundred pages only to reverse course and offer support for even the most imbecilic actions of the martinet in command of the *Caine* (216). Albert Van Nostrand believed that Wouk took his drastic course of action "so that nearly everybody wins" in the end—both those who rebel and those who uphold authority (199).

Harvey Swados, the most strident of the early reviewers, claimed that Wouk wanted to "let us have our cake and eat it too, to stimulate us, without really forcing us to think"; in Swados's view, this is precisely what a lazy reading public wants from popular novels—verification that their smug attitudes about society and its problems are correct (199). A number of critics attacked Wouk's use of the Jewish lawyer Barney Greenwald as the spokesperson for authoritarianism. Allen Guttmann noted that Greenwald's passionate defense of Queeg "reverses" the "emotional vectors" that have all pointed toward the rightness of the mutineers' actions; through the Jewish lawyer Wouk asserts that "the military establishment that fought and defeated Nazi Germany must be affirmed by grateful Jews" (121).

The criticism of *Marjorie Morningstar* was characterized by a series of attacks on Wouk's portrait of Jewish life. Although the novel was cited by Meyer Levin as the novelist's "most solid achievement to date" (10) and acclaimed by John Metcalf as "damned nearly the Great American Novel (Urban Division)" (472), it has been harshly deprecated by Jewish critics who have found the author's portrait of Jewish life vulgar. Once again, Allen Guttmann asserted, Wouk wanted "to have it both ways": to celebrate individualism and rebellion while asserting that ultimately, one must submit to authority in order to achieve true self-actualization (123).

Norman Podhoretz considered Wouk's presentation of American Jewish culture dishonest; the writer cheated readers by giving them "a satisfied sense of having grappled with difficult questions" while actually avoiding the real issues that confronted Jews trying to make their way in a multicultural American society. Podhoretz dismissed the novel and its creator with one of the most stinging denouncements ever leveled at Wouk: "Utterly incapable of rendering the feel of an emotion or a conversation, he points vaguely into space like a blind man trying to locate an object in an unfamiliar room" (188). Such an attitude has persisted among critics, as evidenced by Marc Raphael's pronouncement in 1984 that *Marjorie Morningstar* is little more than "an assemblage of stereotypes—most of negative, indifferent, and ignorant Jews" (66).

The novel is important as a sociological document, however. Meyer Levin and Charles Angoff, editors of *The Rise of American Jewish Literature*, observed that "*Marjorie Morningstar* really catapulted interest in Jewish material to a lofty high" (511). Leslie Fiedler, impresario of American literary criticism for nearly two decades, cited the novel as "the first fictional celebration of the mid-twentieth-century detente between Jews and middle-class America" (258). Even Norman Podhoretz was forced to admit that *Marjorie Morningstar* was "the first novel to treat American Jews intimately as Jews without making them seem exotic" (188).

Wouk's next two novels achieved moderate sales success, but both were critical disasters. Most reviewers rebuked the novelist for his plagiarism of Thomas Wolfe's life story in the bulky but ill-structured *Youngblood Hawke*. *Don't Stop the Carnival* earned even less praise; most critics echoed the sentiments of Samuel Simon, who dismissed the work as "a shoddy and absurd novel" (1749). Fortunately for Wouk, his reputation among critics revived somewhat with the publication of his World War II novels. Pearl Bell had great praise for Wouk's ability to create an exciting plot (71). *Esquire* critic Geoffrey Norman was impressed with Wouk's ability "to make order out of the chaos that was World War II" (96). There have been detractors, as one might expect, among them Paul Fussell, who considered Wouk's effort "a very good popular history" of World War II "in the guise of a very bad novel" (32). Critiques of later novels, all of which deal with issues of Wouk's Jewish heritage, continue the themes developed in reviews of *Marjorie Morningstar*. Wouk is faulted for his monolithic portrait of Judaism and for his stereotyped characters, who strain the limits of readers' credulity.

BIBLIOGRAPHY

Works by Herman Wouk

Fiction

Aurora Dawn. New York: Simon and Schuster, 1947.
The City Boy. Garden City, NY: Doubleday, 1948.
The Caine Mutiny. Garden City, NY: Doubleday, 1951.
Marjorie Morningstar. Garden City, NY: Doubleday, 1955.
Youngblood Hawke. Garden City, NY: Doubleday, 1962.
Don't Stop the Carnival. Garden City, NY: Doubleday, 1965.

The Winds of War. Boston: Little, Brown, 1971.
War and Remembrance. Boston: Little, Brown, 1978.
Inside, Outside. Boston: Little, Brown, 1985.
The Hope. Boston: Little, Brown, 1993.
The Glory. Boston: Little, Brown, 1994.

Drama

The Traitor. New York: Samuel French, 1949.
The Caine Mutiny Court-Martial. Garden City, NY: Doubleday, 1954.
Nature's Way. New York: Samuel French, 1958.

Nonfiction

This Is My God. Garden City, NY: Doubleday, 1959.

Works Cited and Studies of Herman Wouk

Review of *Aurora Dawn. Booklist,* May 1, 1947, 273.
Review of *Aurora Dawn. New York Herald Tribune,* April 20, 1947, 3.
Beichman, Arnold. *Herman Wouk: The Novelist as Social Historian.* New Brunswick, NJ: Transaction Books, 1984.
Bell, Pearl. "Good-Bard & Bud-Bud." *Commentary* 66 (December 1978): 70–73.
Bolton, Richard R. "The Winds of War and Wouk's Wish for the World." *Midwest Quarterly* 16 (1975): 389–408.
Browne, James. "Distortion in *The Caine Mutiny.*" Review of *The Caine Mutiny. College English* 17 (January 1956): 216.
Carpenter, F. I. "Herman Wouk." *College English* 17 (January 1956): 212.
Cohen, Joseph. "Wouk's Morningstar and Hemingway's Sun." *South Atlantic Quarterly* 58 (Spring 1959): 213–24.
Fiedler, Leslie. *Love and Death in the American Novel.* Rev. ed. New York: Stein and Day, 1966.
Fitch, Robert E. "The Bourgeois and the Bohemian." *Antioch Review* 16 (June 1956): 131–45.
Fussell, Paul. Review of *War and Remembrance. New Republic,* October 14, 1978, 32.
Gordis, Robert. "Religion in One Dimension: The Judaism of Herman Wouk." *Midstream* 6 (Winter 1960): 82–90.
Guttmann, Allen. *The Jewish Writer in America.* New York: Oxford University Press, 1971.
Levin, Meyer. Review of *Marjorie Morningstar. Saturday Review,* September 3, 1955, 10.
Charles Angoff, ed. *The Rise of American Jewish Literature.* New York: Simon and Schuster, 1970.
Mazzeno, Laurence W. *Herman Wouk.* New York: Twayne, 1994.
Metcalf, John. Review of *Marjorie Morningstar. Spectator,* October 7, 1955, 472.
Norman, Geoffrey. Review of *War and Remembrance. Esquire,* December 15, 1978, 96.
Podhoretz, Norman. "The Jew as Bourgeois." Review of *Marjorie Morningstar. Commentary,* February 1956, 188.

Raphael, Marc. "From Marjorie to Tevya: The Image of Jews in American Popular Literature, Theater, and Comedy." *American Jewish History* 74 (1984), 66–72.

Simon, Samuel. Review of *Don't Stop the Carnival. Library Journal* 90 (April 1965): 1749.

Swados, Harvey. "Popular Taste and *The Caine Mutiny*." Review of *The Caine Mutiny. Partisan Review* 20 (1953): 199.

Trilling, Diana. Review of *Aurora Dawn. Nation*, May 24, 1947, 636.

Van Nostrand, Albert. *The Denatured Novel*. Indianapolis: Bobbs-Merrill, 1960.

Appendix

Compiled by Dorothy Shatzky

For complete bio-bibliographical listings of the following authors, see *Jewish American Women Writers: A Bio-Bibliographical and Critical Sourcebook*, ed. Ann R. Shapiro. Westport, CT: Greenwood Press, 1994.

Ann Birstein (1927–) B. New York City to Bernard Birstein, Orthodox rabbi. Ed.: B.A., Queens College, 1948; Kenyon School of English; Sorbonne, Paris. M. Alfred Kazin, 1952; divorced, 1982. Daughter, Cathreal, 1955. Major Works: *Star of Glass* (1950); *The Troublemaker* (1955); *The Sweet Birds of Gorham* (1966); *Dickie's List* (1973); *American Children* (1980); *The Last of the True Believers* (1988). Other works: (with Alfred Kazin) *The Works of Anne Frank* (1959); *The Rabbi on Forty-seventh Street* (1982).

E.M. Broner (1930–) B. Detroit to Paul B. and Beatrice Wasserman Masserman, Russian immigrants. Ed.: B.A., Wayne State University, 1950; M.F.A., 1962; Ph.D., Union Institute, 1978. M. Robert Broner; four children. Major Works: *Her Mothers* (1975); *A Weave of Women* (1978). Other Works: (with Cathy Davidson, ed.), *The Lost Tradition: Mothers and Daughters in Literature* (1980).

Rosellen Brown (1939–) B. Philadelphia to David and Blossom Lieberman Brown. Ed.: B.A., Barnard College, 1960; M.A., Brandeis University, 1962. M. Marvin Hoffman, 1963. Taught at Tougaloo College (Mississippi). Major Works: *Some Deaths in the Delta and Other Poems* (1970); *Street Games* (1974); *The Autobiography of My Mother* (1976); *Cora Fry* (1977); *Tender Mercies* (1978); *Civil Wars* (1984); *Before and After* (1992); *A Rosellen Brown Reader: Selected Poetry and Prose* (1992).

Hortense Calisher (1911–) B. New York City to Joseph Henry and Hedwig Lichstern Calisher. Ed.: B.A., Barnard College, 1932. M. Heaton Bennet Hefflefinger, 1935; two children; divorced, 1958. M. Curtis Harnack, 1959. Taught creative writing and literature at various institutions including Barnard College, Brandeis University, Bennington College, Brown University, Columbia University, and the University of Iowa. President of PEN; President of the American Academy of Arts and Letters. Major Works: *In the Absence of Angels* (1951); *False Entry* (1961); *Queenie* (1971); *Herself* (1972); *On Keeping Women* (1977).

Kim Chernin (1940–   ) B. Bronx, NY, to Rose Chernin and Paul Kusnitz. M. 1958; daughter Larissa, b. 1963; divorced 1972. M. 1972, divorced 1978. Career as consultant and writer; social activist and feminist. Major Works: *In My Mother's House* (1983); *The Flame Bearers* (1986); *Sex and Other Sacred Games* (1989); *Crossing the Border* (1994).

Andrea Dworkin (1946–   ) B. Camden, NJ, to Harold and Sylvia Dworkin. Ed.: B.A., Bennington College, 1968. M. 1968; divorced 1974. Writer and public speaker; taught at U of Minnesota. Major Works: *Woman Hating* (1974); *Pornography: Men Possessing Women* (1981); *Right-Wing Women* (1983); *Ice and Fire* (1987); *Intercourse* (1987); *Pornography and Civil Rights* (1988) (with Catharine A. MacKinnon); *Letters from a War Zone* (1989); *Mercy* (1991).

Rebecca Goldstein (1950–   ) B. White Plains, NY. Ed.: B.A., Barnard College; Ph.D., Princeton U. in the philosophy of science. Taught at Barnard College; writer. Awards: Whiting Writers Award, grant from American Council of Learned Societies. Edward Lewis Wallant Award, 1995 for *Mazel*. Major works: *The Mind-Body Problem* (1983); *The Late-Summer Passion of a Woman of Mind* (1989); *The Dark Sister* (1991); *Strange Attractors* (1993); *Mazel* (1995).

Allegra Goodman (1967–   ) B. Brooklyn, NY, to Lenn and Madeline Goodman. Ed.: B.A., Harvard College. M. David Karger, 1989; one son, Ezra. Awards: John Harvard Scholar, Elizabeth Carey Agassiz Scholar, Briggs Prize, Whiting Writer's Award. Major Work: *Total Immersion* (1989); *The Family Moskowitz* (1996).

Joanne Goldenberg Greenberg (1933–   ) B. Brooklyn, NY, to Julius and Rosalie Goldenberg. Ed.: B.A., American University. M. Albert Greenberg, 1955; two sons: David and Alan. Major works: *The King's Persons* (1963); *I Never Promised You a Rose Garden* (1964); *The Monday Voices* (1965); *Summering* (1966); *Rites of Passage* (1972); *High Crimes and Misdemeanors* (1979); *Simple Gifts* (1986); *Age of Consent* (1987); *Of Such Small Differences* (1988); *With The Snow Queen* (1991).

Bette Howland (1937–   ) B. Chicago to Sam Sotonoff and Jesse Berger Sotonoff. Ed.: B.A., U of Chicago 1955. Studied at U of Chicago; Committee of Social Thought, 1960 to 1997. M. Howard Howland; divorced, 1962; two sons, Frank and Jacob. Professor of Literature at U of Chicago and Committee on Social Thought, 1993. Awards: Received grants and fellowships from the Rockefeller Foundation, the Marsden Foundation, the Guggenheim Foundation, and the MacArthur Foundation. Major Works: *W-3* (1974); *Blue in Chicago* (1978); *Things to Come and Go* (1983); *German Lessons* (forthcoming).

Joyce (Glassman) Johnson (1938–   ) B. Queens, NY, to Rosalind Ross Glassman. Acted with the Broadway company of *I Remember Mama*, attended Professional Children's School. Ed.: Barnard College, 1951–1955. M. James Johnson (1962, died 1963). M. Peter Pinchbeck, 1965; later divorced. One son, Daniel. Writer and editor: William Morrow, Dial Press, McGraw-Hill, Atlantic Monthly Press, *Vanity Fair*; visiting prof. American University, SUNY-Purchase, Bennington College, Warren Wilson College; adjunct prof., Columbia University. On Board of Governors for the N.Y.S. Foundation on the Arts (1991–1994). Awards: National Book Critics Circle Award, The John Gardner Memorial Fellowship, O. Henry Award, National Endowment for the Arts Fellowship. Major Works: *Come and Join the Dance* (1962); *Bad Connections* (1978); *Minor Characters* (1983); *In the Night Cafe* (1989); *What Lisa Knew: The Truth and Lies of the Steinberg Case* (1990).

Erica Jong (1942–) B. New York City to Seymour Mann and Eda Minsky Mann. Ed.: B.A., Barnard College, 1963; M.A., Columbia University, 1965. M. Michael Werthman, Allan Jong, Jonathan Fast; one daughter, Molly Miranda Jong-Fast. Instructor, CUNY, Manhattan Com. College, U of Maryland (overseas program). Major Works: Poetry: *Fruits and Vegetables* (1971); *Half-Lives* (1973); *Loveroot* (1975). Fiction: *Fear of Flying* (1973); *How to Save Your Own Life* (1977); *Fanny* (1980); *Parachutes and Kisses* (1984); *Serenissima* (1987); *Any Woman's Blues* (1990).

Johanna Kaplan (1942–) Born New York City to Max and Ruth Duker Kaplan. Ed.: B.A., New York University, 1964; M.A., Teachers College, Columbia, 1966. Teacher of emotionally disturbed children in Mt. Sinai Hospital's Psychiatry Dept. Awards: Recipient of grants from NY State and the National Endowment for the Arts. Freelance book reviewer for *New York Times, Commentary*. Major Works: *Other People's Lives* (1975); *O My America!* (1980).

Ilona Karmel (1925–) B. Cracow to Hirsch and Mita Rosenbaum Karmel. Ed.: B.A., Radcliffe College, 1952. M. Francis Zucker. Major Works: *Stephania* (1953); *An Estate of Memory* (1969).

Edith Konecky (1922–) B. Brooklyn, NY. Ed.: NYU, Columbia U. Married; two sons. Award: N.Y. Foundation for the Arts Fellow (1992). Writer of fiction and critic. Major works: *Allegra Maud Goldman* (1976); *A Place at the Table* (1989).

Rhoda Lerman, née Sniderman (1936–) B. Far Rockaway, NY. Ed.: B. A., English, U of Miami. M. Robert Lerman; three children. Taught at U of Colorado, Syracuse, Hartwick College, SUNY, Buffalo. Major Works: *Call Me Ishtar* (1973); *The Girl That He Marries* (1976); *Eleanor: A Novel* (1979); *The Book of the Night* (1984); *God's Ear* (1989).

Leslea Newman (1955–) B. Brooklyn, NY, to working-class parents. Ed.: B.S. in education, U of Vermont, 1977. Certificate in poetics, Naropa Institute; studied with Allen Ginsberg and Anne Waldman (1980). Career as writer and teacher. Major Works: *Just Looking for My Shoes* (1980); *Good Enough to Eat* (1986); *A Letter to Harvey Milk* (1988); *Heather Has Two Mommies* (1989); *In Every Laugh a Tear* (1992).

Francine Prose (1947–) B. Brooklyn, NY, to Jessie Rubin Prose and Philip Prose. Ed.: B.A., Radcliffe College, 1968; M.A., Harvard, 1969. M. Howard Michels, 1976; two sons. Awards: Jewish Book Council Award (1973), the MLLE Award from *Mademoiselle* (1975), Fulbright Fellowship (1989), Guggenheim Foundation writing grant (1991). Novelist and freelance journalist. Academic career: taught creative writing at Harvard, the U of Arizona, the Iowa Writer's Workshop, Bread Loaf Writers' Workshop, Warren Wilson College, Sarah Lawrence College, the U of Utah. Major Works: *Judah the Pious* (1973); *The Glorious Ones* (1974); *Marie Laveau* (1977); *Household Saints* (1981); *Primitive People* (1992); *The Peaceable Kingdom* (1993).

Nessa Rapoport (1953–   ) B. Toronto, Ont. Ed.: B.A., U of Toronto, 1974. Graduate work in English literature in New York City. Writer and lecturer on Jewish feminism. Awards: Chatelaine Annual Fiction Competition Award for "Katy" (1982). Career in publishing; senior editor, Bantam Books. Major Works: *Preparing for Sabbath* (1981); *The Perfection of the World* (forthcoming).

Anne Roiphe (1935–   ) B. New York, NY, to Eugene Roth and Blanche Phillips Roth. Ed.: B.A., Sarah Lawrence, 1957. M. Jack Richardson, 1958; divorced, 1963. M. Herman Roiphe, 1967. Major Works: *Up the Sandbox!* (1970); *Long Division* (1972); *Torch Song* (1977); *Lovingkindness* (1987); *The Pursuit of Happiness* (1991); *If You Knew Me* (1993).

Norma Rosen (1925–   ) B. New York City, to Rose Miller and Louis Gangel. Ed.: B.A., Mount Holyoke College, 1946; M.A., Columbia, 1953; NYU, studied book designing. M. Robert Samuel Rosen, 1960; two children, Anne Beth, b. 1961; Jonathan Aaron, 1963. Academic career: Taught creative writing at various institutions, among them U of Penn., Harvard, Columbia, NYU Tisch School of Dramatic Writing. Major Works: *Joy to Levine!* (1962); *Touching Evil* (1969); *At the Center* (1982); *John and Anzia, an American Romance* (1989).

Susan Fromberg Schaeffer (1941–   ) B. Brooklyn, NY. Ed.: Ph.D., U of Chicago, 1966. M. Neil Schaeffer. Academic career: teaches creative writing at Brooklyn College. Major Works: *Anya* (1974); *The Madness of a Seduced Woman* (1983), *The Dragons of North Chittendon* (1986); *First Nights* (1993).

Lynne Sharon Schwartz (1939–   ) B. Brooklyn to Jack M. Sharon and Sarah Sharon. Ed.: B.A., Barnard College, 1959; studied at NYU. M. Harry Schwartz, 1957; two daughters, Miranda Ruth and and Rachel Eve. Awards: Vanguard Press; Lamport Foundation; stories anthologized in *Best American Short Stories 1978 and 1979*; O. Henry Prize Stories of 1979; PEN Renato Poggioli Award, 1991. Associate editor, *Writer Magazine*; writer for Operation Open City. Career: writer of fiction. Major Works: *Rough Strife* (1980); *Balancing Acts* (1981); *Disturbances in the Field* (1983); *Leaving Brooklyn* (1989); *A Lynn Sharon Schwartz Reader* (1990).

Lore Segal (1928–   ) B. Vienna, Austria, to Ignatz Groszmann and Franzi Groszmann. M. David Segal, 1961; deceased, 1970; two children, Beatrice and Jacob. Academic career: Taught at U of Illinois, Chicago, and Ohio State U. Major Works: *Other People's Houses* (1964); *Lucinella* (1976); *Her First American* (1995).

Helen Yglesias (1915–   ) B. Brooklyn, NY, to Solomon and Kate Bassine. M. Bernard Cole, 1937; two children, Tamar and Lewis; divorced 1950. M. Jose Yglesias, 1950; one child, Rafael; divorced 1992. Awards: Houghton Mifflin Literary Fellowship, 1972. Career in journalism: cultural editor, *The Daily Worker*; literary editor, *The Nation*. Major Works: *How She Died* (1972); *Family Feeling* (1976); *Sweetsir* (1981); *The Saviors* (1987); *Isabel Bishop* (1989).

Selected Bibliography

Aarons, Victoria. *A Measure of Memory*. Athens: University of Georgia Press, 1996.

Angoff, Charles, and Meyer Levin. *The Rise of American Jewish Fiction*. New York: Simon and Schuster, 1970.

Alter, Robert. *After the Tradition: Essays on Modern Jewish Writing*. New York: Dutton, 1969.

————. *Defenses of the Imagination: Jewish Writers and Modern Historical Crisis*. Philadelphia: Jewish Publication Society of America, 1977.

Baumgarten, Murray. *City Scriptures: Modern Jewish Writing*. Cambridge: Harvard University Press, 1982.

Berger, Alan. *Crisis and Covenant: The Holocaust in American Jewish Fiction*. Albany: State University of New York Press, 1985.

Bilik, Dorothy Seidman. *Immigrant-Survivors: Post-Holocaust Consciousness in Recent Jewish American Fiction*. Middletown, CT: Wesleyan University Press, 1981.

Blacher-Cohen, Sarah. *From Hester Street to Hollywood*. Bloomington: Indiana University Press, 1983.

Chametzky, Jules. *Our Decentralized Literature: Cultural Mediations in Selected Jewish and Southern Writers*. Amherst: University of Massachusetts Press, 1986.

Dembo, L. S. *The Monological Jew: A Literary Study*. Madison: University of Wisconsin Press, 1988.

Eisenberg, Azriel, ed. *The Golden Land: A Literary Portrait of American Jewry, 1654 to the Present*. New York: Yoseloff, 1965.

Ezrahi, Sidra DeKoven. *By Words Alone: The Holocaust in Literature*. Chicago: University of Chicago Press, 1980.

Fiedler, Leslie. *The Jew in the American Novel*. New York: Herzl Institute Pamphlet, 1956.

Finkelstein, Norman. *The Ritual of New Creation: Jewish Tradition and Contemporary Literature*. Albany: State University of New York Press, 1992.

Fishman, Charles. *Blood to Remember*. College Station: Texas Tech University, 1991.

Fishman, Sylvia Barack, ed. *Follow My Footprints: Changing Images of Women in American Jewish Fiction*. Hanover, NH: University Press of New England, 1992.

Fried, Lewis, ed. *Handbook of American-Jewish Literature*. New York: Greenwood Press, 1988.

Girgus, Sam. *The New Covenant: Jewish Writers and the American Idea*. Chapel Hill: University of North Carolina Press, 1984.

Gittleman, Sol. *From Shtetl to Suburbia: The Family in Jewish Literary Imagination*. Boston: Beacon, 1978.

Greenspan, Ezra. *The Schlemiel Comes to America*. Metuchen, NJ: Scarecrow Press, 1983.

Guttmann, Allen. *The Jewish Writer in America: Assimilation and the Crisis of Identity*. New York: Oxford University Press, 1971.

Halperin, Irving. *Messengers from the Dead: Literature of the Holocaust*. Philadelphia: Westminster Press, 1970.

Harap, Louis. *Creative Awakening: The Jewish Presence in Twentieth-Century American Literature, 1900–1940s*. New York: Greenwood Press, 1987.

———. *The Image of the Jew in American Literature from Early Republic to Mass Immigration*. Philadelphia: Jewish Publication Society of America, 1974.

———. *In the Mainstream: The Jewish Presence in Twentieth-Century Literature, 1950s–1980s*. Westport, CT: Greenwood Press, 1987.

Heinemann, Marlene E. *Gender and Destiny: Women Writers and the Holocaust*. Westport, CT: Greenwood Press, 1986.

Howe, Irving. *World of Our Fathers*. New York: Harcourt Brace Jovanovich, 1976.

Kaye, Melanie, et al. *The Tribe of Dina*. Boston: Beacon Press, 1986.

Kamel, Rose Yalow. *Aggravating the Conscience: Jewish-American Literary Mothers in the Promised Land*. New York: Peter Lang, 1988.

Knopp, Josephine Z. *The Trial of Judaism in Contemporary Jewish Writing*. Urbana: University of Illinois Press, 1975.

Kremer, S. Lillian. *Witness through the Imagination: Jewish American Holocaust Literature*. Detroit: Wayne State University Press, 1989.

Langer, Lawrence. *The Holocaust and the Literary Imagination*. New Haven: Yale University Press, 1975.

Lichtenstein, Diane. *Writing Their Nation*. Bloomington: Indiana University Press, 1992.

Liptzin, Sol. *The Jew in American Literature*. New York: Bloch, 1966.

Mazow, Julia. *The Woman Who Lost Her Name*. New York: Harper & Row, 1980.

Malin, Irving, ed. *Contemporary American-Jewish Literature: Critical Essays*. Bloomington: Indiana University Press, 1973.

———. *Jews and Americans*. Carbondale: Southern Illinois University Press, 1965.

Mersand, Joseph. *Traditions in American Literature: A Study of Jewish Characters and Authors*. Port Washington, NY: Kennikat Press, 1968.

Nadel, Ira Bruce. *Jewish Writers of North America: A Guide to Information Sources*. Detroit: Gale, 1981.

Pinsker, Sanford. *Jewish-American Fiction, 1917–1987*. New York: Twayne, 1992.

———. *The Schlemiel as Metaphor: Studies in Yiddish and American Jewish Fiction*. Carbondale: Southern Illinois University Press, 1971. Enlarged and revised ed., 1991.

Rosenfeld, Alvin S. *A Double Dying: Reflections on Holocaust Literature*. Bloomington: Indiana University Press, 1980.

Schulz, Max. *Radical Sophistication: Studies in Contemporary Jewish-American Novelists*. Athens: Ohio University Press, 1969.

Shapiro, Ann R., ed. *Jewish American Women Writers: A Bio-Bibliographical and Critical Sourcebook*. Westport, CT: Greenwood Press, 1994.

Shechner, Mark. *After the Revolution: Studies in the Contemporary Jewish-American Imagination*. Bloomington: Indiana University Press, 1987.

Sherman, Bernard. *The Invention of the Jew: Jewish-American Education Novels (1916–1964)*. New York: Thomas Yoseloff, 1969.

Uffen, Ellen Serlen. *Strands of the Cable: The Place of the Past in Jewish American Women's Writing*. New York: Peter Lang, 1992.

Walden, Daniel. *On Being Jewish: American Jewish Writers from Cahan to Bellow*. Greenwich, CT: Fawcett, 1974.

———, ed. *Twentieth-Century American-Jewish Fiction Writers*. Vol. 28 of *Dictionary of Literary Biography*. Detroit: Gale, 1984.

Wisse, Ruth. *The Schlemiel as Modern Hero*. Chicago: University of Chicago Press, 1971.

Index

Page numbers in **bold type** refer to main entries in the encyclopedia.

About the Editors and Contributors

PIRJO AHOKAS is Associate Professor of Comparative Literature at the University of Turku, Finland. She is the author of *Forging a New Self: The Adamic Protagonist and the Emergence of a Jewish-American Author as Revealed Through the Novels of Bernard Malamud*. She recently organized a Holocaust studies workshop in Warsaw as part of the Biennial Conference of the European Association for American Studies.

EBERHARD ALSEN is Professor of English at the State University of New York, College at Cortland, and has written extensively on American literature. He has published studies of J. D. Salinger, *Salinger's Glass Stories as a Composite Novel* and *Romantic Post-Modernism in American Fiction*.

PETER J. BAILEY is Professor of English at St. Lawrence University in Canton, New York, where he teaches American literature and fiction writing. He has published a book on Stanley Elkin.

SETH BARRON is a graduate student in the English Department at Yale University. He is writing his dissertation on the theatrics of scandal and embarrassment in English Renaissance drama.

JAMES BERGER is Charles Phelps Taft Postdoctoral Fellow at the University of Cincinnati. He is presently under contract for a book entitled *After the End: Representations of Post-Apocalypse*, and has contributed articles to *PMLA, Genre*, and *Postmodern Culture*.

MASHEY BERNSTEIN holds a Ph.D. in American-Jewish literature from the University of California, Santa Barbara, where he currently lectures in composition and film. He has written frequently on Jewish aspects of the media. His articles have appeared in *Midstream, Studies in American Jewish Literature, Christianity and Literature*, and numerous Jewish newspapers and journals nationally and internationally. His most recent article is "My Worst Fears Realized: Woody Allen's Cinematic Use of the Holocaust," to appear in a new book on Allen.

LUDGER BRINKER is Professor of English at Macomb College and a member of the graduate faculty at Wayne State University. His publications include studies of Christopher Marlowe, Alfred Kazin, Ann Birstein, American Jewish gay and lesbian literature, and African-American literature. He is currently at work on a book about Alfred Kazin's autobiographies and an annotated bibliography of American Jewish gay and lesbian literature.

DAVID BUEHRER is Assistant Professor of English at Valdosta State University (Georgia), where he teaches courses in modern and contemporary fiction. His articles on F. Scott Fitzgerald, Saul Bellow, Gabriel García Márquez, Mario Vargas Llosa, Toni Morrison, and Harry Crews have appeared in such journals as *Critique* and *Notes on Teaching English*.

MARTINE CHARD-HUTCHINSON teaches American literature and is a Professor in the English Department at the University of Poitiers. In her main field of research, Jewish-American literature, she has published articles in American, French, and Italian journals that deal with the problematics of identity and its literary forms in Jewish writings. She has also translated into French Bernard Malamud's posthumous work *The People and Uncollected Stories*. Her most recent work, an essay on Cynthia Ozick's shorter fiction, is *Regards sur la fiction brève de Cynthia Ozick*.

JUDY EPSTEIN is an adjunct instructor of English at the State University of New York, College at Cortland.

HANNAH BERLINER FISCHTHAL is Adjunct Assistant Professor of English at Hofstra University and managing editor of both *Yiddish* and *Modern Jewish Studies*. She has published many articles in such periodicals as *Midstream, Jewish Quarterly, Yiddish, Modern Jewish Studies*, and *Jewish Currents*. She also has entries in the *Encyclopedia of World Literature in the Twentieth Century* and the *Handbook of American-Jewish Literature*.

FRANCES FLANNERY-DAILEY is a Ph.D. candidate at the University of Iowa.

ESTHER FRANK teaches Yiddish language and literature at McGill University in Montreal, Quebec. She is presently working on a bio-critical study of the American Yiddish short-story writer Lamed Shapiro.

THOMAS FRANK is a doctoral candidate in American studies at the University of Maryland, College Park. He is writing his dissertation on the cultural function of narrative.

ANDREW FURMAN is Assistant Professor in the English and Comparative Literature and English Department at Florida Atlantic University, specializing in Jewish-American fiction. He has published articles on Philip Roth, Saul Bellow, Anne Roiphe, and Hugh Nissenson in such journals as *Contemporary Literature, MELUS, Midstream*, and *Studies in American Jewish Literature*. His book *Israel through the Jewish-American Imagination: A Survey of Jewish-American Literature on Israel* is scheduled for upcoming publication.

MYRNA GOLDENBERG is Professor of English at Montgomery College and contributing editor to *Belles Lettres: A Review of Books by Women*. She has published over twenty articles and reviews, including ones on Holocaust studies, Rosa Sonnenschein, Annie Nathan Meyer, and Anzia Yezierska.

STEVEN GOLDLEAF is an Associate Professor in the English Department at Pace University. He is coauthor of a critical study of Richard Yates and is completing a book on John O'Hara's short fiction.

IRENE C. GOLDMAN is an Associate Professor in the English Department at Ball State University in Muncie, Indiana. An article of hers on Leslie Epstein has appeared in *Midstream*.

BECKY SPIRO GREEN is a catalog librarian in the rare book department of the Henry E. Huntington Library in San Marino, California.

HAROLD HEFT is an Assistant Professor in the Department of English at the University of Western Ontario in London, Ontario, and Visiting Professor at the Halbert Centre for Canadian Studies at the Hebrew University in Jerusalem in 1997. His area of specialization is North American Jewish writing, and he is currently coediting an edition of *The Collected Letters of A. M. Klein*.

SARA R. HOROWITZ is Director of the Jewish Studies Program and Associate Professor of English Literature at the University of Delaware. She is the author of *Voicing the Void: Muteness and Memory in Holocaust Fiction* (1996). In addition to numerous articles on Holocaust fiction and memoirs, Professor Horowitz has published extensively on Jewish-American literature, Jewish spirituality, feminism, and innovative pedagogy. She is coeditor of *KEREM: A Journal of Creative Explorations in Judaism* and served as a coeditor of *Jewish American Women Writers* (Greenwood Press, 1994), which won the 1995 Judaica Reference Book Award by the Association of Jewish Libraries.

MICHAEL HUFF is a doctoral candidate at the State University of New York at Binghamton.

LISA JUCKNATH teaches English at Framingham High School in Massachusetts and did extensive bibliographical research on Edward Lewis Wallant.

BLOSSOM S. KIRSCHENBAUM is Researcher at Brown University's Department of Comparative Literature. She has translated the works of Giuliana

Morandini, Paola Drigo, and Marina Mizzau as well as other short fiction from Italian, Yiddish, and Slovak works.

SUZANNE KLINGENSTEIN is Assistant Professor of Writing and Humanist Studies at the Massachusetts Institute of Technology. She is the author of *Jews in the American Academy, 1900–1940: The Dynamics of Intellectual Assimilation.*

JEROME KLINKOWITZ is Professor of English at the University of Northern Iowa. He has done annual reviews of books about fiction of the 1950s and 1960s for *American Literary Scholarship* as well as studies of Jewish literature.

RICHARD KOSTELANETZ has authored and edited dozens of books about contemporary literature and art. Entries on his poetry and fiction will appear in an upcoming volume on Jewish-American poets and dramatists, compiled by the editors of this book.

S. LILLIAN KREMER is Assistant Professor of English at Kansas State University and author of *Witness through the Imagination: Jewish-American Holocaust Literature.*

HOLLI LEVITSKY is Assistant Professor and Director of Freshman English at Loyola Marymount University in Los Angeles. She has published articles on William Faulkner and women's studies and is presently at work on a book, *Women Writers of the Holocaust.*

BENNETT LOVETT-GRAFF has held editorial positions at *Chicago Review, Jewish Frontier, Response: A Contemporary Jewish Review,* and *The Research Edition of the Private Papers of James Boswell* at Yale University. He has published articles and reviews on supernatural fiction, the culture wars, Jewish fiction, and hermeneutics in *Paradoxa, Journal of the Fantastic in the Arts, Jewish Book World, Canadian Philosophical Review, Modern Language Studies, Extrapolation* and other journals. He is currently acquisitions editor at the UAHC Press.

SANFORD E. MAROVITZ is Professor of English at Kent State University. He has published widely in American literature as well as in such journals as *Studies in American Jewish Literature, Yiddish,* and *Saul Bellow Journal.*

LAURENCE W. MAZZENO is Academic Vice President at Ursuline College in Cleveland. He is the author of four books, including *Herman Wouk* in the Twayne United States Authors Series. He teaches American literature and seminars on Wouk at the Cleveland College of Jewish Studies.

GABRIEL MILLER is Chairman of the English Department at Rutgers University, Newark. He has published four books; among them is one on Daniel Fuchs for the Twayne series, and a second is on Clifford Odets. He is presently at work on a study of the film director Martin Ritt.

EVAN J. NISONSON is a lecturer, Loyola Marymount University.

LEONARD ORR is Associate Professor of English at Washington State University. His books include *Problems and Poetics of the Non-Aristotelian Novel, Yeats and Postmodernism, Research in Critical Theory since 1965, A Dictionary of Critical Theory,* and *Critical Theory, Cultural Politics, and Latin American Narrative.* In 1994 his *Critical Essays on Samuel Taylor Coleridge* was published, and he is currently writing a book on J. G. Ballard and editing *A Joseph Conrad Companion.*

SANFORD PINSKER is Professor of English at Franklin and Marshall College. His many publications in the area of Jewish studies range from *Jewish-American Fiction, 1917–1987* to *The Schlemiel as Metaphor* as well as studies of Philip Roth, Henry Roth, Saul Bellow, and Bernard Malamud.

KAREN L. POLSTER is a doctoral candidate at the University of California, Riverside. She has contributed a number of articles to *Studies in American Jewish Literature.*

LEONARD ROGOFF's affiliations include Associate Professor at North Carolina Central University. He is presently at work on a history of the Durham–Chapel Hill Jewish community. He has published articles in *American Jewish History* and *The Encyclopedia of Jewish Literature.*

LOIS RUBIN is an Associate Professor of English at Pennsylvania State University at New Kensington. Her publications are mostly in the area of composition pedagogy and research in such journals as *College Teaching* and *Teaching English.*

BRENNA J. RYAN is completing her doctoral dissertation on Carolivia Herron at the University of Alabama in Tuscaloosa.

ELISABETH SANDBERG is Associate Professor of English and Chair of Humanities at Woodbury University in Los Angeles. She has written extensively on the work of Jo Sinclair.

CLAIRE R. SATLOF is a member of the English Department at the University of Pennsylvania and the author of a number of articles on Jewish literature. She is exploring the emergence of a recognizable canon of Jewish feminist fiction.

SABINE SAUTER is a doctoral student at McGill University, where her major field of study is twentieth-century literature and theory.

DOROTHY SHATZKY is a secretary at the J. M. Murray Center in Cortland, New York. She has a B.A. from Barnard College and an M.A. from New York University, both in English, and an M.L.S. from Syracuse University. She contributed all of the biographies and cross-references in the Appendix of this volume for those authors previously listed in *Jewish American Women Writers,* edited by Ann Shapiro.

JOEL SHATZKY is Professor of English at the State University of New York, College at Cortland. He is a frequent contributor to *Jewish Currents* and has published articles in *Studies in American Jewish Literature* and *Jewish Frontier*. He has edited *Theresienstadt: Hitler's Gift to the Jews* by Norbert Troller, translated by Susan Cernyak-Spatz.

MARK SHECHNER is Professor of English at the State University of New York at Buffalo. He is a prolific author of criticism in Jewish-American literature. Among his many works are *After the Revolution: Studies in the Contemporary Jewish American Imagination* and *The Conversion of the Jews and Other Essays*.

MARILYN METZCHER SMITH is a graduate student in the Department of Comparative Literature and English at Florida Atlantic University.

CAROLYN ARIELLA SOFIA serves as faculty advisor/lecturer for the Long Island Center for Jewish Studies. She is a doctoral candidate in English at the State University of New York at Stony Brook, where she is completing her dissertation, "The Rhetoric of Grief in Contemporary Jewish-American and African-American Literature."

DIANE STEVENSON is a poet and lives in the Bronx. She has recently completed a detective novel, *Car Thief.*

MICHAEL TAUB has taught Jewish languages and literature at Binghamton University, Cornell University, and Vassar College. He has written extensively on Yiddish and Hebrew literature and has edited two volumes of drama translated from the Hebrew: *Modern Israeli Drama in Translation* and *Israeli Holocaust Drama*. He is currently completing a volume of essays on the Yiddish theatre and on the Jewish theatre in Poland.

DANIEL WALDEN is Professor Emeritus of American Studies, English, and Comparative Literature at Pennsylvania State University. Among his books are *On Being Jewish: American Jewish Writers from Cahan to Bellow*. He was editor of the Jewish-American writers volume in the *Dictionary of Literary Biography* series and also founder and editor of *Studies in American Jewish Literature*.

HANA WIRTH-NESHER is chair of the Department of English at Tel Aviv University. She is editor of the *Henry Roth Reader* and *What Is Jewish Literature?* She is also the founding editor of *Prooftexts*.

MARK ZAITCHIK teaches English and philosophy at Salem State College. He is a contributor to recent textbooks on ethnicity and is currently preparing a critical introduction to E. L. Wallant's *The Odyssey of a Middleman.*